C Programming for System, Network, and Cloud Engineers

Techniques for Processes, Memory, Network Applications, and Linux Namespaces

Dr Anil Kumar Rangisetti

apress®

C Programming for System, Network, and Cloud Engineers: Techniques for Processes, Memory, Network Applications, and Linux Namespaces

Dr Anil Kumar Rangisetti
Opp G Pullareddy Engineering College
Balaji Villas 3rd Phase, A Blk, Plot A65
Kurnool, Andhra Pradesh, India

ISBN-13 (pbk): 979-8-8688-1804-2   ISBN-13 (electronic): 979-8-8688-1805-9
https://doi.org/10.1007/979-8-8688-1805-9

Copyright © 2026 by Dr Anil Kumar Rangisetti

This work is subject to copyright. All rights are reserved by the Publisher, whether the whole or part of the material is concerned, specifically the rights of translation, reprinting, reuse of illustrations, recitation, broadcasting, reproduction on microfilms or in any other physical way, and transmission or information storage and retrieval, electronic adaptation, computer software, or by similar or dissimilar methodology now known or hereafter developed.

Trademarked names, logos, and images may appear in this book. Rather than use a trademark symbol with every occurrence of a trademarked name, logo, or image we use the names, logos, and images only in an editorial fashion and to the benefit of the trademark owner, with no intention of infringement of the trademark.

The use in this publication of trade names, trademarks, service marks, and similar terms, even if they are not identified as such, is not to be taken as an expression of opinion as to whether or not they are subject to proprietary rights.

While the advice and information in this book are believed to be true and accurate at the date of publication, neither the authors nor the editors nor the publisher can accept any legal responsibility for any errors or omissions that may be made. The publisher makes no warranty, express or implied, with respect to the material contained herein.

Managing Director, Apress Media LLC: Welmoed Spahr
Acquisitions Editor: Melissa Duffy
Editorial Assistant: Gryffin Winkler

Cover designed by eStudioCalamar

Cover image designed by Niklas Bischop on unsplash.com

Distributed to the book trade worldwide by Springer Science+Business Media New York, 1 New York Plaza, New York, NY 10004. Phone 1-800-SPRINGER, fax (201) 348-4505, e-mail orders-ny@springer-sbm.com, or visit www.springeronline.com. Apress Media, LLC is a Delaware LLC and the sole member (owner) is Springer Science + Business Media Finance Inc (SSBM Finance Inc). SSBM Finance Inc is a **Delaware** corporation.

For information on translations, please e-mail booktranslations@springernature.com; for reprint, paperback, or audio rights, please e-mail bookpermissions@springernature.com.

Apress titles may be purchased in bulk for academic, corporate, or promotional use. eBook versions and licenses are also available for most titles. For more information, reference our Print and eBook Bulk Sales web page at http://www.apress.com/bulk-sales.

Any source code or other supplementary material referenced by the author in this book is available to readers on GitHub. For more detailed information, please visit https://www.apress.com/gp/services/source-code.

If disposing of this product, please recycle the paper

To all my teachers, especially Dr. Bheemarjuna Reddy and Shri Badrinadh, for identifying my strengths, giving me wonderful opportunities to work with them, and guiding me to achieve my goals.

To my lovely wife, Sravani, for being a wonderful partner and supporting me in all situations. Without her love and support, I could not have accomplished this work.

—Dr. Anil Kumar Rangisetti

Table of Contents

About the Author xiii

About the Technical Reviewer xv

Acknowledgments xvii

Introduction xix

Chapter 1: Basic Computer System Architecture and Essential Operating System Concepts 1

    Basic Computer System Architecture 2

        CPU Architecture 3

        Memory Hierarchy 5

        CPU and IO Device Interactions 6

        Inspect System Configurations on a Linux OS 7

    Operating System Responsibilities 11

        Users Program Access to OS Services 13

        OS Process Management Activities and Services 16

    Importance of Compiler, Linker, and Loader 23

        Compiler 24

        Compiler Options to Handle Runtime Errors 28

    Runtime Environment of a Process 31

        Process Memory Layout 31

        Process Execution Environment 34

        Process Reliability and Security Issues 40

    C Programmer Powers and Responsibilities 44

        C Programming Powers 45

        C Programmer Responsibilities 47

    Summary 50

TABLE OF CONTENTS

Chapter 2: Quick Revision of Powerful C Constructs 51
Procedure-Oriented Programming 52
Understand C Functions' Memory Layout and Execution Procedure 56
Recursive Functions 71
Nested Functions in GNU C 77
Arrays 81
Powerful Ways for Organizing Array's Data Elements and Accessing 84
Hands-On Activities for Organizing Array's Data Elements and Accessing Them Efficiently 91
Strings and Buffers 100
Strings Processing Hands-On Activities 105
C Structures 112
Passing Structure Variables Between Functions 115
Structure and Its Data Members' Memory Layout 117
Hands-On Activity-1 118
Power of C Structures for Modeling 123
Hands-On Activity-2 128
C Unions 132
An Important Use Case of Unions 134
Hands-On Activity 135
Summary 140
Practice Tasks 141

Chapter 3: Practice C Programming with Important Tools 143
Compilation and Linking Techniques for Enhancing Programming Skills 144
gcc Compilation Options for Performance Tuning 145
gcc Compilation Options for Linking 151
gcc Compilation Options for Secured Code 161
Memory Access Errors Handling Techniques and Tools 172
Memory and Other Important Errors Handling gcc Options for Reliable Code 172
Memory Error Handling Using Valgrind 181

TABLE OF CONTENTS

Code Coverage Analysis for Avoiding Performance Issues 183
    Code Coverage Tools (gcc and gcov) Usage Steps 185
    Hands-On Activity 188

GDB: The GNU Project Debugger 195
    Go Through a Code Execution and Inspect the Code and Data 195
    Inspect the Code and Data Using gdb Commands 202
    Handle Application Runtime Errors 209

Summary 219

Practice Tasks 220

Chapter 4: Power of C: Pointers 223

Importance of Pointer Programming 224
    Basic Concepts of C Pointers 225
    Use Cases of C Pointers 228
    Pointers Flexible Traversals 234

Efficient and Reliable Ways to Access Arrays and Strings Using Pointers 236
    Pointers to Array Subparts 237
    Pointers to Multidimensional Arrays 238
    Pointers to Strings 239
    Hands-On Activities for Organizing Array's Data Elements and Accessing
    Them Efficiently 242

Efficient and Reliable Ways to Access Structures Using Pointers 246
    Basic Pointers Accessing Ways for Structures 247
    Advanced Pointers Accessing Ways for Structures 249
    Hands-On Activity 250

Pointers and Functions for Powerful Programming Techniques 255
    Pointers to a Variety of Functions 256
    C Ways for Polymorphism 261
    Hands-On Activity 262

Summary 267

Practice Tasks 267

TABLE OF CONTENTS

Chapter 5: C Programming for Memory Management 269

Introduction to Dynamic Memory Management 270
- Importance of Dynamic Memory Management 270
- Important C System Calls for Memory Management 271

Important C System Calls for Memory Management 274
- C Library Functions for Basic Dynamic Memory Management 274
- C System Calls for Extending Memory Blocks Dynamically 277
- C System Calls for Handling Multiple Blocks of Memory Allocation 279

Error Handling Programming Techniques for Memory Management 281
- Best Dynamic Memory Management Practices 281
- Memory Error Handling Techniques Using Valgrind 285
- Hands-On Activity Using Valgrind Tools 288

Setting Up Memory Buffers and Accessing Them in a Reliable Manner 293
- Hands-On Activity-1 294
- Hands-On Activity-2 300
- Hands-On Activity-3 306

Summary 312
Practice Tasks 312

Chapter 6: Process and Thread Management Tasks for C Programmers 315

Introduction to Processes and Threads 316
- Process Management Basic Activities Using Fork 317
- Thread Management Basic Activities 319

Explore the Power of Process Management Using C Programming 324
- Developers' Role and Activities in Process Management 324
- Creating a Specific Number of Processes 327
- Control the Multiple Processes Execution Order 331
- Create N Processes and Load Them with Executable Images 335

Safe and Reliable Programming Ways for Process Management 340
- Importance of Parent and Child Processes Exit Order 342
- Handle Carefully Data Sharing Activities Between Parent and Child Processes 345

Reliable Ways of Executing a New Process in a Child Process 354
Importance of Interrupt Handling in Process Management.. 357
Explore Power of Threads Management Using C Programming 363
Developer's Role in Threads Management 363
Hands-On Activity-1... 378
Hands-On Activity-2... 383
Safe and Reliable Programming Ways for Threads Management... 387
Improve the Performance of a Multithreaded Application 387
Multithreading Application Performance Tuning.. 388
Quickly Identify and Handle Threads Synchronization Issues 396
Summary.. 401
Practice Tasks 402

Chapter 7: Handle Interprocess Activities Using C Programming 405
Essential Linux Interprocess Communication (IPC) Approaches... 406
Linux Basic Services for File Handling 407
Importance of dup and dup2 408
PIPEs... 409
FIFO 410
Message Queues 412
Shared Memory 414
Semaphores 416
Explore C Programming and Linux IPC Tools for IPC Management.. 418
Usage of PIPEs in C... 418
Usage of FIFO in C 422
Usage of Message Queues in C 427
Usage of Shared Memory in C 434
Explore C Ways to Implement Service Chaining and Asynchronous Programming.................... 440
Hands-On Activity-1... 441
Hands-On Activity-2... 445
Hands-On Activity-3... 451

TABLE OF CONTENTS

Essential IPC Synchronization Handling Tools 457
Semaphores 458
Usage of Semaphore in C 459
Hands-On Activity-1 461
Hands-On Activity-2 466
Summary 471
Practice Tasks 472

Chapter 8: Essential Network Socket Programming Skills 473
Quick Introduction to TCP/IP Stack and Network Applications 474
TCP/IP Stack 475
TCP/IP Stack and Network Interactions 477
TCP Socket Programming 481
TCP Rules 482
TCP Socket Programming Constructs 486
TCP Socket Programming Practice 501
UDP Socket Programming 515
UDP Socket Programming in C 517
UDP Socket Programming in C 523
Hands-On Activity-1 529
C Programming Ways for Monitoring and Inspecting TCP/UDP Applications Traffic 539
Packet Monitoring and Filtering Activities 539
Hands-On Activity-1 542
Hands-On Activity-2 547
Summary 551
Practice Tasks 551

Chapter 9: Essential Advanced Socket Programming Ways Using C Sockets 553
Important Socket Programming Approaches 554
Multiprocessing and Multithreading 556
Must-Know Socket Options 559
Non-blocking Socket Programming 564

Non-blocking Ways of Socket Programming..565
    Usage of fcntl and select...565
    Hands-On Activity-1..568
    Hands-On Activity-2..578

Handle TCP Client-Server Performance and Reliability Issues 584
    The Reliable TCP Server and Client 587
    Hands-On Activity-1..597
    Hands-On Activity-2..599
    Hands-On Activity-3..602

Handle UDP Client-Server Performance and Reliability Issues.................................604
    Hands-On Activity-1..605
    Hands-On Activity-2..612

Summary...621

Practice Tasks 622

Chapter 10: Learn C Programming Skills for Virtualization 623

Introduction to Linux Namespaces 624
    Linux Namespaces 625
    Linux cgroups 627

Learn How to Program Linux Namespaces and cgroups 630
    Detach a Process from Inherited Namespaces 630
    Attach a Process with Existing Namespaces..636
    Clone New Processes with Suitable Namespaces 643
    Learn Setting Up and Using Control Groups 652

Experiment with Process and Memory Namespaces..655
    Hands-On Activity-1..656
    Hands-On Activity-2..661
    Hands-On Activity-3..666
    Hands-On Activity-4..671
    Hands-On Activity-5..674

TABLE OF CONTENTS

Experiment with Networking Namespaces 679
Learn Setting Up Network Namespaces 679
Various Virtual Networks Setups 682
Hands-On Activity-1 688
Hands-On Activity-2 691
Hands-On Activity-3 694
Summary 699

Index 701

About the Author

Dr. Anil Kumar Rangisetti received his PhD in the field of computer science and engineering from IIT Hyderabad, India. He has 13 years of teaching and research experience in computer science and engineering. During his career, he worked at prestigious Indian institutions, such as IIIT Dharwad, SRM-AP, and GMR, and worked at software development and research labs such as ARICENT and IRL-Delhi. Currently he is working as assistant professor in the Department of CSE, IIITDM, Kurnool. He trained many students in programming languages and in the use of advanced simulators (NS-3), Docker, and networking tools for researching and developing applications at his workplaces. He guided a significant number of undergraduate and postgraduate students for project works.

Broadly, his research interests include Wi-Fi technologies, next-generation mobile networks, SDN, NFV, and cloud computing. He authored a number of novel research publications with IEEE, Springer, Elsevier, and Wiley in the field of a variety of networking technologies such as LTE, SDN and NFV, and Wi-Fi technologies. He authored various practical books related to network simulations, future networking technologies, and programming languages.

He brings with him academic and professional experience, which includes time spent at Aricent and the IBM research lab. Additionally, he enjoys writing and reviewing books on systems and networking technologies, mobile and wireless networks, cloud computing technologies, and programming languages.

About the Technical Reviewer

German Gonzalez-Morris is a polyglot software architect/engineer with 20+ years in the field, with knowledge in Java, SpringBoot, C/C++, Julia, Python, Haskell, and Javascript, among others. He works with cloud (architecture) web-distributed applications and microservices. German loves math puzzles (including reading Knuth, and is proud of solving some of Don's puzzles), swimming, and table tennis. Also, he has reviewed several books, including books on application containers (WebLogic) and programming languages (C, Java, Spring, Python, Haskell, Typescript, WebAssembly, Math for coders, regexp, Julia, data structures and algorithms, and Kafka).

Acknowledgments

First of all, I would like to thank Apress for believing my book idea and giving me this wonderful opportunity. I would especially like to thank Melissa Duffy for keenly going through the book proposal and suggesting to me how to make the book proposal interesting and perfect. Melissa's support and encouragement throughout the book writing process has been wonderful. All of Melissa's suggestions helped in improving the quality of the book's content.

I would like to thank Krishnan Sathyamurthy for his constant support in the entire review and finalization of the book's content. Krishnan's timely help and support helped me to complete all works in time.

A big thanks to the technical reviewer of the book for his valuable time and suggestions in all hands-on activities and technical concepts of the book. His keen observations helped me a lot in correcting all kinds of errors and incorporating necessary topics to improve the quality of the book tremendously.

I would like to thank each and every member of the Apress team for supporting me in writing this wonderful book and completing it successfully and happily. I would love to work with the Apress team again and again.

My heartfelt thanks to all my students for their interest in attending my lectures and working with me. All my students' curiosity, comments, and suggestions helped me to write this wonderful book.

Finally, I would like to thank all my family members, friends, and colleagues for their love and support always.

Introduction

C programming is known for developing systems software (operating systems, databases, network protocol stack, and virtualization technologies) and applications by efficiently utilizing system computational resources. In this book you will be exploring C programming key skills such as handling functions, arrays, strings, unions, pointers, and memory. While learning these key skills, you will be exploring important runtime error handling techniques and best practices to implement reliable and efficient C programs. It is necessary to develop runtime errors and performance handling code in your C applications before deploying them in the runtime environment. Otherwise your programs/applications can crash the system and/or be damaged by other malicious or error-prone applications. In order to help you in thinking of a runtime environment and handling possible issues, this book introduces and discusses how to use important open-source Linux tools (gcc, gdb, gcov, valgrind) for compilation, linking, debugging, code coverage, and handling memory leaks.

This book's chapters are organized in the following logical manner for easy and quick ways of learning complex concepts. In Chapters 1, 2, and 3, we discuss basic computer system architecture and essential operating systems concepts for implementing reliable and efficient C code. Then, you will go through C programming essential skills such as handling arrays, strings, unions, pointers, and memory management using open-source Linux tools (gcc, gdb, gcov, valgrind). In Chapters 4 and 5, you will be dedicatedly practicing runtime error handling and best practices in terms of Pointers usages, dynamic memory allocation handling, and accessing arrays, structures, strings, and buffers. Later you will learn the importance of these concepts while implementing system and network programming.

Later in Chapters 6 and 7, you will explore the power of C programming in terms of system programming and high-performance computing; specifically, you will learn process and thread management for multitasking or multiprocessing through essential system calls. Mainly, you will learn programmer responsibilities in terms of process management tasks such as creating multiple processes, management of process segments, waiting for processes, termination activities, inter-process communication,

INTRODUCTION

synchronization issues, and handling exceptional conditions. These are necessary skills for handling external inputs and runtime errors and offering reliable deployment opportunities for running C applications with multiple processes or threads.

Next, in Chapters 8 and 9, you will explore the power of C socket programming and important system calls to implement TCP/UDP network applications. You will start with a quick introduction of the TCP/IP stack and applications. Specifically, you will learn flexible and error-free ways for handling socket buffers, packets, and fields accessed through C dynamic memory, strings, and pointers concepts. Moreover, we will also discuss essential programming ways (blocking and non-blocking), essential socket options for handling network server/client applications, runtime errors, and performance issues.

Finally, in Chapter 10, you will learn Linux namespaces and their role in virtualization. Specifically, you will learn C programming ways and system calls for handling Linux namespaces and control groups. You will be experimenting with important Linux namespaces such as process, memory, and networking to learn how the popular lightweight virtualization solutions are working. This chapter will help you to explore the importance of virtualization in cloud environments.

CHAPTER 1

Basic Computer System Architecture and Essential Operating System Concepts

Learning about computer system architecture is essential for software developers to implement performance meeting optimized code for system software or applications. Mainly, insights into the underlying system architecture, its components (CPU, memory, cache, registers, I/O devices, system buses), and their interconnections are helpful to tune the application performance metrics such as throughput, latency, reliability, scalability, and security. For instance, knowing details of computer memory hierarchy and organization helps developers to implement suitable codes for minimizing memory access latencies and utilizing the memory optimally. Similarly, learning about the processor architecture in terms of the number of cores and their interconnection helps in writing suitable computational load distribution codes for maximizing CPU core utilization and minimizing communication latencies.

On the other hand, an important system software called operating system (OS) runs over a computer system for simplifying its usage by end users and managing the system's computational, memory, and input/output (IO) resources. OS helps software developers to a greater extent for developing applications and software-specific development tasks without worrying about the underlying system architecture. However, developers must know OS powers, responsibilities, and how to interact with the OS to develop secure and performance-optimized code. For instance, ignoring how the OS is handling a program execution and managing its system memory can lead to access violations and security loopholes in software. In this book, we use Linux OS as a platform for practicing C programming. We discuss necessary Linux OS concepts to help developers to perform their programming activities.

In addition to computer system architecture and OS, system developers must know how to utilize the system software tools such as compilers, debuggers, loaders, and linkers to simplify the software development, debugging, and deployment activities. In this chapter, we discuss the following topics to help C programmers learn and develop C applications and handle performance issues:

- Introduction to basic computer system architecture
- Operating system responsibilities
- Importance of compiler, linker, and loader
- Runtime environment of a process
- C Programmer powers and responsibilities

Basic Computer System Architecture

The heart of any computer system is its central processing unit (CPU). It is interconnected with other important components to process software application inputs, perform computations, and store results.

CHAPTER 1 BASIC COMPUTER SYSTEM ARCHITECTURE AND ESSENTIAL OPERATING SYSTEM CONCEPTS

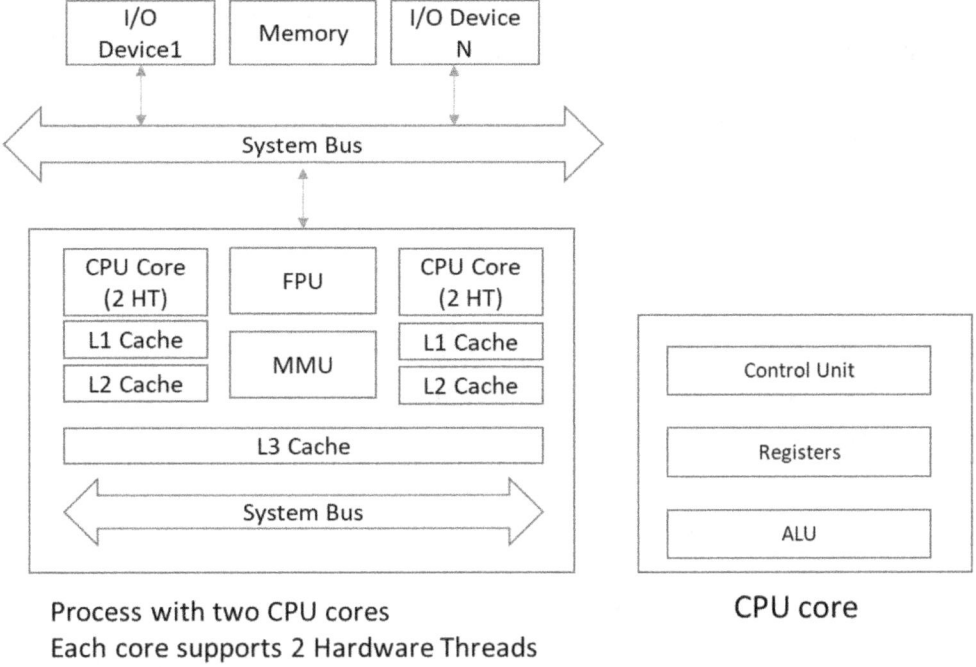

Figure 1-1. Today's general CPU architecture and its internal components

Let's inspect the details of today's standard CPU architecture. From Figure 1-1, check the major components of a CPU architecture.

CPU Architecture

Today's CPU has the following important components:

- Multiple CPU cores with internal caches (L1, L2, and L3)
- Floating point unit (FPU)
- Memory management unit (MMU)
- System buses for interconnecting memory and input/output (IO) devices

Let's check these internal component details for better programming.

The CPU Cores: Today's CPU is equipped with multiple CPU cores (refer to Figure 1-1), and each CPU core can support multiple hardware threads to improve the system processing power in terms of performing the parallel tasks. Most of the modern CPUs, such as Intel's CPU support two hardware-level threads per core through hyperthreading technologies, and high-end or graphics processing units (GPUs) support more than two threads per core, depending on their design and capabilities. Each CPU core is designed to execute the instructions independently from other CPU cores. Moreover, the OS offers multithreading features to use these multiple CPU cores for parallel programming.

Next, another important component of CPU architecture is the floating point unit (FPU). It is useful to perform floating point number calculations. The CPU usually performs integer number calculations using ALU and offloads floating point number calculations to the FPU. Hence, the CPU performance can be improved.

Next, let's discuss internal components of the CPU core (refer to the RHS part of Figure 1-1). The CPU core consists of the following components:

- Controller
- Register
- Arithmetic and logic unit (ALU)

The controller of the CPU core executes an instruction by following the below steps using its internal functional units (for simplicity of the architecture diagram, these units are not included in Figure 1-1):

1. Instruction fetch operation
2. Instruction decode operation
3. Execute
4. Memory access for storing or reading data or instructions
5. Registers access for storing or reading data

Besides hardware-level threads of CPU cores, these internal functional units play an important role in improving the system performance by using instruction pipelining techniques for parallel execution of these steps for independent instructions.

In order to improve the system performance, we must understand the CPU performance affecting bottleneck issues. The CPU carries out instruction execution steps in multiple CPU cycles. As we know, a CPU operates at a specific clock rate, such as 2 GHz, 3 GHz, etc. It means the CPU consumes one or more time cycles of the clock (called CPU cycles) to execute an instruction. For example, a 3 GHz CPU performs 3 billion clock cycles per second. To improve the system performance, it is necessary to utilize CPU clock cycles optimally for executing program instructions. Usually, instructions that require only register access take fewer clock cycles. On the other hand, instructions that require memory access for fetching data take more clock cycles due to memory access latencies.

Next, let's check memory hierarchy and its role in reducing memory access latencies.

Memory Hierarchy

Since memory access is the major bottleneck for instruction execution, CPU cores are equipped with high-speed memories such as cache memories (L1, L2, and L3 caches) to match CPU operating clock cycles. In summary, the impact of the memory access latency depends on the type of memory access that is needed by your program. Usually a system is equipped with the following memory hierarchy, as shown in Figure 1-2:

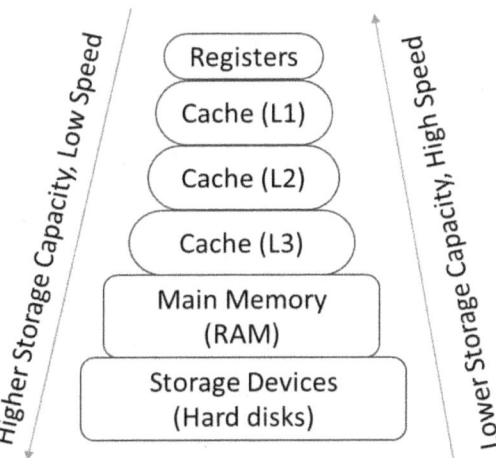

Figure 1-2. *Memory hierarchy containing a variety of memories (top memories are high speed with low storage capacity; bottom memories are low speed with high storage capacity)*

The control unit (CU) of the CPU plays an important role in executing instructions. The CU fetches and decodes an instruction, and integer instructions are executed by the ALU, and floating point instructions are offloaded to the FPU. To perform integer or floating point numbers operations by ALU or FPU, the input data must be placed in CPU core internal registers (high-speed memory and low latency). If input data is readily available in the internal registers, then instruction execution takes fewer CPU cycles. If input data needs to be fetched from the main memory (RAM), then it takes more CPU cycles. Hence, to reduce the latency of instruction execution, CPU cores are connected with internal cache memories such as L1 instruction and L1 data caches. Usually, L1 caches are built to match the speed of CPU clock cycles. Caches help frequently accessed instructions and data to be stored in cache entries, which can be directly accessed by the CPU core.

CPU cores can be equipped with three levels (L1, L2, and L3) of caches to minimize memory access latencies. Usually L1 cache size is smaller (a few KBs) and takes a few CPU clock cycles (<5), and L2 cache size is bigger (hundreds of KBs) and takes more clock cycles (>10). Every cache is accessed at a specific line size, which is a unit of bytes that are stored and retrieved. For instance, the x86 processors cache line size is 64 bytes. Programmers should consider the sizes of caches and line sizes before implementing code to optimally access arrays, frequently accessed instructions, and data of the program. Cache coherency is another important aspect that must be considered for cache access over multiple CPU cores. When one CPU core modifies cache contents, all other CPU cores should be aware that their cached copy is now changed to ensure that CPUs are always accessing the correct state of memory. Cache coherence-related tasks must be handled by programmers carefully in case of parallel programming. Otherwise, it can lead to unnecessary flushing of cache contents.

In case data or instruction is not available in caches, the CPU must communicate with memory to fetch them. It results in higher memory access latencies for instruction execution. There are two important reasons for higher latencies: one is translating CPU-generated instruction or data address to the physical memory accessing address using MMU. Another important latency is accessing address or data buses (system buses) for accessing data from the physical memory. Hence, developers should know how to utilize registers and various caches optimally for minimizing memory access time.

In summary, the impact of the memory access latency depends on the type of memory access that is needed by your program. Next, let's check how memory and various peripherals are interconnected with the CPU.

CPU and IO Device Interactions

The CPU interacts with IO devices using a specific system bus known as the peripheral component interconnect (PCI) bus. It is a hardware interface that connects devices to a computer's motherboard. It's a high-speed bus that allows users to insert expansion cards like video cards, sound cards, and network cards. The CPU issues I/O instructions to control devices.

Moreover, IO devices usually have their own internal registers. Usually devices are managed through device driver software. On an OS these device drivers should be installed before using any IO devices. Nowadays most of the Linux OS comes with default device drivers for mouse, keyboard, audio and video, and network interface cards. Usually programmers can configure device drivers to issue commands for performing device-specific tasks. In general, developers can access devices using specific IO device addresses to read and write data into device registers: data-in register, data-out register, status register, and control register.

We can observe from CPU and IO devices interactions that accessing IO devices from a program, it is necessary to go through system buses and multiple layers such as device drivers and device controllers. Hence, it leads to higher latencies for device access. Developers must play an important role in minimizing IO device access latencies. We discuss it in later sections.

Inspect System Configurations on a Linux OS

We strongly recommend developers inspect their computer system before implementing their applications. It helps developers to know the system resources' capacities and limitations; hence, developers can focus on how to handle limited resources of a system, compatibility, and performance issues.

- **Performance Issues**: Based on underlying system bit processing capabilities, it is necessary to choose the right OS, compiler, and applications to be installed.
- Usually 64-bit computer systems can address larger memory than 32-bit systems; it helps developers to deploy 64-bit OS and large applications for performance improvements.
    - We can install Linux OS systems of 32-bit or 64-bit on a system with 64-bit processing capabilities. A 64-bit OS can handle more memory and is useful for running applications with high performance. On the other hand, 32-bit applications will be poor.
    - We can also choose suitable compilers for 32-bit or 64-bit architectures to generate suitable machine-level instructions.
    - 64-bit applications cannot run on 32-bit systems, and vice versa.
- Let's quickly check your system CPU architecture and its resource details using the following Linux commands:

CHAPTER 1   BASIC COMPUTER SYSTEM ARCHITECTURE AND ESSENTIAL OPERATING SYSTEM CONCEPTS

INSPECTING SYSTEM CONFIGURATION USING LINUX COMMANDS

1. First check your system hardware configuration and note down the following important details for better programming:

    a. Number of CPU cores

    b. Memory size

    c. Cache size

    d. Bit processing capabilities

2. First check your system hardware configuration using the following Linux command:

    ```
    #lscpu
    ```

    ```
    Architecture:              x86_64
    CPU op-mode(s):            32-bit, 64-bit
    Byte Order:                Little Endian
    Address sizes:             39 bits physical, 48 bits virtual
    CPU(s):                    12
    On-line CPU(s) list:       0-11
    Thread(s) per core:        2
    Core(s) per socket:        6
    ..
    Model name:                Intel(R) Core(TM) i7-8700 CPU @ 3.20GHz
    ..
    L1d cache:                 192 KiB
    L1i cache:                 192 KiB
    L2 cache:                  1.5 MiB
    L3 cache:                  12 MiB
    ```

    a. From the above system configuration, we can identify that it is a 64-bit machine, the byte order is little endian, and it has a total of 6 cores.

    b. Its operating speed is 3.20 GHz.

    c. It has three levels of caches (L1, L2, and L3). L1 cache is organized for instructions and data separately.

CHAPTER 1   BASIC COMPUTER SYSTEM ARCHITECTURE AND ESSENTIAL OPERATING SYSTEM CONCEPTS

3. Inspect main memory details using the following Linux command and observe the following details:

   a. Maximum RAM supported on your system.

   b. Address and data bus size.

   ```
   #sudo dmidecode -t memory
   Handle 0x0007, DMI type 16, 23 bytes
   Physical Memory Array
           Location: System Board Or Motherboard
           Use: System Memory
           Error Correction Type: None
           Maximum Capacity: 64 GB
           Error Information Handle: Not Provided
           Number Of Devices: 4

   Handle 0x004B, DMI type 17, 40 bytes
   Memory Device
   ..
           Total Width: 64 bits
           Data Width: 64 bits
           Size: 8192 MB
   ..
           Type: DDR4
           ..
   ```

   c. From the above system, memory configuration details, we should observe that the computer system sports a maximum of 64 GB, but it has only 8 GB RAM. Moreover, it supports 64-bit address and data bus interfaces for memory accessing from the CPU.

4. Inspect various IO devices and their connected system buses details using the following Linux commands. If a command is not available, then install it using `sudo apt install`:

   a. From the below command, you can observe the various IO devices connected to your system, such as the memory controller, RAM, storage disk (SATA), network interface card, video and audio device controllers, etc.

   ```
   #lspci
   00:00.0 Host bridge: Intel Corporation 8th Gen Core Processor Host Bridge/DRAM Registers (rev 07)
   ```

```
00:01.0 PCI bridge: Intel Corporation Xeon E3-1200 v5/E3-1500 v5/6th
Gen Core Processor PCIe Controller (x16) (rev 07)
```
00:02.0 VGA compatible controller: Intel Corporation UHD Graphics 630 (Desktop)

00:12.0 Signal processing controller: Intel Corporation Cannon Lake PCH Thermal Controller (rev 10)

..

00:14.2 RAM memory: Intel Corporation Cannon Lake PCH Shared SRAM (rev 10)

..

00:17.0 SATA controller: Intel Corporation Cannon Lake PCH SATA AHCI Controller (rev 10)

```
00:1f.0 ISA bridge: Intel Corporation Q370 Chipset LPC/eSPI
Controller (rev 10)
```
00:1f.3 Audio device: Intel Corporation Cannon Lake PCH cAVS (rev 10)

..

00:1f.6 Ethernet controller: Intel Corporation Ethernet Connection (7) I219-LM (rev 10)

b. For more details of a specific device, we can use the following command:

```
#lspci -s 00:14.2 -vvv
00:14.2 RAM memory: Intel Corporation Cannon Lake PCH Shared SRAM
(rev 10)
        Subsystem: Hewlett-Packard Company Cannon Lake PCH Shared SRAM
        Control: I/O- Mem+ BusMaster+ SpecCycle- MemWINV- VGASnoop-
        ParErr- Stepping- SERR+ FastB2B- DisINTx-
        Status: Cap+ 66MHz- UDF- FastB2B- ParErr- DEVSEL=fast >TAbort-
        <TAbort- <MAbort- >SERR- <PERR- INTx-
        Latency: 0
        Region 0: Memory at ec132000 (64-bit, non-prefetchable)
        [size=8K]
        Region 2: Memory at 4000106000 (64-bit, non-prefetchable)
        [size=4K]
        Capabilities: <access denied>
```

5. Check OS bit processing capabilities and observe that we are using a compatible OS (64-bit) over the underlying system (64-bit):

   ```
   #uname -m
   x86_64
   ```

6. Check compiler bit version and confirm it can produce compatible code for the underlying system using the following Linux command:

   ```
   #gcc -dumpmachine
   x86_64-linux-gnu
   ```

Well done! Using various Linux commands, we inspected necessary system resources configuration, OS details, and compiler bit (gcc) processing capabilities.

In summary, CPUs and operating systems can support multiple bit sizes (32-bit or 64-bit) and can run applications compiled for suitable bit sizes. However, if your application has been compiled for the smaller bit size, then it may be executed successfully, but its performance will be poor.

Operating System Responsibilities

An operating system (OS) is necessary system software to be installed over a computer system. The OS acts as the brain of the computer system. The OS handles all tasks related to users accessing the system and executing various programs and manages and controls the system hardware resources. In this book, we use Linux OS for all C programming activities. Hence, we discuss all the concepts relevant to Linux OS.

OS mainly offers the following important services to simplify a system's usage by users:

User Interface (UI): It is the primary motivation for users to install the OS. Because UI simplifies the system access by hiding the complexities of the hardware. Most of the OS offer both command line and graphical user interfaces.

User Programs Execution Services: As part of simplification of the system access, it is necessary to free the end user from preparing the program execution steps over the system hardware (CPU, memory). Even at a high level, a program execution over the system hardware involves many complex activities, such as handling multiple program executions simultaneously. Allocating required computational and memory resources safely and optimally managing all system common resources (CPU, memory, I/O) access across the multiple programs. Besides, OS also handles successful termination of program execution tasks, deallocating resources after a program is terminated or aborted and handling various errors during program execution. The OS handles all these tasks on behalf of the users.

I/O Devices Accessing Services: Usually, a system is connected with many external hardware devices (peripherals) to simplify its access as well as utilize it in various interesting use cases. For instance, we use keyboards, mouse, network interface cards, storage devices, etc. The OS manages these external devices through device controllers and simplifies access to end users.

File management: OS offers the file concept as an important abstraction for accessing both system software and hardware resources. For users to access a computer system and execute various tasks, many system files (process files, memory files, device files, storage files) are needed. To simplify accessing these files, OS offers services related to creating, deleting, searching, and updating files.

Processes Communication: OS offers coordination and communication approaches for simplifying multiple programs to accomplish various tasks in a cooperative manner. Specifically, OS offers services for system-level process communication and network-level process communication where systems are connected to the Internet.

OS offers multiple user access services: OS offers creating user accounts, assigning permission, and configuring necessary security profiles.

Computational, Memory, and I/O Hardware Resources Management: OS offers services for sharing the underlying system CPU (cores), physical memory, caches, and I/O devices across multiple programs and multiple users in a safe and efficient manner.

In summary, OS does the following major management activities:

- Process management
- Memory management
- File management
- Device management
- Network management
- Security and protection

Next, let's learn OS services in detail for understanding how to use OS services from a user program.

Users Program Access to OS Services

Software developers must know what the major responsibilities and services of an OS are and how programmers can interact with OS services to interact with system resources for developing applications and ensuring their performance metrics, such as throughput, latency, scalability, reliability, and security.

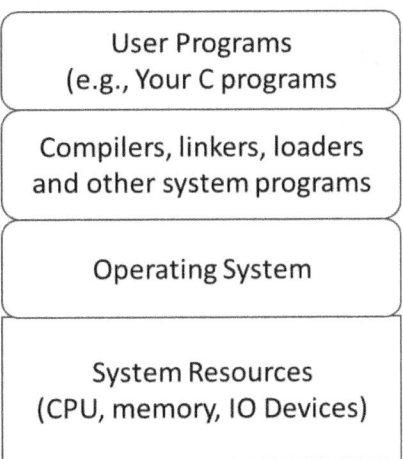

Figure 1-3. *User programs and how they interact with a computer system's resources*

In order to develop any program and execute it over a system, developers must install necessary programming development and deployment tools such as editors, compilers, loaders, linkers, debuggers, and other necessary system programs over the OS (shown in Figure 1-3). Specifically, compilers, loaders, and linkers help developers to create an executable file and load it into system memory for execution.

Then, during a program execution, it can request OS services for computing, memory, IO device resource allocations, and its process and resource management in a protected and secured manner. On the Linux OS, user processes (a program in execution state) access OS services through system calls. A user program and its interaction with Linux OS services are shown in Figure 1-4.

CHAPTER 1 BASIC COMPUTER SYSTEM ARCHITECTURE AND ESSENTIAL OPERATING SYSTEM CONCEPTS

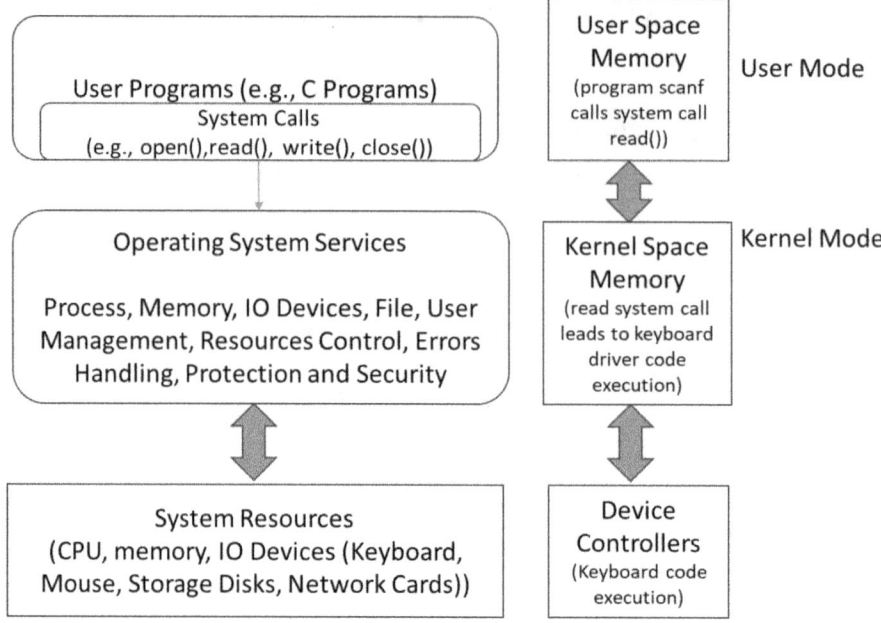

Figure 1-4. *User space, kernel space, and system calls*

From Figure 1-4, we should understand the following details about a user process execution on Linux OS:

- A user process runs in user mode. It means a user executable file is loaded into the user space memory partition of the main memory. On Linux OS to protect the user process from other processes, resource usage control, and securing the OS services from user processes, main memory is divided into two important spaces called user space and kernel space. A user process loads into user space only, but when it needs system resources access or OS service, it must access kernel space. This step is controlled through system calls of the OS.

- In order to access any OS services such as resources, processes, memory, IO devices, files, and network devices, a user process must invoke the respective system calls. All the OS services are loaded only in the kernel space of the main memory. Hence, the process execution mode changes to kernel mode.

- In case of IO devices' access, OS offers another abstraction layer called device drivers. Developers can program IO devices through device driver programming, which means loading necessary input data and commands into devices' specific control registers. Moreover, device drivers can only communicate with specific device controllers. Hence, it provides an additional layer of protection to devices from user programs.

In summary, Linux OS offers the following major services through system calls for accessing them by user programs:

- OS offers the system calls for user programs for performing the following process management operations: processes creating, terminating, aborting, loading, executing, waiting for children processes, and accessing process attributes.

- OS offers the system calls for user programs for performing the following memory management operations: allocation, initialization, and deallocation.

- OS offers the system calls for user programs for performing the following file operations: create, delete, open, close, read, write, file pointer update, and accessing file attributes.

- OS offers the system calls for user programs for performing the following IO device management operations: requesting a device access, releasing a device, reading, writing, attaching or detaching devices, maintaining device information, and accessing device attributes.

- OS offers the system calls for user programs for network programming: host protocol address configuration, host name access, creating network sockets, closing sockets, reading, writing, polling, and non-blocking operations.

- OS offers the system calls for user programs for accessing shared memory for interprocess communication: creating shared memory, attaching, detaching, reading, and writing operations.

- OS offers the system calls for user programs for the following process protection-related tasks: accessing process permissions and allowing or denying user processes access.

- OS offers the system calls for user programs for accessing system date and time.

Among the aforementioned major listed activities of OS, every developer must know the process and related memory, IO devices, and file management activities in detail to handle most of the system applications development activities.

OS Process Management Activities and Services

Users want to run multiple programs on their systems to maximize the system resource utilization. To meet this specific requirement, the OS handles multiple program executions in terms of the management of multiple processes over the system resources such as CPU, memory, devices, etc.

OS defines a program execution activity as creating a process to load the program parts (instructions and data) into the main memory and instructing the CPU to execute the program instructions by allocating necessary resources such as I/O devices and memory. Besides, OS monitors multiple processes' execution states and status (running or terminated or aborted) and deallocates resources at the end of their programs' execution.

To prepare a process, the OS expects the executable program to be converted into machine-level language instructions and assigned with virtual addresses for each of the instructions, known as an executable and linking format (ELF) file. To convert a high-level language program (C, C++) into the ELF file, programmers use program development tools such as compilers, linkers, and loaders over the OS. The compiler converts a high-level language program into machine language instructions, and linker and loader tools help to assign virtual addresses in the ELF file. ELF includes important details such as code region, data region, stack region, and heap region with corresponding virtual addresses. Hence, the OS takes the ELF file and loads the ELF file into physical memory as four important process segments, as shown in Figure 1-5.

A process memory layout contains the following four segments: The code segment holds the program code and process activity-related registers, including the program counter and CPU registers. Data segments hold process global and static variables. Heap segments hold dynamically allocated memory blocks. Then, the stack segment holds function arguments, local variables, and return addresses.

CHAPTER 1　BASIC COMPUTER SYSTEM ARCHITECTURE AND ESSENTIAL OPERATING SYSTEM CONCEPTS

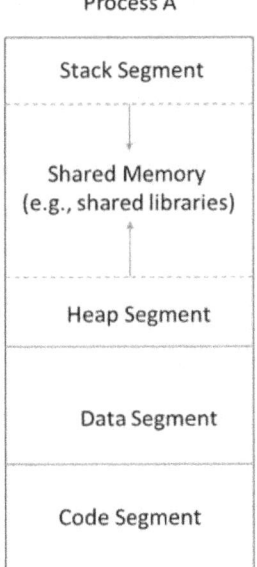

Figure 1-5. *A typical process memory layout*

In between the stack segment and the heap segment, there is a memory hole, which is used for holding shared libraries and allocating a shared memory for interprocess communication. Once a process is created and loaded into memory, the OS manages the process execution as follows.

OS Role in Processes Management

OS executes multiple programs that run them as multiple processes to maximize system resources (CPU, memory, and devices). The OS keeps track of readily available processes to run on a CPU by inserting them into a ready queue data structure. As part of the OS, it always runs scheduling algorithms to select a process from the ready queue to maximize the system throughput and minimize the execution time latencies.

It means to execute a program; the OS creates a process describing the structure and prepares the process for execution by allocating a unique process identifier (PID), virtual memory, files, and devices and maintains details of its parent and the child processes, state (running, waiting, terminated), and scheduling information.

As OS needs to allocate multiple processes over system resources, OS uses scheduling algorithms to interleave multiple processes' execution over available CPUs. Since a process can be interrupted before completion of the execution, the OS saves the process state in the process control block.

CHAPTER 1 BASIC COMPUTER SYSTEM ARCHITECTURE AND ESSENTIAL OPERATING SYSTEM CONCEPTS

Usually, after allocating a process with virtual memory, the Process Control Block (PCB) is inserted into the ready queue of the CPU core. The scheduler based on the scheduling policy selects the process and executes it over the CPU core.

While executing a process over a CPU core, besides memory, scheduling information, and any files or devices allocated, the process-specific registers such as the program counter, stack pointer, and state will be updated and maintained in the process PCB. During execution, a process can be in any of the following states, as shown in Figure 1-6:

- **New**: The process is being created and loaded into main memory.

- **Running**: CPU selects a ready process from its ready queue to execute its instruction. A process is in a running state, if the process instructions are executed by the CPU.

- **Waiting**: A process is in a waiting state. For example, a process requested an IO device access; until the specific operation is completed, the process will be in a waiting state.

  - Developers must play an important role in minimizing these latencies.

- **Ready**: After the process completes its waiting, it can be moved to the CPU ready queue for execution.

- **Terminated**: Once process execution is completed or aborted due to any errors, the process moves to the termination state.

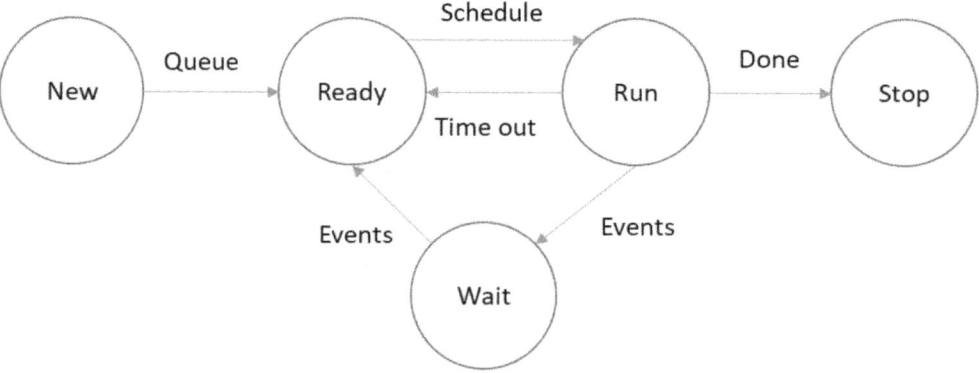

Figure 1-6. *A process state diagram*

CHAPTER 1　BASIC COMPUTER SYSTEM ARCHITECTURE AND ESSENTIAL OPERATING SYSTEM CONCEPTS

A typical OS scheduler selects a process among available processes from the ready queue to execute it on a CPU core. Schedulers usually run a process for a specific time slice (duration) and shift to another ready process to minimize process execution latency. During the shifting from one process to another process, the OS stores the current process information and retrieves ready process information (PCB) to execute over the CPU core. A PCB maintains the following details (refer to Figure 1-7):

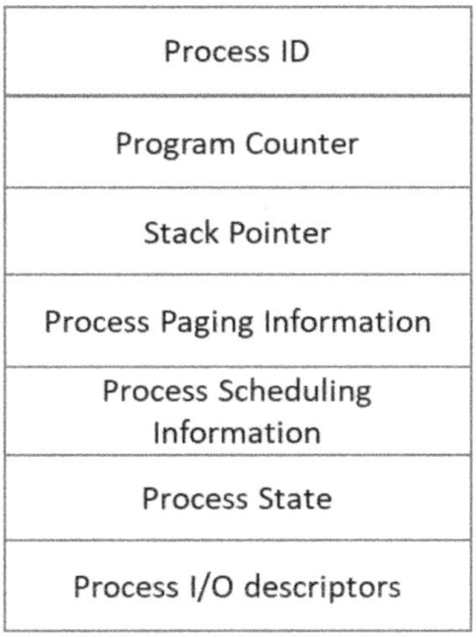

Process ID
Program Counter
Stack Pointer
Process Paging Information
Process Scheduling Information
Process State
Process I/O descriptors

Figure 1-7. *A process state diagram*

Process current state (ready, running, waiting, etc.), address of next instruction to execute, CPU registers, scheduling information priorities, memory allocated to the process, I/O devices allocated to the process, list of open files, and accounting information such as CPU utilization.

Saving and retrieving PCBs by CPU during scheduling of processes is known as context switching delay, which occurs during multiple processes execution. It is one of the important cost systems engineers want to minimize while designing new scheduler algorithms. Next, we will learn which services are offered by OS to programmers for managing user-created processes.

OS Offering Services for User Programs

The Linux OS offers the following important system calls for process management through user programs:

- **Process Creation**: fork() and vfork() system calls allow developers to create their own process and assign suitable tasks for implementing applications.

- **Process Termination**: The exit() system call allows developers to stop a process execution.

- **A New Process Loading into Memory**: The exec() system call allows developers to load a new process into memory for execution.

- **Waiting for Other Processes (Child Processes)**: The wait() system call allows developers to implement process dependencies to implement applications.

- **Aborting**: The abort() system call for stopping or killing a process.

- **Interprocess Communication (IPC)**: shared memory, message queue, pipe, FIFO, semaphore, mutex, etc., related system calls allow developers to implement coordination, communication, and synchronization of tasks among multiple processes in an application.

The OS is responsible for the following activities in connection with its created processes management:

- Creating and deleting both user and system processes, suspending and resuming processes.

- OS keeps track of a process CPU utilization in terms of scheduling information.

- Allocates necessary devices by assigning device descriptors and controls their access through device driver controllers. Hence, the Linux kernel loads and runs necessary device drivers.

- OS maintains the status of a process to dynamically allocate and deallocate resources based on the process running status.

- OS handles system-created process synchronizations, interprocess communication, and deadlock situations.

Next, let's know how the OS helps processes in terms of memory management activities.

OS Role in Memory Management

From a process memory layout, we can understand that to execute a process, all its process segments (code, data, heap, and stack) must be in memory. However, having limited memory, it is not possible to keep entire segments of all processes in main memory.

OS implements a virtual memory management approach to bring necessary parts of a process into a memory frame before its execution. This process is implemented by process segmentation and paging techniques with page replacement algorithms. OS divides a process into segments, and segments are further divided into pages to load into memory on demand. OS divides memory into pages. OS manages multiple processes execution in limited memory by process-level segmentation and page tables. To keep track of which process is loaded into which part of main memory (frames).

In summary, OS memory management activities include the following:

- Dynamically allocating and deallocating memory space for multiple processes through virtual memory management through segmentation and paging techniques.

- Physical memory frames are optimally managed through page replacement algorithms. If a process cannot be placed in memory, the OS uses swapping techniques to move other process pages to the storage device.

- OS is protecting a process memory layout from the other processes by doing the following:
  - A process memory is protected in terms of allocating unique virtual memory address spaces to each of the process segments (Code, Data, Heap, Stack).
  - Assigns and controls segment access by assigning read, write, and execute permissions.

The Linux OS offers the following important system calls for memory management through user programs:

- **Memory Allocation**: `malloc()`, `calloc()`, `alloc()`, `sbrk()`, etc.
- **Memory Deallocation**: `free()`

Next, let's know how the OS helps processes in terms of IO devices, files, and protection.

OS IO Devices, File Management, and Protection Services

OS offers a uniform view of storage disks. OS helps to manage data over storage disks using file concepts. File concepts abstract the underlying storage device structure and accessing complexities. Specifically for the Linux OS, any device access can be viewed in terms of file access. Hence, it abstracts device architectures and accessing methods. For example, in a C program using the same system calls such as open, read, and write, it is possible to manage data over storage disks and exchange messages over network systems.

OS will help the program by doing the following activities for storage devices and file access:

- Creating and deleting files and directories offers system calls to manipulate files and directories.
- Mounting and unmounting devices, and disk free-space management.
- Storage allocation, partitioning, disk scheduling, and protection.

In general, to manage various IO devices access, OS uses the IO management module for doing the following:

- Concurrent execution of CPUs and IO devices.
- Device driver installation in kernel space for controlling specific hardware devices and device-driver accessing interfaces.
- One or more CPUs and device controllers connect through a common bus for providing access to shared memory. Each device controller is in charge of a particular device type.

- Handles CPU moves data from/to main memory to/from devices' local buffers.

- Handles various device controller-generated interrupts to offer reliable services.

OS offers the following protection services to user processes:

- Linux OS assigns unique user identities (user IDs, security IDs) per user. This user ID is assigned to all his files and processes for implementing access control rules by assigning read, write, and execute permissions.

- Linux OS offers group identifiers (group ID) to implement access control rules among a group of users and their resources, such as files and processes.

- Linux OS also offers effective user ID for escalating user privileges to other users for temporarily assigning necessary access rights to complete a task. Later, developers must revoke the effective user ID and permissions.

- Linux OS also allows users to configure application-level profiles and secure computations using Linux security modules: AppArmors and Seccomp.

Next, let's learn important application development, deployment, and debugging-related system tools for developers.

Importance of Compiler, Linker, and Loader

Learning about system architecture makes developers choose the right system resources, their configuration, and optimal resource utilization-related access codes. Moreover, an OS over the system, such as Linux, abstracts the complexity of the underlying system by simplifying the system use through the OS services in terms of GUI, resource management, and offering a reliable and secure execution environment for developing, deploying, and testing developers' applications. Developers use important system programs and tools to implement a variety of system applications and software. In this section, we will discuss the role and importance of rightly using a compiler, linker, and loader in process execution for handling performance, security, and reliability issues.

CHAPTER 1 BASIC COMPUTER SYSTEM ARCHITECTURE AND ESSENTIAL OPERATING SYSTEM CONCEPTS

Compiler

A compiler is the most important tool for developers to carry out their applications' deployment, testing, debugging, and performance handling. The primary role of a compiler is to convert high-level programs (C code) into machine-dependent code (assembly code). Hence, developers must use a suitable compiler for translating their high-level program codes (C, C++, Java) into machine-dependent codes. In this book, we use open-source gcc tools as a C programming compilation toolset for deployment and testing activities. Hence, we discuss major roles and powers of gcc for C developers.

Major roles of a compiler:

- The compiler takes high-level code and converts it into machine-dependent instructions. It means developers must select and install a suitable compiler to prepare their application's executable code over a runtime environment.
  - For example: It is necessary to choose 64-bit or 32-bit machine codes during compilation before deployment of the actual application executable.
- During translation of high-level language codes into machine-dependent code, compilers generate code flow graphs. These code flow graphs are used by the compiler to optimize the code size and execution time. The compiler plays an important role in code optimization in terms of the following dimensions:
  - Reducing the executable code size by eliminating unnecessary expressions, variables, unused variables, functions, and loop optimizations.
  - Reducing execution time of code in terms of loop optimizations such as loop unrolling, tiling, combining, functions optimization, inline functions, etc.
  - The compiler plays an important role in pipelining of instructions execution and parallelizing the instruction execution.

- The compiler plays an important role in improving the reliability and offering runtime error handling capabilities:
  - To warn developers about possible runtime errors before deployment, such as data type range overflows, array index out of bounds, memory address checks, etc.
  - Generate necessary additional code to deal with runtime errors as part of debugging details.
- The compiler plays an important role in improving the security of the code:
  - To disable unnecessary features
  - Enabling necessary security checks
  - Enabling address virtual address randomization features
  - Enabling usage of secured package codes
- The compiler plays an important role in deployment activities such as handling runtime code inspection and errors using debugging information.

Next, let's check a quick overview of important options available with compilers for developers' ready-made usage:

Compiler Options for Application Performance Tuning

In this book, we use open-source gcc tools as a compilation toolset for deployment and testing activities. We discuss gcc compilation options available for applications' code optimization, reducing size, and performance tuning. gcc tools support the following important optimization levels (https://gcc.gnu.org/onlinedocs/gcc/Optimize-Options.html):

- gcc -O0: Developers use this option to debug code easily.
- gcc -Os: Developers use this option to minimize runtime assembly code size.
- gcc -O1: Developers use this option to do basic code optimization tasks such as optimizing execution of common local and global subexpressions and loop invariant expressions.

- `gcc -02`: Developers use this option to perform -O1 code optimizations and do the basic loop optimizations, such as loop unrolling, expanding inline functions, and assembly-level instructions, reordering for improving instruction-level parallelism.

- `gcc -03`: Developers use this option to perform -O2 code optimizations and do the aggressive loop optimization, parallelization of loop iterations, and reordering of assembly instructions aggressively to improve parallelization of code execution.

  - This optimization level is mainly used for improving code performance in terms of reducing execution time; however, it may increase code size and compilation time.

Next, let's check a quick overview of important options available with compilers for handling application code reliability and security:

Compiler Options to Protect Application Code

As part of any application runtime memory layout, the stack segment plays an important role in protecting and securing it from other codes as well as not performing any invalid operations by the application itself. During the compilation process while generating virtual addresses for each segment of a process, `gcc` offers important options to protect and secure a process's runtime memory layout from other processes' memory. Hence, developers must know how to protect their application using compiler options. We discuss these options in terms of application security and reliability options:

- **Stack Protection**: In process layout, runtime stack is the key segment attackers will explore to induce attacks and malicious codes. Since stack size grows dynamically during the program execution, by default `gcc` offers stack crash detection. However, attackers can disable stack protection by compiling the code with the following option: fno-stack-protector. Then, attackers can create buffer overflow attacks and induce their malicious codes for attacking target systems. Hence, as a developer, we must do the following check and compilation options for detecting security loopholes and protecting your code:

CHAPTER 1 BASIC COMPUTER SYSTEM ARCHITECTURE AND ESSENTIAL OPERATING SYSTEM CONCEPTS

- gcc -fstack-protector-strong: This option enables all functions of the compiled code to be included with stack crash detection checks.

- **Using Protected Source Code of Library Functions**: gcc default will not enable using protected source code of library functions. For example, string library functions like strcpy, memcpy, and the standard printf, scanf, and vprintf could lead to crashing of the stacks due to buffer overflows. To enable using protected source codes of library functions in your code, use the following gcc options:

  - gcc -O -D_FORTIFY_SOURCE=2: This option enables use of protected source codes of standard library functions.

Next you will know the following important compilation options to improve the reliability of your code:

- -fsanitize = undefined: Enabling this option allows you to identify the following critical errors in terms of checking arithmetic and shift operations-related errors, data types range checking, range overflow-related errors, and pointers access-related errors.

  - This option will not be enabled by default with gcc. Hence, if you compile your code without this option, it can lead to crashing the system due to invalid arithmetic or shift operations, accessing arrays beyond their sizes, and invalid pointer accesses such as dereferencing NULL pointers.

- -fsanitize = address: This is another important gcc option to check valid dynamic memory allocation usage and runtime stack accesses. Enabling this option allows you to identify the following critical errors, such as runtime stack crashes, accessing invalid pointers, and avoiding invalid dynamic memory access-related operations such as out-of-bounds access, use after free, and double free.

  - This option will not be enabled by default with gcc. Hence, if you don't compile your code without this option, it can lead to program crashes during the deployment environment.

- **-fanalyzer:** This option is available with the gcc-10 version onwards. Unlike the above options, this option allows you to check the potential errors during the compilation stage only. It is very helpful to do static analysis of the code and helps in identifying the following errors during the compilation stage only:

  - Helps in detecting file and memory leaks, possible NULL pointer arguments, dereferencing, possible invalid array indices, double file close, and double memory free operations.

Please note that new versions of compilers (gcc) may provide new warnings. Hence, before using any gcc version, please check its options usage. Next you will know the following important compilation options to improve the reliability of your code:

Compiler Options to Handle Runtime Errors

It is necessary to handle runtime errors of an application during the deployment stage to deal with crashes and confirm suitable runtime environments for application deployment. To handle runtime errors of any application, it is necessary to include debugging-related code before deploying the application. It needs the application to be compiled using debugging options (gcc -g) enabled. Then, developers can do the following activities using gdb:

- Inspect the source code during execution of code for identifying and keeping debugging points at specific lines of code and functions.
- Inspect individual lines of execution using the following commands
- During debugging it is necessary to set specific variables to inspect the code execution and print result variables, data type variables, and pointer variables and watch specific variables' value changes in expressions.
- Inspecting runtime stack, registers, libraries, and assembly code:

After compilation of the application, the next important stage is creating an executable image by linking with necessary library functions. Let's check the important linking and loading options for developers to handle application performance and security issues.

Linking and Loading Options

To support modularity in software development, the individual compiled object files can be linked together using static or dynamic linking approaches for creating a complete executable file. Static linking resolves all symbol addresses at compile time; hence, code size increases but helps in improving execution time. Dynamic linking reduces code size by dynamically loading needed modules at runtime (execution) only. Hence, dynamic linking can reduce the speed of program execution. During compilation time, developers can select static or dynamic linking options based on the requirements.

On Unix or Linux OS platforms, a compiled and linked file to be executed is known as an executable and linking format (ELF) file (refer to Figure 1-8). It is also known as extensible linking format (ELF). During a program execution, the corresponding ELF file will be loaded into physical memory by the loader tool. As we observe, dynamic linking allows few modules to be loaded at runtime and linked with a code for execution; this procedure is beneficial to run the code in a limited memory environment. On the other hand, it needs options for loading external modules into a program runtime environment. In these specific steps, attackers are exploring introducing malicious codes as external modules and exploiting the original code.

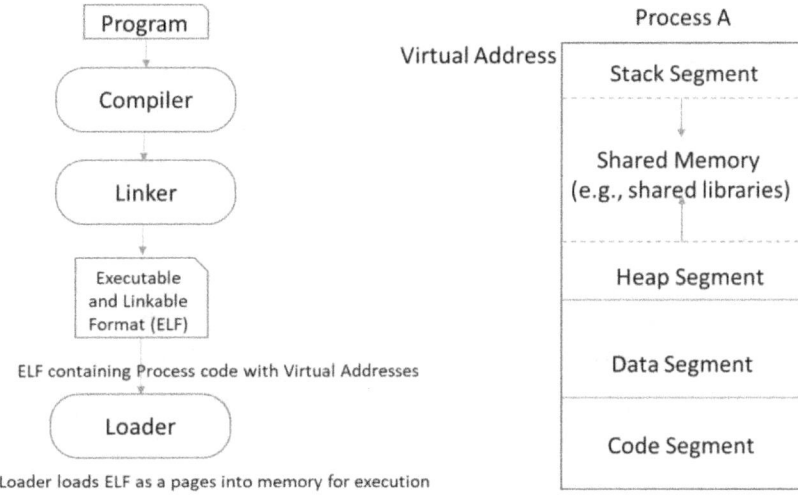

Figure 1-8. *The compiler, linker, and loader's role in process memory layout*

Hence, developers must be responsible for checking the runtime environment and defining the suitable configuration for program execution. Let's discuss the important linking options available for developers:

1. **Static Linking**: Developers can choose this option to load and link all necessary object files for creating a final executable file (ELF) during the compilation time.

   - Static linking helps an ELF to run faster by avoiding linking time cost during the runtime, because all necessary functions' addresses are resolved at compilation time only.

   - Static linking leads to larger-sized ELF files compared to dynamically linkable ELF files.

   - Static linking helps to avoid compatibility issues in linking library functions. Developers decide and use the suitable version of the library before creating an ELF.

2. **Dynamic Linking**: Programmers use this option to reduce ELF storage size and support flexible ways to link the latest version or updated functions from libraries.

   - Dynamic linking leads to smaller-sized ELF files compared to statically created ELF files.

   - Dynamic linking supports shared libraries among multiple programs; it helps in optimally utilizing system memory.

   - Dynamic linking leads to increased execution time due to latency in linking necessary library functions during runtime.

Developers Must Know Linking Options to Handle Runtime Errors

These functions linking plays an important role in the storage size and runtime of an executable file. In the process of loading necessary object files to create a final executable file, there are the following two important options for linking object files.

1. **Process Memory Layout**: A process to be executed on a Linux platform is available in terms of ELF containing code, data, stack, and heap segments with virtual addresses. When a CPU executes a process file (ELF), to load necessary code and other segments, the OS translates the process virtual addresses to physical addresses of the main memory with the memory management

unit. Attackers can exploit this process to observe addresses of the shared libraries' code and other segments to link their malicious codes. Hence, it is necessary to randomize virtual addresses of a process.

2. **Stack Execution**: It is another important feature enabled by default with the gcc linking feature. Stack execution is not really needed by all codes. Usually, a stack stores only local variables and data that are not executable. Hence, the runtime stack segment should have only read and write permissions. But to support inner function definitions in C, a stack execution feature is introduced. Inner function definitions are helpful to easily enable encapsulation and data hiding features in C. However, inner function definitions are not necessary for all C code. To introduce malicious codes and security attacks, attackers use this stack execution feature in addition to virtual address randomization being disabled and stack crash checks being bypassed. We can disable stack execution features using specific gcc options.

Runtime Environment of a Process

In order to handle performance issues of a process, developers must know the following runtime environment details about the process.

- Process memory layout
- Process performance affecting runtime environment
- Process security breaches

Process Memory Layout

As we know, after successful compilation and linking of a program, the process should be loaded into main memory for execution. In Linux, the executable file is known as ELF and loaded into memory in terms of segments.

CHAPTER 1 BASIC COMPUTER SYSTEM ARCHITECTURE AND ESSENTIAL OPERATING SYSTEM CONCEPTS

```
#include<stdio.h>
#include<stdlib.h>
int g;
int processA(int arg1, int arg2)
{
    static int s;
    int local;
    int *p = malloc(sizeof(char)*100);

}
```

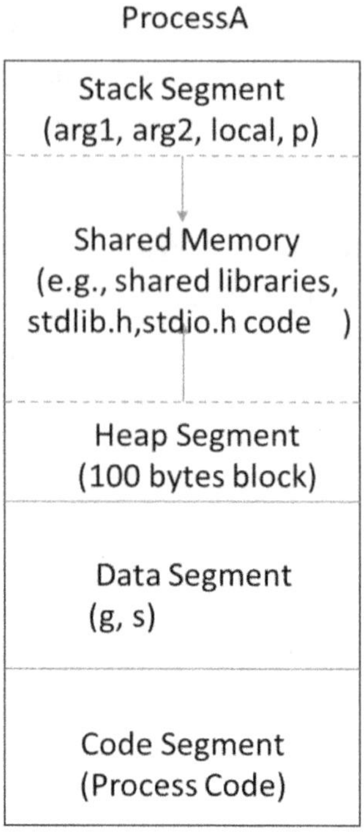

ProcessA

| Stack Segment (arg1, arg2, local, p) |
| Shared Memory (e.g., shared libraries, stdlib.h, stdio.h code) |
| Heap Segment (100 bytes block) |
| Data Segment (g, s) |
| Code Segment (Process Code) |

Figure 1-9. *Sample C program process memory layout*

A process is loaded into main memory in terms of the following segments:

- **Code Segment**: It contains code of the process. It is an executable segment.

- **Data Segment**: The data segment is reserved for storing data of global variables and static variables. It is allocated in memory, and the size of the data segment will not grow.

    - In our example, observe from Figure 1-9 that g and s are kept in the data segment.

- **Heap Segment**: The heap segment is reserved for storing dynamically growable data structures and memory blocks. For instance, in C programs, it is possible to allocate dynamically growable memory blocks using malloc(), calloc(), or realloc(). These dynamically allocated memory blocks are accessed in C programming using pointers. Pointers will be stored in the stack segment, but their pointing memory blocks will be stored in the heap segment to allow expansion or shrinking of the number of memory blocks.

- In our example program, observe from Figure 1-9 that the heap segment contains 100 bytes of memory block, which is allocated through the `malloc()`.

- **Stack Segment**: The stack segment is reserved for keeping function-specific stack frames. Usually, a function's stack frame stores its local variables, arguments, return address, and base address of the function. Stack segment size is dynamic. It grows when function calls are invoked and shrinks when the function execution is completed.

  - In our example program, observe from Figure 1-9 that the stack segment holds the `processA()` function stack frame with its local variables `local,p` and arguments (`arg1, arg2`).

From the process memory layout, developers should understand the following details:

- Every process is loaded into memory in terms of segments.

- Most importantly, stack and heap segments are dynamic in size during the execution of the process. It means developers should know what the maximum sizes allowed for a process are to avoid segment access violation and memory crashes. Developers should analyze their code and identify the following:

  - Specifically recursive functions and maximum recursive call depth

  - Dynamically growable data structures (trees, linked lists, etc.) and their maximum size

- It helps developers to test their applications thoroughly and confirm maximum memory requirements for processing application tasks.

- On the other hand, developers must observe that there is a gap in the stack segment and heap segment. This memory slot will be used by the OS to keep shared libraries of a process and allow other processes to share this specific memory area.

- Developers should know applications using shared libraries and their memory requirements.

- Developers should keep in mind that the OS is finding suitable memory segments to load a user process. Hence, developers should take responsibility in minimizing their overall application size.

Next, we will explore more details about the process execution environment to learn about process performance affecting factors with respect to system resource access.

Process Execution Environment

A process to be executed over a system after loading it with the help of a loader into memory, and its process control block will be stored in the CPU ready queue for the execution. Developers must play an important role in their application development code to enjoy maximum CPU resources for meeting its performance requirements in terms of maximizing throughput (number of instructions executed by CPU in a given unit of time) and minimizing memory access latency for processing application data. Usually an application during its execution can be in the following two important states:

- **Running**: Application instructions are actively executed by the CPU. It means developers should understand how to maximize this duration.

- **Waiting**: On the other hand, the application is waiting for the CPU to get its instruction to be executed. Developers should understand how to minimize the waiting time.

    - Application waiting time depends on the following actions:
    - Memory access
    - IO devices access

In order to improve the application performance, developers should keenly inspect the following details to maximize their application performance:

- **Hot Spots of the Application Code**: Which parts (instructions) of the code are executed heavily, and what application data are these parts accessing?

- **Application Data Accessing Paths**: During process execution, its data can be placed in multiple parts of the memory hierarchy (main memory, registers, cache) to improve accessing speed and reduce application waiting time.

- **Ordering Performance Affecting Parts of the Code**: Developers can change the order of instructions, loop iterations, and inner loops to improve the performance of the code.

- **Coordination with Other Processes or Applications**: In a large application development, it is inevitable to avoid interprocess communication. In this case, developers use OS services such as IPC constructs: shared memory, FIFO, message queues, semaphores, mutex, etc. Hence, developers must inspect and handle interprocess communication-related code to avoid shared data access race conditions, starvation, and deadlocks.

- **External Devices Access Such as Storage**: In many applications to handle large-sized data storage device (disk) access is necessary. In this case, developers must know how to minimize disk accessing delays and manage the main memory buffer to process large amounts of the data.

- **Network Access**: To develop distributed applications and client-server applications, it is necessary to architect the application over networked systems. In this case, network applications access TCP/IP stack services to communicate with other network applications. Hence, network application developers must know how to minimize network access delay to improve application throughput and minimize application accessing delay.

Process and Memory Access-Related Issues

From Figure 1-10, we should observe that a process to be executed must be fetched from the storage device (hard disk) to the main memory. This first point affects an application's performance significantly due to the operating speed mismatch between the CPU and storage devices. The OS handles it by using memory controllers such as DMA. Developers also should play an important role in this point by minimizing the application executable size in terms of segment size. Hence, the OS can find more opportunities to load process segments into main memory frames by converting virtual addresses into physical memory addresses. During this step the CPU interacts with a hardware unit known as the memory management unit (segmentation and paging unit) for translating virtual addresses to physical memory addresses. Here, applications having large segments can lead to the need for many physical frames. If the OS cannot find suitable physical frames in main memory, it needs to replace existing process pages from main memory to storage. It is known as a page replacement approach through the swapping process. The paging and swapping process could add a huge delay in executing an application. Hence, application size must be minimized.

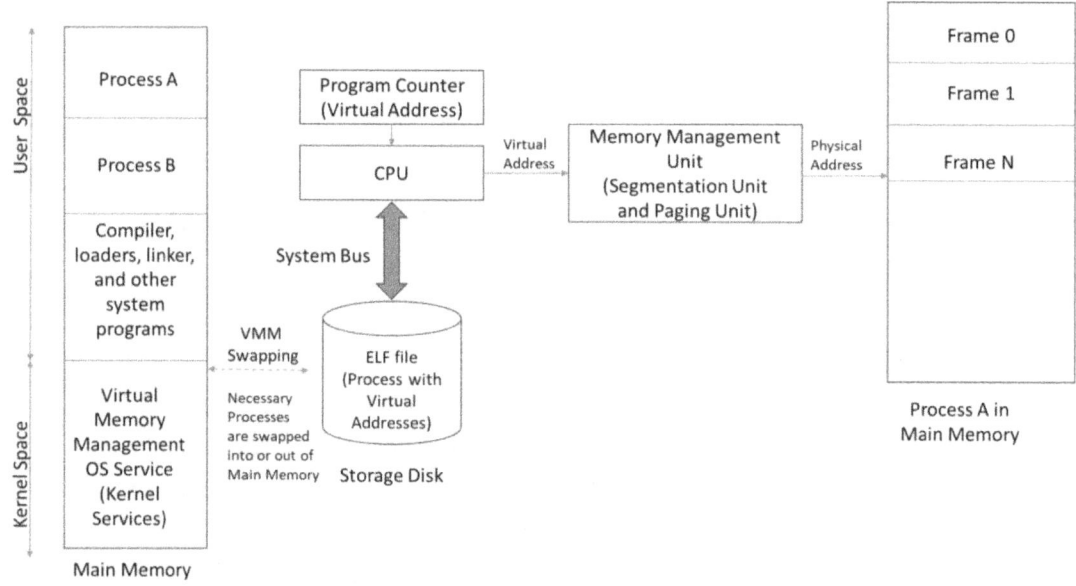

Figure 1-10. *A process runtime execution environment*

Once the OS loads essential pages of your application and it is being executed by the CPU, the following important details are what developers should know about how to maximize their CPU utilization for achieving maximum application throughput and minimizing memory access latencies. From the CPU architecture, we observe there are important CPU internal memories known as cache memories for improving data access speed by reducing physical memory access latency. In this particular aspect, developers should play an important role in organizing his application data in main memory and accessing the data from the memory. For example, a developer should do the following code-level checks in terms of improving application data access and the correct way of accessing memory locations:

- **Array Memory Layout**: Array elements are stored in row-major access or column-major access. In column-major layout, array elements of the columns are stored in contiguous locations in memory. In a row-major layout, array elements of the rows are stored in contiguous locations in memory.
  - Developers must write suitable loop iteration for array accessing code to match with row-major or column-major memory layout. Otherwise, a lot of unnecessary memory read and write access operations will be raised at the system level.
  - Improper accessing code leads to poor utilization of main memory.
  - Improper accessing code leads to poor utilization of CPU internal caches also.
- Know sizes of physical memory frame and CPU internal cache sizes for optimally utilizing the physical memory and cache memories. Otherwise, it could lead to unnecessary page faults, cache misses, poor memory utilization, and longer access delays.
  - For example, knowing a physical frame size helps developers to organize their application data storage in terms of page size and write suitable loops accessing code to minimize page faults.
  - Similarly, knowing internal cache sizes helps developers to organize their application's frequently accessible data storage and write suitable loops accessing code to minimize cache misses.
- Reorder the inner and outer loops of application code for minimizing intermediate data and results and optimally utilizing CPU internal caches.

CHAPTER 1   BASIC COMPUTER SYSTEM ARCHITECTURE AND ESSENTIAL OPERATING SYSTEM CONCEPTS

- Know memory byte organization for consistent access: There are two system-dependent ways of storing multibyte data in memory known as: big endian and little endian. In the case of big-endian memory organization, the most significant byte will be stored at the starting address. On the other hand, little-endian memory organization stores the least significant byte first.

  - Developers must know system memory byte organization to access application data. Specifically, in the case of network application, it could lead to misinterpretation of the data and result in serious bugs.

After knowing process memory access-related issues, developers must check for application-related IO device access requirements for handling its performance issues.

Process and IO Devices Access-Related Issues

In the case of developing large-sized data processing applications, smart applications, and network applications, it is necessary to use a variety of IO devices such as peripherals, disks, and network interface cards. Accessing IO devices leads to longer latencies compared to memory access due to additional layers of overhead in terms of device drivers and device controllers, as shown in Figure 1-11.

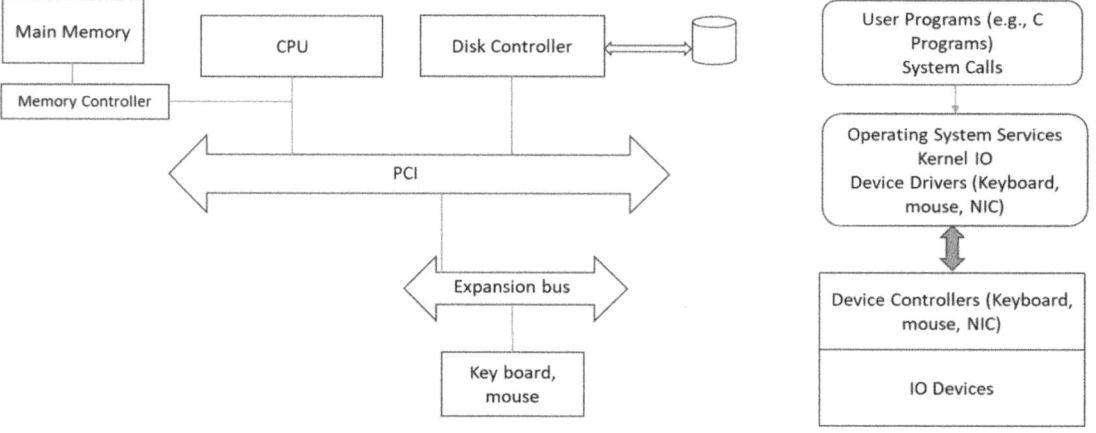

Figure 1-11. *A process and its devices access*

CHAPTER 1 BASIC COMPUTER SYSTEM ARCHITECTURE AND ESSENTIAL OPERATING SYSTEM CONCEPTS

Developers should carefully handle device access for performing application tasks to minimize latencies. Specifically, developers should handle the following tasks with care:

- In order to handle large-sized data, disk access is mandatory. Developers should play an important role in terms of storing and retrieving data over storage disks. Developers should implement suitable data structures to organize and access the application data.

    - Developers may choose to implement constant access time searching algorithms such as B+ tree and hashing.

    - External sorting algorithms such as sort and merge.

- It is also the responsibility of developers to manage main memory buffers for retrieval of disk blocks and accessing them to minimize disk access.

- In case of network application development, developers must handle application network access delay minimization tasks. Usually, network applications are implemented over the standard TCP/IP stack protocol stack using socket programming. Hence, developers must know details of a variety of network sockets to handle reliable data exchange, meeting throughput and latency requirements.

    - For instance, TCP sockets are helpful to guarantee reliable data exchange. However, TCP network applications suffer with additional overhead in terms of connection management, traffic flow control, and congestion control issues.

    - On the other hand, UDP sockets are helpful to handle application-level fine control over data in terms of when to send and what size of data needs to be exchanged. However, UDP network applications suffer from loss of packets and unreliable delivery.

- Moreover, network sockets can work in blocked or non-blocked mode during network application message exchange. Developers must configure a suitable message exchange mode to deal with latency in message exchange.

- Developers during message exchange between network applications must handle internal buffers to avoid intermixing of messages.

- Developers must handle byte ordering related code to handle big-endian and little-endian byte order issues.

• Developers must carefully design network application messages and structure to avoid unnecessary overhead in terms of processing and exchanging over a network of systems.

- Developers must design application message structure with all necessary fields, the order of packing fields, and the order of packing bits.

- Developers must minimize the number of messages to be exchanged between network applications to avoid latencies and offer quick responses.

After knowing how to handle application performance issues, developers must know how to handle common reliability and security issues for deploying an application.

Process Reliability and Security Issues

Developers must consider a multiprocess execution environment during any application development to deal with performance and security issues. As shown in Figure 1-12, there will be multiple processes residing in main memory during a process execution. Although OS offers a secured process execution environment and protection against other processes, developers must check and prevent invalid accesses during a process execution.

- Process memory layout-related access checkpoints
- Shared libraries access-related checkpoints
- Interprocess communication-related access checkpoints
- Network access-related checkpoints

Process Memory Layout-Related Access Checkpoints

From Figure 1-12, we should observe that multiple processes are residing in main system memory during their execution. Developers must write suitable code for executing their application in a reliable and secured manner in a shared environment. In this section, we highlight the developer's precise responsibilities in terms of writing reliable and secure code:

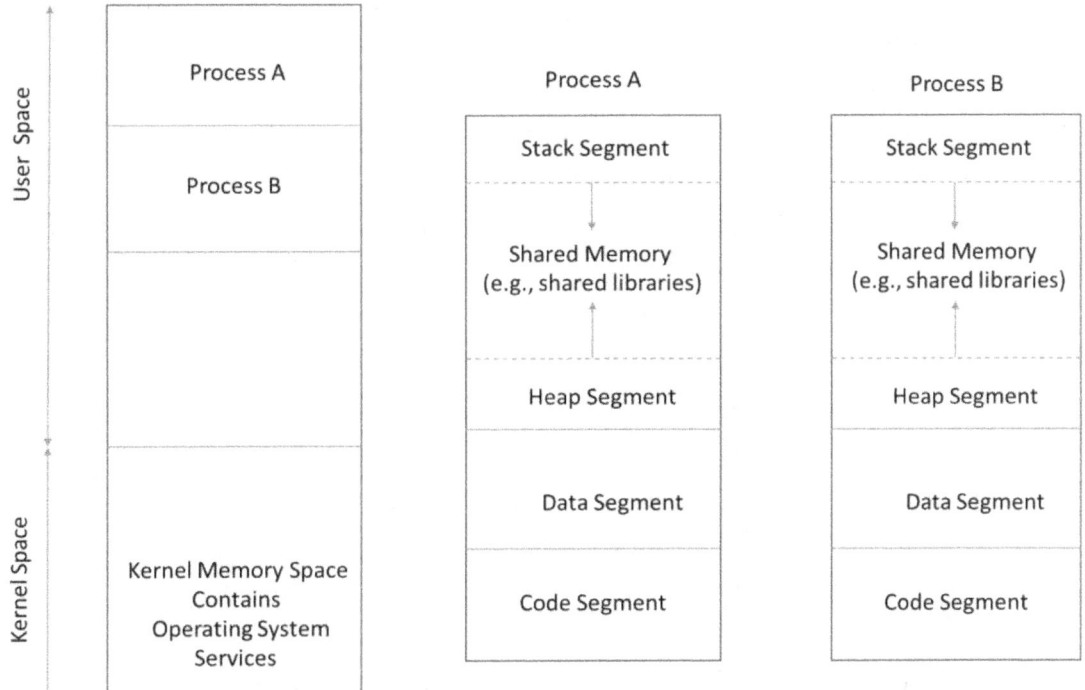

Figure 1-12. *Multiple processes are residing in the main memory layout*

- **Stack Segment-Related Access Checks**: The stack segment is one of the major memory segments developers should handle with utmost care during storing and accessing application data.
    - Never write long, deeper recursive calls in applications without checking stack segment size. Because it can lead to keeping many stack frames inside stack segments and may end up with no space in the stack segment and lead to a stack crash. These errors are not possible to find through compiler options.

- Don't store unnecessary data as local variables in functions to optimally utilize stack segments.

- Check the length of source and destination array values while copying into local arrays of a function. It can lead to buffer overflow problems. It is one of the widely used attack surfaces for malicious users. This problem can be checked with suitable gcc options by developers before deployment.

- Never return local variables' addresses from callee functions to caller functions. Because local variables of a function will be destroyed after the function execution ends, and it can lead to segment access violation.

- Check if the stack needs executable permission or not. By default it is enabled on most of the OS. If it is not required, then disable stack executable permission to avoid buffer overflow attacks. Otherwise malicious users can copy executable codes to stack segments.

- **Heap Segment-Related Access Checks**: Developers use heap segments for handling expandable memory blocks and data structures in their applications. Hence, developers should handle the heap segment carefully by writing suitable heap segment access-related errors:

  - Check in C programs whether pointers are pointing to valid memory blocks and prevent invalid memory reads and writes. Otherwise, it leads to access violations and increases security attack surfaces.

  - Allocate only necessary memory blocks and deallocate them after application-related tasks are completed.

  - Free the dynamically allocated memory blocks after usage carefully to avoid invalid pointer access and double freeing the pointers.

  - These memory accessing and pointer errors can be handled through compilation tools (gcc) and Valgrind tools.

- **Careful About Shared Memory Access Among Processes**: While accessing a stack segment or heap segment, if developers don't check boundaries carefully, then it can lead to access violation and penetration to other process memory access.

Careful About Shared Libraries Access

From Figure 1-12, we should observe that multiple processes are residing in main system memory and sharing memory for accessing shared libraries. Developers should check shared libraries and their paths before accessing any functions from the shared libraries. Attackers can spoof sharelibraries names and function names to redirect genuine calls to malicious function calls. Hence, developers must check the following:

- Include necessary shared libraries only in your code. Otherwise, it can lead to the opening of large attack surfaces for malicious users.

- Before deploying code, cross-check the shared libraries path on your Linux system to avoid library path poisoning attacks.

- Implement your custom dynamic libraries with unique names and save them with the correct library path.

Interprocess Communication-Related Access Checkpoints

From Figure 1-12, we should observe that multiple processes are residing in system memory during their execution and allow communication with other processes using shared memory. It is necessary to communicate with other processes to accomplish many tasks of application in terms of exchanging data and implementing transactions between processes. OS offers IPC constructs such as FIFO, message queues, and shared memory for interprocess communication. And OS offers IPC synchronization-related constructs such as semaphores, mutexes, and condition variables for handling shared critical section parts of the code in reliable manners. These IPC constructs are managed as part of kernel space memory. Developers should handle these IPC constructs carefully as follows:

- Request only suitable IPC constructs from the OS to implement application tasks. For example, to provide interprocess communication between parent and child, it can be done through PIPEs only. If developers request FIFO and forget to release these FIFO constructs from the kernel space, it can lead to security issues and performance issues.

- Release all requested IPC objects after the task is completed.

- Destroy IPC objects created by your application during shutdown of the application.

- In the case of critical section (share data access) code, carefully order semaphore and mutex-related code to request and release locks for accessing the critical section.

- Check for deadlocks possibilities and handle critical section code to avoid deadlocks and starvation situations.

- Developers can take help of Valgrind to identify a few common mistakes in the case of using IPC objects, such as not releasing locks, the wrong way of accessing semaphores, and the wrong order of accessing semaphores.

Before practicing C programming, let's quickly know C programmers' superpowers and responsibilities.

C Programmer Powers and Responsibilities

Unlike many programming languages, C programmers have the following powers to develop a variety of applications and system software. Specifically, C procedure-oriented programming, built-in data structures, and pointer concepts are highly helpful to developers to implement efficient, reliable, and performance meeting code for software:

- C powerful programming ways
- C built-in data structures
- Rich set of C built-in libraries
- C programs can invoke OS services
- C programs can manage system resources

A C programmer should use the above powers with the following responsibilities:

- Optimally utilize system resources such as CPU, memory, and devices.
- Always check for data or resources accessing errors.
- Request and release resources promptly to ensure fairness.
- Avoid runtime access errors by always performing necessary checks to access systems resources and data.
- Use important tools such as `gcc`, `gdb`, and `valgrind` for handling general and well-known issues at deployment time.

Let's get into more details of C programmers' powers and responsibilities for better programming.

C Programming Powers

C programming concepts and features help developers to solve complex system implementation issues by utilizing system resources optimally. In this section, we briefly introduce the following concepts and features of C programming:

- **Procedure-Oriented Programming Approach**: In C programming, developers divide a larger problem into smaller problems called subproblems. Then, to solve each of the subproblems, developers use C functions. C functions offer the following major benefits to developers:
  - Code reusability, simplified coordination, and communication between tasks, and help to easily build larger systems
  - Saves development, deployment, and testing time
- **C Built-In Data Structures**: C programming offers the following powerful built-in data structures to model applications concepts, data, and real-world entities into software solutions easily.
  - **Arrays**: Arrays are powerful linear data structures for storing and accessing application-similar data elements together in memory for efficient access. Arrays' index feature enables developers to

handle memory latency issues significantly. Although arrays are linear data structures, their indexing helps to store and access data in a flexible manner to meet application latency issues.

- Array concepts can be used to create other powerful data structures over C characters, structures, and pointers.
- It is possible to create an array of arrays, an array of characters, an array of structures, and an array of pointers.

- **Structures**: Structures are another important built-in C data structure for modelling most of the real-world entities and concepts into programming space easily. Structures help to combine heterogeneous data type elements together under a variable for offering simplified and efficient access.

  - Structure can hold arrays also.
  - Structures are helpful to model any complex data structures such as trees, graphs, linked lists, databases, etc.
  - Structures are helpful to model any real-world concepts and entities such as employee, student, person, works, takes, descriptions, etc.
  - Structures are helpful to model any complex protocol such as networking protocols, operating system protocols, database protocols, etc.

- **Pointers**: C pointers give wings to developers to access system resources optimally. Specifically, pointers are helpful in managing and accessing memory, devices, files, etc.

  - C pointers play a major role in minimizing memory access time by indirect address-based accessing of memory locations.
  - C pointers help to easily implement and share services across the C software applications.
  - Moreover, C pointers help to implement advanced concepts such as polymorphism, dynamic linking, generic data structures, generic algorithms, etc.

- **C Programs Can Invoke OS Services**: C programming helps developers to easily invoke OS services for handling system-level activities using system call access.
  - C programmers can easily implement multiprogramming and multitasking activities using OS services. C programmers can call process- and thread management-related system calls to perform these activities.
  - C programmers can easily implement memory management activities using memory management-related system calls.
  - C programmers can easily implement IO devices management activities using respective drivers programming.
  - C programmers can easily handle network programming tasks using socket programming.
  - C programmers can easily handle and implement system virtualization activities using namespaces and control groups related system calls.
  - C programmers can easily handle system security-related tasks using Linux secure computing and application armors-related system calls.
  - C programmers using system calls can manage system resources optimally.
- **Rich Set of C Built-In Libraries**: C programming offers developers the use of many built-in functions from standard libraries.
  - stdio, string, stdlib, math, process, net/inet, etc.

C Programmer Responsibilities

C superpowers always come with lots of responsibilities. Hence, C programming developers must use C powers to meet application performance requirements with utmost care to avoid system crashes and utilize system resources optimally in a fair and secure manner.

- **Optimally Utilize System Resources**: C developers are allowed to request system resources such as processes, memory, and device access through system calls. However, developers must request necessary resources only from the OS. Otherwise, it can lead to overall system performance degradation.
  - Requesting many processes unnecessarily from the OS through fork() can lead to a degraded degree of multitasking.
  - Requesting large-sized memory blocks, stack space, and registers unnecessarily from the OS can lead to an unfair memory utilization and cause latency issues as well as overall system performance degradation.
  - Requesting unnecessary IO devices such as files, network programming sockets, etc., can lead to unnecessary blocking of other applications and their performance.
  - In summary, requesting system resources unnecessarily leads to overall system performance degradation as well as the following serious situations.
    - Deadlocks
    - Starvation
- Always check for request grant-related errors: In C programming, developers can request any system resource through OS using system calls. It means a request can be granted or rejected based on the resources' availability. Hence, C developers must write request grant status check code before accessing any of the system resources.
  - File is created or not.
  - Memory block is allocated or not.
  - Network socket creation is successful or not.
- **Request and Release**: C developers must release all requested resources promptly after use. It helps the OS to allocate resources to other applications and improve overall system performance in terms of multitasking, avoiding deadlocks, and starvation situations.

- Free the dynamically allocated memory blocks used by your application after use.

- Close all the files used by your application after completing file access operations.

- Close all devices requested by your application after using them.

• **Avoid Runtime Access Errors**: Never assume your system resources are always available in case of multitasking or multiprocessing OS. It is also possible that resources could be shared by multiple processes in your application itself. Hence, it is necessary to check before accessing any active resource availability by developers writing suitable codes.

- Check memory pointers are pointing to the right and valid locations.

- Check array boundaries before accessing.

- Check the file pointer is pointing to the right location and it has read or write permissions.

- Check the files access permissions.

- Check if a socket is opened or not before accessing it. Check if a file pointer is pointing to a valid file or not. Check if a pointer is pointing to a valid memory block or not.

• **Use the Right Tools for Checking Common Development and Deployment Errors**: In the case of large-sized application development, it is difficult to go through the entire code and confirm all necessary error-checking-related code is included or not. Hence, we recommend using the following tools for identifying common errors and correcting them before deploying your application in the runtime environment.

- Use compiler and important options related to performance tuning, protecting and reliability checking, and code optimization. Example: use gcc with suitable options before finalizing the executable file for deployment.

- Use memory errors, cache utilization, and threads-related errors-checking tools. Example: use `valgrind` with suitable options for identifying common errors and correcting them before deployment of your code.

- Use code coverage tools for confirming complete code coverage and avoiding unnecessary code for fine-tuning the performance of your code. Example: Use `gcov` and `gcc` options to test code coverage and identify hotspots of the code.

Summary

In this chapter, we have discussed essential software development-related concepts such as system architecture, OS powers, services, and C application development tools. These concepts help C developers to carefully handle C application performance in terms of utilizing system resources and handling reliability, security, and runtime errors. Specifically, knowing system configurations helps developers to test their application under resource constraints and identify all possible errors during the development stage only. Further, to carry out any C application development, we understood the importance of using development tools such as `gcc`, `gcov`, `gdb`, and `valgrind` for easily handling system development and performance handling tasks. Finally, we conclude this chapter by introducing a C programmer's powers and responsibility for application development.

In the next chapter, we will introduce essential C programming concepts by revising C functions, arrays, strings, structures, and unions. It helps C developers to quickly carry out C application development activities.

CHAPTER 2

Quick Revision of Powerful C Constructs

In this chapter, we discuss the essential C programming concepts and constructs for implementing C applications. You will be revising the importance of procedure-oriented programming and practicing C functions. You will start with practicing the C functions, recursive functions, and nested functions programming in terms of performance improvement. Mainly, you will be learning C functions' runtime execution environments in detail to handle the performance and security issues at the system level. For instance, it is necessary to learn the details of the runtime memory layout and execution procedure of a program to protect it, optimally manage its resources, and improve the code execution speed. You will be doing related hands-on activities to easily grasp the C functions-related concepts and developing C functions to avoid performance and security issues.

Then, you will be learning the powerful C built-in data structures such as arrays, strings, structures, and unions. Specifically, you will be learning how to use C array features such as indexing and memory layout in various contexts to access application data to meet its performance requirements. Next, you will be practicing how to create C character arrays and C strings to handle data, text, and messages in flexible ways for handling data exchange and processing tasks. Specifically, you will be practicing how to process strings and buffers in C using string library functions easily. Next, you will be learning how to use C structures to model complex concepts such as complex data structures, real-world entities, protocol messages, and handling bits efficiently. Finally, you will be learning the importance of unions to efficiently combine and manage multiple structures for optimal utilization of memory and exchange of information between functions.

© Dr Anil Kumar Rangisetti 2026
Dr A. K. Rangisetti, *C Programming for System, Network, and Cloud Engineers*,
https://doi.org/10.1007/979-8-8688-1805-9_2

Mainly, in this chapter, we will cover the following topics:

1. Procedure-oriented programming
2. Arrays
3. Strings and buffers
4. Structures
5. Unions

Procedure-Oriented Programming

The key principle of procedure-oriented programming is the division of a large task (T) into a specific number of smaller subtasks (t1, t2, ... tn), and solving each subtask separately by coordinating with necessary tasks and communicating with necessary tasks (e.g., ti<->tj, ti<->ti, ti->tj) to complete the complex task. Inherently, procedure-oriented programming approach offers the following benefits:

1. Easy to map real-world problem-solving approaches to programming.
2. Solve a specific subtask of a larger problem, and implement it as a reusable solution.
3. Easy to integrate the smaller solutions to solve the larger problem.
4. Coordinate and reuse solutions to reduce development time.
5. Flexible ways to coordinate and communicate with other solutions by data exchange and invoking existing solutions.

In C programming, procedure-oriented approaches are implemented through functions. In C programming, a function is written for solving a specific problem. A specific function is declared in the C language as follows:

C functions' general syntax:

```
return-type function_name(arguments)
{
    //computations
}
```

From the C function syntax, the following points must be noted:

1. Function signature

    - function_name: Developers must define a function with a unique name. It helps in a reliable way to coordinate with other functions.

    - arguments: Developers should define necessary arguments with a callee function to get inputs from the caller functions and perform all necessary computations to solve a specific task related to the function_name.

        - Example: If the caller function (e.g., main()) needs to pass two numbers and find a maximum of two numbers, the callee function must be defined with necessary arguments: int max(int, int).

        - Example: int main() //Caller function

            ```
            {
                int a;
                    a = max(10,20); //callee
            }
            ```
        - If no arguments are needed from the caller functions to carry out the function's computational tasks, then no arguments will be defined: int max().

    - return type: Developers should define a return type of the function to return computational results from a callee function to a caller function.

        - int max(int, int) { //Function body;}

        - void max(int, int) { //Function body;}

2. Function body: Developers write all necessary code to solve the specific task assigned to the function.

CHAPTER 2   QUICK REVISION OF POWERFUL C CONSTRUCTS

C programming functions related to concepts for implementing procedure-oriented programming principles:

1. In C programming, procedure-oriented programming concepts are implemented through functions. Every C program execution starts with an important default function called `main()`. Inside `main()`, it is possible to call any user-defined functions.

2. A C function communicates with another C function using arguments. These arguments help a caller function to send input data to a callee function. C functions also return values from callee functions to caller functions for exchanging data. If no exchange is needed, then no return value can be specified with C functions.

    - Developers must define only necessary arguments with a function. Because passing arguments means exchanging data between functions through system memory and buses. Passing a higher number of arguments leads to higher overhead in terms of memory and latency. Moreover, it is not advisable to pass many arguments to a function to avoid mistakes during function communication.

    - Developers must play an important role in deciding arguments of a function for meeting performance of a function and reliable programming.

    - C supports a fixed number of arguments and a variable number of arguments. We discuss it in the pointers chapter.

3. C functions offer the following ways to coordinate with other functions:

4. A C function can be independently defined or defined by calling multiple other functions. It means developers can reuse existing functions to save their time.

    - For example: A complex evaluation function (e.g., `compute()`) can call existing mathematical functions (`sqrt()`, `sin()`, `log()`) to perform computations.

5. C supports recursive functions. It means a function can be defined by calling itself recursively.

- Recursive functions enable developers to easily map standard mathematical functions (factorial, Fibonacci, etc.) into C function implementations.

- Recursive functions help developers to easily map complex procedures such as tree and graph traversals, searching, etc., into C programming.

- For example: A factorial function can be defined as a recursive function.

- Example: int fact(int n) //Caller function

    ```
    {
            if (n==0 || n==1) return 1;
            return n*fact(n-1);//callee
    }
    ```

6. GNU C supports nested functions to offer function encapsulation and function data hiding features.

- Example: int GlobalFun(int n) //Caller function

    ```
    {
            int localFun(int x)
            {
            }
            localFun(3);
            ..
            localFun(3);
    }
    ```

- Nested functions (child functions: e.g., `localFun()`) are defined inside a function (parent function: e.g., `GlobalFun()`).

- Nested functions are helpful to hide sensitive function definitions and their data outside of a function.

CHAPTER 2   QUICK REVISION OF POWERFUL C CONSTRUCTS

- Nested functions can be called from their parent functions only. It means localFun() cannot be called from other than GlobalFun().

Next, let's understand a C function execution procedure in detail.

Understand C Functions' Memory Layout and Execution Procedure

C functions are the basic execution units during a C program execution. Hence, it is necessary to understand how a C function definition is stored in main memory. Specifically, we must understand the lifetime and scope of function arguments and local variables.

C functions' general syntax:

```
int glob1=1000;
int sample(int arg1, int arg2)
{
    int loc1, loc2, res1, res2, res3;
    loc1 = 100;loc2=200;
    static int stat1=0;
    res1=arg1+arg2;
    {
        printf("Function local variable:%d ",loc1);
        int loc3 = 10;
        int loc4 = 20;
        res2=loc3+loc4;
        printf(" Inside block:%d ",res2);
    }
    //loc3, loc4 will not be accessible
    res3=loc1+loc2;
    printf(" Outside block:%d ",res2);

    stat1=stat1+500;
    glob1=glob1+1000;
    return stat1;
}
```

```
int main()
{
    //loc1,loc2,stat1,loc3,loc4, res1,res2,res3 will not be accessible
    in main()
    int r;
    printf(" Global: %d ",glob1); //1000
    r = sample(10,20); //r=500
    printf(" Global: %d ",glob1); //2000
    r = sample(30,40); //r=1000;
    printf(" Global: %d ",glob1); //3000
}
```

Every variable in a C program has a specific scope and lifetime.

The scope of a variable defines which parts of the program can access the variable. The lifetime of a variable starts when memory is allocated for the variable in a program during its execution, and ends when memory is deallocated for the variable in a program during its execution. The scope and lifetime of variables differ based on the type of the variables.

1. **Local Variables**: In our sample code, we have function-level local variables and block-level local variables. The local variable's default value will be a garbage value. Local variables will be stored in the stack segment of a C program memory layout.

    - **Function-Level Local Variables**: arg1, arg2, loc1, loc2, res1, res2, and res3. These variables are defined inside the sample(). These local variables can be accessed throughout the function code. Hence, you can observe inside the function there is a block of code where it is printing the function's local variable loc1.

        - However, arg1, arg2, loc1, loc2, res1, res2, and res3 are variables that cannot be accessed from main() or any other function. Because the scope of these variables is limited to the sample() function only.

- **Lifetime of Local Variables**: All local variables' memory of a function will be allocated automatically when the function execution starts. All local variable memory is allocated inside the function stack space only. At the end of the function execution, all local variable memory will be deallocated automatically.
  - It means changes done to local variables in a function's allocated memory area will be lost after the function execution.
  - Hence, it is not possible for returning the memory location address of local variables to other functions for accessing the local variables.
- **Block-Level Local Variables**: `loc3, loc4`. These variables are defined inside the block. These local variables can be accessed inside the specific block only. These block level local variables cannot be accessed outside of the block.
  - Hence, `loc3, loc4` variables cannot be accessed outside of the block.
- **Lifetime of Block-Level Local Variables**: All local variables' memory of a block will be allocated automatically when the block execution starts. At the end of the block execution, all local variable memory will be deallocated automatically. All local variable memory is allocated inside the function stack space only.

2. **Global Variables**: Global variables are defined outside of all functions. These are accessible across all the functions. Global variables' default value will be ZERO. Global variables will be stored in the data segment of a C program memory layout.
   - The scope of a global variable of a program is all functions defined in a program. It means all functions can access the global variables.
   - For example: In our sample code, `glob1` is accessible inside `sample()` and `main()`.

- The lifetime of a global variable starts with main() and ends with the main() execution. That means global variables' memory will be allocated automatically when main() execution is started, and global variables' memory will be deallocated automatically when main() execution is ended.

3. **Static Variables**: Static variables are defined with a static keyword. The static variable's default value will be ZERO. Static variables will be stored in the data segment of a C program memory layout.

    - Scope of static variables is the same as local variables.

    - The lifetime of a static variable starts with the function defined (parent) by the static variable. It means memory allocation will be done at the start of its parent function. In our example code, sample() is the parent function of stat1. It means when the first time sample() is called in a program execution, the stat1 variable will be allocated memory in the data segment of the program memory layout. Then, stat1 lifetime ends with the main() function execution termination.

        - The first sample() call stat1 value will be updated to 500. Moreover, the stat1 variable memory will not be deleted even after sample() execution is ended.

        - Hence, the second sample() call retrieves the existing value 500 and updates it to 1000. Moreover, the stat1 variable memory will not be deleted even after the second sample() execution is ended.

        - stat1 variable memory will be deallocated only after main() execution is ended.

C Function Execution Procedure: Every C function execution needs first allocation of suitable memory. For any C program, there will be four segments to store its functions' data and code.

- **Code Segment:** This is an important memory segment that stores program code. It stores program code that is all function code.

- **Data Segment:** Data segment memory area saves the following details about a function. It will be deallocated only when the main() program execution ends:
  - Function global variables
  - Function static variables
- **Heap Segment:** It is another dynamically allocated memory area for a program execution. It saves dynamically allocated variable memory blocks of a program using system calls such as malloc. These memory block addresses are stored into corresponding pointer variables. We discuss it in the pointers chapter.
- **Stack Segment:** It is an important memory segment where functions' local and argument data gets stored. Usually a callee function execution involves processing local data and its arguments collected from a caller function. Hence, a function needs to store local data and arguments in the stack segment of the program. Technically, these are stored as part of the callee function stack frame. In a program execution, after successful execution of a function, the callee function must return to the caller's next instruction address for continuing the program execution. Hence, the return address is also stored in a callee function stack frame.
  - Functions' stack frames are managed in the stack segment of a program. The stack segment is accessed with a top of stack (ToS) pointer. The ToS points to the highest address of the stack segment memory.
  - When a function is called, its stack frame will be pushed into the stack segment at the current ToS address, and the new ToS pointer address will be updated based on the size of the stack frame.
    - For example: If the ToS pointing address = 1020 and a callee's function stack frame size = 20 bytes, then the new ToS pointing address = 1000.

CHAPTER 2   QUICK REVISION OF POWERFUL C CONSTRUCTS

- As function execution is ended, then the corresponding stack frame is removed from the stack segment. It means the ToS pointer address will be updated to reflect the availability of stack memory space.

- In summary, a function stack frame contains the following details:

  - Local variables, arguments

  - Return address

  - Caller frame pointer

- **Frame Pointer**: Stack segment memory size is dynamic (grows on function calls and shrinks on function returns) in nature. It means until a function call is invoked, no memory is allocated to the function's local variables, and no addresses can be given to function's local variables and arguments (arg1, arg2, loc1, loc2, etc.). But the compiler must generate virtual addresses for every function's local variables and arguments. It is handled by compilers with the help of a CPU register known as the base pointer register (frame pointer). This frame pointer always holds the base address of the current executing function stack frame address. Using the base pointer register, the compiler assigns a unique base address to a function, and it is used to generate addresses for all local variables and arguments of the function.

  - For example: During our program execution, before `main()` calls the `sample()` function, initially the base pointer register (frame pointer) points to the `main()` stack frame base address for addressing the `main()` local variables and its arguments.

    - After `main()` calls the `sample()` function, the `sample()` function stack frame is pushed into the stack segment, and the base pointer register (frame pointer) holds the `sample()` function stack frame base address for addressing its local variables and arguments. Since the `sample()` function stack frame contains the caller function (`main()`) frame pointer holding the address, after `sample()` execution is ended, the base pointer register is restored with the `main()` stack frame base address.

61

- After completing `sample()` execution, if the base pointer register is not restored with the `main()` function base address, then it is not possible to address `main()` local variables and arguments. Hence, it is necessary to keep the caller frame pointer address in a callee stack frame and store it in the stack segment.

- **Developer's Responsibilities:** As we observe, the stack segment plays an important role in function execution in terms of allocating and deallocating function stack frame memory.

  - Although a stack grows and shrinks dynamically based on function calls, usually for a program execution there is a fixed-size memory allocated for the stack segment. For example: On the Linux OS, the default stack segment size is 8 MB. This value can be configured during program execution.

  - It means developers should know how their program execution utilizes this fixed stack segment for efficient utilization and set a suitable runtime stack segment size.

  - Store only necessary local variables and arguments.

  - Access arrays within their boundaries only.

  - Do not return local variable addresses to caller functions.

  - Check array arguments' length while copying them into functions' local arrays.

  - Know how to find a function's stack frame size.

  - Know the maximum number of recursive function calls that are possible.

CHAPTER 2   QUICK REVISION OF POWERFUL C CONSTRUCTS

FUNCTIONS AND REUSABILITY

1. As part of this task, we do the following activities in the `func.c` file: Specifically, we define a few important tasks of robots using the following sample functions.

    a. Give a specific command to Robo for moving in the left direction for n steps and doing an action.

    b. Give a specific command to Robo for moving in the right direction for n steps and doing an action.

    c. Give a specific command to Robo for moving in the up direction for n steps and doing an action.

    d. Give a specific command to Robo for moving in the down direction for n steps and doing an action.

2. For each of these commands in the C language, we define a specific function as follows:

```c
#include<stdio.h>
#define DONE 1
#define NONE 0
int left(int steps, char *action)
{
        for(int i=0;i<steps;i++)
        {
              printf("L <-- ");
        }
        printf("\n");
        if (action!=NULL)
        {
              printf("%s\n",action);
              return DONE;
        }
```

CHAPTER 2 QUICK REVISION OF POWERFUL C CONSTRUCTS

```c
            else
            {
                    return NONE;
            }
    }
    int right(int steps, char *action)
    {
            for(int i=0;i<steps;i++)
            {
                    printf("R --> ");
            }
            printf("\n");
            if (action!=NULL)
            {
                    printf("%s\n",action);
                    return DONE;
            }
            else
            {
                    return NONE;
            }
    }
    int up(int steps, char *action)
    {
            for(int i=0;i<steps;i++)
            {
                    printf("U ^");
            }
            printf("\n");
            if (action!=NULL)
            {
                    printf("%s\n",action);
                    return DONE;
            }
```

```c
        else
        {
            return NONE;
        }
    }
}
int down(int steps, char *action)
{
    for(int i=0;i<steps;i++)
    {
        printf("D .");
    }
    printf("\n");
    if (action!=NULL)
    {
        printf("%s\n",action);
        return DONE;
    }
    else
    {
        return NONE;
    }
}
```

3. Now use these functions for simulating two robots' actions. It means the same functions we are reusing for simulating two robots' actions. It is done through carefully passing necessary arguments to respective functions:

    a. Robot-1 should first move in the left direction for 5 steps, then perform tree planting, then move the robot in the right direction for 3 steps and perform watering activity, then move the robot in the up direction for 4 steps to serve food. Finally, move the robot in the down direction for 5 steps to charge and rest.

    b. Robot-2 should first move in the up direction for 4 steps, then serve food, then move the robot in the right direction for 3 steps and perform watering activity, then move the robot in the left direction for 5 to plant trees. Finally, move the robot in the down direction for 2 steps to charge and rest.

CHAPTER 2 QUICK REVISION OF POWERFUL C CONSTRUCTS

c. These robot activities can be simulated by simply calling left(), right(), up(), and down() functions with suitable arguments for passing the number of steps and action to be performed.

d. Moreover, we can observe that the following left(), right(), up(), and down() functions are reused for performing various robot activities.

```c
int main()
{
        printf("Robo 1:\n");
        unsigned int status;

        left(5,"Trees planting");
        right(3,"Watering");
        up(4,"Serving Food");

        status = down(5,"Charging and Rest");
        if (status==1)
        {
                printf("Robo 1 Successfully at rest place\n");
        }

        printf("Robo 2:\n");
        up(4,"Serving Food");
        right(3,"Watering");
        left(5,"Trees planting");
        down(2,"Charging and Rest");
        printf("Tasks over!\n");
}
```

4. Compile and execute the func.c for simulating two robots' actions using the following commands in order:

```
#gcc -o roboact func.c
#./roboact
Robo 1:
L <-- L <-- L <-- L <-- L <--
Trees planting
```

CHAPTER 2   QUICK REVISION OF POWERFUL C CONSTRUCTS

```
R --> R --> R -->
Watering
U ^U ^U ^U ^
Serving Food
D .D .D .D .D .
Charging and Rest
Robo 1 Successfully at rest place
Robo 2:
U ^U ^U ^U ^
Serving Food
R --> R --> R -->
Watering
L <-- L <-- L <-- L <-- L <--
Trees planting
D .D .
Charging and Rest
Tasks over!
```

a. From the results, we can easily observe two simulated robot actions using our left(), right(), up(), and down().

b. Similarly, we can simulate any number of robots.

c. We recommend extending this code and simulating your favorite robot actions.

However, if you observe the functions' code keenly, there will be redundant code among functions. Specifically to simulate steps and perform action code, there is redundant code among functions. Can we optimize these robots' code? Let's do it in the next activity.

In the next hands-on activity, let's optimize the robot's code by eliminating redundant code among functions.

CHAPTER 2   QUICK REVISION OF POWERFUL C CONSTRUCTS

OPTIMIZED ROBOT COMMANDS SIMULATING FUNCTIONS

1. Observe the func.c code and inspect the left(), right(), up(), and down() functions:

    a. In all these command-related functions, moving is simulated by iterating through a number of steps. Hence, all functions have similar code.

    b. Next, from all these command-related functions, we can notice that simulating action is performed after iterations and checking the command name.

    c. From steps a and b, we can observe that by passing a direction argument in functions, all functions would have the same code.

2. To avoid redundant code and optimize commands related to functions code, we define a single command move() to simulate all commands and implement these functions in impfunc.c.

    a. move() takes all important arguments to simulate robot' actions.

    b. Specifically, in our problem direction, steps and action arguments are sufficient to simulate robots' actions.

    c. We define the move() function as follows to simulate all commands:

    ```
    #define DONE 1
    #define NONE 0
    int move(char direction, int steps, char *action)
    {
        for(int i=0;i<steps;i++)
        {
            if (direction=='L')
                printf("L <-- ");
            else if (direction=='R')
                printf("R -->");
            else if (direction=='U')
                printf("U ^");
    ```

```
                else if (direction=='D')
                    printf("D . ");
        }
        printf("\n");
        if (action!=NULL)
        {
                printf("%s\n",action);
                return DONE;
        }
        else
        {
                return NONE;
        }
}
```

3. Now use the `move()` function for simulating two robots' actions in `main()` as follows:

   a. Robot-1 should first move in the left direction for five steps, then perform tree planting, then move the robot in the right direction for three steps and perform watering activity, then move the robot in the up direction for four steps to serve food. Finally, move the robot in the down direction for five steps to charge and rest.

   b. Robot-2 should first move in the up direction for four steps, then serve food, then move the robot in the right direction for three steps and perform watering activity, then move the robot in the left direction for 5 to plant trees. Finally, move the robot in the down direction for two steps to charge and rest.

   ```
   int main()
   {
           printf("Robo 1:\n");
           unsigned int status;

           move('L',5,"Trees planting");
           move('R',3,"Watering");
           move('U',4,"Serving Food");
   ```

```
            status = move('D',5,"Charging and Rest");
            if (status==1)
            {
                    printf("Robo 1 Successfully at rest place\n");
            }
            printf("Robo 2:\n");
            move('U',4,"Serving Food");
            move('D',3,"Watering");
            move('L',5,"Trees planting");
            move('R',2,"Charging and Rest");
            printf("Tasks over!\n");
    }
```

4. Compile and execute the impfunc.c for simulating two robots' actions using the following commands in order:

```
#gcc -o iroboact impfunc.c

#./iroboact
Robo 1:
L <-- L <-- L <-- L <-- L <--
Trees planting
R --> R --> R -->
Watering
U ^U ^U ^U ^
Serving Food
D .D .D .D .D .
Charging and Rest
Robo 1 Successfully at rest place
Robo 2:
U ^U ^U ^U ^
Serving Food
R --> R --> R -->
Watering
L <-- L <-- L <-- L <-- L <--
Trees planting
```

```
D .D .
Charging and Rest
Tasks over!
```

Well done! You have successfully tested the robot's code using a new function (move) by eliminating redundant code.

Next, let's learn about recursive functions in detail for writing safe and optimized code.

Recursive Functions

In C programming, recursive functions are helpful to easily map real-world solutions to C functions. For instance, to compute Fibonacci numbers, factorials, and greatest common divisors, mathematicians defined standard formulas and algorithms using recurrence relations. Similarly, scientists developed recursive approaches to solve graph and tree problems such as traversals, finding paths, searching elements, etc. In C programming, developers can easily map these algorithms to C functions by carefully observing the following points about recursive solutions or recurrent expression.

Example recursive function:

```
int sample(int arg)
{
    if (arg==0) //Base condition
    //    return 1;
    else  //Recursive procedure condition
    //    do some task;
    sample(arg-1);
}
```

Every recursive solution has the following two parts:

1. Base conditions on input arguments: While solving the problem through recursive procedure, it is necessary to check the base condition to produce intermediate results and terminate the recursive procedure.

- For example-1: To find the factorial of n, base condition: if n == 0, factorial(n) = 1.
- For example-2: To find the Fibonacci of n, base conditions: if n == 0, Fibonacci(n) = 0 and if n == 1, Fibonacci(n) = 1.
- For example-3: To find an element in a sorted list using the binary search algorithm, the base condition to stop the procedure is if list[mid] == element, return found.
- Developers must handle base conditions correctly to avoid infinite recursive calls.

2. Recursive procedure to continue based on input arguments related to conditions: In order to repeat the recursive procedure to solve the problem, it is necessary to check conditions on input arguments to decide which part of the recursive procedure needs to be repeated.
    - For example-1: To find the factorial of n, recursive procedure condition: if n>1, then factorial(n)=n*factorial(n-1).
    - For example-2: To find the Fibonacci of n, recursive procedure condition: if (n>=2), then Fibonacci(n) = Fibonacci(n-1) + Fibonacci(n-2).
    - For example-3: To implement binary search, if a search element is greater than the middle element of the list, then recursively search for the element on the right side part from the middle position of the list. Otherwise, recursively search for the element on the right side part from the middle position of the list.
    - Developers must handle base conditions correctly to avoid infinite recursive calls.

C recursive functions are really helpful to easily convert standard algorithms into C function; however, developers should check the following to handle the performance of the program:

- Handle base conditions and recursive procedure conditions carefully to avoid infinite calls and produce correct results.

- Stack segment utilization: As we discussed in the prior section, stack segment size is limited; hence, while carrying out recursive procedures using C recursive functions, every recursive function call leads to storing function stack frames inside the stack segment.
  - If the input size is larger than the stack size, it can lead to a higher number of recursive calls, and the stack segment gets full. Then, it is not possible to carry out the recursive procedure further. Technically, it is a stack overflow condition and leads to a runtime stack crash. Developers should carefully set input to handle stack overflow conditions by analyzing recursive procedures.
- Developers should also check what contents get stored during recursive calls to optimize stack frame size to execute recursive procedures.
  - Developers should check if it is possible to convert normal recursive procedures into tail recursive procedures.
  - In tail recursive procedures, the recursive call is the final step to carry out. It eliminates the need for storing intermediate results in function stack frames.
  - Converting recursive calls into tail recursive calls helps in using compiler optimization techniques such as eliminating tail recursive calls by converting them into goto labels.
    - It helps in consuming constant stack space instead of dynamic stack space.

CHECK RELIABILITY OF A RECURSIVE FUNCTION

1. In this task, we create a recursive function to access an array's first 10 elements for N times as follows in `recfunc.c`:

```
#include<stdio.h>
int hrecfunc(int n)
{
    int a[1024];
```

CHAPTER 2 QUICK REVISION OF POWERFUL C CONSTRUCTS

```
        if (n==0)
        {
            return 1;
        }
        else
        {
            for (int i=0;i<10;i++)
            {
                a[i]=i*i;
            }
            hrecfunc(n-1);
        }
    }
```

2. Next, create another recursive function to access an array's first 10 elements for N times as follows:

```
int lrecfunc(int n)
{
    int a[10];
    if (n==0)
    {
        return 1;
    }
    else
    {
        for (int i=0;i<10;i++)
        {
            a[i]=i*i;
        }
        lrecfunc(n-1);
    }
}
```

CHAPTER 2 QUICK REVISION OF POWERFUL C CONSTRUCTS

3. Call these two recursive functions with input as 2000:

   ```
   int main()
   {
        lrecfunc(2000);
        printf("Done 1\n");
        hrecfunc(2000);
        printf("Done 2\n");
   }
   ```

4. Test the code using the following commands and observe the results:

   ```
   #gcc recfunc.c
   #./a.out
   Done 1
   Done 2
   ```

   a. Observe that there is no crash; next, change the input to 2020 in lrecfunc() only, and comment out hrecfunc() and test the code:

   ```
   #gcc recfunc.c
   #./a.out
   Done 1
   ```

   b. Observe that there is no crash; next, change the input to 2020 and call both lrecfunc() and hrecfunc(). Then test your code:

   ```
   #gcc recfunc.c
   #./a.out
   Segmentation fault (core dumped)
   ```

   c. Observe that there is a crash. It means hrecfunc() is the cause of the crash.

      i. If you observe hrecfunc(), it contains a local integer array variable of size 1024 elements. Since it is a recursive function, the execution needs 2020*1024*4 bytes.

75

CHAPTER 2   QUICK REVISION OF POWERFUL C CONSTRUCTS

      ii. Check the size of the runtime stack on your Linux system using the following command:

      `#ulimit -s`
      `8192`

      iii. As hrecfunc() needs more than 8 MB size, its execution is resulting in a crash.

5. Next, to avoid crashes of this recursive function, we can update the main() function with the following reliability checks:

```
int main()
{
        int n=20020;
        if (n<20000)
        {
                lrecfunc(n);
        }
        else
        {
                printf(" Error:Large size argument ");
        }
        n=2000;
        if (n<=2000)
        {
                hrecfunc(2000);
        }
        else
        {
                printf(" Error:Large size argument ");
        }
}
```

6. Compile the code with the address option, and run the executable (a.out) for possible errors using the following commands:

   #gcc recfunc.c

   a. Observe that even if you pass higher values to recursive functions, the reliability check at argument size stops the execution of recursive calls and displays the error reason.

      #./a.out
      "Error:Large size argument"

Well done! We successfully tested a recursive function for knowing the stack size and how it can impact the application performance in terms of reliable deployment with limited stack size.

Next, let's learn about nested functions and their importance in C programming.

Nested Functions in GNU C

Nested functions are not supported in ANSI C; these are introduced in GNU C for offering function encapsulation and hiding features. Function encapsulation simplifies function invocation by hiding sensitive functions and complex function calls from the caller functions. A caller function can just call a parent function, then the parent function calls a nested function for carrying out necessary tasks.

Example recursive function:

```
return-type parent_function(arguments)
{
     //define local tasks and data
     return-type child_function(internal arguments)
     {
          //define child tasks and data
     }

     //Only parent can call child function
     child_function(arguments);
     ..
```

```
                //Only parent can call child function
                child_function(arguments);
                ..
                //Only parent can call child function
                child_function(arguments);
}
```

Nested functions are useful to do the following:

- To hide repeated computations outside the parent functions by defining them inside it.
  - Reuse of child functions inside parent function only
  - Possible to hide the secret arguments from external functions
- Secret computations can be done inside parent functions only and hide them from external functions.
  - Function hiding helps in unnecessary exposure of function interfaces.
  - Limits attacking surface from malicious functions and users.
- Offers simplified and limited interfaces to outside functions for carrying out complex tasks.
  - Instead of calling many functions to complete a task, an external function call just comprises the parent function of all child functions to complete the task.

Let's do the following hands-on activity to learn about nested functions.

NESTED FUNCTIONS

1. We define the following activities in nested.c to easily understand the importance of nested functions:

    a. Define a sample secret computation function as a normal function:

    ```
    #include<stdio.h>
    ```

```
int secretCompute1(int n)
{
    int s=0;
    for (int i=0;i<n;i++)
    {
        s=s+i;
    }
    return s;
}
```

b. Then, call the secretCompute1() from the following external function:

```
int Compute(int n)
{
    n=secretCompute1(n);
    return n;
}
```

c. Define a nested function to perform secret computation inside of it:

```
int NestedCompute(int n)
{
    int secretCompute2(int n)
    {
        int s=0;
        for (int i=0;i<n;i++)
        {
            s=s+i;
        }
        return s;
    }
    n=secretCompute2(n);
    return n;
}
```

CHAPTER 2 QUICK REVISION OF POWERFUL C CONSTRUCTS

2. Test the nested functions' importance in `main()` as follows:

   a. First call `Compute()`, then call `secretCompute1()` from the `main()`.

   b. Next, call `NestedCompute()` from `main()`

   c. Next, call `secretCompute1()` from `main()`

```
int main()
{
    int res=Compute(10);
    printf("Compute: %d",res);
    res=secretCompute1(10);
    printf("Compute: %d",res);

    res=NestedCompute(10);
    printf("Compute: %d",res);

    res=secretCompute2(10);
    printf("Compute: %d",res);
}
```

3. Then execute `nested.c`:

```
#gcc nested.c
#./a.out
innerfuncs.c:(.text+0xbf): undefined reference to
`secretCompute'
```

   a. From the results, observe the errors related to `secretCompute2`.

   b. Since `secretCompute2` is a nested function, it cannot be invoked from `main()`. It means we hide the `secretCompute2` successfully from `main()` and any other external functions.

   c. But, `secretCompute1` is successfully invoked from `main()` or any external function, e.g., `compute()`. It means we cannot hide the `secretCompute1()` from external functions.

Well done! We practiced how to implement nested functions in C and the importance of them for implementing data-hiding features in C applications.

In this section, we have learned the importance of procedure-oriented programming and how to use it in C programming using functions. Next, let's learn C default data structures called arrays for efficient data organization and access activities in C applications.

Arrays

Arrays are built-in data structures in C programming. Arrays help developers to organize related data elements as a list and access the list for computational operations. For example, integer data type arrays are helpful to organize a student's 6 subject marks as 6-integer elements array (e.g., int marks[6]) in main memory for better access in terms of reading and writing values. Without arrays it is not possible to relate all 6 subject marks together and access them for any computational tasks.

Array elements are organized in sequential memory locations of the main memory. Moreover to simplify programming activities, in a C program, array elements can be accessed using indexing with respect to the base address of the array.

For example: A character array char a[5] stores its elements in main memory as follows in Figure 2-1:

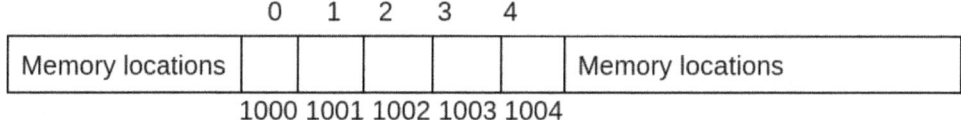

Figure 2-1. Today's general CPU architecture and its internal components

In the above diagram, it is shown that a character array of five elements is stored in five consecutive locations of the memory. Each location size is one byte.

To access these character array elements, we can use the array name and index in array subscripts as follows: a[0]='a';a[1]= 'b'; printf("%c",a[4]);

For example: An integer array int b[5] stores its elements in main memory as follows in Figure 2-2:

CHAPTER 2 QUICK REVISION OF POWERFUL C CONSTRUCTS

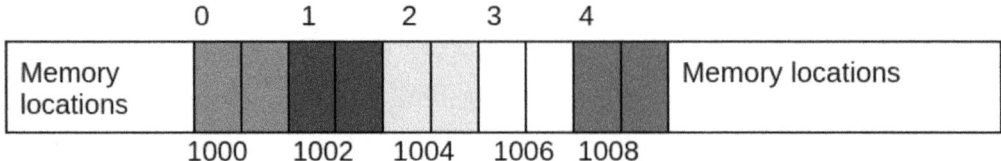

Figure 2-2. *Today's general CPU architecture and its internal components*

In the above diagram, it is shown that an integer array of five elements is stored in ten consecutive locations of the memory since each integer needs two bytes of storage.

To access these character array elements, we can use the array name and index in array subscripts as follows: `b[0]=123;b[1]=456; printf("%d",b[1]);`

`return-type parent_function(arguments)`

Developers should understand the following details about the array while accessing them.

- Array index always starts with 0 and ends with size-1. For example, `int a[5];`, the array size is 5; the first element is stored at `a[0]`, and the last element is stored at `a[4];`

- Once arrays are defined with a fixed size, arrays are not expandable data structures.

- While accessing an array (`int a[5]`), the boundaries of the array must be checked; index <0 and index >size-1 are not allowed; `a[-1]` or `a[5]` are invalid accesses.

- The array starting address can be accessed by printing the address of the first element of the array (`printf("%u", &a[0]);` or `printf("%u",a);`).

- Array element address gives only the starting address of the array element irrespective of the size of the array element. For example, if the integer size is two bytes, then two bytes of an integer will be stored in two consecutive locations as shown in the diagram, and the starting address of an integer is used for accessing the integer.

CHAPTER 2　QUICK REVISION OF POWERFUL C CONSTRUCTS

Developers should understand the following benefits about the array while accessing them.

- Arrays ensure related data elements get stored in consecutive memory locations. It helps in reducing memory access time. Storing data elements sequentially allows the CPU to use system buses, memory, and cache efficiently.

- Storing related data elements in random memory locations leads to inefficient utilization of memory, not being able to fetch related elements together using base address and memory indexing, and related assembly instructions.
    - Inefficient use of system buses and their bandwidth
    - Increased system-level memory read and memory write cycles
    - Inefficient use of memory and caches

As we see, arrays are stored in memory with a starting address; it is possible to access array elements using pointers. In C programming, a pointer is a variable that stores the address of another variable.

```
int *p;
int a[10];
```

We can store the array starting address in a pointer variable as follows:

```
p = &a[0]; or p = a;
```

Now we can assess array elements at the starting address using the pointer variable (p) as follows:

```
*p = 100; //equivalent to a[0]=100;
```

Now we can assess the next array elements using the pointer variable (p) as follows:

```
p=p+1;
*p = 200; //equivalent to a[1]=200;
```

Developers should understand the following details about the array while accessing them using pointers:

- A pointer can store the beginning address of an array; then incrementing the pointer value by 1 allows accessing the next element of the array.
- Pointers allow programmers to specify from which locations of the array can be accessed also.
  - Instead of storing the beginning address of the array, we can store any array element address into the pointer variable. Then, the pointer can access the array from that location.
  - Suppose p = &a[2]; p=p-1;// for accessing the previous element (a[1]) of a[2];
  - Suppose p = &a[2]; p=p+1;// for accessing the next element (a[3]) of a[2];
- However, developers should be careful while accessing arrays using pointers. It can lead to boundaries crossing and access violation errors.

Developers should understand the following details about the array while accessing them.

Powerful Ways for Organizing Array's Data Elements and Accessing

Arrays can also be passed between functions for data exchange. When passing an array to a function, a developer should know the following details:

- In the caller function, a[10] is allocated at a specific memory address at its memory layout. In access(a);, developers pass the base address of the array to the caller function. A caller function can be defined with a pointer argument or array variable arguments as follows:
  - void access(int a[]) or void access(int *p);
  - Passing arguments to functions using the address of the variable is known as the call by reference way.

CHAPTER 2   QUICK REVISION OF POWERFUL C CONSTRUCTS

- Unlike normal variables, arrays are passed to a function using call by reference. In a call by reference way, from the caller function, instead of copying the entire data of a variable to the callee function memory layout, only the address of the variable will be copied.
    - It means the callee function accesses the input array (argument) from the memory layout of the caller function only.
    - No need of reserving memory space for arrays at the callee function.
    - The callee function can directly access the input array of the caller function from the caller function memory space only. Hence, there is no need to return updated values of the array from the callee function to the caller function.
    - Arrays exchange between functions avoids memory copy operations at the system level and reduces memory latency and utilizes system buses efficiently.
- It is a very important feature of arrays for exchanging blocks of data between functions.

By exploring the power of arrays indexing, developers can implement various complex data structures and model complex concepts:

- C arrays are helpful to group related data of the same data type and organize in memory sequential locations for efficient access.
    - `int a[10]; char a[10]; float a[10];`
    - `struct student s[10];`
    - `int *p[10];`
    - Without arrays, data elements are not promised to be stored in sequentially addressable memory locations.
        - For example: `int m1,m2,m3,m4,m5;` // Although all variables are of the same data type, there is no guarantee these variables data will be organized in sequential space of memory.

- - Sequential space of memory is helpful to utilize the system buses efficiently by fetching required data blocks at once for processing.
  - Sequential space of memory is helpful to reduce memory latency by avoiding multiple system read and write cycles.
- Although C arrays are sequentially organized in memory space, C offers flexible ways of accessing individual array location elements using indexing.
  - Array index is helpful to create linear, non-linear data, and circular data structures for organizing data within array allocated memory boundaries.
  - **Linear Data Structures**: Stacks, queues
  - **Circular Data Structures**: Circular queues
  - **Non-linear Data Structures**: Graphs, almost complete binary trees
  - Divide and conquer approaches and parallel algorithms

Next, we will discuss how to create important data structures such as lists, circular lists, matrices, and non-linear data structures such as trees and graphs:

Arrays: Indexing Ways for Accessing Data Structures

Developers can define various arrays and use array indexing wisely for implementing a variety of data structures and improving their access time. Let's check how to implement the following linear list data structure and its accessing ways from Figure 2-3. From the code shown in Figure 2-3, we can observe an array (a[10]) can be accessed in left-to-right traversal or right-to-left traversal within its boundaries.

```
int a[10];                        int a[10];
for (int i=0;i<10;i++)            for (int i=9;i>=0;i--)
{                                 {
    printf("%d",a[i]);                printf("%d",a[i]);
}                                 }
```

Figure 2-3. *Linear list access from both directions using array index*

CHAPTER 2 QUICK REVISION OF POWERFUL C CONSTRUCTS

Next, let's check how to implement the circular list data structure and its accessing ways from Figure 2-4. From the code shown in Figure 2-4, we can observe that an array (a[10]) can be accessed in a circular way using the modulus operator.

```
int a[10];
int i=0;
int j=0;
while (i<20)
{
    printf("%d",a[j]);
    i=i+1;
    j=(j+1)%10;
}
```

Figure 2-4. *Circular list implementation using an array and its accessing using an index*

Next, let's check how to access a list data structure in logarithmic time complexity. From the code shown in Figure 2-5, we can observe that an array (a[10]) can be accessed in a logarithmic time complexity by using the index in terms of dividing the list of array elements to be scanned. For instance, in the following code, we observe in every iteration the size of the list (array) to be scanned is divided by two. Hence, its time complexity is log2(N). Similarly, we can implement logk(N) time complexity accessing ways using arrays.

```
int a[8];                    int a[8];
int i=0;                     int i=0;
int j=0;                     int j=0;
i=7;                         i=0;
while (i!=1)                 while (i<N)
{                            {
    printf("%d",a[i]);           printf("%d",a[i]);
    i=i/2;                       i=2*(i+1);
}                            }
```

Figure 2-5. *Accessing an array using an index in terms of logarithmic time complexity*

87

CHAPTER 2 QUICK REVISION OF POWERFUL C CONSTRUCTS

Next, let's check how to access an array of elements in an interleaved manner. From Figure 2-6, we observe that in every iteration, three elements are accessed together using array index. Hence, developers can decide suitable interleaving steps and skip iterations of a loop for accessing any array.

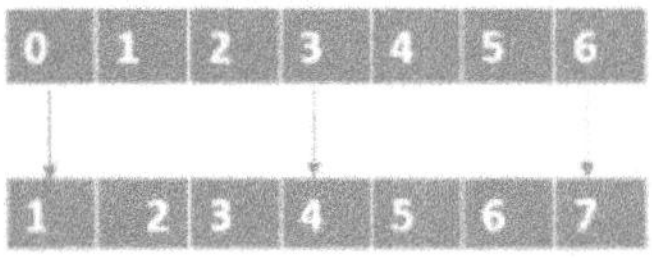

```
int a[7];
int i=0;
while (i<=N)
{
    printf("%d",a[i]);
    printf("%d",a[i+1]);
    printf("%d",a[i+2]);
    i=i+3;
}
```

Figure 2-6. Accessing an array using an index in terms of logarithmic time complexity

Next, let's check a very popular data structure called matrix handling using arrays. C supports N-dimensional data organization in arrays, and these can be simply accessible using matrix accessing ways as follows:

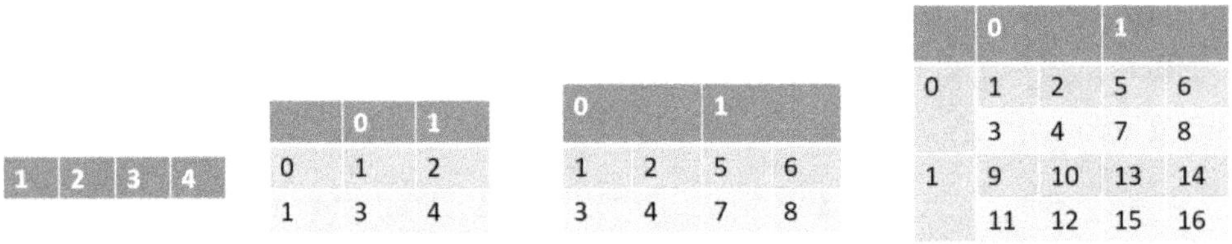

Figure 2-7. 1-D, 2-D, 3-D, and 4-D ways of organizing data elements using arrays

CHAPTER 2 QUICK REVISION OF POWERFUL C CONSTRUCTS

```
int a[2][2];
int i=0;
int j=0;
for (int i=0;i<2;i++)
{
    for (int j=0;j<2;j++)
    {
        printf("%d",a[i][j]);
    }
}
```

```
int a[2][2][2];
int i=0;
int j=0;
for (int k=0;k<2;k++)
{
    for (int i=0;i<2;i++)
    {
        for (int j=0;j<2;j++)
        {
            printf("%d",a[k][i][j]);
        }
    }
}
```

Figure 2-8. *2-D and 3-D data elements accessing using arrays indexing*

From Figure 2-7, we can observe how four data elements of a list can be organized in a simple matrix containing two rows and two columns. Next, we can observe how eight data elements can be organized in 3-D ways containing two 2-D matrices, and each matrix size is 2x2. Similarly, we can observe how 16 elements can be a 4-D way containing four 2-D matrices (2x2), and these four matrices are organized into two rows and two columns.

Next, from Figure 2-8, we can observe how four data elements of a matrix can be accessed in rows, traversing through individual elements of a row. Similarly, in the case of 3-D organization, the outer loop is traversing through a number of inner 2-D matrices for accessing individual matrix data elements. In the case of 4-D organization, we can implement data elements traversing through each row containing nested matrices.

Next, let's discuss how to model non-linear data structures using arrays in C. For example, from Figure 2-9, we can observe how directed graphs can be implemented in C. Vertices of nodes of graphs can be modeled by the number of columns in a row. Then, for every vertex, the corresponding edges can be mapped as rows of the matrix. Every row represents the edges of a vertex. For example, row 1 indicates node-1 and all its edges (1->2, 1->3). In order to process the graph, as shown in Figure 2-9, it is possible to traverse the graph as a matrix and process vertices and their corresponding edges.

CHAPTER 2 QUICK REVISION OF POWERFUL C CONSTRUCTS

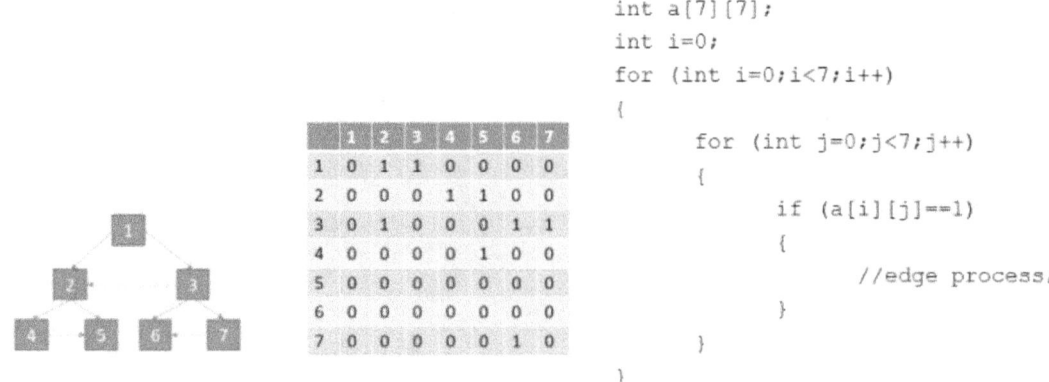

Figure 2-9. Directed graphs implementation and accessing using arrays

Next, let's discuss how to model complete binary trees using arrays in C. For example, from Figure 2-10, we can observe how a complete binary tree can be mapped to a 1-D array and it can be accessed using indexing. In this example, node-1 is having two children: node-2 and node-3. In the 1-D array, a subtree of node-1 (root, left child, right child) elements are stored in consecutive locations. Then, subtrees of node-2 and node-3 elements are stored in order. In a C program, to access these subtrees, developers can use the suitable indexes to traverse the tree. For example, in a complete binary tree, given a node-I, its children are accessible by 2*i+1 and 2*i+2 indices.

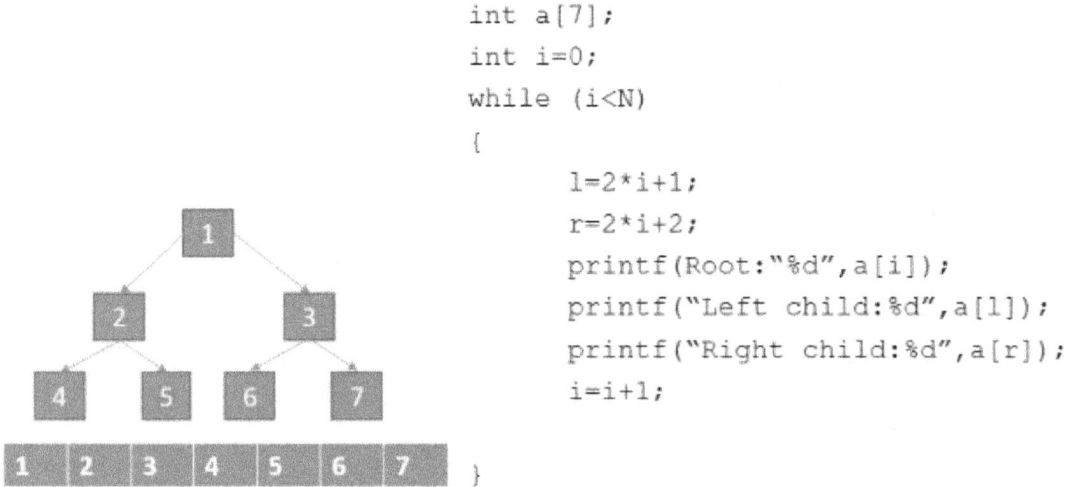

Figure 2-10. Complete binary tree implementation and accessing using arrays

Next, let's discuss important concepts about storing array elements and accessing them wisely.

Hands-On Activities for Organizing Array's Data Elements and Accessing Them Efficiently

In this section, we will discuss the following important concepts about storing array elements and their accessing for meeting performance requirements.

- Array and its individual element sizes in case of 1-D, 2-D, and 3-D arrays: In the last section, we discussed how an N-D dimensional array is organized and its individual elements can be accessed. In this section, we will see the power of C arrays and their indexing in terms of accessing groups of N-D array nested elements traversal together.

  - In a 1-D array a[10], incrementing its index leads to accessing the next element of the array. As we know, array base address is stored in its array name; adding the index i value to the array base index leads to accessing the ith element of the array. Moreover, in a 1-D array, the individual element size is equal to sizeof(data-type of array). sizeof(1-D array) = number of elements X sizeof(data-type)

  - In a 2-D array a[2][2], adding the index i value to the array base index leads to accessing ith element of the array. Since in 2-D arrays individual elements are linear arrays, adding index i value to the array base index leads to accessing the ith linear array of the array. Moreover, a 2-D array individual element size is equal to sizeof(1-D array).

  - Similarly, in the 3-D array a[2][2][2], adding the index i value to the array base index leads to accessing the ith element of the array. Since in 3-D arrays individual elements are 2-D arrays, adding the index i value to the array base index leads to accessing the ith 2-D array of the array. Moreover, a 3-D array individual element size is equal to sizeof (2-D array) = number of 1-D arrays X sizeof(1-D array).

  - We will practice in the following hands-on activity how to find individual element sizes and access N-D arrays.

CHAPTER 2   QUICK REVISION OF POWERFUL C CONSTRUCTS

- **Variable-Size Arrays**: Till now we have seen all array declarations are having fixed size. However, in many cases, it is not possible to know array size during compilation time only. Hence, to define array size during runtime, C supports variable arrays. In this hands-on activity, we will learn how to define variable-size arrays for better storage and memory utilization.

- **Row-Major or Column-Major Access**: In Chapter 1, "Basic Computer System Architecture and Essential Operating System Concepts," we studied the importance of knowing computer memory organization for storing and accessing memory locations. Specifically for storing and accessing arrays, it is necessary that the underlying system memory be organized in row-major access or column-major access.

    - For example, row-major access stores array elements in row-wise order in consecutive memory locations. In this access, developers should access these arrays in row-major access only. Otherwise, it leads to increased memory latency due to improper usage of internal caches, system buses, and many memory access cycles. In this hands-on activity, we will learn how to access arrays in row- and column-major access and evaluate respective accessing costs for deciding the right choice.

- **Optimal Loop Traversals for Better Arrays Accessing**: In many applications development, it is necessary to go through various lists in a nested traversal manner for performing scanning, searching, and computing operations. As developers, we can decide the order of nested loops to minimize memory access latencies to improve application performance.

    - For example, the outer loop size is larger and the inner loop size is smaller. Moreover, inner loop array data elements can be completely kept in main memory or caches for accessing, so there is no need to change the order of nested loops.

CHAPTER 2   QUICK REVISION OF POWERFUL C CONSTRUCTS

- On the other hand, the outer loop size is smaller and the inner loop size is bigger. Moreover, inner loop array data elements cannot be completely kept in main memory or caches for accessing, so there is a need to change the order of nested loops.
- In this hands-on activity, we will learn how to access arrays based on their size in nested loops and evaluate respective accessing costs for deciding the right nested loops order.

Let's practice these activities in the following hands-on activity.

PRACTICE N-DIMENSIONAL ARRAYS AND OPTIMAL ACCESSING CONCEPTS

1. We do the following activities using arraysacces.c. We implement the following functions to learn N-D arrays access and their individual element size identification, accessing nested array elements using array index:

    a. First, to learn 1-D array access, we define the following function. We should observe that individual array elements can be accessed using a simple array index, and their sizes can be computed using the `sizeof` operator as follows:

    ```
    #include<stdio.h>
    #include<time.h>
    int oneDarray(int a[], int n)
    {
        int i;
        for (i=0;i<n;i++)
        {
            printf(" %d",a[i]);
        }
        printf("\n");
        printf("Size of array element a[0]: %ld",sizeof(*a));
        printf("\n");
    }
    ```

93

b. To learn about 2-D array access, we define the following function. We should observe that individual array elements (1-D arrays) of 2-D can be accessed by adding an index to the array base address (a=a+1). Check how to access the 2-D array's individual elements (1-D arrays) and nested elements' sizes.

```c
int twoDarray(int a[][4], int n, int m)
{
    int i,j;
    for (i=0;i<n;i++)
    {
        for (j=0;j<m;j++)
        {
            printf(" %d",a[i][j]);
        }
        printf("\n");
    }

    printf("\nSize of array element a[0]: %ld",sizeof(*a));
    printf("\nSize of inner  array element a[0][0] : %ld", sizeof(**a));
    printf("\n");
    a=a+1;
    for (j=0;j<m;j++)
    {
        printf(" %d",a[0][j]);
    }

}
```

c. To learn about 3-D array access, we define the following function. We should observe that individual array elements (2-D arrays) of 3-D can be accessed by adding an index to the array base address (a=a+1). Check how to access the 3-D array's individual elements (2-D arrays) and nested elements' sizes.

```c
int threeDarray(int a[][2][2], int n, int m, int l)
{
    int i,j,k;
    for (i=0;i<n;i++)
    {
        for (j=0;j<m;j++)
        {
            for (k=0;k<l;k++)
            {
                printf(" %d",a[i][j][k]);
            }
            printf("\n");
        }
        printf("\n");
    }

    printf("\nSize of array element a[0]: %ld",sizeof(*a));
    printf("\nSize of inner  array element a[0][0]: %ld",sizeof(**a));
    printf("\nSize of inner inner  array element a[0][0][0]: %ld",sizeof(***a));
    printf("\n");
    a=a+1;
    for (j=0;j<m;j++)
    {
        for (k=0;k<l;k++)
        {
            printf(" %d",a[0][j][k]);

        }
        printf("\n");
    }
    printf("\n");

}
```

CHAPTER 2   QUICK REVISION OF POWERFUL C CONSTRUCTS

2. We define the following function to evaluate row-major access time vs. column-major access time. First, we define row-major access ways for accessing the given input array. Next, we define column-major access time ways for accessing the given input array. We compute both approaches' access time for our evaluations.

```c
int arrayAccess(int a[1024][1024])
{
    double time1, timedif;

    time1 = (double) clock();
    time1 = time1 / CLOCKS_PER_SEC;

    for (int i=0;i<1024; i++)
    {
        for (int j=0;j<1024;j++)
        {
            a[i][j]=i;
        }
    }
    timedif = ( ((double) clock()) / CLOCKS_PER_SEC) - time1;
    printf("Row Access The elapsed time is %lf seconds\n", timedif);

    time1 = (double) clock();
    time1 = time1 / CLOCKS_PER_SEC;

    for (int i=0;i<1024; i++)
    {
        for (int j=0;j<1024;j++)
        {
            a[j][i]=i;
        }
    }
    timedif = ( ((double) clock()) / CLOCKS_PER_SEC) - time1;
    printf("Column access The elapsed time is %lf seconds\n", timedif);

}
```

3. We define the following function to evaluate array size based on nested loops order. First, we access in the outer loop a large-size array, and in the inner loop, we access the small size array. Next, we access in the outer loop a small-size array, and in the inner loop, we access a large-size array. We compute both approaches' access time for our evaluations.

```c
int arraySizeBasedAccess()
{
      int a[2048];
      int b[8];
      double time1, timedif;
      time1 = (double) clock();
      time1 = time1 / CLOCKS_PER_SEC;
      for (int i=0;i<2048; i++)
      {
            for (int j=0;j<8;j++)
            {
                  if (a[i]==b[j])
                        ;
            }
      }
      timedif = ( ((double) clock()) / CLOCKS_PER_SEC) - time1;
      printf("Inner loop smaller size Access The elapsed time is %lf seconds\n", timedif);

      time1 = (double) clock();
      time1 = time1 / CLOCKS_PER_SEC;
      for (int i=0;i<8; i++)
      {
            for (int j=0;j<2048;j++)
            {
                  if (a[i]==b[j])
                        ;
            }
      }
```

CHAPTER 2   QUICK REVISION OF POWERFUL C CONSTRUCTS

```
            timedif = ( ((double) clock()) / CLOCKS_PER_SEC) - time1;
            printf("Inner loop larger size Access The elapsed time is
            %lf seconds\n", timedif);
    }
```

4. We define the following function to define variable-size arrays and access them.

```
    int variableSize(int n)
    {
        int a[n];
        for (int i=0;i<n;i++)
        {
            a[i]=0;
        }
        printf("Array dynamic size is:%d successfully allocated
        and initialized ",n);
    }
```

5. We will test all the above functions in main() by defining suitable arrays and calling those functions with necessary arguments as follows:

```
    int main()
    {
        int a[8] = {1,2,3,4,5,6,7,8};
        int b[2][4] = {{1,2,3,4},{5,6,7,8}};
        int c[2][2][2] = {{{1,2},{3,4}},{{5,6},{7,8}}};
        int d[2][2][2][2] = {{{{1,2},{3,4}},{{5,6},{7,8}}},
        {{{9,10},{11,12}},{{13,14},{15,16}}}};
        oneDarray(a,8);
        twoDarray(b,2,4);
        threeDarray(c,2,2,2);
        int e[1024][1024];
        arrayAccess(e);
        arraySizeBasedAccess();
        variableSize(1024);
        variableSize(10);
    }
```

CHAPTER 2   QUICK REVISION OF POWERFUL C CONSTRUCTS

6. Compile the code and run it using the following commands:

    ```
    gcc -c arrayaccess.c
    ./a.out
    ```

    a. First, observe the results related to 1-D array access and note down that a 1-D array individual element is an integer, and its size is 4 bytes.

    ```
    1 2 3 4 5 6 7 8
    Size of array element a[0]: 4
      1 2 3 4
      5 6 7 8
    ```

    b. Next, observe the results related to 2-D array access and note down that a 2-D array individual element is a 1-D array (four elements), and its size is 16 bytes. The nested array individual element size is 4 bytes.

    ```
    Size of array element a[0]: 16
    Size of inner  array element a[0][0] : 4
      5 6 7 8 1 2
      3 4

      5 6
      7 8
    ```

    c. Next, observe the results related to 3-D array access and note down that a 3-D array individual element is a 2-D array (four elements), and its size is 16 bytes. In the next level, the nested array individual element is a 1-D array (two elements), and its size is 8 bytes. In the final level, the nested array's individual element is an integer, and its size is 4 bytes.

    ```
    Size of array element a[0]: 16
    Size of inner  array element a[0][0]: 8
    Size of inner inner  array element a[0][0][0]: 4
      5 6
      7 8
    ```

d. Next, observe that row-major access time is much lower than column-major access time, because this program is tested on row-major access memory layout.

```
Row Access The elapsed time is 0.002010 seconds
Column access The elapsed time is 0.011142 seconds
```

e. Next, observe that when the outer loop is accessing a large-size array, the access time is much lower than when the outer loop is accessing a small-size array:

```
Inner loop smaller size Access The elapsed time is
0.000014 seconds
Inner loop larger size Access The elapsed time is
0.000022 seconds
```

f. From the below results, we can observe that we successfully defined an array with dynamic sizes 1024 and 10 and accessed these arrays successfully.

```
Array dynamic size is:1024 successfully allocated and
initialized
```

```
Array dynamic size is:10 successfully allocated and
initialized
```

Well done! You have successfully tested various arrays in C and how to access them to performance requirements specifically in terms of array sizes and row-major or column-major access.

Next, let's learn how to use C arrays for implementing strings and accessing them for important activities.

Strings and Buffers

In C programming, strings are implemented as character arrays. Strings are another important built-in data structure in C for processing large-size data in terms of bytes. C strings are flexible in terms of accessing and searching related programming tasks.

CHAPTER 2 QUICK REVISION OF POWERFUL C CONSTRUCTS

System and network software developers heavily use strings for handling text processing tasks, implementing cryptography algorithms, and handling network application message exchanges. C strings are declared and initialized as a character array as follows:

```c
char str1[10]= {'a','b','c','d','e','f','g','h','i','j'};
```

The C character array will be stored in memory in sequential locations as follows (shown in Figure 2-11):

0	1	2	3	4	5	6	7	8	9
a	b	c	d	e	f	g	h	i	j

Figure 2-11. *Character array memory organization*

C strings defined as character arrays must be accessed as follows by considering the length of the character array; in our example, length of the character array is 10:

```c
printf("String1: %s\n",str1);
for (int i=0;i<10;i++)
{
    printf("%c",str1[i]);
}
```

In programming, developers can use the following flexible definition for C strings. The following definition allocates a C string with a suitable number of storage locations to hold all the characters and includes a special character '\0' to terminate the string. It will be stored in memory in sequential locations as follows. Observe that after the last character, the string termination character is also stored in memory (shown in Figure 2-12):

0	1	2	3	4	5	6	7	8	9	10
a	b	c	d	e	f	g	h	i	j	\0

Figure 2-12. *C string memory organization*

C strings can be accessed as follows:

```c
char *str2 ="abcdefghij";
printf("String2: %s\n",str2);
```

CHAPTER 2 QUICK REVISION OF POWERFUL C CONSTRUCTS

In a C character array, it is necessary to know the length of the character array to process individual characters of str1. In the case of str2, without knowing the length of str2, individual characters of the string can be accessed in a flexible manner using the string-terminating character as follows:

```
int i=0;
while(str2[i]!='\0')
{
    printf("%c",str2[i]);
    i++;
}
```

In the case of str1, accessing individual characters of str1 as follows results in runtime errors. To check this, we can use the following compiler option:

```
i=0;
while(str1[i]!='\0')
{
    printf("%c",str1[i]);
    i++;
}
```

To check this, we can use the following compiler option and observe that during runtime it displays runtime error details:

```
gcc -fsanitize=undefined strings.c
./a.out
strings.c:27:25: runtime error: index 10 out of bounds for type 'char [10]'
strings.c:27:25: runtime error: load of address 0x7ffd2ef699b3 with
insufficient space for an object of type 'char'
0x7ffd2ef699b3: note: pointer points here
 67  68 69 6a 61 62 63 64 65  66 67 68 69 6a 61 62 63  64 65 66 67 68 69 6a
 00  00 f3 41 6e ad 7f 55
```

Hence, it is the responsibility of the developer to include a string-terminating character in C arrays for accessing the strings in a flexible manner as follows:

```c
char str3[11]= {'a','b','c','d','e','f','g','h','i','j','\0'};
i=0;
while(str3[i]!='\0')
{
    printf("%c",str3[i]);
    i++;
}
```

C Strings offers the following benefits to developers:

- Flexible accessing methods of large data in terms of string definition:
    - No need of knowing the length of the string. Hence, applications can construct dynamic-size strings and exchange them for processing activities easily.
- Access individual characters of strings using flexible array indexing ways. It helps in easily implementing substring search, extraction, and individual characters processing activities. Strings play an important role in the following applications:
    - Bioinformatics
    - Cryptography
    - Data processing
    - Network applications message exchanges
    - Many text processing applications
    - Compilers
- C offers `string.h` library functions to easily carry out string copying, concatenation, searching, substring processing, and modifying the individual characters of the C strings.
    - Examples: `strcpy`, `strlen`, `strcat`, `strtok`, `strstr`, `strchr`, etc.

- Since C strings are stored in sequential locations of the memory, it lets developers easily use C strings as buffers to hold input data for various processing tasks.
  - Setting up buffers to process data
  - Queueing operations
  - Temporary storage for processing intermediate results and saving the results
- C strings can be treated as blocks of memory and process them using memory library functions such as `memcpy`, `memset` `memcmp`, etc.
- C strings can be treated as a sequence of bytes. It helps in doing the following important data process and exchange activities in cryptography and network applications:
  - C character occupies one byte, and C strings are stored in memory locations sequentially. It helps in network applications to encode their messages as strings before sending them over the network.
    - Developers can be free from checking byte order (big-endian or little-endian) for processing application messages.
    - Developers can easily parse messages to match with specific fields for processing the message. It simplifies network protocol implementation for developers.
  - Encoding, decoding, encryption, and decryption of messages can be easily implemented using C strings.
    - Cryptography algorithms need to divide the large messages into blocks and process them in various phases to carry out encoding, decoding, encryption, and decryption tasks.

Next, let's practice string processing using string library functions.

Strings Processing Hands-On Activities

In this section, we mainly focus on the following important activities using string library functions:

- Basic definition of C strings and accessing strings using loops.

- String library functions are helpful for implementing bioinformatics, text processing tools, cryptography, and network applications. The following activities can be performed using string library functions easily.

- String copying, concatenation, and management of buffers for applications using the following functions:

    - `strlen, strcpy, strncpy, strcat, and strncat`

- **String Tokenization**: Dividing longer text into smaller texts or strings for performing parsing of longer text, messages, protocol headers, encoding, and decoding of the message:

    - `strtok`

- **String Matching**: Substring searching activities are important to match patterns and protocol implementation based on matching specific fields, password matching activities, finding all possible matching patterns in bioinformatics applications, and many applications. We can do the substring matching activities using the following functions:

    - `strstr, strchr, strrchr, strpbrk, and strspn`

CHAPTER 2   QUICK REVISION OF POWERFUL C CONSTRUCTS

STRINGS PROCESSING ACTIVITIES

1. We do the following activities using `strprocess.c`. We do the following tasks in `strprocess.c`.

2. First define a string, and access it using a loop and print its characters.

   ```
   #include<stdio.h>
   #include<stdlib.h>
   #include<string.h>

   int main()
   {
           char inpStr[] = "Learn c at Apress";

           int N = strlen(inpStr);
           printf("Length of the string:%d\n", N);

           int i=0;
           while (inpStr[i]!='\0')
           {
                   printf("%c",inpStr[i]);
                   i++;
           }
           printf("\n");
           printf("%s\n",inpStr);
   ```

3. Next, perform the following activities:

   a. Copy a source string `inpStr` to `inpStr2` and identify that library functions: `strcpy` and `strncpy` do not copy the string termination character automatically. It is the developer's responsibility to allocate space for the string terminating character.

   ```
   char inpStr2[N+1];
   char inpStr3[N+1];
   strcpy(inpStr2,inpStr);
   printf("Same size copy:%s\n",inpStr2);
   ```

```
strncpy(inpStr3,inpStr,10);
printf("Specific length copy:%s\n",inpStr3);
```

    b. It is the developer's responsibility to copy the terminating character to the destination string at the end of the string. Since we copied only 10 characters into `inpStr3`, we should copy '\0' at the 10th location in `inpStr3`.

```
inpStr2[N]='\0';
inpStr3[10]='\0';
printf("Specific length copy with terminator:%s\n",inpStr3);
```

4. Next, perform the following string concatenation activities:

    a. Use `strcat` to simply concatenate two strings: that is append a string to another string. In the following example, `ext2` is entirely appended to `ext1`.

```
char ext1[11] = "abcd";
char ext2[] = "abcd";
printf("%s\n", ext1);
printf("%s\n", ext2);
strcat(ext1,ext2);
printf("%s\n", ext1);
```

    b. Use `strncat` to append only a specific part of a string to another string. Append only the first two characters of `ext2` to `ext1`.

```
strncat(ext1,ext2,2);
printf("%s\n", ext1);
```

5. Tokenize a given string based on the delimiter " and print all substrings extracted from the `inpStr`:

    a. `strtok` changes the `inpStr` while tokenizing the input string; hence, we should check the `inpStr` after tokenization and before using it again.

```
char * myPtr = strtok(inpStr, " ");
while(myPtr != NULL)
{
    printf("%s\n",myPtr);
```

```
            myPtr = strtok(NULL, " ");
    }

    printf("ORIGINAL:%s\n",inpStr);
    printf("COPY:%s\n",inpStr2);
```

6. Check if a given string ("c at") is present in the input string (inpStr2):

    a. Find the given string ("c at") starting location in the inpStr2 ("Learn c at Apress"). Then, from that matching location in inpStr2 to the end of inpStr2, extract the substring and copy it to the found string.

    ```
    char *found = strstr(inpStr2, "c at");
    if (found != NULL)
    {
        printf("Found string is copied: %s\n", found);
        printf("ORIGINAL string is not changed: %s\n",
        inpStr2);
    }
    ```

7. Search for a substring given an input character from the beginning of inpStr2. Observe that from the matching character ("c") starting location in the input string (inpStr2) ("Learn c at Apress") till the end of the inpStr2 will be copied to the output string found1 ("c at Apress").

    ```
    char * found1 = strchr(inpStr2, 'c');
    ```

8. Search for a substring given an input character from the end of inpStr2. Observe that from the matching character ("r") last location in the input string (inpStr2) ("Learn c at Apress") till the end of the inpStr2 will be copied to the output string found2 ("ress").

    ```
    char * found2 = strrchr(inpStr2, 'r');
    if (found1!=NULL)
            printf("Search From the Start:%s\n",found1);
    if (found2!=NULL)
            printf("Search From the Last:%s\n",found2);
    ```

9. Give a set of characters ("Ars") to match any of these characters in the input string (inpStr2), and collect the matching substring from the beginning to the end of the input string into found3:

```
char *found3 = strpbrk(inpStr2, "Ars");
if (found3 != NULL)
{
    printf("Some Character found from Ars at inpStr2 and from
    the character string is copied into found3:%s\n", found3);
}
```

10. Give a set of characters ("123") to match any of these characters in the input string (inpStr2), and collect the matching substring from the beginning to the end of the input string into found3:

    ```
    found3 = strpbrk(inpStr2, "123");
    if (found3 != NULL)
    {
        printf("Some Character found at:%s\n", found3);
    }
    else
    {
        printf("123 Characters are not found in:%s\n",inpStr2);
    }
    printf("Original String: %s\n", inpStr2);
    ```

11. Give a substring and check what is the longest substring length found in the input string (inpStr2):

    a. In the following test, check for the longest substring length given a matching string "Learn c at" to find in inpStr2.

       ```
       int index = strspn(inpStr2, "Learn c at");
       printf("Length of the longest matching substring found in
       inpStr2 %d\n", index);
       ```

    b. In the following test only part of the "Learn b at" matches in inpStr2.

       ```
       index = strspn(inpStr2, "Learn b at");
       printf("Length of the longest matching substring found in
       inpStr2 %d\n", index);
       ```

CHAPTER 2 QUICK REVISION OF POWERFUL C CONSTRUCTS

c. In the following test no part of the "Yearn b at" matches in inpStr2.

d. These results you can observe while testing it.

```
index = strspn(inpStr2, "Yearn c at");
printf("Length of the longest matching substring found in inpStr2 %d\n", index);

}
```

12. First compile the code and test it:

```
#gcc strporcess.c
#./a.out
```

a. From the following output, first observe the input string length is 17 characters, and we successfully traversed through the loop and printed individual characters.

```
Lenght of the string:17
Learn c at Apress
Learn c at Apress
```

b. From the following output, observe that strncpy does not copy '\0' automatically. Hence, it is displaying random characters after the 10th character.

```
Same size copy:Learn c at Apress
Specific length copy:Learn c ate�
Specific length copy with terminator:Learn c at
```

c. From the following output, next observe that we successfully combined two input strings.

```
abcd
abcd
abcdabcd
abcdabcdab
```

CHAPTER 2 QUICK REVISION OF POWERFUL C CONSTRUCTS

d. From the output, next observe that the input string is tokenized into the following substrings and the original input string was changed.

```
Learn
c
at
Apress
ORIGINAL:Learn
COPY:Learn c at Apress
```

e. From the following output, next observe that from the input string, the matching substring part is copied into the found string, and we print it.

```
Learn c at Apress
Found string is copied: c at Apress
ORIGINAL string is not changed: Learn c at Apress
```

f. From the following output, next observe that from the search character using `strchr`, the search starts at the beginning of the input string and copies the matching substring till the end of the input string into the found string, and we print it.

```
Search From the Start:c at Apress
```

g. From the following output, next observe that from the search character using `strrchr`, the search starts at the end of the input string and copies the matching substring till the end of the input string into the found string, and we print it.

```
Search From the Last:ress
```

h. From the following output, next observe that from the input string ("Ars") using `strpbrk`, the matching substring starts at the r of the input string, and till the end of the input string is successfully copied into the found string, and we print it.

```
Some Character found from Ars at inpStr2 and from the
character string is copied into found3:rn c at Apress
```

111

i. From the following output, next observe that from the input string ("123") using `strpbrk`, no substring match is found.

   ```
   123 Characters are not found in:Learn c at Apress
   ```

j. From the following output, next observe that using `strspn`, it is possible to get the length of the longest substring match found in `inpstr2`:

   ```
   Length of the longest matching substring found in inpStr2 11
   Length of the longest matching substring found in inpStr2 6
   Length of the longest matching substring found in inpStr2 0
   ```

Well done! You have successfully tested important string library functions for handling string processing tasks.

Next, we discuss another powerful C programming construct: structures and how to use them in interesting C applications development.

C Structures

In C programming, structures are another important data structure for organizing and accessing heterogeneous data elements in a flexible way. Due to the power of combining a variety of data elements (`int, float, char,` etc.) under a structure variable, developers have the power to model complex concepts easily. Moreover, structures can be used to model tiny data members such as bits holding data members (`int flag1:2;` it occupies only 2 bits). Hence, structures are very helpful to model real-world concepts into the C programming domain. For example, C structures are useful to model people, devices, features, specifications, characteristics, transactions, protocols, complex concepts, etc.

For example, in the case of developing a users' list for software, developers can easily model users' specific details into a structure as follows.

```
struct user
{
    int id;
    char passwd[10];
    int permission;
};
```

CHAPTER 2　QUICK REVISION OF POWERFUL C CONSTRUCTS

In the above struct definition, struct is a keyword and user is the structure name. Once a structure is defined, developers can use it as a data type for creating variables and accessing the structure variables as follows:

struct user u1;

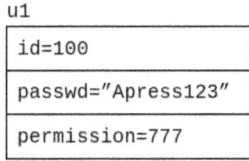

Figure 2-13. *C structure memory layout*

Assign values to a structure variable (u1) and access them as follows:

```
u1.id=100;
strcpy(u1.passwd, "apress123");
u1.permission=777;
printf("%d %s %d", u1.id,u1.passwd,u1.permission);
```

Developers should observe here that the u1 variable is holding all the data members of struct user. It means structure is helping developers to logically combine related data members together and access them in a flexible manner. Moreover, it simplifies defining multiple users as follows:

struct user u2, u3, u4;

Figure 2-14. *C structure variables memory layout*

During program execution, in memory for each of the structure variables, unique memory blocks will be allocated as shown in Figure 2-14. Hence, changes in structure variables are specific to their memory blocks only.

113

Moreover, a list of users can also be easily created using an array of structure variables as follows:

```
struct user userlist[100];
```

Developers must note that, similar to any array, structure arrays are also stored in memory in contiguous locations as follows (shown in Figure 2-15):

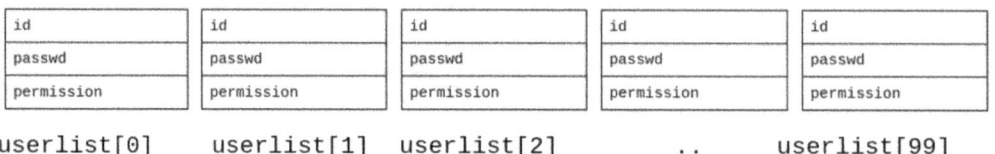

Figure 2-15. *C array of structure variables memory layout*

Developers can use the structures for doing the following important activities:

- To model real-world concepts into a programming domain. Examples: modeling people, devices, concepts, transactions, and protocols.

- To implement a variety of data structures. Structure variables can be modeled as an array of structure variables. It helps in modeling lists of persons, devices, etc.

- To implement important data structures such as linked lists, doubly linked lists, and circular linked lists. Which are important data structures used in OS development for organizing process and files data.

- To implement optimal accessing time-based data structures such as trees, binary trees, binary search trees, B+ trees, B trees, a variety of graphs, and hashing tables. These data structures play an important role in database and file-accessing applications.

- To implement protocol messages. All network protocol messages are implemented in terms of structure with suitable protocol header fields.

CHAPTER 2 QUICK REVISION OF POWERFUL C CONSTRUCTS

- Structures are very flexible for combining bit-level variables also. Hence, in protocol implementation, flags can be easily included as part of the structure.

- Moreover, structure allows combining other structures; hence, it is easy to implement protocol stacks.

Next, let's learn how functions will exchange structure variables for computations.

Passing Structure Variables Between Functions

Structure variables also can be passed between functions for data exchange. When passing a structure variable to a function, a developer should know the following details:

- By default, structure variables are passed to a caller function from a callee function using the call by value approach.

    ```
    void access(struct user u) {u.id=200; strcpy(u.passwd,"12345");u.permission=666; };
    int main()   {struct user u1;
    u1.id=100;strcpy(u1.passwd,"Apress123");
    u1.permission=777; access(u1);}
    ```

- For example, in the above sample code snippet, main() is passing a structure variable u1 to access(). In this case, u1 variable values are copied from the main() memory layout to the access() memory layout. Hence, any changes made in access() memory layout will not be reflected in main() memory layout (shown in Figure 2-16).

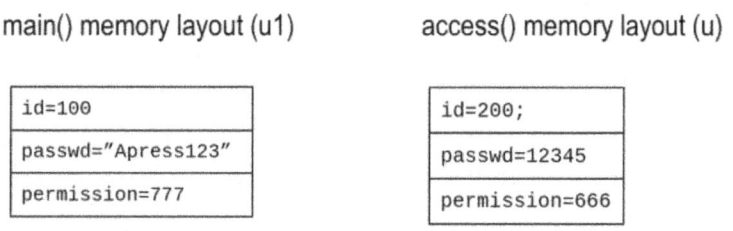

Figure 2-16. *C structure memory layout*

- Hence, in case updating structure variables is needed, developers should pass structure variables using the call by reference approach as follows:

  ```
  void access(struct user *u) {u->id=200; strcpy(u-
  >passwd,"12345");u->permission=666; };
  int main()   {struct user u1;
  u1.id=100;strcpy(u1.passwd,"Apress123");
  u1.permission=777; access(&u1);}
  ```

- From the above code, developers should understand that the structure variable address (&u1) is passed from the callee function (main()) to the caller function (access()). Hence, any changes done to the structure variable's data members in the caller function will be reflected in the caller function.

main() memory layout (u1)

| id=200; |
| passwd=12345 |
| permission=666 |

Figure 2-17. *C structure memory layout*

As shown in Figure 2-17, for u1, memory will be allocated at main() only. Hence, all changes are done in the main() memory layout only.

Since we observe, passing structure variables is a costly operation in terms of memory allocations and updating to structure data members. The developer should take the following responsibilities in case of declaring a structure and passing structure variables to functions:

- Structure variables passing eliminates the need of passing multiple variables to caller functions and tracking them for computations.

- However, developers should define structures with only necessary data members to save memory space.

- If necessary, developers should pass structure variables to the caller function using call by reference approach; it helps in avoiding unnecessary memory copy operations and accesses. Passing structure variables by call by reference helps in meeting performance requirements in terms of saving memory and reducing memory access cost and latencies.

Next, we will discuss more details about the structure data members' memory organization and their issues in terms of optimal use of memory and accessing structure variables efficiently to meet application performance needs.

Structure and Its Data Members' Memory Layout

In the case of C program structure data members' memory allocation, compilers can align structure data members and include necessary padding bytes for efficiently accessing structure variables from the memory by the CPU. In general, a CPU's memory access latency is minimal when a variable memory location address is a multiple of its data processing size. On a 64-bit machine, at a time the CPU can efficiently perform memory read or write operations in terms of 8 bytes by setting up memory banks. Hence, 8-byte alignment is needed for storing data members. Developers must choose necessary byte alignment based on CPU bit processing capabilities while defining structures to offer efficient memory access to structure data members.

Moreover, compilers offer multiple of 2, 4, 8 bytes alignments to meet various applications data access requirements. By default a compiler chooses the largest alignment requirement within the structure based on its internal data members having maximum data type size.

For example, on a 64-bit machine (int (32-bit), char (8-bit), double (64-bit)):

```
struct sample
{
    int i;
    char c;
    double d;
};

struct sample s1;
```

Then, the structure variable s1 will be stored in memory with 8-byte alignment due to double needs 8-byte memory. Hence, structure variable s1 occupies 24 bytes of memory. This can be checked in our upcoming hands-on activity. It means although s1 needs only 13 bytes of memory, it will be stored in a 24-byte memory block with 11 bytes of padding bytes for offering efficient access. Moreover, developers can choose flexible alignment options using the following attribute (__attribute__((aligned(4)))) as follows:

```
struct SampleAligned
{
    int i;
    char c;
    double d;
}__attribute__((aligned(4)));
```

On the other hand, sometimes developers want to optimally utilize the limited memory. Then, it is necessary to organize the structure data members in memory to minimize memory space utilization. It is technically known as packing structure data members. Developers can define structures with the __attribute__((packed)) option to indicate to the compiler to pack the particular structure data members.

```
struct SampleAligned
{
    int i;
    char c;
    double d;
}__attribute__((packed));

struct SampleAligned a1;
```

Now a1 size will be only 13 bytes. The packed option helps in greatly minimizing the memory size to organize structured data elements. However, it results in poor memory access and increased latency. In C programming, it is possible to use both aligned and packed options together for offering better memory access and memory utilization.

Hands-On Activity-1

In this hands-on activity, we do the following activities for learning about structure data member's organization and optimal ways for accessing and storing structure data members:

- First explore the default structure data members memory organization

- Learn programming ways to optimally store structure data members
- **Use Compiler Attribute**: aligned for organizing structure data members to offer better memory access to structure data members
- **Use Compiler Attribute**: packed for organizing structure data members to minimize structure variables data storage

STRUCTURE DATA MEMBERS MEMORY ORGANIZATION

1. We implement this hands-on activity in `structmem.c`. First, we define the following structures for carrying out and learning better structure data members memory organization:

2. Define the following structures to learn about the responsibility of developers in defining a structure by organizing its data members:

```c
#include <stdio.h>
struct BadOrg
{
        char d2;
        int d1;
        char d4;
        int d3;
        char d6;
        int d5;
};
struct GoodOrg
{
        char d2;
        char d4;
        char d6;
        int d1;
        int d3;
        int d5;
};
```

CHAPTER 2   QUICK REVISION OF POWERFUL C CONSTRUCTS

3. Define the following structures to learn about default structure data members' memory layout and how to use the compiler attribute (aligned) to force the structure's data members' memory layout:

   ```
   struct DefAligned
   {
           double d1;
           int i1;
           double d2;
           char c1
   };
   struct ForcedAligned
   {
           double d1;
           int i1;
           double d2;
           char c1
   }__attribute__((aligned(4)));
   ```

4. Define the following structures to learn about how to use compiler attributes (packed and aligned) to minimize memory space and align data members for optimal access:

   ```
   struct Packed
   {
           double d1;
           int i1;
           double d2;
           char c1
   }__attribute__((packed));

   struct ForcedAlignedPacked
   {
           double d1;
           int i1;
           double d2;
           char c1
   }__attribute__((packed,aligned(4)));
   ```

CHAPTER 2　QUICK REVISION OF POWERFUL C CONSTRUCTS

5. Define the following structures to learn about various alignment options to minimize memory space and align data members for optimal access:

   ```
   struct SelectAligned1
   {
        double d1;
        int i1;
        double d2;
        char c1
   }__attribute__((aligned(2)));
   struct SelectAligned2
   {
        double d1;
        int i1;
        double d2;
        char c1
   }__attribute__((packed,aligned(4)));
   ```

6. Define the main() function to test all the above structures' data member organizations and observe their sizes during the program execution:

   ```
   int main()
   {
        struct GoodOrg go;
        struct BadOrg bo;
        struct DefAligned a1;
        struct ForcedAligned a2;
        struct ForcedAlignedPacked pa2;
        struct SelectAligned1 a3;
        struct SelectAligned2 a4;
        Struct Packed p1;
        printf("Good Organization = %lu\n", sizeof(go));
        printf("Bad Organization = %lu\n", sizeof(bo));
        printf("Default Organization = %lu\n", sizeof(a1));
        printf("Forced Organization = %lu\n", sizeof(a2));
        printf("Packed Organization = %lu\n", sizeof(p1));
   ```

CHAPTER 2 QUICK REVISION OF POWERFUL C CONSTRUCTS

```
        printf("Forced and packed Organization = %lu\n",
        sizeof(pa2));
        printf("Choose necessary alignment = %lu\n", sizeof(a3));
        printf("Choose necessary alignment = %lu\n", sizeof(a4));

        return 0;
}
```

7. Save and compile the code and test it using the following command:

```
#./a.out
Good Organization = 16
Bad Organization = 24
```

a. Observe from the above results that having both structure variables, go and bo, with the same data members in the case of the careless way (bo) of defining structures can lead to more memory space utilization than good organization (go).

b. Developers should organize data members as shown in GoodOrg, that is, according to their data members' data type, to minimize memory space utilization.

```
Default Organization = 32
Forced Organization = 24
```

c. Observe from the above results that having both structure variables, a1 and a2, with the same data members, in the case of default memory alignment (a1), the compiler is choosing the largest data type size.

d. However, it is possible to define necessary memory alignments using the aligned attribute.

```
Packed Organization = 21
Forced and packed Organization = 24
Choose necessary alignment = 32
Choose necessary alignment = 24
```

CHAPTER 2   QUICK REVISION OF POWERFUL C CONSTRUCTS

e. Observe from the above results that having all structure variables (p1, pa2, a3, a4) with the same data members, developers can carefully select packed and aligned options:

  i. To minimize memory space, the packed option is helpful.

  ii. To minimize memory space and improve memory access time, both packed and aligned options are helpful.

  iii. Developers can also choose necessary alignment (1, 2, 4, 8) options using aligned.

In summary, developers should play an important role in organizing structure data members for minimizing memory utilization and improving memory access time. Otherwise, applications may suffer with higher memory latencies and high memory utilization.

Next, let's quickly check how to model various data structures and protocols using C structures.

Power of C Structures for Modeling

In C programming, structures allow developers to model real-world entities, concepts, protocols, and data structures. Let's quickly check the following data structure examples for better understanding and modeling details.

Data Structures Modeling

Popular data structures such as linked lists and doubly linked lists can be easily modeled in C using structures. For example, as shown in Figure 2-18, in simple linked lists, a set of nodes are connected in a linear way using pointers. It can be modeled in a C structure containing two important data members: one is the node's data, and another is a pointer to store the next node's memory address. Similarly, in a doubly linked list, a set of nodes are connected together using two pointers for traversing in both directions of the list. Hence, it is implemented in a C structure containing three data members: the node's data and pointers to the left-side and right-side nodes.

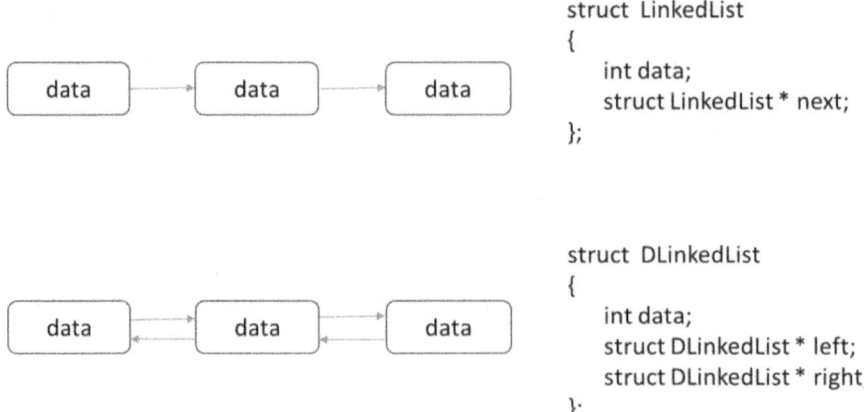

Figure 2-18. *Modeling of linked lists and double-linked C structures*

Similarly, a binary tree can be modeled using a C structure, as shown in Figure 2-19. Observe that the structure contains the node's data and two pointers to point to the left binary tree and right binary tree addresses.

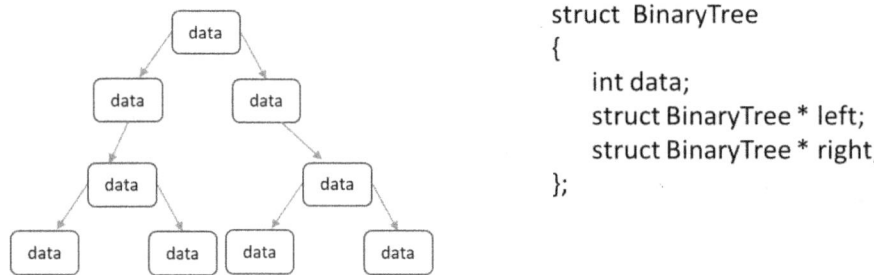

Figure 2-19. *Modeling of binary trees in C structures*

On the other hand, to model a general tree (Figure 2-20), it is necessary to include multiple branches in a tree structure. It can be modeled in a C structure containing the node's data and a double pointer to hold an array of pointers to point to multiple subtrees. We discuss pointers in detail in the pointers chapter.

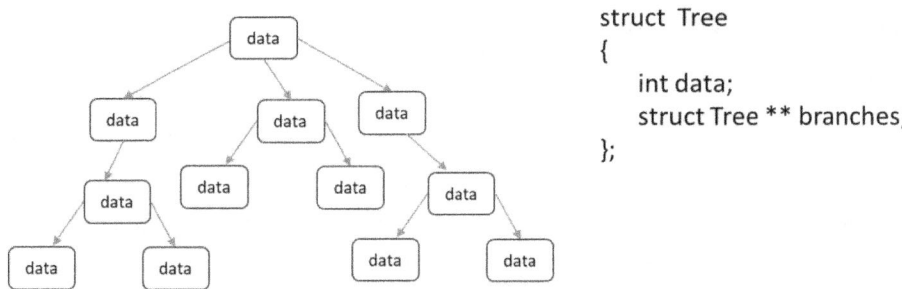

Figure 2-20. *Modeling of general trees in C structures*

```
struct Tree
{
    int data;
    struct Tree ** branches;
};
```

Similar to model multi-key search trees, as shown in Figure 2-21, we can use C structures containing the following data members: a pointer to hold an array of key values and a double pointer to hold matching search trees.

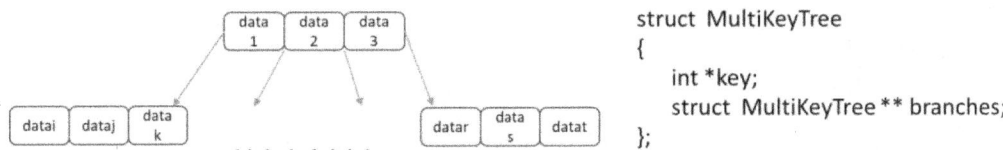

```
struct MultiKeyTree
{
    int *key;
    struct MultiKeyTree ** branches;
};
```

Figure 2-21. *Modeling of multi-key search trees in C structures*

Similarly, graphs can be modeled in C structures containing the following data members: the node's label (vertex) and a double pointer to create multiple edges from vertices, as shown in Figure 2-22.

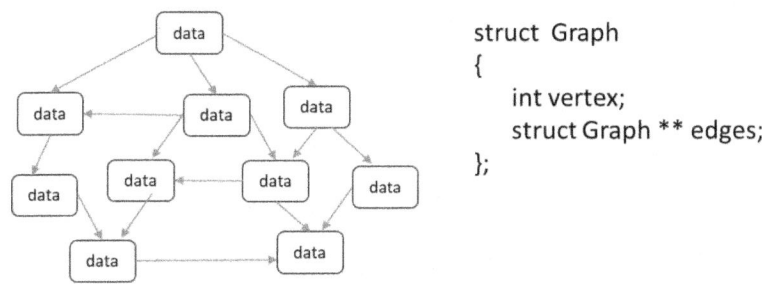

```
struct Graph
{
    int vertex;
    struct Graph ** edges;
};
```

Figure 2-22. *Modeling of graphs in C structures*

Next, we will discuss the power of C structure in terms of implementing protocols and protocol stacks.

CHAPTER 2   QUICK REVISION OF POWERFUL C CONSTRUCTS

Protocols and Protocol Stack Modeling

In order to implement popular system software such as OS, database management systems (DBMS), and network protocols, it is necessary to know how to model protocols and protocol stack-related messages. In this section, we quickly introduce how to model a simple network-related protocol and protocol stack modeling. It helps developers to quickly experiment with network protocols related to C code.

A protocol is nothing but a set of rules for performing a specific task. In computer networks, a protocol is a set of rules to exchange a message between sender and receiver. In protocol implementation, a sender sends a message to a destination by embedding all rules in the message. For example, let's assume a sender is sending a message, and the message should be embedded with the following rules so that the receiver can accept and process the message:

- Every message must be enclosed with a header. Similar to an envelope in the case of mail exchange.

- The header of a message should contain both sender and receiver addresses. So that receiver checks whether the message is destined to it or not.

- To understand and process the message, the sender may impose specific rules in the header by setting specific bits. For example:

    - Starting two bits of the header indicate the type of message.

    - Next, two bits of the header indicate the priority of the message.

    - Next, three bits of the header indicate the size of the message to decode at high priority.

    - Next, bit of the header indicates the request or response message.

In order to implement this simple network protocol between sender and receiver, we understand every message must be included with a header; hence, first we define the `ProtocolHeader` with the necessary fields (structure data members). Observe from Figure 2-23 that the header first byte is encoded to include protocol rules. It helps the receiver in checking the message type, priority, size of the message to decode at priority, and request or response message. Next, observe from Figure 2-23 that to create a suitable network application message using the protocol header, we defined `NetApplication` using the ProtocolHeader.

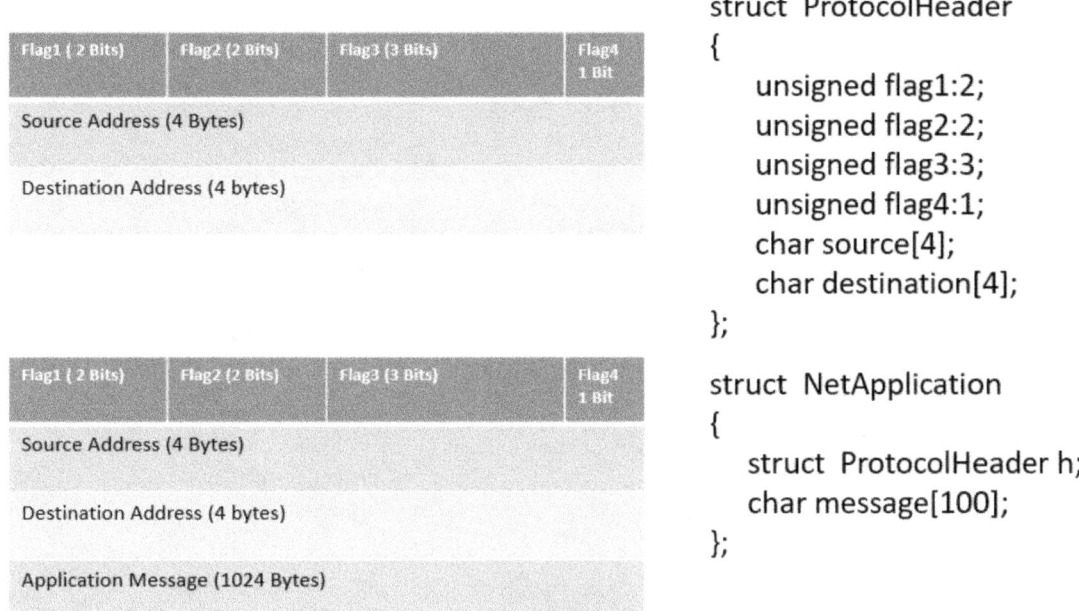

Figure 2-23. Modeling of a protocol in C structures

Similarly, we can use this approach to implement various protocol headers and arrange them in a logical order to create a protocol stack. For example, we can define a simple protocol stack using protocol1 and protocol2 headers as shown in Figure 2-24. Observe from Figure 2-24 that we included two protocol headers (structure variables) in the C protocol stack structure.

CHAPTER 2   QUICK REVISION OF POWERFUL C CONSTRUCTS

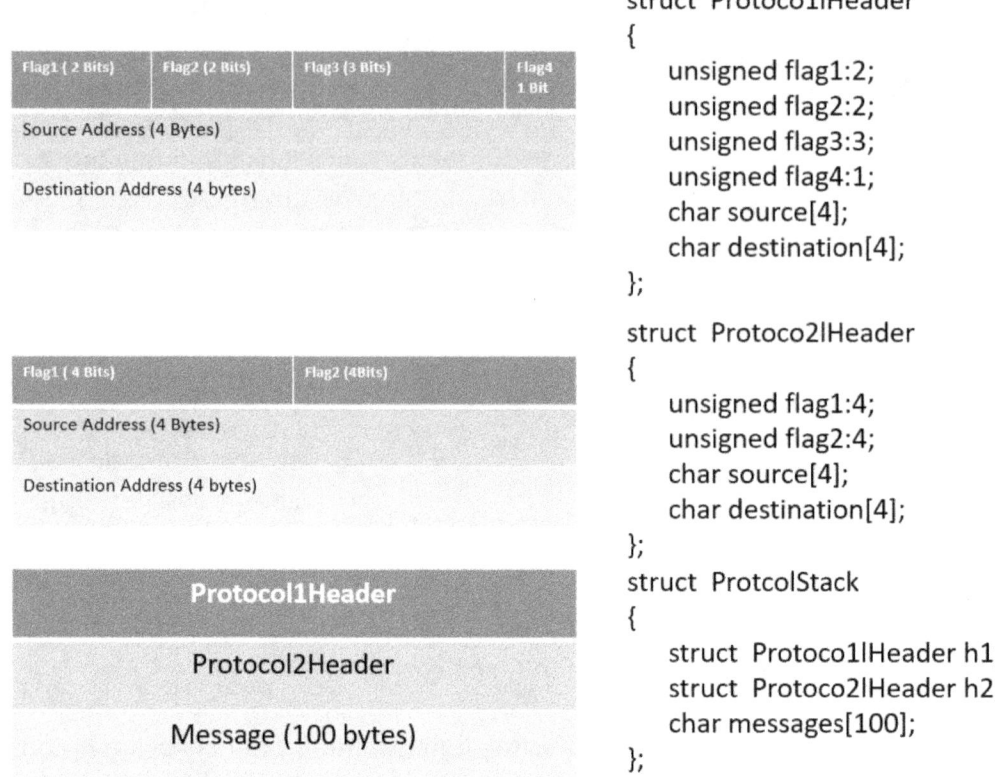

Figure 2-24. *Modeling of a protocol stack in C structures*

Next, let's practice how to implement a simple protocol using C structures.

Hands-On Activity-2

In this hands-on activity, we do the following activities using C structures:

1. Define a packet structure to simulate a protocol message with the following rules:

    a. The message is divided into 4 bytes.

    b. First byte describes four flags in an order (flag1: 1 bit, flag2: 1 bit, flag-3: 3 bits, and flag-4: 3 bits).

    c. Second byte describes the source address.

CHAPTER 2 QUICK REVISION OF POWERFUL C CONSTRUCTS

　　d. Third byte describes the destination address.

　　e. Fourth byte describes the actual message.

2. Create a sample packet using the packet structure

3. Parse the sample packet and print each byte's details

SAMPLE PROTOCOL PACKET IMPLEMENTATION AND TESTING

1. We implement all these hands-on activities in protocol.c:

2. First define the following C structure to implement the protocol messages containing flags, source and destination addresses, and actual data.

```
#include<stdio.h>
#include<stdlib.h>
#include<string.h>
struct Packet
{
        unsigned int f1:1;
        unsigned int f2:1;
        unsigned int f3:3;
        unsigned int f4:3;
        char src;
        char dst;
        char data;
};
```

3. Define the following C code in main() to implement a sample packet:

```
int main()
{
        struct Packet p1;
        printf("Size of packet:%ld\n",sizeof(p1));

        p1.f1=0;
        p1.f2=1;
        p1.f3=7;
```

129

CHAPTER 2   QUICK REVISION OF POWERFUL C CONSTRUCTS

```
p1.f4=4;
p1.src='A';
p1.dst='D';
p1.data='H';
```

4. Print the sample packet contents:

```
printf("Packet contents:\n");
printf("%u %u %u %u %c %c %c\n",p1.f1,p1.f2,p1.f3,p1.f4,p1.src,p1.dst,p1.data);
```

5. Parse the sample packet and print each byte's details:

   a. First, we copy the structure variable into a string buffer using memcpy function. Since each character is one byte in strings, it helps to easily parse the sample packet in terms of bytes.

   ```
   printf("Parsing Packet of 4 bytes\n");
       char buffer[4];
       memcpy(buffer,&p1,4);
   ```

6. Observe that to parse the first byte, we use bitwise operators &, right shift operators.

   a. For example: To parse the flag1 value, we need to check the last bit (0th bit) of the first byte; hence, we do the mask operation over the last bit using 00000001 and the first byte and print the value of the flag.

   b. To parse flag2, we need to check the first bit of the first byte; hence, we do a mask operation over the last 2 bits of the first byte using the binary value 00000010 (in hexadecimal, it is 2). Then right-shift the first byte one time to skip the one bit of flag1 and access the flag2 bit value.

   c. To parse flag3, we need to check the 2nd, 3rd, and 4th bits of the first byte; hence, we do a mask operation over the last 5 bits of the first byte using the binary value 00011110 (in hexadecimal, it is 1C). Then, right-shift the first byte twice to skip two bits of flag1 and flag2 and access the flag3 bit values.

d. To parse flag4, we need to check the 5th, 6th, and 7th bits of the first byte; hence, we do a mask operation over the last 7 bits of the first byte using the binary value 11100000 (in hexadecimal, it is E0). Then, right-shift the first byte five times to skip five bits of flag1, flag2, and flag3, and access the flag4 bit values.

```
for (int i=0;i<4;i++)
{
        if (i==0)
        {
                printf("Flag1: %u Flag2: %u Flag3:%u
                Flag4:%u\n", (buffer[i]&0x01),
                (buffer[i]&0x02) >> 1, (buffer[i]&0x1C) >>
                2, (buffer[i]&0xE0) >> 5);
        }
        if (i==1)
        {
                printf("Source Address: %c \n",buffer[i]);
        }
        if (i==2)
        {
                printf("Destination Address: %c \n",
                buffer[i]);
        }
        if (i==3)
        {
                printf("Data: %c \n",buffer[i]);
        }
}
return 0;
}
```

7. It is simple to access 2nd, 3rd, and 4th bytes directly from the buffer and print individual values:

8. Save the code and compile it for testing using the following commands:

   ```
   #./a.out
   Size of packet:4
   Packet contents:
   0 1 7 4 A D H
   ```

   a. Observe from the results, we successfully created the sample packet and printed its contents:

      ```
      Parsing Packet of 4 bytes
      Flag1: 0 Flag2: 1 Flag3:7 Flag4:4
      ```

   b. Observe from the results, we successfully parsed the flags of the first byte and printed those contents:

      ```
      Source Address: A
      Destination Address: D
      Data: H
      ```

   c. Observe from the results, we successfully parsed source, destination, and data contents.

Well done. We successfully created a sample protocol packet containing flags and addresses. Then, we learned how to parse the packet to access all its internal field values.

In this section, you have learned how to use structure for modeling various data structures, the memory layout of structure data members, and optimally storing and retrieving structure data members. At the end we practiced how to use structure for modeling protocol messages. Next, let's learn another important C programming construct called union for better organizing structure data members and handling optimal memory organization tasks for creating protocol stack messages.

C Unions

C union is helpful to combine a variety of data members and store them in memory for optimally utilizing the memory space. For example, we need to create a sample structure containing three data members, but applications may use at any time only one of the three data members from the structure. If developers organize these data members in C structures, it leads to wastage of memory space. In the case of structures for every data member, memory must be allocated. This problem can be handled by unions as follows:

```
union Sample
{
        int i;
        char c;
        double d;
        double e;
};
union Sample s1;
s1.d = 1.23456;
```

From the above `union` definition, developers should understand the following details:

- `union` is a keyword to define unions in C. Union variables and data members can be accessed in the same way as structure variables. Union variables also can be passed between functions for data exchange. In functions, union variable accessing rules are the same as structure variable accessing rules.

    - By default, union variables are passed by value.

    - Union variables can be passed by reference.

    - Union data members can be accessed using . and pointer operators.

- During program execution, for union `s1` variable, only 8 bytes of memory are allocated on 64-bit machines. In the case of a C `struct` organization, the `s1` variable occupies 13 bytes of memory. It means union variables have memory allocation for only one of its largest-size data members.

- Developers should use `union` variables carefully while assigning data from `union` variable data members.

- Otherwise, accessing `union` variables may give unexpected results. For example, in the case of `s1`, if a value is assigned to data member d.

CHAPTER 2　QUICK REVISION OF POWERFUL C CONSTRUCTS

union variable s1

```
8 bytes of memory holds the value
1.23456
```

- If the developer accesses e, then he also gets 1.23456. He can update e, but e value was never assigned by the developer. It results in unexpected results while accessing d. It is due to the union variable memory layout that is allocating memory for only the largest data size variable. Hence, developers must keep track of which union data members are stored in union variables and how to access them correctly.

- Due to the union unique memory organization, it allows developers to save memory space.

- Union memory layout is very helpful to efficiently pack nested structures in case of protocol messages implementation.

An Important Use Case of Unions

C programming developers must know how to use C unions for efficiently creating nested structures and accessing them in a flexible manner and utilizing memory space optimally for storing nested structures. Let's quickly check the following example for developing protocol message structure implementation.

For example, in the case of developing a protocol stack, it is necessary to include specific protocol headers in a structure to create a protocol message. A standard TCP/IP protocol stack can include multiple protocol layers (l1, l2, l3, … l7), but to support multiple network applications, a network application message needs to include only specific protocol headers. Moreover, to simplify communication between network applications, usually a few standard interfaces will be offered to access the protocol stack. Then, while sending a message using the standard interface, a specific packet (e.g., a routing packet) should include only necessary headers (l1, l2, l3), but the network application packet should include all layers (l1 to l7). To handle this requirement, developers can implement necessary protocol headers as structures as shown in Figure 2-25. Then, to implement the protocol stack using unions, only necessary headers can be included, as shown in Figure 2-25.

CHAPTER 2   QUICK REVISION OF POWERFUL C CONSTRUCTS

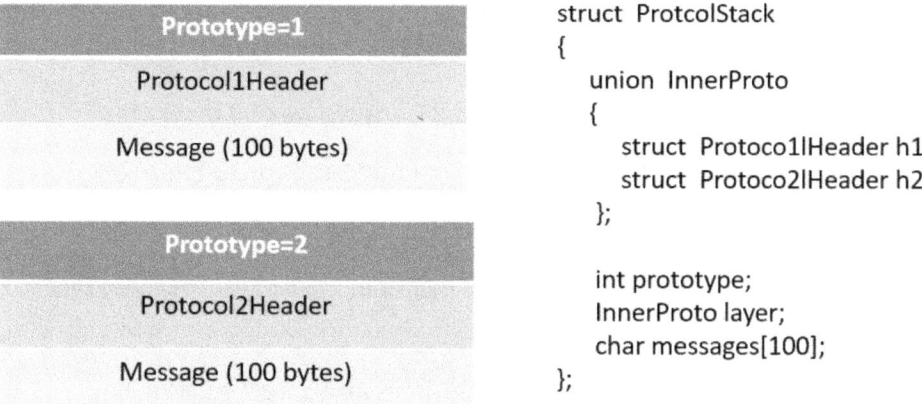

Figure 2-25. *Modeling of a protocol stack using C unions and structures*

Developers must understand the following details from Figure 2-24.

- Developers should first implement independent protocol headers as structures using C struct (`Protocol1Header` and `Protocol2Header`).

- To develop a protocol stack, suppose only one header is used out of two protocol headers at a time; then, it can be handled using a `union` definition as shown in Figure 2-25.

- Developers should include a `type` variable to keep track of which protocol header is going to be included in the protocol stack. In this example, int type is used.

- Because of union, the `ProtocolStack` variable size will be equal to (int type (4 bytes) + message (100 bytes)) + (sizeof(`Protocol1Header`) or sizeof(`Protocol2Header`)). It means developers save memory space optimally while creating a `ProtocolStack` variable.

Next, let's practice unions by developing a simple protocol structure.

Hands-On Activity

We do the following simple protocol stack called MyProto implementation using structures and union concepts in C.

CHAPTER 2   QUICK REVISION OF POWERFUL C CONSTRUCTS

- First, we implement three simple layers of protocol headers that hold source and destination addresses only.
    - Layer1 header includes src and dst addresses of 8 bytes.
    - Layer2 header includes src and dst addresses of 32 bits.
    - Layer3 header includes src and dst addresses of 5 bytes.
- However, while sending a `MyProto` protocol message, only one layer address should be included in it.
- `MyProto` must include the type of address and actual message of 100 bytes.
- Developers should optimally store `MyProto` messages for minimizing memory space.

IMPLEMENT A SAMPLE PROTOCOL USING STRUCT AND UNION

1. We do this hands-on activity in `myproto.c`.
2. First define three layers of protocol headers using C `struct` as follows to store their respective source and destination addresses:

```
#include<string.h>
#include<stdio.h>
struct L1
{
      char src[9];
      char dst[9];
};
struct L2
{
      unsigned int src;
      unsigned int dst;
};
```

136

```
struct L3
{
    char src[5];
    char dst[5];
};
```

3. Define the `MyProto` structure to create protocol messages with necessary headers and a message.

   a. Observe that we use `union` inside the `MyProto` structure to include any one of three layers (`L1`, `L2`, and `L3`) addresses only.

   b. We also include a `type` field in the `MyProto` structure to track layer addresses for creating and parsing `MyProto` messages.

   ```
   struct MyProto
   {
       int type;
       union PacketAddress
       {
           struct L1 l1;
           struct L2 l2;
           struct L3 l3;
       };
       union PacketAddress address;
       char buffer[100];
   };
   ```

4. Define the following function to create a `MyProto` protocol packet:

   a. Observe that based on the type of layer, we include the respective layer structure variable in the `MyProto` packet structure.

   b. To parse correctly `MyProto` packets, we should set the `type` of the packet to the correct protocol header type.

c. After setting up the correct header, we included a sample message in a MyProto packet. We return it to the callee function.

```c
struct MyProto Packet(int t, char *pkt)
{
    struct MyProto p1;
    if (t == 1)
    {
        p1.type = t;
        strcpy(p1.address.l1.src,"aabbccdd");
        p1.address.l1.src[8]='\0';
        strcpy(p1.address.l1.dst,"aabbccde");
        p1.address.l1.dst[8]='\0';
    }
    if (t == 2)
    {
        p1.type = t;
        p1.address.l2.src=12345;
        p1.address.l2.dst=54321;
    }
    if (t == 3)
    {
        p1.type = t;
        strcpy(p1.address.l3.src,"aabb");
        p1.address.l3.src[4]='\0';
        strcpy(p1.address.l3.dst,"aadd");
        p1.address.l3.dst[4]='\0';
    }
    if (pkt!=NULL)
    {
        strcpy(p1.buffer,pkt);
    }
    return p1;
}
```

CHAPTER 2 QUICK REVISION OF POWERFUL C CONSTRUCTS

5. Define the following function to parse the MyProto protocol packet and print its contents:

    a. Observe that based on the type of layer, respective header addresses are accessed.

    b. Note type plays an important role in the correct usage of union data members. Hence, developers should carefully choose a type variable and include it in union-based structures.

    ```
    void PacketDisplay(struct MyProto *p1)
    {
            printf("Type: %d", p1->type);
            if (p1->type == 1)
            {
                    printf("Src: %s", p1->address.l1.src);
                    printf("Dst: %s", p1->address.l1.dst);
            }
            if (p1->type == 3)
            {
                    printf("Src: %s", p1->address.l3.src);
                    printf("Dst: %s", p1->address.l3.dst);
            }
            if (p1->type == 2)
            {
                    printf("Src: %u", p1->address.l2.src);
                    printf("Dst: %u", p1->address.l2.dst);
            }
            printf("Data: %s\n", p1->buffer);
    }
    ```

6. Finally, implement the main() function to create three sample MyProto packets and check their contents correctly.

    ```
    int main()
    {
            struct MyProto p1,p2,p3;
            p1 = Packet(1,"hello");
    ```

```
                p2 = Packet(2,"hello");
                p3 = Packet(3,"hello");
                PacketDisplay(&p1);
                PacketDisplay(&p2);
                PacketDisplay(&p3);
                return 0;
        }
```

7. Compile and run the program using the following command:

   ```
   #./a.out
   Type: 1Src: aabbccddDst: aabbccdeData: hello
   Type: 2Src: 12345Dst: 54321Data: hello
   Type: 3Src: aabbDst: aaddData: hello
   ```

   From the above results, observe that we successfully created three different `MyProto` packets and parsed their contents correctly.

In this section, we have learned how to use C union features to handle implementation of nested structures with optimal memory utilization for handling complex tasks easily.

Summary

In this chapter, we have practiced the important C features such as functions, arrays, strings, structures, and pointers. We discussed each of these concepts using essential examples and figures to quickly understand the C features and how to use them. Specifically, we practiced C features using important hands-on activities and discussed performance, reliability, and security issues while using these features in C application development.

In the next chapter, you will be practicing C programming activities using open-source development, testing, and debugging tools for handling complex C applications. Specifically, you will be learning how to use gcc, gcov, gdb, and valgrind tools for C applications development tasks easily.

Practice Tasks

1. Implement recursive functions for finding the following and check their stack usage:

    - Factorial, Fibonacci, gcd, string reverse, and Towers of Hanoi
    - Identify if you can reduce the stack size to execute recursive functions

2. Implement the cross product of three different lists using C functions and check in which order loops should be written for better performance.

3. Implement the cross product of three different lists and identify common elements from all three lists using C functions and check in which order loops should be written for better performance.

4. Given a long string containing many words, process the string and do the following:

    - Find the number of words in it
    - Find the longest word
    - Match how many words are matching with "Apress"
    - Suppose you need to check "Learning123" in the long string and find all the longest substrings found in the input string
    - Find all substrings of all the words found in the longest string

5. Implement 4-D arrays to store the following details for accessing sensor-generated data:

    - Time, Day, Month, Year
    - Implement the following functions for retrieving data from the data structure:
        - Retrieve values based on day
        - Retrieve values based on year
        - Retrieve values based on time

- Retrieve values based on month
- Retrieve values based on any of the above combination

6. Implement the following protocol message in C:
    - A message can be embedded in three different envelopes.
    - Every message should contain a specific envelope based on the type of message.
    - On envolve -1, the following details should be included before processing the message.
        - 1 bit of information indicating personal or family
        - 2 bits of information indicating parent, grandparent, children, and grandchildren
        - 5 bits of information to read the message on a specific date in a month
    - On envolve -2, the following details should be included before processing the message
        - 3 bits of information indicating any 8 members of family
        - 5 bits of information to read the message on a specific date in a month
    - On envolve -3, the following details should be included before processing the message
        - 1 bit of information indicating personal or team
        - 3 bits of information indicating any 8 members of family
        - 4 bits of information indicating any 16 members of a team

CHAPTER 3

Practice C Programming with Important Tools

In Chapter 2, "Quick Revision of Powerful C Constructs," using C programming constructs, you have practiced the important concepts such as functions, arrays, structures, and unions. In this chapter, you will learn important programming tools for handling performance, reliability, security, and debugging issues. Specifically, you will be using `gcc`, `gdb`, `gcov`, and `valgrind` tools for carrying out the important programming activities.

You will be beginning with understanding the role of compilation and linking activities in improving a program's runtime code performance, reliability, security, and handling of its runtime errors. You will be starting with exploring important `gcc`-related options for doing performance, reliability, security, and debugging activities. Besides compilation options, you will also learn how to use important linking options such as static and dynamic linking for handling code size and faster execution-related tasks.

Next, you will be exploring the important `gcc` options and the `valgrind` memory tool for quick identification of all possible runtime memory access-related errors, such as invalid memory read and write operations and dynamic memory allocation-related programming bugs. Then, you will be learning how to use `gcc` and `gcov` tools for application code profiling to identify hot spots of the code, unreachable code, heavily used functions, etc. Finally, you will be focusing on how to handle various program runtime errors using `gcc` and `gdb` tools. Specifically, you will learn how to inspect variables, functions, runtime stack contents, and assembly code. You will be learning how to use `gdb` for quickly handling runtime errors and application crashes.

CHAPTER 3   PRACTICE C PROGRAMMING WITH IMPORTANT TOOLS

Mainly, in this chapter, we will cover the following topics:

1. Compilation and linking techniques for enhancing programming skills
2. Memory access error handling techniques and tools
3. Code coverage analysis for avoiding performance issues
4. Debugging quick techniques for handling runtime errors

Compilation and Linking Techniques for Enhancing Programming Skills

Compilation is the process of converting a high-level program code (e.g., C, C++) into machine instructions for preparing a runtime machine executable file. In simple terms, the compiled code is associated with virtual addresses for machine-level instructions and symbol tables containing symbolic names with virtual addresses for variables and functions used in the code. In this book, we use gcc tools for compilation activities. The output of the compiler is usually referred to as an object file. During the compilation process, sophisticated compilation tools such as gcc analyze machine-level (assembly) codes by constructing code flow graphs for optimizing the expressions, conditional statements, loops, and functions of the code. Moreover, gcc also helps in sanitizing variables, pointers, and addresses for protecting runtime code, stack, dynamic memory, and data.

To support modularity in software development, the individual compiled object files can be linked together using static or dynamic linking approaches for creating a completely executable file. Static linking resolves all symbol addresses at compile time; hence, code size increases but helps in improving execution time. Dynamic linking reduces code size by dynamically loading needed modules at runtime (execution) only. Hence, dynamic linking can reduce the speed of program execution. During compilation time, developers can select static or dynamic linking options based on the requirements. On Unix or Linux OS platforms, a compiled and linked file to be executed is known as an executable and linking format (ELF) file. During a program execution, the corresponding ELF file will be loaded into physical memory. As we observe, dynamic linking allows few modules to be loaded at runtime and linked with a code for execution; this procedure is beneficial to run the code in a limited memory environment. On the other hand, it needs options for loading external modules into a program runtime environment. In these specific steps, attackers are exploring introducing malicious codes as external modules and exploiting the original code. Hence, developers must be responsible for checking the runtime environment and defining the suitable configuration for program execution.

gcc Compilation Options for Performance Tuning

Compilation tools (gcc) are highly helpful to code optimization. Most of the developers first write the codes for solving the problems and are least bothered about optimizing the code. However, optimizing code is necessary to reduce the code size and/or execution time, improving performance of the code to reduce execution time by minimizing memory accesses, avoiding redundant code, and optimally utilizing the computational and memory resources. In this chapter, we use gcc tools and options for optimizing the code. The gcc tool can be used with various optimization levels to improve the performance of the code during runtime. For instance, we can compile a compiler program with --opt_level=n. The n indicates the level of optimization (0, 1, 2, 3); a higher level indicates highly optimized code, and 0 indicates no optimization. As a developer, we must understand when you choose a higher optimization level, it means the compiler does a lot of work to optimize the code. In most of the cases, higher-level optimization leads to increased compilation time and code sizes. Hence, it is necessary to know a few important details of gcc optimization levels (https://gcc.gnu.org/onlinedocs/gcc/Optimize-Options.html):

- **gcc -O0:** To debug code easily, it is advisable to disable code optimization; hence, developers use this option.

- **gcc -Os:** Developers use this option to minimize runtime assembly code size. Developers may use this option in case memory utilization is a high priority.

- **gcc -O1:** Developers use this option to do basic code optimization tasks such as

    - Optimizing execution of common local and global subexpressions
    - Variables and constant propagation
    - Moving invariant expressions from outside a loop.

- **gcc -O2:** Developers use this option to perform -O1 code optimizations and do the following:
  - Basic loop optimizations such as loop unrolling
  - Expanding inline functions
  - Use protected source code of library functions
  - Assembly-level instruction reordering for improving instruction-level parallelism.
  - This optimization option helps in reducing size as well as improving performance in terms of reducing execution time.

- **gcc -O3:** Developers use this option to perform -O2 code optimizations and do the following:
  - Aggressive loop optimization.
  - Supports parallelization of loop iterations.
  - Function-level optimization is done aggressively.
  - Assembly level instructions are reordered aggressively to improve parallelization of code execution.
  - This optimization level is mainly used for improving code performance in terms of reducing execution time; however, it may increase code size and compilation time.

Next, let's practice using gcc options for code optimization in the following hands-on activity.

GCC OPTIONS FOR CODE OPTIMIZATION

1. As part of this task we do the following activities in `optimization.c`:
   a. We use the following code saved in `optimization.c` to use and test gcc compilation optimization-related benefits.
   b. We mainly test expressions and constant optimization, inline function expansion, and loop optimization-related techniques.

CHAPTER 3   PRACTICE C PROGRAMMING WITH IMPORTANT TOOLS

c. We test gcc -Os, -O1, -O2, -O3 options and compare the code sizes of assembly-level instructions generated for the testing C code.

d. We use the gcc -S option to generate assembly-level code for inspection and comparing code sizes.

   ```
   #include<stdio.h>
   #include<time.h>
   ```

e. The following function contains only one line, and the compiler can optimize this function call with an inline function.

   ```
   void ArrayInfo()
   {
           printf("Accessing elements of the array");
   }
   ```

f. The following function contains arithmetic expressions and loop invariant expressions; these codes can be optimized using compilation options.

   ```
   int ExprsOpt()
   {
           int a=2;
           int b=3;
           int d=4;
           int e=5;
           int f = a*b;
           int g = b+a*b;
           for (int i=0;i<100;i++)
           {
                   d = b*120;
                   int g = d/(i+1);
           }
           return g;
   }
   ```

CHAPTER 3   PRACTICE C PROGRAMMING WITH IMPORTANT TOOLS

g. The following function contains a loop with very few iterations (e.g., 5) only; it can be optimized by the compiler by expanding loop statements of loopOpt1().

```
int loopOpt1()
{
    int d;
    for(int i=0;i<5;i++)
    {
        d = d+i;
    }
    return d;
}
```

h. The following function contains two loops, which can be optimized by the compiler by combining them into a single loop, loopOpt2().

```
void loopOpt2()
{
    int a[50];
    int b[50];
    for(int i=0;i<50;i++)
    {
        a[i]=i;
    }
    for(int i=0;i<50;i++)
    {
        printf("%d",a[i]);
        b[i]=i*2;
        printf("%d",b[i]);
    }
}
int main()
{
    ExprsOpt();
    loopOpt1();
```

CHAPTER 3 PRACTICE C PROGRAMMING WITH IMPORTANT TOOLS

```
        loopOpt2();
        ArrayInfo();
    }
```

2. Start with generating assembly-level code for all code optimization levels (-Os, -O1, -O2, -O3) and no code optimization. Give the following command to generate assembly-level code files:

   a. First generate assembly-level code with no optimization and store the assembly code in the codeop file:

   ```
   #gcc -O0 optimization.c -o  codeop -S
   ```

   b. Generate assembly-level code for all levels and store the corresponding assembly code files:

   ```
   #gcc -Os optimization.c -o  codeops -S
   #gcc -O1 optimization.c -o  codeop1 -S
   #gcc -O2 optimization.c -o  codeop2 -S
   #gcc -O3 optimization.c -o  codeop3 -S
   ```

   c. Test sizes of all the optimized assembly codes using the following command:

   ```
   #ls -lrt codeop*
   -rw-rw-r-- 1 anil anil  3941 Feb 28 11:10 codeop3
   -rw-rw-r-- 1 anil anil  2662 Feb 28 11:13 codeop2
   -rw-rw-r-- 1 anil anil  2577 Feb 28 11:18 codeop1
   -rw-rw-r-- 1 anil anil  2298 Feb 28 11:31 codeops
   -rw-rw-r-- 1 anil anil  3451 Feb 28 12:16 codeop
   ```

From this activity's results, we can observe that codeop3 size is larger (3948 bytes) than all other codes, and codeops size is the lowest (2298 bytes) among all generated assembly codes. It means a higher code optimization level option leads to increased code size.

Next, let's check using gcc options how to inspect assembly language code of C programs for checking optimized code.

CHAPTER 3   PRACTICE C PROGRAMMING WITH IMPORTANT TOOLS

INSPECT COMPILER-GENERATED OPTIMIZED CODES

1. As part of this task, we inspect the optimized codes (optimization.c) of the following gcc options:

    a. First, inspect the codes generated from gcc options: -O0 and -O1.

    b. Then, inspect the codes generated from gcc options: -O0 and -O2.

    c. Then, inspect the codes generated from gcc options: -O0 and -O3.

2. Check the following gcc-generated code-optimized files: codeop and codeop1 files to inspect assembly-level codes using the following commands:

3. Check optimized code differences using the vimdiff command:

    #vimdiff codeop codeop1

    a. From the output of the command, you observe that ExprsOpt- and loopOpt1-related assembly codes have a lot of differences.

    b. In the codeop file, you observe there is a lot of assembly code under the ExprsOpt label; it is due to no code optimization. On the other hand, in the codeop1 file, there is optimized assembly code under the ExprsOpt label containing very few instructions due to code optimization.

    c. In the codeop file, you observe there is a lot of assembly code under the loopOpt1 label; it is due to no code optimization. On the other hand, in the codeop1 file, there is no call to loopOpt1. It is due to loop optimization and expanding loop iterations in the main code itself.

4. Then check the following optimized code differences using the vimdiff command:

    #vimdiff codeop codeop2

    a. From the output of the command, observe that ArrayInfo-related assembly codes for differences in the codeop and codeop2 files.

b. In the codeop file, you observe there is a call to ArrayInfo, whereas in codeop2, there is no call to ArrayInfo.

c. In the codeop file, you observe there is a lot of assembly code under the loopOpt2 label; it is due to no code optimization. On the other hand, in the codeop2 file, there are a lot of code changes in loopOpt2 to loop optimizations.

5. Then check the code for the following optimized code differences using the vimdiff command:

#vimdiff codeop codeop3

a. From the output of the command, observe that ArrayInfo-related assembly codes for differences in the codeop and codeop3 files.

b. In the codeop file you observe, there is a call to ArrayInfo, whereas in codeop3, there is no call to ArrayInfo.

c. In the codeop file you observe, there is a lot of assembly code under the loopOpt2 label; it is due to no code optimization. On the other hand, in the codeop2 file, there are a lot of code changes in the loopOpt2, and moreover, the code size is very high due to loop optimizations.

Well done! You have clearly observed the optimized codes using gcc-generated optimized code files and observed assembly language codes for identifying differences.

Next, let's learn gcc linking options for implementing shared libraries and handling the reusability of the shared libraries in a reliable manner.

gcc Compilation Options for Linking

To support modularity, reuse of code, and sharing of well-tested functions across multiple programs, related C functions are grouped into libraries. For example, in our programs, we use the stdio.h library for printf and scanf functions. These functions linking play an important role in the storage size and runtime of an executable file. In the process of loading necessary object files to create a final executable file, there are the following two important options for linking object files.

CHAPTER 3   PRACTICE C PROGRAMMING WITH IMPORTANT TOOLS

1. **Static Linking**: Developers can choose this option to load and link all necessary object files for creating a final executable file (ELF) during the compilation time.

    - Static linking helps an ELF to run faster by avoiding linking time cost during the runtime, because all necessary functions' addresses are resolved at compilation time only.
    - Static linking leads to larger-sized ELF files compared to dynamically linkable ELF files.
    - Static linking helps to avoid compatibility issues in linking library functions. Developers decide and use the suitable version of the library before creating an ELF.
    - Static linking avoids security issues since all related object files are carefully linked from genuine library files during compilation time itself.
    - Developers can compile all necessary object files and link them during compilation time using the gcc option: Static.
    - Developers can easily create and use static libraries using the ar and rcs commands.

2. **Dynamic Linking**: Developers use this option to reduce ELF storage size and support flexible ways to link the latest version or updated functions from libraries.

    - Dynamic linking leads to smaller-sized ELF files compared to statically created ELF files.
    - Dynamic linking supports shared libraries among multiple programs; it helps in optimally utilizing system memory.
    - Dynamic linking leads to increased execution time due to latency in linking necessary library functions during runtime.
    - Dynamic linking supports updating and revising an ELF in flexible manners. Due to dynamic linking of functions, developers can load the latest version functions containing libraries in the runtime environment and allow ELF to link with the latest version functions seamlessly.

- On Linux platforms, it is simplified by setting dynamically linkable library paths using an environmental variable called LD_LIBRARY_PATH.

- **Note:** Attackers can exploit this environmental variable by poisoning with malicious dynamic library paths.

- Developers can easily create and use dynamic libraries using the gcc tool with compilation and linking options.

Let's do the following activities to practice static linking and dynamic linking concepts:

- Quick test of static linking vs. dynamic linking

- Quickly create and test static and dynamic libraries

- Attacking a dynamic library

QUICK TEST OF STATIC LINKING VS. DYNAMIC LINKING

1. We do the following activities to understand differences between static linking vs. dynamic linking:

    a. Write a C program to use various library functions.

    b. Compile the program with the static linking gcc option and create an executable file to test its size and runtime.

    c. Compile the program with the dynamic linking gcc option and create an executable file to test its size and runtime.

2. Let's write a sample C program that uses various functions from `stdio.h`, `stdlib.h`, `math.h`, `time.h`, and `string.h` as follows and save it in `comlink.c`:

```
#include<stdio.h>
#include<string.h>
#include<stdlib.h>
#include<math.h>
#include<time.h>
```

```
int main()
{
    double time1, timedif;
    time1 = (double) clock();
    time1 = time1 / CLOCKS_PER_SEC;

    char buf[10];
    printf("Hello library\n");
    strcpy(buf,"hello");
    memcpy(buf,"hello",5);
    double d;
    d=sqrt(10);
    printf("SQRT:%lf",d);
    timedif = ( ((double) clock()) / CLOCKS_PER_SEC) - time1;
    printf("The execution time is %lf seconds\n", timedif);
}
```

3. Compile comlink.c with the static linking option (-static) to create an executable file called static and execute it using the following commands:

   ```
   #gcc comlink.c -static -o static
   #./static
   Hello library
   SQRT:3.162278
   The execution time is 0.000050 seconds
   ```

   a. From the results observe the execution time of static: 0.000050 seconds

   b. Then, compile comlink.c with the dynamic linking option (the default gcc uses the dynamic linking option) to create an executable file called dynamic and execute it using the following commands:

      ```
      #gcc comlink.c -o dynamic
      #./dynamic
      Hello library
      SQRT:3.162278Second The elapsed time is 0.000227 seconds
      ```

c. From the results observe that the execution time of dynamic is 0.000227 seconds. It is very high compared to static execution time: 0.000050.

d. Finally, check and compare storage sizes of static and dynamic executable files using the following command and observe that the static file takes up huge storage size compared to the dynamic file:

```
ls -lrt
-rwxrwxr-x 1 iiitdmk iiitdmk 871984 Feb 25 18:34 static
-rwxrwxr-x 1 iiitdmk iiitdmk  16880 Feb 25 18:34 dynamic
```

Well done! From this hands-on activity, we observe how static and dynamic linking options are helpful to reduce code size or execution time. Specifically, static linking will be useful for reducing application executing time, and the dynamic linking option will be useful for reducing application code size.

Next, let's learn how to create static and dynamic libraries using gcc.

QUICKLY CREATE AND TEST STATIC AND DYNAMIC LIBRARIES

1. We do the following activities:

    a. We create a sample file called tools.c with the following two functions to create static and dynamic libraries.

    ```
    int max(int a,int b)
    {
        if (a>b)
        {
            return a;
        }
        else
            return b;
    }
    ```

```
int min(int a, int b)
{
    if (a<b)
    {
        return a;
    }
    else
        return b;

}
```

b. We create a sample file called testtools.c to test the libraries using the following code:

```
#include<stdio.h>
int main()
{
    printf("Min: %d",min(10,20));
    printf("Max: %d",max(10,20));
}
```

2. Create a static library using the tools.c file containing functions by doing the following steps:

   a. Compile the tools.s to create an object file tools.o using the following command:

      #gcc -c tools.c

   b. Include the tools.o object file in your newly created static library file called libstools.a: Give the following command to create the static library in your working directory:

      #ar rcs libstools.a tools.o

   c. Confirm that the library file called libstools.a is successfully created using the following command:

      rw-rw-r-- 1 iiitdmk iiitdmk   1652 Feb 25 18:22 libstools.a

CHAPTER 3   PRACTICE C PROGRAMMING WITH IMPORTANT TOOLS

3. Test your static library using the `testtools.c` file using the following command:

    a. `-L.` : This is a linking option. We are passing the path of the `stools` as your working directory (.)

    b. `-lstools` is your static library name: It is the latter part of the `lib` in the library name: `libstools.a`

    ```
    #gcc -o staticlink1 testtools.c  -L. -lstools
    ```

    c. Execute the `staticlink1` to test the working of the library:

    ```
    #./staticlink1
    Min: 10Max: 20
    ```

    d. From the results we can observe that `testtools` is correctly invoking max and min functions.

4. Next, create a dynamic library using the `tools.c` file containing functions by doing the following steps:

    a. Compile the `tools.s` to create an object file `tools.o` using the following command. We used the Position-Independent Code flag to create tools as a shared library.

    ```
    #gcc -c -fPIC tools.c
    ```

    b. Include the `tools.o` object file in your newly created dynamic shared library file called `libdtools.so`: Give the following command to create the dynamic library in your working directory:

    ```
    #gcc -shared -o libdtools.so tools.o
    ```

    c. Confirm that the library file called `libdtools.so` is successfully created using the following command:

    ```
    #ls -lrt
    -rwxrwxr-x 1 iiitdmk iiitdmk   15664 Feb 25 18:43 libdtools.so
    ```

157

CHAPTER 3　PRACTICE C PROGRAMMING WITH IMPORTANT TOOLS

5. Test your dynamic library using `testtools.c` file using the following command:

    a. `-L.`: This is a linking option. We are passing the path of the `tools` as your working directory (.)

    b. `-ldtools` is your dynamic library name: It is the latter part of the `lib` in the library name: `libdtools.so`

    ```
    #gcc -o dlink1 testtools.c -L. -ldtools
    ```

    c. Execute the `dlink1` to test the working of the library:

    ```
    #./dlink1: error while loading shared libraries: libdtools.so: cannot open shared object file: No such file or directory
    ```

    d. From the results, we can observe that `testtools` is failing to link `libdtools.so,` to resolve this error, and set and export the environment variable LD_LIBRARY_PATH as follows. Setting this flag allows finding your dynamic library from the given path.

    ```
    #export LD_LIBRARY_PATH=.:$LD_LIBRARY_PATH
    ```

    e. Again execute the `dlink1` to test the working of the library:

    ```
    #./dlink1
    Min: 10Max:
    ```

    f. From the results we can observe that `testtools` is correctly invoking `max` and `min` functions using dynamic library. You can also confirm whether your `dlink1` is linked with the `tools` or not using the following command:

    ```
    #ldd dlink1
            linux-vdso.so.1 (0x00007ffe34da0000)
            libdtools.so => ./libdtools.so (0x00007fea795bf000)
            libc.so.6 => /lib/x86_64-linux-gnu/libc.so.6
            (0x00007fea79399000)
            /lib64/ld-linux-x86-64.so.2 (0x00007fea795cb000)
    ```

CHAPTER 3   PRACTICE C PROGRAMMING WITH IMPORTANT TOOLS

Well done! From this hands-on activity, we have learned how to create static and dynamic libraries using gcc compilation and linking options and how to correctly link them with an application by configuring necessary Linux PATH variables.

Next, let's learn about security issues in using dynamic libraries through the following hands-on activity.

ATTACKING A DYNAMIC LIBRARY

1. As part of implementing this task, we do the following activities:

   a. We create malicious min and max functions in mdtools.c under a user directory MDLIB. Create MDLIB first, then create mdtools.c with the following code:

   ```
   int min(int a,int b)
   {
        if (a>b)
        {
             return a;
        }
        else
             return b;
   }
   int max(int a, int b)
   {
        if (a<b)
        {
             return a;
        }
        else
             return b;
   }
   ```

CHAPTER 3   PRACTICE C PROGRAMMING WITH IMPORTANT TOOLS

2. Create a malicious dynamic library with the same name (libdtools.so) using the mdtools.c file in a user directory called MDLIB.

   ```
   #gcc -c -fPIC mdtools.c
   #gcc -shared -o libdtools.so mdtools.o
   ```

3. Then move to the path containing the dlink1 executable file to test it.

   ```
   #./dlink1
   Min: 10Max: 20
   ```

4. From the results, we can observe it correctly linking with the genuine libdtools.so. Next, to attack, it just set the LD_LIBRARY_PATH with the MDLIB path as follows:

   ```
   #export LD_LIBRARY_PATH=./MDLIB:$LD_LIBRARY_PATH
   ```

5. Then test dlink1 again:

   ```
   #./dlink1
   ```

   Min: 20Max: 10

6. From the results, we can observe it is linking with malicious codes (max and min). Hence, we get incorrect results. To identify the cause of it, we can print $LD_LIBRARY_PATH and confirm the reason.

   ```
   #echo $LD_LIBRARY_PATH
   #./MDLIB:.:
   ```

Well done! From this hands-on activity, we have learned security issues in using dynamic libraries. Specifically, we understood the necessity of checking LD_LIBRARY_PATH before using dynamic libraries.

In this section, we have learned various gcc linking options for creating static and dynamic libraries and how to use them in a C application in a reliable manner. Next, let's learn how to use gcc options for handling application runtime environment security checks.

gcc Compilation Options for Secured Code

In the previous section, we checked the code for optimization using important gcc options and linking options and ensured correct dynamic library paths were configured for avoiding malicious code linkage and security breaches. In this section, we will learn how to secure your code from malicious code by closing common security loopholes on a Linux platform. Specifically, we will discuss the important gcc compilation and linking options and kernel parameters to check before deploying your code. During development and testing of your codes, gcc and linking options will help you to overcome serious security issues. For instance, while checking codes, we can observe runtime stack crashes. For attackers, it is also possible to suppress these runtime error messages by using stack protection-related gcc options to carry out well-known security attacks called buffer overflow attacks. Then, attackers can introduce their malicious codes to run over the targeted systems. In this section, we will list out a few popular and important ways to secure your code using gcc, linking, and kernel options.

- **Process Memory Layout**: A process to be executed on a Linux platform is available in terms of ELF containing code, data, stack, and heap segments with virtual addresses. When a CPU executes a process file (ELF), to load necessary code and other segments, the OS translates the process virtual addresses to physical addresses of the main memory with the memory management unit. Attackers can exploit this process to observe addresses of the shared libraries' code and other segments to link their malicious codes. Hence, it is necessary to randomize virtual addresses of a process.

    - The gcc option `-fPIC` helps in generating position-independent code to create shared libraries (as we observed in the dynamic libraries creation steps).

    - In order to enable virtual address space randomization, we also need to enable the following kernel parameter: `kernel.randomize_va_space`

    - These options are not enabled by default or could be changed; hence, it is necessary for developers to set these options before making dynamic libraries and creating ELF.

- **Stack Protection**: In the process memory layout of a C application, the runtime stack is the key segment attackers will explore to induce attacks and malicious codes. Since stack size grows dynamically during the application execution, by default gcc offers stack crash detection. However, attackers can disable stack protection by compiling the code with the following option: fno-stack-protector. Then, attackers can create buffer overflow attacks and induce their malicious codes for attacking target systems. Hence, as a developer, we must do the following check and compilation options for detecting security loopholes and protecting your code:

    - `gcc –fstack-protector-strong`: This option enables all functions of the compiled code to be included with stack crash detection checks.

        - You can observe these by inspecting the assembly language code of your program by compiling your code with the -S option.

        - By default, this option is enabled by the gcc. However, attackers can use `-fno-stack-protector` to bypass these security checks.

    - We can use the `readelf` Linux command to check if an executable is enabled with stack check detection or not using the following Linux command:

        - `readelf -W -s --dyn-syms dlink1 | grep -i _stack_chk_fail`

- **Stack Execution**: It is another important feature enabled by default with the gcc linking feature. Stack execution is not really needed by all codes. Usually, a stack stores only local variables and data of an application that are not executable. Hence, the runtime stack segment of an application should have only read and write permissions. But to support nested function definitions in C, a stack execution feature is introduced. Nested function definitions are helpful to easily enable encapsulation and data hiding features in C applications. However, nested function definitions are not necessary for all C code. To introduce malicious codes and security attacks, attackers use this stack execution feature in addition to virtual address randomization being disabled and stack crash checks. We can disable the stack execution feature using the following linking option and check as follows:

- `gcc -z noexecstack -o <program> <source_code>`: This command disables the stack execution feature. Hence, inside the stack, it is not possible to construct any code dynamically. However, we can execute compile time-generated inner functions.

- `readelf -W -l <program> | grep GNU_STACK`: Using this command, we can see if an executable has read, write, and execute permissions or not.

- **Using Protected Source Code of Library Functions in a C Application**: By default, gcc will not enable using protected source code of library functions. Hence, it is possible that when applications use string library functions like `strcpy, memcpy,` and the standard `printf, vprintf, scanf` could lead to crashing of the stacks due to buffer overflows. To enable using protected source codes of library functions in your code, use the following gcc options:

  - `gcc -O -D_FORTIFY_SOURCE=2`: This option enables use of protected source codes of standard library functions.

  - `gcc -O2`: This code optimization option also enables use of protected source codes of standard library functions. In case the first option is not working, we can use this option on Linux platforms. You can also confirm if an ELF is using the protected source codes or not using the following readelf command:

    - `readelf -W -s – dyn-syms <program> | grep chk@`

Next, let's do the following hands-on activity for checking the security loopholes of application code using gcc options.

CHAPTER 3   PRACTICE C PROGRAMMING WITH IMPORTANT TOOLS

CHECKING SECURITY LOOPHOLES OF A C APPLICATION

1. We do the following activities using an example C code: security.c, and it contains the following functions.

    a. To verify address space randomization, the following asr() function is used. We mainly test addresses of local variables and heap memory.

    ```
    #include<stdio.h>
    #include<stdlib.h>
    #include<string.h>
    void asr()
    {
            //sudo sysctl -w kernel.randomize_va_space=2
            int *p;
            p=(int*)malloc(sizeof(int)*100);
            printf("Address:%p\n",p);
            int a;
            int b;
            printf("Address:%p\n",&a);
            printf("Address:%p\n",&b);
    }
    ```

    b. To verify if the runtime stack is protected or not, the following stackguard function is used. Mainly, we test buffer overflow check by passing large size strings.

    ```
    void stackguard(char *buffer1)
    {
    //      readelf -W -s ./a.out | grep -i _stack_chk_fail
            char buffer2[4];
            strcpy(buffer2,buffer1);
            sprintf(buffer2,"%s",buffer1);
            memcpy(buffer2,buffer1,5);
    }
    ```

c. To verify if the code is using protected library functions or not, the following functions are used to test stdlib.h, string.h, and stdio.h. Mainly, we test buffer overflow checks by passing large-size strings.

```
void strfortify(char *buffer1)
{
//    gcc security.c -O2
      char buffer2[4];
      strcpy(buffer2,buffer1);
}
void printfortify(char *buffer1)
{
      char buffer2[4];
      sprintf(buffer2,"%s",buffer1);
}
void memfortify(char *buffer1)
{
      char buffer2[4];
      memcpy(buffer2,buffer1,5);
}
```

d. To verify if the code is allowing stack execution or not, we use the following stackexec function. Mainly, we test that at runtime, functions can be constructed and invoked using function pointers.

   i. Like variable pointers, function pointers are helpful to store addresses of the functions matching with the function pointer declaration.

```
void stackexec(int i,int j)
{
      int g(int a,int b)
      {
            return a+b;
      }
      int h(int a,int b)
      {
            return a-b;
      }
```

```
            int (*p)(int,int);
            p=&g;
            printf("%d",p(i,j));
            p=&h;
            printf("%d",p(i,j));
    }
```

e. Verify if the code is allowing compile time–generated inner functions to be executed, irrespective of the gcc linking option execstack.

```
void nostackexec(int i,int j)
{
    int g(int a,int b)
    {
        return a+b;
    }
    int h(int a,int b)
    {
        return a-b;
    }
    printf("%d",g(i,j));
    printf("%d",h(i,j));
}
```

f. To test all the aforementioned security loophole-related functions, we call them in the main() function.

```
int main()
{
//      asr();
//      stackguard("abcdef");
//      strfortify("abcdef");
//      printfortify("abcdef");
//      memfortify("abcdef");
//      stackexec(40,30);
//      nostackexec(40,30);
}
```

CHAPTER 3   PRACTICE C PROGRAMMING WITH IMPORTANT TOOLS

2. Start with testing of address space memory layout by calling only asr() in main() and execute the code as follows:

```
#gcc security.c
#./a.out
Address:0x55770c2bb2a0
Address:0x7ffca15c73f8
Address:0x7ffca15c73fc
```

   a. From the above execution, observe the addresses:

   ```
   #./a.out
   Address:0x55e94ac992a0
   Address:0x7ffeabae2ea8
   Address:0x7ffeabae2eac
   ```

   b. Repeat the code execution to check if your application process addresses are randomized or not. We observe that in every execution of the code, random virtual addresses are generated for the process.

   c. Let's disable virtual address randomization using the following Linux command:

   ```
   #sudo sysctl -w kernel.randomize_va_space=0
   ```

   d. Repeat the code execution to check if addresses of a process are randomized or not.

   ```
   #gcc security.c
   #./a.out
   Address:0x5555555592a0
   Address:0x7fffffffde48
   Address:0x7fffffffde4c
   ```

   e. Repeat the code execution to check if process addresses are randomized or not. We observe that in both runs of the code, the same virtual addresses are generated for a process due to the kernel virtual address space generation parameter reset.

167

```
#./a.out
Address:0x5555555592a0
Address:0x7fffffffde48
Address:0x7fffffffde4c
```

3. Next, test that your code is stack protected by calling only the `stackguard` function in main():

```
#gcc security.c
#./a.out
*** stack smashing detected ***: terminated
Aborted (core dumped)
```

   a. From the result, we can observe that stack crashes can be detected.

   b. Next, disable stack protection and execute the code using the following code with the gcc stack no protection option:

```
#gcc -fno-stack-protector security.c
#./a.out
```

   c. From the result, we can observe that stack crashes cannot be detected. It means it is necessary to check if your executable is stack protected or not before deploying it in the runtime environment. You can do this by using the following readelf command:

```
#readelf -W -s ./a.out | grep -i _stack_chk_fail
```

   d. From the result, we can observe whether stack check is included or not.

   e. Repeat the execution by compiling your code with stack protection and generating the executable file:

```
#gcc -fstack-protector-strong security.c
#./a.out
*** stack smashing detected ***: terminated
Aborted (core dumped)
```

   f. From the result, we can observe that the stack check is restored.

CHAPTER 3   PRACTICE C PROGRAMMING WITH IMPORTANT TOOLS

4. Next, testing your code is using protected source code of standard library functions by calling only strfortify, printfortify, and memfortify in main():

   a. First compile your code with default gcc options:

   #gcc security.c

   b. From the results, you can observe no compilation warning. Then, run the executable file:

   ```
   #./a.out
   *** stack smashing detected ***: terminated
   Aborted (core dumped)
   ```

   c. From the execution result, you can observe that there is a system crash. You would have corrected it if corresponding warning messages were displayed during the compilation time. Next, compile code with the code optimization option (O2) as follows:

   #gcc -O2 security.c

   In file included from /usr/include/string.h:495,
                    from security.c:3:
   In function 'memcpy',
   warning: '__builtin___memcpy_chk' writing 5 bytes into a region of size 4 overflows the destination [-Wstringop-overflow=]
      34 | return __builtin__memcpy_chk (__dest, __src, __len, __bos0 (__dest));
   security.c: In function 'main':
   security.c:37:26: warning: '%s' directive writing 6 bytes into a region of size 4 [-Wformat-overflow=]
      37 | sprintf(buffer2,"%s",buffer1);
      36 | return __builtin__sprintf_chk (__s, __USE_FORTIFY_LEVEL - 1,
      ..

169

```
In function 'strcpy',
[-Wstringop-overflow=]
   90 |    return __builtin___strcpy_chk (__dest, __src, __bos
   (__dest));
In function 'memcpy',

[-Wstringop-overflow=]
   34 |    return __builtin___memcpy_chk (__dest, __src, __len,
   __bos0 (__dest));
      |
```

    d. From the execution result (we include necessary warning contents), you can observe warning messages are displayed during the compilation time using the code optimization option (O2).

5. Next, testing your code is enabled with stack execution permission by calling only the `stackexec` function in main:

    a. First compile your code with default gcc options:

```
#gcc security.c
#./a.out
7010
```

    b. From the execution result, you can observe that the code stack is executable; hence, during runtime, inline functions `g()` and `h()` are constructed and executed by `printf()` using pointer-to-function features. Next, execute your code with stack execution permission disabled using the following command with the linking option z noexecstack:

```
#gcc -z noexecstack security.c
#./a.out
Segmentation fault (core dumped)
```

    c. From the execution result, you can observe there is a crash. It means your code runtime stack is not executable. You can confirm it with the following readelf command and observe that ./a.out is enabled with read and write permissions (RW) only:

```
#readelf -W -l ./a.out | grep GNU_STACK
   GNU_STACK    0x000000 0x0000000000000000 0x0000000000000000
0x000000 0x000000 RW  0x10
```

  d. Repeat the code execution with stack execution permission enabled using the following gcc command with the linking option (-z execstack):

```
#gcc -z execstack security.c
#./a.out
7010
```

  e. From the execution result, you can observe the runtime stack of ./a.out is executable.

  f. You can confirm it with the following readelf command and observe that ./a.out is enabled with read and write permissions (RWX):

```
#readelf -W -l ./a.out | grep GNU_STACK
   GNU_STACK    0x000000 0x0000000000000000 0x0000000000000000
0x000000 0x000000 RWE  0x10
```

6. Test if the compile time–generated inner functions can be executed or not irrespective of stack execution permission by calling only nostackexec in main using the following commands in order:

```
#gcc -z noexecstack security.c
#./a.out
7010
#gcc -z execstack security.c
#./a.out
7010
```

  a. From the execution results, you can observe that stack execution permission is not necessary to execute compile time–generated inner functions.

Well done! From this hands-on activity, we have learned how to check common security loopholes on a Linux OS for a C application. Specifically, we have learned how to prote ct the runtime stack environment of an application, randomize virtual address spaces, and use protected codes from library functions.

In this section, we have learned various gcc options for handling security checks of an application. These tasks help you to identify and close security loopholes during development stages only.

Next, we will explore how to handle the most common application errors and memory access errors using the important gcc options and `valgrind` tool.

Memory Access Errors Handling Techniques and Tools

System developers must know how to access program memory in bug-free manners. The gcc offers several compilation options to check and inform important runtime errors such as checking arrays boundaries, addressing sanitization, and analyzing static code for correct usage of arrays, pointers, and dynamic memory access. Besides, the following common errors also can be identified during compilation time, such as data types range overflows and invalid integer or floating-point operations such as division by zero. In a large C programming project development, it is difficult to manually inspect the entire code to identify the aforementioned errors. The gcc tools are offering the various options to automatically check the code and inform of these errors. We had done a lot of C programming experiments and identified the following important options out of a large number of options. These gcc options are used to identify most of the crucial programming errors in a reliable manner during the development stage itself. Hence, we can use these options for improving the reliability of the code. Finally, we quickly introduce a dedicated memory access-related error identification tool known as Valgrind. In the pointers chapter, usage of the `valgrind` tool is discussed in detail.

Memory and Other Important Errors Handling gcc Options for Reliable Code

Specifically, in this section, we will first discuss common application errors such as arithmetic expression errors, data types range overflow errors, and memory access errors related to important operations: allocation, reading, writing, permissions, and deallocation. In the case of large-size application codes, it is very challenging to inspect these common errors and the memory access-related runtime errors. Moreover, memory access-related errors can lead to system crashes and security attacks. In order to simplify identification of common errors and memory access-related errors, we identified the following important gcc options through numerous experiments:

- -fsanitize = undefined: Enabling this option allows developers to identify the following critical errors before deploying your C application code in the runtime environment.
    - This specific option helps in checking arithmetic and shift operations-related errors, data type range checking, and reporting range overflow-related errors.
    - Pointers access checking, pointers valid arithmetic operations, and arrays boundaries checking.
    - This option will not be enabled by default with gcc. Hence, if you compile your C application code without this option, it can lead to data type range overflows, crashing the system due to invalid arithmetic or shift operations, accessing arrays beyond their sizes, and invalid pointer accesses such as dereferencing NULL pointers.
    - Compiling your C application code with this specific option lets you identify and correct critical errors during the development and testing stages only.
- -fsanitize = address: This is another important gcc option to check valid dynamic memory allocation usage and runtime stack accesses. Enabling this option allows developers to identify the following critical errors during development and testing stages:
    - Runtime C application stack crash detection check due to crossing array accessing boundaries (lower limit and higher limit).
    - Accessing invalid pointers in application codes.
    - Avoiding invalid dynamic memory access-related operations such as out-of-bounds access, use after-free, and double-free in C applications.

- This option will not be enabled by default with gcc. Hence, if you don't compile your code without this option, it can lead to crashes during the application deployment environment.

- -fanalyzer: This option is available with the gcc-10 version onwards. Unlike the above options, this option allows you to check the potential errors during the compilation stage only. It is helpful to do static analysis of the code. It helps in identifying the following errors during the compilation stage only:

    - Helps in detecting file and memory leaks of a C application.
    - Helps in detecting use after-free errors of a C application.
    - Helps in detecting possible NULL pointer arguments and dereferencing of a C application.
    - Helps in detecting possible invalid array indices of a C application.
    - Helps in detecting double file close and double memory-free operations of a C application.

CHECK RELIABILITY OF A C APPLICATION CODE

1. In this section, we play with a buggy program called `reliability3.c` and do the following specific activities for identifying all bugs:

    a. First, we compile the program with the undefined option and identify common errors of the code. During execution, if an error message displays a specific line of the code, we comment on the specific line of code and recompile with the undefined option. If no error messages are displayed during the execution of the code, then we stop this activity.

    b. If the error message is not showing any specific line of the code, then we compile with the -fsanitize=address option. Then during the program execution, it shows a specific line of the code or the detailed error message. Then we comment on the specific line of the code and go to step a.

2. We use the following code in reliability3.c:

   a. ArrayAccess(): It is a bug-free function.

   b. StringChecks(char*): It can lead to bugs such as stack and crash and buffer overflow errors based on input arguments.

   c. DataRangesOperations(int): It can lead to arithmetic expression-related bugs, such as division by zero, range overflow, etc., based on input arguments.

   d. ArrayBoundsCheck(int): It can lead to memory access bugs such as invalid read and write errors based on input arguments.

   e. main(): We check all the above functions.

```c
#include<stdio.h>
#include<stdlib.h>
#include<string.h>
int g=100;
void ArrayAccess()
{
        static int variable=0;
        float p=0.1;
        int a[8][8];
        for (int i=0;i<8;i++)
        {
                for (int j=0;j<8;j++)
                {
                        a[i][j]=i*j;
                        p = p*i*j;
                }
        }
        for (int i=0;i<8;i++)
        {
                for (int j=0;j<8;j++)
                {
                        printf("%d",a[i][j]);
                }
        }
```

```c
            for (int i=0;i<8;i++)
            {
                    for (int j=0;j<8;j++)
                    {
                            printf("%d",a[i][j]);
                    }
            }
    }
    void StringChecks(char *buff)
    {
            char ibuff[10];
            strcpy(ibuff,buff);
            printf("Accessing elements of the array %s",ibuff);
    }

    void DataRangesOperations(int N)
    {
            int d;
            d = 100;
            int res;
            for (int i=0;i<N;i++)
            {
                    d = d*1000+d*100+d*10;
            }
            if (d!=0)
            {
                    N = N%d;
                    res = d/N;
            }
    }
    void ArrayBoundsCheck(int N)
    {
            int a[10]={1,2,3,4,5,6,7,8,9,10};
            for (int i=0;i<N;i++)
```

```
        {
                printf("%d ",a[i]);
        }
}

int main()
{
        char *p1 = "abcdefghi";
        ArrayAccess();
        StringChecks(p1);
        DataRangesOperations(1024);
        ArrayBoundsCheck(12);
        char *p2 = (char*)malloc(sizeof(char)*11);
        for (int i=0;i<10;i++)
        {
                p2[i]=i+37;
        }
        p2[10]='\0';
        if (p2!=NULL)
        {
                StringChecks(p2);
                free(p2);
        }
        p2[0]='a';
        free(p2);
}
```

3. Compile the code with the undefined option, and run the executable (a.out) for possible errors using the following commands:

```
#gcc -fsanitize=undefined reliability3.c
#./a.out
reliability3.c:49:5: runtime error: signed integer overflow:
123210000 * 1110 cannot be represented in type 'int'
reliability3.c:53:8: runtime error: division by zero
Floating point exception (core dumped)
```

CHAPTER 3   PRACTICE C PROGRAMMING WITH IMPORTANT TOOLS

   a. From the error message, we can identify lines of code causing the runtime errors: Data type range overflow and divide by zero. (Show in bold case line number 49 and 53.)

   b. You may correct or comment on these lines of code and proceed to the next step to identify more runtime errors.

4. Compile the code with the undefined option, and run the executable (a.out) for possible errors using the following commands:

   ```
   #gcc -fsanitize=undefined reliability3.c
   #./a.out
   reliability3.c:49:5: runtime error: signed integer overflow: 123210000 * 1110 cannot be represented in type 'int'
   ```
   reliability3.c:63:17: runtime error: index 10 out of bounds for type 'int [10]'
   reliability3.c:63:3: runtime error: load of address 0x7fff0e6206f8 with insufficient space for an object of type 'int'

   a. From the error message we can identify lines of code causing the runtime errors: Out of Bounds. (Show in bold case line number 63.)

   b. You may correct or comment on these lines of code and proceed to the next step to identify more runtime errors.

5. Compile the code with the -fsanitize=undefined option, and run the executable (a.out) for possible errors using the following commands:

   ```
   #gcc -fsanitize=undefined reliability3.c
   #./a.out
   Aborted (core dumped)
   ```

   a. From the error message we cannot identify lines of code causing the runtime errors: Aborted (core dumped)

   b. Compile the code with the -fsanitize=address option, and run the executable (a.out) for possible errors using the following commands:

CHAPTER 3   PRACTICE C PROGRAMMING WITH IMPORTANT TOOLS

```
#gcc -fsanitize=address reliability3.c
#./a.out
=============================================================
==5566==ERROR: AddressSanitizer: stack-buffer-overflow
on address
..
  This frame has 1 object(s):
    [32, 42) 'ibuff' (line 37) <==
```
Memory access at offset 42 overflows this variable

- c. From the error message, we can identify lines of code causing the runtime errors: Overflow. (Show in bold case line number 37.)

- d. You may correct or comment on these lines of code and proceed to the next step to identify more runtime errors.

6. Compile the code with the -fsanitize=undefined option, and run the executable (a.out) for possible errors using the following commands:

```
#gcc -fsanitize=undefined reliability3.c
#./a.out
Aborted (core dumped)
```

- a. From the error message we cannot identify lines of code causing the runtime errors: Aborted (core dumped)

- b. Compile the code with the -fsanitize=address option, and run the executable (a.out) for possible errors using the following commands:

```
#gcc -fsanitize=address reliability3.c
#./a.out
=====================================================
==47606==ERROR: AddressSanitizer: 
```
heap-use-after-free
```
on address
```

- c. From the error message we can identify lines of code causing the runtime errors: **heap-use-after-free**. (Show in bold case.)

- d. You may correct or comment on this line of code (p2[0]='a') and proceed to the next step to identify more runtime errors.

179

7. Compile the code with the -fsanitize=undefined option, and run the executable (a.out) for possible errors using the following commands:

   ```
   #gcc -fsanitize=undefined reliability3.c
   #./a.out
   Aborted (core dumped)
   ```

   a. From the error message, we cannot identify lines of code causing the runtime errors: Aborted (core dumped)

   b. Compile the code with the -fsanitize=address option, and run the executable (a.out) for possible errors using the following commands:

   ```
   #gcc -fsanitize=address reliability3.c
   #./a.out
   =========================================================
   ==47658==ERROR: AddressSanitizer: attempting double-free on 0x602000000010 in thread T0:
        #0 0x7f6df386e40f in __interceptor_free
   ```

   c. From the error message we can identify the detailed runtime error message: **double-free**. (Show in bold case.)

   d. You may correct or comment on this line of code (free(p2)) and proceed to the next step to identify more runtime errors.

8. Compile the code with the undefined option, and run the executable (a.out) for possible errors using the following commands:

   ```
   #gcc -fsanitize=undefined reliability3.c
   #./a.out
   ```

   a. No more errors. Well done, we identified all possible errors during the development and testing stage of this code.

   b. If you do not use these compilation options to identify bugs and correct them, then your program will crash during deployment.

Well done! From this hands-on activity, we understand during an application development stage how to use gcc -fsanitize=undefined and address options for detecting runtime errors such as range overflow, divide by zero, and invalid memory access. It helps in improving the reliability of your application code for deployment.

Next, let's check how to use `valgrind` for handling memory access errors.

Memory Error Handling Using Valgrind

Valgrind tools are developed for dynamic code analysis for automatically detecting common memory, cache, and thread-related errors. It is also used as a code profiling tool. On a Linux platform, you need to install it before using it. It helps developers to easily identify common runtime errors during development stages. Hence, it is motivating developers to use Valgrind tools extensively for testing the large code before deploying it in the runtime environment. In this section, we quickly introduce how to use the Valgrind memory tool for identifying memory access-related errors such as invalid read, invalid write, use after free, double free, uninitialized memory blocks, and access permissions violations.

Let's quickly check how to use the Valgrind memory tool:

QUICK INTRODUCTION TO VALGRIND TOOLS USAGE

1. Valgrind tools perform dynamic code analysis; hence, it is necessary to compile your code with debugging details before testing your code with Valgrind.

    a. First, compile your program (e.g., sample_prog.c) with a debugging option.

    ```
    gcc -g sample_prog.c
    ```

    b. Then, you can run your executable code with the `valgrind` tool using the following important options.

    c. Check your `valgrind` tool version using the following command:

    ```
    valgrind --version
    valgrind-3.15.0
    ```

CHAPTER 3   PRACTICE C PROGRAMMING WITH IMPORTANT TOOLS

    d. Check various valgrind options available using the following command:

       valgrind --help |grep 'mem'

```
--tool=<name>                        use the Valgrind tool
named <name> [memcheck]
                        This allows saved stack traces
                        (e.g. memory leaks)
--xtree-memory=none|allocs|full   profile heap memory
in an xtree [none]
--xtree-memory-file=<file>   xtree memory report file
[xtmemory.kcg.%p]
--run-libc-freeres=no|yes free up glibc memory at
exit on Linux? [yes]
--run-cxx-freeres=no|yes  free up libstdc++ memory at
exit on Linux
more sectors may increase performance, but use
more memory.
--aspace-minaddr=0xPP            avoid mapping memory
below 0xPP [guessed]
--leak-check=no|summary|full  search for memory leaks
at exit?  [summary]
```

2. Steps to use the valgrind tool on a sample program (memoryleaks.c):

    a. gcc -g sample_prg.c

    b. valgrind --tool=memcheck --leak-check=full ./a.out

3. Following the important message of Valgrind to observe from the output:

    a. Usually you will be encountering the following error messages when you run your executable file with Valgrind. These messages help developers to easily identify types of memory access errors and lines of the code causing these errors. These error message blocks help in correcting memory access errors quickly:

Invalid read of size
Invalid write of size
Invalid free

CHAPTER 3   PRACTICE C PROGRAMMING WITH IMPORTANT TOOLS

> **Conditional jump or move depends on uninitialised**
> **Access not within mapped region**
>
> b. **Heap Summary:** This summary section helps developers to understand the amount of memory dynamically allocated and freed successfully.
>
>   **Example:** `in use at exit: 0 bytes in 0 blocks`
>   `total heap usage: 2 allocs, 3 frees, 1035 bytes`
>
> c. **Leak Summary:** This summary section helps developers to understand whether all dynamically allocated memory blocks are freed or not. It helps in how many bytes are lost without deallocation.
>
>   **Example:**`definitely lost: 40 bytes in 1 blocks`
>   `indirectly lost: 0 bytes in 0 blocks`
>
> d. **Error Summary:** This summary section helps developers to know the total number of memory access errors.
>
>   **Example:** `2 errors from 2 contexts`
>
> From the above steps we conclude how to use the Valgrind tool on a C application. We discuss Valgrind tool usage in detail in the Pointers and dynamic memory access chapters.

In this section, we introduced the Valgrind tool and how to use it for checking memory access-related errors. In later chapters, we revisit the Valgrind tool in detail for handling memory access-related bugs. Next, let's learn how to use gcc and gcov tools for C application code profiling tasks.

Code Coverage Analysis for Avoiding Performance Issues

In the case of deploying any system software, it is necessary to check source code at various levels, such as individual lines, blocks of code, branches, and functions, for identifying performance issues in terms of handling code size and execution time. Specifically, developers do this code profiling activity for the complete code coverage and static code analysis in terms of identifying hotspots of the code (which are executing most of the time), unused code, and dead codes (not reachable). Further, these statistics help developers to rewrite specific blocks of code to reduce execution time by eliminating redundant code execution, reordering blocks of the code, and parallelizing specific blocks of the code. In case of meeting performance requirements of a code under computational and memory resource constraints, usually developers carry out code coverage activity using automated tools such as gcc and gcov. In this section, we will discuss how to use gcc and gcov tools for carrying out code coverage activity. Specifically, we will do the following activities:

- **Functions Level Statistics Check**: It helps developers to identify highly time-consuming functions quickly. Although it gives high-level statistics of the code, it helps in quickly identifying hotspots of the code with respect to critical and heavily used functions. Besides, developers can quickly work over costly functions in terms of execution time for reducing execution time and identifying possibilities to parallelize specific codes. In summary, function-level statistics help in identifying the following:

    - Costly functions in terms of heavily used functions in a large code

    - Removing unused functions

    - Reducing critical and heavily used function execution cost

    - Parallelizing specific functions' execution

    - Possibility to expand smaller function calls in main code for avoiding function call overhead

- **Conditional Branches Execution Statistics Check**: Next, to check functional-level statistics, it is important to identify which blocks of a function are executing heavily. It helps in identifying the cost of conditional blocks in multiple runs. In most of the software development we observe, conditional branching is necessary. Collecting various branch statement statistics gives insights for rearranging conditional statements and loops, moving redundant codes out of branches and loops to reduce execution time, and rearranging branches of code to parallelize code. This specific activity is highly important for high-performance computing to minimize the time complexity of the code. In summary, it helps in identifying:

    - Hotspots of the code (conditionals, loops, expressions)

CHAPTER 3   PRACTICE C PROGRAMMING WITH IMPORTANT TOOLS

- To move or rearrange the code of various branch statements
- To parallelize the code of various blocks

- **Individual Lines of Code Execution Statistics**: Next to branch-level statements statistics, it is necessary to identify unreachable lines of code, cost of arithmetic, logical, conditional, shift, and assignment operations in individual lines of the code. Since it is tedious work, using automated tools such as gcov helps developers to easily get statistics of individual lines and work on performance metrics quickly. In summary, it helps in identifying the following:

  - Helps in removing unnecessary lines of code and unreachable code
  - Replacing costly expressions with low-cost expressions
    - Multiplication or division operations can be replaced by shift operations
    - Comparison and test operations
  - Rewriting expressions to avoid redundant computations

Next, let's practice the various ways of passing arguments through important activities.

Code Coverage Tools (gcc and gcov) Usage Steps

In this section, you will learn how to use gcc and gcov together for carrying out code coverage and static code analysis tasks. We need to do the following compilation and execution tasks to prepare a program for carrying out code coverage activities:

GCC AND GCOV USAGE

1. First, process your program using gcc code coverage options:

   a. Compile (example file: `important.c`) with code coverage options using gcc:

   ```
   #gcc --coverage important.c
   ```

CHAPTER 3   PRACTICE C PROGRAMMING WITH IMPORTANT TOOLS

    b. Generate an executable file with code coverage options using gcc:

       #gcc --coverage important.c -c

       #gcc --coverage important.o

    c. Must execute at least once your code coverage processed executable file:

       #./a.out

       Trail Runs:83

2. After executing at least once your executable, then only the source file of the executable can be used with the gcov tool.

    a. First, check various gcov options available for you to use: (These are self explanatory options.)

```
#gcov
Usage: gcov [OPTION...] SOURCE|OBJ...

Print code coverage information.
  -a, --all-blocks             Show information for every
                               basic block
  -b, --branch-probabilities   Include branch probabilities
                               in output
  -c, --branch-counts          Output counts of branches taken
                               rather than percentages
  -d, --display-progress       Display progress information
  -f, --function-summaries     Output summaries for each
                               function
  -h, --help                   Print this help, then exit
  -i, --json-format            Output JSON intermediate format
                               into .gcov.json.gz file
  -j, --human-readable         Output human readable numbers
  -k, --use-colors             Emit colored output
  -l, --long-file-names        Use long output file names for
                               included source files
  -m, --demangled-names        Output demangled function names
```

```
-n, --no-output              Do not create an output file
-o, --object-directory DIR|FILE Search for object files in
                             DIR or called FILE
-p, --preserve-paths         Preserve all pathname
                             components
-q, --use-hotness-colors     Emit perf-like colored output
                             for hot lines
-r, --relative-only          Only show data for
                             relative sources
-s, --source-prefix DIR      Source prefix to elide
-t, --stdout                 Output to stdout instead
                             of a file
-u, --unconditional-branches Show unconditional branch
                             counts too
-v, --version                Print version number, then exit
-w, --verbose                Print verbose informations
-x, --hash-filenames         Hash long pathnames
```

b. To collect function-level code coverage statistics, use the following command using your example source code file:

```
#gcov -f important
```

c. To collect branches-level code coverage statistics, use the following command using your example source code file:

```
#gcov -b important
```

d. To collect all blocks-level code coverage statistics, use the following command using your example source code file:

```
#gcov -a important
```

e. To collect individual lines-level code coverage statistics, use the following command using your example source code file:

```
#gcov -l important
File 'important.c'
```

CHAPTER 3   PRACTICE C PROGRAMMING WITH IMPORTANT TOOLS

   f. We can also combine multiple options and collect statistics as follows:

   ```
   #gcov -abclf important
   ```

Well done! From this activity, we have learned how to use gcov tools and its options for inspecting line-level, branch-level, and function-level statistics.

Next, you will learn how to use gcc and gcov together for carrying out code coverage and static code analysis tasks in the following hands-on activity.

Hands-On Activity

In this section, you will learn the following code coverage-related activities:

1. Write two sample functions called search and min functions, and test these functions by calling them a random number of times in the main function for testing.

2. Inspect individual function-level code coverage statistics.

3. Inspect individual branch-level code coverage statistics.

4. Inspect individual lines-level code coverage statistics.

A C APPLICATION CODE COVERAGE AND PROFILING USING GCOV

1. To do code coverage, write the following sample functions: `search`, `min`, `main` in a `important.c` file:

   a. A sample linear `search` function to search for an element present in a given list or not

   ```c
   #include<stdio.h>
   #include<stdlib.h>
   #include<stddef.h>
   int search(int *p, int N, int ele)
   {
       if (p==NULL)
           return -1;
   ```

```
        else
        {
            int i;
            int index=-1;
            for (i=0;i<N;i++)
            {
                if (p[i]==ele)
                {
                    index = i;
                    return index;
                }
            }
            return index;
        }
    }
```

b. Sample `min` function to find a minimum element from the list of numbers:

```
int min(int *p, int N)
{
    if (p==NULL)
        return -1;
    else
    {
        int i;
        int min = p[0];
        int index=-1;
        for (i=0;i<N;i++)
        {
            if (p[i]<=min)
            {
                min = p[i];
                #index = i;
            }
        }
```

CHAPTER 3   PRACTICE C PROGRAMMING WITH IMPORTANT TOOLS

```
            return index;
    }
}
```

c. Test your sample functions in main as follows by calling them a random number of times:

```
int main()
{
    int a[10]={10,2,3,4,5,6,1,8,7,6};
    int r = rand()%100;
    printf("Trail Runs:%d\n",r);
    for (int i=0;i<r;i++)
    {       int x = rand()%10;
            search(a,10,x);
    }
    r = rand()%100;
    printf("Trail Runs:%d\n",r);
    for (int i=0;i<r;i++)
    {
            min(a,10);
    }
    return 0;
}
```

2. Compile the important.c file with the gcc code coverage option and generate an executable file with the gcc code coverage option using the following commands:

```
#gcc --coverage important.c
#gcc --coverage important.c -c
#gcc --coverage important.o
```

3. Execute at least one time your executable file (a.out):

```
#./a.out
Trail Runs:83
Trail Runs:88
```

4. Then, first collect individual function-level code coverage statistics:

   ```
   #gcov -f important
   Function 'main'
   Lines executed:100.00% of 12

   Function 'min'
   Lines executed:90.00% of 10

   Function 'search'
   Lines executed:88.89% of 9

   File 'important.c'
   Lines executed:93.55% of 31
   Creating 'important.c.gcov'
   ```

   a. Observe from the gcov results that in the main() function all lines are executed 100%, whereas in min() 90% of the lines of code got executed, and in search() 88% of the lines of code got executed.

   b. It helps in quickly identifying a function-level individual's stats to find heavily used functions and least used functions.

5. Then, collect individual branch-level code coverage statistics:

   ```
   #gcov -b important
   File 'important.c'
   Lines executed:93.55% of 31
   Branches executed:100.00% of 16
   Taken at least once:87.50% of 16
   Calls executed:100.00% of 7
   Creating 'important.c.gcov'
   ```

   a. Observe from the gcov results that in your code, there are a total of 16 branches, 7 function calls, and 31 lines of code.

   b. It helps in quickly identifying call-level statistics and branch-level statistics.

CHAPTER 3   PRACTICE C PROGRAMMING WITH IMPORTANT TOOLS

6. Then, collect individual line-level code coverage statistics:

```
#gcov -l important
File 'important.c'
Lines executed:93.55% of 31
Creating 'important##important.c.gcov'
```

7. Finally, combine line, branches, functions, block-level options to collect all statistics in a code coverage file using the following command:

```
#gcov -fabcl important
Function 'main'
Lines executed:100.00% of 12
Function 'min'
Lines executed:90.00% of 10
Function 'search'
Lines executed:88.89% of 9
File 'important.c'
Lines executed:93.55% of 31
Branches executed:100.00% of 16
Taken at least once:87.50% of 16
Calls executed:100.00% of 7
Creating 'important##important.c.gcov'
```

  a. From the gcov results you can observe it is printing all levels of statistics together.

  b. However, we still did not observe individual branch-level and line-level actual source codes with statistics. To inspect the source code level, you can observe from the following file: 'important##important.c.gcov'. We inspect it in the next task.

Well done! From this activity, we practiced gcov tools and its options for inspecting line-level, branch-level, and function-level statistics with a sample C application profiling.

Next, let's learn how to check gcov-generated output files for more details about source code with code coverage annotated details.

CHAPTER 3   PRACTICE C PROGRAMMING WITH IMPORTANT TOOLS

INSPECT GCOV-GENERATED OUTPUT FILES

1. Open important##important.c.gcov

   a. First inspect the starting lines of the gcov-generated file:

   ```
   -:      0:Source:important.c
   -:      0:Graph:important.gcno
   -:      0:Data:important.gcda
   -:      0:Runs:1
   -:      1:#include<stdio.h>
   -:      2:#include<stdlib.h>
   -:      3:#include<stddef.h>
   ```

   b. Let's inspect the gcov stats with the search function:

      i. Check for how many times the search function is executed.

      ii. Then, check for individual count and understand as follows:

      83:   6:   if (p==NULL),

      1. The result in the first column indicates how many times the specific line of code got executed.

      2. The second column indicates the actual source code line number.

      3. The third column indicates the actual line of code.

   c. Check the total blocks present in the search function and their statistics. In this case, a total of three blocks are present.

   d. Similarly, check for branch-level statistics.

   ```
   function search called 83 returned 100% blocks executed 89%
          83:         4:int search(int *p, int N, int ele)
           -:         5:{
          83:         6:           if (p==NULL)
          83:         6-block  0
   branch  0 taken   0 (fallthrough)
   ```

193

CHAPTER 3 PRACTICE C PROGRAMMING WITH IMPORTANT TOOLS

```
    branch  1 taken  83
        #####:      7:                  return -1;
        %%%%:       7-block  0
           -:       8:          else
           -:       9:          {
           -:      10:                  int i;
          83:      11:                  int index=-1;
         529:      12:                  for (i=0;i<N;i++)
          83:      12-block  0
         446:      12-block  1
         529:      12-block  2
    branch  0 taken  514
    branch  1 taken  15 (fallthrough)
           -:      13:                  {
         514:      14:                      if (p[i]==ele)
         514:      14-block  0
    branch  0 taken  68 (fallthrough)
    branch  1 taken  446
           -:      15:                      {
          68:      16:                          index = i;
          68:      17:                          return index;
          68:      17-block  0
           -:      18:                      }
           -:      19:                  }
          15:      20:                  return index;
          15:      20-block  0
           -:      21:              }
           -:      22:
           -:      23:}
```

2. Similarly, check for `min` and `main()` functions as a practice task.

Well done! From this activity, we have learned how to check gcov-generated output files for more details about source code with code coverage annotated details.

Next, you will learn how to use gdb for carrying out important C application debugging activities in terms of errors handling, runtime errors, and crashes.

GDB: The GNU Project Debugger

The gdb tool is a handy tool for developers to carry out program debugging activities. In real time, it is highly challenging to confirm a code is passed in all possible test cases, and the code will be executed without any runtime errors in the deployed runtime environment. Specifically, to handle runtime errors of a C application code, it is necessary to go through code execution at individual lines and functions levels for inspecting the data and code carefully. Sometimes it is necessary to inspect the C application crashes using the core dump files. To handle and perform these tasks systematically, learning the gdb tool is essential. In this section, you will learn how to use the gdb tool for performing the following activities.

- Go through a code execution and inspect the C code and data
- Handle C applications crashes easily using gdb
- Inspect C application runtime stack and handle runtime errors using core dump files

Go Through a Code Execution and Inspect the Code and Data

To learn debugging a code, it is necessary to explore important gdb commands for carrying out runtime errors handling activities:

- Inspect the source code during execution for identifying and keeping debugging points at specific lines of code and functions.
  - You will use the following gdb commands: `set listsize`, `list` to display a group of lines for inspecting source code and individual lines or functions to set breakpoints.
  - Set and remove the breakpoints permanently using `break` and `delete` commands. Breakpoints are assigned with numbers; breakpoint numbers are helpful for handling them for removing, enabling, and disabling.

- Enable or disable the breakpoints dynamically using gdb `enable` and `disable` commands.

- **Conditional Breakpoints**: It is also possible to set breakpoints based on specific conditions over lines of code.

• Start debugging and go through lines of execution:

- `run`: This command starts executing the source code in debugging mode and stops at a breakpoint for inspecting the respective code and data. The shortcut for the `run` command is `r`.

- `next`: This command helps to run through individual lines from a breakpoint. The shortcut for the `next` command is `n`.

- `continue`: This command helps to run through a block of lines till the next breakpoint. The shortcut for the `continue` command is `c`.

- **step**: This command helps to run through inside a function, then use n for inspecting individual lines of the function. The shortcut for the `step` command is `s`.

• During debugging, it is necessary to set specific variables to inspect the code execution and print result variables, data type variables, and pointer variables and watch specific variables' value changes in expressions.

- **Setting Variable Values**: `set var variablename=value`. This command helps in changing code behavior during runtime. It also helps in creating temporary variables during runtime.

- **Print Variable Values**: `print variablename`. This command helps in observing data, pointers, and register values during runtime.

- **Watching Variable Values**: watch variablename. This command helps in observing dynamic changes to a variable at a specific expression automatically whenever the specific expression changes the variable.

- **Inspect Breakpoints**: `info break`. This command helps in displaying all available breakpoints and their status. It is very useful to track breakpoint information during a long code debugging with multiple breakpoints.

- Inspecting runtime stack, registers, libraries, and assembly code:
  - `info`: Info is a very important command to inspect runtime stack frames information, registers, and dynamic libraries linked with runtime code. It also helps in displaying function local variables and arguments.
    - During debugging a code, we can use the following info commands: `info locals, info args, info registers, info stack, info sharedlibrary`

- `disassemble`: It is an important command to check assembly-level code of a function during runtime. It helps in inspecting how registers are used at assembly instructions, any stack protection check related code is enabled, and any high-level code is optimized.
  - Expression optimization-related code is also easily inspected in assembly language code.
  - For instance, when you run code with gcc code optimization, divide-by-2 or multiply-by-2 expressions can be converted into shift operations. It can be clearly inspected.
  - **Another Example**: Inline function expansion can be easily checked.
  - Stack local variables and arguments can be easily inspected.
  - Loop optimization-related code also can be easily inspected in a function.

Let's quickly learn how to use gdb commands for common debugging activities.

CHAPTER 3   PRACTICE C PROGRAMMING WITH IMPORTANT TOOLS

WALKTHROUGH OF A C APPLICATION USING GDB

1. We do the following activities by using `reliability3.c`. We assume bugs are not fixed in earlier hands-on activities:

   a. Go through an `ArrayAccess` function and explore all gdb code walkthrough commands.

      i. Set breakpoints at line numbers, functions, and conditional breakpoints.

      ii. Use of continue and ignore commands to skip unnecessary breakpoints inspection and lines of the code during debugging steps.

      iii. End the execution.

2. First compile the code for debugging it using the following commands:

   `#gcc -g reliability3.c`

3. Run the `./a.out` using gdb for debugging the `ArrayAccess` function as follows:

   ```
   gdb ./a.out
   (gdb)
   ```

4. From the result of the above command, you observe the gdb prompt. As we do not know the line number of `ArrayAccess`, let's check where it is by using the following gdb commands in order:

   ```
   (gdb) set listsize 10
   (gdb) list 1
   1       #include<stdio.h>
   2       #include<stdlib.h>
   ..
   5       void ArrayAccess()
   ```

   a. These steps are not necessary, but to check how to use `listsize` and `list` commands, we go through these steps.

CHAPTER 3   PRACTICE C PROGRAMMING WITH IMPORTANT TOOLS

b. Next, directly we set a breakpoint at the `ArrayAccess` function using the following command, and we also set another sample breakpoint at line number 14.

c. We set a conditional break using `if i==7 && j==7`

```
(gdb) b ArrayAccess
Breakpoint 1 at 0x1189: file reliability3.c, line 6.
(gdb) b 14
Breakpoint 2 at 0x11cf: file reliability3.c, line 14.
(gdb) b 22 if i==7 && j==7
Breakpoint 3 at 0x125b: file reliability3.c, line 22.
```

d. We can display all breakpoints information using the following command and observe details such as **Enb**, **type**, and **line numbers**, then set two random breakpoints by executing the following commands in order:

```
gdb) info b
Num      Type              Disp Enb
Address              What
1        breakpoint        keep y    0x0000000000001189 in
ArrayAccess at reliability3.c:6
2        breakpoint        keep y    0x00000000000011cf in
ArrayAccess at reliability3.c:14
3        breakpoint        keep y    0x000000000000125b in
ArrayAccess at reliability3.c:22
         stop only if i==7 && j==7
(gdb) b 29
Breakpoint 4 at 0x12c5: file reliability3.c, line 29.
(gdb) b 30
Breakpoint 5 at 0x1317: file reliability3.c, line 34.
```

e. Then, delete these random breakpoints and check it using the `info` command:

```
(gdb) delete 4
(gdb) disable 5
(gdb) info b
```

199

CHAPTER 3   PRACTICE C PROGRAMMING WITH IMPORTANT TOOLS

```
Num     Type                Disp Enb
Address                What
1       breakpoint          keep y   0x0000000000001189 in
ArrayAccess at reliability3.c:6
2       breakpoint          keep y   0x00000000000011cf in
ArrayAccess at reliability3.c:14
3       breakpoint          keep y   0x000000000000125b in
ArrayAccess at reliability3.c:22
        stop only if i==7 && j==7
5       breakpoint          keep n   0x0000000000001317 in
ArrayAccess at reliability3.c:34
```

f. After setting all breakpoints, let's start runtime execution using the run command (r shortcut):

```
(gdb) r
Starting program: a.out

Breakpoint 1, ArrayAccess () at reliability3.c:6
6       {
```

g. From the result, you can observe that execution stops at breakpoint 1 to inspect code and data. Then go through line-by-line execution using the next command (shortcut n) as follows:

```
(gdb) n
8       float p=0.1;
(gdb) n
10          for (int i=0;i<8;i++)
(gdb) n
12          for (int j=0;j<8;j++)
(gdb) n

Breakpoint 2, ArrayAccess () at reliability3.c:14
14              a[i][j]=i*j;
```

CHAPTER 3   PRACTICE C PROGRAMMING WITH IMPORTANT TOOLS

h. You can observe that every time at line number 14, the program execution is stopping to inspect code and data. You can skip this specific breakpoint number 2 for a specific number of times using the `ignore` command:

```
(gdb) ignore 2 64
Will ignore next 64 crossings of breakpoint 2.
```

i. Now you can observe that breakpoint number 2 is skipping in loop iterations.

j. Next, you can skip a specific number of lines of code to speed up your debugging process using the `until` command:

```
(gdb) n
12              for (int j=0;j<8;j++)
(gdb) n
14                  a[i][j]=i*j;
(gdb) n
15                  p = p*i*j;
(gdb) until 18
ArrayAccess () at reliability3.c:18
```

k. Next, you can skip code execution inspection till the next breakpoint using the `continue` command (c shortcut):

```
(gdb) c
Continuing.
Breakpoint 3, ArrayAccess () at reliability3.c:22
22                      printf("%d",a[i][j]);
(gdb)
```

l. From the result of the continue command, you can observe the next breakpoint 3 is at i==7 and j==7; hence, the code execution got stopped at the specific loop iterations. You can confirm it by printing variable i and j values as follows:

```
(gdb) p i
$1 = 7
```

201

CHAPTER 3   PRACTICE C PROGRAMMING WITH IMPORTANT TOOLS

```
(gdb) p j
$2 = 7
(gdb)
```

m. Finally, you can stop the debugging by giving a continue command to reach execution at the end of the code.

```
(gdb) c
Continuing.
000000000123456702468101214036912151821048121620 2428
05101520253035061218243036420714212835 42490
00000000012345670246810121403691215182104812162024 2805
101520253035061218243036420714212835 4249[Inferior
1 (process 40845) exited normally]
(gdb) Quit
```

Well done! From this hands-on activity, we have all the basic gdb commands for carrying out application debugging activities.

Next, let's learn how to use gdb for inspecting the code and data of an application.

Inspect the Code and Data Using gdb Commands

In this section, we use gdb for inspecting a sample C application code and data thoroughly for quickly performing debugging activities. Specifically, we carry out the following two activities:

1. Inspect a C application code and data using the gdb commands.

2. Inspect a C application stack, registers, and its assembly code using the gdb command.

Let's first inspect the code and data of a C application.

CHAPTER 3   PRACTICE C PROGRAMMING WITH IMPORTANT TOOLS

INSPECT A C APPLICATION CODE AND DATA USING GDB

1. We do the following activities by using reliability3.c. We assume bugs were not fixed in earlier hands-on activity:

    a. Go through the ArrayAccess function and explore the code and data:

       i. Display local variables of the function.

       ii. Set specific variable values to control runtime execution.

       iii. Print variables and pointer variables to inspect their values.

       iv. Watch any loop index variable.

       v. End the execution.

2. First, compile the code for debugging it using the following commands:

    ```
    #gcc -g reliability3.c
    ```

3. Run the ./a.out using gdb for debugging the ArrayAccess function as follows:

    ```
    #gdb ./a.out
    (gdb)b ArrayAccess
    Breakpoint 1 at 0x1189: file reliability3.c, line 6.
    ```

4. After setting all breakpoints, let's start runtime execution using the run command (r shortcut):

    ```
    (gdb) r
    Starting program: a.out
    Breakpoint 1, ArrayAccess () at reliability3.c:6
    ```

    a. Inspect all local variables of the ArrayAccess function using info and print the address of the array variable:

    ```
    6     {
    (gdb) info locals
    j = 0
    ```

CHAPTER 3 PRACTICE C PROGRAMMING WITH IMPORTANT TOOLS

```
i = 0
p = 0.100000001
a = {{896, 896, 896, 896, 896, 896, 896, 896}, {896, 896, 896,
896, 896, 896, 896, 896}, {896, 896, 896, 896, 896, 896, 896,
896}, {896, 896, 896, 896, 0, 0, 256, 64}, {0, 0, 0, 0, 0, 0,
0, 0}, {0, 0,
        0, 0, 0, 0, 0, 0}, {0, 0, 0, 0, 1431650368,
21845, 15775231, 0}, {194, 0, -8761, 32767, -8762, 32767,
1431655677, 21845}}
(gdb) p &a
$3 = (int (*)[8][8]) 0x7fffffffdcb0
```

b. Then go through line-by-line execution as follows:

```
(gdb) n
8          float p=0.1;
(gdb) n
10             for (int i=0;i<8;i++)
(gdb) n
12             for (int j=0;j<8;j++)
(gdb) n
14                 a[i][j]=i*j;
```

c. Then, after going through a few iterations, manually set loop index variable values to control the execution as follows:

```
(gdb) set var i=10
(gdb) set var j=20
```

d. As we set high index values, loops will be terminated after this specific iteration:

```
(gdb) n
15             p = p*i*j;
(gdb) n
12             for (int j=0;j<8;j++)
```

CHAPTER 3 PRACTICE C PROGRAMMING WITH IMPORTANT TOOLS

e. Observe variable p value as follows:

```
(gdb) print p
$1 = 20
```

f. After reaching the end of the current loop, in the next loop, let's watch the loop index j value using the watch command as follows:

```
18                      for (int i=0;i<8;i++)
..
(gdb) n
20                      for (int j=0;j<8;j++)
(gdb) watch j
Hardware watchpoint 2: j

(gdb) n
Hardware watchpoint 2: j

Old value = 0
New value = 1
0x0000555555555294 in ArrayAccess () at reliability3.c:20
20                      for (int j=0;j<8;j++)
(gdb) n
22                              printf("%d",a[i][j]);
(gdb) n
20                      for (int j=0;j<8;j++)
(gdb) n

Hardware watchpoint 2: j

Old value = 1
New value = 2
0x0000555555555294 in ArrayAccess () at reliability3.c:20
20                      for (int j=0;j<8;j++)
```

CHAPTER 3   PRACTICE C PROGRAMMING WITH IMPORTANT TOOLS

5. From the result you can observe as loop iterations go on the j value changes, then the old and new values of j are printed. You may break the debugging using Ctrl-C and quit commands.

Well done! From this hands-on activity, we have learned how to do debugging steps quickly by inspecting necessary code and data of an application.

Next, let's learn gdb options for inspecting a C application runtime stack, registers, and assembly code.

INSPECT A C APPLICATION STACK, REGISTERS, AND ASSEMBLY CODE USING GDB

1. We do the following activities by using reliability3.c. We assume bugs are not fixed in earlier hands-on activities:

   a. Go through an `ArrayAccess` function and explore gdb commands for doing the following tasks:

      i. Inspect runtime stack frames during ArrayAccess function execution

      ii. List out registers and inspect registers' contents

      iii. Inspect if any shared libraries are in use

      iv. Check the starting and end address of the ArrayAccess

      v. Check ArrayAccess corresponding assembly language code

2. First compile the code for debugging it using the following commands:

   ```
   #gcc -g reliability3.c
   ```

3. Run the ./a.out using gdb for debugging the `ArrayAccess` function as follows:

   ```
   #gdb ./a.out
   (gdb)b ArrayAccess
   Breakpoint 1 at 0x1189: file reliability3.c, line 6.
   ```

CHAPTER 3   PRACTICE C PROGRAMMING WITH IMPORTANT TOOLS

4. After setting all breakpoints, let's start runtime execution using the `run` command (r shortcut):

   ```
   (gdb) r
   Starting program: a.out
   Breakpoint 1, ArrayAccess () at reliability3.c:6
   ```

   a. First, inspect runtime stack frames using the `info` command:

   ```
   (gdb) info stack
   #0  ArrayAccess () at reliability3.c:14
   #1  0x00005555555554a6 in main () at reliability3.c:68
   ```

   b. From the result of the stack command, you can observe As ArrayAccess is called from the main function, first the main stack frame is pushed into the runtime stack, then the ArrayAccess frame is pushed.

   c. Next, inspect registers usages and their contents using the following command and observe addresses of the functions and runtime stack:

   ```
   (gdb) info registers
       rax             0x0                     0
       rbx             0x5555555554b0          93824992236720
       rcx             0x5555555554b0          93824992236720
       rdx             0x7fffffffdee8          140737488346856
       rsi             0x7fffffffded8          140737488346840
       rdi             0x1                     1
       rbp             0x7fffffffddc0          0x7fffffffddc0
       rsp             0x7fffffffdc90          0x7fffffffdc90
       ..
       eflags          0x297                   [ CF PF AF SF IF ]
       cs              0x33                    51
       ss              0x2b                    43
       ds              0x0                     0
       es              0x0                     0
       fs              0x0                     0
       gs              0x0                     0
   ```

CHAPTER 3   PRACTICE C PROGRAMMING WITH IMPORTANT TOOLS

d. Print contents of stack pointer, base pointer, and instruction pointers using the following commands.

```
(gdb) p $rsp
$1 = (void *) 0x7fffffffdc90
(gdb) p $rbp
$2 = (void *) 0x7fffffffddc0
(gdb) p $rip
$3 = (void (*)()) 0x5555555551cf <ArrayAccess+70>
```

e. Check if any shared libraries are loaded for your code execution using the following command and observe the few important shared libraries are loaded (libc):

```
(gdb) info sharedlibrary
From                 To                   Syms Read    Shared
Object Library
0x00007ffff7fd0100   0x00007ffff7ff2684   Yes          /lib64/ld-linux-x86-64.so.2
0x00007ffff7dc3630   0x00007ffff7f3827d   Yes          /lib/x86_64-linux-gnu/libc.so.6
```

f. Then, print the start and end addresses of the ArrayAccess function:

```
(gdb) info line
Line 14 of "reliability3.c" starts at address 0x555555555189 <ArrayAccess+70> and ends at 0x5555555551XX <ArrayAccess+115>.
```

g. Then, display assembly code equivalent to ArrayAccess using the disassemble command:

```
(gdb)disassemble ArrayAccess
Dump of assembler code for function ArrayAccess:
   0x0000555555555189 <+0>:    endbr64
   0x000055555555518d <+4>:    push    %rbp
   0x000055555555518e <+5>:    mov     %rsp,%rbp
   0x0000555555555191 <+8>:    sub     $0x130,%rsp
```

```
0x0000555555555198 <+15>:  mov    %fs:0x28,%rax
0x00005555555551a1 <+24>:  mov    %rax,-0x8(%rbp)
0x00005555555551a5 <+28>:  xor    %eax,%eax
```

5. Observe that lines of assembly code are displayed. For simplicity, we displayed only the beginning line of the assembly code of ArrayAccess. Then, you can terminate debugging steps using Ctrl-C and quit commands.

Well done! From this hands-on activity, we have learned important gdb commands to inspect application runtime stack size, registers, and assembly code for deeper inspection of application code for debugging activities.

Next, let's learn gdb options for handling application crashes.

Handle Application Runtime Errors

In this section, we use gdb for handling C application runtime errors. Specifically, we carry out the following three activities:

1. Inspect a C application runtime stack size
2. Handle a C application runtime crash
3. Handle a C application crash from its core dump file

First let's learn how to use gdb for inspecting the application runtime stack and determining stack usage.

INSPECT RUNTIME STACK AND DETERMINE STACK SIZE USAGE

1. We will do the following activities:
   a. We write a recursive function for finding a factorial of a given number.
   b. Inside the recursive function factorial, we include a local array of big size intentionally to show the impact of unnecessary variables on runtime stack usages.
   c. We find the runtime stack size using gdb commands.

CHAPTER 3   PRACTICE C PROGRAMMING WITH IMPORTANT TOOLS

2. First, we write the following C code in a `recfunc.c` and save it:

    ```
    #include<stdio.h>
    long unsigned int fact(long unsigned int n)
    {
        int a[256];
        if (n==0 || n==1)
            return 1;
        else
            return n*fact(n-1);
    }
    int main()
    {
        fact(7);
    }
    ```

3. First, compile the code for debugging it using the following commands:

    ```
    #gcc -g recfunc.c
    ```

4. Run the `./a.out` using gdb for debugging the stack size of the factorial function as follows:

    ```
    #gdb ./a.out
    ```

5. To find the maximum runtime stack size usage, we can directly set a breakpoint at line number 8 to stop execution if n==2:

    ```
    (gdb) list
    1       #include<stdio.h>
    2       long unsigned int fact(long unsigned int n)
    3       {
    4           int a[256];
    5           if (n==0 || n==1)
    6               return 1;
    7           else
    8               return n*fact(n-1);
    9       }
    10
    ```

```
(gdb) b 8 if n==2
Breakpoint 1 at 0x114e: file recfunc.c, line 8.
```

6. Run the code after setting a breakpoint:

   ```
   (gdb) r
   Starting program: a.out

   Breakpoint 1, fact (n=2) at recfunc.c:8
   8            return n*fact(n-1);
   (gdb) info stack
   #0  fact (n=2) at recfunc.c:8
   #1  0x000055555555519c in fact (n=3) at recfunc.c:8
   #2  0x000055555555519c in fact (n=4) at recfunc.c:8
   #3  0x000055555555519c in fact (n=5) at recfunc.c:8
   #4  0x000055555555519c in fact (n=6) at recfunc.c:8
   #5  0x000055555555519c in fact (n=7) at recfunc.c:8
   #6  0x00005555555551cc in main () at recfunc.c:13
   ```

7. To determine the stack size consumed by frame 6 to frame 0, you can give the following commands in order:

   a. First collect the frame 6 bottom-of-the-stack address in use as follows:

      ```
      (gdb) fr 6
            #6  0x00005555555551cc in main () at recfunc.c:13
      13            fact(7);
      ```

   b. Collect the stack pointer address of frame 6 into the gdb variable $1 using the following command:

      ```
      (gdb) p $sp
      ```
      $1 = (void *) 0x7fffffffde10

   c. Then collect the frame 0 top-of-the-stack address in use as follows:

      ```
      (gdb) fr 0
      #0  fact (n=2) at recfunc.c:8
      8            return n*fact(n-1);
      ```

d. Collect the stack pointer address of frame 6 into gdb variable $2 using the following command:

```
(gdb) p $sp
$2 = (void *) 0x7fffffffc4f0
```

e. Total stack space consumed in terms of bytes can be computed using the following command:

```
(gdb) p $1-$2
$3 = 6432
(gdb)
```

Well done! From this hands-on activity, we have learned how to use gdb commands for finding application runtime stack usage details.

Next, let's learn how to handle runtime errors of a C application using gdb.

HANDLE RUNTIME C APPLICATION CRASHES QUICKLY USING GDB

1. We will do the following activities:

    a. We identify potential lines of code causing the program crashes.

    b. Handle the specific lines of code to correct the error.

    c. Repeat steps a and b till all runtime errors are corrected.

2. First compile the code without the debugging option using the following commands:

    ```
    #gcc reliability3.c
    ```

3. Run the ./a.out and observe there is a crash of the program without any clue.

    ```
    #./a.out
    *** stack smashing detected ***: terminated
    Aborted (core dumped)
    ```

4. To quickly identify lines of code causing crashes, first compile the code for debugging it using the following commands:

   ```
   #gcc -g reliability3.c
   ```

5. Run the ./a.out using gdb as follows:

   ```
   #gdb ./a.out
   (gdb) r
   *** stack smashing detected ***: terminated
   Aborted (core dumped)
   ```

   a. To detect the line of code causing this crash, you can simply give the following gdb command called backtrace (shortcut bt):

   ```
   (gdb) bt
   #0  __GI_raise (sig=sig@entry=6) at ../sysdeps/unix/sysv/linux/raise.c:50
   #1  0x00007ffff7dc3859 in __GI_abort () at abort.c:79
   #2  0x00007ffff7e2e26e in __libc_message (action=action@entry=do_abort, fmt=fmt@entry=0x7ffff7f5808f "*** %s ***: terminated\n") at ..
   #3  0x00007ffff7ed0aba in __GI___fortify_fail (msg=msg@entry=0x7ffff7f58077 "stack smashing detected") at fortify_fail.c:26
   #4  0x00007ffff7ed0a86 in __stack_chk_fail () at stack_chk_fail.c:24
   ```
   #5 0x000055555555538d in StringChecks (buff=0x555555556037 "abcdefghijk") at reliability3.c:40
   ```
   #6  0x00005555555554a8 in main () at reliability3.c:69
   ```

   b. Start with observing which function in main() is causing the crash. It is at line 69; the function name is StringChecks.

   c. Then, you can check the specific line of StringChecks causing the program crash. It is not possible due to a runtime stack crash, but you can check inside the function ibuff size is 10 bytes, and we are passing a string of length 12 bytes.

213

CHAPTER 3   PRACTICE C PROGRAMMING WITH IMPORTANT TOOLS

     d. You can change the p1 argument in main() with a new string as follows to correct the error.

        char *p1 = "abcdefghij";

6. After saving changes in reliability3.c, compile the code for debugging it using the following commands:

```
#gcc -g reliability3.c
```

7. Run the ./a.out using gdb as follows:

```
#gdb ./a.out
(gdb) r
Starting program: a.out

Program received signal SIGFPE, Arithmetic exception.
0x00005555555553c6 in DataRangesOperations (N=1024) at reliability3.c:51
51              N = N%d;
```

     a. This time this crash is detected with the line number and function causing the crash: DataRangesOperations (N=1024) at reliability3.c:51

     b. Now we can easily correct it by checking the value of N and d as follows:

```
(gdb) print d
$1 = 0
(gdb) print N
$2 = 1024
```

     c. From the N and d values, we can confirm d should not be zero. We can make corresponding changes in reliability3.c DataRangesOpearions function and save it as below:

```
if (d!=0)
{
    N = N%d;
    res = d/N;
}
```

CHAPTER 3   PRACTICE C PROGRAMMING WITH IMPORTANT TOOLS

8. After saving changes in reliability3.c, compile the code for debugging it using the following commands:

   #gcc -g reliability3.c

9. Run the ./a.out using gdb as follows:

   #gdb ./a.out
   (gdb) r
   (gdb) r
   Program received signal SIGABRT, Aborted.
       __GI_raise (sig=sig@entry=6) at ../sysdeps/unix/sysv/linux/raise.c:50
       50   ../sysdeps/unix/sysv/linux/raise.c: No such file or directory.

   a. This time this crash is detected without the line number and function causing the crash. Use the backtrace (bt) command to get the function call stack details:

      (gdb) bt

      #0 __GI_raise (sig=sig@entry=6) at ../sysdeps/unix/sysv/linux/raise.c:50
      #1 0x00007ffff7dc3859 in __GI_abort () at abort.c:79
      #2 0x00007ffff7e2e26e in __libc_message (action=action@entry=do_abort, ..
      #3 0x00007ffff7e362fc in malloc_printerr (str=str@entry=0x7ffff7f5a5d0 "free(): double free detected in tcache 2") at malloc.c:5347
      #4 0x00007ffff7e37f6d in _int_free (av=0x7ffff7f8db80 <main_arena>, ..
      #5 0x0000555555555554 in main () at reliability3.c:81

   b. From the bt details, we can identify that the error line of code is in main() at line 81. There is also a clue in the trace message saying double free. Hence, we can remove that double free statement and run the code.

      //free(p2);

215

CHAPTER 3   PRACTICE C PROGRAMMING WITH IMPORTANT TOOLS

10. After saving changes in reliability3.c, compile the code for debugging it using the following commands:

    #gcc -g reliability3.c

11. Run the ./a.out using gdb as follows:

    #gdb ./a.out
    (gdb) r
    1 2 3 4 5 6 7 8 9 10 504834048 1585547054 Accessing elements of the array %&'()*+,-.

    a. From the results, we can observe there are no more crashes. Then, we are done with identifying the crash-causing line of code and correcting it. But you may have observed that the array size is 10, but it is displaying 10 elements.

    b. Hence, we discussed first checking all reliability issues using gcc options such as sanitize=undefined, and address to correct these errors during development time.

12. We can also run -analyzer to detect a few possible runtime errors at the compilation time itself as follows:

    gcc-10 -fanalyzer reliability3.c
    reliability3.c: In function 'StringChecks':
    reliability3.c:38:2: warning: use of possibly-NULL 'buff' where non-null expected [CWE-690] [-Wanalyzer-possible-null-argument]
       38 | strcpy(ibuff,buff);

    reliability3.c: In function 'main':
    reliability3.c:83:7: warning: use after 'free' of 'p2' [CWE-416] [-Wanalyzer-use-after-free]
       83 | p2[0]='a';

13. Correct these errors as shown in the code below and save the file for an error-free program:

    ```
    if (p2!=NULL)
    {
         StringChecks(p2);
    ```

```
        free(p2);
}
//      p2[0]='a';
```

Well done! From this hands-on activity, we have learned how to use gdb for handling application crashes in quick time.

Next, let's learn how to handle a C application crash from its core dump file.

HANDLE RUNTIME CRASHES OF A C APPLICATION USING A CORE DUMP FILE

1. We will do the following activities:

    a. We write the sample code in segfaults.c to generate a core dump file and use it for debugging.

    ```c
    #include<stdio.h>
    #include<stdlib.h>
    #include<string.h>
    void StrProcess1(char *p)
    {
            int i;
            char a[10];
            strcpy(a,p);
            for (i=0;i<strlen(p);i++)
            {
                    printf("String Access %c",a[i]);
            }
            printf("\n");
    }
    int main()
    {
            char *p1; char *p2;
            p1=(char*)malloc(sizeof(char)*10);
            memset(p1,'a',10);
    ```

```
            StrProcess1(p1);
            StrProcess1(p2);
            StrProcess1("abcdefghijk");
}
```

2. To generate a core dump file, it is necessary to set the following stack limits using the `ulimit` command:

   ```
   #ulimit -c unlimited
   ```

3. Then compile the code with debugging enabled and run the executable `./a.out`:

   ```
   #gcc -g segfaults.c
   #./a.out
   Core was generated by `./a.out'.
   ```

4. From the result, you can observe there is a core dump file generated; let's inspect these details using the following command:

   ```
   #ls
   -rw------- 1 iiitdmk iiitdmk 389120 Feb 25 16:04 core
   ```

5. Next, directly use the core dump file to detect the line of code causing the crash as follows:

   ```
   #gdb ./a.out core
   #0  __strcpy_avx2 () at ../sysdeps/x86_64/multiarch/strcpy-avx2.S:301
   301    ../sysdeps/x86_64/multiarch/strcpy-avx2.S: No such file or directory.
   ```

6. You can use the `backtrace` command to detect the line of code causing the crash as follows:

   ```
   (gdb) bt
   #0  __strcpy_avx2 () at ../sysdeps/x86_64/multiarch/strcpy-avx2.S:301
   #1  0x0000564e8cc1923c in StrProcess1 (p=0x0) at segfaults.c:8
   #2  0x0000564e8cc192ee in main () at segfaults.c:22
   ```

CHAPTER 3   PRACTICE C PROGRAMMING WITH IMPORTANT TOOLS

7. You can even check the stack frame for inspecting the local variables and arguments details to get more details about bug:

```
(gdb) fr 1
#1  0x0000564e8cc1923c in StrProcess1 (p=0x0) at segfaults.c:8
8             strcpy(a,p);
(gdb) info locals
i = 10
a = "aaaaaaaaaa"
(gdb) info args
p = 0x0
```

8. From the argument details, we can easily identify the crash as due to the passing of a NULL pointer variable.

Well done! From this hands-on activity, we have learned how to use gdb for handling a C application crash from its core dump file.

In this section, we have learned various gdb commands for handling debugging application activities such as inspecting code and data during runtime, quickly traversing code, and identifying crash-related lines of code. Specifically, we have learned how to determine application runtime stack size and how to find reasons for crashes using core dump files. These hands-on tasks help you to improve application debugging skills.

Summary

In this chapter, we have practiced C programming using the important tools gcc, gdb, gcov, and valgrind for handling C application's code optimization, reliability, runtime bugs, and security-related tasks. Specifically, we have practiced well-designed hands-on activities specific to these open-source tools' usage for handling complex tasks of C applications such as performance tuning, checking reliability and security, and handling runtime crashes. This chapter's activities help C developers to easily handle large-sized C applications development and deployment activities.

CHAPTER 3   PRACTICE C PROGRAMMING WITH IMPORTANT TOOLS

In the next chapter, we introduce a powerful C tool: Pointers for implementing various sample system development activities such as memory management, accessing data, handling complex data structures, and exchanging huge data between functions optimally in C programming.

Practice Tasks

1. Use gcc code optimization options and check the following functions' execution time:
   - Factorial, Fibonacci, gcd, string reverse, and Towers of Hanoi
   - Identify if you can reduce the stack size to execute recursive functions
2. Use gcc code optimizations and check the loop orders in the following activities and compare their execution times:
   - Implement the cross product of three different lists using C functions and check in which order loops should be written for better performance.
   - Implement the cross product of three different lists and identify common elements from all three lists using C functions and check in which order loops should be written for better performance.
3. Create a static and dynamic shared library that contains sample string functions such as string reverse, isPalindrome, string duplicate, etc.
   - Test libraries in terms of code and execution time
4. Use gcc compiler security and other options for doing reliability checks for problem-1, problem-2, and problem-3.

5. Code coverage analysis for avoiding performance issues

    - Implement the bubble sort function and test it by doing code coverage analysis for performance improvement.

    - Implement a binary search function and test it by doing code coverage analysis for performance improvement.

    - Implement matrix multiplication and test it by doing code coverage analysis for performance improvements.

CHAPTER 4

Power of C: Pointers

In Chapter 2, "Quick Revision of Powerful C Constructs," we discussed the essential C programming concepts such as functions, arrays, strings, structures, and unions. In this chapter, we discuss the most important concepts of C programming, called pointers. In C programming, pointers help developers to implement efficient codes to meet the performance of C applications in terms of minimizing latencies in memory access and energy consumption. Pointers offer flexibility in terms of implementing and accessing complex data structures such as linked lists, trees, hash tables, and protocol messages. Moreover, pointers to functions and generic pointer concepts are helpful for developers to implement advanced programming approaches such as generic algorithms, generic data structures, and polymorphism concepts.

Specifically, in this chapter, we discuss basic usages of pointers and advanced use cases of pointers. You will be starting with revising how to use pointers, then exploring advanced concepts in terms of accessing C arrays, strings, and structures for learning efficient and reliable techniques. You will be learning generic pointers and pointers to function concepts in detail to implement advanced programming approaches such as generic functions, data structures, and polymorphism concepts.

In order to quickly learn and practice C pointers programming, you will be doing the important hands-on activities related to how to use pointers with arrays and structures for reliable and flexible accessing techniques. These hands-on activities help developers to explore C pointers for efficient, reliable, and flexible programming techniques in terms of using C arrays, structures, and functions.

Mainly, in this chapter, we will cover the following topics:

1. Importance of Pointer programming
2. Efficient and reliable ways to access arrays and strings using Pointers
3. Efficient and reliable ways to access structures using Pointers
4. Pointers and functions for powerful programming techniques

CHAPTER 4   POWER OF C: POINTERS

Importance of Pointer Programming

Pointers is a powerful programming concept for developers for implementing efficient code in terms of memory accessing, optimally utilizing memory, and minimizing memory access latencies. Hence, pointers will help in efficiently utilizing system resources such as CPU and memory. For instance, we will observe the following important use cases of the pointers:

- Minimizing functions communication overhead
  - Pointers offer a call-by-reference approach to pass arguments from a caller function to a callee function. In the call by reference approach, the callee function accesses the caller function's supplied arguments directly from the caller function's memory spaces only.
  - Pointers addressing approach eliminates the need of copying a caller function's arguments to a callee function's memory space.
  - Pointers accessing approaches save the main memory space as well as offer faster access to a program's data memory locations.
  - Pointers-related code minimizes system memory read or write cycles and system bus access. Hence, pointers-related code is called optimized code as well as energy-efficient code.
- Pointers are the key concept behind the dynamic memory concepts implementation.
  - Dynamic memory allocation allows developers to utilize the limited memory in optimal manners.
  - Dynamic memory allocation concepts are implemented by pointers. When a function requests a block of memory from the OS using library/system calls, then the OS returns the starting address of a memory block to the caller function. Developers use pointers to store the memory block addresses and access these dynamically allocated memory blocks and release the memory blocks after use.
  - Pointers offer flexible approaches in terms of addressing and accessing to manage the dynamically allocated memory blocks.

- Pointers are the basis for implementing data structures to offer efficient data accessing techniques.
  - All popular data structures implementations are based on pointers only. Because, pointers help in connecting scattered memory blocks in a flexible manner and simplifies their accessing approaches.
  - **Examples**: linked lists, doubly linked lists, trees, search trees, multilevel search trees, graphs, hash tables, etc.
- Pointers are the key concept behind the advanced concepts such as polymorphism concepts.
  - C developers can implement function overloading concepts using pointers to function concepts.
  - C developers can implement generic data structures for managing a variety of elements using void pointers.
  - C developers can implement generic algorithms using void pointers and function pointers. It means developers can implement one algorithm to work on a variety of data type elements.

Let's start exploring basic pointers concepts in C to quickly understand pointers usage in C applications development.

Basic Concepts of C Pointers

In C programming, a pointer is a variable, and it can store the address of another variable. In this section, first we will learn how to declare and use pointers such as basic pointers and multilevel pointers.

Basic Pointers

For instance, as shown in Figure 4-1, an integer basic pointer variable (int* ptr) will be defined to store another integer variable (var) memory address.

CHAPTER 4   POWER OF C: POINTERS

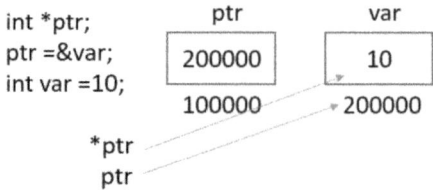

Figure 4-1. Pointer declaration and its memory layout

To declare C basic pointers, we use the following syntax: data_type *variable;

For example, to define an integer pointer (p) to store an integer variable (i) address, we do the following steps:

int *p; int i; p=&i;
i=100;

To use the pointer p and access the variable (i):

printf("%u ", &i); // to print variable i address
printf("%u ", p); // to print variable i address using p
*p = *p+100; //Write variable i using pointer p, and update i to
printf("%d ", *p); // to read variable i value using p and print it.

Similarly, developers can define any data type pointer variables to store a respective data type variable address as follows:

char *p1; char c; p1=&c; double *p2; double d; p2=&d;
float *p3;float f; p3=&f;

Moreover, pointers can store addresses of any data type variable (any basic data types (int, float, char, etc.), arrays, structures, and pointers).

Multilevel Pointers

Multilevel pointers are helpful to pass pointers between functions and access multidimensional arrays, strings, and structures. As shown in Figure 4-2, we can define a double pointer (int **dptr) to store the address of another pointer (int *ptr). Then, we can access the ptr's value and address using dptr as shown in Figure 4-2.

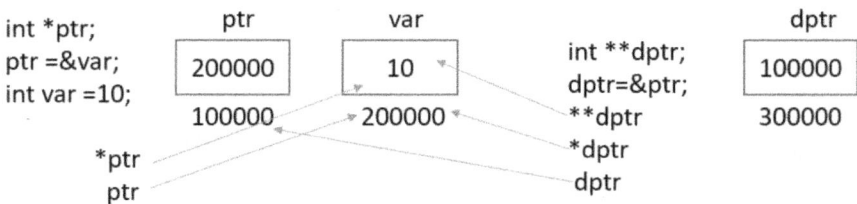

Figure 4-2. Double pointer declaration and its memory layout

Let's define double pointer variables to store another pointer variable using the following code snippet:

```
int *p; int i; p=&i;
int **dp; dp=&p;
i=100;
printf("%u ",dp);//To print pointer p address
printf("%u ",*dp);//To print variable i address
**dp = **dp+100;//To access (update) variable i value
printf("%d ",**dp);//To read (update) variable i value
```

Similarly, it is possible to define any multiple levels of pointers (a triple pointer int ***tp to store the address of double pointers (int **dp), and a int ****qp to store the address of the triple pointer (tp), etc.).

Multilevel pointers are helpful in the context of accessing pointers among functions. For instance, a PtrAccess wants to pass its pointer p to another function, Forward2Fun.

Then Forward2Fun must be defined with a double pointer argument as follows:

```
#include<stdio.h>
void Forward2Fun(int **dp)
{
    printf("Actual Variable x address:%u\n",*dp);
    printf("Intermediate Ptr Variable address:%u\n",dp);
    printf("Double Ptr Variable address:%u\n",&dp);
    printf("Actual Variable value:%d\n",**dp);
    **dp = **dp+200;
    printf("Updated Variable value:%d\n",**dp);
    Pass2NextFun(&dp);
}
```

Hence, Forward2Fun can be called from the PtrAccess as follows:

```
void PtrAccess(int *p)
{
    printf("Actual Variable x address:%u\n",p);
    printf("Ptr Variable address:%u\n",&p);
    printf("Actual Variable value:%d\n",*p);
    *p = *p+100;
    printf("Updated Variable value:%d\n",*p);
    Forward2Fun(&p);
}
```

Similarly, Forward2Fun wants to pass its double pointer dptr to another function, Pass3NextFun; then it must be defined with a triple pointer argument as follows:

```
void Pass2NextFun(int ***tp)
{
    printf("Actual Variable x address:%u\n",**tp);
    printf("Intermediate Ptr Variable address:%u\n",*tp);
    printf("Double  Ptr Variable address:%u\n",tp);
    printf("Triple Ptr Variable address:%u\n",&tp);
    printf("Actual Variable value:%d\n",***tp);
    ***tp = ***tp+200;
    printf("Updated Variable value:%d\n",***tp);
}
```

Next, we will discuss the important use cases of C pointers for quick understanding using the pointers in the right tasks.

Use Cases of C Pointers

C pointers help developers to use them in the following major use cases:

- Efficient communication approach for functions.
- Flexible data accessing approaches.
- Pointers to data structures.
- Pointers are flexible ways for data structure traversals.

In this section, we quickly introduce how pointers are helpful in the above use cases.

CHAPTER 4 POWER OF C: POINTERS

Efficient Communication Approach for Functions

To offer efficient communication among functions, C pointers will be used as function arguments to implement call-by-reference parameter-passing approach. Call-by-reference approach allows accessing the caller function by passing variables from the caller function's memory layout itself. Hence, it avoids allocating memory for function arguments in the callee memory layout and saves memory as well as minimizes memory access latencies for function arguments.

For example, let's discuss the following scenario: We define a function incr, and from the main, it is called using a call-by-reference approach. Observe the arguments of incr; it is taking a pointer variable (int *a) as an argument.

```
int incr(int *a) {*a=*a+100;}
```

Next, to call incr, main is passing the address of a variable (int i) as follows:

```
int main() {int i=200; incr(&i); printf("i: %d",i);}
```

During this program, the following details should be understood by developers:

```
//Caller main() only has memory location for i
//Callee incr() has no memory allocated for i,
//incr() access i through pointer *a
```

It means main is passing the address of a variable (i) to the incr, and incr is accessing the variable (i) from the memory space of the main only. In the above scenario, main on passing i to incr, it gets the updated value (300) in incr memory space only. Hence, there is no need to access system buses and do memory copy operations. Hence, pointers are helpful in optimizing code and minimizing energy in terms of memory accessing and reducing memory access time.

Let's check the overhead of the call-by-value parameter-passing approach using the following scenario:

```
void CallByValue1(int a)
{
    a=a+1;
}
```

229

CHAPTER 4   POWER OF C: POINTERS

```
int CallByValue2(int a)
{
    a=a+1;
    return a;
}
int main()
{
    int x=10;
    printf("Actual Variable x address: %u\n",&x);
    printf("Actual Variable x value: %d\n",x);
    CallByValue1(x);
    printf("Actual Variable x value: %d\n",x);
    x=CallByValue2(x);
    printf("Actual Variable x value: %d\n",x);
}
Actual Variable x value: 10
Actual Variable x value: 10
Actual Variable x value: 11
```

   In the above scenario, main updates its variable x value using CallByValue1, but the main variable x value will not be updated. It is due to main memory space not being accessible to CallByValue1, and x is allocated in CallByValue1 memory space also. Hence, the copy of x is updated in CallByValue1 memory space.

   In the above scenario, main updates its variable x value if it calls CallByValue2; then, the main variable x can receive the updated value from the return values of CallByValue2.

   But returning a variable involves copying the main's x variable value to CallByValue2 memory space (a variable). In this approach, developers should observe the memory copy operations overheads as well as the exchange of data between functions. Hence, the call by value approach leads to poor code and higher memory access latencies.

CHAPTER 4 POWER OF C: POINTERS

Flexible Data Accessing Approaches

Moreover, to simplify communication between functions and writing optimized code, it is also possible to define an array of pointers to store and handle independent variables together using a pointer array, as shown in Figure 4-3. We can observe that three independent variables' (y, w, and z) addresses are stored in an array of pointers (ptrArr).

Then ptrArr can be used to access the variables as shown in Figure 4-3. For instance, ptrArr[0] is used to access variable y.

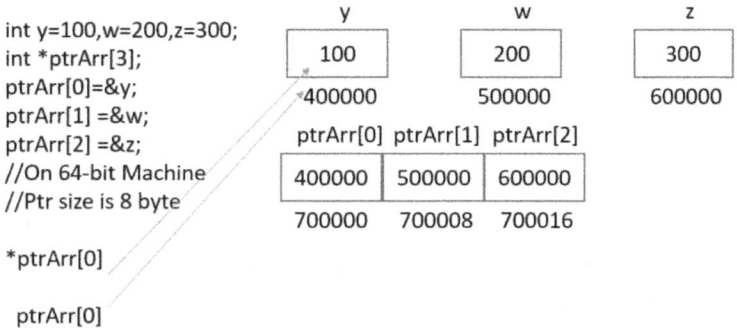

Figure 4-3. *Array of pointers and usage*

Observe from the figure that ptrArr stores all three variables' addresses in three consecutive locations of the ptrArr as shown in Figure 4-3. Moreover, we can use loops and access the ptrArr in a flexible manner to access the independent variables (y, w, z).

For example, define an integer pointer array of size 3 (int *pa[3]) to store the addresses of three variables and access them as follows using pa:

```
int *pa[3]; //Define an integer pointer array of size 3
// store 3 int variables addresses in the pointer array
int i1,i2,i3; pa[0]=&i1; pa[1]=&i2; pa[2]=&i3;
```

```
// access the int variables values using pointer array as follows
*pa[0]=*pa[0]+100; *pa[1]=*pa[1]+100; *pa[1]=*pa[1]+100;
```

CHAPTER 4   POWER OF C: POINTERS

```
// Flexible code using loops
for (int i=0;i<3;i++)
{ *pa[i]=*pa[i]+100;}

// Read the int variables values using pointer array as follows
printf("%d %d %d ", *pa[0],*pa[1],*pa[2]);
```

Next, we will discuss how to use pointers to access various data structures.

Pointers to Data Structures

It is also possible to define a pointer to built-in data structures such as an array or structure in C applications.

Pointers to Arrays

In order to efficiently pass large-sized lists to functions, it is necessary to pass arrays to the functions. Then, pointers will help developers to access the lists in flexible manners. For example, a pointer to an array variable (ptr2Arr) can hold the address of arrays (int a[10]). Then, we can use ptr2Arr to access the array (a).

This accessing approach reduces memory access latency and energy significantly. In this example, the pointer to an array (ptr2Arr) stores the base address of the array (a). It offers flexible ways to access the array using the pointer. For example, by incrementing the ptr2Arr variable, it is possible to access the array elements in a sequence as shown in Figure 4-4 with solid arrows:

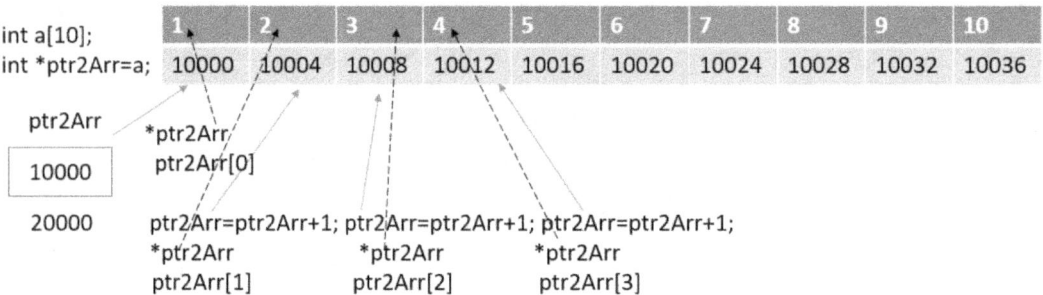

Figure 4-4.   Pointer to an array and usage

Let's check alternative ways for accessing an array using a pointer to an integer variable using the following code snippets to understand the flexibility of pointers to access the data structures.

CHAPTER 4 POWER OF C: POINTERS

```
//Define pointer variable to store a 1-D array address
int *ap;   int a[10]; ap=a;
```

```
//access the first element of the array using various approaches
*ap = 1; ap[0]=1; *(ap+0)=1;
```

```
//access the second element of the array using various approaches
ap=ap+1; *ap=2; ap[1]=2; *(ap+1)=2;
```

```
int a[15]={1,2,3,4,5,6,7,8,9,10,11,12,13,14,15};
```

```
int *p2a = a;
printf("%d\n",p2a[0]);
p2a=p2a+1;
printf("%d\n",p2a[0]);
p2a=p2a+1;
printf("%d\n",p2a[0]);
```

Further, pointers can be defined to subparts of a large array and access them in a flexible manner is possible. For instance, using a pointer to an array of a given size (int (*ptr)[5]), it is possible to access subarrays of size 5 from the array a[10]. Pointers' flexibility is not limited to 1-D arrays alone; it can be extended to any dimension. We will discuss these details as part of arrays and pointers concepts.

Pointers to Structures

In order to handle complex data structures and protocol messages in a flexible manner, we will use structures. Hence, it is possible to easily create a structure to store a variety of data elements to model any complex data structure and possible to pass these structure variables to functions. Besides, to access these structure variables in flexible and efficient manners, respective pointers can be defined. For example, we can define a sample structure as follows:

```
struct User { int id; int permission; };
struct User u1; u1.id=1; u1.permission=777;
```

Then, we can define a pointer (p2s) to struct user as follows:

```
struct User *p2s; //Declare a pointer struct User
p2s = &u1;// Store struct User u1 address in p2s
```

CHAPTER 4   POWER OF C: POINTERS

Then, using p2s, structure data members can be accessed as follows:

```
p2s->id=2; or (*p2s).id=2; //access the u1 using p2s
p2s->permission=666; or (*p2s).permission=666;
```

Next, we will learn how to use pointers for traversing data structures in flexible manners.

Pointers Flexible Traversals

In order to handle complex data structures and protocol internal fields in a flexible manner, pointers are very helpful. Suppose we have the following sample data structures:

```
struct ABC { int a; float b;char c;};
int a[10] = {1,2,3,4,5,6,7,8,9,10};
float f[10] = {1.1,2.2,3.3,4.4,5.5,6.6,7.7,8.8,9.9,10.10};
struct ABC abc[3] = {{1,2.0,'a'},{2,3.0,'b'},{3,4.0,'c'}};
```

Then, it is possible to define pointers to the above data structures as follows:

```
int *ip = a;
float *fp = f;
struct ABC *sp = abc;
```

Now incrementing a pointer variable can help in traversing those data structures in flexible ways as follows. Incrementing the ip is sufficient to traverse the integer array data structure and access its elements as follows:

```
printf("Int Array ele:%d\n",*ip);
ip=ip+1;
printf("Int Array ele:%d\n",*ip);
```

Similarly, incrementing the fp is sufficient to traverse the float array data structure and access its elements as follows:

```
printf("Float Array ele:%f\n",*fp);
fp=fp+1;
printf("Int Array ele:%f\n",*fp);
```

CHAPTER 4 POWER OF C: POINTERS

Now let's see the power of the pointer; incrementing the sp is sufficient to traverse the array of structure variables and access its elements as follows:

```
printf("Struct Array eles:%d %f %c\n",sp->a,sp->b,sp->c);
sp=sp+1;
printf("Struct Array eles:%d %f %c\n",sp->a,sp->b,sp->c);
On testing these code snippets, we can observe the following output:
Int Array ele:1
Int Array ele:2
Float Array ele:1.100000
Int Array ele:2.200000
Struct Array eles:1 2.000000 a
Struct Array eles:2 3.000000 b
```

In this section, we have learned how pointers are flexible to traverse the arrays, structures, and variety of elements. Next, let's see how void pointers (generic pointers) are powerful and flexible to implement generic data structures and traversals.

Void Pointers to Implement Generic Data Structures

In the above scenario, we observed how a pointer is helpful to traverse built-in data structure elements such as arrays. In this section, we will learn how to use void pointers to implement generic data structures and access them. For instance, we can define a generic pointer using a void pointer as follows:

```
void *gp;
```

Then, it is possible to use gp for accessing any data type array as follows. Developers can store an integer array address in the gp and then access its elements in a flexible way.

```
gp =a;
```

However, in order to traverse and access the elements through generic pointers, it is necessary to type cast the void pointer to the respective data type pointer. In this example, gp should be type casted to an integer pointer as follows:

```
printf("Int Array ele:%d\n",*(int*)gp);
gp=(int*)gp+1;
printf("Int Array ele:%d\n",*(int*)gp);
```

235

Similarly, gp should be type casted to a float pointer to access the float array as follows:

```
gp =f;
printf("Float Array ele:%f\n",*(float*)gp);
gp=(float*)gp+1;
printf("Float Array ele:%f\n",*(float*)gp);
```

Similarly, gp should be type casted to a structure pointer to access the array of structures as follows:

```
gp = abc;
printf("Struct Array eles:%d %f %c\n",((struct ABC*)gp)->a,((struct ABC*)gp)->b,((struct ABC*)gp)->c);
gp=(struct ABC*)gp+1;
printf("Struct Array eles:%d %f %c\n",((struct ABC*)gp)->a,((struct ABC*)gp)->b,((struct ABC*)gp)->c);
```

We recommend readers test the above sample codes in a main program to check the correctness and practice these basic concepts. Next, we will learn how to use pointers in reliable manners to avoid accidental access and crashes.

Efficient and Reliable Ways to Access Arrays and Strings Using Pointers

Arrays are built-in data structures in C programming. Arrays help developers to organize related data elements as a list and access the list for computational operations. In the previous section, we have learned how to define an array of pointers to store and handle independent variables together using a pointer array as shown in Figure 4-3. We have learned how to access independent variables using an array of pointers. Moreover, we have also learned how pointers (ptr2Arr) help to store the address of an array (int a[10]) and access the array (a) to reduce memory access latency and energy consumption. In this section, we will learn advanced approaches to access an array, its subparts, and multidimensional arrays using pointers.

- Pointer to subarrays
- Pointers to multidimensional arrays

CHAPTER 4 POWER OF C: POINTERS

- Pointers to strings
- Hands-on activities

Pointers to Array Subparts

Declaring pointers to array subparts is an important and flexible approach for easily traversing large-sized lists. It helps in easily partitioning a large list among multiple tasks and running them in parallel. For example, we define a pointer (ptr2ArrB) to subparts of a large array, and accessing them in a flexible manner is possible, as shown in Figure 4-5.

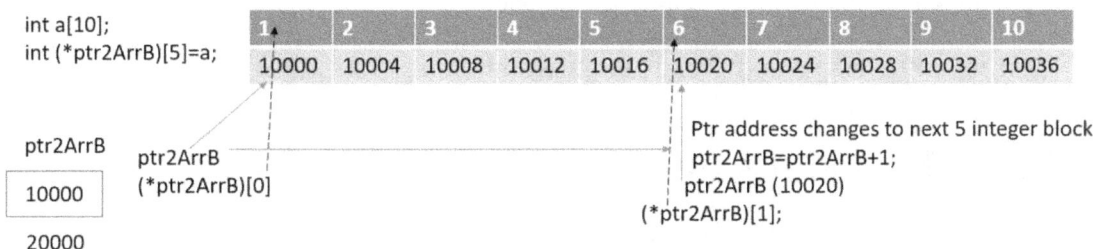

Figure 4-5. Pointers to subarrays and usage

Observing from Figure 4-5, we defined a pointer (int (*ptr2ArrB)[5]) to a subarray of size 5 (a[10]). Then, we access subarrays in a flexible manner by incrementing the ptr2ArrB variable for accessing specific subarrays as follows:

```
int (*ptr2ArrB)[5] = a;
printf("%d\n",(*ptr2ArrB)[0]);
```

Then, the next five elements can be accessed by incrementing the pointer ptr2ArrB.

```
ptr2ArrB=ptr2ArrB+1;
printf("%d\n",(*ptr2ArrB)[0]);
```

In this example, incrementing ptr2ArrB leads to accessing subarrays of size 5 from the array a[10]. It means a pointer to a subarray enables developers to access any size group of element traversals by simply incrementing the pointer. For instance, (int (*ptr2ArrB)[100]) then ptr2ArrB can be used to traverse 100 elements in a flexible manner.

CHAPTER 4　POWER OF C: POINTERS

However, these pointers to subarrays can also lead to the following reliability issues:

- Crossing array boundaries and attempting to access wrong elements of the other subarrays
- Segmentation faults due to crossing original array boundaries

Hence, developers must do the following:

- Check the end size of the array while traversing and avoid subarray boundary crossing as well as original array boundary crossing.
- Necessary to use valgrind, compilation with -fsanitize options to check any array addressing-related issues.

Next, we will learn how to declare and use pointers to multidimensional arrays.

Pointers to Multidimensional Arrays

Pointers' flexibility is not limited to 1-D arrays alone; it can be extended to any dimension. Especially pointers to multidimensional arrays are helpful to easily partition matrices, 3-D data, and other complex data structures easily. For example, having the following 2-D array with two 1-D arrays:

```
int m[2][2] = {{1,2},{3,4}};
int (*p2da)[2];
p2da=&m[0];
```

It is possible to access the first 1-D subarray of a using the following pointer:

```
printf("%d\n",(*p2da)[0]); // prints 1
printf("%d\n",(*p2da)[1]); // prints 2
```

Incrementing the pointer now leads to accessing the next subarrays of a:

```
p2da=p2da+1;
printf("%d\n",(*p2da)[0]); //prints 3
printf("%d\n",(*p2da)[1]); //prints 4
```

Similarly, pointers can be defined to 2-D subarrays of a 3-D array, and accessing them in a flexible manner is possible, as shown in Figure 4-6.

CHAPTER 4 POWER OF C: POINTERS

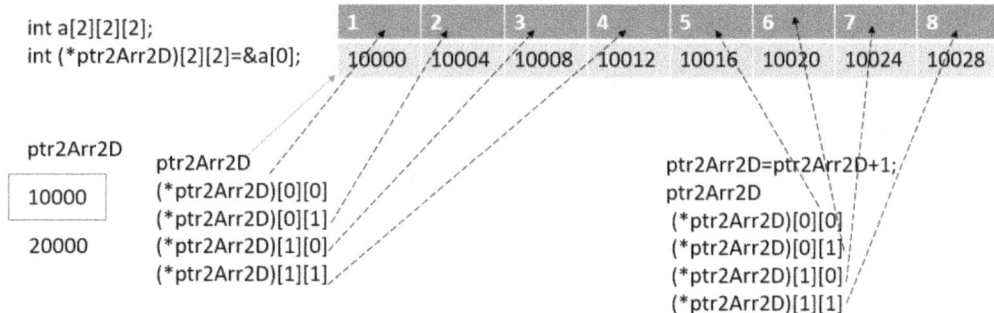

Figure 4-6. *Pointers to subarrays and usage*

Observing from Figure 4-6, we defined a pointer (int (*ptr2Arr2D)[2][2]) to a subarray of size ([2][2]). Then, we can access the 2-D subarrays of a in a flexible manner by incrementing the ptr2Arr2D variables.

In this example, incrementing ptr2Arr2D leads to accessing the 2-D subarrays of size [2][2] from the 3-D array a[2][2][2].

However, these pointers to subarrays can also lead to the following reliability issues:

- Crossing array boundaries and attempting to access wrong elements of the arrays
- Segmentation faults due to crossing original array boundaries

Hence, developers must check the end size of the list to traverse and avoid subarrays boundary crossing as well as original array boundary crossing.

Next, we will learn how to declare and use pointers to strings and multidimensional arrays of strings.

Pointers to Strings

Strings are also character arrays. Hence, all benefits associated with accessing arrays using pointers are applicable to accessing strings too. In this section, we will learn how to use pointers to access the following:

- Simple string (character arrays)
- Array of strings
- Array of array of strings

239

CHAPTER 4   POWER OF C: POINTERS

Pointers to Simple Strings

As we discussed in Chapter 2, "Quick Revision of Powerful C Constructs," in C character, arrays are known as strings. To access a simple string, let's check the following example by defining a string and finding its length by traversing it using a pointer.

```
char *str = "exec";
```

Now, we can define a function to find the length of the string using a pointer as follows:

```
int strLength(char *cmd)
{
    int len = 0;
    while (cmd[len] != '\0')
    {
        len++;
    }
    return len;
}
```

In the above code, we traverse the character array using a pointer (*cmd) and check termination of the string using '\0'.

First cmd points to the base address of the input string, then we access the individual characters of the string using cmd[len], and traverse the individual characters of the string using len++;

You can test the function using the following code:

```
int len = strLength(str);
printf ("Command length %d\n", len);
```

Next, we will learn how to declare pointers to an array of strings.

Pointers to Array of Strings

To access an array of strings, let's check the following example by defining a sample array of strings and initializing at the end of the array of strings using NULL as follows:

```
char *cmd[] = {"wc", "-l", NULL};
```

Then, cmd is an array of pointers, and each pointer is helpful to store the address of a string. For example, to count the number of strings defined in an array of strings, we define the following function:

```
int countArgs(char *cmd[])
{
     int noa = 0;
     while (cmd[noa] != NULL)
     {
          noa++;
     }
     return noa;
}
```

The above function traverses the individual string using an array of pointers (*cmd[]) and checks termination of the array using NULL;

First cmd points to the base address of the first string, then we access the subsequent string using cmd[noa], and traverse all the strings using noa++;

We can use the above code for testing a command and its arguments count. You can test the function using the following code:

```
int noa  = countArgs(cmd);
printf ("Total number of arguments %d\n", noa);
```

Next, we will learn how to declare pointers to an array of array of strings.

Pointers to Array of Array of Strings

An array of array of strings is helpful for handling complex text processing tasks such as arrays of lines, and each line contains an array of words to process and compute results. For example, to process variable commands and their arguments by the Unix shell, it needs to handle an array of array of strings.

To access an array of array of strings, let's check the following example by defining a sample array of array of strings and initializing the end of the array of strings using NULL and the end of the array of array of strings also NULL, as follows:

```
#define N 30
char *cmds[][N] = {{"ls", NULL}, {"grep", "fork", NULL}, {"wc", "-l", NULL}, {NULL}};
```

Since we defined the sample array of array of strings as a list of commands, to count the number of commands, we use the following function:

```
int countCmds(char *cmds[][N])
{
    int noc = 0;
    while (cmds[noc][0] != NULL)
    {
        noc++;
    }
    return noc;
}
```

You can test the function using the following code:

```
int noc = countCmds(cmds);
printf ("Total number of commands %d\n", noc);
```

The above function traverses the individual cmd (contains array of strings such as a command and its arguments) using an array of array of pointers (*cmd[][N]) and checks the termination of the array using NULL;

First cmd points to the base address of the first command, then we access the subsequent commands using cmd[noc] and traverse all the strings using noc++;

Next, we will practice how to use pointers for accessing 1-D, 2-D, 3-D, and subparts of the arrays in reliable manners.

Hands-On Activities for Organizing Array's Data Elements and Accessing Them Efficiently

In this section, we will understand the importance of pointers in terms of flexibility and efficiency in accessing multidimensional arrays. We do the following hands-on activities to understand and practice pointers in accessing arrays:

- Test accessing time of arrays using simple indexing vs. pointers
- Access 1-D subarrays of 2-D arrays using pointers
- Access 2-D subarrays of 3-D arrays using pointers

CHAPTER 4 POWER OF C: POINTERS

ACCESS MULTIDIMENSIONAL ARRAYS USING POINTERS

1. We define the following tasks in `arraysnptr.c`:

    a. We define the following function to test the accessing time of a 1-D array using a simple indexing versus pointers approach.

    b. We calculate the total time to access an array of size 2048 elements using the clock() function.

    ```
    #include<stdio.h>
    #include<time.h>
    void array1()
    {
        int a[2048];
        double time1, timedif;
        time1 = (double) clock();
        time1 = time1 / CLOCKS_PER_SEC;
        for (int i=0;i<2048;i++)
        {
            a[i]=i;
            a[i]=a[i]+1;
        }
        timedif = ( ((double) clock()) / CLOCKS_PER_SEC) - time1;
        printf("Arrays The elapsed time is %lf seconds\n",
        timedif);
        time1 = (double) clock();
        time1 = time1 / CLOCKS_PER_SEC;

        int *p=a;
        for (int i=0;i<2048;i++)
        {
            *p=i;
            *p=*p+1;
            p++;
        }
    ```

243

CHAPTER 4 POWER OF C: POINTERS

```
        timedif = ( ((double) clock()) / CLOCKS_PER_SEC) - time1;
        printf("Pointers The elapsed time is %lf seconds\n",
        timedif);
    }
```

2. Next, we define the following function to access 1-D subarrays of a 2-D array:

    a. We define a pointer ((*p)[4]), which holds a pointer to a 1-D array of size 4 of a 2-D array containing multiple 1-D arrays of size 4.

    b. We access the individual 1-D arrays of the 2-D array using pointer traversals of p. On incrementing p, we access a 1-D array of whole elements.

    ```
    void array2()
    {
        int a[2][4]={{1,2,3,4},{5,6,7,8}};
        int (*p)[4];
        p=&a[0];
        for (int i=0;i<2;i++)
        {
            printf("%d ",(*p)[0]);
            printf("%d ",(*p)[1]);
            printf("%d ",(*p)[2]);
            printf("%d ",(*p)[3]);
            printf("\n");
            p=p+1;
        }
    }
    ```

3. Next, we define the following function to access 2-D subarrays of a 3-D array:

    a. We define a pointer ((*p)[2][2]), which holds a pointer to a 2-D array of size 2x2 of a 3-D array containing multiple 2-D arrays of size 4.

    b. We access the individual 2-D arrays of the 3-D array using pointer traversals of p. On incrementing p, we access a 2-D array of whole elements.

```c
void array3()
{
    int a[4][2][2]={{{1,2},{3,4}},{{5,6},{7,8}},{{9,10},
    {11,12}},{{13,14},{15,16}}};
    int (*p)[2][2];
    p=&a[0];
    for (int i=0;i<4;i++)
    {
        printf("%d ",(*p)[0][0]);
        printf("%d ",(*p)[0][1]);
        printf("\n");
        printf("%d ",(*p)[1][0]);
        printf("%d ",(*p)[1][1]);
        printf("\n");
        p=p+1;
    }
}
```

4. We test all the above functions in main() as follows:

```c
int main()
{
    array1();
    array2();
    array3();
}
```

5. Compile the code and run it using the following commands:

```
#gcc  arraysnptr.c
#./a.out
```

6. Observe the following details from the results:

   a. Pointers-based array access time (**0.000022**) is much lower compared to the array indexing approach (0.000031):

   Arrays The elapsed time is 0.000031 seconds
   Pointers The elapsed time is **0.000022** seconds

b. It is flexible to access the entire 1-D array of a 2-D array using a suitable pointer as follows:

1 2 3 4
5 6 7 8

c. Similarly, it is flexible to access the entire 2-D array of a 3-D array using a suitable pointer as follows:

1 2
3 4
5 6
7 8
9 10
11 12
13 14
15 16

Well done! You have successfully tested how to use suitable pointers to access subparts of multidimensional arrays in a flexible manner. Moreover, we observed pointers access time is much lower than the array indexing approach. Hence, we recommend developers define suitable pointers to access multidimensional arrays for flexibility and efficiency.

In this section, we have learned how to use pointers to access arrays, multidimensional arrays, and subparts of arrays in a flexible and efficient manner. Next, we will learn how to use pointers to access structures in flexible and efficient manners.

Efficient and Reliable Ways to Access Structures Using Pointers

In C programming, structures are very important built-in data structures for modeling real-world entities and a variety of data structures such as lists, trees, and graphs. In this section, we will learn how pointers are helpful to access the structure in flexible and efficient manners. Mainly, we will learn the following concepts:

- Basic pointers accessing ways for structures
- Advanced pointers accessing ways for structures
- Hands-on activities

Basic Pointers Accessing Ways for Structures

After defining real-world entities, complex data structures, and protocol messages using structures, it is necessary to learn how to access them using pointers to get the following benefits:

- Efficient ways to pass structure variables to functions using the call by reference approach

- Flexible ways to access structure members and arrays of structures by easily traversing them using pointers traversals

- Flexible ways to access nested structures and internal members

Efficient Ways for Structure Variables Passing to Functions

In order to exchange complex data structures and protocol messages between functions in a flexible and efficient manner, pointers to structs should be defined. In this section, first we will learn how to declare suitable pointers to access basic structures.

For example, we have as struct user:

```
struct User { int id; int permission; };
struct User u1; u1.id=1; u1.permission=777;
```

Then, to pass the structure variable u1 to any function and access its internal data members (id, permission), it is necessary to understand the following details, such as declaring pointers to structure variables as follows:

```
struct User *p2s; //Declare a pointer struct User
p2s = &u1;// Store struct User u1 address in p2s
```

Then using p2s, structure variable u1 internal data members are accessed as follows:

```
p2s->id=2; or (*p2s).id=2; //access the u1 using p2s
p2s->permission=666; or (*p2s).permission=666;
```

Moreover, developers can use typedef to give aliases for simplifying the complex data type syntax. For instance, struct Sample pointer declaration and accessing it can be simplified using typedef as follows:

```
typedef struct Sample
{
    double d;
    int i;
    char c;
}Sample;
```

First, we rename struct Sample to Sample. Then, it gives flexibility to developers to declare structure variables or pointers to structure variables using Sample as follows:

```
void StructAccess(Sample s)
{
    s.d=1.5;
    s.i=5;
    s.c='a';
}
void StructAccThrPtr(Sample *s)
{
    (*s).d=1.5;
    s->i=5;
    s->c='a';
}
```

From the above code snippet, StructAccThrPtr is defined to pass structure variables through the call by reference approach. It helps in avoiding unnecessary copying of structure variables from caller functions to callee functions. Moreover, developers should observe that accessing struct variables is through C operators such as -> or (*). Next, to test the above functions, we can call them from main as follows:

```
Sample *sptr;
Sample s;
StructAccess(s);
sptr=&s;
StructAccThrPtr(sptr);
```

CHAPTER 4 POWER OF C: POINTERS

From the above code snippets, developers have learned the usage of simple struct variables and how to access them using pointer declarations. Next, we will learn how pointers to structures can be flexible in terms of accessing nested structures and their internal members.

Advanced Pointers Accessing Ways for Structures

In this section, we will learn how to use pointers for accessing complex structures such as nested structures in flexible manners. It is necessary to use nested structures for implementing real-world entities, complex data structures (trees, graphs, hash tables, etc.), and protocol messages (database protocols, OS protocols, and network protocols). For example, to model a protocol message containing a packet structure and suitable number of nested structures for embedding various rules to process or exchange the message. For example, as shown in Figure 4-7, it is possible to access a packet structure containing nested structures using pointers:

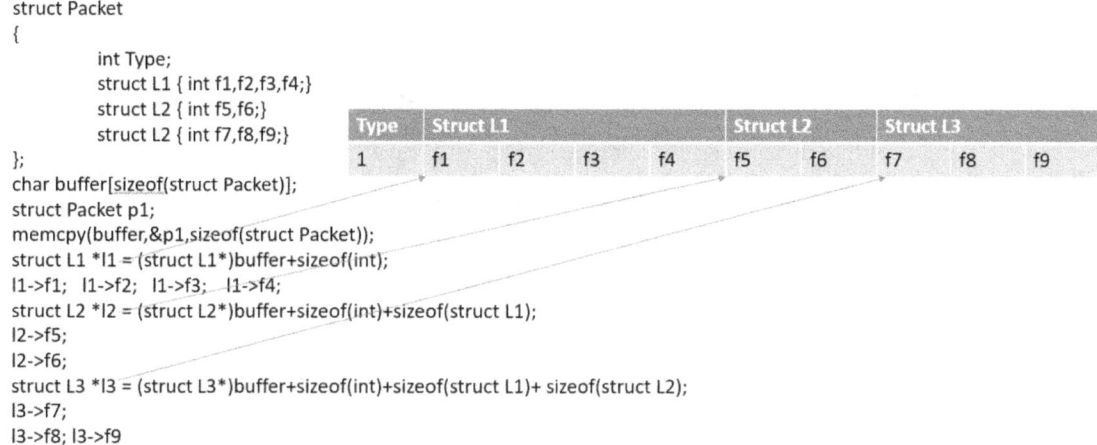

```
struct Packet
{
        int Type;
        struct L1 { int f1,f2,f3,f4;}
        struct L2 { int f5,f6;}
        struct L2 { int f7,f8,f9;}
};
char buffer[sizeof(struct Packet)];
struct Packet p1;
memcpy(buffer,&p1,sizeof(struct Packet));
struct L1 *l1 = (struct L1*)buffer+sizeof(int);
l1->f1;  l1->f2;  l1->f3;  l1->f4;
struct L2 *l2 = (struct L2*)buffer+sizeof(int)+sizeof(struct L1);
l2->f5;
l2->f6;
struct L3 *l3 = (struct L3*)buffer+sizeof(int)+sizeof(struct L1)+ sizeof(struct L2);
l3->f7;
l3->f8; l3->f9
```

Figure 4-7. *Pointer to access protocol message structure*

In case of no pointers to structures, inner structures of the struct Packet should be accessible as follows:

struct Packet p1;

To access data members of struct L1 l1, developers should access them through p1.l1.f1, p1.l1.f2, and so on.

249

CHAPTER 4   POWER OF C: POINTERS

To access data members of struct L2 l2, developers should access them through `p1.l2.f5`, `p1.l2.f6`, and so on.

In case of using pointers to structures to access p1, it can be simplified as follows.

Because of pointers to struct, it is possible to typecast the packet `buffer` to `struct L1` type and access its internal data members directly using the pointer variable l1 variable (`l1->f1`), as shown in Figure 4-7.

Similarly, to access the internal data members of structs L2 and L3, it is possible to typecast `buffers` to respective structure types and access the internal data members in flexible manners as shown in Figure 4-7.

Developers must note the following details while accessing internal structures and their data members of a protocol message using pointers:

- First copy the entire message into a character buffer of packet structure size (`struct Packet`). This step simplifies developers' ability to easily convert the message into a suitable structure type and traverse each of the structure and its internal data members easily.

    - For example, to access `struct Packet p1;`, then

    `memcpy(buffer, &p1,sizeof(struct Packet));`

- In case of the outer structure containing any data members prior to a target internal structure variable access, then it is necessary to declare a pointer to store the address from the exact beginning of the target structure variable location as follows:

    - Suppose Packet contains a Type (int) field prior to the `struct L1`; then to access internal data members of the L1,

    `struct L1 *ptr=(struct L1*)buffer+sizeof(int);`

Next, let's practice more details of how to access nested structures and their internal data members using pointers in the following hands-on activity.

Hands-On Activity

In this section, we mainly do the following important activities to define a sample protocol message and access it using pointers:

- Define a sample protocol message containing the following fields:
  - Type, setting type=1 means L1 message, type=2 means L2 message, and type=3 means L3 message
  - Three internal structures (struct L1, struct L2, struct L3) to create three types of messages
  - Based on the type set suitable src and destination addresses using suitable structures
  - A message
- Parse each message based on type of the message and print the message contents such as
  - Source address
  - Destination address
  - message

PROTOCOL MESSAGE PARSING USING POINTERS

1. We do these hand activities in parsing.c.
2. First define the following sample internal structure to create our protocol message.

   a. Each structure contains their unique source and destination addresses holding fields.

   b. Use typedef to simplify the structure variable declaration using simplified names.

   ```
   #include<stdio.h>
   #include<string.h>
   typedef struct Layer1
   {
        char src[3];
        char dst[3];
   }L1;
   typedef struct Layer2
   ```

CHAPTER 4 POWER OF C: POINTERS

```
    {
        char src[5];
        char dst[5];
    }L2;
    typedef struct Layer3
    {
        char src[7];
        char dst[7];
    }L3;
    struct Application
    {
        int type;
        L1 h1;
        L2 h2;
        L3 h3;
        char message[17];
    };
```

3. Define the following parsing function to parse the structure L1 internal fields and print those values.

   a. Copy the application message into a character buffer of suitable size.

   b. Declare the L1 pointer and assign it with the struct L1 starting address as shown in the code by adding sizeof (int) bytes to the starting address of the buffer.

   c. Print L1 internal fields.

   ```
   void parseL1(struct Application *a)
   {
       printf("Parsing Layer1\n");
       char buffer[sizeof(struct Application)];
       memcpy(buffer,a,sizeof(struct Application));
       L1 *ptr=(L1*)(buffer+sizeof(int));
       printf("L1 src:%s ",ptr->src);
       printf("\n");
       printf("L1 dst:%s ",ptr->dst);
   }
   ```

CHAPTER 4   POWER OF C: POINTERS

4. Define the following parsing function to parse the structure of L2 internal fields and print those values.

   a. Copy the application message into a character buffer of suitable size.

   b. Declare the L2 pointer and assign it with the struct L2 starting address as shown in the code by adding sizeof (int) + sizeof (struct L1) bytes to the starting address of the buffer.

   c. Print L2 internal fields.

   ```
   void parseL2(struct Application *a)
   {
           printf("Parsing Layer2\n");
           char buffer[sizeof(struct Application)];
           memcpy(buffer,a,sizeof(struct Application));
           L2 *ptr=(L2*)(buffer+ sizeof(L1)+sizeof(int));
           printf("L2 src:%s ",ptr->src);
           printf("\n");
           printf("L2 dst:%s ",ptr->dst);
   }
   ```

5. Define the following parsing function to parse the struct L1 internal fields and print those values.

   a. Copy the application message into a character buffer of suitable size.

   b. Declare L3 pointer and assign it with struct L3 starting address as shown in code by adding sizeof (int) + sizeof (struct L1)+ sizeof(struct L2) bytes to the starting address of the buffer.

   c. Print L3 internal fields.

   ```
   void parseL3(struct Application *a)
   {
           printf("Parsing Layer3\n");
           char buffer[sizeof(struct Application)];
           memcpy(buffer,a,sizeof(struct Application));
           L3 *ptr=(L3*)(buffer+ sizeof(L1)+ sizeof(L2)+sizeof(int));
   ```

CHAPTER 4   POWER OF C: POINTERS

```
            printf("L3 src:%s ",ptr->src);
            printf("\n");
            printf("L3 dst:%s ",ptr->dst);
        }
```

6. In main(), test all parse functions as follows:

   a. Define a sample application message.

   b. Set the type of the message.

   c. Set suitable source and destination addresses for the application message.

   d. Call respective parse functions to test each of them.

   ```
   int main()
   {
           struct Application a1;
           a1.type=1;
           strcpy(a1.h1.src,"aa");
           strcpy(a1.h1.dst,"bb");
           a1.type=2;
           strcpy(a1.h2.src,"1234");
           strcpy(a1.h2.dst,"5678");

           strcpy(a1.h3.src,"0x1234");
           strcpy(a1.h3.dst,"0x9090");
           a1.type=3;
           strcpy(a1.message,"abcdefghabcdefgh");
           parseL1(&a1);
           printf("\n");
           parseL2(&a1);
           printf("\n");
           parseL3(&a1);
           printf("\n");
           printf("Application Message: %s",a1.message);
   }
   ```

7. Test parsing.c by executing it using the following commands:

   ```
   #gcc parsing.c
   #./a.out
   Parsing Layer1
   L1 src:aa
   L1 dst:bb
   Parsing Layer2
   L2 src:1234
   L2 dst:5678
   Parsing Layer3
   L3 src:0x1234
   L3 dst:0x9090
   Application Message: abcdefghabcdefgh
   ```

8. Observe from the above results the following details:

   a. All messages are correctly decoded.

   b. Each layer's internal fields are correctly displayed.

   c. The application message is correctly displayed.

Well done! We have successfully created a sample protocol message structure with nested structures. Moreover, we accessed this sample protocol message using pointers in reliable and flexible manners.

Next, we discuss another power of function pointers and how developers use pointers to functions for implementing polymorphism concepts in C.

Pointers and Functions for Powerful Programming Techniques

Pointers are not limited to variables only. Pointer variables can be defined to hold addresses of functions and use them for invoking (or calling) functions. In this section, first we will learn how to declare a variety of function pointers and use them in interesting use cases. Next, we will learn how to use pointers to function concepts for implementing polymorphism concepts in the C language. Polymorphism means one

CHAPTER 4   POWER OF C: POINTERS

name and many forms. It is helpful to minimize the number of interfaces to access an application. For example, to copy any type of data on an operating system, we simply use the COPY command. In this section, we will do relevant hands-on activities to implement polymorphism concepts. In summary, we will learn the following concepts in this chapter:

- Pointers to a variety of functions
- C ways for polymorphism
- Hands-on activities

Pointers to a Variety of Functions

Pointers are not limited to variables only. Pointers variables can be defined to hold addresses of any type of function and use them for invoking (or calling) functions. In this section, we will learn the following type of function pointers:

- Basic function pointers
- Advanced function pointers

Basic Function Pointers

First we will learn how to declare a pointer to simple functions and access them using function pointers. For example, we have the following function:

```
int add(int a, int b) {return a+b;}
```

Then, we can define a pointer to the add function variable as follows:

- First define a pointer to the function name: (*p2fun). You can choose any valid function name in c.
- Next, since add is taking two integer variables as arguments, we should include the type of these arguments to the p2fun as follows: (*p2fun)(int,int)
- Finally, we should include the return type to the p2fun as follows:

    ```
    int (*p2fun)(int,int)
    ```

CHAPTER 4 POWER OF C: POINTERS

Now we can use this pointer to function (p2fun) to assign the address of the add function as follows:

```
int (*p2fun)(int,int); //Declare a pointer to add function
p2fun=&add; //Assign add address to the p2fun
```

Next we can use this pointer to function (p2fun) to call the add function as follows:

```
int res=(*p2fun)(10,20);//call the add function using the p2fun pointer
```

Finally, the result can be printed using the res variable.

In the next section, we will learn how to declare function pointers to any complex functions easily.

Advanced Function Pointers

In basic function pointers, we have learned how to declare pointers to functions that return basic data type variables. In this section, we will learn the following important concepts to handle any complex function pointers declaration and usage.

- Declaring a pointer to a function that returns pointer
- Declaring an array of function pointers
- Declaring a pointer to function which returning array of function pointers
- Declaring a pointer to a function that can store the address of a pointer to a function that returns an array of function pointers

First we will check the following example to see how to declare a pointer to a function that returns a pointer. It helps you to declare pointers to functions that return arrays or dynamically allocated memory blocks or any complex data structure pointer.

For example, given the following function:

```
#include<stdlib.h>
int * getMemBlock(int s)
{
    int *p=(int*)sizeof(malloc(int)*s);
    return s;
}
```

257

CHAPTER 4   POWER OF C: POINTERS

To declare a pointer to the getMemBlock:, we do the following steps:

- Declare a pointer to a function: (*p2memf)
- Include arguments to the p2memf as follows: (*p2memf)(int)
- Finally, include the return type to the p2memf as follows: int *(*p2memf)(int)

We can use the p2memf to assign the getMemBlock address as follows:

```
int *(*p2memf)(int);
p2memf = getMemBlock;
```

To invoke the getMemBlock using the p2memf as follows:

```
int *p = (*p2memf)(10);
```

We can access the resultant memory block using pointer p. Next, we will learn how to use typedef to simplify declaring pointers to functions.

Typedef

The typedef keyword is used to create a simplified name for a complex data type. For example, we use typedef heavily in renaming structure data types.

```
struct user {int id; char name[10];}
```

We should use struct user u1, u2; to declare structure variables, but using typedef, we can do the following:

```
typedef struct user {int id; char name[10];} User;
```

Using the new data type name (**User**), we can create structure variables as follows: User u1, u2;

When we use typedef using pointers as follows: typedef int* ptr;

Then, we can simply declare pointer variables as follows: ptr a,b,c;. It is equivalent to int *a,*b,*c;

Declare Array of Function Pointers

For example, in the following declaration: char (*ptr)(); ptr is a pointer to a function returning a character.

258

Suppose we want to declare an array of such function pointers, typedef simplifies it. First, typedef the pointer to the function returning character as follows:

typedef char (*ptr)();

Now ptr is a new data type created using typedef. Hence, to declare an array of function pointers, we can simply do the following to create an array of function pointers as follows:

ptr a[2];

Now we can assign the following functions addresses to these pointers as follows:

```
char getA() { }
char getB() { }
a[0] = getA;
a[1] = getB;
```

We can call these functions using the function pointers as follows:

```
(*a[0])();
(*a[1])();
```

Declare a Pointer to a Function Returning an Array of Function Pointers

We do the following tasks to learn this concept:

- Declare the following sample functions: char getCH(), char getCH()

- Declare a test() function to return the address of the above two functions. We use an array of function pointers (ptr func[2];) inside the test function to assign the address of the getCH() and getSym()

- Finally, test returns the func to return an array of function pointers

    ```
    #include<stdio.h>
    #include<stdlib.h>
    typedef char (*ptr)();
    char getCH()
    ```

CHAPTER 4   POWER OF C: POINTERS

```
{
        return 'a';
}
char getSym()
{
        return '*';
}
ptr* test()
{
        static ptr func[2];
        func[0]=getCH;
        func[1]=getSym;
        printf("CH: %c\n",(*func[0])());
        printf("SYM: %c\n",(*func[1])());
        return func;
}
```

Next, we do the following tasks to test it:

- Declare an array of function pointers (`ptr* fptr`) to collect the `test` returning array of function pointers.

- Invoke `getCH()` and `getSym()` using `fptr`.

- Declare a pointer to a function (`ptr* (*ptr2frafptr)();`) to hold the address of a function (`test`) that returns an array of function pointers.

- Finally, collect the `test` returning array of function pointers using `fptr` and invoke them.

```
int main()
{
        ptr* fptr=test();//returns array of function pointers
        printf("%c\n",(fptr[0])());//invokes getCh();
        printf("%c\n",(fptr[1])());//invokes getSym();
```

CHAPTER 4 POWER OF C: POINTERS

```
        ptr* (*ptr2frafptr)();// a pointer to function to hold
        address of a function (test) which returns array of function
        pointers

        ptr2frafptr = test;// assign test address to the ptr2frafptr
        fptr=(*ptr2frafptr)(); //returns array of function pointers

        printf("%c\n",(fptr[0])());//invokes getCh();
        printf("%c\n",(fptr[1])());//invokes getSym();
}
```

In this section, we have learned how to handle complex function pointers using typedef declarations easily. In the next section, we will learn how to implement polymorphism concepts in C.

C Ways for Polymorphism

Pointers to functions feature enable developers to implement generic functions and dynamic linking of suitable functions at runtime. Specifically, dynamically linking a function code with a function call helps in implementing generic interfaces to access a variety of functions with the same signature. It is a very helpful feature for software development in terms of deploying easy-to-use software. Pointers to the function feature help in implementing polymorphism concepts in the C language.

A Quick Example

Next, let's check how to use the same pointer to the function interface (*p2fun) for calling add, div, and mul functions using the following code snippets:

```
int mul(int a, int b) {return a*b;}
int div(int a, int b) {return a/b;}

p2fun=&mul; //Assign a suitable function to pointer

(*p2fun)(10,20);//call the mul function using the p2fun pointer

p2fun=&div; //Assign a suitable function to pointer

(*p2fun)(10,20);//call the div function using the p2fun pointer

printf("Ptr2Fun calling:%d\n",(*p2fun)(10,20));
```

261

From the above code snippets, developers should observe the flexibility of linking a suitable function by assigning a suitable function address to the function pointer (p2fun). It helps in implementing dynamic linking of functions. Moreover, using the same interface (p2fun) for invoking a variety of functions (mul, div) helps in implementing polymorphism concepts such as one function name and multiple tasks.

Use typedef to Simplify Interface Name

Moreover, developers use typedef to simplify complex pointers to function declarations as follows:

```
typedef int (*PTR2FUN)(int,int);

PTR2FUN p2f;
p2f=&add;
printf("Ptr2Fun calling using typedef:%d\n",p2f(10,20));
```

From the above code snippet, developers should observe calling any of the add, mul, or div done using the simple interface p2f. In the next section, let's implement a sample polymorphism application in C.

Hands-On Activity

In this hands-on activity, we do the following activities for implementing polymorphism concepts and testing:

- We define three sample functions: sum, mul, div
- We test the sample functions invocation without polymorphism concepts
- We test the sample functions invocation using function pointer concepts
- We use function pointer concepts to implement polymorphism concepts and test it

CHAPTER 4 POWER OF C: POINTERS

POLYMORPHISM IN C

1. We implement this hands-on activity in polymorph.c

2. First define the following three sample functions:

    a. Observe that we defined the following three functions with the same function signatures:

        i. All three functions are taking three arguments of the same type in the same order.

        ii. All three functions are returning void.

    b. All three function names are unique:

    ```
    #include<stdio.h>
    void sum(void *a, void *b, int type)
    {
            if (type==1)
            {
                    int r=*(int*)a+*(int*)b;
                    printf("SUM: %d\n",r);
            }
            if (type==2)
            {
                    float r = *(float*)a+*(float*)b;
                    printf("SUM: %f\n",r);
            }
    }
    void mul(void *a, void *b, int type)
    {
            if (type==1)
            {
                    int r=*(int*)a * *(int*)b;
                    printf("MUL: %d\n",r);
            }
    ```

263

```
        if (type==2)
        {
                float r = *(float*)a * *(float*)b;
                printf("MUL: %f\n",r);
        }
}

void div(void *a, void *b, int type)
{
        if (type==1)
        {
                int r=*(int*)a / *(int*)b;
                printf("DIVISION: %f\n",r);
        }
        if (type==2)
        {
                float r = *(float*)a / *(float*)b;
                printf("DIVISION: %f\n",r);
        }
}
```

3. Define the following common interface to invoke add, mul, and div using the same interface:

   a. Observe we use a generic function pointer (void (*arithOp) (void *,void *, int))

   b. We assign the suitable function address to the function pointer based on the option (op)

```
void CommonInteface(int op, int type, void *a, void *b)
{
        void (*arithOp)(void *,void *, int);
        if (op==1)
        {
                arithOp=sum;
                (*arithOp)(a,b,type);
        }
```

```c
        if (op==2)
        {
                arithOp=mul;
                (*arithOp)(a,b,type);
        }
        if (op==3)
        {
                arithOp=div;
                (*arithOp)(a,b,type);
        }
}
```

4. Test these functions in main() as follows:

   a. First test sum, mul, and div without using the function pointer concepts as follows and observe that we should call the respective function name to correctly invoke these functions.

   ```c
   int main()
   {
           int a=1,b=2;
           float c=1.2,d=2.2;
           sum(&a,&b,1);
           sum(&c,&d,2);

           mul(&a,&b,1);
           mul(&c,&d,2);

           div(&a,&b,1);
           div(&c,&d,2);
   ```

   b. Declare a generic function and assign the suitable function address to test it.

   ```c
           void (*arithOp)(void *,void *, int);
           arithOp=sum;
           (*arithOp)(&a,&b,1);
           (*arithOp)(&c,&d,2);
           arithOp=mul;
           (*arithOp)(&a,&b,1);
   ```

CHAPTER 4   POWER OF C: POINTERS

```
            (*arithOp)(&c,&d,2);
            arithOp=div;
            (*arithOp)(&a,&b,1);
            (*arithOp)(&c,&d,2);
```

5. Finally, use CommonInteface to test sum, mul, and div. Observe that we pass the suitable option to invoke the correct function using the function pointer inside the CommonInteface.

```
            CommonInteface(1,1,&a,&b);
            CommonInteface(1,2,&c,&d);

            CommonInteface(2,1,&a,&b);
            CommonInteface(2,2,&c,&d);

            CommonInteface(3,1,&a,&b);
            CommonInteface(3,2,&c,&d);
    }
```

6. Save and compile the code and test it using the following command:

```
#gcc polymorph.c
#./a.out

Sum: 3
Sum: 3.400000
MUL: 2
MUL: 2.640000
DIVISON: 2.640000
DIVISON: 0.545455
Sum: 3
Sum: 3.400000
MUL: 2
MUL: 2.640000
DIVISON: 2.640000
DIVISON: 0.545455
Sum: 3
Sum: 3.400000
MUL: 2
```

```
MUL: 2.640000
DIVISON: 2.640000
DIVISON: 0.545455
```

From the results, we observe that the correct function is invoked using a common interface with the help of generic function pointers and generic pointers. In summary, developers should understand that function pointers and generic pointers are key building blocks to implement polymorphism concepts.

Overall in this section, we have learned the basics of function pointers and learned how to declare complex function pointers easily using typedef. Finally, we explored the C ways to implement polymorphism concepts through a hands-on activity.

Summary

In summary, we have learned the basics of pointers, how to use pointers for efficiently accessing data, and C built-in data structures such as arrays and structures. We understood the power of pointers to minimize the memory access time and improve the efficiency of the C applications. Moreover, we have explored flexible approaches of pointers to access the multidimensional arrays and nested structures. Finally, we have explored the power of function pointers and learned how to declare complex function pointers easily using typedef. We also explored the C ways to implement polymorphism concepts easily.

In the next chapter, we will learn the power of C pointers and how to use them for dynamic memory management tasks in a reliable manner using OS system calls.

Practice Tasks

1. Define an array of 100 elements in a function, then check how to pass it to another function. Use pointers and storage classes to solve the task.

2. Define a multidimensional data structure called a 4-D data structure to enter data of equipment [Year][Months][Days][Hours]

    - Pass your data structure to a function and access it in a flexible manner using pointers.

- Write a function to access Year-wise data.
- Write a function to access Year and Month-wise data.
- Write a function to access Year-, Month-, Day-wise data.
- Write a function to access Year-, Month-, Day-, and Hours-wise data.

3. Given a large 2-D matrix, write a partitioning function to return various possible square matrices from the 2-D matrix.

4. Define a sample protocol to simulate exchanging emails containing the following headers.
   - Header (From, To addresses, Type of message (Personal, Family))
   - Personal (Text message)
   - Family (Invitation, Venue, Message)
   - Implement sender and receiver functions to exchange these sample email messages
   - Use structures and pointers to access the specific message in a flexible manner

5. Implement polymorphism concepts for the following sample application
   - Implement search, replace, and delete operations over a list of elements
   - Use function pointers to minimize the number of interfaces to access the variety of lists (integers, float, char, etc.)

CHAPTER 5

C Programming for Memory Management

In Chapter 4, "Power of C: Pointers," we discussed the importance of pointers and how pointers help developers to implement efficient code and flexible ways to access data structures and polymorphism concepts in C. In this chapter, we discuss how C developers can manage application memory during runtime efficiently in terms of allocation, deallocation, and accessing. We discuss the importance of dynamic memory management for C applications to utilize the limited memory efficiently. Specifically, we discuss important library functions such as `malloc, calloc, realloc,` and `free` to manage application memory efficiently.

Moreover, in this chapter, we discuss reliable programming techniques for application memory management to avoid C application crashes during runtime. We discuss how to write necessary dynamic memory allocation code in a bug-free manner to avoid application crashes, memory access violation errors, memory leaks, security breaches, and efficient utilization of limited memory. As part of practice, you do hands-on activities using the `valgrind` tool to quickly handle memory access-related errors of a C application.

In order to use memory allocation system calls in suitable use cases, you will be doing the important hands-on activities related to `malloc, calloc,` and `realloc.` These hands-on activities help developers to implement dynamic memory allocation-related code in a reliable manner.

Mainly, in this chapter, we will cover the following topics:

1. Introduction to dynamic memory management
2. Important C system calls for memory management

3. Error-handling programming techniques for memory management

4. Setting up memory buffers and accessing them in a reliable manner

Introduction to Dynamic Memory Management

Dynamic memory management is all about allocation, deallocation, and accessing the main memory of an application. It involves developers requesting OS for allocating system memory blocks using system calls. Hence, the OS must offer suitable system calls for memory management tasks. In C programming, developers use the `stdlib.h` library for accessing memory management-related system calls using library functions and interact with the OS for allocation and deallocation of memory blocks. Since developers are requesting the OS for memory blocks, they must be managing these memory blocks carefully to avoid application crashes, protection, and performance issues in accessing the memory blocks. We discuss these concepts in upcoming sections.

Importance of Dynamic Memory Management

We have learned from Chapter 1, "Basic Computer System Architecture and Essential Operating System Concepts," the importance of memory and its role in an application's performance. Moreover, memory is one of the system resources that must be utilized in an optimal way for offering improved access time to applications. It means an application should use its memory in an efficient manner in terms of consumption and accessing techniques. For instance, C developers may use many variables, arrays, and structures for performing various computations. During the corresponding application execution, memory allocation and deallocation activities for the application data are involved. This task is simplified in case the developers know well in advance the actual amount of memory is required to execute the application. In this case, C developers can define necessary data type variables, arrays, and structure accessing variables in the application to perform computations. However, in real-time applications execution, it is not possible to restrict applications with limited memory and determine an application's required memory well in advance. Moreover, allocating memory statically can result in underutilization or insufficient memory for handling dynamic requirements. Developers cannot implement scalable applications in case of fixing the memory requirements at the initialization of the applications. Hence, developers must decide the suitable memory size and allocate memory blocks during the application execution on a system. In order to support these runtime memory allocation requirements, the OS must offer necessary system calls for allocation and deallocation. Fortunately, C applications can use the important system calls using library function calls such as `malloc`, `calloc`, `realloc`, and `free` for dynamic memory management requirements of a C application. Dynamic memory management activities offer the following benefits to developers:

- Able to run large-size applications within limited memory.
- Avoids unnecessary memory allocation for application.
- Improves underlying system memory utilization.
- Developers can implement scalable applications in terms of dynamically resizing memory blocks.
- Developers can implement customized memory allocation techniques for applications and their internal modules.
- Developers can prioritize an application execution time in terms of minimizing its size.

In order to offer dynamic memory management benefits to applications, besides OS services in terms of system calls, developers should take responsibility in terms of enjoying dynamic memory benefits. Otherwise, dynamic memory management features can negatively impact the application performance and lead to security issues and poor utilization of memory. Next, let's learn C developer roles in dynamic memory management for a variety of C application developments.

Important C System Calls for Memory Management

C developers have the power to manage C applications memory by interacting with the OS memory management services. It means C developers can write C memory management codes related to memory allocation, deallocation, and accessing by calling OS services through system calls. Memory management of a C application gives power and responsibility to C developers. First we discuss the powers associated with memory management tasks:

- C developers have access to OS memory management services in terms of memory management-related system call access.

- **Allocate the Necessary Memory Blocks in a Flexible Manner:** Developers request necessary-size memory blocks from the OS using library functions such as `malloc`, `calloc`, and `realloc`. Then developers manage memory block utilization within C applications in a flexible way. It offers the following benefits:

  - Guaranteed memory allocation from the custom memory blocks
  - Speed up memory access
  - Possible to prioritize the application module demands and manage internally within the application
  - Less dependency on other processes running on a system

- **Improve Application Performance by Minimizing the Memory Access Latency:** Once suitable blocks are granted by OS to a C application, then memory access will be faster due to the following reasons:

  - There will be no memory access contention with other processes.
  - Optimally allocate the memory blocks by writing suitable application codes and data structures to manage the application-acquired memory blocks.
  - Moreover, pointer usage helps developers to minimize memory access latency and energy consumption.

- **Efficient Utilization of Limited Memory:** Developers request and release memory blocks during runtime based on the application demands. It is highly useful for efficient utilization of limited memory due to the following reasons:

  - No need of reserving memory blocks unnecessarily
  - Possible to allocate and deallocate memory blocks as per application requirements

- Possible to manage memory blocks internally through implementing suitable data structures

- **Protect Application Data Using Customized Techniques:** It is possible for developers to protect the memory blocks by writing reliable accessing code. Specifically, developers impose suitable memory accessing checks before carrying out any computations. For instance, developers can do the following to protect the internal memory access of application:

  - Set suitable read, write, and execute permissions
  - Lock-based access control techniques can be implemented
  - Do suitable checks for allowing or denying memory accesses by the application

Next, we discuss the C developers' responsibilities associated with memory management tasks:

- Developers should confirm successful allocation of memory blocks from the OS before accessing any location of the memory block. Developers should do the following:

  - Must check memory blocking pointers' addresses and their contents because OS may fail to allocate requested memory blocks.
  - Developers should check pointers corresponding to dynamically allocated memory blocks and manage them.
  - Must set suitable read, write, and execute permission for each memory block.
  - Must write suitable locking and unlocking codes for accessing specific memory blocks.

- Developers should keep track of all dynamically allocated blocks of memory and their accessing pointers. Developers should do the following:

  - Keep track of pointers and their allocated memory blocks

- Must check the right pointer being used for accessing the right memory block

- Should not cross the boundaries of the memory blocks during access and must write suitable code checks to avoid memory boundary crossing

- Developers should release the memory blocks after use. Developers should do the following:

  - Deallocate memory blocks after use.

  - Once a memory block is deallocated, the corresponding pointer must not be used again.

  - Invalidate the addresses of the deallocated blocks.

Next, let's learn about dynamic memory allocation-related system calls and their usage in C programming.

Important C System Calls for Memory Management

C developers have access to `stdlib.h` for implementing dynamic memory management tasks using `malloc`, `calloc`, `realloc`, and `free`. Let's discuss more details about these library functions.

C Library Functions for Basic Dynamic Memory Management

First, we discuss the following basic library functions: `malloc` and `free`. Developers use `malloc` to request a memory block of size n bytes from the OS. In case the OS allocates the requested block successfully, it returns the starting address of the memory block. If allocation fails, OS returns `NULL`. Developers collect these return addresses into a pointer variable and access the dynamically allocated memory block. For example, in Figure 5-1, we show allocating a 10-integer memory block from the OS and collecting its address into the pointer variable m1. We can also observe that the memory block can be accessed by incrementing a pointer variable or accessing it using the array indexing approach.

CHAPTER 5 C PROGRAMMING FOR MEMORY MANAGEMENT

```
int *m1;
m1=(int*)malloc(sizeof(int)*10);   1000                    1040

                                   m1, m1+1, m1+2 ...      m1+9
                                   m1[0], m1[1],m1[2], ... m1[9]
```

Figure 5-1. *Dynamic memory allocation using malloc*

Developers should observe the following details to access the successfully allocated memory blocks:

- Observe malloc arguments and return type:

    - **Size of Memory Block**: 10-integer block

    - **Return Type Pointer**: (int*) to access the memory block from its starting address using an integer array

- On successful allocation of a memory block by malloc(), the default contents of cells contain random values.

- Allocating a 10-integer memory block resulting in 10-integer cells for accessing integer data elements. Similarly, it is possible to allocate any data type size cells in memory blocks. That means developers can allocate the following:

    - Allocate an N-byte (characters) memory block and access its individual bytes (character)

    ```
    int *c = (char*)malloc(sizeof(char)*N);
    c=c+1;
     c='a' or c[i]='a';
    ```

    - Allocate an N double data type element memory block and access its individual double element

    ```
    double *d = (double*)malloc(sizeof(double)*N);
    d=d+1; *d=1.2 or d[i]=1.2;
    ```

CHAPTER 5   C PROGRAMMING FOR MEMORY MANAGEMENT

- Allocate an N structure type elements memory block and access its individual struct element

  ```
  struct User {int id; float score;};
  struct User *su = (struct User*)malloc(sizeof
  (struct User)*N);
  su=su+1; *(su.id)=1;*(su.score)=1.2; or su->id=1;
  or su->score=1.2; or su[i].id=1;su[i].score=1.2;
  ```

- Developers must define suitable data-type pointers to store memory block starting addresses.

- Incrementing the memory block pointer results in traversing individual cells of the memory block. It helps in accessing contents of the memory block through loops.

- Developers have flexibility to access memory blocks using the index approach also.

In case the OS fails to allocate a memory block, then by checking the pointer address of the block, developers should handle the memory accessing errors.

On the other hand, developers should manage these memory blocks in terms of accessing them in an application, and after use, these blocks should be released from the application using another important library function: free. Using free developers releases the memory blocks pointed to by the pointer variable as follows. Then, the OS manages the freed memory blocks. Otherwise, these memory blocks will be wasted, and the OS cannot allocate these blocks to any other application.

```
free(m1);
```

After freeing the memory block (m1), developers should take care of the following:

- Assign m1 to NULL to avoid reusing the pointer.

- Then, don't use the m1 again without allocating a new memory block.

These simple activities after freeing the memory can help in avoiding access violation errors and security loopholes and in protecting your application.

CHAPTER 5   C PROGRAMMING FOR MEMORY MANAGEMENT

From malloc and free, we observe that developers have the flexibility to allocate necessary memory blocks, flexible ways of accessing memory blocks, and the ability to deallocate the blocks after use. More than these dynamic memory management tasks, developers can extend or shrink the old memory blocks in a flexible way. We discuss it in the next section.

C System Calls for Extending Memory Blocks Dynamically

Developers use realloc to resize a memory block of size from n bytes to m bytes dynamically. It means developers can implement C applications to request the OS to extend the size of an old memory block or shrink the size of the old memory block as per requirements. On successful request fulfillment of extending or shrinking a memory block, the OS returns an address to the memory block. It is possible that the new memory block can be allocated from any new address or from the old address itself. Moreover, realloc handles copying the old contents to new memory block locations. Hence, developers need not worry about memory copying activities. However, developers should check the return value of the realloc for success or failure.

For example, let's extend the memory block of m1 from size 10 to size 15 using realloc, as shown in Figure 5-2. Observe from realloc argument, we pass the old memory block pointing address, and new block size.

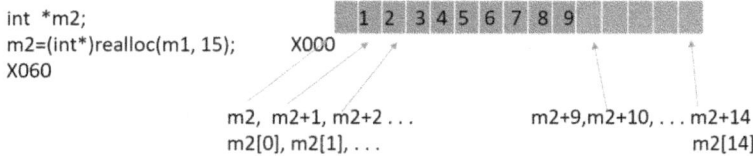

Figure 5-2. Extending an old memory block (m1) size using realloc

Similarly, it is possible to shrink the memory block of m1 from size 10 to size 5 using realloc as shown in Figure 5-3. Observe from the realloc argument that we pass the old memory block pointing address and the new block size 5.

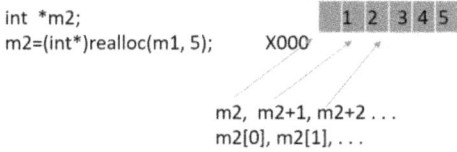

Figure 5-3. Shrinking an old memory block (m1) size using realloc

277

CHAPTER 5 C PROGRAMMING FOR MEMORY MANAGEMENT

Developers should observe the following details to successfully access the extended memory blocks using `realloc`:

- Observe `realloc` arguments and return type:
  - Old memory block accessing pointer (`m1`)
  - **Size of Memory Block**: integers block
  - **Return Type Pointer**: (int*) to store the address and access the memory block as an integer array
- Allocating a 15-integer memory block resulting in extending the old memory block to 15-integer cells for accessing integer data elements. On successful allocation of a 15-integer memory block, the OS returns the memory block address. Developers can collect this address and use the memory block.
- Allocating a 5-integer memory block resulting in shrinking the old memory block to 5-integer cells for accessing integer data elements. On successful allocation of a 5-integer memory block, the OS returns the memory block address. Developers can collect this address and use the memory block.
- Since reallocation of memory blocks is done seamlessly by `realloc()`, developers need not copy the memory cell contents from old blocks to new blocks.
- Developers must define suitable data-type pointers to store memory block starting addresses.
- Incrementing the memory block pointer results in traversing individual cells of the memory block. It helps in accessing contents of the memory block through loops.
- Developers have flexibility to access memory blocks using the index approach also.

In case the OS fails to allocate the memory block, then by checking the pointer address, developers should handle the memory accessing errors.

Next, we will discuss how to allocate multiple blocks of memory simultaneously and access them in flexible ways.

C System Calls for Handling Multiple Blocks of Memory Allocation

Developers use `calloc` to allocate n memory blocks, each with a block size of m, dynamically. For example, developers can request the OS to create a 2-D block of memory, as shown in Figure 5-4. In this example, the C application is requesting four memory blocks, and each block size is 4-integer data elements using `calloc`. Then, in case of successful allocation of these multiple blocks, `calloc` returns a pointer to this 2-D block. This pointer holds the starting address of the block, and the application can traverse through each block (four blocks) and each cell of the block (four cells) using a nested loop, as shown in Figure 5-4. On the other hand, since the memory block contains 16-integer cells, the application can access it using a single loop containing 16 iterations to access individual elements of the memory block.

```
int *p = (int*)calloc(4,sizeof(int)*4);
for (int i=0;i<4;i++)
{
    for(int j=0;j<4;j++)
    {
        p[j]=j;
    }
}
```

	p,	p+1,	p+2,	p+3
	0	1	2	3
p+4	0	1	2	3
p+8	0	1	2	3
	0	1	2	3
	p+12,	p+13,	p+14,	p+15

Figure 5-4. *Allocating a 2-D memory block of size 4x4 integers using calloc*

Moreover, developers can also implement applications requesting multiple blocks, and each block size can be variable, as shown in Figure 5-5. However, developers should handle this case carefully using double pointers. Why do double pointers exist? Because it is necessary to first allocate an array of pointers (**dp) to hold memory blocks of varying sizes. Then, each pointer can hold a specific size memory block. For example, in this figure, we show how to allocate 4-integer blocks of memory, and the first block holds 1-integer cell, the next block holds 2-integer cells, and so on.

CHAPTER 5   C PROGRAMMING FOR MEMORY MANAGEMENT

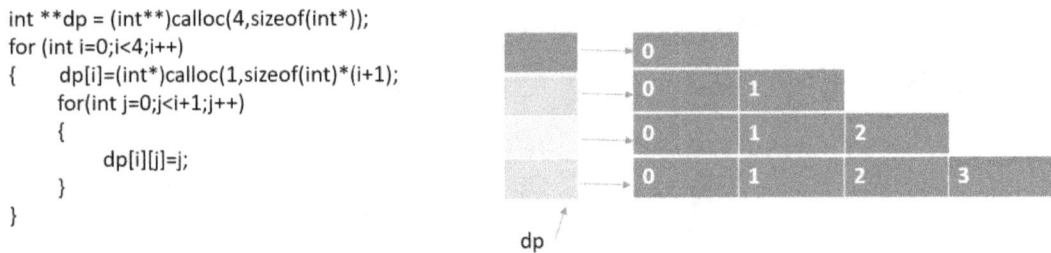

```
int **dp = (int**)calloc(4,sizeof(int*));
for (int i=0;i<4;i++)
{    dp[i]=(int*)calloc(1,sizeof(int)*(i+1);
     for(int j=0;j<i+1;j++)
     {
         dp[i][j]=j;
     }
}
```

Figure 5-5. *Allocating a 2-D memory block of size 4 rows with variable sizes using calloc*

Developers should observe the following details from Figure 5-5 to access the successfully allocated multiple memory blocks:

- Observe calloc arguments and return type:
  - Number of blocks.
  - Data type of a block and size of the block.
  - **Return Type Pointer**: (int*) holds address to access a memory block as an integer array, (int **) holds address to access the pointer array memory block.
- Calloc allocation results in memory blocks cells being initialized with zero by default.
  - Developers can assign new values to memory blocks later.
- It is allocating a 16-integer memory block containing 4-integer blocks and each block holding 4-integer elements.
  - Developers can simply collect the starting address of the block using a single pointer and access the individual elements of the memory block using the arrays approach.
- Developers must define suitable data-type pointers to store a memory block starting addresses.
  - Developers must define a double pointer (int **dp) to allocate an array of pointers and allocate each pointer with a necessary block memory size.

- It is the developer's responsibility to deallocate both pointer block memory and individual pointer-holding memory blocks using free.

In this section, we have learned how to use various dynamic memory allocation library functions for meeting application dynamic memory needs, such as allocation of fixed-size memory blocks, variable-size memory blocks, and extending old memory blocks. Next, we will learn how to handle dynamic memory allocation tasks in a reliable manner and important error-handling techniques and tools.

Error Handling Programming Techniques for Memory Management

C developers must know how to access application memory in bug-free manners. Specifically, in this section first we will discuss common memory access errors related to important operations: allocation, reading, writing, and deallocation. Next, we discuss how these errors can be handled by the developers with a few good practices. In the case of dynamic memory allocation in large-size applications, it is very challenging to inspect the memory access-related runtime errors. Moreover, memory access-related errors can lead to application crashes and security attacks. In order to simplify identification of common memory access-related errors, we introduce quick usage of the valgrind tool. You will be specifically practicing the use of the valgrind memory tool for identifying memory access-related errors quickly. In this section, we will learn the following:

- Best dynamic memory management practices
- Memory error handling techniques using valgrind
- Hands-on activities related to memory management

Best Dynamic Memory Management Practices

We will learn the best dynamic memory management practices through the following sample function code. Basically, we will learn the common dynamic memory access-related errors and how to handle them in reliable manners.

CHAPTER 5   C PROGRAMMING FOR MEMORY MANAGEMENT

For example:

```
void memoryAccess(int N)
{
      int *p=(int*)malloc(sizeof(int)*10);
      int i;
      for (i=0;i<N;i++)
      {
            p[i]=p[i]+1;
      }
}
```

Developers, on executing the memoryAccess(), may not throw any errors in case of default gcc compilation and execution steps. However, in a runtime environment, this memoryAccess() can lead to the following critical runtime errors and crashes:

1. memoryAccess() is requesting the OS to allocate 10 bytes of memory during runtime using the malloc() library function. Since it is a request, if the OS fails to allocate the requested block of memory, it returns a NULL pointer.

    a. **Possible Error**: Since there is no error-checking code written after memory allocation, it could lead to runtime errors.

    b. **Best Practice**: Hence, developers must check the pointer variable after a memory allocation request is made. Developers must check the pointer variable and write the code in the safe block as follows:

    ```
    if (p!=NULL)
    {
          //access pointer p
    }
    ```

2. memoryAccess() is written by assuming the memory block will be allocated successfully and the respective locations can be accessed directly (p[i]=p[i]+1) without any errors.

CHAPTER 5   C PROGRAMMING FOR MEMORY MANAGEMENT

a. **Possible Error**: On any system, usually memory is shared by multiple processes, and an OS dynamically allocates and deallocates memory blocks. However, the OS may not guarantee the contents of the memory locations are cleared. It means developers may access random values from the memory locations, and it could lead to serious bugs during execution. Hence, developers cannot assume any default values inside dynamically allocated memory locations.

b. **Best Practice**: Before using the dynamically allocated memory locations, initialize them. Developers should initialize the memory locations as follows:

```
for (i=0;i<10;i++)
{
      p[i]=0;
}
```

3. memoryAccess() is requesting the OS to allocate the specific size memory blocks. It means that on successful allocation of the memory blocks by the OS to the function, it is the function's responsibility after its use to inform the OS when it can release the allocated memory block.

   a. **Possible Error**: Wastage of the unused memory blocks. After the memory block usage, the function did not inform the OS to deallocate the memory block; hence, the OS cannot deallocate the memory block from the function. However, the function is not using the memory block.

   b. **Possible Errors**: Attackers can exploit the unused memory blocks for loading malicious codes, sniffing and stealing data from the memory locations, etc.

   c. **Possible Errors**: Inefficient usage of limited memory, which leads to performance issues. Because of multitasking, high-performance computing needs large memory to improve the system performance.

d. **Best Practice**: Deallocate the memory after usage and initialize the respective pointer with NULL. Initializing the pointer with NULL after deallocation will help to avoid double free or dereferencing NULL pointers. Developers should free the memory locations as follows:

```
free(p);
p=NULL;
```

4. memoryAccess(int N) is checking boundaries of memory access locations in the wrong manner. In case the user passes an N value>10, then it can lead to the following two important memory access errors:

    a. **Possible Error**: If N>10, then it can lead to an invalid memory read operation. Invalid memory read operations lead to crossing boundaries of your program data region. It can lead to security issues too.

    b. **Possible Error**: If N>10, then it can lead to an invalid memory write operation. Invalid memory write operations lead to crossing boundaries of your program data region. It can lead to security issues such as buffer overflow attacks.

    c. **Best Practice**: Always check boundaries of memory blocks to do read or write operations. Developers should allocate sufficient memory block sizes for performing any calculations.

    ```
    int *p=(int*)malloc(sizeof(int)*N);
    ```

5. It is also possible to set read, write, and execute permissions for the memory blocks. Developers must check any access permission violations in those specific cases.

6. Other common mistakes during dynamic memory allocation:

    a. **Uninitialized Pointer Access**: It means developers try to access pointers containing random addresses or NULL. These kinds of memory access lead to system crashes and segmentation faults.

b. **Use After Free**: It means developers may try to access already freed memory blocks.

c. **Dereferencing NULL Pointers**: Pointers initialized with NULL cannot be accessed.

d. **Double-Free Operation**: It means developers may try to deallocate already freed memory blocks.

e. **Best Way to Avoid the Aforementioned Errors**: Check pointers before using them. Developers can check it as follows:

```
if (p!=NULL)
{
        //access p
        //dereference
        //free
}
```

In this section, we have learned common memory access errors and best practices. Next, we will learn how to handle these errors using the `valgrind` tool.

Memory Error Handling Techniques Using Valgrind

`Valgrind` tools are developed for dynamic code analysis for automatically detecting common memory, cache, and thread-related errors. It is also used as a code profiling tool. On a Linux platform, you need to install it before using it. It helps developers to easily identify common runtime errors during development stages. Hence, it is motivating organizations to use valgrind tools extensively for testing the large code before deploying them in the runtime environment. In this section, we are revisiting how to use the valgrind memory tool for identifying memory access-related errors such as invalid read, invalid write, use after free, double free, uninitialized memory blocks, and access permissions violations.

CHAPTER 5   C PROGRAMMING FOR MEMORY MANAGEMENT

QUICK INTRODUCTION TO VALGRIND TOOLS USAGE

1. Valgrind tools perform dynamic code analysis; hence, it is necessary to compile your code with debugging details before testing your code with `valgrind`.

    a. First, compile your program with a debugging option.

    e.g., `gcc -g sample.c`

    b. Then, you can run your executable code with the `valgrind` tool using the following important options.

    c. Check your `valgrind` version using the following command:

    ```
    valgrind --version
    valgrind-3.15.0
    ```

    d. Check various `valgrind` options available using the following command:

    ```
    valgrind --help |grep 'mem'
    ```

    ```
                    --tool=<name>              use the Valgrind tool
                    named <name> [memcheck]
                                        This allows saved stack traces
                                        (e.g. memory leaks)
    --xtree-memory=none|allocs|full    profile heap memory
    in an xtree [none]
    --xtree-memory-file=<file>    xtree memory report file
    [xtmemory.kcg.%p]
    --run-libc-freeres=no|yes  free up glibc memory at exit
    on Linux? [yes]
    --run-cxx-freeres=no|yes   free up libstdc++ memory at
    exit on Linux
    more sectors may increase performance, but use
    more memory.
    --aspace-minaddr=0xPP          avoid mapping memory
    below 0xPP [guessed]
    --leak-check=no|summary|full   search for memory leaks
    at exit? [summary]
    ```

286

2. Steps to use valgrind tool on a sample program (sample.c):

   a. `gcc -g sample.c`

   b. `valgrind --tool=memcheck --leak-check=full ./a.out`

3. The following important messages of valgrind should be observed:

   a. Usually you will be encountering the following error messages when an application is executed using valgrind. These messages help developers to easily identify types of memory access errors and lines of the code causing these errors. These error messages help in correcting memory access errors quickly:

   Invalid read of size
   Invalid write of size
   Invalid free
   Conditional jump or move depends on uninitialised
   Access not within mapped region

   b. **Heap Summary:** This summary section helps developers to understand the amount of memory dynamically allocated and freed successfully.

   Example: `in use at exit: 0 bytes in 0 blocks`
   `total heap usage: 1 allocs, 1 frees, 40 bytes`

   c. **Leak Summary:** This summary section helps developers to understand whether all dynamically allocated memory blocks are freed or not. It helps in how many bytes are lost without deallocation.

   Example: `definitely lost: 40 bytes in 1 blocks`
   `indirectly lost: 0 bytes in 0 blocks`

   d. **Error Summary:** This summary section helps developers to know the total number of memory access errors.

   Example: `2 errors from 1 contexts`

In summary, before using the valgrind tool, the C application should be compiled with the gdb option, and during the execution, developers should check the important error messages to improve the reliability of the applications.

Next, let's practice using the `valgrind` tool to correct various memory accessing errors.

Hands-On Activity Using Valgrind Tools

In this hands-on activity, we will learn how to identify and correct the following important memory accessing errors:

- Invalid memory read operations
- Invalid memory write operations
- Memory initialization errors
- Invalid memory access permissions
- Memory leaks

> **HANDS-ON ACTIVITY USING VALGRIND MEMORY TOOL**

1. We do the following activities to learn how to use the `valgrind` tool to identify and correct memory access-related errors:

   a. First, we use the following memory access functions in a `memoryleaks.c` to test with `valgrind` tools for identifying all possible memory access errors:

   b. We intentionally introduced various memory access errors such as invalid read, invalid write, uninitialized memory blocks, access permissions, and memory leaks in the following functions of `memoryleaks.c`.

   c. We use this code to test with `valgrind` for identifying and correcting the aforementioned errors.

   ```
   #include<stdio.h>
   #include<stdlib.h>
   #include<string.h>
   ```

```c
void ivr() //invalid read operation
{
    int *p=(int*)malloc(sizeof(int)*10);
    int i;
    for (i=0;i<10;i++)
    {
        p[i]=0;
    }
    for (i=0;i<12;i++)
    {
        printf("%d",p[i]);
    }
    free(p);
}
void ivw() //invalid write operation
{
    int *p=(int*)malloc(sizeof(int)*10);
    int i;
    for (i=0;i<10;i++)
    {
        p[i]=0;
    }
    for (i=0;i<12;i++)
    {
        p[i]=0;
    }
    free(p);
}
void uninitialize() //Memory initialization errors
{
    int *p=(int*)malloc(sizeof(int)*10);
    if (p!=NULL)
    {
        memset(p,0,10);
        for(int i=0;i<10;i++)
```

CHAPTER 5   C PROGRAMMING FOR MEMORY MANAGEMENT

```
                    {
                            printf("%d",p[i]);
                    }
            }
    }
    int *accesserr() //Memory access permissions
    {
            int a=100;
            return &a;
    }
    int* leak() //Memory leaks
    {
            int *p=(int*)malloc(sizeof(int)*10);
    }
    int main()
    {
            char *p;
    //      ivr();
    //      ivw();
    //      uninitialize();

     //     int *p1=accesserr();
     //     *p1=300;

     //     int *q=leak();
     //     free(q);
     //     q[0]=100;
    }
```

2. First, compile your code by uncommenting `ivr()` as follows:

    #gcc -g memoryleaks.c

3. Test your code executable file using valgrind; you will observe the **Invalid read error** with lines of code causing errors:

   ```
   #valgrind --tool=memcheck --leak-check=full ./a.out
   ==43107== Invalid read of size 4
   ==43107==    at 0x10922D: ivr (memoryleaks.c:16)
   ==43107==    by 0x1093CE: main (memoryleaks.c:65)
   ==43107==  Address 0x4a73068 is 0 bytes after a block of
   ```

4. Correct the invalid read errors shown in valgrind output (memoryleaks.c) of the function ivr() and compile the code using gdb by uncommenting ivw().

5. Test your code executable file using valgrind, you will observe the **Invalid write error** with lines of code causing errors. In your code, due to commenting and blank lines, line numbers may slightly vary:

   ```
   #valgrind --tool=memcheck --leak-check=full ./a.out
   ==43208== Invalid write of size 4
   ==43208==    at 0x1092BF: ivw (memoryleaks.c:31)
   ==43208==    by 0x1093CE: main (memoryleaks.c:66)
   ```

6. Correct the invalid write errors shown in line 31 (memoryleaks.c) of function ivw() and compile the code using gdb by uncommenting uninitialize().

7. Test your code executable file using valgrind; you will observe the uninitialised value(s) errors.

   ```
   #valgrind --tool=memcheck --leak-check=full ./a.out
   ==44206== Conditional jump or move depends on uninitialised value(s)
   ==44206==    at 0x48F5958: __vfprintf_internal (vfprintf-
                internal.c:1687)
   ==44206==    by 0x48DFD3E: printf (printf.c:33)
   ==44206==    by 0x109310: uninitialize (memoryleaks.c:44)
   ==44206==    by 0x10938C: main (memoryleaks.c:66)
   ```

8. Correct the errors shown in uninitialize function and compile the code using gdb by uncommenting accesserr() and related code.

CHAPTER 5 C PROGRAMMING FOR MEMORY MANAGEMENT

9. Test your code executable file using valgrind; you will observe the **Invalid write and Access** not within mapped region at address 0x0

   ```
   #valgrind --tool=memcheck --leak-check=full ./a.out
   ==43508== Invalid write of size 4
   ==43508==    at 0x1093DB: main (memoryleaks.c:71)
   ==43508==    Address 0x0 is not stack'd, malloc'd or (recently) free'd
   ==43508== Process terminating with default action of signal 11 (SIGSEGV): dumping core
   ==43508==    Access not within mapped region at address 0x0
   ```

10. Correct the errors shown in the main function at line number 71 and execute code with valgrind.

11. Test your code executable file using valgrind; you will observe the **Invalid write and Access** not within mapped region at address 0x0

    ```
    valgrind --tool=memcheck --leak-check=full ./a.out
    ==43802== LEAK SUMMARY:
    ==43802==    definitely lost: 40 bytes in 1 blocks
    ==43802==    indirectly lost: 0 bytes in 0 blocks
    ```

12. Correct the errors shown in the main function at line number 71 and compile the code using gdb by uncommenting leak() and related code.

13. Test your code executable file using valgrind; you will observe the errors at line numbers 74 and 75. In your code, due to commenting and blanklines, line numbers may slightly vary:

    ```
    #valgrind --tool=memcheck --leak-check=full ./a.out
    ==44016== Memcheck, a memory error detector
    ==44016== Command: ./a.out
    ==44016== Invalid write of size 4
    ==44016==    at 0x1093DB: main (memoryleaks.c:75)
    ==44016==    Address 0x4a73040 is 0 bytes inside a block of size 40 free'd
    ==44016==    at 0x483CA3F: free (in /usr/lib/x86_64-linux-gnu/valgrind/vgpreload_memcheck-amd64-linux.so)
    ==44016==    by 0x1093D6: main (memoryleaks.c:74)
    ```

```
==44016==   Block was alloc'd at
==44016==    at 0x483B7F3: malloc (in /usr/lib/x86_64-linux-gnu/
valgrind/vgpreload_memcheck-amd64-linux.so)
==44016==    by 0x1093A6: leak (memoryleaks.c:57)
==44016==    by 0x1093C6: main (memoryleaks.c:73)
==44016== HEAP SUMMARY:
==44016==    in use at exit: 0 bytes in 0 blocks
==44016==    total heap usage: 1 allocs, 1 frees, 40 bytes allocated
==44016== All heap blocks were freed -- no leaks are possible
==44016== For lists of detected and suppressed errors, rerun with: -s
==44016== ERROR SUMMARY: 1 errors from 1 contexts (suppressed: 0 from 0)
```

14. Correct the errors shown in the `main` function at line numbers 74 and 75 and execute code with `valgrind`.

From the results, you can observe that all memory access-related errors are detected and corrected successfully using `valgrind`.

In this section, we have learned how to identify and correct various memory access errors using the `valgrind` tool quickly. Next, let's practice doing dynamic memory allocation tasks in reliable manners.

Setting Up Memory Buffers and Accessing Them in a Reliable Manner

In this section, we do the following hands-on activities to practice dynamic memory allocation using `malloc`, `calloc`, and `realloc` in reliable manners:

- In hands-on activity-1, we are going to practice how to use `malloc` and `realloc` in reliable manners for dynamic memory allocation tasks. Specifically, you will learn the importance of realloc in extending memory blocks.

CHAPTER 5   C PROGRAMMING FOR MEMORY MANAGEMENT

- In hands-on activity-2, we are going to practice how to use `calloc` for handling 2-D memory block allocations and accessing them using the array indexing approach. More importantly, you will learn using `calloc` how to allocate multiple blocks, each block with a variable size.

- In hands-on activity-3, we are going to practice how to use `calloc` and `realloc` for extending 2-D memory block allocations and accessing them using an array indexing approach.

Let's start with a hands-on activity in the upcoming section.

Hands-On Activity-1

In this hands-on activity, we do the following activities related to the usage of `malloc`, `realloc`, and `free`. From the following activity, first, we learn how to use `malloc` to get the required size of memory blocks from the OS and access it. Then, specifically, we will learn the importance of `realloc` to extend the size of an existing buffer seamlessly. Finally, we release the dynamically allocated memory blocks using `free` system calls. Moreover, to handle dynamic memory allocation, extending, and deallocation activities in a reliable manner, we implement the suitable reliability checks code in all the required functions.

- Implement a function to allocate a memory buffer using `malloc` of a given size to handle integer data elements. The function should return a pointer to access the buffer.

- Implement a function to copy contents of one memory buffer to another buffer.

- Learn how to extend an existing memory buffer using `malloc` only. In this task, you will observe the overhead in terms of copying contents from the old buffer to the new buffer and deallocation activities.

- Implement a function to extend an existing buffer using `realloc`. In this task, you will observe the flexibility of realloc in terms of avoiding overhead tasks such as copying memory contents and deallocation of the old memory blocks.

CHAPTER 5 C PROGRAMMING FOR MEMORY MANAGEMENT

USAGE OF MALLOC, REALLOC, AND FREE

1. We implement this hands-on activity in memalloc1.c. Define the following function to allocate a memory buffer of a given size and return the pointer to caller functions:

   ```
   #include<stdio.h>
   #include<stdlib.h>
   int* GetBuffer(int n)
   {
           int *p = (int*)malloc(sizeof(int)*n);
           return p;
   }
   ```

2. Define the following function to copy contents from the source memory buffer to the destination buffer:

   ```
   int* BufferCopy(int *src, int m, int *dst, int n)
   {
           for (int i=0;i<m;i++)
           {
                   dst[i]=src[i];
           }
           return dst;
   }
   ```

3. Define the following function to extend an existing buffer from size m to new size n. Then, on successful extension of the existing buffer, initialize the extended location with a given character ch.

   ```
   int* extendBuff(int *src,int m,int n,int ch)
   {
           int *tbuf;
           tbuf=realloc(src,n*sizeof(int));
           if (tbuf==NULL)
   ```

295

CHAPTER 5 C PROGRAMMING FOR MEMORY MANAGEMENT

```
        {
                printf("exteding failed\n");
                        return src;
        }
        else
        {
                for (int i=m;i<n;i++)
                {
                        tbuf[i]=ch;
                }
                        return tbuf;
        }
}
```

4. We test the above implemented function in main by doing the following activities:

   a. Allocate a memory buffer of size 10-integer data elements. Collect the buffer address into pointer m1. On successful allocation of the buffer, initialize the buffer contents with 1 to 10 numbers.

   ```
   int main()
   {
           int *m1 = GetBuffer(10);
           if (m1!=NULL)
           {
                   printf("Dynamically allocated memory block contents\n");
                   for (int i=0;i<10;i++)
                   {
                           m1[i]=i;
                           printf("%d ", m1[i]);
                   }
                   printf("\n");
           }
   ```

```
        else
        {
            return 0;
        }
```

b. Extend the old buffer from size 10-integer data elements to 20-integer data elements using `malloc` only.

c. Since malloc cannot be used to extend the memory blocks, we first allocate a new buffer of size 20 data elements and collect the new buffer address into pointer m2.

d. Then, we copy the old buffer (m1) contents to the new buffer (m2) in a reliable manner by checking pointer addresses and sizes of the respective buffers.

e. After copying the old buffer integer data elements to the new buffer, deallocate the old buffer (m1) and initialize the old buffer pointer (m1) to NULL.

f. After accessing the new buffer (m2) elements, deallocate the buffer and initialize the buffer pointer (m2) to NULL.

```
        int *m2 = GetBuffer(20);
        if (m2!=NULL)
        {
            m2 = BufferCopy(m1,10,m2,20);
            free(m1);
            m1=NULL;
            printf("Copied memory block contents\n");
            for (int i=10;i<20;i++)
            {
                m2[i]=i;
                printf("%d ", m2[i]);
            }
            printf("\n");
            for (int i=0;i<20;i++)
```

CHAPTER 5   C PROGRAMMING FOR MEMORY MANAGEMENT

```
        {
                printf("%d ", m2[i]);
        }
        printf("\n");
        free(m2);
        m2=NULL;
    }
```

5. Then, we again allocate 10-integer data elements holding the memory buffer and hold its address in pointer (p). To extend the buffer size of pointer p, we use realloc-based extendBuff function with p as an argument and the new size of the buffer.

   a. Observe from the below code that we need not copy the old buffer contents to the new buffer. It is handled by realloc seamlessly.

   b. We need to collect the new buffer address into a pointer variable for accessing the new buffer data elements.

   c. On successful extension of the buffer and accessing the buffer contents, deallocate the memory using free.

```
int *p = GetBuffer(10);
if (p!=NULL)
{
        printf("Dynamically allocated memory block contents\n");
        for (int i=0;i<10;i++)
        {
                p[i]=i;
                printf("%d ", p[i]);
        }
        printf("\n");
        p=extendBuff(p,10,20,1);
        printf("Extended memory block contents\n");
        for (int i=0;i<20;i++)
        {
                printf("%d ", p[i]);
        }
```

```
            printf("\n");
            free(p);
            p=NULL;
        }
    }
```

6. Compile and test the memalloc1.c using the following commands:

   ```
   #gcc memalloc1.c
   #./a.out
   Dynamically allocated memory block contents
   0 1 2 3 4 5 6 7 8 9
   Copied memory block contents
   10 11 12 13 14 15 16 17 18 19
   0 1 2 3 4 5 6 7 8 9 10 11 12 13 14 15 16 17 18 19
   Dynamically allocated memory block contents
   0 1 2 3 4 5 6 7 8 9
   Extended memory block contents
   0 1 2 3 4 5 6 7 8 9 1 1 1 1 1 1 1 1 1 1
   ```

7. Compile the memalloc1.c using -fanalyzer and observe that there will be no possible memory access errors and memory leaks:

   ```
   #gcc-10 -fanalyzer memalloc1.c
   ```

8. Test this executable using valgrind and observe that there will be no memory access errors and memory leaks:

9. Next, do the following using valgrind after changing the following lines of code:

   a. Change buffer sizes

   b. Remove deallocation-related code

   c. Remove pointers and their addresses checking code

From the results, observe that we successfully allocated a memory buffer, accessed its contents, and deallocated the buffer in reliable manners.

Next, let's learn how to use calloc for allocating multiple memory blocks and access their contents using a simple array indexing approach.

Hands-On Activity-2

In this hands-on activity, we do the following activities related to the usage of calloc and free. From the following activity, first, we learn how to use calloc to get the multiple memory blocks, and every block size is fixed as shown in Figure 5-6 (e.g., 10 rows containing 20 elements) from the OS, and access them using the 2-D array indexing approach.

Figure 5-6. *Allocating a 2-D memory block of size 10x20 integers using calloc*

Then, specifically, we will learn the importance of calloc to allocate an array of pointers, and each pointer is holding a specific size of memory block. For example, the first row contains one memory cell, the next row contains two memory cells, and so on, as shown in Figure 5-7.

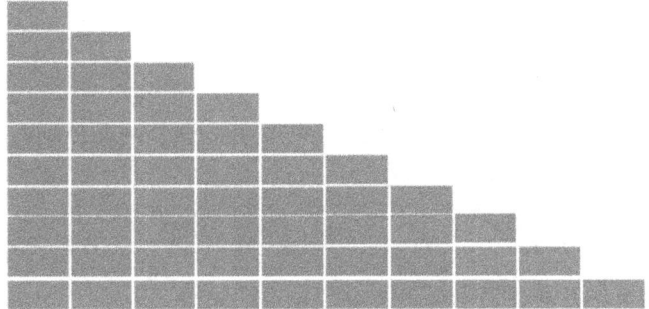

Figure 5-7. *Allocating a 2-D memory block of size 10 rows, and each row size is variable*

Finally, we release the dynamically allocated multiple memory blocks using free. Moreover, to handle dynamic memory allocation, extend and deallocate activities in a reliable manner, we implement the suitable reliability checks code in all the required functions.

- Implement a function to allocate a 2-D memory buffer with n rows, and each row contains m cells using calloc. The function should return a pointer to access the buffer using the 2-D array indexing approach.

- Implement a function to allocate a 2-D memory buffer with n rows, and each row size can vary. The function should return a double pointer to access the buffer using the 2-D array indexing approach.

USE CALLOC TO ALLOCATE 2-D MEMORY BUFFERS

1. We implement the following functions in memalloc2.c:
2. Define the following function to return a 2-D memory block containing each row with an equal number of elements holding the memory buffer.

    a. Observe the calloc function taking two important arguments: number of blocks and each block size.

    b. We simply access the 2-D memory block using the pointer returned by the calloc.

    c. The 2-D memory block locations are traversed using a nested loop.

    ```
    #include<stdio.h>
    #include<stdlib.h>
    int* arrayofBlocks(int n, int s)
    {
        int *p=(int*)calloc(n,sizeof(int)*s);
        for (int i=0;i<n;i++)
        {
            int k=0;
            for (int j=0;j<s;j++)
    ```

CHAPTER 5 C PROGRAMMING FOR MEMORY MANAGEMENT

```
                {
                        p[k]=k++;
                }
        }
        for (int i=0;i<n;i++)
        {
                int k=0;
                for (int j=0;j<s;j++)
                {
                        printf("%d ",p[k]);
                        k++;
                }
                printf("\n");
        }
        return p;
}
```

3. Define the following function to return a 2-D memory block containing each row with a variable number of elements holding the memory buffer.

   a. Observing the outer loop, `calloc is` allocating an array of pointers (N) to hold addresses of N memory blocks.

   b. Since we are allocating an array of pointers, we are collecting it using a double pointer.

   c. Then, in the inner loop, `calloc` is allocating a block of memory for each row, and these addresses are stored in the array of pointers.

   d. The function is returning the double pointer to caller functions.

```
int** arrayofVarSizeBlocks(int n)
{
        int **p=(int**)calloc(n,sizeof(int*));
        if (p!=NULL)
        {
                for (int i=0;i<n;i++)
                {
                        p[i] = (int*)calloc(1,sizeof(int)*(i+1));
```

```c
            if (p[i]!=NULL)
            for (int j=0;j<i+1;j++)
            {
                    p[i][j]=j;
            }
        }
        for (int i=0;i<n;i++)
        {
            for (int j=0;j<i+1;j++)
            {
                    printf("%d ",p[i][j]);
            }
            printf("\n");
        }
        return p;
    }
    return NULL;
}
```

4. Define the following C code in main() to allocate a 2-D memory block containing 10 rows, and each row contains 20-integer data elements.

    a. Observe that we are checking the successful allocation of the 2-D memory blocks (blocks) and deallocating it using the pointer blocks after use.

    ```c
    int main()
    {
        printf("Equal size memory blocks\n");
        int *blocks=arrayofBlocks(10,20);
        if (blocks!=NULL)
        {
            free(blocks);
            blocks=NULL;
        }
    ```

CHAPTER 5 C PROGRAMMING FOR MEMORY MANAGEMENT

5. Allocate a 2-D memory block containing 10 rows, and each row size is variable. For example, we allocate the first row with one element, the second row with two elements, and so on.

    a. Observe that after usage of the 2-D memory block, first we are deallocating individual memory blocks' memory, then we deallocate the array of pointers' memory.

    b. We also assign NULL addresses to the pointers after deallocating the respective memory blocks.

    ```
    printf("Variable size memory blocks\n");
    int **ap = arrayofVarSizeBlocks(10);
    if (ap!=NULL)
    {
        for (int i=0;i<10;i++)
        {
            free(ap[i]);
            ap[i]=NULL;
        }
        free(ap);
        ap=NULL;
    }
    ```

6. Compile the code and test it using the following commands:

    ```
    #gcc memalloc2.c
    #./a.out
    Equal size memory blocks
    0 0 1 2 3 4 5 6 7 8 9 10 11 12 13 14 15 16 17 18
    0 0 1 2 3 4 5 6 7 8 9 10 11 12 13 14 15 16 17 18
    0 0 1 2 3 4 5 6 7 8 9 10 11 12 13 14 15 16 17 18
    0 0 1 2 3 4 5 6 7 8 9 10 11 12 13 14 15 16 17 18
    0 0 1 2 3 4 5 6 7 8 9 10 11 12 13 14 15 16 17 18
    0 0 1 2 3 4 5 6 7 8 9 10 11 12 13 14 15 16 17 18
    0 0 1 2 3 4 5 6 7 8 9 10 11 12 13 14 15 16 17 18
    0 0 1 2 3 4 5 6 7 8 9 10 11 12 13 14 15 16 17 18
    ```

```
0 0 1 2 3 4 5 6 7 8 9 10 11 12 13 14 15 16 17 18
0 0 1 2 3 4 5 6 7 8 9 10 11 12 13 14 15 16 17 18
Variable size memory blocks
0
0 1
0 1 2
0 1 2 3
0 1 2 3 4
0 1 2 3 4 5
0 1 2 3 4 5 6
0 1 2 3 4 5 6 7
0 1 2 3 4 5 6 7 8
0 1 2 3 4 5 6 7 8 9
```

7. Compile the memalloc2.c using -fanalyzer and observe that there will be no possible memory access errors and memory leaks:

    #gcc-10 -fanalyzer memalloc2.c

8. Test this executable using valgrind and observe that there will be no memory access errors and memory leaks:

9. Next, do the following activities using valgrind tool after changing the following lines of code:

    a. Change buffer sizes

    b. Remove deallocation-related code

    c. Remove pointers and their addresses checking code

From the results, observe that we successfully allocated multiple memory buffers, such as 2-D memory blocks with fixed elements and variable elements. Moreover, we accessed these buffers through simple 2-D array indexing approaches and deallocated the buffers in reliable manners.

CHAPTER 5   C PROGRAMMING FOR MEMORY MANAGEMENT

Next, let's learn how to use calloc and realloc for allocating multiple memory blocks, extending the memory blocking, and accessing their contents using a simple array indexing approach.

Hands-On Activity-3

In this hands-on activity, we do the following activities related to the usage of calloc and free. From the following activity, we learn how to use realloc to extend the multiple memory blocks allocated by calloc and access them using the 2-D array indexing approach. For instance, we first allocate 10 memory blocks using calloc as shown in the LHS shown memory blocks of Figure 5-8. Then, we extend these multiple memory blocks using realloc and append five more memory blocks as shown in the RHS of the figure.

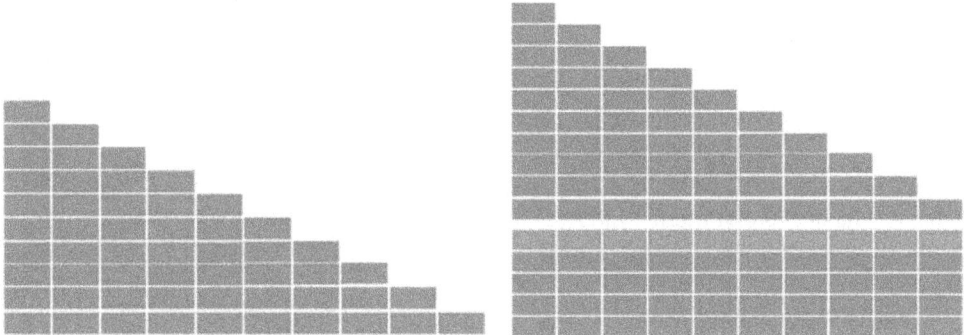

Figure 5-8. *Allocating a 2-D memory block of size 10 rows, where each row size is variable, and then extending it by adding five more rows of size 10 integers*

Finally, we release the dynamically allocated multiple memory blocks using the free system call. Moreover, to handle dynamic memory allocation, extend and deallocate activities in a reliable manner, we implement the suitable reliability checks code in all the required functions.

- Implement a function to allocate a 2-D memory buffer with 10 rows, and each row size varies as follows: the first row contains 1-integer element, the second row contains 2-integer elements, and so on. The function should return a double pointer to access the buffer using the 2-D array indexing approach.

- Implement a function to extend the above 2-D memory buffer by appending the buffer with five rows, and each row contains 10-integer elements of storage.

CALLOC AND REALLOC USAGE

1. We implement these hands-on activities in `memalloc3.c`:
2. Define the following function to return a 2-D memory block containing each row with a variable number of elements holding the memory buffer.

```c
#include<stdio.h>
#include<stdlib.h>
int** arrayofVarSizeBlocks(int n)
{
    int **p=(int**)calloc(n,sizeof(int*));
    if (p!=NULL)
    {
        for (int i=0;i<n;i++)
        {
            p[i] = (int*)calloc(1,sizeof(int)*(i+1));
            if (p[i]!=NULL)
            {
                for (int j=0;j<i+1;j++)
                {
                    p[i][j]=j;
                }
            }
            else
            return NULL;
        }
        return p;
    }
}
```

```
            else
            {
                    return NULL;
            }
    }
```

3. Define the following function to extend a given memory block containing m rows with n rows, and each row contains k-integer data elements.

   a. Observe from the below code, we need not copy the old 2-D memory blocks' contents to the new 2-D blocks of memory. It is handled by realloc seamlessly.

   b. We need to collect the new buffer address into a pointer variable for accessing the new buffer data elements.

   c. On successful extension of the buffer, access the buffer contents using simple 2-D array accessing approaches.

```
int** extendVarSizeBlocks(int **p,int m,int n,int k)
{
        int **tvb;
        if (p==NULL)
        {
                return NULL;
        }
        else
        {
                tvb=(int**)realloc(p,n*sizeof(int*));
                if (tvb==NULL)
                {
                        return NULL;
                }
                else
                {
                        printf("Old memory block contents\n");
                        for (int i=0;i<m;i++)
                        {
                                for (int j=0;j<i+1;j++)
```

```c
            {
                    printf("%d ",tvb[i][j]);
            }
            printf("\n");
        }
        printf("New memory block contents\n");
        for (int i=m;i<n;i++)
        {
            tvb[i] = (int*)
            calloc(1,sizeof(int)*(k));
            if (tvb[i]!=NULL)
            for (int j=0;j<k;j++)
            {
                    tvb[i][j]=j;
                    printf("%d ",tvb[i][j]);
            }
            else
            {
                    return NULL;
            }
            printf("\n");
        }
        return tvb;
    }
  }
}
```

4. Define the following C code in main() to test the above functions by doing the following tasks:

   a. First, allocate a 2-D memory block containing 10 rows, and each row contains a variable number of cells.

   b. Collect the 2-D memory block address into a double pointer (ap).

   ```c
   int main()
   {
           int **ap = arrayofVarSizeBlocks(10);
   ```

```
            if (ap==NULL)
            {
                    printf("Allocation is failed\n");
                    return 0;
            }
```

5. Then extend the 2-D memory block pointed to by ap with five rows, and each row contains 10-integer data element storage.

    a. Observe that after usage of the 2-D memory block, we are first deallocating individual memory blocks' memory, then we deallocate the array of pointers' memory.

    b. We also assign NULL addresses to the pointers after deallocating the respective memory blocks.

```
            else
            {
                    int **dp = extendVarSizeBlocks(ap,10,15,10);
                    if (dp==NULL)
                    {
                            printf("Allocation is failed\n");
                            return 0;
                    }
                    if (dp!=NULL)
                    {
                            for (int i=0;i<15;i++)
                            {
                                    free(dp[i]);
                                    dp[i]=NULL;
                            }
                            free(dp);
                            dp=NULL;
                    }
            }
    }
```

6. Compile the code and test it using the following commands:

```
gcc memalloc3.c
./a.out
Old memory block contents
0
0 1
0 1 2
0 1 2 3
0 1 2 3 4
0 1 2 3 4 5
0 1 2 3 4 5 6
0 1 2 3 4 5 6 7
0 1 2 3 4 5 6 7 8
0 1 2 3 4 5 6 7 8 9
New memory block contents
0 1 2 3 4 5 6 7 8 9
0 1 2 3 4 5 6 7 8 9
0 1 2 3 4 5 6 7 8 9
0 1 2 3 4 5 6 7 8 9
0 1 2 3 4 5 6 7 8 9
```

7. Compile the memalloc3.c using -fanalyzer and observe that there will be no possible memory access errors and memory leaks:

    `#gcc-10 -fanalyzer memalloc3.c`

8. Test this executable using valgrind and observe that there will be no memory access errors and memory leaks:

9. Next, do the following using valgrind after changing the following lines of code:

    a. Change buffer sizes

    b. Remove deallocation-related code

    c. Remove pointers and their addresses checking code

From the results, observe that we successfully extended the multiple memory buffers, such as 2-D memory blocks. Moreover, we accessed these buffers through simple 2-D array indexing approaches and deallocated the buffers in reliable manners.

In this section, we have practiced how to use `malloc`, `calloc`, and `realloc` for handling various dynamic memory management tasks in a reliable manner.

Summary

In this chapter, we have learned best practices to manage dynamic memory of C applications in reliable manners. Specifically, we used `stdlib` functions such as `malloc`, `calloc`, and `realloc` to carry out dynamic memory management tasks. We have learned the basics of each of the aforementioned library functions to handle memory blocks' allocations and deallocation after use. In order to practice, we implemented suitable hands-on activities in C and explored `valgrind` tool usage for detecting and correcting errors quickly.

In the next chapter, we will learn how to use C programming skills to implement high-performance applications using multiprocessing and multithreading concepts.

Practice Tasks

1. Dynamically allocate a list of strings based on user-specified list size using `calloc` and print the list of strings.

   - Use valgrind to check all possible errors and correct them if any

2. Extend or shrink the list of strings allocated in the previous task and print the list of strings.

   - Use valgrind to check all possible errors and correct them if any

3. Implement a 2-D matrix of size NxM. Where N and M can be any user-defined sizes, allocate 2-D matrices using dynamic memory library functions, and initialize them with sample values. Print the matrices in a reliable manner.

   - Use valgrind to check all possible errors and correct them if any

CHAPTER 5   C PROGRAMMING FOR MEMORY MANAGEMENT

4. Take a long input string of dynamic size, divide it into various tokens, and print each token and its frequency in the string.

    - Use valgrind to check all possible errors and correct them if any

5. Take N lists of variable size and join them into a single list; use dynamic memory allocation functions to allocate memory to lists.

    - Use valgrind to check all possible errors and correct them if any

6. Take N strings of variable size and join them into a single string; use dynamic memory allocation functions to allocate memory to strings

    - Use valgrind to check all possible errors and correct them if any

CHAPTER 6

Process and Thread Management Tasks for C Programmers

In this chapter, we discuss the powerful programming techniques in the C language for implementing high-performance computing-related applications. Specifically, we discuss the multiprocessing and multithreading programming techniques to implement parallel processing applications. First, we discuss how to create and manage multiple processes in a reliable manner using Linux system calls such as `fork, exec,` and `wait`. It helps you in implementing parallel processes, assigning specific jobs to each process, and handling performance and reliability-related issues of process management.

Next, we will discuss lightweight process management techniques for implementing parallel executable multitasking applications. On Linux, lightweight processes are created and managed through multithreading concepts. In order to learn multithreading programming to implement high-performance computing-related applications, we will discuss the following concepts. For example, partitioning complex tasks of an application as subtasks that can run in parallel. Besides, we discuss how to assign specific tasks to individual threads, dividing input data among threads to maximize parallel execution, and sharing data among multiple threads in a reliable manner. Specifically, you will be using the posix threads library (`pthreads`) for implementing threads and threads synchronization tasks in C programming.

In this chapter, we will revisit the `valgrind` (`helgrind`) tool for handling specific issues in processes and thread management. You will be practicing relevant hands-on activities of multiple processes management. Mainly, in this chapter, we will cover the following topics:

1. Introduction to processes and threads
2. Explore the power of process management using C programming
3. Safe and reliable programming ways for process management
4. Explore the power of threads management using C programming
5. Safe and reliable programming ways for threads management

Introduction to Processes and Threads

On Linux systems, every program execution is carried through process creation in terms of setting up process memory layout (stack, heap, data, and code segments) and CPU registers, as we discussed in Chapter 1, "Basic Computer System Architecture and Essential Operating System Concepts." Process creation is considered a heavy task in OS since it involves processes' dynamic memory management, CPU resources management, and IO resources management, besides handling of security and protection tasks. OS manages multiple processes in a reliable manner for executing multiple applications in parallel and offering high performance in terms of system resources such as CPU, memory, and IO utilization. In case developers need to implement high-performance computing applications, they must know how to access process management-related services from the OS. On Linux OS, process management-related tasks such as process creation, assigning specific jobs to processes, and collecting processes' execution status can be done through using the important system calls such as `fork, exec,` and `wait.` We will discuss the following important process management concepts with respect to developers' role in handling high-performance computing applications.

On the other hand, to implement multitasking applications at low overheads on Linux systems, lightweight processes called threads are introduced. Multiprocesses involve a lot of overhead due to creating separate processes and managing their process memory layouts (stack, heap, data, and code segments) and computational and IO resources. Threads are part of a process, and threads share the main process code, data, heap segments, and resources. Hence, w.r.t. to a thread, the OS needs to manage only its stack space and execution state. However, developers must manage threads in terms of allocating tasks, data, and necessary resources in a reliable manner.

Process Management Basic Activities Using Fork

On Linux systems using the fork system call, developers can create new processes in C. For example, to create two parallel processes in C (mproc.c), the following code snippet is helpful:

```
#include <unistd.h>
#include <sys/wait.h>
int main()
{
      pid_t ret;
      ret = fork();
      if (ret<0)
      {
            perror("fork failed");
      }
      if (ret==0)
      {
            printf("child process created %d\n",getpid());
            printf("Parent process id %d\n",getppid());
      }
      if (ret>0)
      {
            printf("Parent process\n");
      }
      printf("Task to be done\n");
}
#gcc -o twoproc mproc.c
#./twoproc
child process created 5403
Parent process id 5402
```

Parent process

Task to be done
Task to be done

From the above code snippet execution, the following points must be noted down by developers:

- The `twoproc` execution starts with a single process.
- After the `fork` system call, the `twoproc` (parent) creates another process called the child process. Then, both parent and child processes are executed simultaneously.
- Developers must check the return value of the `fork` to classify parent and child processes.
  - If the `ret` value is zero, then the process is a child process. Developers should assign a specific task in `if` block to carry out a specific task by the child process. In this sample code, the child process is printing its process id and parent process id.
  - If the `ret` value is greater than zero, then the process is the parent process. Developers should assign a specific task in `if` block to carry out the task by the parent process. In this sample code, the parent process is printing a sample statement only.
  - If the `ret` value is negative, then `fork` failed to create a child process. Developers check this error and handle it by printing suitable messages.
- On successful creation of parent and child processes, both processes will be executed in parallel. It means `twoproc` execution interleaves between carrying out parent tasks and child tasks simultaneously.
- Finally, developers should observe that the code placed after the parent and child blocks is executed by both parent and child processes. It means

CHAPTER 6   PROCESS AND THREAD MANAGEMENT TASKS FOR C PROGRAMMERS

- Both parent and child processes are still active and executing the rest of the code.

- Developers should explicitly decide and terminate the parent and the child process executions. It can be done by calling `exit` system calls in respective processes.

Besides these basic observations about the multiple processes' execution, developers should handle process termination, waiting, and coordination activities. These topics will be discussed in later sections. Next, you will learn thread management activities using the pthreads library.

Thread Management Basic Activities

On Linux systems using the pthreads library, developers create new threads in C. We use the following library function to create the threads and assign tasks to the threads. The pthread_create() creates a new thread from the calling process, and the thread executes its assigned specific task with given input arguments:

```
int pthread_create(pthread_t *thread, const pthread_attr_t *attr,
            void *(*start_routine) (void *), void *arg);
```

pthread_create takes the following arguments and creates threads:

- `pthread_t *thread`: This pointer points to the thread id.
- `void *(*start_routine) (void *)`: It is the address of a specific function or task to be executed by a thread. In the C language, it is a generic function pointer capable of holding the address of any function matching with the following specific function signature: A function name (thread task) takes input arguments as void * and returns void *.
  - During thread creation the address of the function (thread task) is passed to the function pointer.
  - For example: `void* task(void *){ printf ("job..");}` is the user-defined function. Then, the `task` is the address of the function to be passed to this argument.

CHAPTER 6 PROCESS AND THREAD MANAGEMENT TASKS FOR C PROGRAMMERS

- `void *arg`: It is a generic pointer. Using this pointer, it is possible to pass any type of data to the thread task.
    - Usually to pass multiple input variables, developers define a structure (e.g., `struct minputs i1;`) to hold multiple input variables and pass the address of the structure variable (`&i1`) as an argument.
- `const pthread_attr_t *attr`: Passing a NULL value to this argument creates threads with default resources and characteristics. This is an important argument for customizing the following thread resources and characteristics:
    - To define custom stack size as per application requirements
    - To configure specific stack address space
    - To define a type of thread, such as a joinable or detachable thread
        - **Joinable Threads**: In `main()`, developers must wait for the threads' execution completion using pthread_join and release threads resources.
        - **Detachable Threads**: In `main()`, developers need not wait for the threads' execution completion, and resources are automatically released at the end of the threads' execution.
        - Use detached threads when the main application need not maintain order of threads' execution and resources of the threads.
        - Use joinable threads when the main application needs to maintain order of threads' execution and resources of the threads.

For example, to wait for thread execution in C, the following code snippet is helpful: `int pthread_join(pthread_t thread, void **retval);` It is helpful to wait for a thread execution to be completed and collect its return value in a calling function.

- `pthread_t *thread`: This pointer points to the thread id.
- `void **retval`: It is a generic double pointer capable of holding the address of any pointer variable that is returning from the thread's task.

For example, to create two joinable threads, assign specific tasks to the threads, pass specific input arguments, and collect threads' return values in main, the following code snippet is helpful:

```c
#include <stdio.h>
#include <stdlib.h>
#include <pthread.h>
void *task1(void *arg)
{
    int n1 = *(int*)arg;
    int i;
    for (i=0;i<n1;i++)
    {
        printf("Task1: %d\n",i);
    }
    int *ret =(int*)malloc(sizeof(int));
    *ret=i;
    return (void*)ret;
}
void *task2(void *arg)
{
    int n2 = *(int*)arg;
    int i;
    for (i=0;i<n2;i=i+10)
    {
        printf("Task2: %d\n",i);
    }
    int *ret =(int*)malloc(sizeof(int));
    *ret=i;
    return (void*)ret;
}
int main()
{
    pthread_t t1,t2;
    int *ret1,*ret2;
```

```
        printf("Main Process\n");
        int n1=100;
        int n2=1000;
        pthread_create(&t1, NULL, task1, &n1);
        pthread_create(&t2, NULL, task2, &n2);

        if(pthread_join(t1, (void**)&ret1)!=0)
        {
                perror("Thread join error");
        }
        printf("Thread1 return value %d",*ret1);
        free(ret1);
        if(pthread_join(t2, (void**)&ret2)!=0)
        {
                perror("Thread join error");
        }
        printf("Thread2 return value %d",*ret2);
        free(ret2);

        printf("Main ends");
        return 0;
}
#gcc -o twotasks mthread.c -lpthread
#./twotasks
Main Process
..
Task1: 13
Task1: 14
Task2: 0
Task2: 10
Task2: 20

Thread1 return value 100Thread2 return value 1000Main ends
```

From the above code snippet and its execution, the following points must be noted down by developers:

- We created two threads, and specific tasks were assigned to the threads by passing the addresses of the specific functions, such as task1 and task2.

- Input arguments to a specific thread task are passed via the address of an input variable, and inside task1 and task2, the input variable (arg) is type casted to a specific data type (int).

- Since a thread task is a function, once function execution is over, the function stack memory will be automatically deallocated. Hence, to return any value from the thread task, developers must allocate dynamic memory inside the thread task and return the address (e.g., ret1) of the dynamically allocated memory block.

From the above code execution, the following points must be noted down by developers:

- The twotasks execution starts after the main process starts.

- After two threads are created, both threads are executed simultaneously. Hence, the results of Task1 and Task2 are overlapped in the display.

- The main process should wait for the two threads' execution to be completed using pthred_join. This step is helpful in the following ways:

  - To coordinate with threads and collect results (return values) from the threads.

  - To release thread resources in a reliable manner.

  - To avoid error-prone code in case of a greater number of threads to be managed.

- Threads share main process code, data, and heap segments. For instance, even if we allocated dynamic memory inside the thread tasks, the memory block is deallocated from the main.

- We can create two threads and assign the same task to both threads; then, both threads share the same code.

- For example: pthread_create(**&t1,** NULL, **task1,** &n1); and pthread_create(**&t2,** NULL, **task1,** &n2);

- Threads have their own stack segment only. Hence, it is necessary to pass input arguments (e.g., arg) to threads and return values (e.g., ret1) from threads to the calling function.

Explore the Power of Process Management Using C Programming

C developers can enjoy the power of creating multiple processes using fork() system calls and implement high-performance computing applications. First, we will discuss the following basic process management activities with respect to developers' role in handling parallel processing applications.

- Developer's role and activities in process management
- Creating a specific number of processes
- Control the multiple processes' execution order
- Create N processes and load them with executable images

Developers' Role and Activities in Process Management

On Linux systems using the fork system call, multiple-process applications are implemented. For example, to implement an application with n parallel processes, developers implement it by calling the fork system call a suitable number of times. Moreover, managing these processes must also be done by developers. Developers should decide the following basic activities in managing these multiple processes:

- **Assigning Specific Jobs to Each of the Processes**: Developers should carefully plan the number of processes to be created and assign them with suitable jobs. Every fork() call creates a child process from a parent process. Hence, it is necessary to track every parent process and child process carefully for assigning them with specific tasks.

Otherwise, OS resources such as processes and related resources will be wasted and lead to poor performance of the system. Developers should do the following activities for managing N processes:

- Ensure only one parent process exists.
- Create N children processes.
- Assign every child process with a specific task.
- The parent process should be waiting for each child process termination and collect the child process exit status.

- **Order in Which Multiple Processes Must Be Executed**: After the fork() call, both parent and child processes will be executed simultaneously. Hence, developers should decide the order of these multiple processes to be executed to avoid process coordination issues. Developers should do the following activities for controlling process execution order:

  - Identify process dependencies in terms of results collection and passing one process result to another process.
  - Use wait() and related system calls to control the order in which processes are to be created.
  - Collect termination status of child processes in their parent process.

- **Handling Process Exit Activities**: Every process is a heavy task, and it consumes various computational, memory, and IO resources. When multiple processes are created using fork, developers must take care of process exit activities in terms of handling process resource release activities in a graceful manner. Developers should do the following activities:

  - Free dynamically allocated memory
  - Close all opened files
  - Close network sockets
  - Collect process exit status to carry out any specific tasks

- **Handling Process Errors**: Processes created through fork() may generate various errors. Since these processes are created by developers, developers must handle these runtime errors for reliable process management. Otherwise the process behavior is unpredictable and leads to system or application crashes. Developers should do the following activities:
  - Write error handling code for failure of a process creation, termination, and waiting.
  - Write error handling code for failure of a process resource allocation, usage, and release activities.
  - Display suitable error messages for handling a variety of errors.

- **Handling Process Interrupts**: Interrupts are asynchronous events generated during process execution. In case a user-defined process does not handle these events, handling them improperly can lead to missing important events or unnecessary process termination. In C programs, these interrupts are known as signals. Developers should do the following activities:
  - Catch all possible signals to be generated in a specific application.
  - Specifically, catch all signals that can terminate user-defined processes to avoid process termination in an abrupt manner.
  - Handle all possible signals by writing custom signal handling code to ensure reliability of the application.

Besides the aforementioned basic process management activities, developers also decide the following important coordination activities in terms of managing multiple processes.

- How to share any data among the multiple processes?
- Setting up necessary interprocess communication resources.
- How to handle data race conditions during sharing of the data for ensuring reliable data sharing?

CHAPTER 6 PROCESS AND THREAD MANAGEMENT TASKS FOR C PROGRAMMERS

- How to coordinate and collect the results for any aggregation operations such as average, standard deviations, min, and max elements finding?

- How to avoid deadlocks among the processes in case of process dependencies?

- How to ensure high performance metrics for parallel applications in terms of throughput and latency?

We will discuss these interprocess coordination topics in detail in the upcoming Chapter 7, "Handle Interprocess Activities Using C Programming." Next, we will practice how to create a specific number of processes and handle them in a C program.

Creating a Specific Number of Processes

In this section, we will quickly learn how to create N processes, assign them with specific tasks, and run all N processes simultaneously. We do, specifically, the following activities:

- Create N processes as N child processes using the fork() system call

- Assign each child process with a sample task such as generating 20 numbers

- All N child processes run in parallel to generate the numbers

- Parent process should wait for all N children process to be terminated and collect their exit status

---
CREATE A SPECIFIC NUMBER OF PROCESSES

---

1. We implement the following activities in fork1.c:

    a. Take input to create a specific number of children processes.

    b. Assign each child process to generate 20 integer numbers.

    c. At the end of the 20 integer number generation, terminate each child process using exit with return status 0.

CHAPTER 6   PROCESS AND THREAD MANAGEMENT TASKS FOR C PROGRAMMERS

d. Handle process creation errors in a reliable manner.

e. On successful creation of a child process, collect the child process id into a child process id array.

```c
#include <stdio.h>
#include <stdlib.h>
#include <unistd.h>
#include <sys/wait.h>

int main()
{
    int ncp;
    printf("Enter number of child processes to be created");
    scanf("%d",&ncp);
    pid_t cpids[ncp];
    int i;
    for (i=0;i<ncp;i++)
    {
        cpids[i] = fork();
        if (cpids[i]<0)
        {
            perror("fork");
            return 1;
        }
        else if (cpids[i]==0)
        {
            for (int j=0;j<20;j++)
            {
                printf("Child process %d (PID: %d) generating: %d\n", i+1, getpid(),j);
            }
            printf("Child process %d (PID: %d) done\n", i + 1, getpid());
            exit(0);
        }
    }
```

CHAPTER 6   PROCESS AND THREAD MANAGEMENT TASKS FOR C PROGRAMMERS

2. Next, inside the parent process, we do the following activities:

   a. Wait for all child processes to be terminated.

   b. Collect each child's process termination status.

   c. After all child processes are terminated, the parent process can terminate automatically (without exit()).

   ```
   printf("Parent process (PID: %d) waiting for children...\n",
   getpid());
   for (i = 0;i<ncp;i++)
   {
           int status;
           pid_t pid = wait(&status);
           if (pid==-1)
           {
                   perror("wait");
                   return 1;
           }
           if (WIFEXITED(status))
           {
                   printf(" Child process %d exit status %d\n",
                   pid,WEXITSTATUS(status));
           }
   }
   printf("Parent process (PID: %d) Done\n", getpid());
   return 0;
   }
   ```

3. Save the fork1.c and execute it to observe the following results:

   a. All child processes are generating 20 integers.

   b. Child processes are executing simultaneously.

   c. After every child processes termination, the parent process is collecting exit status.

CHAPTER 6 PROCESS AND THREAD MANAGEMENT TASKS FOR C PROGRAMMERS

d. After all child processes terminate, the parent process also dies in a reliable manner.

```
#gcc fork1.c
#./a.out
Enter number of child processes to be created 3
Child process 1 (PID: 12817) generating: 1
Child process 1 (PID: 12817) generating: 2
..
Parent process (PID: 12816) waiting for children...
Child process 1 (PID: 12817) generating: 5
..
Child process 2 (PID: 12818) generating: 0
Child process 1 (PID: 12817) generating: 13
Child process 2 (PID: 12818) generating: 1
Child process 1 (PID: 12817) generating: 14
Child process 2 (PID: 12818) generating: 2
Child process 3 (PID: 12819) generating: 9
Child process 2 (PID: 12818) generating: 19
Child process 3 (PID: 12819) generating: 10
Child process 2 (PID: 12818) done
..
Child process 12817 exit status 0
 Child process 12818 exit status 0
 Child process 12819 exit status 0
Parent process (PID: 12816) Done
```

From the above overlapping processes' results, you can observe that N children processes are executed in parallel. It means using the `fork` system call; it is possible to create multiple processes and execute them in parallel in a reliable manner.

In this section, we have learned how to create a suitable number of processes using fork, assigning them a specific task, and waiting for their execution to be completed in a reliable manner. Next, we will learn how to control multiple processes' execution order in a reliable manner using `fork()` and `wait()` system calls.

Control the Multiple Processes Execution Order

In this section, we will learn the basics of how to order process execution termination orders and collect their return status using wait-related system calls:

pid_t waitpid(pid_t pid, int *wstatus, int options);

By default, waitpid() waits for a child process (pid) to be terminated. To change this default behavior, the following arguments can be passed:

- WNOHANG: To return immediately without waiting for the child to be exited.

- WCONTINUED: To return if an already stopped child process has been continued because of the signal (SIGCONT).

- WUNTRACED: To return if an untraced child process has been stopped.

It is also possible to wait for a specific child process or any child process by passing the suitable values to pid.

- pid: > 0 wait for a child process whose ID is equal to pid to be terminated.

- pid: < -1 wait for any child process to be terminated.

- pid: 0 wait for any child process group ID to be equal to the calling process group ID.

In this section, we will quickly learn how to create N processes, assign them with specific tasks, and control these N processes' order using waitpid. We do, specifically, the following activities:

- Create N processes as N child processes using the fork() system call.

- After a child process is terminated, then only the next child process should be created.

- Assign each child process with a sample task such as generating 20 numbers.

- Parent process waits for all N children processes to be terminated and collects their exit status

CHAPTER 6   PROCESS AND THREAD MANAGEMENT TASKS FOR C PROGRAMMERS

CONTROL PROCESSES ORDER OF EXECUTION

1. We implement the following activities in fork2.c:

    a. Take input to create a specific number of children processes, and create each child process in a specific order.

    b. Handle process creation errors in a reliable manner.

    c. On successful creation of a child process, collect its PID into a child process id array and assign the child process to generate 20 integer numbers.

    d. At the end of the 20 integer numbers generated by a process only, a new child process should be created.

    e. Terminate each child process using exit with return status 0.

    ```c
    #include <stdio.h>
    #include <stdlib.h>
    #include <unistd.h>
    #include <sys/wait.h>
    #include <stdio.h>
    #include <stdlib.h>
    #include <unistd.h>
    #include <sys/wait.h>

    int main()
    {
            int ncp = 3;
            pid_t cpids[ncp];
            int i;

            for (i=0;i<ncp;i++)
            {
                    cpids[i] = fork();
                    if (cpids[i]<0)
                    {
                            perror("fork");
                            return 1;
                    }
    ```

CHAPTER 6   PROCESS AND THREAD MANAGEMENT TASKS FOR C PROGRAMMERS

```
            else if (cpids[i]==0)
            {
                for (int j=0;j<20;j++)
                {
                    printf("Child Process%d (PID: %d)
                    generating: %d\n", i+1, getpid(),j);
                }
                printf("Child Process%d (PID: %d) done\n", i + 1,
                getpid());
                exit(0);
            }
```

2. Next, inside the parent process, we do the following activities:

   a. Use the child process id array (cpid), and pass the child process id to waitpid (cpid[i]) for waiting for the child process to be terminated.

   b. Collect each child's process termination status.

   c. After all child processes terminate, then only the parent process can terminate automatically (without exit()).

```
            else
            {
                printf("Parent process (PID: %d) waiting for
                children...\n", getpid());
                int status;
                pid_t pid = waitpid(cpids[i],&status,0);
                if (pid==-1)
                {
                    perror("wait");
                    return 1;
                }
                if (WIFEXITED(status))
                {
                    printf(" Child process%d exit status %d\n",
                    pid,WEXITSTATUS(status));
                }
            }
        }
```

```
            printf("Parent process (PID: %d) Done\n", getpid());
            return 0;
    }
```

3. Save the fork2.c and execute it to observe the following results:

    a. After a child process generates 20 integers completely, then only a new child process starts.

    b. Child processes are executed in a sequential manner.

    c. After every child processes termination, the parent process is collecting exit status.

    d. After all child processes terminate, the parent process also dies in a reliable manner.

    ```
    #gcc fork2.c
    #./a.out
    Parent process (PID: 13193) waiting for children...
    Child Process1 (PID: 13194) generating: 0
    Child Process1 (PID: 13194) generating: 1
    Child Process1 (PID: 13194) done
      Child process13194 exit status 0
    Parent process (PID: 13193) waiting for children...
    Child Process2 (PID: 13195) generating: 0
    Child Process2 (PID: 13195) generating: 1
    Child Process2 (PID: 13195) done
      Child process13195 exit status 0
    Parent process (PID: 13193) waiting for children...
    Child Process3 (PID: 13196) generating: 0
    Child Process3 (PID: 13196) generating: 1
    Child Process3 (PID: 13196) generating: 19
    Child Process3 (PID: 13196) done
      Child process13196 exit status 0
    Parent process (PID: 13193) Done
    ```

From the above results, you can observe that children processes are executed in a sequential order. It means using `waitpid`, it is flexible to control multiple processes' execution in a reliable manner.

In this section, we have learned how to control multiple processes' execution order in a reliable manner using fork() and wait() system calls. Next, we will learn how to load new processes with executable images in a flexible manner using fork()- and exec()-related system calls.

Create N Processes and Load Them with Executable Images

In this section, we use another important system call exec to load process images at runtime. On Linux, after calling fork, developers can use the following system calls to load parent or child processes' images with new executable images: execl, execlp, execle, execv, execvp, and execvpe. Developers are recommended to explore differences among these exec variants. Developers must understand the following details while using any exec variant to load existing executable images (e.g., ls, wc, or any executable program) in a new process:

- Fork creates a child process from a parent process, and developers confirm it by collecting the return value of fork(), which is zero. Moreover, the child process image is a duplicate of the parent process. It means both parent and child processes have their own copies of the following memory segments: stack, heap, data, and code.

- Using exec system calls, it is possible to load a new executable image memory stack, heap, data, and code segments into a process.

- For example: In the case of the ls command, its executable file contains its own code, data, heap, and stack segments. Then, after a child process is created using an exec-related system call, developers can pass the ls command executable file to load it in the child process. Hence, the child process executes the ls command using ls's code, data, heap, and stack memory segments.

  - Since the child process is loaded with a completely new process executable image, the child process cannot return to the parent process.

  - Developers must know exec status using perror and print the exit status for reliable execution.

CHAPTER 6   PROCESS AND THREAD MANAGEMENT TASKS FOR C PROGRAMMERS

In this book, we use the most reliable system call, execvp, to load process images into newly created processes using fork.

`int execvp(const char *file, char *const argv[]);` It takes the following important arguments:

- `const char *file`: It points to the path of the specific process image file (ls, ps, etc.) to be loaded. The default executable file search path includes /bin, /usr/bin, and the current working directory in order.
  - For example: If a developer wants to load the ls command using execvp, then execvp first searches for the ls command executable file in the /bin directory, then /usr/bin, then the current working directory.
- The `char *const argv[]` argument is an array of pointers to null-terminated strings such as a command and its arguments.
  - Developers should assign the first argument to the executable filename associated with a new process to be executed, then assign input arguments to be passed to the process, and finally assign a NULL pointer to terminate the list of input arguments.
  - For example, to load the ls command, then developers should assign arguments to argv as follows: `{"/bin/ls","-l",NULL}`. The first argument is the path of the ls command, then its input argument, finally terminated by NULL.

In this section, we will quickly learn how to create N processes, load each of these processes with unique commands using execvp. We do, specifically, the following activities:

- Create N processes as N child processes using the fork() system call.
- Assign each child process with a unique command to be executed.
- Allow all child processes to execute commands in parallel.
- Parent process waits for all N children processes to complete their commands execution and collect their exit status.

CHAPTER 6   PROCESS AND THREAD MANAGEMENT TASKS FOR C PROGRAMMERS

EXECUTE MULTIPLE COMMANDS PARALLELY USING EXECVP

1. We implement the following activities in fork3.c:

    a. Take input to create a specific number of children processes, which is 3, and create each child process in a specific order.

    b. Handle process creation errors in a reliable manner.

    c. On successful creation of a child process, collect its PID into a child process id array.

    d. Assign the following three commands to three child processes to execute in parallel

        i. Listing all files in the current working directory with option -l

        ii. Listing all processes executing with option -a

        iii. Listing various partitions of the hard disk with option -h

    e. Terminate each child process using exit with return status 0.

```c
#include <stdio.h>
#include <stdlib.h>
#include <unistd.h>
#include <sys/wait.h>
// int execv(const char *pathname, char *const argv[]);
int main()
{
    int ncp = 3;
    pid_t cpids[ncp];
    int i;

    char *cmds[][10] = {{"/bin/ls","-l",NULL},{"/bin/ps","-a",
    NULL},{"/bin/df","-h",NULL}};
    for (i=0;i<ncp;i++)
    {
        cpids[i] = fork();
        if (cpids[i]<0)
        {
            perror("fork");
```

```
                    return 1;
            }
            else if (cpids[i]==0)
            {
                    sleep(2);
                    execvp(cmds[i][0],cmds[i]);
                    perror("execvp ");
                    exit(0);
            }
    }
```

2. Next, inside the parent process, we do the following activities:

   a. Wait for all child processes to be terminated.

   b. Collect each child's process termination status.

   c. After child processes terminate, the parent process can terminate automatically (without exit()).

   ```
           printf("Parent process (PID: %d) waiting for children...\n",
           getpid());
           for (i = 0;i<ncp;i++)
           {
                   int status;
                   pid_t pid = wait(&status);
                   if (pid==-1)
                   {
                           perror("wait");
                           return 1;
                   }
                   if (WIFEXITED(status))
                   {
                           printf(" Chile %d exit status %d\n",
                           pid,WEXITSTATUS(status));
                   }
           }
           printf("Parent process (PID: %d) Done\n", getpid());
           return 0;
   }
   ```

CHAPTER 6　PROCESS AND THREAD MANAGEMENT TASKS FOR C PROGRAMMERS

3. Save the fork3.c and execute it to observe the following results:

   a. All child processes are executing their assigned commands.

   b. All child processes are executing commands in parallel.

   c. After every child processes termination, the parent process is collecting exit status.

   d. After all child processes terminate, the parent process also dies in a reliable manner.

   ```
   #gcc fork3.c
   #./a.out
   Parent process (PID: 16458) waiting for children...
   total 312
   prw-r--r-- 1 iiitdmk iiitdmk      0 Apr 29 12:13 american_maid
   -rwxrwxr-x 1 iiitdmk iiitdmk  17056 May  7 10:58 a.out
   -rw-rw-r-- 1 iiitdmk iiitdmk    645 Apr 29 15:18 fifo1.c
   -rw-rw-r-- 1 iiitdmk iiitdmk    970 Apr 29 15:22 fifo2.c

     Chile 16459 exit status 0
   Filesystem   Size  Used Avail Use% Mounted on
   udev         3.8G     0  3.8G   0% /dev
   tmpfs        774M  3.4M  771M   1% /run
   /dev/sda8    572G   86G  458G  16% /
   tmpfs        3.8G   12K  3.8G   1% /dev/shm
   tmpfs        5.0M  4.0K  5.0M   1% /run/lock
   tmpfs        3.8G     0  3.8G   0% /sys/fs/cgroup

     Chile 16461 exit status 0
       PID TTY          TIME CMD
      2295 tty1     00:00:04 Xorg
      3113 tty1     00:00:00 dbus-run-sessio
      3114 tty1     00:00:00 dbus-daemon
      3115 tty1     00:00:00 gnome-session-b
      3135 tty1     00:00:00 at-spi-bus-laun
      3140 tty1     00:00:00 dbus-daemon
   ```

CHAPTER 6   PROCESS AND THREAD MANAGEMENT TASKS FOR C PROGRAMMERS

```
     16458 pts/0     00:00:00 a.out
     16460 pts/0     00:00:00 ps
  Chile 16460 exit status 0
  Parent process (PID: 16458) Done
```

From the above results, you can observe that developers can use `fork` and `execvp` to load new processes at runtime in flexible manners. Hence, it is possible to easily create multiprocessing jobs in C using OS system calls such as `fork, exec, and wait`.

In this section, we have learned how to use well-known process management system calls and do the basic activities. In the next section, we are going to learn various issues to be handled during multiple processes' creation and handle them in a safe manner to achieve reliable results.

Safe and Reliable Programming Ways for Process Management

In this section, specifically, we will learn the importance of the following process management activities and how developers can handle these tasks in a reliable manner using safer codes:

- **Importance of Parent and Child Processes Exit Order**:
  The order of parent and child process termination is very important to handle the respective process-related resources management. For example, if a parent process is not waiting for its children process to terminate or not collecting children process termination status, it can lead to improper process resources handling from the system-wide perspective.
  It can lead to improper utilization of the following resources:

  - **Process Table**: During process management, it is a major resource used by OS to maintain processes entries for managing their information such as process id, state, scheduling information, and file descriptors. If a process entry exists in the process table, then the process resources are also available. Hence, when a process exits, the process entry must be removed from the process table

- When the OS creates processes, then the OS waits for termination of processes and takes care of removing entries of all exited processes.

- Developers are responsible for exiting and collecting the exit status of all processes created in an application. Otherwise, the application suffers from performance and security issues.

  - Memory
  - IO resources

- **Carefully Handle Data Sharing Activities Between Parent and Child Processes**: It is necessary for developers to handle how parent and child processes are using stack, heap, data, and code segments and how file descriptors are shared. Otherwise, it can lead to serious issues in terms of

  - Incorrect and inconsistent results
  - Data leakage and corruption
  - Security issues due to leakage of file or network socket descriptors

- **Reliable Ways of Executing a New Process in a Child Process**: It is necessary for developers to carefully load child processes with new process images to be executed and collect their execution exit status. Otherwise, it can lead to serious issues in terms of

  - Unpredictable results
  - No clues in terms of newly loaded process execution errors
  - May lead to creating unnecessarily new processes and wasting process-related resources

- **Importance of Interrupt Handling in Process Management**: It is necessary for developers to handle asynchronous events such as interrupts generated toward processes. Otherwise, it can lead to serious issues in terms of

  - Missing of handling important events
  - Termination of process by external interrupts

CHAPTER 6   PROCESS AND THREAD MANAGEMENT TASKS FOR C PROGRAMMERS

- Crashes of processes
- Unable to handle unexpected errors

Importance of Parent and Child Processes Exit Order

In earlier sections, we have learned how to ensure processes termination orders and collect their return status using `wait` system calls. Specifically using the `waipid` system call, it is possible to wait for a specific child process or any child process by passing the suitable values to pid. Waiting for a child process in its parent process is mandatory to handle child process termination gracefully and to release child process resources or any shared resources between them in a reliable manner. If a parent process does not wait for children processes, it can lead to

- Handling of orphan processes
- Handling of zombie processes

Orphan Process

On Linux OS, if a parent process dies (or execution is completed) before its children processes execution, then active children processes become orphan processes. All these orphan processes are handled by a special process in the Linux OS called the init process (PID 1). The Linux `init` process handles the orphan processes. For example, the following code leads to orphan processes, because in the following code, the child process is waiting for 4 seconds; during this time, the parent process will be exited, then the child processes become orphan processes.

```
#include <stdio.h>
#include <stdlib.h>
#include <unistd.h>
int main()
{
    pid_t ret;
    ret = fork();
    if (ret<0)
```

```c
    {
        perror("fork failed");
    }
    if (ret==0)
    {
        printf("child process created %d\n",getpid());
        printf("child process parent %d\n",getppid());
        sleep(4);
        printf("orphan process parent %d\n",getppid());
        exit(0);
    }
    if (ret>0)
    {
        printf("Parent process%d\n",getpid());
        sleep(1);
        exit(0);
    }
}
```

An orphan process can lead to the following issues:

- OS may not handle orphan processes immediately and release their resources. Hence, during this period,
  - Child processes holding resources can be leaked to other processes.
  - Improper handling of child resources can lead to performance degradation issues especially if child processes are consuming heavy computational, memory, and network resources.
  - Security issues can arise due to malicious processes can sniff the orphan processes and their processes.
- Debugging an orphan process is a challenging task.

CHAPTER 6   PROCESS AND THREAD MANAGEMENT TASKS FOR C PROGRAMMERS

Zombie Process

If a parent process creates a child process, then the parent process must wait for the child process termination using wait or waitpid and handle the child process resources in a reliable manner. After all child processes of a parent process are terminated, then only the parent process should exit; otherwise, the child processes become zombie processes. Zombie processes are also known as defunct processes on Linux OS.

Zombie processes are more dangerous than orphan processes. Because these processes will not be handled by either parent or the Linux process (init). A zombie process will be created when the parent process is not waiting for a child process to be terminated and not collecting the child process exit status. For example, the following code leads to zombie processes. Because in the following code, the child process dies before the parent process, and the parent process is not waiting for its child process.

```c
#include <unistd.h>
#include <stdio.h>
#include <stdlib.h>
int main()
{
    pid_t ret;
    ret = fork();
    if (ret<0)
    {
        perror("fork failed");
    }
    if (ret==0)
    {
        printf("child process created %d\n",getpid());
        exit(0);

    }
```

```
        if (ret>0)
        {
            int stat;
            sleep(3);
            printf("Parent process\n");
        }
        printf("Task to be done\n");
}
```

Using the following command, we can check for zombie processes: `ps aux | grep Z`.

A zombie process can lead to the following issues:

- OS does not handle zombie processes and release their resources.

- Child process-related process table entries will not be removed automatically.

- Hence, it is not possible to automatically release process table entries and related process resources, file descriptors, and socket descriptors. It means leakage of computational resources; files and network sockets are possible. Hence, security issues are also possible.

- Performance issues can arise due to a large number of zombie processes. OS may not be able to create new child processes due to the lack of process table entries and inability to allocate computational and other necessary resources.

- Debugging a zombie process is a challenging task.

Handle Carefully Data Sharing Activities Between Parent and Child Processes

In this section, we discuss the following concepts related to parent and child process resource sharing:

- Parent and child processes' segments (code, data, heap, and stack)

- Sharing of file descriptors between parent and child processes

Parent and Child Processes' Segments

In this section, we will learn the basics of data sharing between parent and child processes. We define sample variables in the below program to allocate sample data in the data segment (global), stack segment (local), and heap segment (p allocated dynamic memory) of parent and child processes.

```c
//sharing1.c
#include <unistd.h>
#include <sys/wait.h>
#include <stdio.h>
#include <stdlib.h>
int global=100;
int main()
{
    pid_t ret;
    ret = fork();
    int local=200;
    int *p=(int*)malloc(sizeof(int));
    *p=300;
    if (ret<0)
    {
        perror("fork failed");
    }
    if (ret==0)
    {
        printf("child process created %d\n",getpid());
        printf("Parent process id %d\n",getppid());
        printf("Parent copy global %d\n",global);
        printf("Parent copy local %d\n",local);
        global=100*10;
        local=local*10;
        *p=600;
        printf("Child copy global %d\n",global);
        printf("Child copy local %d\n",local);
        printf("Child heap copy %d\n",*p);
```

```c
//      free(p);
        exit(0);
    }
    if (ret>0)
    {
        int stat;
        printf("Parent process\n");
        printf("Inside Parent copy global %d\n",global);
        printf("Inside Parent copy local %d\n",local);
        global=100*5;
        local=local*5;
        *p=800;
        printf("Inside Parent copy global %d\n",global);
        printf("Inside Parent copy local %d\n",local);
        printf("Inside Parent heap copy %d\n",*p);
        pid_t cpid;
        cpid=waitpid(ret,&stat,0);
        if (cpid==-1)
        {
            perror("wait");
            return 1;
        }
        if (WIFEXITED(stat))
        {
            printf(" Child process %d exit status %d\n",
                cpid,WEXITSTATUS(stat));
        }
//      free(p);
    }
    printf("Task to be done\n");
}
```

Then, we executed updated code as follows:

```
#gcc sharing1.c
#./a.out
Parent process
```

```
Inside Parent copy global 100
Inside Parent copy local 200
Inside Parent copy global 500
Inside Parent copy local 1000
Inside Parent heap copy 800

child process created 23487
Parent process id 23486
Parent copy global 100
Parent copy local 200
Child copy global 1000
Child copy local 2000
Child heap copy 600

 Child process 23487 exit status 0
Task to be done
```

From the above code snippet execution, the following processes' data sharing details must be noted down by developers:

- Both parent and child have their own copies of code, data, stack, and heap segments.

- Parent and child processes have their own copies of stack segments; hence, both processes set their own values to `local` variables and access their private copies, respectively.

- Similarly, parent and child processes have their own copies of data segments; hence, both processes set their own values to `global` variables and access their private copies, respectively.

- Even parent and child processes have their own copies of heap segments; hence, both processes set their own values to pointer variables (p) allocated memory blocks and access their private copies, respectively.

Next, let's check if there are any invisible errors, such as memory leaks, in the above code using the `valgrind` tool:

Use Valgrind to Check Processes for Memory Leaks

Let's execute the above code using the following commands:

`#gcc -g sharing1.c`

Use the following `valgrind` command with the `trace-children` option to track children's process memory and file leaks:

`#valgrind --tool=memcheck --trace-children=yes --track-fds=yes ./a.out`

```
==32713== HEAP SUMMARY:
==32713==    in use at exit: 4 bytes in 1 blocks
==32713==    total heap usage: 2 allocs, 1 frees, 1,028 bytes allocated
==32713==
==32713== LEAK SUMMARY:
==32713==    definitely lost: 0 bytes in 0 blocks
==32713==    indirectly lost: 0 bytes in 0 blocks
==32713==    possibly lost: 0 bytes in 0 blocks
==32713==    still reachable: 4 bytes in 1 blocks
==32713==         suppressed: 0 bytes in 0 blocks
```

From the above results, we can observe that there are memory leaks due to dynamic memory allocation and not releasing the dynamically allocated memory blocks. We should release these memory blocks using the `free` system call in both parent and child processes. (Before testing this code, uncomment free() in the source code.)

Let's execute the corrected code using the following commands:

`#gcc -g sharing1.c`

Then, use `valgrind` to quickly check any memory leaks using the following command:

```
#valgrind --tool=memcheck --trace-children=yes --track-fds=yes ./a.out
==32818== HEAP SUMMARY:
==32818==    in use at exit: 0 bytes in 0 blocks
==32818==    total heap usage: 2 allocs, 2 frees, 1,028 bytes allocated
==32818==
==32818== All heap blocks were freed -- no leaks are possible
```

Now, we can observe that both parent and child processes are not causing any memory leaks. Hence, this application terminated in a graceful manner.

Sharing of File Descriptors Between Parent and Child Processes

In this section, we will learn how parent and child processes share file descriptors for accessing files by implementing the following code in `sharing2.c`:

- First in the main process, a file will be opened in read mode only.

- After successfully opening the file, in the main process, `fork` is called to create a child process.

- Now two processes are executing simultaneously.

- Then, both the parent and child processes share file descriptors opened prior to the `fork()` call, since a file is opened and its descriptor is available to both the child and parent processes.

- In the child process, it reads 4 bytes from the file descriptor and writes on the standard output descriptor. Then it will be exited using `exit()`. Do not close the file.

- The parent process waits for the child process to exit and then reads 4 bytes from the file descriptor and writes on the standard output descriptor. After reading from the file, close the file.

```
#include <stdio.h>
#include <stdlib.h>
#include <fcntl.h>
#include <unistd.h>
#include <sys/stat.h>
#include <sys/wait.h>
int main()
{
    const char *filename = "fork1.c";
    int fd;
    ssize_t bytes_read;
    char buffer[1024];
```

```c
fd = open(filename, O_RDONLY);
if (fd == -1)
{
    perror("Error opening file");
    return 1;
}
pid_t ret=fork();
if (ret==-1)
{
    perror("fork");
    return 1;
}
if (ret==0)
{
    bytes_read = read(fd, buffer, 4);
    if (bytes_read == -1)
    {
        perror("Error reading file");
        close(fd);
        return 1;
    }
    write(1, buffer, bytes_read);
//    close(fd);
    exit(0);
}
if (ret>0)
{
    waitpid(ret,NULL,0);
    bytes_read = read(fd, buffer, 4);
    if (bytes_read == -1)
    {
        perror("Error reading file");
        close(fd);
        return 1;
    }
    write(1, buffer, bytes_read);
```

```
                if (close(fd) == -1)
                {
                        perror("Error closing file");
                        return 1;
                }
        }
        return 0;
}
#gcc sharing2.c
#./a.out
```

On executing the above program, we can observe the following message and details:

#include

- First the child process reads the first 4 bytes (**#inc**) and prints them onto the output screen.

- Then, the parent process reads from the same file the next 4 bytes (**lude**), and it prints on to the output screen.

- Since both processes are sharing the same file descriptor, when one process updates the file descriptor value, it is visible to the other process. In this example, since the child process changed the file descriptor by reading the first 4 bytes, the parent process is reading the subsequent 4 bytes from the same file.

Next, let's check if there are any invisible errors, such as file and memory leaks, in the above code using the `valgrind` tool:

Use Valgrind to Check File Descriptor Leaks

Let's execute the above code using the following commands:

```
#gcc -g sharing2.c
```

Use the `valgrind` tool to quickly check if any memory and file leaks are possible in the above code with the `trace-children` and `track-fds` options:

```
#valgrind --tool=memcheck --trace-children=yes --track-fds=yes ./a.out

==31997== FILE DESCRIPTORS: 4 open at exit.
==31997== Open file descriptor 3: fork1.c
==31997==    at 0x498BD3B: open (open64.c:48)
==31997==    by 0x10926D: main (sharing2.c:11)
==31997==
==31997== Open file descriptor 2: /dev/pts/0
==31997==    <inherited from parent>
==31997==
==31997== Open file descriptor 1: /dev/pts/0
==31997==    <inherited from parent>
==31997==
==31997== Open file descriptor 0: /dev/pts/0
==31997==    <inherited from parent>
==31997==
```

Ideally at the end of the program execution, only standard input, output, and error descriptors should be open. But it is showing four descriptors. This behavior is due to the child process not closing its file, and hence, valgrind showing four descriptors is open.

Next, let's close the file in the child process and run the program again to observe the correct results:

```
//    close(fd);
```

```
#valgrind --tool=memcheck --trace-children=yes --track-fds=yes ./a.out
==32285== FILE DESCRIPTORS: 3 open at exit.
```

Now from the output, we can observe that only standard input, output, and error descriptors are open. Hence, using valgrind, it is easier to detect and correct file descriptor leakages and correct them in a graceful manner.

CHAPTER 6   PROCESS AND THREAD MANAGEMENT TASKS FOR C PROGRAMMERS

Reliable Ways of Executing a New Process in a Child Process

In this section, we will learn the possible issues during a child process executing a new process from the executable file:

- We create parent and child processes. Then, assign the parent process to execute the ps command and the child process to execute the ls commands.

- If the parent and child processes execute the given commands successfully, there are no issues to be handled.

- If the parent or child process fails to execute the given commands, then it is necessary to collect exit status and print the error messages. Otherwise, there is no clue about the failure of executing those commands. It leads to difficulty in debugging applications.

- To solve these issues in a reliable manner, we use perror and exit system calls after execvp. These system calls help to correctly track execvp errors and the process exit status.

To do this task, we use the following code in reliableps.c by commenting out perror and exit system calls and passing the correct commands to parent and child processes:

```
#include <sys/wait.h>
#include <stdio.h>
#include <stdlib.h>
int main()
{
    pid_t ret;
    ret = fork();
    if (ret<0)
    {
        perror("fork failed");
    }
```

```c
        if (ret==0)
        {
                char *cmd[] = {"ls", "-l", NULL};
                execvp(cmd[0],cmd);
                // perror("execvp");
                // exit(EXIT_FAILURE);
        }
        if (ret>0)
        {
                int stat;
                printf("Parent process\n");
                pid_t cpid;
                cpid=waitpid(ret,&stat,0);
                if (cpid==-1)
                {
                        perror("wait");
                        return 1;
                }
                if (WIFEXITED(stat))
                {
                        printf(" Child process %d exit status %d\n",
                        cpid,WEXITSTATUS(stat));
                }
                char *cmd[] = {"ps", "-a", NULL};
                execvp(cmd[0],cmd);
                // perror("execvp");
                //exit(EXIT_FAILURE);
        }
}
```

Then, we executed updated code as follows:

```
#gcc reliableps.c
#./a.out
Parent process
total 356
```

CHAPTER 6   PROCESS AND THREAD MANAGEMENT TASKS FOR C PROGRAMMERS

```
prw-r--r-- 1 iiitdmk iiitdmk      0 Apr 29 12:13 american_maid
-rwxrwxr-x 1 iiitdmk iiitdmk  16968 May 13 15:07 a.out
-rw-rw-r-- 1 iiitdmk iiitdmk   1624 May  8 11:44 cmd3p.c
-rw-rw-r-- 1 iiitdmk iiitdmk   2151 May  9 15:39 cmdnpic.c
 Child process 29591 exit status 0
   PID TTY          TIME CMD
  2314 tty1     00:00:04 Xorg
  3128 tty1     00:00:00 dbus-run-sessio
  3129 tty1     00:00:00 dbus-daemon
  3136 tty1     00:00:00 gnome-session-b
  3145 tty1     00:00:00 at-spi-bus-laun
  3150 tty1     00:00:00 dbus-daemon
```

From the above code snippet execution, the following details must be observed by developers:

- No issues are found, and processes are terminated properly.
- Next, we pass the incorrect commands, such as aps and bls, to parent and child processes, respectively.

Then, we execute the code, and developers should observe that there is no clue about failures of child or parent processes. Moreover, it is showing the child process executed successfully without errors by returning exit status 0. It can lead to wrong assumptions about the application code and difficult to handle these bugs.

```
#gcc reliableps.c
#./a.out
Parent process
 Child process 21298 exit status 0
```

Then, we execute the above code by using perror and exit system calls in parent and child processes after execvp to track errors and exit status in a reliable manner. After executing the code, developers should observe that it is showing execvp failure reasons and the correct exit status = 1 (fail to execute the command) for the child process.

```
#gcc reliableps.c
#./a.out
```

```
Parent process
execvp: No such file or directory
 Child process 29663 exit status 1
execvp: No such file or directory
```

In this section, we have learned how to track process errors and exit status in reliable manners. Next, we will learn how to handle various asynchronous events generated toward processes in reliable manners using signals.

Importance of Interrupt Handling in Process Management

In this section, we will learn how to handle asynchronous events (interrupts) toward processes in a reliable manner using Linux signal handling concepts. It is important to handle interrupts in an application due to the following reasons:

- Interrupts are helpful in terms of handling high-priority tasks on an urgent basis. When a process receives an interrupt, the process addresses it by executing the corresponding interrupt-related service code.

- On Linux OS, interrupts are implemented using signals and related system calls. Linux supports a long list of signals; we discuss the following important, commonly used signals related to reliable process termination and asynchronous events and errors handling:

    - SIGINT: It is generated when a user presses Ctrl+C or by the system call kill (SIGINT, pid) to terminate a process. The default action to handle this signal is terminating the process.

    - SIGTERM: This signal is generated toward a process to terminate it. It can be generated by the system call kill (SIGTERM, pid). Default action to handle this signal is terminating the process.

    - SIGPIPE: It is generated toward a process when it attempts to write to a file descriptor (pipe or socket) and the descriptor read end is closed. The default action to handle this signal is terminating the process.

- Developers can register for these signals and handle them as per application needs, such as terminating the process by a suitable message or ignoring the signal and continuing the process execution.
- It is important to handle these signals in applications to avoid unwanted termination of processes by malicious processes generated signals (SIGINT, SIGPIPE, or SIGTERM).

- SIGCHLD: When a child process terminates, then the parent process receives this signal. The default action to handle this signal is ignoring the signal, and the parent process can continue its execution.
  - Developers can register for this signal and handle all child processes' exit status in a reliable manner.

- SIGSEGV: When a process executes invalid read or write operations against memory, then this signal is generated. The default action to handle this signal is generating a core dump file and terminating the process.
  - Developers can register for this signal and terminate the process in a graceful manner.

- SIGKILL: This signal is useful to terminate a process immediately in a forceful manner. The default action to handle this signal is terminating the process.
  - Developers cannot register for this signal. Hence, it cannot be caught or ignored.

- SIGUSR1 and SIGUSR2: These signals are known as user-defined interrupts. Default action to handle these signals is terminating the process.
  - Developers can register for these signals and define customized application behavior to handle these signals.

CHAPTER 6   PROCESS AND THREAD MANAGEMENT TASKS FOR C PROGRAMMERS

In C programs, developers can implement signal handling tasks using the following system call from the library: #include <signal.h>

int sigaction(int signum, const struct sigaction *act, struct sigaction *oldact);

This system call is used to change the default signal behaviors and execute customized signal handling tasks. However, the following signals' default behavior cannot be changed: SIGKILL and SIGSTOP. It takes the following important arguments:

- int signum: We should pass the signal number or corresponding macros such as SIGINT, etc., to be registered in our application.
- const struct sigaction *act: We should pass a sigaction structure by filling the following fields:
  - sa_handler: Set a pointer to the address of a signal handling function (fun_name). This function signature should be as follows: void fun_name (int signum);
  - sa_mask: Set list of signals to be masked or blocked.
  - sa_flags: Possible to set flags while handling signals. For example, setting the flags as SA_RESTART to restart an interrupted system call.
  - Example: struct sigaction sa;

    sa. = signal_handler;
    sigemptyset(&sa.sa_mask);
    sa.sa_flags = 0;
    sa.mask = 0;
- struct sigaction *oldact: We should pass the NULL to this pointer for overriding the default behavior to handle the signal.
- In our testing, we generate a signal using the kill system call:
  - Example: kill(pid,SIGTERM);

CHAPTER 6 PROCESS AND THREAD MANAGEMENT TASKS FOR C PROGRAMMERS

We use the reliableps.c and do the following tasks to handle the following signals:

- SIGTERM, SIGINT, and SIGPIPE: On receiving these signals, instead of terminating the process, we print customized messages and continue the process execution. It means if any malicious process generated these signals, we are ignoring them and handling them in a reliable manner.

- SIGSEGV: On receiving this signal, we print the customized message and exit the process in a reliable manner.

- To handle these signals, we include the following code snippets in the existing code of reliableps.c

```c
#include <unistd.h>
#include <sys/wait.h>
#include <stdio.h>
#include <stdlib.h>
void signal_handler(int signum)
{
    printf("Signal %d received by process %d\n", signum, getpid());
    if (signum == SIGTERM)
    {
        printf("Process interrupted\n");
    }

    if (signum == SIGINT)
    {
        printf("Process interrupted\n");
    }
    if (signum == SIGPIPE)
    {
        printf("Pipe error\n");
    }
```

```c
        if (signum == SIGSEGV)
        {
            printf("Process segfault handled\n");
            exit(1);
        }
    }
}
int main()
{
    struct sigaction sa;
    sa.sa_handler = signal_handler;
    sigemptyset(&sa.sa_mask);
    sa.sa_flags = 0;
    if (sigaction(SIGINT, &sa, NULL) == -1)
    {
        perror("sigaction");
        exit(1);
    }
    if (sigaction(SIGTERM, &sa, NULL) == -1)
    {
        perror("sigaction");
        exit(1);
    }
    if (sigaction(SIGSEGV, &sa, NULL) == -1)
    {
        perror("sigaction");
        exit(1);
    }
    if (sigaction(SIGPIPE, &sa, NULL) == -1)
    {
        perror("sigaction");
        exit(1);
    }
    ..
}
```

Then, we executed updated code as follows:

```
#gcc reliableps.c
#./a.out
Parent process
Signal 15 received by process 30877
Process interrupted
Signal 13 received by process 30878
Pipe error

total 356
prw-r--r-- 1 iiitdmk iiitdmk        0 Apr 29 12:13 american_maid
-rwxrwxr-x 1 iiitdmk iiitdmk    16968 May 13 15:07 a.out
-rw-rw-r-- 1 iiitdmk iiitdmk     1624 May  8 11:44 cmd3p.c
-rw-rw-r-- 1 iiitdmk iiitdmk     2151 May  9 15:39 cmdnpic.c
    PID TTY          TIME CMD
   2314 tty1     00:00:04 Xorg
   3128 tty1     00:00:00 dbus-run-sessio
   3129 tty1     00:00:00 dbus-daemon
   3136 tty1     00:00:00 gnome-session-b
   3145 tty1     00:00:00 at-spi-bus-laun
   3150 tty1     00:00:00 dbus-daemon
```

From the above code snippet execution, the following points must be noted down by developers:

- Both parent and child processes are executed successfully.
- All signals (SIGINT, SIGTERM, and SIGPIPE) are handled in a reliable manner without terminating the process. It means we can stop unwanted termination signals toward a process.
- We suggest generating a segmentation fault by doing invalid read or write memory operations in reliableps.c, executing it, and observing the results of catching SIGSEGV as a learning task.

In this section, we have learned how to manage multiple processes in a reliable manner. Next, we will learn how to manage multiple threads using C programming in a reliable manner and ensure high performance.

… CHAPTER 6　PROCESS AND THREAD MANAGEMENT TASKS FOR C PROGRAMMERS

Explore Power of Threads Management Using C Programming

In C programming, threads can be created and managed in a flexible manner using the pthreads library. C functions, arrays, structures, and pointers play an important role in managing multiple threads. For instance, functions are the key blocks in assigning tasks to threads. Developers can define a function and implement a specific task before assigning it to a thread. Moreover, functions can be easily tested and verified for implementing multitasking applications in a modular way. Further, C built-in data structures arrays are very helpful in carefully partitioning and assigning data to multiple threads simultaneously. Structures and pointers are very helpful in passing input data and collecting results from thread tasks in flexible and efficient manners. In this section, we will start with discussing the developer's role in threads management tasks in detail and then carry out important hands-on activities for practicing implementation of multithreading applications.

Developer's Role in Threads Management

C developers must know how to implement a suitable number of threads and manage them in reliable and efficient manners to implement high-performance multitasking applications. We discuss the following key roles of developers to implement multithreading applications:

- Creating threads and assigning tasks
- Challenges in assigning tasks and respective data to threads
- Common threads of performance issues and solutions

Creating Threads and Assigning Tasks

In order to achieve maximum benefits from threads, it is necessary to allow threads to run independently and complete their execution in reliable manners. Hence, developers must plan for dividing a large task into smaller independent tasks and allocate them with suitable input data. C programmers can do it by using the following important C features:

- **Functions**: Functions are helpful to implement smaller independent tasks and assign them to threads. Mainly functions are helpful in careful partitioning of a complex task and implementing it as independently executable subtasks.
  - Implement a suitable number of functions.
  - Assign each function to a specific thread for parallel execution.
  - Execute the same function by multiple threads for further parallel execution:
    - It needs carefully partitioning input data among multiple threads and handling threads coordination and communication issues.
- **Arrays**: In order to pass a large-size list of elements, arrays are very helpful due to their call by reference passing approach to functions. Moreover, arrays' flexible indexing approaches help in carefully partitioning a large input list of elements among threads.
  - Arrays indexing simplifies partitioning and assigning data to threads. For example, an N-element list is divided among K threads by assigning **start** and **end** indices to threads by passing the array by its name and its start and end indices to the thread function arguments.
- **Structures**: Structures are helpful in easily handling complex data structure implementation and passing them to threads for efficient data access.
  - Useful to combine multiple logical arguments under a structure variable and pass it to a thread function using call by reference approach.
- **Pointers**: Pointers offer flexibility and power to pass arguments and functions and access threads' data in efficient manners.

In case of developing a multitasking application in a parallel manner, it is necessary to first partition the complex or large task as N smaller tasks and implement them using C functions as follows:

```
void *task1(void *arg)
{
      ..
}
void *task2(void *arg)
{
      ..
}
void *taskN(void *arg)
{
      ..
}
```

Then, the main() process can create a suitable number of threads and assign each of the tasks to specific threads and wait for the threads to complete their tasks as follows:

```
int main()
{
      pthread_create(&t1, NULL, task1, &n1);
..
      pthread_create(&tN, NULL, task2, &n2);
      if(pthread_join(t1, (void**)&ret1)!=0)
      {
            perror("Thread join error");
      }
      printf("Thread1 return value %d",*ret1);
..
      free(ret1);
      if(pthread_join(tN, (void**)&ret2)!=0)
      {
            perror("Thread join error");
      }
}
```

CHAPTER 6   PROCESS AND THREAD MANAGEMENT TASKS FOR C PROGRAMMERS

Next, it is necessary to partition the input list of elements carefully among n threads. This task can be handled by using structures, arrays, and indexing approaches. For example, a list of elements needs to be divided among N threads, then we need to partition the list and pass necessary arguments to threads executing functions for accessing their specific partition. It can be handled by creating a `struct` containing the following data elements to access the specified partition by a thread:

```c
typedef struct
{
        int* list; //Address of the list
        int start; //Starting index of the list w.r.t thread
        int end;//End of the list w.r.t thread

} FunArgs;
```

Next, based on the number of threads (`nthrds`), divide the list size (n) uniformly as follows:

```c
int npt = n / nthrds;
```

In case of any elements remaining after uniform division, assign them to the last thread as follows:

```c
int remels = n % nthrds;
```

Finally, we can go through the list of threads and pass the respective partition to the threads' specific Task as follows:

```c
FunArgs args[nthrds];
int start = 0;
for (int i = 0; i < nthrds; i++)
{
        ..
        args[i].list = list;
        args[i].start = start;
        args[i].end = start + npt;
        if (i == nthrds - 1)
        {
                args[i].end += remels;
        }
```

```
    pthread_create(&threads[i], NULL, Task, &args[i]);
    start = args[i].end;
    ..
}
```

In the next section, we will discuss the various problems to handle and suitable solutions during the implementation of multithreaded applications.

Challenges in Assigning Specific Tasks and Data to Threads

Threads should run as independently as possible to maximize parallel execution. It means coordination between threads should be minimized. It is easier to carry out a variety of tasks in parallel that are not accessing (write operation) shared data elements. For instance, given the following tasks:

- Find an element from a list of n elements
- Compute mean value of n elements
- Find the maximum element from a list of n elements

We can parallelize the given three tasks' execution by creating independent functions and assigning them to three threads.

However, in the case of parallelizing each task (e.g., finding the mean) using N threads, then the following challenges arise:

- **Data Dependencies**: It is necessary to divide the input list among N threads, wait for each thread's results, and collectively take a decision or compute the final result.
  - For instance, to compute the mean of N elements, we used k threads in main, then the main process should wait for all k threads, then
    - Collect k threads of intermediate sum results and then find the mean value
- **Critical Sections Access**: Sometimes due to code and data sharing activities, multiple threads need to execute the shared code and data in a reliable manner.

- For instance, in the case of computing the mean value of a list of n elements, intermediate sum computations can be done using simply a global sum variable. But it leads to race conditions for thread computations and leads to inconsistent results.
  - It demands converting shared code and data into critical sections and accessing it through synchronization approaches such as mutex locks or semaphores.
- **Synchronization Approaches**: Necessary to use locks (mutex or semaphore) over shared resources or data for controlling critical section code access. Synchronization approaches to access a critical section must offer the following properties:
  - **Mutual Exclusion**: At a time only one process should access the critical section code.
  - **Progress**: Once a process leaves the critical section, then one of the waiting processes should enter into the critical section and access the code.
  - **Bounded Waiting**: No process should wait indefinitely to access a critical section.
- Synchronization approaches such as mutex locks ensure reliable access to a critical section, but the following overheads are possible:
  - Necessary to handle locking issues and latencies.
  - Starvation issues must be handled to offer fair access chances of shared resources or data to all threads.
  - An incorrect way of implementing locking approaches could lead to the following conditions while executing multiple threads
    - **Mutual Exclusion**: Once a thread acquires a specific lock, all other threads that need the lock must wait until the thread releases the lock.
    - **Hold and Wait**: It is possible that a thread can acquire a lock (l1) and wait for another lock (l2) to acquire.

- **No Preemption**: Usually, it is not possible to stop a thread while it is executing in the critical section.

- **Circular Wait**: Multiple threads may wait for shared locks in a circular fashion. For example, thread-1 acquired lock-1 and simultaneously thread-2 acquired lock-2, then it is possible for thread-1 to be waiting for lock-2 and thread-2 to be waiting for lock-1.

- Because of the incorrect way of implementing locks, if multiple threads while accessing a critical section face all the above conditions, it leads to deadlock. It means no thread among the multiple threads is able to continue its execution. Hence, it is necessary to carefully check locking-related codes and correct these issues.

- **Organize Data Carefully**: Organizing the shared data carefully to avoid inefficient utilization of shared cache lines and memory

  - Improper division of a large array among N threads can lead to poor cache and memory utilization

  - False sharing of cache lines

  - Unnecessary padding of arrays

  - Unnecessary locking approaches implementation overheads for handling global arrays in reliable manners

- **Flow Dependencies**: Waiting for other threads' tasks to complete before proceeding further with computation or decision-making steps.

  - For instance, if we want to implement a binary search algorithm over N elements, then we create K+1 threads. One thread to sort elements and k threads to search the list of elements.

    - All k-searching threads must wait for the sorting thread to complete.

In the next section, we will discuss important solutions to these common issues.

CHAPTER 6   PROCESS AND THREAD MANAGEMENT TASKS FOR C PROGRAMMERS

Common Threads Issues and Respective Solutions

In case of implementing a multitasking application, developers must handle the following tasks to ensure reliable and high-performance results:

Critical Section and Synchronization Issues Handling Tasks

In this section, we will discuss how to handle data dependency issues among multiple threads. In case of implementing a multitasking application, it is necessary to share some data and coordinate data and results among threads. However, if multiple threads are accessing shared data, their read and write operations over the shared data could lead to the following conflict operations:

- **Read Write or Write Read**: Simultaneously, one thread is reading shared variable data, and the other thread is writing to the shared data
- **Write Write**: Both threads are writing data into shared variable simultaneously

Developers must handle these conflict operations carefully to get reliable results from multiple threads' execution. For example, in the case of multiple threads accessing a global variable counter simultaneously, it can lead to incorrect results. For example, when two threads access the global counter variable in the following shared code snippet, it can result in incorrect results:

```
int counter=0;
void task()
{
     counter = counter+1;
}
```

If two threads execute the task() for 1000 times simultaneously, at the end of the threads' execution, the resultant value of the counter must be equal to the serial execution of the two threads. Since the counter is updated by each of the threads by 1000 times, the final value of the counter must be 2000. But the counter updating instruction at assembly-level code is similar to the following code snippet:

```
move reg, counter;
Add reg, 1;
move counter, reg;
```

In this case, developers must understand these three assembly instructions are simultaneously executed by the two threads, and due to the possibility of interleaving of these instructions, execution can lead to inconsistent results. It is known as threads' race **conditions**.

- For example, using **move reg, counter** instruction thread-1 copied the **counter** value 0 to **reg** and incremented the **register** value to 1 using the next instruction **Add**.

- Before thread-1 executes **move counter, reg** instruction if thread-2 starts executing **move reg, counter**, then it sets the **reg** value to 0.

- Then, if thread-1 starts executing its next instruction **move counter, reg**, then it results in the **counter** value being 0 which is incorrect.

  - Since thread-1 executed its entire code, and at the end of the thread-1 execution, the **counter** value must be 1. But due to incorrect interleaving, the **counter** value is 0, and it is incorrect.

The above sample code is technically called **critical section** code. While accessing critical sections, threads suffer from race conditions, and it must be handled by developers to guarantee parallel execution results of N threads are equal to one of the serial executions of N threads. Hence, threads must execute the critical section code in a reliable manner to ensure consistent and correct results by using synchronization tools such as locking.

Pthreads Mutex Objects for Locking and Synchronization

In pthreads for safe interleaving, read and write conflict operations of critical section code issues are solved by using mutex locks. For example, in the case of sharing the counter variable among multiple threads, threads must acquire a lock to enter into the critical section and release the locks after exiting the critical section of the code.

For example, C developers use a mutex lock variable to access the critical section by using the following mutex-related accessing functions:

- First define and initialize a mutex variable using the following library function. It is helpful to allocate storage space for a mutex object and initialize it with a suitable value.

    ```
    int pthread_mutex_init(pthread_mutex_t *mutex,
        const pthread_mutexattr_t *attr);
    ```

    - The first argument is a mutex object pointing pointer; it is used to lock and unlock a mutex object.
    - The second argument is helpful to initialize mutex attributes such as priority inversion and sharing with processes.

- Then, the following two functions are used for requesting a lock against a mutex object:

    ```
    int pthread_mutex_lock(pthread_mutex_t *mutex);
    ```

    - On success of acquiring a lock over the mutex object by a thread, the thread continues its execution.
    - On failure of acquiring a lock over the mutex object by a thread, the thread waits.

- The following two functions are used for releasing a lock from a mutex object:

    ```
    int pthread_mutex_unlock(pthread_mutex_t *mutex);
    ```

    - A thread releases its already acquired lock over the specific mutex object. Then, other threads waiting over the specific mutex object may acquire the lock.
    - On failure of acquiring a lock over the mutex object by a thread, the thread waits.

- Finally, the following function is used for destroying a specific mutex object:

    ```
    int pthread_mutex_destroy(pthread_mutex_t *mutex);
    ```

    - It releases storage allocated to the mutex object.

For example, in the case of sharing the counter variable among multiple threads, using mutex locks acquiring and releasing can be handled as follows:

Define and initialize a mutex object for accessing the counter variable as follows:

```
pthread_mutex_t crits;
pthread_mutex_init(&crits, NULL);
```

Then, before accessing the counter variable from a thread task, acquire a lock over the mutex object crits, and after accessing the counter variable from a thread task, release the lock over the mutex object crits after use as follows:

```
pthread_mutex_lock(&crits);
counter++;
pthread_mutex_unlock(&crits);
```

All the instructions placed between mutex lock and unlock instructions are executed as atomic instructions. Atomic instructions mean all these instructions are executed or none of these instructions are executed by a thread. Hence, critical section execution is serialized and guarantees consistent results to threads.

Mutex and Conditional Variable for Synchronization

In this section, we will discuss how to handle threads flow dependencies and synchronization issues. In many multitasking applications implementations, it is necessary to depend on other threads' execution order and result conditions for resuming dependent threads to continue. These use cases can be handled using the following important functions:

- The following function is used for waiting against a specific mutex object until a specific condition becomes true:

    ```
    int pthread_cond_wait(pthread_cond_t *cond, pthread_mutex_t *mutex);
    ```

- Then, the following function is used for signaling any thread that is waiting over a specific mutex object to indicate the condition has become true:

    ```
    int pthread_cond_signal(pthread_cond_t *cond);
    ```

- The following function is used for signaling a group of threads that are waiting over a specific mutex object to indicate the condition has become true:

    ```
    int pthread_cond_broadcast(pthread_cond_t *cond);
    ```

- Next, let's say two threads are running task-1 and task-2 in parallel, then if task-1 completes then immediately task-1 executing thread should convey the status to task-2 executing thread. To handle this scenario,

First initialize necessary mutex and conditional variables as follows:

```
pthread_mutex_t mutex = PTHREAD_MUTEX_INITIALIZER;
pthread_cond_t condition = PTHREAD_COND_INITIALIZER;
int status = 0;
```

For example, Task-2 is waiting for a specific status update to continue further; then, it can be handled by waiting over the particular mutex condition variable (condition) as follows:

```
void* Task2(void* arg)
{
    //check status variable in reliable manner;

    while (status == 0)// Wait over status variable
    {
        pthread_cond_wait(&condition, &mutex);
    }
    ..resume task 2..
}
```

Task-1 must update the specific status variable and signal the waiting thread to continue over the condition variable as follows:

```
void* Task1(void* arg)
{
    ..
    //update status variable in reliable manner;
    printf("Task1 is Completed %d\n", status);
```

```
        pthread_cond_signal(&condition);
        ..
}
```

Further, it is also possible to implement use cases such as notifying a group of waiting threads at once using pthread_cond_broadcast, as in the following example:

```
void* Task1(void* arg)
{
        ..
        //update status variable in reliable manner;
        status=status+1;
        if (status==5)
        {
                pthread_cond_broadcast(&condition);
        }
        ..
}

#define NUM_THREADS 5

pthread_mutex_t mutex = PTHREAD_MUTEX_INITIALIZER;
pthread_cond_t cond = PTHREAD_COND_INITIALIZER;
int status = 0;

void * mutitasks(void *arg)
{
        .. check status in a reliable manner..
        while (status < NUM_THREADS)
        {
                pthread_cond_wait(&cond, &mutex);
        }
}
```

However, mutex locks involve waiting for acquiring locks and carefully ordering lock acquiring and release operations. Locking operations can lead to increased latencies and deadlocks for executing multiple threads simultaneously.

Hence, developers should carefully check lock acquiring and releases-related code. Fortunately, to some extent, these issues can be quickly identified using the valgrind tool. We discuss in later sections how to use valgrind for identifying lock-related issues quickly.

Common Data Sharing Issues and Threads Performance

In this section, we will discuss major issues in organizing common data across the threads and allow threads to execute independently and run with high performance. In the previous section, we observe that although mutex and conditional variables are helpful in handling data dependency, flow dependency, and critical section access issues, mutex object-based synchronization approaches are costly in terms of latency and the necessity to handle other issues such as deadlocks and starvation due to locking approaches.

In some situations, by carefully inspecting the critical section code and data, it is possible to convert the critical section code into a non-critical section by using arrays and private variables. These approaches are helpful in terms of avoiding lock management overhead and related issues:

- For example, in the case of computing the mean of N elements using K threads, then intermediate sum results can be stored in an array of size K (e.g., `int result[K]`). Then, in a main process, after joining all threads, the final sum can be computed from the `result` array.

- On the other hand, using common arrays is dangerous among independent threads in terms of memory and cache utilization because of false sharing issues.

False Sharing

False sharing problems arise when two threads are accessing a global array of size n, and thread-1 is updating the first part (0, n/2) of the array, and thread-2 is updating the second part (n/2+1, n) of the array simultaneously, and the array is stored within the same cache line of size n. False sharing is due to the following reasons:

- Thread-1 is actually updating the first part of the array (a) only. But when thread-2 needs to access the second part of the same array (a), the cache line will be unnecessarily replaced from the memory again to copy the array (a) contents due to a new thread accessing the cache line.

- Unnecessary copying of contents from memory to cache and cache to memory leads to poor utilization of cache as well as memory. It leads to increased latency and poor performance.

To mitigate false sharing of global arrays, developers can do the following:

- If cache line size is N, then do not partition an array of size N among threads. It can be done by adding padding bytes to the array. Hence, each thread gets allocated with a unique cache line to store its array.

  - It may lead to poor utilization of cache lines but avoids unnecessary cache content replacements and higher latencies.

  - Padding of arrays will be a useful solution in case lower-size padding is needed.

  - Padding of arrays will be a poor solution in case higher-size padding is needed.

The above approach has the following drawbacks:

- Necessary to set up large-size global arrays
- Necessary to use synchronization approaches for reliable computations
- Necessary to carefully handle locking overheads and minimize latencies
- Necessary to check for deadlocks and starvation issues

To mitigate false sharing, it is also possible to revise the code by eliminating global arrays and introducing local private variables per thread to store intermediate results.

```
typedef struct
{
    int* list; //Address of the list
```

```
        int start; //Starting index of the list w.r.t thread
        int end;//End of the list w.r.t thread
        int res;// Private variable per thread to store intermediate results
} FunArgs;
```

This solution has the following benefits:

- This solution avoids usage of global arrays.
- Avoids unnecessary cache lines replacement, memory copy, and memory utilization.
- This solution is very useful in case of storing lower-sized intermediate results.
- Avoid unnecessary locking overhead and related latencies.
- More reliable code in terms of avoiding deadlocks and starvation issues.

This solution has the following drawbacks:

- This solution is not useful in case of storing large-size intermediate results.
- Allocating private arrays per thread is costly in terms of memory utilization and cache utilization.

Next, we will do important hands-on activities to practice multithreading programming.

Hands-On Activity-1

In this hands-on activity, we implement three important functions to run in parallel over a common input list of elements. Specifically, we do the following:

- Implement search, min, and mean functions. And assign these functions to three unique threads.
- Execute these three functions in parallel over a list of size N using the three threads.

BASIC THREADS USAGE

1. We implement this hands-on activity in `basicthreads.c`. First, we define the important arguments to thread tasks as follows:

2. Define the following structure to pass the important arguments to execute the search function using a thread task:

   a. List of elements, start of the list, end of the list

   b. Search element and result (found or not)

   ```
   #include <stdio.h>
   #include <stdlib.h>
   #include <pthread.h>
   #include <math.h>
   #include <limits.h>
   typedef struct
   {
       int* list;
       int start;
       int end;
       int ele;
       int result;
   } FunArgs1;
   ```

3. Define the following structure to pass the important arguments to execute the minimum element finding function using a thread task:

   a. List of elements, start of the list, end of the list

   b. Minimum element holding variable

   ```
   typedef struct
   {
       int* list;
       int start;
       int end;
       int min;
   } FunArgs2;
   ```

CHAPTER 6   PROCESS AND THREAD MANAGEMENT TASKS FOR C PROGRAMMERS

4. Define the following structure to pass the important arguments to execute the minimum element finding function using a thread task:

   a. List of elements, start of the list, end of the list

   b. Mean variable to hold the result

   ```
   typedef struct
   {
       int* list;
       int start;
       int end;
       float mean;
   } FunArgs3;
   ```

5. Define the following function to implement linear search over an input list of elements and find the given search element:

   ```
   void* Search(void* arg)
   {
       FunArgs1* data = (FunArgs1*)arg;
       for (int i = data->start; i < data->end; i++)
       {
           if (data->list[i] == data->ele)
           {
               data->result=1;
               break;
           }
       }
   }
   ```

6. Define the following function to implement the minimum element finding procedure over an input list of elements.

   ```
   void* MinElement(void* arg)
   {
       FunArgs2* data = (FunArgs2*)arg;
       int min=data->list[data->start];
       for (int i = data->start; i < data->end; i++)
       {
           if (data->list[i] <= min)
   ```

```
            {
                    min = data->list[i];
            }
        }
        data->min = min;
    }
```

7. Define the following function to implement the mean value over an input list of elements.

```
void* Mean(void* arg)
{
        FunArgs3* data = (FunArgs3*)arg;
        float sum=0.0;
        for (int i = data->start; i < data->end; i++)
        {
                sum = sum+data->list[i];
        }
        data->mean = (float)(sum)/(data->end-data->start);
}
```

8. Implement the main() process to allocate a list of size N and assign sample elements to the list:

```
int main()
{
        int n, s, nthrds;
        printf("Enter the number of elements in the listay: ");
        scanf("%d", &n);
        int* list = (int*)malloc(n * sizeof(int));
        printf("Enter the elements of the listay:\n");
        for (int i = 0; i < n; i++)
        {
                scanf("%d", &list[i]);
        }
```

9. Create three threads and assign each thread with a unique function and list of elements to process:

```
pthread_t threads[3];
FunArgs1 args1;
args1.list = list;
args1.start = 0;
args1.end = n-1;
args1.ele = s;
pthread_create(&threads[0], NULL, Search, &args1);
FunArgs2 args2;
args2.list = list;
args2.start = 0;
args2.end = n-1;
pthread_create(&threads[1], NULL, MinElement, &args2);
FunArgs3 args3;
args3.list = list;
args3.start = 0;
args3.end = n-1;
pthread_create(&threads[2], NULL, Mean, &args3);
```

10. Wait for all threads to complete their execution and collect the results:

```
for (int i = 0; i <3; i++)
{
    pthread_join(threads[i], NULL);
}
printf("Search Result %d\n", args1.result);
printf("Minimum Element %d\n", args2.min);
printf("Mean %f\n", args3.mean);
```

11. Finally, delete the dynamically allocated list to free the memory:

```
free(list);
return 0;
}
```

12. Compile and test the thread1.c using the following commands:

    ```
    #gcc basicthreads.c -lpthread
    #./a.out
    Enter the number of elements in the listay: 10
    Enter the elements of the listay:
    1
    2
    ..
    10
    Search Result 1
    Minimum Element 1
    Mean 5.000000
    ```

From the results, we can observe that all three threads executed their tasks successfully in parallel.

Next, let's practice how to divide a list of size N elements among k threads in a reliable manner to execute a specific task in parallel.

Hands-On Activity-2

In this hands-on activity, we do the following activities related to implementing parallel linear search algorithms.

- Allocate a list of elements using dynamically allocated memory and pass it to threads.

- Divide the given input list of size N among a given number of threads, such as k.

- Execute k threads in a reliable manner and collect the results.

PARTITION A LIST OF SIZE N AMONG K THREADS

1. We implement the following thread tasks in `parallelsearch.c` to implement the parallel search algorithm:

2. Define the following structure to pass the important arguments to execute the search function using a thread task:

   a. List of elements, start of the list, end of the list

   b. Search element and result (found or not)

   ```
   #include <stdio.h>
   #include <stdlib.h>
   #include <pthread.h>
   #include <math.h>
   #include <limits.h>
   typedef struct
   {
       int* list;
       int start;
       int end;
       int key;
       int result;
   } FunArgs;
   ```

3. Define the following function to implement linear search over a given input list, partition elements, and find the given search element:

   ```
   void* ParallelSearch(void* arg)
   {
       FunArgs* data = (FunArgs*)arg;
       for (int i = data->start; i < data->end; i++)
       {
           if (data->list[i] == data->key)
           {
               data->result=1;
               break;
           }
       }
   }
   ```

4. Do the following tasks in main: first, allocate a list of size N using dynamic memory and initialize with N elements.

   ```
   int main()
   {
           int n, s, nthrds;
           printf("Enter the number of keyments in the listay: ");
           scanf("%d", &n);
           int* list = (int*)malloc(n * sizeof(int));
           printf("Enter the keyments of the listay:\n");
           for (int i = 0; i < n; i++)
           {
                   scanf("%d", &list[i]);
           }
           printf("Enter the search element: ");
           scanf("%d", &s);
   ```

5. Create a given number of threads and assign to each thread a unique partition of the list to search:

   ```
           printf("Enter the number of threads: ");
           scanf("%d", &nthrds);
   ```

   a. Divide the list elements uniformly into a number of partitions:

   ```
   int npt = n / nthrds;
   ```

   b. Assign remaining elements of the list to the last partition:

   ```
   int remels = n % nthrds;
   int start = 0;
   pthread_t threads[nthrds];
   FunArgs args[nthrds];
   ```

   c. Assign each partition to a unique thread in the following loop:

   ```
   for (int i = 0; i < nthrds; i++)
   {
           args[i].list = list;
           args[i].start = start;
           args[i].end = start + npt;
           args[i].key = s;
   ```

```
            if (i == nthrds - 1)
            {
                args[i].end += remels;
            }
            pthread_create(&threads[i], NULL, ParallelSearch, &args[i]);
            start = args[i].end;
    }
```

6. Wait for all threads to complete their execution and collect the results:

```
    for (int i = 0; i < nthrds; i++)
    {
        pthread_join(threads[i], NULL);
    }
    for (int i = 0; i < nthrds; i++)
    {
        if (args[i].result == 1)
        {
            printf("Element found");
            break;
        }
    }
```

7. Finally, delete the dynamically allocated list to free the memory:

```
        free(list);
        return 0;
    }
```

8. Compile the code and test it using the following commands:

```
#gcc parallelsearch.c -lpthread
#./a.out
Enter the number of keyments in the listay: 10
Enter the keyments of the listay:
1
2
..
10
Enter the search element: 10
```

CHAPTER 6   PROCESS AND THREAD MANAGEMENT TASKS FOR C PROGRAMMERS

```
Enter the number of threads: 4
Element found
```

From the results, observe that we successfully partitioned a list of size N among k threads and executed a parallel search.

In this section, we have learned how to do basic multithreading tasks. Next, let's learn how to handle thread issues such as critical sections, avoiding false sharing, and handling locks in a reliable and efficient manner.

Safe and Reliable Programming Ways for Threads Management

In this section, we will learn the important thread management skills to improve the performance of multithreaded applications and identify any key issues related to safe and reliable threads executions. We do the following activities:

- Improve the performance of a multithreaded application
- Quickly identify and handle threads synchronization issues

Improve the Performance of a Multithreaded Application

In order to improve the performance of a multithreaded application, it is necessary to check the following details:

- **How Do Threads Share Their Input Data**: It helps in identifying possible critical sections and race conditions among threads. Developers can reorganize the code and share variables to eliminate critical sections and race conditions.

  - It helps in improving the performance of the multithreaded application by eliminating usage of synchronization tools and approaches such as mutex locks and semaphores.

  - It helps in improving the reliability of the multithreaded application due to avoiding wrong ways of using synchronization tools.

- **How Input Data Is Partitioned Among Threads**: It helps in identifying any false sharing of input data, so developers can reorganize the input data and improve the performance.
  - False sharing of arrays can lead to poor utilization of memory and caches; hence, developers can carefully reorganize input data to eliminate false sharing issues.
  - It helps in improving memory access time by reducing latencies.
  - It helps in improving the overall performance of multithreaded application.
- **How Do Threads Synchronize Their Tasks Execution**
  - It helps in identifying locking issues and correcting them.
  - It helps in identifying deadlocks and starvation-causing codes.
  - It improves the reliability of the multithreaded application.

In the next section, we will discuss how to inspect a multithreaded application to improve its performance and execute it in a reliable manner.

Multithreading Application Performance Tuning

We implement the following sample multithreaded application (`parallelsum.c`) to compute the parallel sum using a global `result` variable over a list of size N using k threads. Then, we do the following tasks to improve its reliability and performance:

- **First Approach**: We identify the critical section of the application (accessing `result`) and handle critical section issues using mutex locks.
- **Second Approach**: We reorganize the code to eliminate the critical section and synchronization tools using global arrays to store intermediate results.
- **Third Approach**: Next, we reorganize the code to eliminate the false sharing using local variables to store intermediate results.
- Compare these three approaches' performance and identify the best approach to implement this multithreaded application.

```c
#include <stdio.h>
#include <stdlib.h>
#include <pthread.h>
#include <math.h>
#include <limits.h>
#define ARRAY_SIZE 50000
#define NofT 200

typedef struct
{
    int tid;
    int* list;
    int start;
    int end;
} FunArgs;

int result=0;
void* ParallelSum(void* arg)
{
    FunArgs* data = (FunArgs*)arg;

    for (int i = data->start; i < data->end; i++)
    {
        result = result+data->list[i];
    }

    printf("Total: %d\n",result);
}
int main()
{
    int* list = (int*)malloc(ARRAY_SIZE * sizeof(int));
    for (int i = 0; i < ARRAY_SIZE; i++)
    {
        list[i]=i;
    }
    pthread_t threads[NofT];
    FunArgs args[NofT];
```

```c
        int npt = ARRAY_SIZE / NofT;
        printf("NoElePerThread %d\n",npt);
        int remels = ARRAY_SIZE % NofT;
        int start = 0;
        for (int i = 0; i < NofT; i++)
        {
            args[i].tid = i;
            args[i].list = list;
            args[i].start = start;
            args[i].end = start + npt;
            if (i == NofT - 1)
            {
                args[i].end += remels;
            }
            pthread_create(&threads[i], NULL, ParallelSum, &args[i]);
            start = args[i].end;

        }
        for (int i = 0; i < NofT; i++)
        {
            pthread_join(threads[i], NULL);
        }
        unsigned int total=0;
        printf("Total: %d",result);

        free(list);
        return 0;
}
```

On executing the parallelsum.c, we can observe the following issues:

- On multiple runs, you observe the different results
- This program's results are inconsistent and incorrect on many runs
- It means threads are facing race condition issues due to critical section

```
#gcc parallelsum.c -lpthread
./a.out
Total: 1246820665
./a.out
Total: 1249204847
./a.out
Total: 1249975000
```

Let's solve these issues using mutex locks in our first approach:

First Approach

We update the parallelsum.c with the following `ParallelSum` function to update the result variable in a reliable manner using mutex locks to solve race conditions as follows:

```
pthread_mutex_t mutex;

void* ParallelSum(void* arg)
{
    FunArgs* data = (FunArgs*)arg;
    for (int i = data->start; i < data->end; i++)
    {
        pthread_mutex_lock(&mutex);
        result = result+data->list[i];
        pthread_mutex_unlock(&mutex);
    }
    printf("Total: %d\n",result);
}
```

We update the `main` function to collect the final `result` as follows, and we also compute the total duration to complete this task using clock functions as follows:

```
int main()
{
..
    pthread_mutex_init(&mutex, NULL);
```

```
    double time1, timedif;
    time1 = (double) clock();
    time1 = time1 / CLOCKS_PER_SEC;

    printf("Total: %d",result);
    timedif = ( ((double) clock()) / CLOCKS_PER_SEC) - time1;
    printf("Mutex time is %lf seconds\n", timedif);

    free(list);

    pthread_mutex_destroy(&mutex);
}
```

On executing the parallelsum.c, we can observe the following issues:

- On multiple runs, you observe the same results.
- This program's results are consistent and correct on many runs.

```
#gcc parallelsum.c -lpthread
./a.out
otal: 1249975000Mutex time is 0.032943 seconds
./a.out
Total: 1249975000Mutex time is 0.035864 seconds
./a.out
Total: 1249975000Mutex time is 0.035627 seconds
```

Next, in our second approach, instead of mutex locks, use global arrays to store threads' intermediate results.

Second Approach

We update the parallelsum.c with the following ParallelSum function to update the result variable in a reliable manner using the global array (result) to solve race conditions as follows:

```
typedef struct
{
    int tid;
    int* list;
```

```
    int start;
    int end;
} FunArgs;
```

We use the following global array `result` of size equal to the number of threads to store intermediate results of each thread.

```
int result[NofT]={0};
void* ParallelSum(void* arg)
{
    FunArgs* data = (FunArgs*)arg;
    for (int i = data->start; i < data->end; i++)
    {
        result[data->tid] = result[data->tid]+data->list[i];
    }
}
```

We update the `main` function to collect the final result using the global `result` array as follows, and we also compute the total duration to complete these tasks using `clock` functions as follows:

```
int main()
{
..
    unsigned int total=0;
    for (int i = 0; i < NofT; i++)
    {
        total=total+result[i];
    }
    printf("Total: %d",total);
}
```

On executing the `parallelsum.c`, we can observe the following issues:

- On multiple runs, you observe the same results.
- This program's results are consistent and correct on many runs.

CHAPTER 6   PROCESS AND THREAD MANAGEMENT TASKS FOR C PROGRAMMERS

```
#gcc parallelsum.c -lpthread
./a.out
Total: 1249975000Result Array is 0.010054 seconds
./a.out
Total: 1249975000Result Array is 0.010008 seconds
./a.out
Total: 1249975000Result Array is 0.010628 seconds
```

From the above results, we can observe that the global array approach takes less time (0.010054) to complete the task than mutex locks time (0.032943). It is due to avoiding locking overhead and latencies. Next, in our third approach, instead of using global arrays, we use thread-private variables to store threads' intermediate results.

Third Approach

As we discussed in previous sections, global arrays could result in false sharing of data among threads and lead to poor utilization of memory and cache. Hence, we update the parallelsum.c with the following ParallelSum function to update the result variable in a reliable manner using the private thread variable (result) to solve race conditions and false sharing issues as follows:

```
typedef struct
{
    int* list;
    int start;
    int end;
    int result;
} FunArgs;
void* ParallelSum(void* arg)
{
    FunArgs* data = (FunArgs*)arg;
    data->result=0;
    for (int i = data->start; i < data->end; i++)
    {
        data->result = data->result+data->list[i];
    }
    printf("Total: %d\n",data->result);
}
```

394

CHAPTER 6   PROCESS AND THREAD MANAGEMENT TASKS FOR C PROGRAMMERS

We update the `main` function to collect the final result using individual threads' private variables as follows, and we also compute the total duration to complete these tasks using clock functions as follows:

```
int main()
{
..
    unsigned int total=0;
    int nhrds;
    for (int i = 0; i < nthrds; i++)
    {
        printf("%d",args[i].result);
        total=total+args[i].result;
    }
}
```

On executing the `parallelsum.c`, we can observe the following issues:

- On multiple runs, you observe the same results.
- This program's results are consistent and correct on many runs.

```
#gcc parallelsum.c -lpthread
./a.out
Total: 1249975000Result Private Vriable is 0.009764 seconds
./a.out
Total: 1249975000Result Private Vriable is 0.007051 seconds
./a.out
Total: 1249975000Result Private Vriable is 0.009992 seconds
```

From the above results, we can observe that the private variable approach takes less time (0.007051) to complete the task than the first (mutex locks (0.032943)) and second approaches (global array (0.010054)). It is due to avoiding locking overhead and latencies due to false sharing of arrays. In summary, it is necessary for developers to check critical section codes and reorganize them to avoid locking approaches and false sharing situations to implement high-performance applications.

In the next section, we will learn how to identify threads synchronization issues quickly using the `valgrind (helgrind)` tool.

CHAPTER 6   PROCESS AND THREAD MANAGEMENT TASKS FOR C PROGRAMMERS

Quickly Identify and Handle Threads Synchronization Issues

In this section, we will learn how to identify the following multithreading application-related issues using the `valgrind` tool with `helgrind` options:

- Identify critical sections
- Identify locking order issues
- Identify deadlock situations

Identify Data Race Conditions Quickly

In this section, we will test a sample program that creates two threads and accesses a global variable simultaneously.

- We compile the sample program datarace.c with the debugging option to use it with the valgrind tool.
- Then, using the helgrind option by executing the code, we quickly identify possible data race issues and respective lines of the code.

IDENTIFY MULTITHREADING ISSUES

---

1. We use the following sample multithreading application to identify critical section, locking order, and deadlock issues.

2. We define a critical section in the sample application (`datarace.c`). This critical section will be accessed by two threads simultaneously.

   ```
   #include <stdio.h>
   #include <pthread.h>
   int counter = 0;
   ```

CHAPTER 6   PROCESS AND THREAD MANAGEMENT TASKS FOR C PROGRAMMERS

3. Define the following functions to access the global variable counter by two threads using critSecAccess.

```
void *critSecAccess(void *arg)
{
    for (int i = 0; i < 100000; i++)
    {
        counter++;
    }
    return NULL;
}
int main()
{
    pthread_t tr1, tr2;
    pthread_create(&tr1, NULL, critSecAccess, NULL);
    pthread_create(&tr2, NULL, critSecAccess, NULL);
    pthread_join(tr1, NULL);
    pthread_join(tr2, NULL);
    printf("Counter value: %d\n", counter);
    return 0;
}
```

4. Compile the datarace.c using the -g option to execute it using valgrind and helgrind to quickly identify possible data race conditions and to spot the code quickly:

```
#gcc -g datarace.c -lpthread
#valgrind --tool=helgrind ./a.out
==17183== Possible data race during read of size 4 at 0x10C024 by thread #3
==17183== Locks held: none
==17183==    at 0x1091FE: critSecAccess (datarace.c:11)
==17183== Possible data race during write of size 4 at 0x10C024 by thread #3
==17183== Locks held: none
==17183==    at 0x109207: critSecAccess (datarace.c:11)
=20442== ERROR SUMMARY: 2 errors from 2 contexts (suppressed: 0 from 0)
```

CHAPTER 6   PROCESS AND THREAD MANAGEMENT TASKS FOR C PROGRAMMERS

5. From the `valgrind` results, the developer should observe the following statements to quickly spot the data race issues:

    a. Possible data race during read of size

    ==17183== at 0x1091FE: critSecAccess (datarace.c:11)

    b. Possible data race during write of size

    ==17183== at 0x109207: critSecAccess (datarace.c:11)

From the results, developers can identify from datarace.c that line number 11 is a critical section code, and it is possible to solve the data race issue quickly.

Identify Locking Issues Quickly

In this section, we will test a sample program that creates two threads and accesses a global variable from two critical sections simultaneously.

- We compile the sample program lockingissues.c with the debugging option to use it with the `valgrind` tool.
- Then, using the helgrind option by executing the code, we quickly identify possible locking issues and deadlock-related issues.

IDENTIFY MULTITHREADING ISSUES

1. We use the following sample multithreading application to identify critical section, locking order, and deadlock issues

2. We define two critical sections in the sample application (`lockingissues.c`), and they implement mutex locks to access the global variable counter.

    a. Observe that in both functions to access the counter, two locks are acquired, then two locks are released.

    b. We will test this code by changing the order of locks and not unlocking specific mutex variables to simulate locking issues.

    ```
    #include <stdio.h>
    #include <pthread.h>
    ```

```c
int counter = 0;
pthread_mutex_t crits1;
pthread_mutex_t crits2;
void *critSecAccess1(void *arg)
{
    pthread_mutex_lock(&crits1);
    pthread_mutex_lock(&crits2);
    for (int i = 0; i < 100000; i++)
    {
        counter++;
    }
    pthread_mutex_unlock(&crits2);
    pthread_mutex_unlock(&crits1);
    return NULL;
}
void *critSecAccess2(void *arg)
{
    pthread_mutex_lock(&crits1);
    pthread_mutex_lock(&crits2);
    for (int i = 0; i < 100000; i++)
    {
        counter++;
    }
    pthread_mutex_unlock(&crits2);
    pthread_mutex_unlock(&crits1);
    return NULL;
}
```

3. Define two threads in main, and assign them with `critSecAccess1` and `critSecAccess2`, respectively.

```c
int main()
{
    pthread_t tr1, tr2;
    pthread_mutex_init(&crits1, NULL);
    pthread_mutex_init(&crits2, NULL);
    pthread_create(&tr1, NULL, critSecAccess1, NULL);
    pthread_create(&tr2, NULL, critSecAccess2, NULL);
    pthread_join(tr1, NULL);
```

CHAPTER 6   PROCESS AND THREAD MANAGEMENT TASKS FOR C PROGRAMMERS

```
        pthread_join(tr2, NULL);
        printf("Counter value: %d\n", counter);
        pthread_mutex_destroy(&crits1);
        pthread_mutex_destroy(&crits2);
        return 0;
}
```

4. First, we test the above code by commenting out the unlock code (crits1, crits2).

   ```
   #gcc -g lockingissues.c -lpthread
   #valgrind --tool=helgrind ./a.out
   ==18054== Thread #3: Exiting thread still holds 2 locks
   ==18054==    at 0x488C6C6: start_thread (exit-thread.h:33)
   ==18054==    by 0x49C6132: clone (clone.S:95)
   ==18054== Use --history-level=approx or =none to gain increased speed, at
   ==18054== the cost of reduced accuracy of conflicting-access information
   ..
   ==18054== ERROR SUMMARY: 5 errors from 5 contexts (suppressed: 4 from 4)
   ```

5. From the valgrind results, the developer should observe the following statements to quickly spot the locking issues:

   a. Exiting thread still holds 2 locks

   b. ERROR SUMMARY: 5 errors from 5 contexts (suppressed: 4 from 4)

6. Next, we change the code as follows:

   a. critSecAccess1: first acquire crits1, then crits2. Next release crits2 first, then release crits1.

   b. critSecAccess2: first acquire crits2, then crits1. Next release crits1 first, then release crits2.

   c. These changes are dangerous because they may lead to circular waiting of threads over the crits1 and crits2.

   d. It can also lead to a deadlock situation.

CHAPTER 6   PROCESS AND THREAD MANAGEMENT TASKS FOR C PROGRAMMERS

7. Let's execute the updated code and identify locking issues using `valgrind` and `helgrind` tools quickly as follows:

```
#gcc -g lockingissues.c
#valgrind --tool=helgrind ./a.out
Thread #3: lock order "0x10C040 before 0x10C080" violated
==18489==
==18489== Observed (incorrect) order is: acquisition of lock at
0x10C080
..
==18489==    by 0x1092B0: critSecAccess2 (lockingissues.c:23)
==18489==    by 0x4842B1A: ??? (in /usr/lib/x86_64-linux-gnu/valgrind/
vgpreload_helgrind-amd64-linux.so)
==18489==    by 0x488C608: start_thread (pthread_create.c:477)
```

8. From the `valgrind` results, the developer should observe the following statements to quickly spot the locking issues:

    a. `=18489== Observed (incorrect) order is: acquisition of lock`

    b. `==18489== by 0x1092B0: critSecAccess2 (lockingissues.c:23)`

From the results, observe that the application is acquiring locks in the incorrect order, and developers can quickly identify lines of code to change (`lockingissues.c:23`).

In this section, we have learned how to handle critical sections and locking issues using the `valgrind` tool. It helps developers to handle the multithreaded application issues in a reliable manner quickly.

Summary

In this chapter, we have learned the basics of how to implement high-performance applications in C using multiprocessing and multithreading concepts. Specifically, we have learned how to use `fork-`, `exec-`, `wait`-related system calls and practiced implementing sample multiprocessing programs. Then, we have learned how to improve the reliability of multiprocessing applications by handling various errors during

CHAPTER 6   PROCESS AND THREAD MANAGEMENT TASKS FOR C PROGRAMMERS

ensuring correct process order, executing new programs, termination, and responding to interrupts in reliable manners. As part of implementing multitasking applications, we have explored pthreads and synchronization tools. We have learned the best approaches to implement high-performance and reliable multithreaded applications. Specifically, we have learned how to handle thread race conditions, synchronization issues, and false sharing issues for improving multitasking application performance and reliability.

In the next chapter, we will learn how to handle interprocess communication tasks in C using Linux IPC tools.

Practice Tasks

1. Implement a multiprocessing application to execute N commands using N child processes in a reliable manner.

   - Handle possible interrupts to avoid unnecessary terminations

   - Use the valgrind tool to identify process errors, memory errors, and file-sharing errors

2. Implement a multiprocessing application to execute N commands in a specific order using N child processes in a reliable manner. The user should give the order of commands to be executed.

   - Handle possible interrupts to avoid unnecessary terminations

   - Use the valgrind tool to identify process errors, memory errors, and file-sharing errors

3. Implement a multiprocessing application to find a list of words from a given file. Each process should execute searching tasks over the file in parallel and print results (found/not found).

   - Based on the list size, a number of processes should be created

   - Handle possible interrupts to avoid unnecessary terminations

   - Use the valgrind tool to identify process errors, memory errors, and file-sharing errors

CHAPTER 6 PROCESS AND THREAD MANAGEMENT TASKS FOR C PROGRAMMERS

4. Implement a multitasking application to process a long list of integer elements and find the minimum element from the list using k threads.

    - Every thread should get an equal portion of the work in terms of searching list
    - Avoid false sharing among threads
    - Avoid locking approaches
    - Use valgrind tool to identify any data races possible in your implementation

5. Implement a multitasking application to find a list of words from a given file. Each thread should execute searching tasks over the file in parallel and print results (found/not found).

    - Based on the list size, a number of threads should be created
    - Use the valgrind tool to identify any data races possible in your implementation
    - Use the valgrind tool to identify any possible locking issues in your implementation
    - Correct all threads issues of the application to improve the reliability of the application

CHAPTER 7

Handle Interprocess Activities Using C Programming

In Chapter 6, "Process and Thread Management Tasks for C Programmers," we have learned how to implement multiprocessing applications in C using Linux system calls such as `fork`, `wait`, and `exec`. In this chapter, we will learn how to implement processes coordination activities using Linux services. Specifically, we will learn various Linux interprocess communication (IPC) approaches and services for implementing multiprocess coordination activities. In this chapter, first, you will be learning how to implement synchronous multiprocess coordination activities using IPC approaches such as pipes and named pipes (also known as FIFO). Next, you will be learning how to implement asynchronous multiprocess coordination activities using IPC approaches such as message queues and shared memory. Finally, you will be learning how to handle interprocess coordination activities in a reliable manner using an IPC approach called semaphores.

As part of practicing, you will be doing relevant hands-on activities in C. For instance, you will be learning how to use FIFO for implementing service chaining applications and message queues for implementing asynchronous ways of exchanging data between processes. Then, you will practice how to use IPC semaphores to handle reliable data sharing between multiple processes. Mainly, in this chapter, we will cover the following topics:

1. Essential Linux interprocess communication (IPC) approaches
2. Explore C programming and Linux IPC tools for IPC management

3. Explore ways to implement service chaining and asynchronous programming

4. Essential IPC synchronization handling tools

Essential Linux Interprocess Communication (IPC) Approaches

We know that on a computer system, an OS manages process creation, execution, coordination, resources management, and access control activities. Moreover, the OS also allows developers to handle these activities using suitable system calls. In Chapter 6, "Process and Thread Management Tasks for C Programmers," on a Linux OS, we have learned how to create a suitable number of processes using `fork` and control their execution using important system calls such as `wait`, `exec`, `exit`, and `signal`. Next, it is necessary to learn Linux-related system calls and their usage for enjoying the power of handling interprocess activities. Mainly, Linux OS handles IPC activities by implementing suitable data structures and offering suitable accessing methods, checking process access permissions, and scheduling processes to handle synchronization issues. Interprocess coordination activities are complex, and these are handled through the Linux kernel; moreover, it is possible for C applications to request Linux IPC services using suitable system calls. In this section, we will learn the following Linux IPC approaches:

- Linux basic services for file handling
- PIPE
- FIFO
- Message Queues
- Share Memory
- Semaphores

Linux Basic Services for File Handling

Before going into details of Linux IPC approaches, it is necessary to know Linux basic concepts for handling files on a computer system. Linux processes, resources, and devices are implemented in terms of files only, and files are the major means to provide interprocess communication. On a Linux OS, every process is allotted a file table data structure. By default, the OS assigns the following three file descriptors per process inside its file table for providing access to the standard input device, output device, and error handling.

- STDIN: During a process execution, the process is allowed to access the keyboard for accepting inputs using the STDIN file descriptor. It is a standard input descriptor, and its index value is 0 in the file table.

- STDOUT: During a process execution, it allows the process to access display devices such as monitors for displaying results using the STDOUT file descriptor. It is a standard output descriptor, and its index value is 1 in the file table.

- STDERR: During a process execution, the process errors or warning messages are redirected to display devices such as monitors using the STDERR file descriptor. It is a standard error descriptor, and its index value is 2 in the file table.

After filling the basic three file descriptor entries in the file table at indices 0, 1, and 2, the next available index is 3 for any new file. During the process execution, if the process opens any new file, then the OS enters a new file pointing descriptor (3) in the next free index of the file table. Then, using file descriptor 3, the process accesses the new file for performing any read or write operations. The next available file table index entry is 4, and there is a limit on the maximum entries allowed per file table. Hence, developers should check the maximum entries allowed per file table while implementing applications to avoid any issues. For example, on an Ubuntu Linux system, the per-process maximum file entries limit is 1024.

During a process execution to track its file accessing positions, permissions, and allowable operations, the file descriptor will be useful. For example, when a process accesses a file using its descriptor, then the file accessing position will be updated in the file table entry pointed to by the file descriptor. Moreover, if the same file is opened twice in a process, then two file descriptors will be assigned inside the process's file table, both pointing to the beginning of the file only. For example, if the first descriptor writes 4 bytes into the file from the beginning, then only the first descriptor file accessing location will be updated. Hence, the second file descriptor still points to the beginning of the file only, and if it writes anything into the file, the old contents at the beginning will be overwritten. It means the first descriptor and second descriptor can be used independently to access the file.

Importance of dup and dup2

In many situations, it is necessary to share files for performing interprocess coordination activities. For example, two processes, p1 and p2, can open a sample file; then if p1 writes some contents into the file, then p2 should be able to write into the file from the position where p1 ends. It means two file descriptors should be pointing to the same file table entry to access the file pointer location. On Linux OS, these situations are handled using dup and dup2 system calls.

- dup: For example, a file descriptor fd1 points to a file (sample.txt), then dup(fd1) returns a new file descriptor (fd2). These two file descriptors point to the same file (sample.txt).

  - Both file descriptors share the same file offset.

  - Closing one file descriptor does not close the sample.txt; the file is closed when both file descriptors are closed.

- dup2(int fd1, int fd2): For example, a file descriptor fd1 points to a file (sample.txt), and then dup2(0,fd1) results into

  - fd1 is closed first.

  - Then, the standard input descriptor(0) is duplicated and assigned with the fd1.

  - Both the standard input descriptor and fd1 now refer to the sample.txt; hence, if we use read(0,buff,4), then it results in reading four characters from the sample.txt file and copying them into buff.

PIPEs

On a Linux OS, pipes are the basic IPC approach to handle related processes' (parent and child) coordination activities. It means unrelated processes cannot use Linux pipes IPC to exchange data. We can view a pipe as a communication channel (data sharing page) between two related processes (such as parent and child). Once a pipe is created, it must relate to both parent and child processes, and one should do a write operation and the other should do a read operation over the pipe. Hence, usually pipes are used for synchronous communication between related processes. For example, in Linux commands, pipelining such as ls | wc is done through IPC pipes only.

Basically, on a Linux OS, pipe data structures are implemented through two file tables. One file table has a file descriptor for read operations over the pipe, and another file table has another file descriptor for write operations over the pipe. Once a pipe is created on a Linux OS using a system call pipe, it returns these two descriptors to the program. The first descriptor (0) of the pipe allows only read operations to be performed over the pipe communication channel and the second descriptor (1) of the pipe allows only write operations to be performed over the communication channel. For example, a parent process should relate to the pipe using the second descriptor (1) for writing over the communication channel, then a child process should relate to the pipe using the first descriptor (0) for reading over the communication channel.

OS Role in Pipes Management

While parent and child processes are accessing a pipe for data exchange, the OS handles the following:

- OS sets up a pipe channel on calling the pipe system call and offers read and write system calls to access it.

- Allows only related processes to use a pipe.

- While writing onto a pipe, if there is no related process connected for reading to it, then the writing process is blocked.

  - While writing onto a pipe, if there is no space available, the process is blocked

CHAPTER 7 HANDLE INTERPROCESS ACTIVITIES USING C PROGRAMMING

- While reading from a pipe, if there is no related process connected for writing to it, then the reading process is blocked.
  - While reading from a pipe, if there is no data available the process is blocked
- Handles parent and child processes communication synchronization issues.
- After closing the both read and write descriptors of a pipe, the pipe data structures and resources will be freed automatically.

Use Case of PIPEs

Linux IPC pipes are typically used in the following scenarios:

- To establish a small communication channel of size 8K between parent and child processes to exchange data.
- To implement related processes chaining:
  - **Example**: Unix or Linux Shell uses pipes to implement redirecting one command output to another command (ls |wc)
- To establish race-condition-free communication channels between related processes (parent and child) for accessing shared data. Developers need not handle synchronization uses.
- To set up a small-sized shared memory for synchronous access between parent and child processes and manage it automatically in terms of memory allocation and release by OS.

Next, we will discuss how to establish a communication channel for any two processes for coordination activities using Linux IPC FIFO.

FIFO

On a Linux OS, FIFOs are nothing but named pipes only. Hence, the OS handles the FIFOs, also managed through similar data structures of pipes such as file tables and file descriptors. Moreover, most of the pipes' accessing rules are applicable to FIFO files also. Uniquely, FIFOs are important IPC approaches to handle non-related processes coordination activities. It means any two processes can be connected to a FIFO and access it for implementing coordination activities. We can view a FIFO as a named file for sharing data between any two processes. Like pipes, once a FIFO is created by a process with a unique name for writing operations, then the other process must connect with the same FIFO name for reading operations. FIFOs are flexible in terms of establishing communication channels between any two processes. It is also possible to control access of the FIFO file using the FIFO name and access permissions such as read and write.

In order to access a FIFO file between two processes, like pipes, developers can use read and write system calls. By default, after setting up a FIFO file, a process can access the FIFO file using read or write operation in a blocking mode for synchronous communications. However, developers can change the mode of read and write operations to non-blocking mode to implement polling approaches in applications.

OS Role in FIFO Management

While two processes are accessing a FIFO file for data exchange, the OS handles the following:

- OS sets up a FIFO file on calling mkfifo system call and offers read and write system calls to access it.

- Two processes can communicate with a FIFO only if both processes open the same named FIFO file.

- While writing to a named FIFO file, if there is no process connected for reading from it, then the writing process is blocked.

  - While writing onto the FIFO file, if there is no space available, the process is blocked

- While reading from a FIFO file, if there is no process connected for writing to it, then the reading process is blocked.

  - While reading from the FIFO file, if there is no data available, the process is blocked

- Handles synchronization issues between any two processes connected with a FIFO file.

- After closing both the read and write descriptors of a FIFO file, the FIFO file still exists. It is the developer's responsibility to remove the unused FIFO files.

Use Case of FIFOs

Linux IPC FIFOs are typically used in the following scenarios:

- To establish a file type of small communication channel of size 8K between any two processes to exchange data.

- To implement related services or processes chaining.
    - **Example**: Any two processes can coordinate using FIFOs

- To establish race-condition-free communication channels between any two processes for accessing shared data. Developers need not handle synchronization uses.

Next, we will discuss how to establish an asynchronous communication channel for any two processes for coordination activities using Linux IPC Message Queues.

Message Queues

On a Linux OS, a message queue is implemented as a kernel memory data structure for organizing a list of messages. Usually, Linux OS manages multiple message queues, which are created by users or processes. Message queues are helpful to implement asynchronous communication between any two processes. Message queues play an important role in implementing event-driven programming. For example, in event-driven programming, there are producers and consumers. Usually, producers generate a variety of messages or events. In order to manage these messages or events, message queues are the widely used data structure. Once message queues are set up, producers can generate events, and these events will be stored in message queues; then, consumers access these events and react.

Basically, message queues play an important role in decoupling producers and consumers and allowing them to coordinate with each other using message queues. Moreover, message queues also enable asynchronous ways of exchanging messages and offer prioritized ways of accessing messages.

In Linux, once a message queue is created in the kernel, then a unique queue identifier (ID) will be assigned to it. If a process wants to access a message queue, it must have access permission and know the message queue key for accessing it. Having a message queue ID, a process can access it for sending or retrieving messages to other processes in an asynchronous manner. It means a source process need not wait for a destination process to connect with the message queue either for reading or writing messages. Moreover, Linux message queues store messages using a specific structure describing the type of the message and the actual message. Hence, it enables processes to read messages from the message queue using the type of message in a priority manner.

OS Role in Message Queues Management

While two processes are accessing a message queues for data exchange, the OS handles the following:

- OS sets up a kernel memory data structure for implementing a message queue on calling the `mstctl` system call and offers `msgsnd` and `msgrcv` system calls to access it.

- Multiple processes can communicate with a message queue if they have access permissions to the message queue only.

- Multiple processes can communicate with a message queue only if these processes use the same message queue ID for sending or receiving messages.

- While sending a message to a message queue, it is not necessary that the receiver should connect with the message queue.

- Similarly, while receiving a message from a message queue, it is not necessary that the sender should relate to the message queue.

- While sending a message to a message queue, if there is no space available, the process is blocked by default. However, developers can set it to non-blocking mode.

- While reading a message from a message queue, if there is no message available for reading, then the reading process is blocked. However, developers can set it to non-blocking mode.

- Once message queues usage is over, then it is the developer's responsibility to delete them; otherwise, they occupy kernel memory space, and it leads to performance issues.

Use Case of Message Queues

Linux IPC Message Queues are typically used in the following scenarios:

- To establish a small-sized asynchronous communication channel among multiple processes
- To implement event-driven programming
  - **Example**: IoT applications, smart applications
- To implement producer- and consumer-related applications
- To implement publisher- and subscriber-related applications
- To implement a variety of protocols
  - OS protocols
  - Network protocols

Next, we will discuss how to establish a large-size asynchronous communication channel or buffer for multiple processes' coordination activities using Linux IPC shared memory segments.

Shared Memory

On a Linux OS, shared memory IPC is helpful to establish large-size (e.g., in GB) shared buffers for implementing multiprocess coordination activities. Shared memory is implemented in the Linux OS by setting up and sharing memory pages between multiple processes through their virtual address space. In the shared memory IPC approach, once a shared memory is set up, the OS checks process access rights and keys to allow any memory read or write operations. One of the benefits of shared memory is that applications can access the shared memory by attaching pointers in the process spaces. Moreover, shared memory size can be huge, and they can be accessed like any arrays by the programs. Hence, the OS does not provide any specific system calls to read or write into shared memory.

OS implements shared memory as an array of shared memory segments. Most importantly, a process should access shared memory in a reliable manner; OSs do not handle any synchronization issues while sharing shared memory among multiple processes. Hence, developers should implement process synchronization procedures in applications for reliable data exchange between multiple processes.

OS Role in Shared Memory Management

While two processes are accessing a shared memory for data exchange, the OS handles the following:

- OS sets up a shared memory page on calling the shmctl system call.

- OS does not provide any specific system calls to read or write a shared memory. Applications can access a shared memory by attaching a pointer to the shared memory and accessing it.

- Multiple processes can communicate with a shared memory only if both processes are attached to the same shared memory key.

- Multiple processes can communicate with a shared memory if they have access permissions only.

- While reading data from a shared memory, it is not necessary that the writer should connect with the shared memory.

- Similarly, while writing data to a shared memory, it is not necessary that a reader should connect with the shared memory.

- OS allows extending the shared memory size dynamically.

- Once shared memory usage is over, then it is the developer's responsibility to detach their applications from the shared memory; then, the OS can free the unused shared memory.

Use Case of Shared Memory

Linux IPC Message Queues are typically used in the following scenarios:

- To establish a large-sized shared buffer among multiple processes

- Good fit for multiple processes sharing the shared memory for read operations only

- To implement database applications

- To implement network protocols and applications

- To implement a variety of protocols

  - OS protocols

  - Network protocols

Next, we will discuss how to handle synchronization issues using semaphores while accessing shared data by multiple processes.

Semaphores

In this section, we will quickly introduce the importance of semaphores. In the IPC synchronization handling tools section, we discuss semaphores in detail. Mainly, semaphores are used by developers to handle synchronization issues during multiple processes sharing global data. It means using semaphores over a shared variable to synchronize its access even if N processes are simultaneously accessing the shared variable. It means, at the end of N processes, parallel execution over the shared variable result will be equal to the serial execution result of N processes. Hence, semaphores ensure consistent and correct results during multiple processes' coordination activities. On the Linux OS, semaphores are implemented as shared lock variables stored in memory, and for processes to access the lock variable, the OS provides test (or wait) and set (or post) operations. Mainly, wait and post operations are atomic operations. It means while executing these operations, processes will not be interrupted.

OS Role in Semaphores Management

While two processes are accessing a message queue for data exchange, the OS handles the following:

- OS sets up a semaphore variable on calling the `semactl` system call and offers `semapost` and `semawait` system calls to access it.

- Usually, a semaphore variable is initialized with a count variable (max count). This count indicates the number of processes that can simultaneously access the semaphore.

- If a semaphore variable is positive, then only a process can apply the semaphore wait operation over the semaphore variable.
  - If a semaphore variable value is 0, then OS blocks the process until the semaphore variable becomes > 0
  - `semawait` operation decrements the semaphore variable
- If a semaphore variable is lower than the max count, then only a process can apply a semaphore post operation over the semaphore variable.
  - If a semaphore variable value reaches the max of 0, then the OS blocks the process until the semaphore variable value is lower than the max count.
  - `semapost` operation increments the semaphore variable.
- Developers must release the semaphore variable after use.

Use Case of Semaphores

Linux IPC semaphores are typically used in the following scenarios:

- To ensure synchronized access to global data or resources among multiple processes
- To handle synchronization issues while accessing shared memory or buffers
- To implement producer- and consumer-related buffer-sharing applications
- To implement any multiple-process synchronization coordination activities
- To implement a variety of protocols for synchronization issues
  - OS protocols
  - Network protocols

Next, we will learn how to use these Linux IPC approaches in C applications using Linux system calls.

CHAPTER 7   HANDLE INTERPROCESS ACTIVITIES USING C PROGRAMMING

Explore C Programming and Linux IPC Tools for IPC Management

C developers can enjoy the power of Linux IPC approaches using system calls for implementing large software applications involving multiprocess coordination activities. In this section, we will learn how to use the following Linux IPC approaches in C programming.

- Usage of PIPEs in C
- Usage of FIFOs in C
- Usage of Message Queues in C
- Usage of Shared Memory in C

Usage of PIPEs in C

As we understood in Linux, all IPC approaches are basically implemented through suitable data structures with accessing functions. In this section, we will learn how to use PIPEs in C applications in the following ways.

- Creating a PIPE
- Accessing a PIPE
- Responsibilities of developers in accessing a PIPE

First, we will learn how to create a pipe from a C application to establish a communication channel between related processes such as parent and child processes. In a C application, using a `pipe` system call, a pipe communication channel will be created, and it returns read and write file descriptors. In C programming, these file descriptors are easily accessible using an array of size 2 as follows:

```
int pipefd[2]; //index-0 for read and index-1 for write
if (pipe(pipefd) == -1)
{
    perror("Pipe failed");
    return 1;
}
```

CHAPTER 7   HANDLE INTERPROCESS ACTIVITIES USING C PROGRAMMING

Next, we will learn how to access a pipe between a parent and child process. If two processes are created as follows: `pid = fork();`

Suppose a child process wants to read data from the pipe; then, it must first close the write descriptor of the pipe (pipefd[1]), then it can use the `read` system call over the read descriptor to read data bytes into a character array as follows:

```
..
if (pid == 0)
{
    char buf[100];
    close(pipefd[1]);
    read(pipefd[0], buf, sizeof(buf));
    close(pipefd[0]);
}
```

Finally, after completing the read operation, the read descriptor of the pipe should be closed.

Similarly, suppose a parent process wants to write data bytes into the pipe; then, it must first close the read descriptor for the pipe (pipefd[0]), then it can use the `write` system call over the write descriptor to write data bytes using a character array as follows:

```
if (pid>0)
{
    char msg[10];
    close(pipefd[0]);
    write(pipefd[1], msg, strlen(msg) + 1);
    close(pipefd[1]);
}
```

Next, let's implement a sample C program using a pipe.

Sample C Program Using a Pipe

We will implement a sample C program to do the following things using a pipe to communicate between parent and child processes.

- Create a parent and a child process using fork
- Set up a pipe

CHAPTER 7 HANDLE INTERPROCESS ACTIVITIES USING C PROGRAMMING

- The parent process should send a message (sample) using the pipe to the child process
- Child process should receive the message from the piper and print it

```c
#include <stdlib.h>
#include <string.h>
#include <unistd.h>
int main()
{
    int pipefd[2];
    pid_t pid;
    if (pipe(pipefd) == -1)
    {
        perror("Pipe failed");
        return 1;
    }
    pid = fork();
    if (pid == 0)
    {
        printf("Child is waiting for parent to receive data");
        char buf[10];
        close(pipefd[1]);
        read(pipefd[0], buf, sizeof(buf));
        printf("Child: Data received over pipe is: %s\n", buf);
        close(pipefd[0]);
    }
    else
    {
        close(pipefd[0]);
        char *buf = "sample";
        write(pipefd[1], buf, strlen(buf) + 1);
        close(pipefd[1]);
    }
    return 0;
}
```

```
#gcc pipe1.c
#./a.out
Parent sent data
Child is waiting for parent to receive data
Child: Data received over pipe is: sample
```

On executing the above code, developers should observe the following:

- Since the parent process is writing into the pipe, it is closing the read descriptor of the pipe at the beginning of the parent process execution.
  - After the writing operation is over, the write descriptor is also closed by the parent process.
- Since the child process is reading from the pipe, it is closing the write descriptor of the pipe at the beginning of the child process execution.
  - After the reading operation is over, the read descriptor is also closed by the child process.
- Both child and parent processes are running in parallel.
- No waiting system call is used, but still the child process is waiting for the parent process to send data.
  - It is due to the blocking nature of the read system call to read data from the file.

Developers Role in Case of Pipe Usage

While parent and child processes are accessing a pipe for data exchange, the following things must be understood by developers:

- Both parent and child processes share the pipe communication channel and pipe's read and write file descriptors.
- Developers should decide which process is reading from the pipe and which process is writing into the pipe. Then, in the respective processes, unused file descriptors must be closed to avoid errors.

- Both read and write operations over a pipe are blocking operations; hence, until data is ready, the reading process execution blocks similarly until memory space is available over the pipe writing process execution blocks. The OS automatically handles blocking and synchronization activities of processes while accessing pipes; developers need not implement any code.

- After completing usage of the pipe, the respective process must close the respective file descriptor of the pipe. Otherwise, the pipe resources will not be released by the OS unless all processes accessing the pipe are terminated.

- Since it is possible to occur pipe access-related interrupts, developers should handle the SIGPIE signal.

Next, let's learn how to implement any two process coordination activities using named pipes.

Usage of FIFO in C

In this section, we will learn how to use FIFOs in C applications in the following ways.

- Creating a named pipe (FIFO)
- Accessing a FIFO
- Responsibilities of developers in accessing a FIFO

First, we will learn to create a named pipe (FIFO). In a C application (fifocreate.c), using `mkfifo` system call, a named pipe is created as follows:

```
#define OUTQ "sample.txt"
if (mkfifo(OUTQ, 0666) == -1)
{
    perror("mkfifo");
    exit(EXIT_FAILURE);
}
```

Next, we will learn how to access a FIFO file between two processes as follows.

CHAPTER 7   HANDLE INTERPROCESS ACTIVITIES USING C PROGRAMMING

Suppose process-1 (process1.c) wants to write data into a sample OUTQ FIFO file, then it must open the FIFO file in write-only mode as follows for writing data bytes of a character array into the FIFO file using the `write` system call:

```
#define OUTQ "sample.txt"
..
int num, fd;
fd = open(OUTQ, O_WRONLY);
char buf[100]
if ((num = write(fd, buf, strlen(buf))) == -1)
{
      perror("write");
}
close(fd);
```

After the write operation is completed over the OUTQ FIFO file, it must be closed. Similarly, suppose process-2 (process2.c) wants to read from the OUTQ FIFO file; first, it must open the FIFO file in read-only mode for reading data into a character array as follows:

```
#define OUTQ "sample.txt"
..
int num, fd;
fd = open(OUTQ, O_RDONLY);
char buf[100]
if ((num = read(fd, buf, strlen(buf))) == -1)
{
      perror("read");
}
close(fd);
```

After the read operation is completed over the OUTQ FIFO file, it must be closed. Next, let's implement a sample C program using a FIFO file.

Sample C Program Using a FIFO

We will implement the following sample C programs to do the following things using FIFO to communicate between two processes.

CHAPTER 7   HANDLE INTERPROCESS ACTIVITIES USING C PROGRAMMING

- Create a process1.c and do the following:
  - Set up a sample FIFO file called sample.txt
  - Open the FIFO file in write-only mode
  - Write sample data into FIFO file
  - Close the FIFO file
- Create a process2.c and do the following:
  - Open the sample.txt FIFO file in read-only mode
  - Read data from FIFO file and print it
  - Close the FIFO file

```c
process1.c
#include <stdlib.h>
#include <stdio.h>
#include <fcntl.h>
#include <stdlib.h>
#include <string.h>
#include <fcntl.h>
#include <unistd.h>
#define OUTQ "sample.txt"
int main(void)
{
    char *s="sample";
    int num, fd;

    mkfifo(OUTQ, 0644);
    printf("P1 waiting for P2\n");
    fd = open(OUTQ, O_WRONLY);
    if ((num = write(fd, s, 7) == -1))
    {
        perror("write");
    }
    else
    {
```

```
                printf("P1 sent data %s\n",s);
        }
        close(fd);
        return 0;
}
gcc process1.c -o p1
./p1
P1 waiting for P2
P1 sent data sample
```

On executing the process1.c, developers should observe the following:

- Since FIFOs are also used for synchronous communication, until p2 connects to the OUTQ FIFO file, p1 execution blocks

- As soon as P2 started,
  - P1 execution unblocks and sends its data

```
process2.c
#include <stdio.h>
#include <stdlib.h>
#include <string.h>
#include <fcntl.h>
#include <unistd.h>
#define OUTQ "sample.txt"
int main(void)
{
        char s[10];
        int num, fd;
        printf("P2 waiting for P1\n");
        fd = open(OUTQ, O_RDONLY);
        if ((num = read(fd, s, 7) == -1))
        {
                perror("write");
        }
```

```
        else
        {
               printf("P2 received data %s\n",s);
        }
        close(fd);
        return 0;
}
gcc process2.c -o p2
./p2
P2 waiting for P1
P2 received data sample
```

On executing the process2.c, developers should observe the following:

- Since FIFOs also used for synchronous communication, until p1 connects to the OUTQ FIFO file, p2 execution blocks.
- As soon as P1 sends data
  - P2 execution unblocks and receives data from the FIFO file.

Developers' Role in Case of FIFO Usage

While two processes are accessing a FIFO file for data exchange the following things must be understood by developers:

- First, it is necessary to create a named FIFO as a file using the `mkfifo` system call with the following important arguments:
  - Unique FIFO filename
  - Suitable permissions such as read, write, and execute (666)
  - Handle the errors during FIFO setup
- Two processes use a FIFO for data exchange; both should share the same FIFO file
- Developers should decide which process is reading from the FIFO and which process is writing into the FIFO. Then, in the respective processes, FIFO should be opened in the respective mode, such as RDONLY or WRONLY.

CHAPTER 7 HANDLE INTERPROCESS ACTIVITIES USING C PROGRAMMING

- Both read and write operations are blocking operations; hence, until data is ready, the reading process blocks similarly until memory space is available over the FIFO writing process blocks. The OS automatically handles blocking and synchronization activities while accessing FIFO; developers need not implement any code.

- After completing usage of FIFO, the respective process must close the respective file descriptor of the FIFO file. After usage, developers should decide when to remove FIFO files.

Using pipes and FIFOs, we have learned how to establish synchronous communication between processes. Next, let's learn how to implement any two process coordination activities using message queues in an asynchronous manner.

Usage of Message Queues in C

In this section, we will learn how to use message queues in C applications in the following ways:

- Creating a message queue
- Accessing a message queue
- Responsibilities of developers in accessing a message queue

First, we will learn to create a message queue using a unique key with the `ftok` and `msgget` system calls as follows:

```
key_t key;
if ((key = ftok("msgsndr.c", 'B')) == -1)
{
    perror("ftok");
    exit(1);
}
if ((msqid = msgget(key, 0644 | IPC_CREAT)) == -1)
{
    perror("msgget");
    exit(1);
}
```

427

CHAPTER 7 HANDLE INTERPROCESS ACTIVITIES USING C PROGRAMMING

In the above code snippet, we should observe first that a unique key should be generated using ftok before creating a message queue. Then, a message queue is created using the msgget system call with read/write permissions.

Next, we will learn how to access the message queue between any processes using the unique key generated in the previous code snippet. First, we should define a message structure describing the message type and actual message using a C struct as follows:

```c
struct Message
{
     long mtype;
     char mtext[200];
};
```

Create two sample messages using the struct Message as follows:

```c
struct Message msg[2] = {{1,"Sample A"}, {2,"Sample B"}};
```

Next, suppose a message sender process (msgsndr.c) wants to send a message to a message queue using a msgsnd system call as follows:

```c
if (msgsnd(msqid, &msg[0], 9, 0) == -1)
{
     perror("msgsnd");
}
```

Next, suppose a message receiver process (msgrcvr.c) wants to read a message from a message queue using msgrcv system call as follows:

```c
struct Message msg;
int msqid;
key_t key;
if ((key = ftok("msgsndr.c", 'B')) == -1)
{
     perror("ftok");
     exit(1);
}
if ((msqid = msgget(key, 0644)) == -1)
{
     perror("msgget");
```

```
        exit(1);
}
if (msgrcv(msqid, &msg, 9, i, 0) != -1)
{
        printf("Msg Type: %d %s \n",msg.mtype, msg.mtext);
}
```

Next, let's implement a sample C program using a message queue.

Sample C Program Using a Message Queue

We will implement the following sample C programs to do the following things using a message queue to communicate between two processes.

- Create an msgsndr.c and do the following:
    - Set up a sample message queue using msgnsdr.c and 'B' as keys.
    - It sends two types (1 and 2) of sample messages to the message queue.
- Create an msgrcvr.c and do the following:
    - Open the sample message queue using msgnsdr.c and 'B' as keys
    - It tries to receive two types of messages from the message queue
    - Finally, remove the message queue (if you want to test it multiple times, do not remove the message queue in the code).

```
msgsndr.c
#include <stdio.h>
#include <stdlib.h>
#include <errno.h>
#include <string.h>
#include <sys/types.h>
#include <sys/ipc.h>
#include <sys/msg.h>
struct Message
{
        long mtype;
```

```c
        char mtext[200];
};
int main(void)
{
        struct Message msg[2] = {{1,"Sample A"}, {2,"Sample B"}};
        int msqid;
        key_t key;
        if ((key = ftok("msgsndr.c", 'B')) == -1)
        {
                perror("ftok");
                exit(1);
        }
        if ((msqid = msgget(key, 0644 | IPC_CREAT)) == -1)
        {
                perror("msgget");
                exit(1);
        }
        for (int i=0;i<2;i++)
        {
                int len = strlen(msg[i].mtext);
                if (msgsnd(msqid, &msg[i], len+1, 0) == -1)
                {
                        perror("msgsnd");
                }
                else
                {
                        printf("%s sent\n",msg[i].mtext);
                }
        }
        return 0;
}
#gcc msgsndr.c
#./a.out
Sample A sent
Sample B sent
```

CHAPTER 7   HANDLE INTERPROCESS ACTIVITIES USING C PROGRAMMING

On executing the msgsndr.c, developers should observe the following:

- Message sender successfully creates a message queue,

- Then, the message sender simply inserts two messages into the message queue and exits. No need for a message-receiving process to be active.

    - You may repeat testing the program by sending very large messages of size > 8K bytes and check what happens.

    - Change the last argument of msgsnd to IPCNOWAIT instead of 0 and test it by sending the large message of size > 8K bytes.

msgrcvr.c
```
#include <stdio.h>
#include <stdlib.h>
#include <errno.h>
#include <sys/types.h>
#include <sys/ipc.h>
#include <sys/msg.h>
struct Message
{
      long mtype;
      char mtext[9];
};
int main(void)
{
      struct Message msg;
      int msqid;
      key_t key;
      if ((key = ftok("msgsndr.c", 'B')) == -1)
      {
            perror("ftok");
            exit(1);
      }
```

CHAPTER 7 HANDLE INTERPROCESS ACTIVITIES USING C PROGRAMMING

```
        if ((msqid = msgget(key, 0644)) == -1)
        {
                perror("msgget");
                exit(1);
        }
        printf("Receiver Waiting for Messages\n");
        for(int i=1;i<3;i++)
        {
                if (msgrcv(msqid, &msg, 9, i, 0) != -1)
                {
                        printf("Msg Type: %d %s \n",msg.mtype, msg.mtext);
                }
        }
        msgctl(msqid, IPC_RMID, NULL);
        return 0;
}
#gcc msgsndr.c
#./a.out
Receiver Waiting for Messages
Msg Type 1: Sample A
Msg Type 2: Sample B

#gcc msgrcvr.c
#./a.out
Receiver Waiting for Messages
..
```

On executing the `msgrcvr.c`, developers should observe the following:

- Message receiver successfully accesses the existing message queue.

- Then, the message receiver simply extracts two types of messages from the message queue and exits. Observe that the message sending process need not be running while the message receiver receives messages from the message queue.

  - On re-execution of the program, observe that the process is blocking. Why? Because the messages will be deleted from the message queue once read from the queue.

432

- You may test the program by trying to access message types other than 1 and 2.

  - Observe that msgrcv blocks in case no matching type message exists in the message queue

  - Change the last argument of msgrcv to IPCNOWAIT and test it. Observe that msgrcv exists without waiting for messages

Developers' Role in Case of Message Queue Usage

While two processes are accessing a message queue for data exchange, the following things must be understood by developers:

- First, it is necessary to create a message queue using a unique key with the following system calls:

  - ftok
  - msgget

- Any two processes can exchange messages using the message queue. Moreover, processes can exchange messages using a message queue in an asynchronous way.

- By default, the msgsnd system call works in blocking mode. Hence, when a process is trying to read a message from the message queue, if the specific message does not exist, then the process execution blocks.

- By default, the msgrcv system call works in blocking mode. Hence, when a process is trying to write a message into the message queue, if the specific message size cannot be inserted in the message queue, then the process execution blocks.

- Message queues created by developers should be deleted after their use in case they are no longer needed.

The major limitation of pipes, FIFOs, and message queues is the size of data to be exchanged between processes. Next, let's learn how to implement large size buffers for exchanging and sharing large data between any two processes coordination activities using shared memory IPC.

CHAPTER 7　HANDLE INTERPROCESS ACTIVITIES USING C PROGRAMMING

Usage of Shared Memory in C

In this section, we will learn how to use shared memory in C applications in the following ways.

- Creating a shared memory
- Accessing a shared memory
- Responsibilities of developers

First, we will learn to create a shared memory using the shmget system call.

```
int shmid;
int *share;

shmid = shmget(KEY, size, 0666 | IPC_CREAT);
if (shmid == -1)
{
    perror("shmget failed");
    return 1;
}
```

From the above code snippet, we should understand that a shared memory segment should be created using a unique key, then it can be used to share the shared memory segment among multiple processes. Next, let's learn how a process can access the shared memory set up in the previous code as follows:

```
share = (int *)shmat(shmid, NULL, 0);

if (share == (int *)-1)
{
    perror("shmat failed");
    return 1;
}
```

From the above code, before using a shared memory by a process, we should observe that the process should attach to the shared memory using the unique shared memory id and collect the suitable pointer. For example, in the above shared memory segment is set up for integer data elements; hence, it is accessed using the integer-type pointer. Then it is possible to access the shared memory as follows:

```
*share=100; or printf("%d",*share);
```

CHAPTER 7   HANDLE INTERPROCESS ACTIVITIES USING C PROGRAMMING

After shared memory has been used and is no longer required, then the process can detach from the shared memory as follows:

```
if(shmdt(shm_ptr) == -1)
{
     perror("shmdt");
     exit(1);
}
```

Finally, after shared memory has been used and is no longer required, then the process created can also delete the shared memory as follows:

```
if (shmctl(shmid, IPC_RMID, NULL) == -1)
{
     perror("shmctl");
     exit(1);
}
```

Next, let's implement a sample C program using a shared memory for sharing between processes.

Sample C Program Using a Shared Memory

We will implement the following sample C programs to do the following things using shared memory to communicate between two processes.

- Create a sharedmem1.c and do the following:
    - Set up a shared memory for the integers buffer using a unique key
    - Attach its process to the shared memory using an integer pointer
    - Set a value inside the shared memory using the attached pointer
    - Detach from the shared memory
- Create a sharedmem2.c and do the following:
    - Get the shared memory for accessing the integers buffer using its unique key.
    - Attach its process to the shared memory using integer pointer.
    - Read a value from the shared memory using the attached pointer.

435

CHAPTER 7   HANDLE INTERPROCESS ACTIVITIES USING C PROGRAMMING

- Detach from the shared memory.
- Remove the shared memory after use. (If you want to test it multiple times, do not remove the shared memory in the code.)

Next, we will learn how to access a FIFO file between two processes that are created as follows:

sharedmem1.c
```c
#include <sys/ipc.h>
#include <sys/shm.h>
#include <sys/wait.h>
#include <stdio.h>
#include <unistd.h>
#include <fcntl.h>
#include <stdlib.h>
#define KEY 7860
int main()
{
    int shmid;
    int *share;
    int size = sizeof(int);
    shmid = shmget(KEY, size, 0666 | IPC_CREAT);
    if (shmid == -1)
    {
        perror("shmget failed");
        return 1;
    }
    share = (int *)shmat(shmid, NULL, 0);
    if (share == (int *)-1)
    {
        perror("shmat failed");
        return 1;
    }
```

```
        *share=100;
        printf("P1 Successfully written sample contents into shared memory:
        %d \n",*share);
        if (shmdt(share) == -1)
        {
                perror("shmdt");
                 exit(EXIT_FAILURE);
        }
        return 0;
}
#gcc sharedmem1.c -o p1
#./p1
P1 Successfully written sample contents into shared memory: 100
```

On executing the sharedmem1.c, developers should observe the following:

- The process p1 successfully set up the shared memory using the unique shared key.

- Then, process p1 attached to the shared memory using the shared key and collected the integer-type pointer to access it.

- Then, process p1 access the shared memory by setting value inside the share memory using the integer pointer.

    - However, it is not guaranteed safe access.

- We suggest changing the type of shared memory in the above program to string type and accessing it using a character pointer.

```
sharedmem2.c
#include <sys/ipc.h>
#include <sys/shm.h>
#include <sys/wait.h>
#include <stdio.h>
#include <unistd.h>
#include <fcntl.h>
#include <stdlib.h>
#define KEY 7860
```

```c
int main()
{
    int shmid;
    int *share;
    int size = sizeof(int);
    shmid = shmget(KEY, size, 0666 | IPC_CREAT);
    if (shmid == -1)
    {
        perror("shmget failed");
        return 1;
    }
    share = (int *)shmat(shmid, NULL, 0);
    if (share == (int *)-1)
    {
        perror("shmat failed");
        return 1;
    }
    printf("P2 read shared memory contents %d",*share);
    if (shmdt(share
    {
        perror("shmdt");
        exit(EXIT_FAILURE);
    }
    shmctl(shmid, IPC_RMID, NULL);
    return 0;
}
#gcc sharedmem2.c -o p2
#./p2
P2 read shared memory contents 10
```

On executing the sharedmem2.c, developers should observe the following:

- The process p2 gets the shared memory using the unique shared key.
- Then, process p2 attached to the shared memory using the shared key and collect the integer type pointer to access it.

- Then, process p2 accesses the shared memory by reading the value inside the shared memory using the integer pointer.
  - However, it is not guaranteed safe access.
- We suggest changing the type of shared memory in the above program to string type and accessing it using a character pointer.

Developers' Role in Case of Shared Memory Usage

While two processes are accessing a shared memory for data exchange the following things must be understood by developers:

- First, it is necessary to create a unique shared memory accessing id using the following arguments:
  - Unique key.
  - Size of the shared memory.
  - Suitable permissions such as read, write, and execute (666).
- Any process to access the shared memory must attach to the shared memory and use a suitable type pointer to access it.
  - For example, if we set a character buffer of size 1024, then it is necessary to attach to the shared memory using a character pointer.
- Accessing the shared memory is simple in terms of using the shared pointer.
- Shared memory access simultaneously by multiple processes can lead to data race conditions; hence, it is necessary to implement a synchronized way to access the shared memory using synchronization tools such as semaphores.
- A process after using the shared memory must be detached from it.
- After shared memory usage is over (after detaching from all processes), the developer should remove the shared memory.

CHAPTER 7   HANDLE INTERPROCESS ACTIVITIES USING C PROGRAMMING

Explore C Ways to Implement Service Chaining and Asynchronous Programming

System developers must learn the synchronous programming and asynchronous programming approaches for handling complex software. Synchronous programming is nothing but handling issues involved in the case of sender and receiver processes exchanging data in active mode. It means both sender and receiver processes need to connect with the communication channel for the entire data exchange duration. For example, if a sender wants to send data to a receiver, then the receiver must be actively waiting to receive data. Usually, synchronous ways of exchanging messages involve waiting for the other process to be ready. In programming, it is handled through blocking of sending and receiving processes while exchanging data. As developers we must use the right communication channel and accessing methods for implementing synchronous programming activities in a reliable manner. In C programming, using Linux IPC approaches such as pipes and FIFOs is helpful to implement synchronous programming tasks. Synchronous programming will be helpful in the case of exchanging continuous data between active processes in a reliable manner.

On the other hand, asynchronous programming plays an important role in offering reliable data exchange between offline processes. Moreover, asynchronous programming is the key to implementing current popular software development approaches such as microservices and function as a service. In these recent software development approaches to handle popular problems such as producer-consumer and publisher-subscriber event-driven programming is necessary. It means a process (producer or publisher) generates application-related messages or events at any time. Then, consumer or subscriber processes must handle or process these messages (or events) later in reliable manners. In programming, these use cases are usually handled through asynchronous programming approaches. In Linux, using IPC approaches such as message queues and shared memory, it is possible to implement asynchronous approaches for handling data exchange between processes.

In this section, specifically, we will practice synchronous and asynchronous programming using IPC approaches using the following hands-on activities.

- Service chaining implementation using pipes
- Service chaining implementation using FIFOs
- Asynchronous programming implementation using message queues

CHAPTER 7   HANDLE INTERPROCESS ACTIVITIES USING C PROGRAMMING

Hands-On Activity-1

In this hands-on activity, we will implement Linux commands chaining using pipes in c; specifically, we will do the following:

- Define a list of valid commands with their options, which can be chained together
    - For example: ls | wc -l
- Set up the number of processes required using the fork system call
- Execute the list of commands using execvp system calls
- Handle errors related to pipes, fork, and execvp system calls

LIST OF COMMANDS CHAINING

1. We implement this hands-on activity in ncmdschain.c.

2. First include the following necessary header files to do this hands-on activity:

    ```
    #include <stdio.h>
    #include <stdlib.h>
    #include <unistd.h>
    #include <sys/wait.h>
    ```

3. We define the following for:

    a. Creating a list of valid commands (cat, grep, and wc) with options. For example, we are chaining these commands as follows:

        i. cat ncmdshain.c |grep 'fork'|wc -l

        ii. You may replace these with valid commands and do the hands-on activity

    b. Set up a suitable number of pipes. For example, to chain N commands, N-1 pipes are needed.

CHAPTER 7   HANDLE INTERPROCESS ACTIVITIES USING C PROGRAMMING

    c. Define an array of N to collect processes IDs.

```
#define MAX_COMMANDS 10
int main()
{
        char *cmds[MAX_COMMANDS][100] = {{"cat", "ncmdschain.c",
        "ncmdschain.c",NULL}, {"grep", "fork", NULL}, {"wc",
        "-l", NULL}, {NULL}};
        int noc = 3;
        int pipes[noc-1][2];
        pid_t cpids[noc];
```

4. Set up n-1 pipes to chain n commands using pipe system call:

```
for (int i=0; i<noc-1; i++)
{
        if (pipe(pipes[i]) == -1)
        {
                perror("pipe");
                exit(EXIT_FAILURE);
        }
}
```

5. Create N processes using child processes to execute the N commands as follows:

```
for (int i=0; i<noc; i++)
{
        cpids[i] = fork();
        if (cpids[i] == -1)
        {
                perror("fork");
                exit(EXIT_FAILURE);
        }
```

CHAPTER 7   HANDLE INTERPROCESS ACTIVITIES USING C PROGRAMMING

6. Then, for the first process, using the dup2 system call redirects its standard output to the pipe connecting it to the next process as follows:

   ```
   if (cpids[i] == 0)
   {
       if (i == 0)
       {
           dup2(pipes[i][1], STDOUT_FILENO);
       }
   ```

7. Then, for the next process (or intermediate process), using dup2 connects its standard input descriptor using the previous process pipe, and using dup2 redirects its standard output descriptor to the pipe connecting it to the next process as follows:

   ```
   else if (i>0 && i<noc-1)
   {
       dup2(pipes[i-1][0], STDIN_FILENO);
       dup2(pipes[i][1], STDOUT_FILENO);
   }
   ```

8. Then, for the last process, using dup2 connects its standard input descriptor using the previous process pipe as follows:

   ```
   else if (i == noc-1)
   {
       dup2(pipes[i-1][0], STDIN_FILENO);
   }
   ```

9. After redirecting the pipes using dup system call, close all n-1 pipes' read and write descriptors to avoid redirection errors:

   ```
   for (int j=0; j<noc-1; j++)
   {
       close(pipes[j][0]);
       close(pipes[j][1]);
   }
   ```

CHAPTER 7   HANDLE INTERPROCESS ACTIVITIES USING C PROGRAMMING

10. Finally, execute a command using a child process in a reliable manner using execvp as follows:

    ```
                    execvp(cmds[i][0], cmds[i]);
                    perror("execvp");
                    exit(EXIT_FAILURE);
                }
            }
    ```

11. Because both parent and child processes are sharing the pipes, after child processes are assigned with commands and chained their execution with pipes, it is also necessary to close all n-1 pipes read and write descriptors to avoid redirection errors in the parent process.

    ```
            for (int i=0; i<noc-1; i++)
            {
                    close(pipes[i][0]);
                    close(pipes[i][1]);
            }
    ```

12. Finally, the parent process should wait for all child processes to complete their execution as follows:

    ```
            for (int i=0; i<noc; i++)
            {
                    wait(NULL);
            }
            return 0;
    }
    ```

13. Compile and test the ncmdschain.c using the following commands:

    ```
    #gcc ncmdschain.c
    #./a.out
    6
    ```

From the results, we can observe that all three commands (cat, grep, wc) chaining is done correctly and observed correct results. You may repeat the test case by chaining different commands and observing the results.

Next, let's practice how to chain nonrelated processes using FIFO.

Hands-On Activity-2

In this hands-on activity, we will implement any process services chaining using FIFO; specifically, we will do the following:

- Set up three sample processes (p1, p2, and p3)
- **First Process (p1)**: It sends three sample messages to p2
- Second Process (p2): On processing the three messages, it sends the results to process (p3)
- **Third Process**: After processing p2 results, it prints process-3 results.
- Set up a suitable number of FIFO files

SERVICE CHAINING USING FIFO

1. Implement process-1 in (fifo1.c) as follows:
2. First include the following necessary header files to do this hands-on activity:

    ```c
    #include <stdio.h>
    #include <stdlib.h>
    #include <errno.h>
    #include <string.h>
    #include <fcntl.h>
    #include <sys/types.h>
    #include <sys/stat.h>
    #include <unistd.h>
    #define OUTQ "P1P2"
    ```

3. Set up a FIFO file using `mkfifo` with the name P1P2 and open it in write-only mode:

    ```c
    int main(void)
    {
        char s[300];
        int num, fd;
    ```

CHAPTER 7   HANDLE INTERPROCESS ACTIVITIES USING C PROGRAMMING

```
mkfifo(OUTQ, 0644);

printf("P1 waiting for P2\n");
fd = open(OUTQ, O_WRONLY);
```

4. Define three sample messages to be sent from p1 to p2 using a string array:

```
printf("P2 ready then sending commands\n");
char *str[3] = {"READ", "COMPRESS", "SEND"};
```

5. Write the three sample messages into the FIFO file as follows:

```
for (int i=0;i<3;i++)
{
    if ((num = write(fd, str[i], strlen(str[i]))) == -1)
    {
        perror("write");
    }
    else
    {
        printf("P1: Command %d size in bytes\n", num);
    }
}
```

6. Finally, close the FIFO file:

```
close(fd);
return 0;
}
```

7. Compile the code and test it using the following commands:

```
#gcc fifo1.c -o p1
#./p1
P1 waiting for P2
```

From the results, observe that p1 is waiting for process p2 to get connected with FIFO file to read messages.

8. Next, implement process-2 in (fifo2.c) as follows:

9. Open the FIFO file (P1P2) in read-only mode, and set up a new FIFO file (P2P3) and open it in write-only mode:

```c
#include <stdio.h>
#include <stdlib.h>
#include <errno.h>
#include <string.h>
#include <fcntl.h>
#include <sys/types.h>
#include <sys/stat.h>
#include <unistd.h>
#define INPQ "P1P2"
#define OUTQ "P2P3"
int main(void)
{
    char s[300];
    int num, fd1, fd2;
    mkfifo(OUTQ, 0644);

    printf("P2 started to process P1 commands but it is waiting for P3 to be ready...\n");
    fd1 = open(INPQ, O_RDONLY);
    fd2 = open(OUTQ, O_WRONLY);
```

10. Using the loop, read the messages from the FIFO file P1P2 after sample processing and send them to FIFO file P2P3:

```c
    printf("P3 ready to receive...\n");
    do
    {
        if ((num = read(fd1, s, 300)) == -1)
        {
            perror("read");
        }
```

CHAPTER 7 HANDLE INTERPROCESS ACTIVITIES USING C PROGRAMMING

```
                else if (num>0)
                {
                        s[num] = '\0';
                        printf("P2: processed %d commnad: %s\n",
                        num, s);
                        int num1;
                        if ((num1 = write(fd2, s, strlen(s))) == -1)
                        {
                                perror("write");
                        }
                        else
                        {
                                printf("P2: send %d command to
                                P3\n", num);
                        }
                }
        }while (num > 0);
```

11. Finally, close both FIFO files:

```
        close(fd1);
        close(fd2);
        return 0;
}
```

12. While p1 is running, compile the code (fifo2.c) and test it using the following commands:

```
#gcc fifo2.c -o p2
#./p2
P2 started to process P1 commands but it is waiting for P3 to be
ready...
```

Observe the p1 results window:

```
P1 waiting for P2
P2 ready then sending commands
P1: Command 4 size in bytes
```

CHAPTER 7 HANDLE INTERPROCESS ACTIVITIES USING C PROGRAMMING

```
P1: Command 8 size in bytes
P1: Command 4 size in bytes
```

From the results, observe that p1 sent all his messages successfully as soon as p2 connected to it.

However, p2 is waiting for process-3 to get started for sending its messages.

13. Next, implement process-3 in (fifo3.c) as follows:

14. Open the FIFO file (P1P2) in read-only mode, and open the FIFO file (P2P3) in write-only mode:

    ```c
    #include <stdio.h>
    #include <stdlib.h>
    #include <errno.h>
    #include <string.h>
    #include <fcntl.h>
    #include <sys/types.h>
    #include <sys/stat.h>
    #include <unistd.h>
    #define INPQ "P2P3"
    int main(void)
    {
        char s[300];
        int num, fd1;
        printf("P3 waiting for P2 commands...\n");
        fd1 = open(INPQ, O_RDONLY);
        printf("P3 can receive P2 commands...\n");
    ```

15. In a loop, read the data from the P2P3 FIFO file and print it:

    ```c
    do
    {
        if ((num = read(fd1, s, 300)) == -1)
        {
            perror("read");
        }
    ```

```
            else if (num>0)
            {
                    s[num] = '\0';
                    printf("P3: executed the commands of P2 %d :
                    \"%s\"\n", num, s);
            }
    }while (num > 0);
```

16. After writing, close the FIFO file:

    ```
    close(fd1);
    return 0;
    }
    ```

17. While p2 is running, compile the code (fifo3.c) and test it using the following commands:

```
#gcc fifo3.c -o p3
#./p3
P3 waiting for P2 commands...
P3 can receive P2 commands...
P3: executed the commands of P2 16 : "READCOMPRESSSEND"
```

Observe the p2 results window:

```
P2 started to process P1 commands but it is waiting for P3 to be
ready...
P3 ready to receive...
P2: processed 16 commnad: "READCOMPRESSSEND"
P2: send 16 command to P3
```

From the results, observe that p2 sent all his messages successfully as soon as p3 connected to the FIFO file.

Then, process-3 read all messages successfully and exited.

From the results of p1, p2, and p3, we can observe that these processes are exchanging data in a synchronous manner. Moreover, FIFOs are helpful in easily setting up service chaining among processes.

Next, we will learn how to set up message queues and implement asynchronous programming tasks.

Hands-On Activity-3

In this hands-on activity, we will implement asynchronous programming using message queues, and specifically, we will do the following activities:

- We set up a message queue to process messages in priority order in an asynchronous manner. It means the sender need not wait for the receiver to send messages. Moreover, a message receiver can start at any point in time and read messages from the message queue in priority order.
- The message sender sends three types of messages, and it assumes the following priority order to process these messages.
  - Type-3 highest priority, type-2 medium priority, type-1 low priority
- Message receiver waits in a forever loop.
  - It processes messages from the message queue in priority order.
  - On exiting the receiver, remove the message queue in a reliable manner using signals. (If you want to test it multiple times, do not remove the message queue in the code.)

SERVICE CHAINING USING FIFO

1. Implement the message sender process in (sendr.c) as follows:
2. First, include the following necessary header files to do this hands-on activity:

```
#include <stdio.h>
#include <stdlib.h>
#include <errno.h>
#include <string.h>
#include <sys/types.h>
#include <sys/ipc.h>
```

CHAPTER 7   HANDLE INTERPROCESS ACTIVITIES USING C PROGRAMMING

```
#include <sys/msg.h>
struct Message
{
        long type;
        char messg[200];
};
```

3. Define five sample messages with different priorities as follows:

```
int main(void)
{
        struct Message msg[5] = {{1,"A"}, {3,"B"},{3,"C"},
        {1,"D"},{2,"C"}};
```

4. Set up a message queue with a unique key using ftok and msgctl system calls in a reliable manner:

```
int msqid;
key_t key;
if ((key = ftok("sendr.c", 'B')) == -1)
{
        perror("ftok");
        exit(1);
}
if ((msqid = msgget(key, 0644 | IPC_CREAT)) == -1)
{
        perror("msgget");
        exit(1);
}
```

5. After setting up the message queue, send all five sample messages using msgsnd:

```
for (int i=0;i<5;i++)
{
        int len = strlen(msg[i].messg);
        if (msgsnd(msqid, &msg[i], len, 0) == -1)
```

```
            {
                    perror("msgsnd");
            }
            else
            {
                    printf("%s sent\n",msg[i].messg);
            }
        }
        return 0;
}
```

6. Compile the code and test it as follows:

   ```
   #gcc sendr.c
   #./a.out
   A sent
   B sent
   C sent
   D sent
   C sent
   ```

   Observe from the above results that the message sender process is not waiting for any receiver, and it simply sends all its messages and exits. Next, let's implement the message receiver process as follows:

7. Include the following necessary header files to do this hands-on activity in rcvr.c:

   ```
   #include <stdio.h>
   #include <stdlib.h>
   #include <errno.h>
   #include <string.h>
   #include <sys/types.h>
   #include <sys/ipc.h>
   #include <sys/msg.h>
   #include <signal.h>
   ```

CHAPTER 7 HANDLE INTERPROCESS ACTIVITIES USING C PROGRAMMING

8. Set up a signal handler to handle the exit of the message receiver in a reliable manner. The message receiver exits after removing the message queue only.

    ```c
    int gmqid;
    void signal_handler(int signum)
    {
            printf("Signal %d received \n", signum);
            if (signum == SIGINT)
            {
                    printf("Process interrupted\n");
                    msgctl(gmqid, IPC_RMID, NULL);
                    exit(0);
            }
    }
    ```

9. Define a message structure like message sender for receiving messages correctly as follows:

    ```c
    struct Message
    {
            long type;
            char messg[200];
    };
    ```

10. Access the already set up message queue using the unique key (sendr.c):

    ```c
    int main(void)
    {
            struct Message msg;
            int msqid;
            key_t key;
            if ((key = ftok("sendr.c", 'B')) == -1)
            {
                    perror("ftok");
                    exit(1);
            }
    ```

CHAPTER 7 HANDLE INTERPROCESS ACTIVITIES USING C PROGRAMMING

```
if ((msqid = msgget(key, 0644)) == -1)
{
    perror("msgget");
    exit(1);
}
gmqid=msqid;
```

11. Register with a signal handler to handle the Ctrl+C command. Specifically, before existing, it removes the message queue. In case you want to repeat the testing without removing the message queue, do not register with the signal handler:

```
struct sigaction sa;
sa.sa_handler = signal_handler;
sigemptyset(&sa.sa_mask);
sa.sa_flags = 0;
if (sigaction(SIGINT, &sa, NULL) == -1)
{
    perror("sigaction");
    exit(1);
}
printf("Receiver Processing Messages in Priority.\n");
```

12. Wait for messages to be received from the message queue in a forever loop. Inside the loop, to process messages in priority order (Type-3, Type-2, and Type-1), use IPC_NOWAIT and read messages from the message queue using msgrcv using loops in order as follows:

```
for(;;)
{
    while (msgrcv(msqid, &msg, sizeof msg.messg, 3, IPC_
    NOWAIT) != -1)
    {
        printf("Type-3: \"%s\"\n", msg.messg);
    }
    while (msgrcv(msqid, &msg, sizeof msg.messg, 2, IPC_
    NOWAIT) != -1)
```

CHAPTER 7 HANDLE INTERPROCESS ACTIVITIES USING C PROGRAMMING

```
                {
                        printf("Type-2: \"%s\"\n", msg.messg);
                }
                while (msgrcv(msqid, &msg, sizeof msg.messg, 1, IPC_
                NOWAIT) != -1)
                {
                        printf("Type-1: \"%s\"\n", msg.messg);
                }
        }
        return 0;
}
```

13. After running message sender, compile the code and test it using the following commands:

    ```
    #gcc rcvr.c -o msgrcvr
    #./msgrcvr
    Receiver Processing Messages in Priority.
    Type-3: "B"
    Type-3: "C"
    Type-2: "C"
    Type-1: "A"
    Type-1: "D"
    ```

    From the results, observe that the message receiver processes the message in priority order (3, 2, and 1). Moreover, it is waiting infinitely.

    a. You may test it again by running a message receiver and observing no messages are available due to all messages already being processed from the message queue.

    b. After the message sender sends a sample message again, you may test it again by running a message receiver and observing messages will be processed in priority order.

From the results, observe that the message sender and receiver processes are exchanging data in an asynchronous manner. Moreover, message queues are helpful to implement processing messages in priority also. We recommend extending these codes to include more priority messages and changing the order of messages to be processed for better learning.

Next, we will learn how to set up message queues and implement asynchronous programming tasks.

Essential IPC Synchronization Handling Tools

In this section, we will discuss how to handle synchronization issues among multiple processes. In the case of implementing a multiprocessing application, it is necessary to share data and exchange results among multiple processes using IPC approaches. For example, since OS is not handling process synchronization issues, in case of sharing data using the shared memory IPC approach, the following conflict operations are possible:

- **Read/Write or Write/Read:** When one process is trying to read data from the shared memory and another process is trying to update the data from the shared memory simultaneously
- **Write/Write:** Both processes are writing data into shared variables simultaneously

Developers must handle these conflict operations carefully to get reliable and consistent results from multiple executions of processes. For example, when two processes are updating the shrdres=0 variable, which is attached to a shared memory in the following shared code snippet, it can result in incorrect results:

```
for(int k=0;k<10000;k++)
    *shrdres = *shrdres+1;
```

If two processes (p1 and p2) execute the code simultaneously, at the end of the execution, the resultant value of the shrdres must be equal to the serial execution of the two processes (p1 p2 or p2 p1). Since the shrdres is updated by each of the processes 1000 times, the final value of the shrdres must be 2000. But the shrdres updating instruction at assembly-level code is like the following code snippet:

```
move reg, *shrdres;
Add reg, 1;
move *shrdres, reg;
```

In this case, developers must understand that these three assembly instructions are simultaneously executed by the two processes, and due to the possibility of interleaving of these instructions, execution can lead to inconsistent results. It is known as data access race **conditions**.

- For example, using **move reg, *shrdres** instructions, process-1 copied the **counter** value 0 to **reg** and incremented **register** value to 1 using the next instruction, **Add**.

- Before process-1 executes **move counter, reg** instruction, if process-2 starts executing **move reg, *shrdres**, then it sets the **reg** value to 0.

- Then, if process-1 starts executing its next instruction **move counter, reg**, then it results in ***shrdres** value being 0. Since process-1 executed its entire code, and at the end of the process-1 execution, the **counter** value must be 1. But due to incorrect interleaving, the ***shrdres** value is 0, and it is incorrect.

The above sample code is technically called **critical section** code. While accessing critical sections, processes suffer from race conditions, and it must be handled by developers to guarantee the parallel execution results of N processes are equal to one of the serial executions of N processes (p1, p2, ... pN). In order to address the critical section issues, Linux supports IPC approaches called semaphores. We discuss it in the coming section.

Semaphores

On a Linux OS, semaphores are nothing but shared memory variables only. However, to access these shared variables (semaphores), Linux OS offers atomic operations called wait (v) and post (p). Usually, a semaphore variable is considered as a key variable to access the critical section, and it should be initialized with a counter value.

To enter a critical section, a process must do a **wait** operation over the semaphore variable. If semaphore variable is > 0, then the wait operation decrements the semaphore variable and allows the process to enter the critical section. If the semaphore variable is < 0, then the process gets blocked by the OS until the semaphore variable is > 0.

On the other hand, before leaving a critical section, a process must do a **post** operation over the semaphore variable. If semaphore variable is less than the initialized count value, then the post-operation increments the semaphore variable and the process exits the critical section. If the semaphore variable equals the initialized count, then the process gets blocked by the OS until the semaphore variable is less than the initialized count. Semaphore synchronization approaches are advantageous due to the following reasons:

- **Mutual Exclusion:** At a time, only one process can access the critical section code.

- **Progress:** Once a process leaves the critical section, then one of the waiting processes can enter the critical section and access the code.

- **Bounded Waiting:** No process waits indefinitely to access a critical section.

Next, we will learn how to set up and access semaphore variables in C programming tasks.

Usage of Semaphore in C

We will learn the following in case of using FIFO in C:

- Creating a semaphore
- Accessing a semaphore
- Responsibilities of developers

First, we will learn to create a semaphore IPC in Linux. In C applications, using the sem_open system call, it is possible to create a new semaphore or get an existing semaphore using suitable flags. For example, in case we want to create a new semaphore with initial count 1 and create it only if the given semaphore name exists, then we set the O_CREAT and O_EXCL flags:

```
sem_t *semkey = sem_open("/mysemlock", O_CREAT | O_EXCL, 0644, 1);
if (semkey == SEM_FAILED)
{
    perror("sem_open failed");
    exit(EXIT_FAILURE);
}
```

CHAPTER 7 HANDLE INTERPROCESS ACTIVITIES USING C PROGRAMMING

Then, to access the semaphore, the following two important operations are used. First, operation is sem_wait; it decrements the semaphore value if and if the value is > 1. Otherwise, the process calling sem_wait blocks until the semaphore value becomes >0. Usually, sem_wait is used before accessing the critical section.

On the other hand, after accessing the critical section, it is necessary to signal the OS to allow other waiting processes to schedule in the critical section. It is done through the sem_post operation. The sem_post operation increments the semaphore value if its value is less than the semaphore initialized value. Usually, the sem_post is used after exiting from the critical section code.

For example, to update a shared resource by multiple processes, the following code snippet describes the usage of sem_wait and sem_post operations:

```
sem_wait(semkey);
for(int k=0;k<10000;k++)
      *shrdres = *shrdres+1;
sem_post(semkey);
```

Finally, after semaphore usage is completed, it is necessary to close the semaphore and remove the semaphore using the following two operations.

```
sem_close(semkey);
sem_unlink("/mysemlock");
```

Next, we will learn the developers' role in the usage of a semaphore.

Developers' Role in Case of Shared Memory Usage

While two processes are accessing a semaphore for critical section access in a mutually exclusive way, the following things must be understood by developers:

- First, it is necessary to create a unique semaphore object using the following arguments:
  - Semaphore name
  - Suitable permissions such as read, write, and execute (666)
  - Suitable flags
  - Initial value (count)

- Sharing memory access simultaneously by multiple processes can lead to data race conditions; hence, it is necessary to implement a synchronized way to access the shared memory using synchronization tools such as semaphores.

- Before accessing the critical section, first it needs to acquire a semaphore key by decrementing the semaphore value using sem_wait.

- After accessing the critical section, any process needs to release the semaphore key by incrementing the semaphore value using sem_post.

- Incorrect usage of sem_wait or sem_post can lead to incorrect results; hence, do not change the meaning of the semaphore operations usage.

- The order of the sem_wait and sem_post must be followed in the correct order.
    - Changing the order of wait and post-operation can lead to deadlock situations

- In case of a fixed number of processes to enter a critical section, then counting semaphore should be used. It means initialize the semaphore value to >1.

Next, we will do the following hands-on activities to practice semaphore usage in terms of handling data race conditions and controlling the number of processes to enter a critical section simultaneously.

Hands-On Activity-1

In this hands-on activity, we will learn how to access a shared memory resource in a reliable manner using semaphores. Specifically, we do the following:

- Set up a shared memory of an integer size in a reliable manner.
- Set up 1 parent and 10 child processes using the fork system call in a reliable manner.

CHAPTER 7   HANDLE INTERPROCESS ACTIVITIES USING C PROGRAMMING

- All 10 child processes simultaneously update the shared memory contents by 10000 times.

- Use semaphore to update the shared memory contents in a reliable manner to achieve consistent results.

- Use semaphores in a reliable manner.

- After 10 child processes' execution is over, the parent process should print the updated value of the shared memory.

- At the end of the program, remove semaphores and the shared memory.

SAFE WAYS TO ACCESS SHARED MEMORY USING SEMAPHORE

1. We implement this hands-on activity in safesharing.c.

2. First include the following necessary header files to do this hands-on activity:

   ```
   #include <sys/ipc.h>
   #include <sys/shm.h>
   #include <sys/wait.h>
   #include <stdio.h>
   #include <unistd.h>
   #include <fcntl.h>
   #include <stdlib.h>
   #include <semaphore.h>
   #define KEY 7860
   ```

3. First create a semaphore using sem_open in a reliable manner to protect the shared resource access in a safe manner.

   a. Give a unique semaphore name to create it

   b. Initialize it with 1 to ensure only one process can enter the critical section at a time

   ```
   int main()
   {
       pid_t pid;
   ```

CHAPTER 7 HANDLE INTERPROCESS ACTIVITIES USING C PROGRAMMING

```
int shmid;
int *shrdres;
int size = sizeof(int);
sem_t *semkey = sem_open("/mysemlock", O_CREAT | O_EXCL,
0644, 1);
if (semkey == SEM_FAILED)
{
    perror("sem_open failed");
    exit(EXIT_FAILURE);
}
```

4. Set up a shared memory using a unique key in a reliable manner:

   ```
   shmid = shmget(KEY, size, 0666 | IPC_CREAT);
   if (shmid == -1)
   {
       perror("shmget failed");
       return 1;
   }
   ```

5. Attach to the shared memory using its id in a reliable manner:

   ```
   shrdres = (int *)shmat(shmid, NULL, 0);
   if (shrdres == (int *)-1)
   {
       perror("shmat failed");
       return 1;
   }
   ```

6. Let's create 10 child processes using fork as follows:

   a. First create 10 child processes using fork in a reliable manner.

   b. Observe that both shared memory and semaphore are shared among all child processes and the parent process.

CHAPTER 7   HANDLE INTERPROCESS ACTIVITIES USING C PROGRAMMING

c. Hence, inside child processes it is possible to access the shared memory and semaphore.

```
for (int i = 0; i < 10; i++)
{
    pid = fork();
    if (pid == -1)
    {
        perror("fork failed");
        exit(EXIT_FAILURE);
    }
```

d. Specifically, observe that while accessing the shared memory, first obtain a semaphore key using `sem_wait`. If any process has already acquired the semaphore key, then the current process gets blocked.

e. After accessing the shared memory, the process should release the semaphore key using `sem_post`.

```
    else if (pid == 0)
    {
        sem_wait(semkey);
        for(int k=0;k<10000;k++)
            *shrdres = *shrdres+1;
        sem_post(semkey);
        if (shmdt(shrdres) == -1)
        {
            perror("shmdt");
            exit(EXIT_FAILURE);
        }
        exit(EXIT_SUCCESS);
    }
}
```

CHAPTER 7 HANDLE INTERPROCESS ACTIVITIES USING C PROGRAMMING

7. Parent process waits for all children processes to complete their execution in a reliable manner and exit:

   ```
   for (int i = 0; i < 10; i++)
   {
       wait(NULL);
   }
   ```

8. The parent process prints the final value of the shared resource:

   ```
   printf("Final shared variable value: %d\n", *shrdres);
   ```

9. Finally, the parent process closes the semaphore key and removes the semaphore object:

   ```
   sem_close(semkey);
   sem_unlink("/mysemlock");
   ```

10. Detach the parent process from the shared memory and remove the shared memory:

    ```
    if (shmdt(shrdres) == -1)
    {
        perror("shmdt");
        exit(EXIT_FAILURE);
    }
    shmctl(shmid, IPC_RMID, NULL);
    return 0;
    }
    ```

11. Compile and test the safesharing.c using the following commands:

    ```
    #gcc safesharing.c -lpthread
    #./a.out
    Final shared variable value: 100000

    #./a.out
    Final shared variable value: 200000
    ```

465

From the results, we can observe that all 10 processes are accessing the shared memory in a reliable manner. Hence, all processes' updates are correctly reflected in the results. We recommend you remove sem_wait and sem_post and test the code. Then, we will observe the unpredictable results due to race conditions.

Next, let's learn how to control the number of processes to enter into a critical section using a counting semaphore.

Hands-On Activity-2

In this hands-on activity, we will learn how to control the number of processes accessing a shared memory resource for read operations in a reliable manner using semaphores. Specifically, we do the following:

- Set up a shared memory of an integer size in a reliable manner.
- Set up 1 parent process and 10 child processes using the fork system call in a reliable manner.
- Set up a semaphore variable and initialize it with a suitable count to control the number of processes to enter the critical section simultaneously.
- All 10 child processes try simultaneously reading the shared memory contents; however, the parent process should control the number of processes to enter the critical section simultaneously.
- Use semaphores in a reliable manner to control the access of the shared memory.
- At the end of the program remove semaphores and the shared memory.

CHAPTER 7 HANDLE INTERPROCESS ACTIVITIES USING C PROGRAMMING

CONTROL NUMBER OF PROCESSES TO ACCESS SHARED MEMORY USING SEMAPHORE

1. We implement this hands-on activity in ctrlacces.c.

2. First include the following necessary header files to do this hands-on activity:

   ```
   #include <sys/ipc.h>
   #include <sys/shm.h>
   #include <sys/wait.h>
   #include <stdio.h>
   #include <unistd.h>
   #include <fcntl.h>
   #include <stdlib.h>
   #include <semaphore.h>
   #define KEY 7860
   ```

3. First create a semaphore using sem_open in a reliable manner to protect the shared resource access in a safe manner

   a. Give a unique semaphore name to create it

   b. Initialize it with 1 to ensure only one process can enter into the critical section at a time

   ```
   int main()
   {
           pid_t pid;
           int shmid;
           int *shrdres;
           int size = sizeof(int);
           sem_t *semkey = sem_open("/mysemlock", O_CREAT |
           O_EXCL, 0644, 2);
           if (semkey == SEM_FAILED)
           {
                   perror("sem_open failed");
                   exit(EXIT_FAILURE);
           }
   ```

CHAPTER 7 HANDLE INTERPROCESS ACTIVITIES USING C PROGRAMMING

4. Set up a shared memory using a unique key in a reliable manner:

    ```
    shmid = shmget(KEY, size, 0666 | IPC_CREAT);
    if (shmid == -1)
    {
        perror("shmget failed");
        return 1;
    }
    ```

5. Attach to the shared memory using its id in a reliable manner:

    ```
    shrdres = (int *)shmat(shmid, NULL, 0);
    if (shrdres == (int *)-1)
    {
        perror("shmat failed");
        return 1;
    }
    ```

6. Let's create 10 child processes using fork as follows:

    a. First create 10 child processes using fork in a reliable manner.

    b. Observe that both shared memory and semaphore are shared among all child processes and the parent process.

    c. Hence, inside child processes, it is possible to access the shared memory and semaphore.

    ```
    for (int i = 0; i < 10; i++)
    {
        pid = fork();
        if (pid == -1)
        {
            perror("fork failed");
            exit(EXIT_FAILURE);
        }
    }
    ```

    d. Specifically, observe that while accessing the shared memory, first obtain a semaphore key using sem_wait. If any process has already acquired the semaphore key, then the current process gets blocked.

e. After accessing the shared memory, the process is not releasing the semaphore key, because here the parent process controls the number of processes to enter the critical section.

```c
        else if (pid == 0)
        {
                printf("%d process trying to enter\n ",i);
                sem_wait(semkey); // Acquire semaphore
                printf("%d process entered and read shared
                memory %d \n",i,*shrdres);
                sleep(2);
                printf("%d process exited\n ",i);
                if (shmdt(shrdres) == -1)
                {
                        perror("shmdt");
                        exit(EXIT_FAILURE);
                }
                exit(EXIT_SUCCESS);
        }
}
```

7. The parent process first releases the semaphore and allows waiting processes to enter the critical section. Then it also waits for all children processes to complete their execution and exit:

```c
for (int i = 0; i < 10; i++)
{
        sem_post(semkey);
        wait(NULL);
}
```

8. The parent process prints the final value of the shared resource:

```c
printf("Final shared variable value: %d\n", *shrdres);
```

CHAPTER 7 HANDLE INTERPROCESS ACTIVITIES USING C PROGRAMMING

9. Finally, the parent process closes the semaphore key and removes the semaphore object:

   ```
   sem_close(semkey); // Close the semaphore
   sem_unlink("/mysemlock"); // Remove the se
   ```

10. Detach the parent process from the shared memory and remove the shared memory:

    ```
    if (shmdt(shrdres) == -1)
    {
            perror("shmdt");
            exit(EXIT_FAILURE);
    }
    shmctl(shmid, IPC_RMID, NULL);
    return 0;
    }
    ```

11. Compile and test the ctrlacces.c using the following commands:

    ```
    #gcc ctrlacces.c -lpthread
    #./a.out
    0 process trying to enter
     0 process entered and read shared memory 0
    1 process trying to enter
    2 process trying to enter
     1 process entered and read shared memory 0
    3 process trying to enter
    4 process trying to enter
    5 process trying to enter
    6 process trying to enter
    7 process trying to enter
    8 process trying to enter
     2 process entered and read shared memory 0
    9 process trying to enter
    0 process exited
    1 process exited
       2 process exited
    ```

```
4 process entered and read shared memory 0
3 process entered and read shared memory 0
5 process entered and read shared memory 0
4 process exited
3 process exited
  5 process exited
  6 process entered and read shared memory 0
7 process entered and read shared memory 0
8 process entered and read shared memory 0
6 process exited
7 process exited
8 process exited
  9 process entered and read shared memory 0
9 process exited
  Final shared variable value: 0
```

From the results, we can observe that at a time, only a maximum of two processes are accessing the shared resources, and the remaining processes are waiting for their turn. As soon as the parent process releases the semaphore key, waiting processes enter into the critical section.

In this section, we have practiced how to use Linux IPC synchronization tools for handling issues such as data race conditions between multiple processes. It helps developers to implement reliable applications to produce consistent results in case of shared resources accessed by multiple processes.

Summary

In this chapter, we have learned about important Linux IPC constructs and synchronization issues handling tools. Specifically, we have learned which IPC constructs to be used in which contexts. Hands-on activities discussed in this chapter help developers to use pipes, FIFOs, message queues, and shared memory in a reliable and efficient manner. Moreover, developers can easily handle large-sized applications and global resource sharing among multiple process tasks in a flexible manner using Linux IPC constructs and synchronization tools.

In the next chapter, we will learn Linux socket programming to implement TCP- and UDP-based network applications.

Practice Tasks

1. Implement a simple custom shell for handling the following:
   - Multiple commands execution in a reliable manner
   - Commands sequencing
   - Redirecting command outputs to files
   - Redirecting inputs for commands from files

2. Simulate the following application in a reliable manner using message queues.
   - Implement publisher and subscriber processes
   - Publishers publish sample events such as input data for performing the following: processing, sorting, and counting tasks
   - The subscriber should handle input data processing, sorting, and counting tasks in a specific priority order.

3. Simulate the following application in a reliable manner using shared memory and other necessary IPC constructs.
   - Implement publisher and subscriber processes
   - Publishers publish sample events such as input data for performing the following: processing, sorting, and counting tasks
   - The subscriber should handle file data processing, sorting, and searching tasks in a specific priority order

CHAPTER 8

Essential Network Socket Programming Skills

In Chapter 7, "Handle Interprocess Activities Using C Programming," we have learned how to implement inter process communication activities on a system using Linux IPC constructs in C programming. In this chapter, we will learn how to implement network applications using Linux socket programming in C. We will start this chapter by introducing Internet, the TCP/IP protocols stack, and network application architectures. Next, you will be learning how to implement network applications using fundamental transport protocols such as transmission control protocol (TCP) and user datagram protocol (UDP). Specifically, you will learn how to use TCP/UDP sockets for implementing client-server network applications in C.

You will start with learning TCP/UDP client and server application structures before implementing network applications. Next, you will be learning to implement reliable network applications using TCP sockets by exploring TCP details. Then, you will explore the importance of UDP and experiment with UDP socket programming. You will practice TCP/UDP socket programming through basic hands-on activities.

Finally, you will learn how to implement applications related to inspecting TCP/UDP traffic using open-source C libraries such as `libpcap`. You will practice implementing basic TCP traffic inspection and UDP traffic inspection hands-on activities in C programming. Mainly, in this chapter, we will cover the following topics:

1. Quick Introduction to TCP/IP stack and network applications

2. TCP socket programming

3. UDP socket programming

4. C programming ways for monitoring and inspecting TCP/UDP applications traffic

CHAPTER 8   ESSENTIAL NETWORK SOCKET PROGRAMMING SKILLS

Quick Introduction to TCP/IP Stack and Network Applications

The Internet comprises a network of networks. Broadly, Internet comprises access networks, enterprise networks, and Internet service provider (ISP) networks. Access networks are nothing but your home networks and Wi-Fi/mobile networks. Users connect to the Internet using access networks such as Wi-Fi networks (home networks) and mobile networks. On the other hand, enterprise networks are helpful to provide a variety of services for a large set of users. For example, universities, multinational companies, set up larger networks for catering user Internet services and deploying various services such as web service, e-mail, e-commerce servers. These servers should be accessible over the Internet means they must be reachable from any access networks. Here come ISP networks, such as regional and global ISP networks, which interconnect all the networks. For example, home Wi-Fi networks or enterprise LANs connect with regional ISP networks, and cellular or mobile networks connect with global ISP networks.

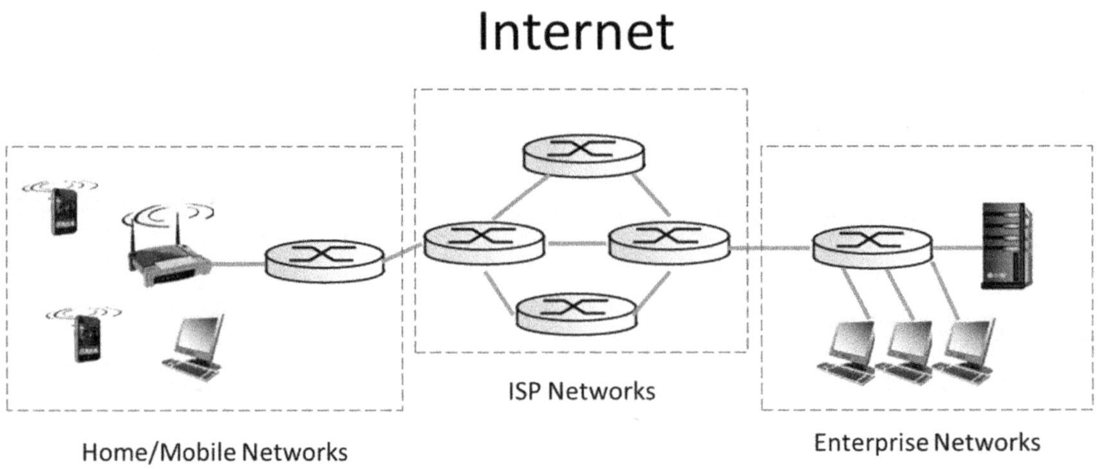

Figure 8-1. A simplified Internet

From Figure 8-1, observe a simplified Internet infrastructure and components.

- End devices are nothing but mobile phones, laptops, computers, and servers. These devices are helpful to deploy and access Internet services. For instance, mobile phones or laptops are helpful to access the Internet, whereas physical servers host a variety of Internet services such as e-mail, webservers, e-commerce servers.

CHAPTER 8 ESSENTIAL NETWORK SOCKET PROGRAMMING SKILLS

- Interconnecting devices such as switches, Wi-Fi access pointers, and routers are helpful to forward or route users' traffic over the Internet. These devices are helpful to connect a variety of networks together. Specifically, routers are helpful to interconnect larger networks as part of setting up the Internet.

- Communication channels such as wireless spectrum, Ethernet, fiber, and optical cables are helpful to establish connections between devices.

Next, we will learn necessary Internet protocol stack basics for implementing network applications in C.

TCP/IP Stack

The Internet is a complex infrastructure, network applications in order to exchange data traffic have lots of rules that are needed to be followed. Here comes the Internet standard TCP/IP protocol stack at rescue for exchanging traffic over the Internet. Fathers of the Internet: Vinton Cerf and Robert Kahn, designed TCP/IP protocol stack for data transmission over Internet.

TCP/IP Layers

TCP/IP protocol suite handles the complexities of network applications data exchange by the following five important layers with necessary rules for data exchange as shown in Figure 8-2.

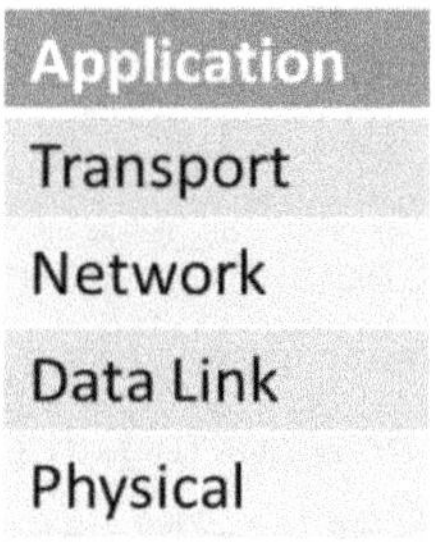

Application
Transport
Network
Data Link
Physical

Figure 8-2. *TCP/IP protocol stack*

CHAPTER 8   ESSENTIAL NETWORK SOCKET PROGRAMMING SKILLS

It is important to understand the order of the protocol stack processing on a host. On the sender side, data is transmitted by enforcing rules from the top layer (application) to the bottom layer (physical). On the other hand, on the receiver side, data is received from the bottom layer (physical) to the top layer (application) by checking rules.

- **Application Layer**: Define application-specific rules such as message types, message structure, order of messages exchange, and error handling over the Internet.
  - It uses high-level and user-readable addresses, such as hostnames, for addressing sender or receiver network applications.
  - **Example**: HTTP is designed to handle web applications' messages exchange
  - **Example**: SMTP is designed to handle e-mail message exchange
- **Transport Layer**: Defines source process to destination process message exchange rules over Internet. It takes an application message from the application layer and creates a transport layer specific message structure to handle message exchanges in reliable manners between source network application and destination network application. Usually, transport layer message structure defines source and destination port numbers of network applications as addresses; it sets sequential and acknowledgment numbers for reliability checks, receives buffer sizes for flow control, and flags for connection and control message types.
  - It uses a 16-bit port number as source or destination process address.
  - TCP is defined as a connection-oriented protocol for reliable message exchange between network applications. Mainly, it handles error control, flow control, and congestion control activities for reliable messages exchange between source and destination network applications.
  - UDP is defined as a connection-less protocol for network applications to have fine grain control over message exchange in terms of message size, exchange interval, and quick delivery

with less overhead. It does not need connection procedures and reliability algorithms for data transmission. However, it does not offer reliable message exchange services as TCP does.

- **Network Layer**: Defines source host to destination host messages exchange rules over the Internet. It takes transport layer messages and creates a network layer datagram to transmit over the Internet from source host to destination host. It mainly defines rules related to network devices addressing, datagrams routing over the Internet, and error handling.

  - IP is defined for handling Internet devices addresses management and routing of IP packets for Internet messages exchange.

    - It uses a 36-bit number as a source or destination IP address
    - Internet control message protocol (ICMP) is defined for handling errors during source host to destination host message exchange

- **Data Link Layer**: Defines link (or channel) access rules and node to next node messages exchange rules over Internet. It takes a network layer datagram and creates a data link layer frame to transmit from one node to next node during data transmission from source to destination over the Internet.

  - It uses a 48-bit number as a source or destination medium access control (MAC) address
  - It defines channel access rules

- **Physical Layer**: Defines rules related to transmitting data over physical channels such as wireless or wired medium.

TCP/IP Stack and Network Interactions

Next, we will learn how TCP/IP layers work over Internet infrastructure. Any host (mobile or laptop or computer or server) and network devices that need to connect with the Internet must install a TCP/IP stack.

Network Devices and Their TCP/IP Stack Layers

Network applications running over the hosts can exchange messages over the Internet using TCP/IP layers services (shown in Figure 8-3) and rules. For example, a web browser installed on a phone wants to access web servers; it needs to communicate through a TCP/IP stack to enjoy HTTP services, TCP services, IP services, and channel access services. Usually, network applications connect with TCP/IP stack using network socket as end point for sending or receiving messages over the Internet.

Similarly, interconnecting devices such as routers and switches also need to run a partial stack of TCP/IP (shown in Figure 8-3) to support the end host messages to forward over the Internet. For example, network switches are designed to set up LAN. To exchange messages within a LAN, there is no need of routing services; however, it needs channel access and node-to-next-node message delivery services. To handle these services, switches are installed with data link layer (DLL) and physical layer (PL) protocols.

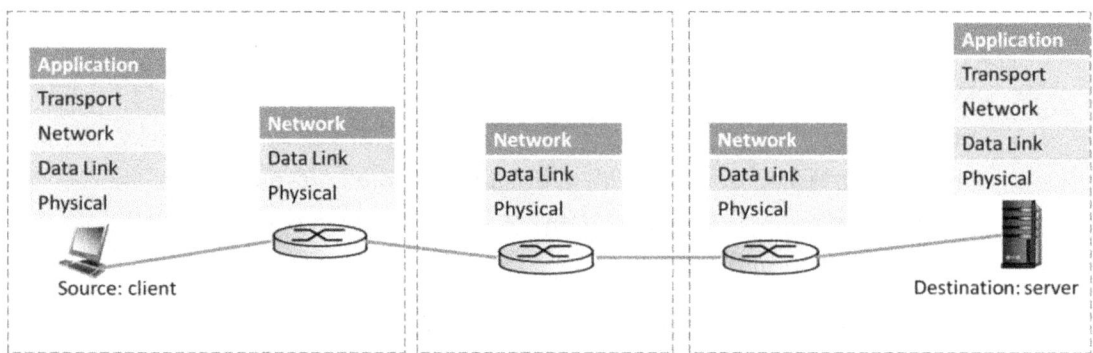

Figure 8-3. Source and destination network traffic exchange over multiple networks

On the other hand, to interconnect multiple networks, routing services are necessary besides DLL and PL. Hence, routers are installed with network layer (NL), DLL, and PL.

Basics of Protocol Address

A protocol address is a combination of an IP address (32-bit) and a port number (16-bit). IP address is for uniquely identifying network devices (hosts or servers) over the Internet. On the other hand, port number is useful to uniquely identify network applications (or process) on the network host. In socket programming, we call it a socket address. Socket

CHAPTER 8 ESSENTIAL NETWORK SOCKET PROGRAMMING SKILLS

is an API for network applications to send and receive messages over the network. When a network application sends a message, it traverses over the network using the IP address to reach the network and the specific host, and the port number is useful on the host to identify a unique network application to deliver the message. Usually, to assign a port number to a network application, we should choose a unique number > 1024. Because port numbers <1024 are reserved and privileged port numbers. Next, we will discuss IP address details.

IP Address

Any device that wants to connect with the Internet and exchange traffic, it must be assigned with an IP address. To simplify IP addresses assignment tasks to network devices, DHCP (Dynamic Host Configuration Protocol) client and server applications are helpful. A network device runs a DHCP client to get a unique IP address to be configured by contacting the DHCP server. An IPv4 address is a 32-bit unique address assigned to a network device. Besides the IP address, the DHCP server supplies the following important configuration details to a network device to access the Internet:

- **An Unique IP Address and Subnet Mask:** In IPv4 addressing, a block of IP addresses is denoted as a.b.c.d/n in which a.b.c.d defines one of the addresses and the /n defines the subnet mask.

- **For Example**: 205.24.37.39/28 indicates device IP: 205.24.37.39 and subnet mask is 28 bits.

- **Default Router IP Address:** It helps to reach route host traffic to the Internet or other networks.

- **DNS Server Address**: It helps to translate hostnames to IP addresses.

Let's inspect an IP address in detail to calculate subnet, host addresses from a classless IP address as shown in Figure 8-4.

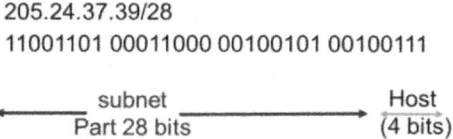

Figure 8-4. *Extracting subnet and host ID from a classless IP address*

CHAPTER 8   ESSENTIAL NETWORK SOCKET PROGRAMMING SKILLS

Subnet length "n" indicates starting from the MSB of the 32-bit IP address to n bits are used for calculating the subnet address. It means from the IP (205.24.37.39), the MSB 28 bits indicate the subnet of the IP address (205.24.37.32), and the remaining 4 bits of 32 bits are used to calculate the host identifier (7).

It is also possible to calculate the total number of IP addresses belonging to a subnet using the following formula: $2^{(32-n)}$. In our example, $2^{(32-28)} = 16$ addresses.

The first address of the subnet can be computed by setting the rightmost $32 - n$ bits to 0s and do AND operation with the given IP as follows:

11001101 00011000 00100101 00100111
11001101 00011000 00100101 00100000

The first address of the subnet is 205.24.37.32. However, this IP address cannot be used to configure any host of the network. It indicates the network ID.

The last address of the subnet can be computed by setting the rightmost $32 - n$ bits to 1s and doing an AND operation with the given IP as follows:

11001101 00011000 00100101 00100111
11001101 00011000 00100101 00101111

The last address of the subnet is 205.24.37.47. However, this IP address cannot be used to configure any host of the network. It indicates a subnet-directed broadcast address. It helps to send broadcast messages in the network.

It is also necessary to know details of public and private IP addresses of the Internet.

Public IP addresses are limited and these need to be purchased from ISP. We use public IP addresses to host services over the Internet.

On the other hand, private IP addresses (shown in Figure 8-5) are free to all networks to use them for their internal network devices. These are helpful to handle addressing for large numbers of devices that belong to local or internal networks.

Private Network	Private IP Address Ranges
10.0.0.0/24	10.0.0.0 to 10.255.255.255
172.16.0.0/20	172.16.0.0 to 172.31.255.255
192.168.0.0/16	192.168.0.0 to 192.168.255.255

Figure 8-5. *Private IP networks and addresses*

Private IP addresses are used to assign network addresses to LAN or internet devices. In case these private IP address hosts need to contact an Internet public server, routers of the private network with network address translation (NAT) configuration helps in translating these private IP addresses to a public IP. The following are the available private IP address blocks for internet or LAN devices.

TCP Socket Programming

Transmission Control Protocol (TCP) is implemented as part of a transport layer to offer reliable data exchange over the Internet. TCP offers reliable services; it enforces the following important rules between network applications.

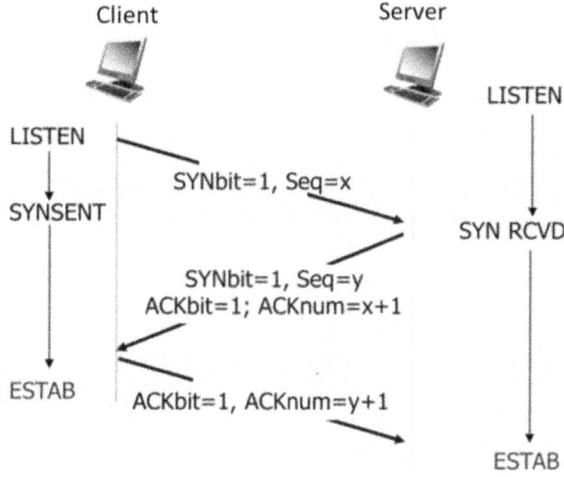

Figure 8-6. *TCP connection establishment: 3-way handshake procedure*

For example, a TCP client and a TCP server application need to exchange data in a reliable manner shown in Figure 8-6; the following three high-level rules are imposed by TCP:

1. Connection set up rules between the TCP client and the TCP server

2. Data exchange rules through acknowledgments

3. Connection shutdown rules between the TCP client and the TCP server

CHAPTER 8　ESSENTIAL NETWORK SOCKET PROGRAMMING SKILLS

TCP Rules

Data exchange between TCP network applications involves a number of rules to be followed for reliable transmission over the network. In this section, we will discuss these rules. First, we discuss TCP connection setup rules.

TCP Connection Setup

TCP connection set up involves a three way handshaking procedure between the TCP client and TCP server as shown in Figure 8-6. This procedure helps in setting up reliable data exchange configurations (agreeing on sequence numbers for data exchange, receiver buffer sizes for flow control, estimating suitable retransmission timeouts) between the client and server. From Figure 8-6, we should inspect the following details from three-way handshake messages:

1. TCP client will be in LISTEN state initially. TCP client starts establishing connection with the TCP server by sending a SYN segment with sequence number (x). Then, the TCP client moves to SYNSENT state.

2. TCP server also will be in LISTEN state initially. The TCP server, upon accepting the connection, moves to the SYN RCVD state. And it confirms the TCP client sequence number by sending acknowledgement (ACK) as x+1, and the server also sending its starting sequence number as y.

3. TCP client on receiving TCP server ACK moves to connection established (ESTAB) state. TCP client confirms the TCP server sequence number by sending acknowledgement (ACK) as y+1. Then, the TCP server, on receiving ACK from the TCP client, also moves to the connection established (ESTAB) state.

On successful connection establishment of both client and server, they agree on sequence numbers and receiver buffer sizes. Moreover, it also helps in estimating round trip time between client and server, and sets suitable retransmission timeouts for handling retransmission of missing TCP segments.

Then, both client and server can start exchanging data in a reliable manner. Hence, in case of missing any TCP data or ACK, the TCP handles by filling gaps through retransmissions and reordering based on sequence numbers in case of wrong sequence delivery.

TCP Connection Shutdown

As we observed, TCP needs to manage important details such as sequence numbers, timers, and buffers; hence, on successful exchange of data, the TCP connection must be shutdown by the respective TCP application. Hence, TCP gracefully releases these connection-related resources on respective TCP hosts to optimally utilize computational and memory resources.

The TCP connection shutdown procedure involves four-way handshaking, as shown in Figure 8-7:

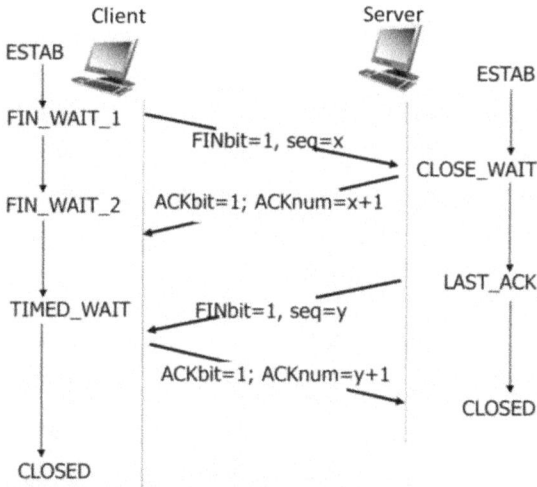

Figure 8-7. *TCP connection shutdown: 4-way handshake procedure*

1. The TCP client will be in a connection established state initially. The TCP client wants to shutdown the connection with the TCP server by sending a FIN segment with a sequence number (x). Then, the TCP client moves to FIN_WAIT_1 state, indicating connection shutdown in progress. In this state, the TCP client cannot send any more data to the TCP server. However, it can receive data while connection shutdown is in progress.

CHAPTER 8   ESSENTIAL NETWORK SOCKET PROGRAMMING SKILLS

2. The TCP server also will be in a connection established state initially. The TCP server, on accepting the FIN, it moves to CLOSE_WAIT state. And it acknowledges the TCP by sending acknowledgement (ACK) as x+1, and the TCP server can still send any pending data. On receiving the ACK, the TCP client enters into FIN_WAIT_2 state to allow the TCP server to send any remaining data.

3. After sending the remaining data, the TCP server closes the connection by sending a FIN segment with a sequence number (y) and it moves to the LAST_ACK sent state. Then, the TCP server cannot send any more data to the TCP client.

4. The TCP client, on receiving the FIN, moves to the TIMED_WAIT state. The TCP client confirms the TCP server sequence number by sending acknowledgement (ACK) as y+1. Then, the TCP server, on receiving ACK from the TCP client, also moves the connection CLOSED state.

    - The TCP client moves to connection to be CLOSED state after waiting two times the maximum segment lifetime. It helps in handling lost ACKs and preventing duplicate segment issues from any new immediate connections.

Next, we will learn how these connection setup, shutdown, and reliability-related rules are embedded in the TCP protocol using its header, as shown in Figure 8-8. The standard TCP header size is 20 bytes.

Source Port (16 bit)						Destination Port (16 bit)
Sequence Number (32 bit)						
Acknowledgment Number (32 bit)						
Hdr len (4 bit)	NU	A	P	R	S	F	Receive window (16 bit)
Checksum (16 bit)						Urgent Pointer (16 bit)
Options (variable length)						
Application Data (variable length)						

Header (20 bytes)

Figure 8-8. *TCP header and its fields*

CHAPTER 8　ESSENTIAL NETWORK SOCKET PROGRAMMING SKILLS

The TCP header shown in Figure 8-8 consists of the following important field's information to handle connection setup, shutdown, reliability, flow control, and congestion control tasks:

- **Source Port (16 Bits)**: It indicates the sender's network application process port number.

- **Destination Port (16 Bits)**: It indicates the receiver's network application process port number.

- **Sequence Number (32 Bits)**: It indicates the starting byte address of the receiving TCP segment. It helps the TCP receiver to handle missing segments and reordering of data.

- **Acknowledgement Number (32 Bits)**: It indicates the next sequence number of the TCP segment to receive in order.

- **Header Length (4 Bits)**: TCP header length can vary between a minimum of 20 bytes to the maximum of 60 bytes. The value of header length is used to compute actual header length. It helps in computing the actual offset of the data.

- **NU (7 Bits)**: Not used bits for future extensions.

- **ACK (Acknowledgment) Flag (1 Bit)**: A indicates that the TCP segment is an ACK segment, and the acknowledgment number confirms the receipt of data.

- **P (PUSH) Flag (1 Bit)**: It indicates the receiver TCP to deliver buffered data immediately to the application.

- **SYN (Synchronize) Flag (1 Bit)**: S indicates that the TCP segment is a connection setup segment called the SYN segment.

- **FIN (Finish) Flag (1 Bit)**: F indicates that the TCP segment is a connection close segment called the FIN segment.

- **RST (Reset) Flag (1 Bit)**: R indicates that the TCP segment is a connection reset segment called an RST segment. It is used to terminate an ongoing TCP connection when an error is detected.

- **Receiver Window Size (16 Bits)**: It helps in handling flow control between the TCP sender and receiver. It specifically indicates the size of maximum data the TCP receiver can accept.

- **Checksum (16 Bits)**: Used for error detection to ensure data integrity during transmission.

- **Urgent Pointer (16 Bits)**: Used in conjunction with the Urgent flag to point to urgent data within the segment.

- **Options (Variable Length)**: TCP options are helpful for high-bandwidth networks to configure higher window sizes, and enable selective acknowledgments during data exchange. For example:

  - **Window Scaling**: In high-bandwidth networks, it is possible to exchange data segments of size > 65535; in this case, TCP can set a suitable window scaling factor to multiply the actual receiver window size.

  - **Selective Acknowledgments (SACK)**: It helps in retransmitting only lost segments.

  - **Timestamps**: To compute round trip times, timestamps will be used.

  - **End of Option List**: To indicate the end of the options list.

  - **No Operation (NOP)**: To align TCP segment size on a 32-bit boundary.

TCP Socket Programming Constructs

TCP client-server application implementation involves the following important system calls. First, we will discuss common and TCP client-side-specific system calls.

TCP clients need to set up a connection with the TCP server before data exchange to establish a TCP connection, the following system calls are used in sequence. First, we use the following system call to create a TCP socket as follows:

```
int tcp_ls = socket(AF_INET, SOCK_STREAM, 0);
```

CHAPTER 8　ESSENTIAL NETWORK SOCKET PROGRAMMING SKILLS

socket system call takes the following arguments:

- **Domain (or Protocol Family)**: AF_INET for IPv4, AF_INET6 for IPv6, or AF_UNIX for Unix domain sockets.

- **Type**: SOCK_STREAM for reliable, connection-oriented communication (TCP) or SOCK_DGRAM for connectionless communication (UDP).

- **Protocol**: Specifies the specific protocol to be used within the domain.
  - For example: Setting 0 under SOCK_STREAM, means TCP socket
  - For example: Setting 0 under SOCK_DGRAM, means UDP socket
  - When we create raw sockets, it is necessary to specify specific protocol packets the socket will receive.

The socket() system call returns a new TCP socket descriptor; it is used by TCP network applications for sending/receiving data through the TCP/IP stack and to get access to all the underlying protocol stack layers' services in a transparent manner. Hence, network application messages can be exchanged in a reliable manner over the Internet.

After creating a socket, it is necessary to assign a unique protocol address (IP plus port number) to it. To assign an IP address, the following C socket address structure is used:

```
struct sockaddr_in {
    short sin_family;
    unsigned short sin_port;
    struct in_addr sin_addr;
    char sin_zero[8];
};
```

For example, to assign a TCP protocol address to a server, then we should define it as follows:

```
struct sockaddr_in server;
bzero(&server, sizeof(server));
server.sin_family = AF_INET;
```

CHAPTER 8 ESSENTIAL NETWORK SOCKET PROGRAMMING SKILLS

To assign a specific port number to a server, then we should define it as follows:

`server.sin_port = htons(12345);`

To assign a specific IP address to a server, then we should define it as follows:

`server.sin_addr.s_addr = inet_addr("127.0.0.1");`

In the case of a multihomed host with more than one network interface, if the server is to listen over all IP addresses, we should define it as follows:

```
server.sin_addr.s_addr = INADDR_ANY;
server.sin_port = htons(12345);
```

Here, we observe htons or htonl functions usage while assigning protocol addresses. These are used to handle network byte ordering and host byte ordering mismatch issues. Usage of these functions converts host data to network byte order before transmitting over the network.

Next, using the bind system call, the socket protocol address is assigned to the socket descriptor:

bind system call takes the following arguments:

- **Socket Descriptor**: The socket descriptor returned by the socket().
- A pointer to a sockaddr structure: sockaddr_in for IPv4 or sockaddr_in6 for IPv6
- **Address Length**: Size of address structure

The bind() call fails when binding to a protocol address (IP+port) already in use, or using a reserved port such as port number <1024. Hence, we should handle these errors as follows:

```
if (bind(tcp_ls, (const struct sockaddr *)&server,
sizeof(server)) < 0)
{
    perror("Socket binding failed");
    close(tcp_ls);
    exit(EXIT_FAILURE);
}
```

Next, let's check how to connect to a TCP server using the connect system call. The connect system call is used by the TCP clients to connect with the TCP server for establishing a reliable communication channel set up by performing 3-way handshake messages exchange as shown in Figure 8-7.

```
int connect(int sockfd, const struct sockaddr *addr, socklen_t addrlen);
```

connect system call takes the following arguments:

- sockfd: The socket descriptor returned by TCP client socket() system call.

- addr: Pointer to socket address structure containing TCP server protocol address.

- addrlen: The size of the server address structure.

By default, connect works in blocking mode. It means until 3-way handshake completes between the TCP client and the TCP server, this system call blocks. It returns the following:

- On successful connection establishment, connect() returns 0.

- On failure, connect() returns -1 and sets the errno variable to indicate the specific error. Following are the common errors we should handle:

  - ETIMEDOUT: On connection timeout, this error will be raised.

  - ECONNREFUSED: When no TCP server is listening on the specified port address, this error will be raised.

  - EHOSTUNREACH: When no TCP server exists with a specified IP address, this error will be raised.

  - ENETUNREACH: When no route exists to the TCP server IP network, this error will be raised.

  - EINPROGRESS: In case of non-blocking sockets, if a 3-way handshake is in progress between the TCP server and TCP client, this error will be returned.

In the case of UDP applications also, UDP clients can call the connect system call. However, it does not result in any handshake message exchange between UDP client and UDP server. Hence, UDP clients can use send() and recv() or read and write() system calls without needing to specify the destination address for each operation.

Next, we will discuss the specific system calls to set up a TCP server: The first system call is listen. The listen system takes a TCP server socket, and puts it in a passive state and prepares the server to accept connections from the TCP clients.

The listen() system call takes the following arguments:

- sockfd (Socket File Descriptor): This is a TCP socket descriptor.

- **Backlog**: The TCP server manages two queues for handling TCP connections. On arriving at any new TCP client connection request, first the client connection request is placed in the incomplete connection queue; after completing a 3-way handshake, the connection completion socket will be placed in the complete connection queue. Backlog value indicates total queue length of complete and incomplete queues.

Next, we will discuss the system calls to accept TCP client connections from a TCP server to handle a 3-way handshake procedure:

```
int accept(int sockfd, struct sockaddr *addr, socklen_t *addrlen);
```

The accept system call takes the following arguments:

- sockfd: The TCP server listening socket descriptor

- addr: A pointer to a client sockaddr structure to copy clients protocol address into it

- addrlen: Stores the actual size of the client's address

The accept returns the following three important values:

- Connected socket: on successful completion of the 3-way handshake with the TCP client, it returns the connected socket

- addr: Client protocol address copied to this pointer

- addrlen: Client protocol address length

CHAPTER 8 ESSENTIAL NETWORK SOCKET PROGRAMMING SKILLS

The `connect` system call from a TCP client initiates a 3-way handshake to the TCP server. Then, the TCP server accepts the handshaking procedure through the `accept()` system call. Once the 3-way handshake completes, it returns a connected socket descriptor for exchanging data with the client. By default, `accept()` is a blocking call; it blocks until the 3-way handshake completes between the TCP client and TCP server.

If the listening socket is configured in non-blocking mode and no connections are pending, `accept()` will return an error (e.g., `EWOULDBLOCK` or `EAGAIN`).

Next, let's discuss the system calls to exchange data over sockets. First, let's discuss how to send data over a TCP socket:

```
ssize_t send(int sockfd, const void *buf, size_t len, int flags);
```

The `send` system call takes the following arguments to exchange data over the connection socket. By default, it works in blocking mode. It means, until sending a few bytes send blocks, on successful return, it indicates the number of bytes sent. Hence, to send a specific length message, it is necessary to call multiple times the `send` system with the remaining data. In the case of listening socket sets in non-blocking mode, it is also possible to use it in non-blocking mode. The `send` system call takes the following arguments:

- sockfd: The connected socket descriptor
- buf: A pointer to the character buffer containing the message to be transmitted.
- len: The length of the message in bytes.
- flags: A bitmask of flags that modify the behavior of the send() call. For example:
  - Sending out-of-band data, the MSG_OOB flag should be set
  - Preventing the generation of a SIGPIPE signal if the connection is broken, the MSG_NOSIGNAL should be set

Return value of send system call:

- On success, send() returns the number of bytes actually sent
  - On returning -1, it sets the errno variable to indicate the specific error

The following common errors we should handle while using send():

- EPIPE: This error will be returned when the peer has closed its TCP connection
- EAGAIN or EWOULDBLOCK: This error will be returned in case of a non-blocking mode set, and there is no send buffer space available to send any data
- ECONNRESET: This error will be returned in case the peer TCP connection closes
- EDESTADDRREQ: This error will be returned in case of connectionless sockets and if no peer address is set
- ENOTCONN: This error will be returned in case of connectionless sockets and the socket is not connected
- EBADF: On passing invalid socket descriptor

For example:

```c
#include <errno.h>
#include <sys/types.h>
#include <sys/socket.h>
ssize_t sc = send(sockfd, buf, len, 0);
if (sc == -1)
{
    if (errno == EPIPE)
    {
        //handle peer TCP connection close error
    }
    else if (errno == EAGAIN || errno == EWOULDBLOCK)
    {
        //handle error in case of non blocking mode
    }
    else
    {
        //handle connection-less socket error
    }
} else if (sc < len)
```

```
{
    //handle partial data sent logic
} else
{
    //handle complete data sent logic
}
```

The recv() system call is used to receive data from a connected socket. By default, it works in blocking mode. It means, until receiving a few bytes, the recv blocks; on successful return, it indicates the number of bytes received. Hence, to receive a specific length message, it is necessary to call multiple times the recv system call with remaining data. In the case of listening socket sets in non-blocking mode, it is also possible to use them in non-blocking mode.

```
ssize_t recv(int sockfd, const void *buf, size_t len, int flags);
```

The recv system call takes the following arguments:

- sockfd: The connected socket descriptor
- buf: A pointer to a buffer to hold received data
- len: Size of data to receive into the buffer
- flags: Optional flags that modify the behavior of the call
    - MSG_WAITALL to block until the full amount of data is received

Return value of recv system call:

- On success, recv() returns the number of bytes actually received.
    - On returning 0 indicates the connection is closed
    - On returning -1, it sets the errno variable to indicate the specific error.
    - Waiting for the full amount to be received, in case MSG_WAITALL flag is specified.

We should handle the following common errors while using `recv()`:

- EAGAIN or EWOULDBLOCK: This error will be returned in case of a non-blocking mode set, and there is no data available in the receive buffer.
- ECONNRESET: This error will be returned in case the peer TCP connection closes.
- ENOTCONN: This error will be returned in case of connectionless sockets and the socket is not connected.
- EBADF: On passing invalid socket descriptor.
- EINTR: The recv() call was interrupted by a signal before any data could be received. The application should typically retry the recv() call in this case.

For example:

```
ssize_t sc = recv(sockfd, buf, len, 0);
if (sc == -1)
{
      if (errno == EINTR)
      {
            //retry to receive data
      }
      else if (errno == EAGAIN || errno == EWOULDBLOCK)
      {
            //handle error in case of non blocking mode
      }
      else
      {
            //handle connection reset or bad descriptors error
      }
} else if (sc < len)
{
      //handle partial data received logic
} else
```

```
{
    //handle complete data received logic
}
```

After data exchange is over, it is necessary to close the socket to release connection resources. `close()` decrements a socket descriptor reference count (number of processes sharing the socket descriptor), and the TCP 4-way handshake will be initiated when all processes close the socket and its reference count reaches zero.

The `close()` call takes the following arguments:

- sockfd: The file descriptor of the socket to be shut down

On close, the TCP connection termination 4-way shutdown handshake sequence will be initiated by sending a FIN segment to the peer. While a 4-way handshake is in progress, the close initiator can send any remaining buffered data before the connection is fully closed. However, using the socket option SO_LINGER with a zero timeout, any remaining buffered data can be discarded, and the connection can be reset. In case of using socket option SO_LINGER with a specific timeout value, the close waits until the remaining buffered data is sent or the timeout expires. We discuss various TCP socket options in the next chapter.

The `shutdown()` system call is used to disable sends, receives, or both on a socket. The `shutdown()` call takes the following arguments:

- sockfd: The file descriptor of the socket to be shut down.

- SHUT_RD: Disables further receives on the socket.

- SHUT_WR: Disables further sends on the socket.

- SHUT_RDWR: Disables both further sends and receives on the socket

---

Note As part of error handling, in a few places we call exit() system call. The exit system call ends the process and releases all its resources such as memory, file, and socket descriptors too. Then, there is no need to call close().

Next, we will learn TCP server and client program structures before practicing TCP socket programming:

CHAPTER 8   ESSENTIAL NETWORK SOCKET PROGRAMMING SKILLS

General TCP Server Program Structure

First, we will introduce a general TCP server program structure. This TCP server structure is an iterative server structure. It means it handles multiple clients in an iterative manner, not in parallel.

- Create a TCP socket
- Bind the TCP socket with the server IP and port number
- Listen over the TCP socket
- In an infinite loop, do the following:
  - Accept TCP client connections and return client-connected socket descriptors
  - Use TCP-connected sockets for exchanging traffic with TCP clients
  - Handle errors during data exchange
  - Close the client connections after data exchange

```c
//Include network, socket, and addressing related header files
#include <arpa/inet.h>
#include <netinet/in.h>
#include <sys/socket.h>
#include <sys/types.h>
#include <string.h>
#include <stdio.h>
#define PORT 12345
#define BUF_SIZE 10

int main()
{
    int tcp_ls, tcpc_cs;
    struct sockaddr_in server, client;
    socklen_t slen;
    char buf[BUF_SIZE];
    //create a TCP socket
    tcp_ls = socket(AF_INET, SOCK_STREAM, 0);
```

```c
if (tcp_ls < 0)
{
    //handle socket errors
}
//bind IP and port
bzero(&server, sizeof(server));
server.sin_family = AF_INET;
server.sin_addr.s_addr = INADDR_ANY; // Listen on all available interfaces
server.sin_port = htons(PORT);
if (bind(tcp_ls, (const struct sockaddr *)&server, sizeof(server)) < 0)
{
    //handle bind errors
}
//Listen over socket
if (listen(tcp_ls, 10) < 0)
{
    //handle listen errors
}
printf("Server listening on port %d...\n", PORT);
slen = sizeof(client);

//Wait for client connections
while (1)
{
    //collect connected socket
    tcpc_cs = accept(tcp_ls, (struct sockaddr *)&client, &slen);
    if (tcpc_cs < 0)
    {
        //handle accept errors
    }
    printf("Connection accepted from %s:%d\n", inet_ntoa(client.sin_addr), ntohs(client.sin_port));
    //Use connected socket for data exchange
    while(1)
```

```
            {
                    ssize_t rcnt = recv(tcpc_cs, buf, sizeof(buf) - 1, 0);
                    //handle receive errors and connection termination
                    ssize_t scnt = send(tcpc_cs, buf, strlen(buf), 0);
                    //handle send errors and connection termination
            }
    }
    close(tcp_ls);
    return 0;
}
```

Next, we will learn how to handle multiple clients in parallel using a multiprocess TCP server.

Multiprocess TCP Server Program Structure

First, we will introduce a general TCP server program structure:

- Create a TCP socket
- Bind the TCP socket with the server IP and port number
- Listen over the TCP socket
- In an infinite loop, do the following:
  - Accept TCP client connections and return client-connected socket descriptors
  - Start a new process using fork to handle the new client request
    - In the parent process, close client-connected socket, and in child process, close the listening socket
    - In the child process, use TCP connected sockets for exchanging traffic with TCP clients
    - Handle errors during data exchange
    - Close the client connections after data exchange
  - Close the server socket on exit

Example: Here, we have shown the connection handling part only since the remaining things are common.

```
while (1)
{
        tcp_cs = accept(tcp_ls, (struct sockaddr *)&client, &client_len);
        if (tcp_cs < 0)
        {
                //handle accept errors
        }
        printf("Connection accepted from %s:%d\n", inet_ntoa(client.
        sin_addr), ntohs(client.sin_port));
        //Create a new process to handle new client requests
        pid_t cpid=fork();
        if (cpid<0)
        {
                //handle fork errors
        }
        else if (cpid==0)
        {
                close(tcp_ls);
                while(1)
                {
                        //handle client data exchange
                }
        }
        else  //parent process
        {
                close(tcp_cs);
                wait(NULL); //wait for client to terminate
        }
}
close(tcp_cs);
close(tcp_ls);
return 0;
}
```

CHAPTER 8   ESSENTIAL NETWORK SOCKET PROGRAMMING SKILLS

General TCP Client Program Structure

We will introduce a general TCP client program structure:

- Create a TCP socket to connect with a TCP server
- Bind the TCP socket with the server IP and port number
- Send the connection request to the TCP server protocol address
- In an infinite loop, do the following:
  - Use TCP server sockets for exchanging traffic with TCP clients
  - Handle errors during data exchange
  - Close the client connections after data exchange

```c
#include <arpa/inet.h>
#include <netinet/in.h>
#include <sys/socket.h>
#include <sys/types.h>
#define BUF_SIZE 10
#define SERVER_IP_ADDRESS 127.0.0.1
#define PORT_NUMBER 12345
int main()
{
    int tcp_cs;
    struct sockaddr_in server_address;
    char buf[BUF_SIZE];
    //create a TCP socket
    tcp_cs = socket(AF_INET, SOCK_STREAM, 0);
    if (tcp_cs == -1)
    {
        //handle socket errors
    }
    //Bind IP and port address of TCP server
    server_address.sin_family = AF_INET;
    server_address.sin_port = htons(PORT_NUMBER);
    server_address.sin_addr.s_addr = inet_addr(SERVER_IP_ADDRESS);
```

```
    //Connect to the TCP server
    if (connect(tcp_cs, (struct sockaddr *)&server_address,
    sizeof(server_address)) == -1)
    {
        //handle connect errors
    }
    printf("Connected to server %s:%d\n", SERVER_IP_ADDRESS, PORT_
    NUMBER);
    //Use connected socket for data exchange
    while(1)
    {
        ssize_t scnt = send(tcp_cs, buf, strlen(buf), 0);
        //handle send errors and connection termination
        ssize_t rcnt = recv(tcp_cs, buf, sizeof(buf) - 1, 0);
        //handle receive errors and connection termination
    }
    close(tcp_cs);
    return 0;
}
```

Next, we will practice TCP socket programming:

TCP Socket Programming Practice

In this section, we will do the following hands-on activity:

- Implement TCP client and TCP server programs to exchange messages continuously

- Messages should be read from sample text files

- Handle errors related to data exchange such as end of file, socket connection, accept, send, and recv

CHAPTER 8   ESSENTIAL NETWORK SOCKET PROGRAMMING SKILLS

TCP Server Program for Waiting for Messages

First, we will introduce the TCP server program structure:

- The TCP server will do the following tasks:
  - Set up a TCP socket and bind with a protocol address
  - Open a sample.txt file (Sample contents: abcdefghij\nabcdefghij\nabcdefghij\nabcdefghij\n)
  - In a loop, wait for TCP client connection requests
    - Displays connected client protocol address (IP+port)
    - In an infinite loop, wait to receive a message from a TCP client
      - Then, the TCP server reads a text message from the sample.txt of specific length (e.g., 10).
      - Send the text as a reply to TCP client.
      - The above process is repeated until the file contents are over.
      - Once the file contents are over, it closes the TCP client connection.
  - On exit, close the TCP server socket

We implement the below program in `itcps.c`:

```
#include <arpa/inet.h>
#include <netinet/in.h>
#include <stdio.h>
#include <stdlib.h>
#include <string.h>
#include <sys/socket.h>
#include <sys/types.h>
#include <sys/wait.h>
#include <unistd.h>
#define BUF_SIZE 10
#define PORT 12346
```

CHAPTER 8 ESSENTIAL NETWORK SOCKET PROGRAMMING SKILLS

```c
int main()
{
    int tcp_ls, tcpc_cs;
    struct sockaddr_in server, client;
    socklen_t slen;
    FILE *fptr;
    char buf[BUF_SIZE];
    tcp_ls = socket(AF_INET, SOCK_STREAM, 0);
    if (tcp_ls < 0)
    {
        perror("Socket creation failed");
        exit(EXIT_FAILURE);
    }
    bzero(&server, sizeof(server));
    server.sin_family = AF_INET;
    server.sin_addr.s_addr = INADDR_ANY;
    server.sin_port = htons(PORT);
    if (bind(tcp_ls, (const struct sockaddr *)&server,
    sizeof(server)) < 0)
    {
        perror("Socket binding failed");
        close(tcp_ls);
        exit(EXIT_FAILURE);
    }
    if (listen(tcp_ls, 10) < 0)
    {
        perror("Listen failed");
        close(tcp_ls);
        exit(EXIT_FAILURE);
    }
    printf("Server listening on port %d...\n", PORT);
    slen = sizeof(client);
    while (1)
    {
        tcpc_cs = accept(tcp_ls, (struct sockaddr *)&client, &slen);
```

```c
        if (tcpc_cs < 0)
        {
              perror("Accept failed");
              close(tcp_ls);
              exit(EXIT_FAILURE);
        }
        printf("Connection accepted from %s:%d\n", inet_ntoa(client.
        sin_addr), ntohs(client.sin_port));

        fptr = fopen("sample.txt", "r");

        if (fptr == NULL)
        {
              printf("Error: Could not open file.\n");
              return 1;
        }

        while(1)
        {
              bzero(buf, BUF_SIZE);
              ssize_t rcnt = recv(tcpc_cs, buf, sizeof(buf), 0);
              if (rcnt <= 0)
              {
                    printf("Client disconnected or error occurred.\n");
                    break;
              }
              buf[rcnt] = '\0'; // Null-terminate the received data
              printf("Client: %s\n", buf);
              bzero(buf, BUF_SIZE);
              if (fread(buf,1, BUF_SIZE, fptr)>0)
              {
                    if (send(tcpc_cs, buf, strlen(buf), 0) == -1)
                    {
                          perror("Error sending data");
                          break;
                    }
```

```
                    printf("Sent: %s\n", buf);
                }
                else
                {
                    printf("File closed\n");
                    fclose(fptr);
                }
            }
        }
        close(tcpc_cs);
        close(tcp_ls);
        return 0;
}
```

Compile the code and execute it using the following commands:

```
#gcc itcps.c -o its
#./its
Server listening on port 12346...
Connection accepted from 127.0.0.1:41244
Client: abcdefghij 10
Sent: abcdefghij
Client:
abcdefghi 10
Sent:
abcdefghi
Client: abcdefghij 10
Sent: j
abcdefgh
Client: j
abcdefgh 10
Sent: ij
abcdefg
Client:
abcdefghi 10
Sent: hij
```

```
Client: ij
abcdefg 10
File closed
Client disconnected or error occurred.
```

Observe the following details:

- When a client connects, it displays the client IP +port
- Once clients started sending messages, the server sent a reply for each message until sample.txt contained text messages
- On file close, client connection will be closed

TCP Client Program for Messages Exchange

The TCP client program structure:

- The TCP client will do the following tasks:
  - Set up TCP socket and bind with protocol address
  - Open a sample.txt file (Sample contents:abcdefghij\nabcdefghij\nabcdefghij\nabcdefghij\n)
  - Connect with the TCP server
  - In an infinite loop:
    - Client reads a text message from the sample.txt of specific length (e.g., 10).
    - Send the text as a request message to the TCP client.
    - Receive the response from the TCP server and display it.
    - The above process is repeated until the file contents are over.
    - Once file contents are over, then close the TCP client connection.

We implement the below program in `itcpc.c`:

```c
#include <stdio.h>
#include <stdlib.h>
#include <string.h>
```

```c
#include <sys/socket.h>
#include <sys/wait.h>
#include <arpa/inet.h>
#include <unistd.h>
#include <netinet/tcp.h>
#include <errno.h>

#define PORT_NUMBER 12346
#define SERVER_IP_ADDRESS "127.0.0.1"
#define BUF_SIZE 10

int main()
{
    int tcp_cs;
    struct sockaddr_in server_address;

    FILE *fptr;
    char buf[BUF_SIZE];
    char buf2[10];
    fptr = fopen("sample.txt", "r");
    if (fptr == NULL)
    {
        printf("Error: Could not open file.\n");
        return 1;
    }
    tcp_cs = socket(AF_INET, SOCK_STREAM, 0);
    if (tcp_cs == -1)
    {
        perror("Error creating socket");
        exit(EXIT_FAILURE);
    }

    server_address.sin_family = AF_INET;
    server_address.sin_port = htons(PORT_NUMBER);
    server_address.sin_addr.s_addr = inet_addr(SERVER_IP_ADDRESS);

    if (connect(tcp_cs, (struct sockaddr *)&server_address,
    sizeof(server_address)) == -1)
```

CHAPTER 8   ESSENTIAL NETWORK SOCKET PROGRAMMING SKILLS

```c
    {
            perror("Error connecting to server");
            exit(EXIT_FAILURE);
    }
    printf("Connected to server %s:%d\n", SERVER_IP_ADDRESS, PORT_NUMBER);

    while (fread(buf,1, BUF_SIZE, fptr)>0)
    {
            printf("Line1:%s", buf);
            if (send(tcp_cs, buf, strlen(buf), 0) == -1)
            {
                    perror("Error sending data");
                    break;
            }
            printf("Sent: %s\n", buf);
            ssize_t rcnt = recv(tcp_cs, buf2, sizeof(buf2), 0);
            if (rcnt == EINTR)
            {
                    perror("Error receiving data");
                    continue;
            }
            if (rcnt == 0)
            {
                    perror("closing connection");
                    exit(EXIT_FAILURE);
            }
            buf2[rcnt] = '\0';
            printf("Received: %s %d\n", buf2,rcnt);
    }
    fclose(fptr);
    printf("End of the file");
    close(tcp_cs);

    return 0;
}
```

CHAPTER 8 ESSENTIAL NETWORK SOCKET PROGRAMMING SKILLS

Compile the code and execute it using the following commands in another terminal:

```
#gcc itcpc.c -o itc
#./itc
Connected to server 127.0.0.1:12346
Sent: abcdefghij
Received: abcdefghij 10
Sent:
abcdefghiabcdefghij
Received:
abcdefghi 10
Sent: j
abcdefgh
abcdefghi
Received: j
abcdefgh 10
Sent: ij
abcdefgj
abcdefgh
Received: ij
abcdefg 10
End of the file
```

Observe the following details:

- When a client connects, it displays the client IP +port
- Once clients started sending messages, the server sent a reply for each message until sample.txt contained text messages
- On file close, client connection will be closed

The itcps.c is implemented for supporting an iterative way of handling clients' requests. Hence, if you run two TCP clients in two terminals in parallel, still you will observe the TCP server processes requests in sequential order only. We recommend readers test it for better learning.

Next, let's learn how to handle multiple client requests in parallel using a multiprocess TCP server.

CHAPTER 8   ESSENTIAL NETWORK SOCKET PROGRAMMING SKILLS

Multiprocess TCP Server Program

Multiprocess TCP server program tasks:

- The TCP server will do the following tasks:
    - Set up TCP socket and bind with protocol address
    - Open a sample.txt file
    - In a loop waits for TCP clients connection requests; for each new TCP client connection request
        - Display connected client protocol address (IP+port)
        - Create a new process using fork
        - After the fork, the listening and connected sockets are shared by both parent and child processes.
        - Parent process closes the connected socket and waits for child processes to be terminated in non-blocking mode using `waitpid`
        - The child process closes the listen socket and uses the connected socket to handle the TCP client messages exchange as follows:
        - In an infinite loop, wait to receive a message from a TCP client
            - Then, the TCP server reads a text message from the sample.txt of specific length.
            - Send the text as a reply to the TCP client.
            - The above process is repeated until the file contents are over.
            - Once the file contents are over, it closes the TCP client connection.
    - On exit close the TCP server socket

CHAPTER 8 ESSENTIAL NETWORK SOCKET PROGRAMMING SKILLS

- To implement it, we will do the following major changes to the itcps.c and save it in mtcps.c.
- Use the following code to replace the iterative server while (1) loop code:

```
while (1)
{
      tcpc_cs = accept(tcp_ls, (struct sockaddr *)&client,
      &client_len);
      if (tcpc_cs < 0)
      {
            perror("Accept failed");
            close(tcp_ls);
            exit(EXIT_FAILURE);
      }
      printf("Connection accepted from %s:%d\n", inet_ntoa(client.
      sin_addr), ntohs(client.sin_port));
      if (fork()==0)
      {
            close(tcp_ls);
            fptr = fopen("sample.txt", "r");
            if (fptr == NULL)
            {
                  printf("Error: Could not open file.\n");
                  return 1; // Indicate a n error
            }
            while(1)
            {
                  bzero(buf, BUF_SIZE);
                  ssize_t rcnt = recv(tcpc_cs, buf,
                  sizeof(buf) - 1, 0);
                  if (rcnt <= 0)
                  {
                        printf("Client disconnected or error
                        occurred.\n");
```

511

```c
                    break;
                }
                buf[rcnt] = '\0'; // Null-terminate the
                received data
                printf("Client: %s\n", buf);
                bzero(buf, BUF_SIZE);
                if (fread(buf,1, BUF_SIZE, fptr)>0)
                {
                    printf("Line1:%s", buf);
                    if (send(tcpc_cs, buf, strlen(buf),
                    0) == -1)
                    {
                        perror("Error sending data");
                        break;
                    }
                    printf("Sent: %s\n", buf);
                    ssize_t rcnt = recv(tcpc_cs, buf,
                    sizeof(buf) - 1, 0);
                    if (rcnt == 0)
                    {
                        printf("Client disconnected or error
                        occurred.\n");
                        break;
                    }
                }
                else
                {
                    printf("File closed\n");
                    fclose(fptr);
                    exit(0);
                }
            }
        }
        else
        {
            close(tcpc_cs);
```

```
            int stat;
            waitpid(-1,&stat,WNOHANG);
        }
    }
```

Test the multiprocess TCP server as follows:

- First start the multiprocess TCP server
- Observe the following after starting two TCP clients:
    - Server accepts second TCP client while processing first TCP client.
    - Server responds to both clients using two processes in parallel.
    - On termination of TCP clients, the server is still running and waiting for new clients.

```
#gcc mtcps.c -o mts
#./mts

Server listening on port 12346...
Connection accepted from 127.0.0.1:55962
Client: abcdefghij
Sent: abcdefghij
Client: abcdefghij
Sent:
abcdefghi
Connection accepted from 127.0.0.1:55966
Client: abcdefghij
Sent: abcdefghij
Client:
abcdefghi
Sent: j
abcdefgh
Client: abcdefghij
Sent:
abcdefghi
Client: j
```

CHAPTER 8 ESSENTIAL NETWORK SOCKET PROGRAMMING SKILLS

```
abcdefgh
Sent: ij
abcdefg
Client:
abcdefghi
Sent: j
abcdefgh
Client: ij
abcdefg
Sent: hij

Client: j
abcdefgh
Sent: ij
abcdefg
Client disconnected or error occurred.
Accept failed: Socket operation on non-socket
Client: ij
abcdefg
Sent: hij

Client disconnected or error occurred.
Accept failed: Socket operation on non-socket
```

After starting the multiprocess TCP server, change the TCP client code by introducing sleep() before printing received messages. Then start two TCP clients as follows using the gcc commands:

- Observe the following after starting two TCP clients in two terminals:
  - Server accepts second TCP client while processing first TCP client
  - Server responds to both clients using two processes in parallel
  - Clients are terminated after file contents are over

Client-1:
```
#gcc itcpc.c -o itc
#./itc
Connected to server 127.0.0.1:12346
```

```
Sent: abcdefghij
Received: abcdefghij 10
..
Received: hij
 4
End of the file
```
Client-2:
```
#./itc
Connected to server 127.0.0.1:12346
Sent: abcdefghij
Received: abcdefghij 10
..
Received: hij
 4
End of the file
```

In this section, we have learned how to implement basic TCP client-server applications. We implemented and tested both iterative and multiprocess TCP servers successfully. Coming to reliability tests and more TCP options, we will explore in the next chapter. Next, we will explore UDP socket programming.

UDP Socket Programming

UDP protocol is implemented as part of the transport layer as a lower overhead protocol. Unlike TCP, UDP is known as a connection-less protocol. UDP applications need not set up connections before sending data. Hence, UDP applications can send data immediately without suffering from connection setup delays. Moreover, during UDP applications, data exchange, there is no need to wait for acknowledgements. These features enable UDP network applications to have fine control over data exchange in terms of when and what size of data to send. Many interesting network applications, such as domain name system (DNS), DHCP, simple network management protocol (SNMP), broadcast, and multicast applications, use UDP. We can summarize the following benefits related to UDP protocol usages:

CHAPTER 8   ESSENTIAL NETWORK SOCKET PROGRAMMING SKILLS

- Less overhead in terms of connection management
- Suitable for short messages delivery in quick time
- No latency issues from acknowledgments waiting and flow control tasks
- Lesser size header overhead (only 8 bytes) due to no overhead in protocol
- UDP servers can handle a greater number of clients
- Suitable for loss-tolerant applications such as multimedia network applications

However, due to a lack of reliability protocol implementation details, the UDP protocol suffers from the following major drawbacks:

- Unreliable data exchange
- UDP applications can flood the network with huge traffic
- UDP application can lead to security attacks

Due to UDP simplicity, its protocol overhead is very low compared to TCP. UDP protocol mainly offers the following services to its applications:

- Source network process to destination network process message delivery
- Sending or receiving messages as datagrams (as a whole unit)
- Source and destination application addressing
- Error checking on receiving data

UDP protocol rules are represented in its header as shown in Figure 8-9.

Source Port (16 bit)	Destination Port (16 bit)	Header (8 bytes)
Length (16 bit)	Checksum (16bit)	
Application Data (variable length)		

Figure 8-9.   *UDP header and its fields*

Let's discuss the UDP header field details:

- **Source Port**: It is a 16-bit length and identifies the source UDP process address.

- **Destination Port**: It is a 16-bit length and identifies the destination UDP process address.

- **Length**: It is a 16-bit length and used to check the total length of the UDP message (header+application data or payload).

- **Checksum**: It is a 16-bit length and used for detecting corruption of the UDP message (header and data). The checksum is computed and sent by the UDP sender, and UDP receiver uses it for verifying the integrity of the data during transmission.

UDP Socket Programming in C

In this section, we will learn system calls related to UDP socket programming. The following are the basic system calls needed to implement UDP network applications:

- Creating a UDP socket
- Assigning UDP protocol address to UDP sockets
- Use connection-less or connection-oriented sockets for data exchange
- Send and receive UDP datagrams using UDP socket

Create a UDP socket using the socket system call as follows:

```
int ufd;
if ((ufd = socket(AF_INET, SOCK_DGRAM, 0)) < 0)
{
    perror("socket creation failed");
    exit(EXIT_FAILURE);
}
```

On successful creation of a UDP socket, it returns a UDP datagram socket descriptor, which will be used by network applications for exchanging UDP datagrams.

CHAPTER 8   ESSENTIAL NETWORK SOCKET PROGRAMMING SKILLS

Next, assign the protocol address (IP address and port number) using the socket address structure to the UDP socket as follows:

```
struct sockaddr_in server;
memset(&server, 0, sizeof(server));
server.sin_family = AF_INET;
server.sin_addr.s_addr =inet_addr("172.16.80.34");
server.sin_port = htons(12345);
```

Next, bind the protocol address (IP address and port number) to the UDP socket as follows:

```
if (bind(ufd, (const struct sockaddr *)&server, sizeof(server)) < 0)
{
    perror("bind failed");
    exit(EXIT_FAILURE);
}
```

An UDP application can communicate with another UDP peer using connect or without connect. Let's understand the differences between connection-oriented and connection-less UDP applications' data exchange.

Importance of Connection-Oriented Socket for UDP Clients

Like TCP applications, UDP applications can also use connect, send, and recv system calls for data exchange. But there are the following significant differences compared to TCP usage of the connect system call:

- When UDP client usage connects with the UDP server protocol address, there will be no handshaking procedure and reliability guarantee for data exchange.

- Connect helps UDP clients to receive and handle ICMP errors such as connection reset.

- Connect helps faster data exchange in case of communicating with the same server by eliminating unnecessary routing table lookups.

CHAPTER 8   ESSENTIAL NETWORK SOCKET PROGRAMMING SKILLS

- Moreover, UDP applications can call connect again for disconnecting with a previous peer protocol address or connecting with a new peer protocol address.

- UDP client on usage of connect with a UDP server protocol address: the UDP client can receive data from the UDP server address only, and it cannot receive data from any other protocol address.

An UDP client exchanges data with a UDP server; there is no need for a connection. However, to exchange data with a peer UDP network application, it is necessary to fill the destination protocol address (IP+port). Hence, instead of using send and recv for UDP applications data exchange, it is necessary to handle data exchange between network applications using sendto and recvfrom system calls.

We will discuss these system calls in the next section.

UDP Traffic Exchange System Calls

If a UDP client is using a connection-oriented socket, then it can use send and recv system calls like TCP applications. On the other hand, if the UDP client is using a connection-less socket, then it should use the following system calls by filling the destination protocol address.

The sendto() system call is used to send data over a socket. Specifically, it is used to send data as datagrams with destination IP address and port number over UDP sockets or raw sockets. By default, it works in blocking mode; it can also be set to work in non-blocking mode. It means, until sending a few bytes to sendto blocks on successful return, it indicates the number of bytes sent. Hence, to send a specific length message, it is necessary to call the sendto system call multiple times with the remaining data.

```
ssize_t sendto(int sockfd, const void *buf, size_t len, int flags,
         const struct sockaddr *dest_addr, socklen_t addrlen);
```

The sendto() takes the following arguments:

- sockfd: The UDP socket descriptor configured with the destination protocol address

- buf: Address of the buffer containing data to be send

- len: Size of data to be send

CHAPTER 8   ESSENTIAL NETWORK SOCKET PROGRAMMING SKILLS

- flags: To modify the default behavior of the `sendto`, we can set suitable flags
  - Set MSG_DONTWAIT for non-blocking operation
- dest_addr: A pointer to a socket address structure containing the destination address and port.
- addrlen: The size of the dest_addr structure.

The `sendto() return value:`

- On success, it returns the number of bytes sent.
- On failure or errors, it returns -1 and sets the error code in errno.

The `sendto() the following errors should be handled:`

- EAGAIN or EWOULDBLOCK: This error will be returned in case of a non-blocking mode set, and there is no send buffer space available to send any data.
- EMSGSIZE: This error will be raised when exceeding the maximum UDP packet size.
- EAFNOSUPPORT: This error will be raised when the address family is not supported by the socket (e.g., trying to send to an IPv6 address on an IPv4-only socket).
- EINVAL: On passing invalid socket descriptor or length
- EACCES: This error will be raised when using unprivileged port numbers as part of the protocol address without permissions.
  - For example, port numbers < 1024 are reserved
- EHOSTUNREACH: When no UDP peer exists with a specified IP address, this error will be raised.
- ENETUNREACH: When no route exists to the UDP peer IP network, this error will be raised.

For example, to send a UDP message from the client to the UDP server socket, the following code snippet is useful:

```
while (1)
{
    ..
    char msg[10];

    printf("Enter Server Message\n");
    scanf("%s",msg);
    strcat(msg,"\n");
    msg[strlen(msg)]='\0';

    sendto(ufd, (const char *)msg, strlen(msg), 0,
            (const struct sockaddr *)&server, len);
    ..
}
```

Next, check how to receive data over UDP sockets from network applications. The recvfrom() is used to receive data from a UDP socket or a raw socket. Network applications can also receive the source IP address and port number of the datagram and copy it to a socket address structure. By default, it works in blocking mode; it can also be set to work in non-blocking mode. It means, until receiving a few bytes, recvfrom blocks; on successful return, it indicates the number of bytes received. Hence, to receive a specific length message, it is necessary to call multiple times the recvfrom system call with remaining data or with suitable flags MSG_WAITALL.

```
ssize_t recvfrom(int sockfd, void *buf, size_t len, int flags,
            struct sockaddr *src_addr, socklen_t *addrlen);
```

The recvfrom() takes the following arguments:

- sockfd: The UDP socket descriptor to receive data
- buf: Address of the buffer to store received data
- len: Size of data to be received
- flags: To modify the default behavior of the recvfrom, we can set suitable flags
    - Set MSG_WAITALL to wait until the specified length of data is received

CHAPTER 8 ESSENTIAL NETWORK SOCKET PROGRAMMING SKILLS

- src_addr: A pointer to a socket addresses structure containing source address and port to copy
- addrlen: The size of the src_addr structure

The recvfrom() return value:

- On success, it returns the number of bytes received.
- On failure or errors, it returns -1 and sets the error code in errno.

The recvfrom() the following errors should be handled:

- **Return Value**:

  On success, it returns the number of bytes received. On error, it returns -1 and sets errno to indicate the error.

- EAGAIN or EWOULDBLOCK: This error will be returned in case of non-blocking mode set, and there is no data available in the buffer to read.

- ECONNRESET: In the case of connection-oriented sockets, while receiving data, if the peer connection was closed, then this error will be raised.

- ETIMEDOUT: Based on socket option: SO_RCVTIMEO, maximum timeout while waiting to receive data.

- EINTR: The recvfrom() call was interrupted by a signal before any data could be received. The application should typically retry the recvfrom() call in this case.

- EBADF: The provided socket descriptor is not valid.

- ENOMEM or ENOBUFS: When sufficient memory or buffer space is not available for handling the receive operation, this error will be raised.

For example, to receive UDP messages from the UDP server address, the following code snippet is useful:

```
while (1)
{
    ..
```

```
        len = sizeof(server);
        mlen = recvfrom(ufd, (char *)buffer, 10, 0,
              (struct sockaddr *)&server, &len);
        if (mlen < 0)
        {
              perror("recvfrom failed");
              exit(EXIT_FAILURE);
        }
        buffer[mlen] = '\0';

        printf("Server message from %s:%d: %s\n",
        inet_ntoa(server.sin_addr), ntohs(server.sin_port), buffer);
        ..
}
```

Finally, after data exchange, UDP sockets can be closed as follows:

```
close(ufd);
```

UDP Socket Programming in C

First we will discuss general UDP server and client program structures before practicing UDP programming.

General UDP Server Program Structure

A general UDP server program structure contains the following steps:

- Create a UDP socket
- Bind the UDP socket with the server IP and port number
- In an infinite loop do the following
  - Use UDP sockets for exchanging traffic with UDP clients
  - Handle errors during data exchange
  - Close the client connections after data exchange

CHAPTER 8 ESSENTIAL NETWORK SOCKET PROGRAMMING SKILLS

```c
#include <stdio.h>
#include <stdlib.h>
#include <string.h>
#include <unistd.h>
#include <arpa/inet.h>
#include <sys/socket.h>
//Define server port and buffer size
#define SRV_PORT 12345
#define BUF_SIZE 1024

int main()
{
    int ufd;
    struct sockaddr_in server, client;
    char buffer[BUF_SIZE];
    //create a UDP socket
    if ((ufd = socket(AF_INET, SOCK_DGRAM, 0)) < 0)
    {
        perror("socket creation failed");
        exit(EXIT_FAILURE);
    }
    //bind IP and port number to UDP server
    memset(&server, 0, sizeof(server));
    server.sin_family = AF_INET;
    server.sin_addr.s_addr = INADDR_ANY;
    server.sin_port = htons(SRV_PORT);

    if (bind(ufd, (const struct sockaddr *)&server, sizeof(server)) < 0)
    {
        perror("bind failed");
        exit(EXIT_FAILURE);
    }
    //wait for incoming messages and respond
    printf("UDP Server listening on port %d...\n", SRV_PORT);
    socklen_t len;
    ssize_t mlen;
```

```
    while (1)
    {
        len = sizeof(client);
        mlen = recvfrom(ufd, (char *)buffer, BUF_SIZE - 1, 0,
                    (struct sockaddr *)&client, &len);
        //handle recv data errors
        ..
        char msg[1024];

        sendto(ufd, (const char *)msg, strlen(msg), 0,
                    (const struct sockaddr *)&client, len);
        //handle send data errors
        ..

    }
    close(ufd);
    return 0;
}
```

General UDP Connection-Less Client Program Structure

A general UDP client program structure contains the following steps:

- Create a UDP socket
- Assign UDP socket with server IP and port number in server socket address structure
- In an infinite loop, do the following:
  - Use UDP sockets for exchanging traffic with UDP clients using sendto and recvfrom system calls
  - Handle errors during data exchange
  - Close the client socket after data exchange

```
#include <stdio.h>
#include <stdlib.h>
#include <string.h>
#include <sys/socket.h>
```

CHAPTER 8   ESSENTIAL NETWORK SOCKET PROGRAMMING SKILLS

```c
#include <arpa/inet.h>
#include <unistd.h>
//Assign UDP server IP and port
#define SRV_IP "127.0.0.1"
#define SRV_PORT 12345
#define BUFFER_SIZE 1024

int main()
{
    int ufd;
    ssize_t scnt,rcnt;
    struct sockaddr_in server;
    char buffer[BUFFER_SIZE];
    socklen_t server_len = sizeof(server);
    //create a UDP socket
    ufd = socket(AF_INET, SOCK_DGRAM, 0);
    if (ufd < 0)
    {
        perror("Error creating socket");
        exit(EXIT_FAILURE);
    }
    //Assign UDP server IP and port in server address structure
    memset(&server, 0, sizeof(server));
    server.sin_family = AF_INET;
    server.sin_port = htons(SRV_PORT);
    if (inet_pton(AF_INET, SRV_IP, &server.sin_addr) <= 0)
    {
        perror("Invalid address/ Address not supported");
        close(ufd);
        exit(EXIT_FAILURE);
    }
    //In a infinite loop exchange data
    while(1)
    {
        ..
```

```
            scnt = sendto(ufd, buffer, strlen(buffer), 0,
                                        (const struct sockaddr *)&server,
                                        sizeof(server));
            //handle send data errors

            rcnt = recvfrom(ufd, buffer, BUFFER_SIZE - 1, 0,
                        (struct sockaddr *)&server, &server_len);
            //handle receive data errors

    }
    close(ufd);
    printf("Socket closed.\n");
    return 0;
}
```

Next, we will learn how to access a FIFO file between two processes as follows.

General UDP Connection-Oriented Client Program Structure

A general UDP client program structure contains the following steps:

- Create a UDP socket
- Assign UDP socket with server IP and port number in server socket address structure
- Connect to the UDP server IP
- In an infinite loop, do the following:
  - Use UDP sockets for exchanging traffic with UDP clients using send and recv system calls
  - Handle errors during data exchange
  - Close the client socket after data exchange

```
#include <stdio.h>
#include <stdlib.h>
#include <string.h>
#include <sys/socket.h>
#include <arpa/inet.h>
```

```c
#include <unistd.h>
//Assign UDP server IP and port
#define SRV_IP "127.0.0.1"
#define SRV_PORT 12345
#define BUFFER_SIZE 1024

int main()
{
    int ufd;
    ssize_t scnt,rcnt;
    struct sockaddr_in server;
    char buffer[BUFFER_SIZE];
    socklen_t server_len = sizeof(server);
    //create a UDP socket
    ufd = socket(AF_INET, SOCK_DGRAM, 0);
    if (ufd < 0)
    {
        perror("Error creating socket");
        exit(EXIT_FAILURE);
    }
    //Assign UDP server IP and port in server address structure
    memset(&server, 0, sizeof(server));
    server.sin_family = AF_INET;
    server.sin_port = htons(SRV_PORT);
    if (inet_pton(AF_INET, SRV_IP, &server.sin_addr) <= 0)
    {
        perror("Invalid address/ Address not supported");
        close(ufd);
        exit(EXIT_FAILURE);
    }
    //Connect to the UDP server
    if (connect(ufd, (const struct sockaddr *)&server,
    sizeof(server)) < 0)
    {
```

CHAPTER 8   ESSENTIAL NETWORK SOCKET PROGRAMMING SKILLS

```
            perror("connect failed");
            exit(EXIT_FAILURE);
    }

    //In a infinite loop exchange data
    while(1)
    {
        ..
        scnt = send(ufd, buffer, strlen(buffer), 0);

        //handle send data errors

        rcnt = recv(ufd, buffer, BUFFER_SIZE - 1, 0);

        //handle receive data errors

    }
    close(ufd);
    printf("Socket closed.\n");
    return 0;
}
```

Next, let's UDP socket programming by implementing a simple chat network applications.

Hands-On Activity-1

In this hands-on activity, we will implement a simple chat application by doing the following tasks:

- We will implement basic UDP server and UDP connection-less client applications
- UDP server application will do the following major tasks
  - Bind to the specific server IP and port numbers
  - Waiting for any client messages
  - Sends response to the client message

529

CHAPTER 8   ESSENTIAL NETWORK SOCKET PROGRAMMING SKILLS

UDP SERVER

1. We implement this hands-on activity in budps.c.

2. First include the following necessary header files to do this hands-on activity:

   ```
   #include <stdio.h>
   #include <stdlib.h>
   #include <string.h>
   #include <unistd.h>
   #include <arpa/inet.h>
   #include <sys/socket.h>
   ```

3. In the main, we do the following:

   a. Assign specific server port

   b. Define specific buffer size for messages handling

   c. Create a UDP socket and bind the server protocol address

   ```
   #define SRV_PORT 12345
   #define BUF_SIZE 1024
   int main()
   {
       int ufd;
       struct sockaddr_in server, client;
       char buffer[BUF_SIZE];
       if ((ufd = socket(AF_INET, SOCK_DGRAM, 0)) < 0)
       {
           perror("socket creation failed");
           exit(EXIT_FAILURE);
       }

       memset(&server, 0, sizeof(server));
       server.sin_family = AF_INET;
       server.sin_addr.s_addr = INADDR_ANY;
       server.sin_port = htons(SRV_PORT);
   ```

CHAPTER 8 ESSENTIAL NETWORK SOCKET PROGRAMMING SKILLS

```
        if (bind(ufd, (const struct sockaddr *)&server,
        sizeof(server)) < 0)
        {
                perror("bind failed");
                exit(EXIT_FAILURE);
        }
```

4. Next, the UDP server waits in an infinite loop to receive messages from a UDP client and sends a reply to it:

```
        printf("UDP Server listening on port %d...\n", SRV_PORT);
        socklen_t len;
        ssize_t mlen;

        while (1)
        {
                len = sizeof(client);
                mlen = recvfrom(ufd, (char *)buffer, BUF_SIZE - 1, 0,
                            (struct sockaddr *)&client, &len);
                if (mlen < 0)
                {
                        perror("recvfrom failed");
                        exit(EXIT_FAILURE);
                }
                buffer[mlen] = '\0';

                printf("Client message from %s:%d: %s\n",
                inet_ntoa(client.sin_addr), ntohs(client.sin_port),
                buffer);
                char msg[BUF_SIZE];

                printf("Enter Server Message\n");
                scanf("%s",msg);
                strcat(msg,"\n");
                msg[strlen(msg)]='\0';
                sendto(ufd, (const char *)msg, strlen(msg), 0,
                            (const struct sockaddr *)&client, len);
        }
```

CHAPTER 8 ESSENTIAL NETWORK SOCKET PROGRAMMING SKILLS

5. On exit of the server, close the UDP socket to release the resources of the UDP socket:

   ```
   close(ufd);
   return 0;
   }
   ```

6. Compile and test the insptcp.c using the following commands:

   a. Wait for UDP client to send data

   b. On receiving hi, send hello

   c. Exit by giving CTRL+C

   ```
   #gcc budps.c -o bus
   #./bus
   UDP Server listening on port 12345…
   Client message from 127.0.0.1:45948: hi
   Enter Server Message
   hello
   ```

Next, let's implement a UDP client application and send data to test the data exchange between the UDP server and the UDP client.

Next, we will implement the following tasks in UDP client applications:

- UDP client application will do the following major tasks
  - Bind to the specific server IP and port numbers
  - Waiting for any client messages
  - Sends response to the client message

CHAPTER 8   ESSENTIAL NETWORK SOCKET PROGRAMMING SKILLS

UDP CLIENT

1. We implement this hands-on activity in budpc.c.

2. First include the following necessary header files to do this hands-on activity:

   ```
   #include <stdio.h>
   #include <stdlib.h>
   #include <string.h>
   #include <unistd.h>
   #include <arpa/inet.h>
   #include <sys/socket.h>
   #include <unistd.h>
   ```

3. In the main, we do the following:

   a. Define server IP and port

   b. Define specific buffer size for messages handling

   c. Create a UDP socket

   d. Define a UDP server address structure and assign server IP and port to it

   ```
   #define SRV_IP "127.0.0.1"
   #define SRV_PORT 12345
   #define BUFFER_SIZE 1024
   int main()
   {
       int ufd;
       ssize_t scnt,rcnt;
       struct sockaddr_in server;
       char buffer[BUFFER_SIZE];
       socklen_t server_len = sizeof(server);
       ufd = socket(AF_INET, SOCK_DGRAM, 0);
       if (ufd < 0)
       {
           perror("Error creating socket");
           exit(EXIT_FAILURE);
       }
   ```

```
            memset(&server, 0, sizeof(server));
            server.sin_family = AF_INET;
            server.sin_port = htons(SRV_PORT);

            if (inet_pton(AF_INET, SRV_IP, &server.sin_addr) <= 0)
            {
                perror("Invalid address/ Address not supported");
                close(ufd);
                exit(EXIT_FAILURE);
            }
```

4. Next, the UDP client sends a message to the UDP server:

```
            while(1)
            {
                char msg[100];
                printf("Enter message");
                scanf("%s",msg);
                strcat(msg,"\n");
                msg[strlen(msg)]='\0';
                scnt = sendto(ufd, msg, strlen(msg), 0,
                                    (const struct sockaddr *)
                                    &server, sizeof(server));
                if (scnt < 0)
                {
                    perror("Error sending message");
                    close(ufd);
                    exit(EXIT_FAILURE);
                }
                printf("Message sent: \"%s\" (%zd bytes)\n",
                msg, scnt);
```

5. Waiting to receive messages from the UDP server:

```
server_len = sizeof(server);
rcnt = recvfrom(ufd, buffer, BUFFER_SIZE - 1, 0,
            (struct sockaddr *)&server, &server_len);
printf("Rcvd from %s:%d\n", inet_ntoa
(server.sin_addr), ntohs(server.sin_port));
if (rcnt < 0)
{
    perror("Error receiving response");
    close(ufd);
    exit(EXIT_FAILURE);
}
else if (rcnt == 0)
{
    printf("No data received\n");
}
else
{
    buffer[rcnt] = '\0';
    printf("Response from server: \"%s\"
    (%zd bytes)\n", buffer, rcnt);
}
}
```

6. On exit, finally release the UDP socket resource by closing the UDP socket.

```
close(ufd);
return 0;
}
```

7. Compile and test the budpc.c using the following commands:

   a. While the UDP server is running, send a message hi
   b. Wait for getting reply

c. Send another message hi and observe that it waits forever (due to the UDP server shutdown)

```
#gcc budpc.c
#sudo ./a.out
./a.out
Enter messagehi
Message sent: "hi
" (3 bytes)
Rcvd from 127.0.0.1:12345
Response from server: "hello
" (6 bytes)
Message sent: "hi" (3 bytes)
```

From the results, we observe both UDP server and client applications exchange their data successfully when the UDP server is online. However, on exit of the UDP server, the UDP client blocks to receive replies. It means on shutdown of the UDP server, UDP client is not getting any error message to handle. Actually ICMP sends an error message to indicate the server is not available. These error developers should handle. Next, we will check how to handle these errors using connection-oriented sockets.

Next, we will implement the following tasks in UDP client applications:

- UDP client application will do the following major tasks
  - Bind to the specific server IP and port numbers
  - Waiting for any client messages
  - Sends response to the client message

UDP CONNECTION-ORIENTED CLIENT

1. We implement this hands-on activity in cbudpc.c.
2. In the main, we do the following major changes:
   a. Define server IP and port
   b. Define specific buffer size for messages handling
   c. Create a UDP socket

CHAPTER 8   ESSENTIAL NETWORK SOCKET PROGRAMMING SKILLS

d. Define a UDP server address structure and assign server IP and port to it
e. Then, connect to the UDP server using the connect system call with the UDP server address
f. Replace sendto and recvfrom with send and recv, respectively.

```
..
int main()
{
        ..
        if (inet_pton(AF_INET, SRV_IP, &server.sin_addr) <= 0)
        {
            perror("Invalid address/ Address not supported");
            close(ufd);
            exit(EXIT_FAILURE);
        }
        if (connect(ufd, (const struct sockaddr *)&server, sizeof(server)) < 0)
        {
            perror("connect failed");
            exit(EXIT_FAILURE);
        }

        ..
        while(1)
        {
            ..
            msg[strlen(msg)]='\0';
            scnt = send(ufd, msg, strlen(msg), 0);
            ..
            rcnt = recv(ufd, buffer, BUFFER_SIZE - 1, 0);
            ..
        }
        close(ufd);
        return 0;
}
```

CHAPTER 8 ESSENTIAL NETWORK SOCKET PROGRAMMING SKILLS

3. Compile and test the cbudpc.c using the following commands:

    a. First start a UDP server.

    b. Send a message hi.

    c. Wait for getting reply.

    d. Stop UDP server.

    e. Then, send another message hi and observe that it gets an error message due to the UDP server shutdown.

```
#gcc cbudpc.c -lpcap
#sudo ./a.out
./a.out
Enter messagehi
Message sent: "hi
" (3 bytes)
Rcvd from 127.0.0.1:12345
Response from server: "hello
" (6 bytes)
Message sent: "hi" (3 bytes)
Rcvd from 127.0.0.1:12345
Error receiving response: Connection refused
```

From the results, we observe both UDP server and client applications exchange their data successfully when the UDP server is online. On exit of the UDP server, ICMP sends an error message to indicate the server is not available, and the UDP client, able to receive that message, prints it.

Next, let's learn and practice how to implement TCP and UDP traffic inspection network applications.

C Programming Ways for Monitoring and Inspecting TCP/UDP Applications Traffic

In previous sections, we have learned how to implement basic TCP/UDP network applications in C programming. In this section, we will learn how to monitor and inspect TCP/UDP network application traffic in C programming. Network application traffic inspection activities are essential skills for network engineers to deal with network application debugging and security activities. In order to quickly focus on network applications traffic activities, we will use a standard open-source packet capturing library (pcap.h) for doing hands-on activities. First, we will learn how to use the pcap.h library functions for conducting network applications traffic inspection activities.

Packet Monitoring and Filtering Activities

First we will check the pcap.h important library functions for conducting network applications traffic inspection activities.

- pcap_open_live(dev, snaplen, promisc, to_ms, errbuf): This function helps in opening a network device for packet capturing. We should pass the suitable values for the following arguments to access this function:
  - dev: Name of network device (e.g., eth0).
  - snaplen: Maximum size of a packet to be captured.
  - promisc: Setting 1 to this enables promiscuous mode over the network device to capture all network traffic received over the device.
  - to_ms: The maximum timeout value in milliseconds before pcap_loop waits before returning.
  - errbuf: A character array to capture any error or warning message.
- pcap_close(handle): At the end of the packet capturing, we should close the packet capture handle to release resources associated with the device.

- **pcap_loop**: This function loops over the network device to monitor and collect packets, then it can be processed using the user-specific callback function. We should pass the suitable values to the following arguments to access this function:
  - handle: The pcap handle returned from the pcap_open_live file.
  - N: The packet count.
    - Captures N packets
    - E.g., passing 0 means capturing packets continuously until an error occurs or pcap_breakloop() is called.
  - packet_handler: Callback function to process the collected packets
  - *args: The user inputs pointer passed to the packet_handler.
- packet_handler: Actual user-defined packet inspection function pointed to this pointer executed on each captured packet.

Next, we will discuss a common program structure for implementing network traffic inspection applications:

Basic Traffic Monitoring and Inspecting Program Structure

For implementing most of the traffic monitoring and inspection applications, the following general program structure is used:

- First define a specific network application packet inspection function with the following arguments:
  - Custom input arguments holding pointer: u_char *args
  - A pointer of type const struct pcap_pkthdr
  - A character pointer to hold a buffer containing a captured raw packet
    - Convert the pointer to a specific packet type (e.g., TCP or UDP)
    - Inspect headers and their fields using pointer traversals

CHAPTER 8   ESSENTIAL NETWORK SOCKET PROGRAMMING SKILLS

Example:

```
void tcp_inspect(u_char *args, const struct pcap_pkthdr *hdr, const u_char *tpkt)
{
    ..
    //inspect captured packets
    struct ip *iphdr;
    struct tcphdr *tcph;
    u_int ipsz;
    u_int tcpsz;
    iphdr = (struct ip*)(tpkt + 14);
    ipsz = iphdr->ip_hl * 4;
    ..
}
```

- Next, in main(), do the following steps:
  - Open your network device (e.g., eth0) using pcap_open_live before capturing packets using the suitable arguments:
    - Network device
    - Enable promiscuous mode to capture all network packets
    - Set maximum timeout in milliseconds to wait for capturing packets
    - Collect any warning or error messages using a character buffer
- Handle errors during opening of network device
- Capture packets over network device using pcap_loop by passing the following important arguments:
  - Device handle
  - Count of packets to capture: 0 indicates continuously capture packets
  - Function pointer to packet inspecting function
  - Any custom input argument

- Close the handle at the end of the packet capturing activities to release the resources

Example:

```c
int main()
{
    char *dev = "eth0";

    pcap_t *handle;
    char errbuf[PCAP_ERRBUF_SIZE];

    handle = pcap_open_live(dev, BUFSIZ, 1, 1000, errbuf);

    if (handle == NULL)
    {
        fprintf(stderr, "Couldn't open network device %s: %s\n", dev,
        errbuf);
        return 1;
    }

    pcap_loop(handle, 0, tcp_inspect, NULL);
    pcap_close(handle);
    return 0;
}
```

Next, we will do the following hands-on activities:

- Inspect TCP connection open and shutdown messages
- Inspect UDP messages that belong to DNS or have a message length greater than 64 bytes
- Monitor particular TCP connection details

Hands-On Activity-1

In this hands-on activity, we will implement a simple packet capture C program for doing the following tasks:

- Capture network traffic continuously on an Ethernet interface
- Specifically capture and inspect only TCP connection packets
  - Inspect source and destination IP addresses
  - Inspect source and destination port numbers
  - Sequence and acknowledgment numbers
  - Receiver window
- Specifically, capture and inspect only TCP connection shutdown packets

INSPECT TCP TRAFFIC

1. We implement this hands-on activity in insptcp.c.
2. First include the following necessary header files to do this hands-on activity:

   ```
   #include <pcap/pcap.h>
   #include <stdio.h>
   #include <stdlib.h>
   #include <netinet/in.h>
   #include <netinet/ip.h>
   #include <netinet/tcp.h>
   #include <arpa/inet.h>
   ```

3. We define the following callback function for inspecting TCP connection open and shutdown messages:

   a. Display each TCP connection open and shutdown packets: source IP, source port, destination IP, and destination port details

   b. Display each TCP connection sequence numbers, acknowledgement numbers, receiver window

   ```
   void tcp_inspect(u_char *args, const struct pcap_pkthdr *hdr,
   const u_char *tpkt)
   {
   ```

CHAPTER 8　ESSENTIAL NETWORK SOCKET PROGRAMMING SKILLS

    c. Define pointers to the TCP and IP headers to inspect the respective protocol details.

```
struct ip *iphdr;
struct tcphdr *tcph;
u_int ipsz;
u_int tcpsz;
```

    d. Traverse through the IP header starting byte using the pointer as follows:

```
iphdr = (struct ip*)(tpkt + 14);
ipsz = iphdr->ip_hl * 4;
if (ipsz < 20)
{
    printf("   * Invalid IP hdr length: %u bytes\n", ipsz);
    return;
}
if (iphdr->ip_p != IPPROTO_TCP)
{
    return;
}
```

    e. Traverse through TCP header starting byte using the pointer as follows:

```
tcph = (struct tcphdr*)(tpkt + 14 + ipsz);
tcpsz = tcph->th_off * 4;
if (tcpsz < 20)
{
    printf("   * Invalid TCP hdr length: %u bytes\n", tcpsz);
    return;
}
```

4. Filter TCP open connection messages by checking the SYN flag and display connection segment details:

```
int syn = (tcph->th_flags & TH_SYN) ? 1 : 0;
if (syn==1)
{
```

```
        printf(" TCP new connection\n");
        printf("   Source IP: %s\n", inet_ntoa(iphdr->ip_src));
        printf("   Destination IP: %s\n", inet_ntoa(iphdr->
        ip_dst));
        printf("   Source Port: %d\n", ntohs(tcph->th_sport));
        printf("   Destination Port: %d\n", ntohs(tcph->
        th_dport));
        printf("   Sequence Number: %u\n", ntohl(tcph->th_seq));
        printf("   Acknowledgement Number: %u\n", ntohl(tcph->
        th_ack));
        printf("   Header Length: %d\n", tcph->th_off * 4);
        printf("   Window Size: %d\n", ntohs(tcph->th_win));
        printf("   Checksum: %d\n", ntohs(tcph->th_sum));
        printf("   Urgent Pointer: %d\n", ntohs(tcph->th_urp));
    }
```

5. Filter TCP connection shutdown messages by checking the FIN flag and display connection segment details:

```
        int fin = (tcph->th_flags & TH_FIN) ? 1 : 0;
        int rst = (tcph->th_flags & TH_RST) ? 1 : 0;
        if (fin==1 || rst==1)
        {
            printf(" TCP connection close or abort\n");
            printf("   Source IP: %s\n", inet_ntoa(iphdr->ip_src));
            printf("   Destination IP: %s\n", inet_ntoa(iphdr->
            ip_dst));
            printf("   Source Port: %d\n", ntohs(tcph->th_sport));
            printf("   Destination Port: %d\n", ntohs(tcph->
            th_dport));
        }
    }
```

6. In main, do the following for inspecting TCP traffic:

    a. Capture network traffic over your Ethernet device by waiting for 1000 ms using pcap library functions

CHAPTER 8 ESSENTIAL NETWORK SOCKET PROGRAMMING SKILLS

    b. Process the TCP messages using the callback function (tcp_inspect)

    c. Close the packet processing handle

```
int main()
{
    char *dev = "enx00e04d6df09d"; //use your eth device
    char errbuf[PCAP_ERRBUF_SIZE];
    pcap_t *handle;
    handle = pcap_open_live(dev, BUFSIZ, 1, 1000, errbuf);
    if (handle == NULL)
    {
        fprintf(stderr, "Couldn't open network device %s: %s\n", dev, errbuf);
        return 2;
    }
    pcap_loop(handle, 0, tcp_inspect, NULL);
    pcap_close(handle);
    return 0;
}
```

7. Compile and test the insptcp.c using the following commands:

```
#gcc insptcp.c -lpcap
#sudo ./a.out
TCP new connection
  Source IP: 172.16.80.34
  Destination IP: 142.250.206.3
  Source Port: 37560
  Destination Port: 443
  Sequence Number: 1309084086
  Acknowledgement Number: 0
  Header Length: 40
  Window Size: 64240
  Checksum: 22879
  Urgent Pointer: 0
```

CHAPTER 8 ESSENTIAL NETWORK SOCKET PROGRAMMING SKILLS

```
    ..
    TCP connection close or abort
      Source IP: 172.16.80.34
      Destination IP: 142.250.206.3
      Source Port: 37560
      Destination Port: 443
```

From the results, we can observe that TCP connection and shutdown segments are filtered from the network traffic and displayed with details.

Next, let's practice how to implement a UDP traffic inspection application.

Hands-On Activity-2

In this hands-on activity, we will implement a simple packet capture C program for doing the following tasks:

- Capture network traffic continuously on an Ethernet interface
- Specifically, capture and inspect only UDP packets of type DNS or message length > 64 bytes
  - Inspect source and destination IP addresses
  - Inspect source and destination port numbers
  - Message length
  - Payload

INSPECT UDP TRAFFIC

1. We implement this hands-on activity in `inspudp.c`

2. First include the following necessary header files to do this hands-on activity:

   ```
   #include <pcap/pcap.h>
   #include <stdio.h>
   #include <stdlib.h>
   #include <netinet/if_ether.h>
   #include <netinet/in.h>
   ```

CHAPTER 8   ESSENTIAL NETWORK SOCKET PROGRAMMING SKILLS

```
#include <netinet/ip.h>
#include <netinet/tcp.h>
#include <netinet/udp.h>
#include <arpa/inet.h>
```

3. We define the following callback function for inspecting UDP messages of DNS or message length > 64 bytes:

   a. Display each UDP packets: source IP, source port, destination IP, and destination port details

   b. Display UDP packet payload bytes

   ```
   void udp_inspect(u_char *user_data, const struct pcap_pkthdr
   *pkthdr, const u_char *upkt)
   {
   ```

   c. Define pointers to Ethernet and IP headers to inspect the respective protocol details.

   ```
   struct ethhdr *eth_header = (struct ethhdr *)upkt;
   if (ntohs(eth_header->h_proto) != ETHERTYPE_IP)
   {
        return; // Not an IP upkt
   }
   struct iphdr *ip_header = (struct iphdr *)(upkt + ETH_HLEN);
   if (ip_header->protocol != IPPROTO_UDP)
   {
        return; // Not a UDP upkt
   }
   ```

4. Traverse through the UDP header starting byte using the pointer as follows:

   ```
   struct udphdr *udp_header = (struct udphdr *)(upkt + ETH_HLEN +
   (ip_header->ihl * 4));
   u_char *contents = (u_char *)(upkt + ETH_HLEN + (ip_header->
   ihl * 4) + sizeof(struct udphdr));
   int contents_len = ntohs(udp_header->len) - sizeof(struct
   udphdr);
   ```

5. Specifically capture and inspect only UDP packets of type DNS or message length > 64 bytes:

```
if (ntohs(udp_header->dest)==53 || contents_len>64)
{
    printf("UDP Packet (DNS or message len>64) \n");
    printf("Src IP: %s\n", inet_ntoa(*(struct in_addr *) &ip_header->saddr));
    printf("Dst IP: %s\n", inet_ntoa(*(struct in_addr *) &ip_header->daddr));
    printf("Src Port: %d\n", ntohs(udp_header->source));
    printf("Dst Port: %d\n", ntohs(udp_header->dest));
    printf("UDP Length: %d\n", ntohs(udp_header->len));
    printf("Contents Length: %d\n", contents_len);
    printf("Contents: ");
    for (int i = 0; i < contents_len ; i++)
    {
        printf("%02x ", contents[i]);
    }
    printf("\n\n");
    }
}
```

6. In main, do the following for inspecting UDP traffic:

    a. Capture network traffic over your Ethernet device by waiting for 1000 ms using pcap library functions

    b. Process the UDP messages using the callback function (udp_inspect)

    c. Close the packet processing handle

```
int main()
{
    char *dev = "enx00e04d6df09d";  // use your interface
    char errbuf[PCAP_ERRBUF_SIZE];
    pcap_t *handle;
    handle = pcap_open_live(dev, BUFSIZ, 1, 1000, errbuf);
```

```
            if (handle == NULL)
            {
                fprintf(stderr, "Couldn't open network device %s:
                %s\n", dev, errbuf);
                return 2;
            }
            pcap_loop(handle, 0, udp_inspect, NULL);
            pcap_close(handle);
            return 0;
    }
```

7. Compile and test the inspudp.c using the following commands:

```
#gcc inspudp.c -lpcap
#sudo ./a.out
..
UDP Packet (DNS or message len>64)
Src IP: 172.16.40.3
Dst IP: 172.16.80.34
Src Port: 53
Dst Port: 36276
UDP Length: 106
Contents Length: 98
Contents: 4d 85 81 80 00 01 00 00 00 01 00 01 08 61 63 63 6f 75 6e
74 73 06 67 6f 6f 67 6c 65 03 63 6f 6d 00 00 41 00 01 c0 15 00 06
00 01 00 00 00 07 00 26 03 6e 73 31 c0 15 09 64 6e 73 2d 61 64 6d
69 6e c0 15 2f 36 4c 56 00 00 03 84 00 00 03 84 00 00 07 08 00 00
00 3c 00 00 29 0f a0 00 00 00 00 00 00
..
```

From the results, we can observe that UDP messages of type DNS or message length >64 bytes are filtered from the network traffic and displayed with details.

In this section, we have learned how to implement basic TCP/UDP traffic monitoring and inspecting applications. It helps you to design and implement various network traffic filtering activities.

Summary

In this chapter, we have learned the basics of the Internet, the TCP/IP stack, and TCP/UDP network application structures. We have practiced implementation of iterative and multiprocess TCP servers in C. We have learned how to test TCP client-server applications. We also explored UDP programming and implemented connection-oriented or connection-less UDP client applications. Finally, we have explored network packet monitoring and inspection application implementation using C open-source libraries such as pcap. You have done a significant number of hands-on activities to practice TCP/UDP socket programming and traffic inspection applications in C.

In the next chapter, we will learn how to handle reliability issues of TCP/UDP applications, important socket options, and non-blocking socket programming.

Practice Tasks

1. Implement a TCP client-server programs to do the following:
   - TCP server does the following:
     - It handles the following options: 1. Checking prime number or not; 2. Generate prime numbers below given N; 3. Exit
     - Handles multiple TCP clients in parallel
   - TCP client does the following:
     - Displays following options: 1. Check if N is prime number or not; 2. Get me prime numbers below N; 3. Exit
     - Sends request to the TCP server
     - Collect results and display at client side
2. Implement UDP client-server programs to do the following:
   - UDP server does the following:
     - It handles the following options: 1. Search for a word in a given file; 2. Count the number of words, lines, and character; 3. Exit
     - Handles multiple UDP clients

- UDP client does the following:
    - Displays the following options: 1. Search for a word in a given file; 2. Count the number of words, lines, and character; 3. Exit
    - Sends request to the UDP server
    - Collect results and display at client side
    - Handle errors
3. Implement the following network traffic monitoring and inspection application:
    - For every 10 seconds, do the following tasks:
        - Print total number of TCP packets sent
        - Print total number of TCP packets received
        - Print total number of UDP packets received
        - Print total number of UDP packets sent
        - Print total number of DNS messages generated
        - Print total number of TCP connection requests generated
        - Print total number of TCP connections closed
        - Print total number of UDP messages of length > 512 generated

CHAPTER 9

Essential Advanced Socket Programming Ways Using C Sockets

In Chapter 8, "Essential Network Socket Programming Skills," we have learned how to implement network TCP/UDP applications using Linux socket programming in C. In this chapter, you will learn advanced socket programming approaches for handling TCP/UDP network applications. You will start with understanding the importance of non-blocking socket programming ways. Non-blocking socket programming is helpful to minimize network applications latencies and offer better response time. Mainly, we discuss how to use `fcntl, select` system's call for implementing non-blocking approaches in TCP/UDP network applications.

Then, you will learn various important socket options for handling network applications issues in reliable manners. Specifically, you will learn how to use socket options for handling TCP server tasks such as reliable data transmissions confirmation and handling server crashes. In the case of UDP, we will learn socket options related to fault tolerance, load balancing, and broadcast messaging implementation tasks in UDP servers. Then, you will practice implementing TCP/UDP applications to meet reliability, scalability, and performance. This chapter helps you to implement reliable techniques for developing network applications using socket programming.

Mainly, in this chapter, we will cover the following topics:

1. Important socket programming approaches
2. Non-blocking ways of programming
3. Handle TCP client-server performance and reliability issues
4. Handle UDP client-server performance and reliability issues

CHAPTER 9   ESSENTIAL ADVANCED SOCKET PROGRAMMING WAYS USING C SOCKETS

Important Socket Programming Approaches

In Chapter 8, "Essential Network Socket Programming Skills," we have learned how to implement basic network applications using TCP and UDP socket programming. In this chapter, we will learn the important socket programming approaches to deal with network applications for meeting the following requirements:

- **Performance**: Network applications performance is mainly measured in terms of throughput and latency. In general, network application-level throughput is measured in terms of the number of requests handled per second, and latency is measured as the duration between request arrival and response sent. It is necessary to improve application-level throughput and minimize latency for improving application performance. In the case of implementing network applications, to meet application performance requirements, the following approaches are also helpful:

    - **Multiprocessing**: As discussed in Chapter 6, "Process and Thread Management Tasks for C Programmers," using fork, it is necessary to design network applications to handle multiple clients and requests in parallel. Hence, compared to iterative ways using parallel processing, more requests can be handled in a given duration. It also improves response time for individual clients by interleaving with other clients. As an example, in Chapter 8, "Essential Network Socket Programming Skills," we implemented multiprocessing TCP server using fork.

    - **Multithreading**: As discussed in Chapter 6, "Process and Thread Management Tasks for C Programmers," it is possible to identify parallel tasks of network applications and handle them using multiple threads. Hence, like multiprocessing, it is possible to minimize latency as well as improve the throughput of a network application.

    - **Non-blocking Approaches**: In Chapter 8, "Essential Network Socket Programming Skills," we observed by default socket connection, read, and write operations are performed in blocking mode. It means until the operation completes, the application cannot progress further. It leads to huge delays in network applications. Hence, it is necessary to learn how to implement non-blocking approaches for handling socket connections read and write operations. In this chapter, we will learn how to implement non-blocking approaches in socket programming to minimize unnecessary waiting time of a network application.

- **Reliability**: While implementing a network application, another important aspect we should consider is reliability in terms of handling network application tasks such as connection handling, shutdown, and read and write operations. Specifically, the following major issues can be observed while deploying network applications related to reliability:

    - **Client or Server Crashes**: It is so common to observe failure of network applications in terms of client's side or server-side crashes. Server-side crashes are very important to handle in quick time to minimize loss and performance degradation of network applications. It needs a quick restart of servers and running redundant servers as backup servers to seamlessly handle failures. On the other hand, client crashes are very important to be identified by the server in a quick time to notify with suitable warning messages and to stop any ongoing transactions immediately.

        - In this chapter, we will learn how to handle TCP and UDP applications' reliability tasks using important socket options.

    - Failure of read or write operations over sockets: It is necessary to handle all failures of socket operation with suitable warning messages to ensure reliability of the applications.

- **Scalability**: Besides reliability, it is another important aspect that must be considered while designing and implementing network applications. In order to scale network applications to handle ever-growing demands from huge numbers of clients and their requests, it is necessary to implement network applications as lightweight servers and run multiple servers to handle load distribution activities. This can be achieved by incorporating the following important features in network applications:

- Prefer multithreading for network application microtasks over multiprocessing and use multiprocessing to run only longer jobs.

- Prefer non-blocking approaches for performing socket read and write operations to minimize network applications latencies.

- Deploy multiple servers and distribute load uniformly or based on network application requirements.

  - In this chapter, we will discuss how to implement fault-tolerant and load distribution activities in a UDP server's context.

In summary, to meet these important network applications requirements, the following socket programming approaches we will discuss in this chapter with suitable hands-on activities:

- Multiprocessing and multithreading
- Must know socket options
- Non-blocking socket programming

Multiprocessing and Multithreading

To meet network applications' performance and scalability, it is necessary to adapt multiprocessing or multithreading programming approaches. For instance, in Chapter 8, "Essential Network Socket Programming Skills," we discussed how to handle multiple TCP clients' requests in parallel by a multiprocessing TCP server using the fork system call. Multiprocessing enables network applications to carry out parallel processing and improves application-level throughput, such as the number of requests handled per unit of time, and minimizes response time for handling requests. However, developers should take care of the following important issues while using multiprocessing:

- Handle process creation errors and any runtime errors

- Wait for child processes to collect return status or results in a suitable order

CHAPTER 9 ESSENTIAL ADVANCED SOCKET PROGRAMMING WAYS USING C SOCKETS

- Assign suitable jobs to processes
- Decide what to be shared between parent and child process
- Decide what to be copied between parent and child process
- Implement a reliable data exchange between parent and child processes
- Handle child process termination gracefully
- Handle multiprocess coordination activities

Similarly, as part of lightweight solutions while implementing multitasking using multithreading network applications, the following relevant issues should be handled:

- Handle threads creation errors and any runtime errors
- Wait for threads to collect return status or results in a suitable order
- Divide network application tasks carefully and assign them to individual threads to offer improved parallelism of executing multiple tasks
- Implement reliable data exchange between threads and the main process
- Handle multiple threads coordination activities

In Chapter 8, "Essential Network Socket Programming Skills," we already discussed how to implement multiprocess network applications in this section, we quickly discuss how to implement multithreaded servers using the following code snippet, for example, to handle each TCP client request with a specific thread:

First implement a sample TCP client task handling function as follows (it is sample code only):

```
void *handle_tcp_client(void *csock)
{
    int socket = *(int *)csock;
    char ibuffer[1024];
    char obuffer[1024];

    //read data into ibuffer from the socket
    recv(socket, ibuffer, 1024, 0);
```

CHAPTER 9 ESSENTIAL ADVANCED SOCKET PROGRAMMING WAYS USING C SOCKETS

```
        //process the input data and copy output to obuffer

        //send result over the socket
        send(socket, obuffer, strlen(obuffer), 0);
        //close the socket as task is completed

        close(socket);
        return NULL;
}
```

Then, on accepting a new TCP client connection, set up a new thread, assign it with the task of implementing function, and pass the connection socket descriptor for handling the client as follows:

```
while (1)
{
    // Accept a new connection
    csocket = accept(tcpsock, (struct sockaddr *)&address, (socklen_t *)&addrlen);
    if (csocket < 0)
    {
        //handle errors
    }

    // Create a new thread to handle new TCP client
    pthread_t tid;
    //Connection socket argument to pass it to the thread
    int *ptr = malloc(sizeof(int));
    *ptr = csocket;
    // Assign task with thread and pass connection socket
    if (pthread_create(&tid, NULL, handle_tcp_client, (void *)ptr) != 0)
    {
        //handle errors
    }
    else
    {
```

```
            pthread_detach(tid);
    }
}
```

In summary, it is developers' responsibility to partition a complex network application as independently runnable processes and tasks. Then, assign partitions to suitable processes and threads to improve parallelism and achieve higher throughput and minimize latency of network applications.

As a practice task, we recommend readers implement a multithreaded TCP server by modifying Chapter 8, "Essential Network Socket Programming Skills," mtcps.c. Next, we will discuss the important socket options for handling network applications' performance, reliability, and scalability requirements.

Must-Know Socket Options

It is important to learn about how to use various socket options for addressing important issues of network applications. Socket options are helpful to give more power to network applications by interacting with the kernel and using important network-related features such as address binding, reusing addresses and port numbers, routing, enabling broadcasting and multicasting, and kernel features. Besides using important kernel-level network features, it is also possible to configure suitable socket send and receive buffer sizes, timer values for polling operations, and data send or receive operation timeout values. Configuring these options allows tuning the performance of the network applications and enables optimization of network application performance. By default, some of the important network operations are disabled, such as address reuse, routing, broadcast, and multicast operations. To use these socket options and configure socket parameters, in socket programming the following functions are helpful: setsockopt and getsockopt.

Here, we discuss the few important socket options developers can use to enable network applications with special features:

- **Routing and Related Features**:
    - SO_BROADCAST: By default, the broadcast messaging feature is disabled for network applications. Specifically, it is allowed for only UDP network applications.

CHAPTER 9 ESSENTIAL ADVANCED SOCKET PROGRAMMING WAYS USING C SOCKETS

- IP_MULTICAST_IF: By default, the multicast messaging feature is disabled for network applications. To implement multicast applications, to set the network interface, this option will be used.

- IP_TTL: It is a helpful feature to implement routing network applications. To enable setting of time-to-live (TTL) for IP packets, use this option.

- **Socket General Options**:

  - SO_SNDBUF: To change the default socket send buffer size, use this option. It is possible to change the socket send buffer size for both TCP and UDP applications.

  - SO_RCVBUF: To change the default socket receive buffer size, use this option. It is possible to change the socket receive buffer size for both TCP and UDP applications.

  - SO_SNDTIMEO: This option is helpful for both TCP and UDP applications to set maximum timeouts for socket send operations over blocking sockets.

  - SO_RCVTIMEO: This option is helpful for both TCP and UDP applications to set maximum timeouts for socket receive operations over blocking sockets.

  - SO_RCVLOWAT: This option is helpful for both TCP and UDP applications in non-blocking socket receive operation. Usually, the socket polling system calls `select()/poll()`, which returns true if any data is available for reading over the socket. On the other hand, it is possible to specify the minimum amount of data that must be available in the receive buffer to return from the blocking `recv()`.

  - SO_SNDLOWAT: This option is helpful for both TCP and UDP applications in non-blocking socket send operation. It is possible to set a specific threshold, such as the minimum amount of available space in the socket send buffer, to indicate the socket is writable.

- **SO_LINGER**: Usually on closing a socket, if there is data in the socket buffer, the remaining data will be sent and the socket is closed. To change this behavior, SO_LINGER is helpful to limit the amount of remaining data to be sent based on the timeout value. This option is specific to TCP only.

- **Address Reuse Options**:
  - **SO_REUSEADDR**: This option is helpful in the case of binding a socket with an address that is already in use. It is helpful for restarting servers with multiple processes in case of crashes.
  - **SO_REUSEPORT**: This option is helpful to run multiple servers to bind with the same IP and port address. It helps in enabling fault-tolerance and load distribution features for UDP servers. In Linux (kernel version 3.9 and later versions), the kernel handles the distribution of request packets among servers seamlessly.

- **TCP-Related Options**:
  - **SO_KEEPALIVE**: This option is helpful to identify idle TCP clients by the TCP server and close their connections. It is possible to set a suitable timeout, the number of keep-alive messages to be sent, and the duration between consecutive keep-alive messages using related socket options.
  - **TCP_NODELAY**: To disable the TCP Nagle algorithm, this option should be set. It helps in minimizing network latency for interactive applications implementation.
  - **TCP_MAXSEG**: To set the maximum segment size for TCP, this option should be set. It is helpful in high-bandwidth networks.
  - **SO_OOBINLINE**: This option should be enabled to check if any out-of-band (urgent) data is received inline with regular data.

Next, we will discuss how to set and use socket options:

For setting socket options, the following function is used:

```
#include <sys/socket.h>
int setsockopt(int sockfd, int level, int optname, const void *optval, socklen_t optlen);
```

It takes the following arguments:

- sockfd: The socket descriptor to set a given socket option name
- Level: It is possible to set socket options at socket level or protocol level; the following levels can be specified:
  - SOL_SOCKET: Socket level options
  - IPPROTO_IP: IP protocol level options only
  - IPPROTO_TCP: TCP protocol level options only
  - IPPROTO_UDP: UDP protocol level options only
- optname: Socket option name macro
  - E.g., SO_REUSEADDR
- optval: It is a generic pointer variable. In order to enable or disable a specific socket option, a specific value needs to be passed. To pass a specific configurable value for option names such as timeout, count, etc., then it is possible to pass the address of the variable holding the value to this pointer.
- optlen: Option length in terms of the size of the option value.

It is necessary to check default option values before setting socket option values. For retrieving socket option values, the following function is used:

```
#include <sys/socket.h>
int getsockopt(int sockfd, int level, int optname, void *optval, socklen_t *optlen);
```

It takes the following arguments:

- sockfd: The socket descriptor to query its option default values
- Level: It is possible to query socket options at the following levels:
  - SOL_SOCKET: Socket level options
  - IPPROTO_IP: IP protocol level
  - IPPROTO_TCP: TCP protocol level
  - IPPROTO_UDP: UDP protocol level

CHAPTER 9   ESSENTIAL ADVANCED SOCKET PROGRAMMING WAYS USING C SOCKETS

- optname: Socket option name macro
    - For example, SO_REUSEADDR
- optval: It is a generic pointer variable to collect a socket option value and store it. We must convert this pointer to a suitable data type of the option value to read the value from the pointer.
- optlen: Option length in terms of the size of the option value.
- On success getsockopt() returns 0; on any errors, it returns -1, and errno is set to indicate the error.

Next, we will give a sample code snippet on how to use these functions:

For example, to know the default value of SO_REUSEADDR option value:

```
int sockfd;
int optval;
socklen_t optlen = sizeof(optval);
..
if (getsockopt(sockfd, SOL_SOCKET, SO_REUSEADDR, &optval, &optlen) == -1)
{
      //handle errors
}
printf("Default SO_REUSEADDR value: %d\n", optval);
```

For example, to enable SO_REUSEADDR option value, we should set it to one as follows:

```
optval = 1;
if (setsockopt(sockfd, SOL_SOCKET, SO_REUSEADDR, &optval, optlen) == -1)
{
      //handle errors
}
```

Next, we will discuss the importance of non-blocking socket programming:

CHAPTER 9   ESSENTIAL ADVANCED SOCKET PROGRAMMING WAYS USING C SOCKETS

Non-blocking Socket Programming

By default, TCP/UDP sockets work in blocking mode only. In blocking mode, network applications block while reading or writing data from the sockets till those operations return or complete. It means network applications cannot proceed further until the operation completes while reading or writing data from the blocking sockets. For instance, while a TCP/UDP server is waiting to receive data from a socket, it cannot process new client connections and any other client requests till the operation completes. Blocking sockets results in significant delay to network applications performance; hence, it is necessary to learn how to use non-blocking approaches for using TCP/UDP sockets to perform socket read or write operations.

For example, if a network application is trying to receive data from two independent sockets, whichever socket is ready, it can process it and send it to the other peer immediately. If it is implemented in blocking sockets as follows:

```
recv(socket1, ibuffer1, 1024, 0);
recv(socket2, ibuffer2, 1024, 0);
//process either buffer and send results to output socket

//send result over the socket
send(socket, obuffer, strlen(obuffer), 0);
//close the socket as task is completed
```

Here, the network application first tries to read data from socket1 and then socket2. In case even the socket2 data is ready, the application cannot process it immediately. It is necessary to handle them as non-blocking sockets by polling both sockets and checking which one is ready for processing.

Not only this case, but it is also possible that sometimes unnecessary application blocks occur over a socket for independent operations such as read and write operations. In this case, over non-blocking sockets, it is possible to check if the socket is ready for read or write through polling, and the respective ready operation can be performed immediately.

To deal with these situations, it is necessary to poll over sockets and do the operations using non-blocking socket programming. In the following section, on how to implement non-blocking socket programming using polling functions, we discuss suitable hands-on activities in detail.

Non-blocking Ways of Socket Programming

In this section, we primarily focus on practicing non-blocking ways of socket programming. We will learn how to implement non-blocking TCP/UDP servers, which handle multiple clients in interactive ways without blocking while doing read or write operations over sockets. As part of non-blocking socket programming, we will learn how to use `fcntl` to convert blocking sockets into non-blocking sockets for doing read or write operations. Then, we will learn how to use the `select` system call for polling over the blocking sockets and perform connection handling and read or write over sockets.

Usage of fcntl and select

By default, all sockets work in blocking mode only, as we discussed in Chapter 8, "Essential Network Socket Programming Skills." For example, `tcp_bsd` is a TCP socket, then let's check how to convert it into a non-blocking socket.

First, get the flags of the socket descriptor using the fcntl as follows:

```
int flags = fcntl(tcp_bsd, F_GETFL, 0);
if (flags == -1)
{
    perror("fcntl(F_GETFL)");
    return -1;
}
```

Then, set the non-blocking flags over the socket descriptor using the fcntl as follows to convert it into non-blocking socket:

```
if (fcntl(tcp_bsd, F_SETFL, flags | O_NONBLOCK) == -1)
{
    perror("fcntl(F_SETFL)");
    return -1;
}
```

In this example, we are converting a TCP listening socket into a non-blocking socket for accepting a TCP client's connection in non-blocking mode. Similarly, if we want to convert a client-connected socket into non-blocking mode, we should set its flag as a non-blocking socket.

Next, we will learn how to poll sockets for performing connection handling or reading/writing operations over sockets. For example, let's check how to do a read operation over a TCP listening socket in non-blocking mode using the select system call. Select system call takes the following important arguments:

- Maximum number of descriptors to be polled in terms of maximum descriptor number.
  - It is necessary to update this to avoid unnecessary polling over closed socket descriptors.
- Read socket descriptor set: It holds a list of socket descriptors to be polled for checking readiness for a read operation to be performed over sockets. It is necessary to include a socket descriptor to be polled for a read operation in this set using FD_SET.
- Write socket descriptor set: It holds a list of socket descriptors to be polled for checking readiness for a write operation to be performed over sockets. It is necessary to include a socket descriptor to be polled for a write operation in this set using FD_SET.
- Exception socket descriptor set: It holds a list of socket descriptors to be polled for checking error status over the sockets. It is necessary to include a socket descriptor to be polled for reading error messages in this set using FD_SET.
- Waiting time before returning from the select operation.

For example, to poll two listening sockets, we will do the following tasks:
Declare the read socket set as follows:

```
fd_set rfds;
```

Then, initialize the read socket descriptor set with the list of socket descriptors:

```
FD_ZERO(&rfds);
FD_SET(tcp_ls[0], &rfds);
FD_SET(tcp_ls[1], &rfds);
```

Then, find the maximum descriptor over the list of socket descriptors as follows:

```
int maxfd = tcp_ls[0]>tcp_ls[1]?tcp_ls[0]:tcp_ls[1];
```

Then, configure the maximum waiting time over the polling operation as follows:

```
struct timeval waitime;
waitime.tv_sec = 1; // 1 second
waitime.tv_usec = 0;
```

Finally, use the select with all necessary arguments as follows for polling; it returns when any socket descriptor is ready for a read operation, the maximum waiting time is over, or any error during poll operations. We can handle these cases as follows:

```
int rval = select(maxfd + 1, &rfds, NULL, NULL, &waitime);
if (rval < 0 && errno != EINTR)
{
    perror("select error"); exit(EXIT_FAILURE);
}
```

If polling is success and returned one of the ready socket from the list of socket descriptors, then we can classify which socket descriptor is ready as follows:

```
if (FD_ISSET(tcp_ls[i], &rfds))
{
    ..perform connection handling task..
}
if (FD_ISSET(tcp_ls[i], &rfds))
{
    ..perform connection handling task..
}
```

Next, we will practice non-blocking socket programming by doing the following hands-on activities.

CHAPTER 9 ESSENTIAL ADVANCED SOCKET PROGRAMMING WAYS USING C SOCKETS

Hands-On Activity-1

In this hands-on activity, we implement a non-blocking server and do the following tasks:

- Implement two TCP servers, which run in non-blocking mode
  - Poll both TCP servers continuously; on receiving any connection request for any of these TCP servers, handle it in non-blocking mode.
  - TCP servers, on receiving an input message from a TCP client, echo the message to the client.
  - TCP servers handle requests in non-blocking mode.
  - TCP connection requests and TCP client's inputs are handled in non-blocking mode.
- We will test the TCP servers using netcat TCP clients
  - Test TCP server with multiple netcat TCP clients.
  - TCP clients should generate messages in an interleaving manner.

Note As part of the hands-on activity, we use the netcat tool for running TCP or UDP client applications. If it is not installed, we can install it using the command apt-get install netcat.

NON-BLOCKING TCP SERVERS

---

1. We implement this hands-on activity in nonbtcp.c.
2. First include the following necessary header files to do this hands-on activity:

   ```
   #include <stdio.h>
   #include <stdlib.h>
   #include <string.h>
   #include <errno.h>
   ```

CHAPTER 9 ESSENTIAL ADVANCED SOCKET PROGRAMMING WAYS USING C SOCKETS

```
#include <sys/socket.h>
#include <arpa/inet.h>
#include <netinet/in.h>
#include <sys/select.h>
#include <fcntl.h>
#include <unistd.h>
```

3. Define the TCP server port number and buffer size:

```
#define SRV_PORT 12345
#define BUF_SIZE 1024
```

4. Define the following function to convert a blocking TCP socket into non-blocking TCP socket:

```
int block2nonblock(int tcp_bsd)
{
    int flags = fcntl(tcp_bsd, F_GETFL, 0);
    if (flags == -1)
    {
        perror("fcntl(F_GETFL)");
        return -1;
    }
    if (fcntl(tcp_bsd, F_SETFL, flags | O_NONBLOCK) == -1)
    {
        perror("fcntl(F_SETFL)");
        return -1;
    }
    return 0;
}
```

5. In main(), declare the necessary variables to access TCP listening sockets, connected sockets, and server and client addresses.

    a. We assume a maximum of two TCP servers and ten TCP clients will be connected (it is possible to change these limits).

    b. Define variable for message handling through buffer, read socket descriptor set, and waiting time before returning from the polling activity:

CHAPTER 9   ESSENTIAL ADVANCED SOCKET PROGRAMMING WAYS USING C SOCKETS

```
int main()
{
    int tcp_ls[2], tcp_cs[10];
    struct sockaddr_in server[2], client[2];
    socklen_t client_len;
    char buf[1024];
    fd_set rfds;
    struct timeval waitime;
```

6. Set up two non-blocking TCP servers by doing the following:

   a. Create two TCP sockets.

   b. Configure the sockets as non-blocking listening sockets.

   c. Configure a unique server protocol address for each of the servers.

   d. Bind server protocol addresses with the respective two sockets.

   e. Listen over the sockets.

```
        for(int i=0;i<2;i++)
        {
            tcp_ls[i] = socket(AF_INET, SOCK_STREAM, 0);
            if (tcp_ls[i] < 0)
            {
                perror("socket"); exit(EXIT_FAILURE);
            }
            if (block2nonblock(tcp_ls[i]) < 0)
            {
                close(tcp_ls[i]); exit(EXIT_FAILURE);
            }

            memset(&server[i], 0, sizeof(server[i]));
            server[i].sin_family = AF_INET;
            server[i].sin_addr.s_addr = INADDR_ANY;
            server[i].sin_port = htons(SRV_PORT+i);
            if (bind(tcp_ls[i], (struct sockaddr *)&server[i],
            sizeof(server[i])) < 0
```

CHAPTER 9 ESSENTIAL ADVANCED SOCKET PROGRAMMING WAYS USING C SOCKETS

```
        {
            perror("bind"); close(tcp_ls[i]); exit(EXIT_
            FAILURE);
        }
        if (listen(tcp_ls[i], 5) < 0)
        {
            perror("listen"); close(tcp_ls[i]); exit(EXIT_
            FAILURE);
        }
    }
```

7. We are assuming a total of ten clients will be connected to TCP servers, and initialize the ten connection descriptors:

    ```
    for (int i=0;i<10;i++)
    {
        tcp_cs[i] = -1;
    }
    ```

8. Do the following tasks for polling two TCP servers to accept connections and collecting the connected clients' sockets

    a. Initialize read socket descriptors with listening socket descriptors and connection socket descriptors to poll.

    b. Find the maximum descriptor value from all socket descriptors. It helps to poll all the socket descriptors that are less than or equal to the maximum descriptor.

    c. Configure maximum poll waiting time as 1 second before `select` returns from polling over socket descriptors.

    d. Call `select` to poll over listening and connected socket descriptors.

        ```
        int c=0;
        while (1)
        {
            FD_ZERO(&rfds);
            int maxfd = tcp_ls[0]>tcp_ls[1]?tcp_ls[0]:tcp_ls[1];
        ```

```
                FD_SET(tcp_ls[0], &rfds);
                FD_SET(tcp_ls[1], &rfds);
                for (int i=0;i<10;i++)
                if (tcp_cs[i] != -1)
                {
                        FD_SET(tcp_cs[i], &rfds);
                        if (tcp_cs[i] >= maxfd) maxfd = tcp_cs[i];
                }
                printf("TCP Servers listening on ports 12345 and 12346
                ...\n");
                waitime.tv_sec = 1; // 1 second
                waitime.tv_usec = 0;
                int rval = select(maxfd + 1, &rfds, NULL, NULL,
                &waitime);
                if (rval < 0 && errno != EINTR)
                {
                        perror("select error"); exit(EXIT_FAILURE);
                }
                if (rval == 0)
                {
                        continue;
                }
```

9. Do the following tasks for checking any connection request is ready over the two listening TCP sockets

   a. Collect connected clients' socket descriptors from both TCP servers by accepting connections.

   b. Convert the blocking connected socket descriptors to non-blocking connected socket descriptors.

   c. Handle errors during accepting connections.

```c
            for (int i=0;i<2;i++)
            if (FD_ISSET(tcp_ls[i], &rfds))
            {
                    client_len = sizeof(client);
                    tcp_cs[c] = accept(tcp_ls[i], (struct sockaddr *)
                    &client[i], &client_len);
                    if (tcp_cs[c] < 0)
                    {
                            if (errno == EAGAIN || errno == EWOULDBLOCK)
                            {
                                    ;
                            }
                            else
                            {
                                    perror("accept");
                                    exit(EXIT_FAILURE);
                            }
                    }
                    else
                    {
                            if (block2nonblock(tcp_cs[c]) < 0)
                            {
                                    close(tcp_cs[c]); tcp_cs[c] = -1; continue;
                            }
                            printf("New connection accepted from %s:%d\n", inet_
                            ntoa(client[i].sin_addr), ntohs(client[i].sin_port));
                            c++;
                    }
            }
```

10. Do the following tasks for checking if any TCP client's connected sockets are ready for reading data

    a. Check all ten TCP clients' connected sockets descriptors for readiness of reading data.

CHAPTER 9 ESSENTIAL ADVANCED SOCKET PROGRAMMING WAYS USING C SOCKETS

b. If any TCP client connection descriptor is ready, read data from the connected socket and send a reply by echoing the received message to the client.

c. If any TCP client connection is closed, then close the corresponding connection descriptor and initialize with -1 to avoid checking for readiness.

d. Handle any read errors during reading data from the TCP clients.

```c
for (int i=0;i<10;i++)
if (tcp_cs[i] != -1 && FD_ISSET(tcp_cs[i], &rfds))
    {
        ssize_t rcnt = read(tcp_cs[i], buf,
        sizeof(buf) - 1);
        if (rcnt < 0)
        {
            if (errno == EAGAIN || errno == EWOULDBLOCK)
            {
                // No data available to read yet
            }
            else
            {
                perror("read");
                close(tcp_cs[i]);
                tcp_cs[i] = -1;
            }
        }
        else if (rcnt == 0)
        {
            printf("Client disconnected.\n");
            close(tcp_cs[i]);
            tcp_cs[i] = -1;
        }
        else
        {
            buf[rcnt] = '\0';
```

```
                        printf("Received from client: %s\n", buf);
                        ssize_t wcnt = write(tcp_cs[i], buf, rcnt);
                }
        }
```

11. In case TCP servers exited, end the program by closing both TCP servers' sockets.

    ```
            }
            close(tcp_ls[0]);
            close(tcp_ls[1]);
            return 0;
    }
    ```

12. Next, we will test these non-blocking TCP servers.

13. Start TCP servers using the following command:

    a. In a terminal, run the following command and observe that two TCP servers are listening on unique ports.

    b. After TCP clients are connected to these servers, the following TCP client messages will be observed:

    ```
    #gcc nonbtcp.c -o nonbtcps
    #./nonbtcps
    TCP Servers listening on ports 12345 and 12346 ...
    New connection accepted from 127.0.0.1:39470
    New connection accepted from 127.0.0.1:39608
    New connection accepted from 127.0.0.1:39472
    New connection accepted from 127.0.0.1:39610
    Received from client: hi
    Received from client: hi
    Received from client: hi
    Received from client: hi
    Received from client: hi
    ```

CHAPTER 9   ESSENTIAL ADVANCED SOCKET PROGRAMMING WAYS USING C SOCKETS

```
Received from client: hi
Received from client: hi
Received from client: hi
```

14. We will test these two TCP servers with four TCP clients.

15. Open four more terminals and start four netcat TCP clients:

    a. In terminal one, run the following command:

       i.   Send the first message hi, and observe that the TCP client receives hi

       ii. Then, before sending a second hi message from the client, check the server-side message.

       iii. After three TCP clients connect to the server, then send the second message from the client.

       iv. This procedure helps you to check that interleaving of TCP clients and servers can handle all TCP clients' messages in blocking mode.

       ```
       #nc 127.0.0.1 12345
       hi
       hi
       hi
       hi
       ```

    b. In terminal two, run the following command:

       i. After the first client, connect the second TCP client and send its message one after one.

       ii. Observe that the client receives replies immediately without any waiting.

       ```
       #nc 127.0.0.1 12346
       hi
       hi
       hi
       hi
       ```

c. In terminal three, run the following command:

   i. After the second client, connect the third TCP client and send its message one after one.

   ii. Observe that the client receives replies immediately without any waiting.

```
#nc 127.0.0.1 12345
hi
hi
hi
hi
```

d. In terminal four, run the following command:

   i. After the third client, connect the third TCP client and send its message one after one.

   ii. Observe that the client receives replies immediately without any waiting.

```
#nc 127.0.0.1 12346
hi
hi
hi
hi
```

From the results, we can observe that both TCP servers are handling their TCP client connections without blocking. Moreover, all four TCP clients can exchange their messages with their TCP servers in an interleaving manner without any blocking.

Next, let's do another hands-on activity related to implementing non-blocking UDP servers.

CHAPTER 9   ESSENTIAL ADVANCED SOCKET PROGRAMMING WAYS USING C SOCKETS

Hands-On Activity-2

In this hands-on activity, we implement a non-blocking server and do the following tasks:

- Implement two UDP servers, which run in non-blocking mode.
  - Poll both UDP servers continuously; on receiving any request for any of the UDP servers, handle it in non-blocking mode.
  - UDP servers, on receiving an input message from a UDP client, echo the message to the client.
  - UDP servers handle requests in non-blocking mode.
- We will test the UDP servers using netcat UDP clients.
  - Test the UDP server with multiple netcat UDP clients.
  - UDP clients should generate messages in an interleaving manner.

NON-BLOCKING UDP SERVERS

1. We implement this hands-on activity in nonbudp.c.
2. First include the following necessary header files to do this hands-on activity:

   ```
   #include <stdio.h>
   #include <stdlib.h>
   #include <string.h>
   #include <errno.h>
   #include <sys/socket.h>
   #include <arpa/inet.h>
   #include <netinet/in.h>
   #include <sys/select.h>
   #include <fcntl.h>
   #include <unistd.h>
   ```

CHAPTER 9 ESSENTIAL ADVANCED SOCKET PROGRAMMING WAYS USING C SOCKETS

3. Define the TCP server port number and buffer size:

   ```
   #define UDP_PORT 12345
   #define BUF_SIZE 1024
   ```

4. Define the following function to convert a blocking TCP socket into nonblocking TCP socket:

   ```
   int block2nonblock(int udp_bsd)
   {
       int flags = fcntl(udp_bsd, F_GETFL, 0);
       if (flags == -1)
       {
           perror("fcntl(F_GETFL)");
           return -1;
       }

       if (fcntl(udp_bsd, F_SETFL, flags | O_NONBLOCK) == -1)
       {
           perror("fcntl(F_SETFL)");
           return -1;
       }
       return 0;
   }
   ```

5. In main(), declare the necessary variables to access UDP sockets, server and client addresses, buffer, read socket descriptor set, and waiting time:

   ```
   int main()
   {
       int uds[2];
       struct sockaddr_in server[2], client[2];
       socklen_t client_len = sizeof(client[0]);
       char buf1[BUF_SIZE];
       char buf2[BUF_SIZE];
       int maxsd, rval;
       fd_set rfds;
   ```

CHAPTER 9   ESSENTIAL ADVANCED SOCKET PROGRAMMING WAYS USING C SOCKETS

6. Set up two UDP servers by doing the following:

   a. Create two UDP sockets.

   b. Configure them as non-blocking listening sockets.

   c. Configure server protocol address.

   d. Bind server protocol addresses with sockets.

   ```
   for (int i=0;i<2;i++)
   {
           uds[i] = socket(AF_INET, SOCK_DGRAM, 0);
           if (uds[i] < 0)
           {
                   perror("UDP socket creation failed");
                   exit(EXIT_FAILURE);
           }
           if (block2nonblock(uds[i]) < 0)
           {
                   close(uds[i]); exit(EXIT_FAILURE);
           }

           memset(&server[i], 0, sizeof(server[i]));
           server[i].sin_family = AF_INET;
           server[i].sin_addr.s_addr = INADDR_ANY;
           server[i].sin_port = htons(UDP_PORT+i);

           if (bind(uds[i], (struct sockaddr *)&server[i],
           sizeof(server[i])) < 0)
           {
                   perror("UDP socket bind failed");
                   exit(EXIT_FAILURE);
           }
   }
   ```

7. Do the following tasks for polling two UDP servers to accept connections and read data from the connected client's sockets:

a. Initialize read socket descriptors.

b. Find the maximum descriptor value from all socket descriptors. It helps to poll all the socket descriptors that are less than or equal to the maximum descriptor.

c. Configure maximum waiting time as 1 second before `select` returns from polling over socket descriptors.

d. Call `select` to poll over UDP socket descriptors.

```
printf("UDP servers are waiting on port numbers 12345 and 12346\n");
while (1)
{
        FD_ZERO(&rfds); // Clear the socket set
        FD_SET(uds[0], &rfds); // Add UDP socket
        FD_SET(uds[1], &rfds); // Add UDP socket

        maxsd = (uds[0] > uds[1]) ? uds[0] : uds[1];

        rval = select(maxsd + 1, &rfds, NULL, NULL, NULL);

        if ((rval < 0) && (errno != EINTR))
        {
                perror("select error");
        }
```

8. Do the following tasks for checking if any UDP server sockets are ready for reading data

   a. Check two UDP server sockets descriptors for readiness for reading data.

   b. If any descriptor is ready, read data from the corresponding socket and send a reply by echoing the received message.

   c. Handle any read errors.

```c
        if (FD_ISSET(uds[0], &rfds))
        {
            int n = recvfrom(uds[0], buf1, BUF_SIZE, 0, (struct
            sockaddr *)&client[0], &client_len);
            if (n < 0)
            {
                perror("UDP recvfrom failed");
                exit(EXIT_FAILURE);
            }
            buf1[n] = '\0';
            printf("Received UDP message from %s:%d: %s\n",
            inet_ntoa(client[0].sin_addr), ntohs(client[0].sin_
            port), buf1);
            sendto(uds[0], buf1, strlen(buf1), 0, (const struct
            sockaddr *)&client[0], client_len);
        }
        if (FD_ISSET(uds[1], &rfds))
        {
            int n = recvfrom(uds[1], buf2, BUF_SIZE, 0, (struct
            sockaddr *)&client[1], &client_len);
            if (n < 0)
            {
                perror("UDP recvfrom failed");
                exit(EXIT_FAILURE);
            }
            buf2[n] = '\0';
            printf("Received UDP message from %s:%d: %s\n",
            inet_ntoa(client[1].sin_addr), ntohs(client[1].sin_
            port), buf2);
            sendto(uds[1], buf2, strlen(buf2), 0, (const struct
            sockaddr *)&client[1], client_len);
        }
    }
```

9. End the program by closing both UDP servers' sockets.

    ```
    close(uds[0]);
    close(uds[1]);
    return 0;
    }
    ```

10. Next, we will test these non-blocking UDP servers.

11. Start UDP servers using the following command:

    a. In a terminal, run the following command and observe that two UDP servers are listening on unique ports.

    b. After UDP clients connect to these servers, the following TCP client messages will be observed:

    ```
    #gcc nonbudp.c -o nonbudps
    #./nonbudps
    UDP servers are waiting on port numbers 12345 and 12346
    Received UDP message from 127.0.0.1:49240: hi
    Received UDP message from 127.0.0.1:38464: hi
    Received UDP message from 127.0.0.1:38464: hi
    Received UDP message from 127.0.0.1:49240: hi
    ```

12. Open two more terminals and start two netcat UDP clients:

    a. In terminal one, run the following command:

        i. Send the first message hi, and observe the UDP client receives hi.

        ii. Then, before sending a second hi message, check the server-side message.

        iii. After the second UDP client exchanged its first message, send a second message from the client.

        iv. This procedure helps you to check that interleaving of UDP clients and servers are able to handle all UDP clients' messages in blocking mode.

CHAPTER 9   ESSENTIAL ADVANCED SOCKET PROGRAMMING WAYS USING C SOCKETS

13. Open two more terminals and start two UDP clients:

    a. In terminal one, run the following command:

    b. Observe that the client receives replies immediately without any waiting.

    ```
    #nc -u 127.0.0.1 12345
    hi
    hi
    hi
    hi
    ```

    c. Next, in terminal two, run the following command to start another UDP client:

    d. Observe that the client receives replies immediately without any waiting.

    ```
    #nc -u 127.0.0.1 12346
    hi
    hi
    hi
    hi
    ```

From the results, we can observe that both UDP servers are handling their connections without blocking. Moreover, two UDP clients are able to exchange their messages with their UDP servers in an interleaving manner without any blocking.

Next, we will learn how to handle reliability issues of TCP servers.

Handle TCP Client-Server Performance and Reliability Issues

In this section, we will learn how to handle the reliability and performance affecting TCP client-server exchange issues in socket programming. Primarily, we will handle the following important issues that affect performance as well as reliability of data exchange:

CHAPTER 9   ESSENTIAL ADVANCED SOCKET PROGRAMMING WAYS USING C SOCKETS

- **Crashes of TCP Servers:** While running TCP client-server applications, it is common to encounter servers crashing events. To handle server crashes, the most common solution is quick restart of the server. In the case of TCP servers, usually TCP servers run with a unique protocol address (IP+port). Moreover, to handle multiple TCP clients in parallel, it is necessary to spawn multiple TCP servers using multiple processes or multiple threads.

    - In this case, while child processes handle their respective TCP clients, if a child process crashes, these issues can be handled by the parent process by waiting for the child process's termination status. Moreover, a child process crash will not affect entire server processing tasks. But if the parent process crashes, it can result in the entire server down and no more clients can be handled; it leads to poor performance of the TCP server. In case the parent process dies, it is important to restart the TCP server in a quick time. However, during the restart of the server, there is a protocol address reuse issue to bind with the new TCP socket. It is due to the same protocol address in use by child processes. To handle this particular issue in socket programming, we should set the TCP server socket option with SO_REUSEADDR. Then, it is possible to restart the TCP server with a new socket with an existing protocol address even though the address is in use by other processes.

        - In this section, we will do a relevant hands-on activity to show how to restart a server during crashes without any protocol addressing reuse issues.

- **Crashes of TCP Clients:** While running TCP client-server, another common issue is crashes of TCP clients. When a TCP client exits or crashes, it is necessary to be identified by the TCP server. Because TCP server reserves socket resources for handling each of its TCP clients to offer reliable data transmissions. Ignoring TCP clients crashes by the TCP servers could lead to serious performance issues, such as unable to handle more TCP clients due to lack of socket resources. Hence, it is necessary to identify TCP clients crashes by the

TCP servers. Moreover, it is also necessary to identify idle TCP clients by the TCP servers to optimally manage TCP server resources by closing the idle TCP clients connections.

- In socket programming TCP clients crash issues can be handled by TCP servers by checking errors during send and receive operations.

  - In this section, we will do a relevant hands-on activity to identify idle TCP clients.

- Moreover, to identify idle TCP clients as per TCP client-server requirements, it is possible to poll idle TCP clients with the help of keep-alive probe messages. To use this feature in socket programming, we should set a TCP socket with SO_KEEPALIVE option and configure the necessary parameters.

  - In this section, we will do a relevant hands-on activity to identify idle TCP clients.

- **TCP Connection, Send and Receive Errors**: While TCP client-server applications exchange data, it is also necessary to identify various possible errors and handle them in a reliable manner. For example, it is possible that during data exchange one of the TCP peers may exit or crash, then it results in connection reset or connection close errors. It is necessary to identify these errors and handle them gracefully; otherwise, it can lead to the crash of the other peer or unnecessary data transmissions.

  - In this section, we will do a relevant hands-on activity to identify possible errors and how to handle them gracefully in socket programming.

- **Confirmation of Reliable Delivery at Application Level:** It is another important issue during TCP client-server applications data exchange. Although TCP protocol is promising reliable data exchange, it is at protocol-level only. When a TCP peer sends data to another TCP peer in a reliable manner, it means the data is delivered to the peer TCP socket buffer only. But the data is not yet read by the TCP application running over the peer TCP socket. It means to confirm the TCP application read the data from the socket buffer entirely; the TCP server application should check it explicitly. Otherwise, it can lead to reliability issues in terms of confirmation of reliable delivery at the TCP application level. In socket programming, it is possible to address this issue by sending application-level ACKs, and the other party can wait for receiving these application-level ACKs.

- In this section, we will do a relevant hands-on activity to identify reliable delivery at the application level gracefully in socket programming.

The Reliable TCP Server and Client

In order to handle the following reliability issues of the TCP server, we first implement the TCP server by enabling important socket options and handling errors related to connection handling and data exchange:

- Seamlessly allow TCP server restart during crashes
  - Configure SO_REUSEADDR option to allow TCP server restarts seamlessly by reusing the TCP server protocol address.
- Check idle TCP clients' status
  - Configure SO_KEEPALIVE option to poll idle TCP clients and know the live status of TCP clients.
- Confirm that the TCP client application read entire data
  - Shutdown write operations and check whether TCP clients read the entire data or not.
- Handle TCP clients' connection intermediate termination errors
  - Handle TCP clients' normal connection close procedure.
  - Handle TCP clients' termination due to crashes.

CHAPTER 9 ESSENTIAL ADVANCED SOCKET PROGRAMMING WAYS USING C SOCKETS

RELIABLE TCP SERVER

1. We implement this hands-on activity in rtcps.c

2. First include the following necessary header files to do this hands-on activity:

   ```c
   #include <arpa/inet.h>
   #include <netinet/in.h>
   #include <stdio.h>
   #include <stdlib.h>
   #include <string.h>
   #include <sys/socket.h>
   #include <sys/types.h>
   #include <sys/wait.h>
   #include <unistd.h>
   #include <netinet/tcp.h>
   #include <errno.h>
   ```

3. In main, we do the following:

   a. Assign specific server port

   b. Define specific buffer size for messages handling

   c. Create a TCP socket and bind it with a unique server protocol address (IP+port)

   ```c
   #define BUF_SIZE 1024
   #define PORT 12345
   int main()
   {
           int tcp_ls, tcpc_cs;
           struct sockaddr_in server, client;
           socklen_t slen;

           FILE *fptr;
           char buf[BUF_SIZE];
           tcp_ls = socket(AF_INET, SOCK_STREAM, 0);
           if (tcp_ls < 0)
   ```

```
{
    perror("Socket creation failed");
    exit(EXIT_FAILURE);
}
```

4. Set SO_REUSEADDR option to enable rebinding of the protocol address to the server socket during restart of the server due to crashes:

```
int sopt = 1;
socklen_t soplen = sizeof(sopt);
if (setsockopt(tcp_ls, SOL_SOCKET, SO_REUSEADDR, &sopt, soplen) < 0)
{
    perror("setsockopt(SO_REUSEADDR) failed");
    exit(EXIT_FAILURE);
}
```

5. Set SO_KEEPALIVE option to probe idle clients for checking live status by configuring the following parameters:

   a. TCP_KEEPIDLE: waiting time before sending first keep-alive probe.

   b. TCP_KEEPCNT: Count of keep-alive probes to be sent for declaring the client is dead. It means if the TCP client is not responding for any of these probes, the TCP server confirms the client is dead and closes the client connection.

   c. TCP_KEEPINTVL: interval between keep-alive messages for sending consecutive keep-alive probes.

```
if (setsockopt(tcp_ls, SOL_SOCKET, SO_KEEPALIVE, &sopt, soplen) < 0)
{
    perror("Error setting SO_KEEPALIVE");
    close(tcp_ls);
    exit(EXIT_FAILURE);
}
printf("SO_KEEPALIVE enabled.\n");
```

CHAPTER 9   ESSENTIAL ADVANCED SOCKET PROGRAMMING WAYS USING C SOCKETS

```
sopt = 10;
if (setsockopt(tcp_ls, IPPROTO_TCP, TCP_KEEPIDLE, &sopt,
soplen) < 0)
{
    perror("Error setting TCP_KEEPIDLE");
    close(tcp_ls);
    exit(EXIT_FAILURE);
}
printf("TCP_KEEPIDLE set to %d seconds.\n", sopt);

sopt = 1;
if (setsockopt(tcp_ls, IPPROTO_TCP, TCP_KEEPCNT, &sopt,
soplen) < 0)
{
    perror("Error setting TCP_KEEPCNT");
    close(tcp_ls);
    exit(EXIT_FAILURE);
}
printf("TCP_KEEPCNT set to %d probes.\n", sopt);

sopt = 1;
if (setsockopt(tcp_ls, IPPROTO_TCP, TCP_KEEPINTVL, &sopt,
soplen) < 0)
{
    perror("Error setting TCP_KEEPINTVL");
    close(tcp_ls);
    exit(EXIT_FAILURE);
}
printf("TCP_KEEPINTVL set to %d seconds.\n", sopt);
bzero(&server, sizeof(server));
```

6. Configure TCP server protocol address and bind it to the TCP socket:

```
server.sin_family = AF_INET;
server.sin_addr.s_addr = INADDR_ANY; // Listen on all
available interfaces
server.sin_port = htons(PORT);     // Convert port to
network byte order
```

```c
if (bind(tcp_ls, (const struct sockaddr *)&server,
sizeof(server)) < 0)
{
    perror("Socket binding failed");
    close(tcp_ls);
    exit(EXIT_FAILURE);
}
```

7. Listen over the TCP socket:

```c
if (listen(tcp_ls, 10) < 0)
{
    perror("Listen failed");
    close(tcp_ls);
    exit(EXIT_FAILURE);
}

printf("Server listening on port %d...\n", PORT);

slen = sizeof(client);
printf("Parent PS server PID:%d\n",getpid());
```

8. TCP server waiting in an infinite loop to accept connection requests from TCP clients:

```c
while (1)
{
    tcpc_cs = accept(tcp_ls, (struct sockaddr *)
    &client, &slen);
    if (tcpc_cs < 0)
    {
        perror("Accept failed");
        close(tcp_ls);
        exit(EXIT_FAILURE);
    }
    printf("Connection accepted from %s:%d\n", inet_ntoa
    (client.sin_addr), ntohs(client.sin_port));
```

CHAPTER 9   ESSENTIAL ADVANCED SOCKET PROGRAMMING WAYS USING C SOCKETS

9. Handle each TCP client request with a new child process for sending the entire contents of the sample.txt file (include any sample text inside of it):

    a. Handle connection errors.

    b. Handle connection close in a reliable manner.

    c. Handle connection reset errors.

```
if (fork()==0)
{
    close(tcp_ls);
    fptr = fopen("sample.txt", "r");

    if (fptr == NULL)
    {
        printf("Error: Could not open file.\n");
        return 1;
    }
    bzero(buf, BUF_SIZE);
    ssize_t rcnt = recv(tcpc_cs, buf, sizeof(buf) - 1,0);
    if (rcnt <= 0)
    {
        printf("Client disconnected or error occurred.\n");
        continue;
    }
    buf[rcnt] = '\0';
    printf("Client: %s %d\n",buf,rcnt);
    while (fread(buf,1, BUF_SIZE, fptr)>0)
    {
        int sc;
        sc=send(tcpc_cs, buf, strlen(buf),0);
        if (errno==ECONNRESET)
        {
```

CHAPTER 9   ESSENTIAL ADVANCED SOCKET PROGRAMMING WAYS USING C SOCKETS

```
                    perror("Peer closed the
                    connection");
                    exit(1);
            }

            printf("Sent: %s %d\n", buf, sc);
        }
```

d. After sending the entire file contents, before closing the client socket, confirm whether the TCP client application received the entire contents and display the confirmation message:

```
            printf("File closed\n");
            shutdown(tcpc_cs,SHUT_WR);
            bzero(buf, BUF_SIZE);
            ssize_t bytes_received = recv(tcpc_cs, buf,
            sizeof(buf), 0);
            if (bytes_received == 0)
            {
                    printf("Client successfully
                    closed.\n");
            }

            fclose(fptr);
        }
```

e. Wait for the child process to exit and collect the return status in the parent process:

```
        else
        {
            close(tcpc_cs);
            int stat;
            waitpid(-1,&stat,WNOHANG);
        }
    }
```

CHAPTER 9   ESSENTIAL ADVANCED SOCKET PROGRAMMING WAYS USING C SOCKETS

10. On exit of the server, close the TCP socket to release the resources of the socket:

    ```
    close(tcp_ls);
    return 0;
    ```
}

We will test this TCP server in later hands-on activities for handling server restart, idle clients, client connection errors, and confirming the TCP client application reads the entire data.

Next, we will implement the following TCP client application to test the above reliable TCP server. We do the following tasks in the TCP client:

- TCP client connects to the TCP server

  - Send a sample message.

  - Waits and receives the sample.txt contents from the server.

  - Exits after receiving the complete contents from the server.

RELIABLE TCP CLIENT

1. We implement this hands-on activity in rtcpc.c.

2. First include the following necessary header files to do this hands-on activity:

   ```
   #include <stdio.h>
   #include <stdlib.h>
   #include <string.h>
   #include <sys/socket.h>
   #include <sys/wait.h>
   #include <arpa/inet.h>
   #include <unistd.h>
   #include <netinet/tcp.h>
   ```

3. In main, we do the following:

   a. Define server IP and port

   b. Define specific buffer size for messages handling

CHAPTER 9   ESSENTIAL ADVANCED SOCKET PROGRAMMING WAYS USING C SOCKETS

    c. Create a TCP socket

    d. Define a TCP server address structure and assign server IP and port

```c
#define PORT_NUMBER 12345
#define SERVER_IP_ADDRESS "127.0.0.1"
#define BUF_SIZE 1024

int main()
{
    int tcp_cs;
    struct sockaddr_in server_address;
    char buf[BUF_SIZE];
    tcp_cs = socket(AF_INET, SOCK_STREAM, 0);
    if (tcp_cs == -1)
    {
        perror("Error creating socket");
        exit(EXIT_FAILURE);

    }
    server_address.sin_family = AF_INET;
    server_address.sin_port = htons(PORT_NUMBER);
    server_address.sin_addr.s_addr = inet_addr(SERVER_IP_ADDRESS);
```

4. Connect to the TCP server:

```c
            if (connect(tcp_cs, (struct sockaddr *)&server_address,
            sizeof(server_address)) == -1)
            {
                perror("Error connecting to server");
                exit(EXIT_FAILURE);
            }
            printf("Connected to server %s:%d\n", SERVER_IP_ADDRESS,
            PORT_NUMBER);
```

CHAPTER 9   ESSENTIAL ADVANCED SOCKET PROGRAMMING WAYS USING C SOCKETS

5. Sends a sample message to receive sample.txt contents from the TCP server:

    ```c
    printf("Enter sample text\n");
    scanf("%s",buf);
    if (send(tcp_cs, buf, strlen(buf), 0) == -1)
    {
        perror("Error sending data");
        exit(EXIT_FAILURE);
    }
    printf("Sent: %s\n", buf);
    ```

6. Waiting in a loop to receive contents from the TCP server:

    ```c
    while(1)
    {
        ssize_t rcnt = recv(tcp_cs, buf, sizeof(buf) - 1, 0);
        if (rcnt == -1)
        {
            perror("Error receiving data");
            exit(EXIT_FAILURE);
        }
        if (rcnt == 0)
        {
            perror("closing connection");
            break;
        }
        buf[rcnt] = '\0';
        printf("Received: %s %d\n", buf,rcnt);
    }
    ```

7. After receiving the contents from the server, close the socket to release the resources:

```
        close(tcp_cs);
        return 0;
}
```

Save this TCP client application in rtcp.c to test with the reliable TCP server (rtcps.c).

We will use this TCP client application with the reliable TCP server to conduct the following hands-on activities.

Hands-On Activity-1

In this hands-on activity, we will test rtcps.c with rtcpc.c for doing the following tasks:

- Start a reliable TCP server.
- Start a TCP client and connect to the server and start receiving sample.txt contents.
- While receiving data from the TCP server child process
  - Crash the main TCP server parent process.
    - Kill the parent process for simulating crashing of the server
  - After killing the process, restart the TCP server and observe that the TCP server will restart successfully and handle the new TCP client connections.

RESTART TCP SERVER IN A RELIABLE MANNER

1. First change the following lines of code in rtcpc.c
   a. Include sleep(1) while receiving data from the TCP server for allowing more time to receive data. You may also set a higher sleep value also for testing.
   b. During receiving data, it is possible to kill the TCP server parent process.
2. Comment SO_KEEPALIVE-related code in rtcps.c

3. Compile and create an executable file for a reliable TCP server (rctps.c) using the following command:

   ```
   #gcc rtcps.c -o rs
   ```

4. Then, start the TCP server using the following command:

   a. Note down the parent process id (marked in bold) to kill it.

   ```
   # ./rs
   SO_REUSEADDR enabled.
   Server listening on port 12346...
   Parent PS server:13167
   ```

5. Next, test the TCP server with the TCP client (rtcpc.c) executable, using the following commands in a new terminal:

   ```
   #gcc rtcpc.c -o rc
   #./rc
   Connected to server 127.0.0.1:12346
   Enter sample text
   Get
   ```

6. Once you enter sample text, the TCP client starts receiving data from the TCP server.

7. While receiving data from the TCP server, do the following:

   a. Open a new terminal and kill the parent process

   b. Observe that the TCP client is able to receive sample.txt from the child process

   ```
   #sudo kill -9 13167
   ```

   c. Then, restart the TCP server from its executable using the following command:

   - Observe that the TCP server restarts successfully

```
# ./rs
SO_REUSEADDR enabled.
Server listening on port 12346...
Parent PS server:14040
```

8. Open a new terminal and test it by connecting a new TCP client as follows:

```
#./rc
Connected to server 127.0.0.1:12346
Enter sample text
Get
```

From these results, we can observe that using the socket reuse address option, it is possible to restart the TCP server with the same protocol address while its address is already in use by its children processes. Do this hands-on activity without the SO_REUSEADDR option and observe that restarting the TCP server fails after the server crash.

Next, we will do another hands-on activity using rtcps.c and rtcpc.c for checking the idle TCP client's status.

Hands-On Activity-2

In this hands-on activity, we will test the reliable TCP server in the context of checking its idle TCP clients' status by doing the following tasks:

- Start the reliable TCP server with SO_KEEPALIVE option
- Connect a TCP client with the reliable TCP server
  - While waiting for entering sample text from the TCP client
    - Don't enter any text
    - Open a new terminal and start the Wireshark tool for observing TCP keep-alive probe messages and acknowledgments

CHAPTER 9 ESSENTIAL ADVANCED SOCKET PROGRAMMING WAYS USING C SOCKETS

Note As a part of this hands-on activity, check whether the Wireshark tool is installed or not. Wireshark is useful for inspecting network traffic; in our hands-on activity, we inspect TCP data exchange between TCP client and server applications. If it is not installed, we can install it with the command: sudo apt-get install Wireshark.

CHECK IDLE TCP CLIENTS STATUS

1. Un comment SO_KEEPALIVE-related code in rtcps.c:

2. Compile and create an executable file for a reliable TCP server (rctps.c) using the following command:

   ```
   #gcc rtcps.c -o rs
   ```

3. Then, start the TCP server using the following command:

   ```
   # ./rs
   SO_REUSEADDR enabled.
   Server listening on port 12346...
   Parent PS server:13167
   ```

4. Next, test the TCP server with the TCP client (rtcpc.c) executable, using the following commands in a new terminal:

   ```
   #gcc rtcpc.c -o rc
   #./rc
   Connected to server 127.0.0.1:12346
   Enter sample text
   ```

5. Don't enter any input message, open a new terminal and do the following:

   a. Now the TCP client is idle; hence, our TCP server probes it using a TCP keep-alive message.

CHAPTER 9   ESSENTIAL ADVANCED SOCKET PROGRAMMING WAYS USING C SOCKETS

b. Start Wireshark tool using the following command and select the loopback interface to capture traffic for inspecting TCP client and server data exchange:

#sudo wireshark

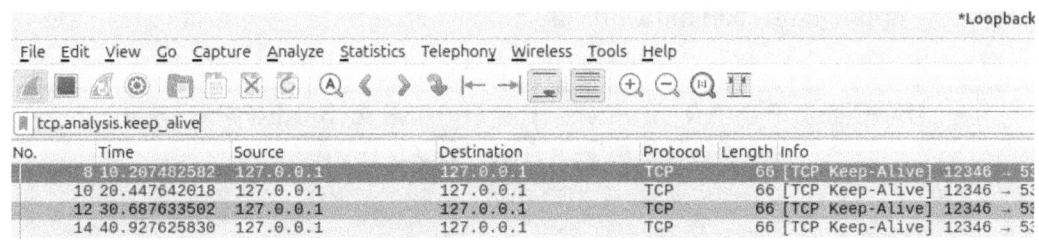

c. Then, in the filter tab, enter tcp.analysis.keep_alive to monitor probe message exchange between the idle TCP client and reliable TCP server (as shown in the below screenshot).

#sudo wireshark

From the Wireshark results, we can observe that our reliable TCP server is probing idle TCP clients by sending KEEP ALIVE messages.

Next, we will do another hands-on activity using rtcps.c and rtcpc.c for checking TCP client connection closing errors and confirming that the TCP client application reads the data entirely.

601

Hands-On Activity-3

In this hands-on activity, we will test the reliable TCP server in the context of TCP client connection errors and confirmation of receiving data by the TCP client application by doing the following tasks:

- TCP client connects with the reliable TCP server.
- While exchanging data, the TCP client exits after receiving only partial data.
  - Then, our reliable TCP server detects it and stops sending further data.
- Next, we test the following scenario:
  - TCP clients receive entire data from the reliable TCP server, then the TCP client sleeps for one second and exits.
  - Our reliable TCP server, after receiving TCP client application connection close confirmation, only confirms the TCP client application read data entirely.

HANDLE TCP CLIENT CONNECTION ERRORS AND CONFIRM THAT CLIENT APPLICATION READ DATA

---

1. First include the following lines of code in rtcpc.c to exit after receiving partial data: exit(1);

2. Compile and create an executable file for a reliable TCP server (rctps.c) using the following command:

   ```
   #gcc rtcps.c -o rs
   ```

3. Then, start the TCP server using the following command:

   ```
   # ./rs
   SO_REUSEADDR enabled.
   Server listening on port 12346...
   Parent PS server:13167
   ..
   ```

CHAPTER 9   ESSENTIAL ADVANCED SOCKET PROGRAMMING WAYS USING C SOCKETS

```
abcdefghijklmno 10000
Peer closed the connection: Connection reset by peer
```

4. Next, test the TCP server with the TCP client (rtcpc.c) executable, using the following commands in a new terminal:

```
#gcc rtcpc.c -o rc
#./rc
Connected to server 127.0.0.1:12346
Enter sample text
Get
..
```

5. Observe in the TCP client running terminal that it exits after receiving partial data.

6. Observe from the TCP server running terminal that it confirms intermediate connection termination by displaying the connection reset message (Peer closed the connection: Connection reset by peer).

7. Stop the TCP server and restart the TCP server:

```
# ./rs
SO_REUSEADDR enabled.
Server listening on port 12346...
Parent PS server:14040
..
abc 10000
File closed
```
Client successfully closed

8. Next, test the TCP server with the TCP client (rtcpc.c) executable, using the following commands in a new terminal:

```
#gcc rtcpc.c -o rc
#./rc
Connected to server 127.0.0.1:12346
Enter sample text
Hi
```

CHAPTER 9   ESSENTIAL ADVANCED SOCKET PROGRAMMING WAYS USING C SOCKETS

```
..
abcdefghijklmnopqrstuvwxyz
abc 159
```
closing connection: Success

9. Observe from the TCP client running terminal that the TCP client exits after one second on receiving complete data from the TCP server, and it displays: (**closing connection: Success**)

10. Observe from the TCP server running terminal that the TCP server displays the following message after the TCP client connection success only: (**Client successfully closed**)

From the results, it can be observed that our reliable TCP server stops sending data when the TCP client crashes. Then, the TCP server confirms the TCP client received the entire data only when the client exits after reading the entire data.

Next, let's learn and practice how to implement a reliable UDP server for handling fault-tolerance and load-balancing activities using socket options.

Handle UDP Client-Server Performance and Reliability Issues

In this section, we will learn the following important features implementation related to UDP servers.

- **Reliability:** It is necessary to set up multiple UDP servers to handle failures of UDP servers in a network. In this section, we will learn how to use default kernel supporting features such as distributing requests to UDP servers uniformly for implementing reliable UDP servers. Specifically, by enabling SO_REUSEPORT option over the UDP socket, the kernel allows multiple UDP servers to run with the same protocol address. Hence, it is possible to run multiple UDP servers for implementing reliability features.

CHAPTER 9   ESSENTIAL ADVANCED SOCKET PROGRAMMING WAYS USING C SOCKETS

- **Load Balancing**: Using SO_REUSEPORT and running multiple UDP servers, besides reliability feature, it is possible to implement load balancing between UDP servers by distributing UDP clients' messages across the multiple UDP servers with the help of the kernel. Moreover, the kernel distributes these packets between multiple UDP servers in round-robin fashion.

- **Broadcasting Applications**: Usually, it is not possible to send broadcast messages over sockets. However, UDP sockets are useful to send broadcast messages by enabling the SO_BROADCAST option. In this section, we will learn how to implement sample broadcast messages processing UDP server and broadcast messages sending UDP client.

In this section, we will learn these features by doing the following hands-on activities.

Hands-On Activity-1

In this hands-on activity, we will learn how to enable fault-tolerance and load-balancing features for UDP servers using SO_REUSEPORT option by doing the following tasks:

- Implement a UDP server with the SO_REUSEPORT option, and it does the following activities:

  - It receives messages from UDP clients, and as a reply, it echoes the same message.

- We test this UDP server with netcat UDP clients.

- We conduct this hands-on activity in two phases: In the first phase we test UDP servers' reliability by doing the following tasks:

  - Start two UDP servers (server-1 and server-2).

  - Start two UDP clients (client-1 and client-2): client-1 exchange messages with server-1 and client-2 exchange messages with server-2.

  - Later, stop one of the UDP servers (server-2) and observe that client-2 starts message exchange with server-1 seamlessly.

- In the second phase, we test UDP server load balancing by doing the following tasks:
    - Start two UDP servers (server-1 and server-2).
    - Start four UDP clients (client-1 to client-4).
    - While exchanging messages between UDP clients and servers, we can observe load distribution as follows:
        - Observe that two clients exchange messages with server-1, and two other clients exchange messages with server-2 automatically.

RELIABLE UDP SERVER (FIRST PHASE)

1. We implement this hands-on activity in rudps.c.
2. First include the following necessary header files to do this hands-on activity:

```
include <stdio.h>
#include <stdlib.h>
#include <string.h>
#include <unistd.h>
#include <arpa/inet.h>
#include <sys/socket.h>
```

3. Define the UDP server port number and buffer size:

```
#define SRV_PORT 12345
#define BUF_SIZE 1024
```

4. In main(), create a UDP socket:

```
int main()
{
    int ufd;
    struct sockaddr_in server, client;
    char buf[BUF_SIZE];
```

CHAPTER 9   ESSENTIAL ADVANCED SOCKET PROGRAMMING WAYS USING C SOCKETS

```c
if ((ufd = socket(AF_INET, SOCK_DGRAM, 0)) < 0)
{
    perror("Socket creation error");
    exit(EXIT_FAILURE);
}
```

5. Set socket option and reuse port on UDP socket; it helps in starting multiple UDP servers with the same protocol address (IP+port):

```c
int optval = 1;
socklen_t optlen = sizeof(optval);
if (setsockopt(ufd, SOL_SOCKET, SO_REUSEPORT, &optval,
optlen) < 0)
{
    perror("Set REUSE port option error");
    exit(EXIT_FAILURE);
}
```

6. Then, set the UDP server protocol address (IP+port) and bind the protocol address with the UDP socket:

```c
memset(&server, 0, sizeof(server));
server.sin_family = AF_INET;
server.sin_addr.s_addr = INADDR_ANY;
server.sin_port = htons(SRV_PORT);

if (bind(ufd, (const struct sockaddr *)&server,
sizeof(server)) < 0)
{
    perror("bind error");
    exit(EXIT_FAILURE);
}
```

CHAPTER 9   ESSENTIAL ADVANCED SOCKET PROGRAMMING WAYS USING C SOCKETS

7. Do the following tasks for accepting UDP clients' messages and sending replies:

   a. Continuously do the following:

      i. Wait for receiving a message from a UDP client.

      ii. Then, send a reply to the UDP client, echoing the same message.

         ```
         socklen_t len;
         ssize_t mlen;
         printf("UDP Server listening on port %d...\n", SRV_PORT);

         while (1)
         {
             len = sizeof(client);
             mlen = recvfrom(ufd, (char *)buf, BUF_SIZE - 1, 0,
                         (struct sockaddr *)&client, &len);
             if (mlen < 0)
             {
                 perror("recvfrom error");
                 exit(EXIT_FAILURE);
             }
             buf[mlen] = '\0';

             printf("Client message from %s:%d: %s\n",
             inet_ntoa(client.sin_addr), ntohs(client.sin_port), buf);
             char msg[BUF_SIZE];

             printf("Server Message:\n");
             scanf("%s",msg);
             strcat(msg,"\n");
             msg[strlen(msg)]='\0';
             sendto(ufd, (const char *)msg, strlen(msg), 0,
                         (const struct sockaddr *)&client, len);
         }
         ```

CHAPTER 9   ESSENTIAL ADVANCED SOCKET PROGRAMMING WAYS USING C SOCKETS

```
        close(ufd);
        return 0;
}
```

8. Compile and create the executable of the rudps.c using the following commands:

    ```
    #gcc rudps.c -o rudps
    ```

9. Start two UDP servers in separate terminals:

    a. In terminal one, run the following command:

    ```
    #./rudps
    UDP Server listening on port 12345...
    Client message from 127.0.0.1:40267: hi
    Server Message:
    hi
    ```
    Client message from 127.0.0.1:37989: hello
    Server Message:
    hello

    b. In terminal two, run the following command:

    ```
    #./rudps
    UDP Server listening on port 12345...
    Client message from 127.0.0.1:37989: hello
    Server Message:
    hello
    ```

10. Open two more terminals and start two UDP clients:

    a. In terminal one, run the following command:

    ```
    #nc -u 127.0.0.1 12345
    hi
    hi
    ```

CHAPTER 9 ESSENTIAL ADVANCED SOCKET PROGRAMMING WAYS USING C SOCKETS

b. In terminal two, run the following command:

```
#nc -u 127.0.0.1 12345
hello
hello
```

11. Then, kill one of the UDP servers; let's stop terminal two running the UDP server by issuing Ctrl+C command.

12. From the second UDP client:

a. Send hello message and observe that the message goes to the backup UDP server automatically

```
#nc -u 127.0.0.1 12345
hello
hello
hello
hello
```

From the results, we can observe that although one of the UDP servers goes down, the other UDP server is handling active UDP client messages. Since we set the socket reuse port option on the UDP socket, the kernel is handling redirecting UDP client messages to the active UDP server. This default feature is like implementing fault-tolerance features of UDP servers to offer improved reliability of UDP servers.

Next, let's test how the socket reuse port option is helpful in implementing load balance features for UDP servers.

TESTING LOAD BALANCING OF UDP SERVERS (SECOND PHASE)

1. We use the same code of `rudps.c` and do the following:

    a. We run two UDP servers in two terminals.

    b. We start four UDP clients in four terminals.

    c. We observe how the socket reuse port option is useful for getting the benefit of load balancing from the kernel.

2. Compile and create the executable of the rudps.c using the following commands:

   #gcc rudps.c -o rudps

3. Start two UDP servers in separate terminals:

   a. In terminal one, run the following command:

   ```
   #./rudps
   ```

   b. In terminal two, run the following command:

   ```
   #./rudps
   ```

4. Open four more terminals and start four UDP clients:

   a. In terminal one, run the following command:

   ```
   #nc -u 127.0.0.1 12345
   one
   one
   ```

   b. In terminal two, run the following command:

   ```
   #nc -u 127.0.0.1 12345
   two
   two
   ```

   c. In terminal three, run the following command:

   ```
   #nc -u 127.0.0.1 12345
   three
   three
   ```

   d. In terminal four, run the following command:

   ```
   #nc -u 127.0.0.1 12345
   four
   four
   ```

5. Observe two UDP servers are receiving requests almost equally:

    a. In terminal one, observe the following:

    ```
    #./rudps
    UDP Server listening on port 12345...
    Client message from 127.0.0.1:50964: two
    Server Message:
    two
    Client message from 127.0.0.1:50012: three
    Server Message:
    three
    ```

    b. In terminal two, observe the following:

    ```
    #./rudps
    UDP Server listening on port 12345...
    Client message from 127.0.0.1:46510: one
    Server Message:
    one
    Client message from 127.0.0.1:43854: four
    Server Message:
    four
    ```

From the results, we can observe that from the two UDP servers, each UDP server is handling two UDP clients. Since we set the socket reuse port option on the UDP socket, the kernel is distributing UDP client messages to all the active UDP servers for offering the load distribution feature. This default feature is like implementing load balancing features of UDP servers.

Next, let's test how to implement a broadcast messages processing UDP server and test it.

Hands-On Activity-2

In this hands-on activity, we will implement a broadcast messages processing server and a broadcast messages sending client.

CHAPTER 9   ESSENTIAL ADVANCED SOCKET PROGRAMMING WAYS USING C SOCKETS

- The broadcast message processing server does the following:

  - It is configured with a broadcast IP and a unique port number.

  - In an infinite loop, it does the following:

    - It waits for receiving broadcast messages (Hello).

    - On receiving a broadcast message, it replies with a Hi message.

BROADCAST UDP SERVER

1. We implement this hands-on activity in bcastserver.c.

2. First include the following necessary header files to do this hands-on activity:

   ```
   #include <stdio.h>
   #include <stdlib.h>
   #include <string.h>
   #include <unistd.h>
   #include <arpa/inet.h>
   #include <sys/socket.h>
   ```

3. Define the broadcast UDP server port number and buffer size:

   ```
   #define SRV_PORT 12345
   #define BUF_SIZE 1024
   ```

4. In main(), create a UDP socket:

   ```
   int main()
   {
       int ufd;
       struct sockaddr_in server, client;
       char buffer[BUF_SIZE];
       if ((ufd = socket(AF_INET, SOCK_DGRAM, 0)) < 0)
       {
   ```

```
            perror("Socket creation error");
            exit(EXIT_FAILURE);
    }
```

5. Set socket option and reuse port on UDP socket; it helps in starting multiple UDP servers with the same protocol address (IP+port):

   ```
   int optval = 1;
   socklen_t optlen = sizeof(optval);
   if (setsockopt(ufd, SOL_SOCKET, SO_REUSEPORT, &optval,
   optlen) < 0)
   {
           perror("Set REUSE port option error");
           exit(EXIT_FAILURE);
   }
   ```

6. Then, set the UDP server protocol address (broadcast IP address+port) and bind the protocol address with the UDP socket:

   ```
   memset(&server, 0, sizeof(server));
   server.sin_family = AF_INET;
   server.sin_addr.s_addr = INADDR_BROADCAST;
   server.sin_port = htons(SRV_PORT);

   if (bind(ufd, (const struct sockaddr *)&server,
   sizeof(server)) < 0)
   {
           perror("bind error");
           exit(EXIT_FAILURE);
   }
   ```

7. Do the following tasks for accepting UDP clients' messages and sending replies:

   a. Continuously do the following:

      i. Wait for receiving a message from a UDP client.

ii. Then, send a reply to the UDP client as HI message to confirm the existence of the broadcast server.

```
socklen_t len;
ssize_t mlen;
printf("UDP broadcast Server listening on port %d...\n",
SRV_PORT);
while (1)
{
    len = sizeof(client);
    mlen = recvfrom(ufd, (char *)buffer, BUF_SIZE - 1, 0,
            (struct sockaddr *)&client, &len);
    if (mlen < 0)
    {
        perror("recvfrom failed");
        exit(EXIT_FAILURE);
    }
    buffer[mlen] = '\0';
    printf("Client message from %s:%d: %s\n",
    inet_ntoa(client.sin_addr), ntohs(client.sin_port),
    buffer);
    char msg[BUF_SIZE];
    sendto(ufd, "HI\n", strlen("HI\n"), 0,
            (const struct sockaddr *)&client, len);
}
close(ufd);
return 0;
}
```

8. Compile and create the executable of the rudps.c using the following commands:

```
#gcc bcastserver.c -o bs
```

CHAPTER 9   ESSENTIAL ADVANCED SOCKET PROGRAMMING WAYS USING C SOCKETS

9. Start a broadcast UDP server:

   a. In terminal one, run the following command:

   ```
   #./bs
   UDP broadcast Server listening on port 12345...
   Client message from 172.16.80.104:40876: Hello
   Client message from 172.16.80.104:40876: Hello
   ```

From the results, we can observe that it receives broadcast messages continuously.

Next, let's implement broadcast messages sending client applications.

- Broadcast messages sending client to do the following:
  - Its UDP socket is set with the broadcast option to send broadcast messages.
  - In a loop it sends a broadcast message to the broadcast server protocol address and waits for 1 second to get a reply, if no reply comes:
- It sends another broadcast message (Hello).
  - Until a reply comes, it repeatedly sends broadcast messages every one second to the broadcast server.
  - On receiving a reply (Hi), it exits.

BROADCAST UDP CLIENT

1. We implement this hands-on activity in bcastclient.c.

2. First include the following necessary header files to do this hands-on activity:

   ```c
   #include <stdio.h>
   #include <stdlib.h>
   #include <string.h>
   #include <unistd.h>
   ```

```
#include <arpa/inet.h>
#include <sys/socket.h>
#include <fcntl.h>
#include <errno.h>
```

3. Define the UDP server port number and buffer size:

```
#define SRV_PORT 12345
#define BUF_SIZE 1024
```

4. In main(), create a UDP socket:

```
int main()
{
    int ufd,rcnt;
    struct sockaddr_in server, client;
    char buffer[BUF_SIZE];
    if ((ufd = socket(AF_INET, SOCK_DGRAM, 0)) < 0)
    {
        perror("Socket creation error");
        exit(EXIT_FAILURE);
    }
```

5. Convert the UDP blocking socket into a non-blocking UDP socket to enable non-blocking send and receive operations:

```
    if (fcntl(ufd, F_SETFL, O_NONBLOCK) < 0)
    {
        perror("fcntl failed");
        close(ufd);
        exit(EXIT_FAILURE);
    }
```

6. Set the socket option broadcast option on the UDP socket; it helps in sending broadcast messages:

```
    int optval=1;
    if (setsockopt(ufd, SOL_SOCKET, SO_BROADCAST, &optval,
    sizeof(optval)) < 0)
```

```
        {
                perror("setsockopt (SO_BROADCAST) failed");
                close(ufd);
                exit(EXIT_FAILURE);
        }
```

7. Then, set the UDP server protocol address (broadcast IP+port):

    ```
    memset(&server, 0, sizeof(server));
    server.sin_family = AF_INET;
    server.sin_addr.s_addr = INADDR_BROADCAST;
    server.sin_port = htons(SRV_PORT);
    socklen_t len;
    ssize_t mlen;
    ```

8. Do the following tasks for accepting UDP clients' messages and sending replies:

    a. Continuously do the following

    i. Send a broadcast message Hello.

    ii. If no reply comes in one second, send another broadcast message.

    iii. If a reply message comes, read the message and exit.

    ```
    printf("UDP broadcast Server listening on port %d...\n", SRV_PORT);

    while (1)
    {
            if (sendto(ufd,"Hello\n", strlen("Hello\n"), 0,
                        (struct sockaddr *)&server,
                        sizeof(server)) < 0)
            {
                    perror("sendto failed");
                    close(ufd);
                    exit(EXIT_FAILURE);
            }
            printf("Message sent\n");
    ```

```c
            socklen_t server_len = sizeof(client);
            rcnt = recvfrom(ufd, buffer, BUF_SIZE, 0,
                            (struct sockaddr *)&client,
                            &server_len);
            printf("Rcvd from %s:%d\n", inet_ntoa(client.sin_addr), ntohs(client.sin_port));

            if (rcnt < 0)
            {
                if (errno == EAGAIN || errno == EWOULDBLOCK)
                {
                    sleep(1);
                }
                else
                {
                    perror("Error receiving response");
                    close(ufd);
                    exit(EXIT_FAILURE);
                }
            }
            else
            {
                buffer[rcnt] = '\0';
                printf("Response from server: \"%s\" (%zd bytes)\n", buffer, rcnt);
                break;
            }
        }

    close(ufd);
    return 0;
}
```

CHAPTER 9   ESSENTIAL ADVANCED SOCKET PROGRAMMING WAYS USING C SOCKETS

9. Compile and create the executable of the rudps.c using the following commands:

   ```
   #gcc bcastclient.c -o bc
   ```

10. While the broadcast server is running, start a broadcast UDP client:

    a. In terminal one, run the following command:

    ```
    #./bc
    Message sent
    Rcvd from 0.0.0.0:0
    Message sent
    Rcvd from 172.16.80.104:12345
    Response from server: "HI
    " (3 bytes)
    ```

11. Kill the broadcast server and observe the following from the client:

    a. Sending broadcast messages every one second until receiving a reply message from the broadcast server.

    ```
    #./bc
    Message sent
    Rcvd from 0.0.0.0:0
    Message sent
    Rcvd from 0.0.0.0:0
    Message sent
    Rcvd from 0.0.0.0:0
    Message sent
    ```

12. Restart the broadcast server in a terminal and observe the following from the client:

    a. Stops sending broadcast messages after receiving a reply message from the broadcast server.

    ```
    #./bc
    Message sent
    Rcvd from 0.0.0.0:0
    ```

```
Message sent
..
Message sent
Rcvd from 0.0.0.0:0
Message sent
..
Rcvd from 172.16.80.104:12345
Response from server: "HI
" (3 bytes)
```

From the results, we can observe that it sends broadcast messages continuously until it gets a reply. Moreover, due to enabling the socket reuse option, even if the broadcast messages processing server is down for a while, once the server restarts, it can get a reply to its broadcast message.

Summary

In this chapter, we discussed advanced socket programming techniques to implement reliable network applications and improve their performance. Specifically, we have practiced how to implement non-blocking socket programming approaches for polling TCP or UDP servers to handle multiple clients simultaneously. Next, we have explored how to use socket options for handling TCP server issues such as restarting in case of crashes, checking idle TCP clients' status, and confirming TCP application-level message delivery. Finally, we practiced how to handle UDP server issues such as failures and enabling load balancing features using socket options. We also implemented a simple UDP broadcast message application.

In the next chapter, we will learn how to implement important virtualization concepts by programming Linux features such as namespaces and control groups in C.

CHAPTER 9   ESSENTIAL ADVANCED SOCKET PROGRAMMING WAYS USING C SOCKETS

Practice Tasks

1. Implement a proxy TCP server; it should hide the background multiprocessing-capable TCP servers. Every background TCP server should do the following:

   - On receiving a number, it should send as a reply whether the number is prime or not

   - Incorporate reliability and load balancing features to TCP server

2. Implement a multithread UDP server for handling the following:

   - To convert and send a given text into capitalized text

   - Incorporate reliability and load balancing features to UDP server

3. Implement a multicast UDP server for handling the following:

   - It should generate a file with 10 random numbers and send it to all UDP clients who subscribed with the server

CHAPTER 10

Learn C Programming Skills for Virtualization

In Chapters 5, "C Programming for Memory Management," and 6, "Process and Thread Management Tasks for C Programmers," we have learned how to use C programming concepts and Linux features such as multiprocessing and interprocess communication for handling large and high-performance applications. In this chapter, you will understand the importance of Linux features such as namespaces and control groups (cgroups) in implementing lightweight virtualization concepts over the systems. Namespaces and cgroups are key building blocks for realizing today's widely used containerization technologies such as Docker. Moreover, most of the popular public cloud platforms (such as Google Cloud, AWS, Azure) are also built over the containerization technologies only.

Interestingly, Linux offers programming of virtualization concepts using important system calls related to namespaces and cgroups. In this chapter, you will be learning how to implement virtualization concepts such as process, memory, and network virtualization using C programming and Linux features such as namespaces and cgroups. As part of practice, you will do hands-on activities related to setting up namespaces such as users, processes, memory, IPC, and networks for implementing suitable virtualized environments for processes.

Specifically, in this chapter, we will cover the following topics:

1. Introduction to Linux namespaces
2. Learn how to program Linux namespaces
3. Experiment with process and memory namespaces
4. Experiment with networking namespaces

CHAPTER 10 LEARN C PROGRAMMING SKILLS FOR VIRTUALIZATION

Introduction to Linux Namespaces

Virtualization technologies are key building blocks of today's popular public cloud platforms. Usually system administrators deploy database, web, proxy, and cache servers using suitable virtual machines over the physical servers (computational servers) running an operating system. Virtual machines (VMs) help to pack and deploy software applications with their own OS and configurations to hide the complexities of the underlying physical server and its OS for sharing the resources. Actually, VMs run over the hypervisors (VMware, VirtualBox), and hypervisors (refer to Figure 10-1) handle the complexity by partitioning, sharing, and controlling the underlying physical server resources such as CPU, memory, storage and network bandwidth.

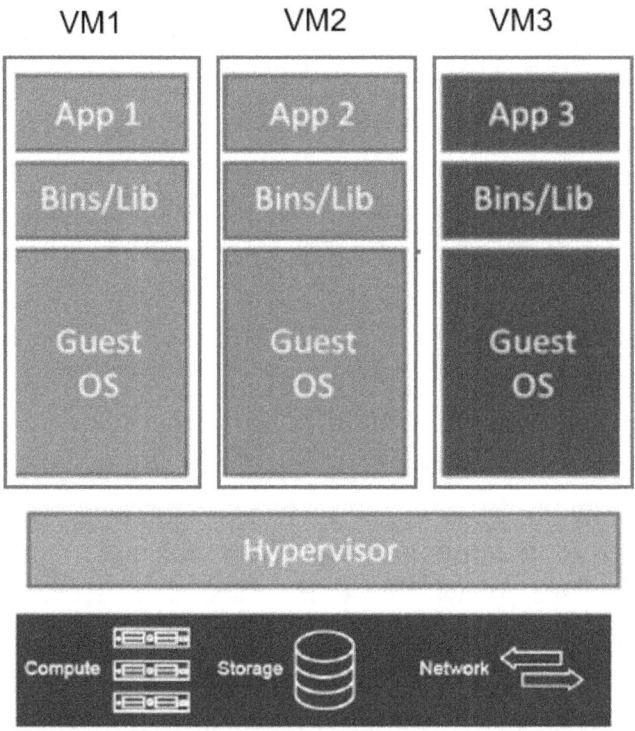

Figure 10-1. Virtual machines deployment

On the other hand, in many scenarios software applications can run within an isolated execution environment by sharing the underlying kernel instead of a dedicated OS. This concept is known as lightweight virtualization. In a lightweight virtualization environment, applications are deployed over the underlying physical server using containers (refer to Figure 10-2).

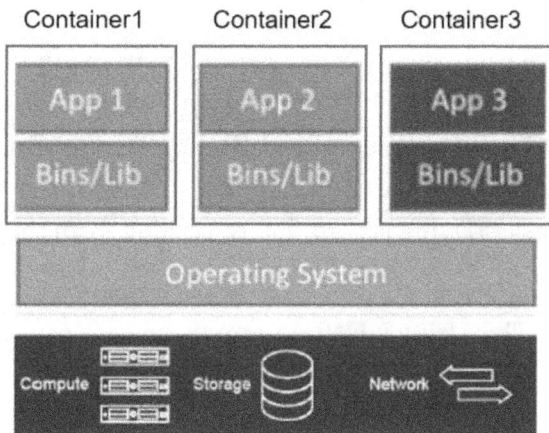

Figure 10-2. *Containers deployment*

A container provides a packed, isolated execution environment for an application over a physical server. While a container is running, the kernel virtualization features, such as namespaces, provide dedicated computational, memory, and network resources in terms of virtualized process, memory, and network stack. Moreover, a container can be configured with necessary CPU, memory, storage, and network bandwidth resource limits. Then, while the container is running, the underlying kernel feature cgroups monitor and control the container resources. In this section, first we will learn the details of Linux namespaces and cgroups.

Linux Namespaces

Linux namespace is nothing but partitioning kernel resources such as process, virtual memory, and network stack. For example, the Linux kernel offers the following namespaces: process hierarchy namespace, virtual memory namespace, user groups namespace, network namespace, etc. These Linux namespaces can be packed with a process and offer the process its own virtualized execution environment over a physical server running a Linux kernel. As part of hands-on activities, we will learn how to associate a process with the following important Linux kernel namespaces:

- CLONE_NEWPID: On a Linux system, attaching a process with a new PID namespace, it is possible to run the process with its own process hierarchy containing unique parent and children process IDs, which do not conflict with any of the existing processes running over the physical server.

- For example, on Linux OS, the process hierarchy tree starts with PID (1) as a root, and its children process trees contain unique PIDs. To virtualize the PID namespace, a new process can attach with the NEWPID namespace, then the new process tree can have its own unique PIDs containing PID 1 and the other PIDs. The new process PID tree is completely isolated from the Linux OS main PID tree.

- CLONE_NEWUTS: Using NEWUTS namespaces, a process can be configured with its own unique hostname and domain name to avoid collisions with the underlying system.

  - For example, a web server running with a NEWUTS namespace on a physical system isolates the underlying physical system hostname and domain name to avoid collisions.

- CLONE_NEWUSER: It is very important to configure a process to run it with a new user namespace for detaching the underlying physical system root and users' privileges and isolating the process.

  - For example, under a root user login, if we are running a process with NEWUSER, then the new process cannot access the root user-accessible files.

    - It means if root is not allowing read and write permissions over its sample.txt to other users then even with a root login, a process running with the NEWUSER namespace cannot access the sample.txt.

- CLONE_VM: Usually on creating a child process using `fork`, then parent and child processes run with their own copies of virtual memory. Hence, they cannot share the underlying virtual memory. When a process combined with a VM namespace enables sharing of the virtual memory, hence the process is able to directly access its parent process's virtual memory.

  - For example, use VM namespace with a process to enable direct sharing of virtual memory of the parent process without any IPC approach.

- CLONE_NEWIPC: It is important to run a new process with the NEWIPC namespace for disabling access to the use of IPC constructs such as shared memory, FIFO, and message queues set up by the parent process. Moreover, the new process can set up its own IPC constructs, such as shared memory, FIFO, and message queues, which are isolated from the parent process.

  - For example, it is possible to set up unique IPC constructs for a process group running with the NEWIPC namespace.

- CLONE_NEWNET: It is helpful to run a process with a NEWNET namespace to configure the process with its own network accessing interfaces, bridges, subnetworks, IP addresses, routing tables, and firewall rules.

  - For example, it is possible to run a group of processes with their own virtual networks, which are isolated from the physical system network.

In this section, we have understood the details of various namespaces to set up for a process to run in a virtualized execution environment over a physical server with a Linux kernel. While namespaces are helpful for setting up a virtualized environment, cgroups help in implementing the configuring of physical server resources limits, monitoring, and controlling approaches. Next, we will learn about various cgroups supported by Linux.

Linux cgroups

Control groups (cgroups) are the important concepts to realize lightweight virtualization concepts to the full extent. While namespaces ensure processes are executed in their own isolated environment over a physical system, cgroups concepts help in monitoring resources (CPU, memory, bandwidth) usage and controlling or restricting resources usage to the processes as per the respective cgroups rules. On Linux OS, control groups (cgroup) are created for CPU, memory, IO devices, etc. Once a cgroup is created for a resource (CPU, memory, etc.) with specific rules, the cgroup acts like a controller to monitor and enforce rules over the processes assigned to the cgroup. For example, on Linux OS the following cgroups are allowed to be implemented:

- **Memory Control Groups**: On Linux, it is possible to set up various memory control groups by configuring main memory limits, and processes can join these memory control groups.
  - After creating a memory cgroups, the following important parameters should be set up to limit the user space memory, kernel memory, and TCP buffer memory usage by process:
    - `memory.limit_in_bytes`
    - `memory.kmem.limit_in_bytes`
    - `memory.kmem.tcp.usage_in_bytes`
  - While running a process under memory control groups, the following important metrics, such as total usage, max usage, and failure count, can be monitored:
    - `memory.stat`
    - `memory.usage_in_bytes`
    - `memory.max_usage_in_bytes`
    - `memory.failcnt`
    - `memory.kmem.failcnt`
    - `memory.kmem.tcp.failcnt`
- **CPU Control Groups**: On Linux, it is possible to set up various CPU control groups by configuring CPU resources limits, and processes can join these CPU control groups.
  - After creating a CPU cgroup, the following important parameters can be set up to limit the CPU scheduling time usage by process:
    - `cpu.rt_period_us, cpu.cfs_period_us`: Max scheduling period in microseconds
    - `cpu.cfs_quota_us, cpu.rt_runtime_us`: Percentage of allowed CPU time over the max scheduling period
    - `cpu.shares`: Possible to set

CHAPTER 10   LEARN C PROGRAMMING SKILLS FOR VIRTUALIZATION

- While running a process under CPU control groups, the following important metrics, such as CPU usage, can be monitored:

  - `cpuacct.usage`:

    Reports the total CPU time consumed by all tasks in the cgroup in nanoseconds.

  - `cpuacct.usage_percpu`:

    Reports the CPU time consumed by all tasks in the cgroup on each individual CPU core in nanoseconds.

- **IO Control Groups (BLKIO)**: On Linux, it is possible to set up various IO devices operations control groups by configuring blkio resources, and processes can join these blkio control groups.

  - After creating a blkio cgroup, the following important parameters can be set up to limit the IO devices' read or write operations usage by process:

    - `blkio.throttle.read_bps_device` and `blkio.throttle.write_bps_device`: To limit IO operations based on bits per second

    - `blkio.throttle.read_iops_device` and `blkio.throttle.write_iops_device`: To limit based on IO operations per second

  - While running the processes under IO control groups, the following important metrics, such as IO usage, can be monitored:

    - `blkio.io_serviced` and `blkio.io_service_bytes`

- **Network Control Groups**: On Linux, using cgroups controllers, `net_cls` and `net_prio`, it is possible to set limits over network resources.

  - `net_cls`: Using this controller, a network process can be assigned with a network class ID. Then, traffic generated by the process can be classified based on this class ID to control traffic network resources such as bandwidth utilization.

- net_prio: Using this controller, a network process can be assigned with a priority. Then, traffic generated by the process can be treated by the IP layer based on priority for routing and scheduling of packets.

Next, we will learn how to use Linux namespaces and cgroups in C applications using Linux system calls.

Learn How to Program Linux Namespaces and cgroups

C developers can enjoy the power of implementing virtualization concepts such as setting up an isolated process execution environment with its own features such as process tree hierarchy, user groups, UNIX Time-sharing System (UTS), virtual memory, and network stack using Linux namespaces related system calls such as unshare, setns, and clone. Moreover, the Linux cgroups feature will help developers to enforce suitable resources controllers for process groups to monitor and control important resources such as CPU, memory, IO, and network. In this section, we will learn the following concepts:

- Detach a process from inherited namespaces
- Attach a process with existing namespaces
- Clone a new process with suitable namespaces
- Learn setting up and using control groups

Detach a Process from Inherited Namespaces

When a process is created using fork, then both parent and child processes will be associated and share the following namespaces:

- PID namespace
- IPC namespace
- User namespace
- UTS namespaces

- Mount namespaces
- Network namespaces

It means the child process directly accesses the parent process execution environment. Hence, the child process can directly update the parent process execution environment. This approach will not be helpful in case the parent process wants its child process to be executed in a separate isolated execution environment. For example, a child process should not access private files, network configuration, or IPC constructs that are inherited from the parent process, then just creating a new process from the parent process with a fork is not helpful.

On keen observation, it is necessary to execute both parent and child processes in their own isolated environment over the physical server. It means the necessity of implementing virtualization concepts for keeping processes in their own execution environment and controlling their respective resources utilization.

On Linux, using the unshare system call, it is possible to detach namespaces from a process. Let's first learn how to use the unshare system call.

Unshare System Call Usage

Developers use the unshare system call with the following flags to disassociate a child process from its parent's namespace and associate it with a corresponding new namespace.

- CLONE_NEWPID
- CLONE_NEWUSER
- CLONE_NEWUTS
- CLONE_NEWIPC
- CLONE_NEWNET

For example, in a program to separate its existing network namespace and run with a new network namespace, then the following code snippet is useful:

```c
#define _GNU_SOURCE
#include <sched.h>
#include <fcntl.h>
#include <stdio.h>
```

```
#include <stdlib.h>
#include <sys/types.h>
#include <unistd.h>
#include <sys/wait.h>
int main() {
    system( ip a ");
    if (unshare(CLONE_NEWUTS) == -1)
    {
        perror("unshare");
        exit(EXIT_FAILURE);
    }
    system( ip a ");// it is possible to execute the program with a new
    network namespace from this point onwards.
};
```

In the above example, the program shares all other namespaces with the parent process; only the network namespace will be disassociated from the parent, and the program execution will attach to the new network namespace.

It is also possible to disassociate multiple namespaces (e.g., network and UTS) using the bitwise OR operator with suitable namespace flags as follows:

```
if (unshare(CLONE_NEWUTS|CLONE_NEWNET) == -1)
{
    perror("unshare");
    exit(EXIT_FAILURE);
}
```

In summary, unshare helps in carefully disassociating with unnecessary namespaces and implementing suitable isolated execution environments for process execution. This is one of the basic steps in implementing virtualization concepts in Docker technology. Next, we will learn the basic implementation of detaching from specific namespaces using unshare.

Detach from the UTS Namespace Using unshare

In this example, we will run a process by disassociating with the inherited UTS namespace from the parent. Then, the process runs with a completely new UTS namespace and changes its hostname to newhost. In the following program, we use the gethostname to display the hostname of the process, and the `system function` will be used to change the hostname.

```c
#define _GNU_SOURCE
#include <sched.h>
#include <fcntl.h>
#include <stdio.h>
#include <stdlib.h>
#include <sys/types.h>
#include <unistd.h>
#include <sys/wait.h>

int main()
{
    char hostname[256];
    int result = gethostname(hostname, sizeof(hostname));
    printf("Before Unshare the current process%d hostname %s\n",getpid(),
    hostname);

    if (unshare(CLONE_NEWUTS) == -1)
    {
        perror("unshare");
        exit(EXIT_FAILURE);
    }
    system("hostname newname");
    result = gethostname(hostname, sizeof(hostname));
    printf("After Unshare the current process%d hostname %s\n",getpid(),
    hostname);

    return 0;
}
```

Save the above code in unshare1.c and execute it using the following commands:

```
#gcc unshare1.c
#sudo ./a.out
Before Unshare the current process46083 hostname iiitdmk-HP-
ProDesk-600-G5-MT
After Unshare the current process46083 hostname newname
```

Then, to confirm the original hostname is not changed, we can check with the following command:

```
#hostname
iiitdmk-HP-ProDesk-600-G5-MT
```

Next, let's check how to detach a process from the user namespace of the parent process.

Detach from the User Namespace Using unshare

In this example, we will run a process by disassociating with its parent user namespace and running it with a completely new user namespace.

```c
int main()
{
    printf("Before Unshare the current process%d uid %d\n",getpid(), getuid());

    if (unshare(CLONE_NEWUSER) == -1)
    {
        perror("unshare");
        exit(EXIT_FAILURE);
    }

    printf("After Unshare the current process%d uid %d\n",getpid(), getuid());

    return 0;
}
```

Save the above code in unshare2.c and execute it using the following commands:

```
#gcc unshare2.c
#./a.out
Before Unshare the current process46398 uid 1000
After Unshare the current process46398 uid 65534
```

Then, to confirm the original parent process user id is not changed, we can check with the following command:

```
$ id
uid=1000(iiitdmk) gid=1000(iiitdmk) groups=1000(iiitdmk)
```

Detach from the Network Namespace Using unshare

In this example, we will run a process with a completely new network namespace and test the ip address configuration of the process before and after unshare.

```c
int main()
{
    printf("Before Unshare the current process%d \n",getpid());
    system("ip a");

    if (unshare(CLONE_NEWNET) == -1)
    {
        perror("unshare");
        exit(EXIT_FAILURE);
    }

    printf("After Unshare the current process%d \n",getpid());
    system("ip a");

    return 0;
}
```

Save the above code in unshare3.c and execute it using the following commands:

```
#gcc unshare3.c
#./a.out
```
Before Unshare the current process46650
```
1: lo: <LOOPBACK,UP,LOWER_UP> mtu 65536 qdisc noqueue state UNKNOWN group default qlen 1000
    link/loopback 00:00:00:00:00:00 brd 00:00:00:00:00:00
    inet 127.0.0.1/8 scope host lo
    valid_lft forever preferred_lft forever
    inet6 ::1/128 scope host
```

```
        valid_lft forever preferred_lft forever
2: eno1: <NO-CARRIER,BROADCAST,MULTICAST,UP> mtu 1500 qdisc fq_codel state
DOWN group default qlen 1000
        link/ether 84:a9:3e:71:80:39 brd ff:ff:ff:ff:ff:ff
        altname enp0s31f6
3: enx00e04d6df09d: <BROADCAST,MULTICAST,UP,LOWER_UP> mtu 1500 qdisc fq_
codel state UP group default qlen 1000
        link/ether 00:e0:4d:6d:f0:9d brd ff:ff:ff:ff:ff:ff
        inet 172.16.80.34/23 brd 172.16.81.255 scope global dynamic
        noprefixroute enx00e04d6df09d
        valid_lft 672216sec preferred_lft 672216sec
        inet6 fe80::60b7:8bb4:d85:ee1f/64 scope link noprefixroute
        valid_lft forever preferred_lft forever
```

After Unshare the current process46650

```
1: lo: <LOOPBACK> mtu 65536 qdisc noop state DOWN group default qlen 1000
        link/loopback 00:00:00:00:00:00 brd 00:00:00:00:00:00
```

Observe from the above output that before unsharing the process using the parent process network interfaces and configuration, after unsharing, the process runs with completely new network interfaces and configuration. Hence, we don't find many interfaces for the child process.

Next, let's learn how to join a process with existing namespaces using setns.

Attach a Process with Existing Namespaces

Using unshare, we have learned how to disassociate from the parent namespaces and associate with the corresponding new namespace. In this section, we will learn how to attach a process with an existing namespace using setns system calls. For example, using unshare, it is possible to set up the following new namespaces:

- PID namespace
- IPC namespace
- User namespace
- UTS namespaces

CHAPTER 10 LEARN C PROGRAMMING SKILLS FOR VIRTUALIZATION

- Mount namespaces
- Network namespaces

Next, we will learn how to set up namespaces using unshare commands and how to join these namespaces by processes using setns.

Set Up a New Namespace Using unshare and Attach It with setns

For example, to set up a new UTS namespace and run a shell, the following command is useful:

```
sudo unshare --uts /bin/bash
```

Then, observe the shell runs with a new UTS namespace to confirm it changes the hostname using the following command and verify it:

```
#hostname newnshost
```

```
#hostname
newnshost
```

On the other terminal, to confirm it, check the hostname using the following command and verify it:

```
#hostname
anil-XXX..
```

Next, learn how to access this namespace for associating with a process. First, we need to note down the unshared bash/shell commands' executing process id using the following command:

```
..
#ps -ax
47201 pts/1    S       0:00 sudo unshare --uts /bin/bash
47204 pts/1    S+      0:00 /bin/bash
```

CHAPTER 10   LEARN C PROGRAMMING SKILLS FOR VIRTUALIZATION

Note down the bash/shell commands executing process id, and then to access its UTS namespace from a process, the process should open the following namespace file in its program:

```
/proc/47204/ns/uts
int fd;
fd = open(exist_ns, O_RDONLY | O_CLOEXEC);
```

Then, to attach a process with the namespace, the setns system call should be used as follows:

```
        if (setns(fd, CLONE_NEWUTS) == -1)
        {
                perror("setns");
                close(fd);
                exit(EXIT_FAILURE);
        }
```

Next, let's learn how to set up the following namespaces using unshare and attach with them in a process using setns:

- UTS namespace
- User namespace
- Network namespace

Attach with an Existing UTS Namespace Using setns

For example, to set up a new UTS namespace and run a shell, the following command is useful:

```
sudo unshare --uts /bin/bash
```

Next, note down the unshared bash/shell commands executing process id using the following command:

```
..
#ps -ax
47201 pts/1     S       0:00 sudo unshare --uts /bin/bash
47204 pts/1     S+      0:00 /bin/bash
```

638

Next, in the following program, the existing UTS namespace will be open: /proc/**47204**/ns/uts to set the namespace for a program as follows:

```
#define _GNU_SOURCE // Required for setns()
#include <stdio.h>
#include <stdlib.h>
#include <unistd.h>
#include <fcntl.h>
#include <sched.h>
#include <errno.h>
#include <string.h>
int main(int argc, char *argv[])
{
    const char *exist_ns = argv[1];
    int fd;

    printf("Before Unshare the current process%d \n",getpid());
    system("hostname");
    fd = open(exist_ns, O_RDONLY | O_CLOEXEC);
    if (fd == -1)
    {
        perror("open");
        exit(EXIT_FAILURE);
    }

    if (setns(fd, CLONE_NEWUTS) == -1)
    {
        perror("setns");
        close(fd);
        exit(EXIT_FAILURE);
    }

    printf("Successfully the process %d attached with the existing namespace: %s\n", getpid(), exist_ns);
    system("hostname");
```

```
        close(fd);
        return 0;
}
```

Save the above code in setns1.c and execute it using the following commands:

```
#gcc setns1.c
#sudo ./a.out /proc/47204/ns/uts
Before Unshare the current process47563
iiitdmk-HP-ProDesk-600-G5-MT
Successfully the process 47563 attached with the existing namespace: /
proc/47204/ns/uts
newnshost
```

From the above output, we can observe the child process before setting the namespace running with the inherited UTS namespace; after setting ns, it joined successfully with the completely new existing UTS namespace.

Attach with Existing User and Network Namespaces

For example, to set up a new network namespace (testns1), the following command is useful:

```
ip netns add testns1
```

For example, to set up a new user namespace and run a shell the following command is useful:

```
unshare -U
```

Next, note down the unshared bash/shell commands executing process id using the following command:

```
..
#ps -ax
49355 pts/1    S+       0:00 -bash
```

Next, in the following program, the existing user namespace file will be open: /proc/**49355**/ns/user and to set the existing network namespace (testns1), the following network namespace file will be open: /var/run/netns/testns1

```c
int main(int argc, char *argv[])
{
    const char *exist_ns1 = argv[1];
    const char *exist_ns2 = argv[2];
    int fd1,fd2;

    printf("Before Unshare the current process%d \n",getpid());
    system("ip a");
    system("id");
    fd1 = open(exist_ns1, O_RDONLY | O_CLOEXEC);
    if (fd1 == -1)
    {
        perror("open");
        exit(EXIT_FAILURE);
    }

    if (setns(fd1, CLONE_NEWNET) == -1)
    {
        perror("setns");
        close(fd1);
        exit(EXIT_FAILURE);
    }

    fd2 = open(exist_ns2, O_RDONLY | O_CLOEXEC);
    if (fd2 == -1)
    {
        perror("open");
        exit(EXIT_FAILURE);
    }

    if (setns(fd2, CLONE_NEWUSER) == -1)
    {
        perror("setns");
        close(fd2);
        exit(EXIT_FAILURE);
    }
```

```
        printf("Successfully the process %d attached with the existing
        namespaces: %s %s\n", getpid(), exist_ns1, exist_ns2);
        system("ip a");
        system("id");
        close(fd1);
        close(fd2);
        return 0;
}
```

Save the above code in setns2.c and execute it using the following commands:

#gcc setns2.c

#sudo ./a.out /var/run/netns/testns1 /proc/49355/ns/user

Before Unshare the current process49517

```
1: lo: <LOOPBACK,UP,LOWER_UP> mtu 65536 qdisc noqueue state UNKNOWN group
default qlen 1000
     link/loopback 00:00:00:00:00:00 brd 00:00:00:00:00:00
     inet 127.0.0.1/8 scope host lo
     valid_lft forever preferred_lft forever
     inet6 ::1/128 scope host
     valid_lft forever preferred_lft forever
2: eno1: <NO-CARRIER,BROADCAST,MULTICAST,UP> mtu 1500 qdisc fq_codel state
DOWN group default qlen 1000
     link/ether 84:a9:3e:71:80:39 brd ff:ff:ff:ff:ff:ff
     altname enp0s31f6
3: enx00e04d6df09d: <BROADCAST,MULTICAST,UP,LOWER_UP> mtu 1500 qdisc
fq_codel state UP group default qlen 1000
     link/ether 00:e0:4d:6d:f0:9d brd ff:ff:ff:ff:ff:ff
     inet 172.16.80.34/23 brd 172.16.81.255 scope global dynamic
noprefixroute enx00e04d6df09d
     valid_lft 669925sec preferred_lft 669925sec
     inet6 fe80::60b7:8bb4:d85:ee1f/64 scope link noprefixroute
     valid_lft forever preferred_lft forever
```

```
uid=0(root) gid=0(root) groups=0(root)
```
Successfully the process 49517 attached with the existing namespaces: /var/run/netns/testns1 /proc/49355/ns/user
```
1: lo: <LOOPBACK> mtu 65536 qdisc noop state DOWN group default qlen 1000
    link/loopback 00:00:00:00:00:00 brd 00:00:00:00:00:00
```
uid=65534(nobody) gid=65534(nogroup) groups=65534(nogroup)

From the above output, we can observe the child process before setting the namespace running with the inherited user id and network stack. After setting ns, it joined successfully with the existing user and network namespaces (testns1).

Next, let's learn how to start a process in its new virtualized environment using specific namespaces.

Clone New Processes with Suitable Namespaces

Using unshare we have learned how to disassociate a process from the parent process namespaces and using setns system calls we have learned how to associate a process with an existing namespace. Both approaches are very helpful in terms of handling virtualization concepts precisely after processes have been created. In this section, we will learn how to start a process using clone with new namespaces configurations, and change namespaces during execution. Unlike fork, clone is helpful to run specific tasks as virtualized processes by attaching them with necessary namespaces. The clone is a more flexible system call in terms of handling process virtualization tasks. Let's learn how to use clone using the following code snippets:

First define a sample process (process1) to run in parallel with its own virtualized execution environment:

```c
static int process1(void *arg)
{
    printf("PID: %ld\n", (long)getpid());
    system("ip a");
    return 0;
}
```

CHAPTER 10   LEARN C PROGRAMMING SKILLS FOR VIRTUALIZATION

Then, to set up virtualized execution environment for the process (process1), it is necessary to do the following in the main:

clone(process1, tos1, CLONE_NEWPID | SIGCHLD, NULL);

Finally, to set up virtualized execution environment for the process (process1), it is necessary to do the following in the main:

- Allocate necessary stack memory for process executions
- Set up suitable namespaces

```
int main()
{
    ..
    char *stm1;
    char *tos1;
    ..
    stm1 = malloc(1024 * 1024);
    if (stm1 == NULL)
    {
        perror("malloc");
        exit(1);
    }
    tos1 = stm1 + (1024 * 1024);
    ..
    pid1 = clone(process1, tos1, CLONE_NEWPID | SIGCHLD, NULL);
}
```

In this section, we will learn the following approaches to set up new processes in a virtualized environment using C programming:

- Start multiple processes with necessary new namespaces
- Start a process with multiple namespaces
- Start a process with limited namespaces and attach new namespaces later

Start Multiple Processes with Necessary New Namespaces

In this example, we will run two processes using a clone system call. The first process runs with its own new PID namespace; on the other hand, the second process runs with its own new network namespaces. Both processes inherit other namespaces from the calling process. We do this activity using the following code:

```
#define _GNU_SOURCE
#include <sched.h>
#include <stdio.h>
#include <stdlib.h>
#include <sys/wait.h>
#include <unistd.h>
static int process1(void *arg)
{
    printf("PID: %ld\n", (long)getpid());
    system("ip a");
    return 0;
}
static int process2(void *arg)
{
    printf("PID: %ld\n", (long)getpid());
    system("ip a");
    return 0;
}
int main()
{
    char *stm1, *stm2;
    char *tos1,*tos2;
    pid_t pid1, pid2;

    stm1 = malloc(1024 * 1024);
    if (stm1 == NULL)
```

```c
    {
        perror("malloc");
        exit(1);
    }
    tos1 = stm1 + (1024 * 1024);
    stm2 = malloc(1024 * 1024);
    if (stm2 == NULL)
    {
        perror("malloc");
        exit(1);
    }
    tos2 = stm2 + (1024 * 1024);

    pid1 = clone(process1, tos1, CLONE_NEWPID | SIGCHLD, NULL);
    if (pid1 == -1)
    {
        perror("clone");
        exit(1);
    }
    printf("Parent PID: %ld\n", (long)getpid());
    printf("Clone PID: %ld\n", (long)pid1);
    waitpid(pid1, NULL, 0);
    pid2 = clone(process2, tos2, CLONE_NEWNET | SIGCHLD, NULL);
    if (pid2 == -1)
    {
        perror("clone");
        exit(1);
    }
    printf("Parent PID: %ld\n", (long)getpid());
    printf("Clone PID: %ld\n", (long)pid2);
    waitpid(pid2, NULL, 0);

    free(stm1);
    free(stm2);
    return 0;
}
```

Save the above code in clone1.c and execute it using the following commands:

```
#gcc clone1.c
#sudo ./a.out
```
Parent PID: 50346
Clone PID: 50347
Child PID: 1
```
1: lo: <LOOPBACK,UP,LOWER_UP> mtu 65536 qdisc noqueue state UNKNOWN group default qlen 1000
    link/loopback 00:00:00:00:00:00 brd 00:00:00:00:00:00
    inet 127.0.0.1/8 scope host lo
    valid_lft forever preferred_lft forever
    inet6 ::1/128 scope host
    valid_lft forever preferred_lft forever
2: eno1: <NO-CARRIER,BROADCAST,MULTICAST,UP> mtu 1500 qdisc fq_codel state DOWN group default qlen 1000
    link/ether 84:a9:3e:71:80:39 brd ff:ff:ff:ff:ff:ff
    altname enp0s31f6
```
Parent PID: 50346
Clone PID: 50350
Child PID: 50350
```
1: lo: <LOOPBACK> mtu 65536 qdisc noop state DOWN group default qlen 1000
    link/loopback 00:00:00:00:00:00 brd 00:00:00:00:00:00
```

From the above output, we can observe the following details:

- Process-1 runs with its own PID namespace; we observe its clone PID is 1, and it is sharing a network namespace with its calling process. Hence, we observe it displays all network interfaces of the calling process host network configuration.

- Process-2 runs with its own network interfaces and configuration; we observe only one interface detail. Moreover, process-2 is sharing the PID namespace of the calling process; hence, we observe that both the clone PID and child PID are the same.

CHAPTER 10   LEARN C PROGRAMMING SKILLS FOR VIRTUALIZATION

Start a Process with Multiple Namespaces

In this example, we will run a process with multiple namespaces using a clone system call. Specifically, while cloning a process, we attach new PID and network namespaces. We do this activity using the following code:

```
#define _GNU_SOURCE
#include <sched.h>
#include <stdio.h>
#include <stdlib.h>
#include <sys/wait.h>
#include <unistd.h>
static int process1(void *arg)
{
      printf("Child PID: %ld\n", (long)getpid());
      system("ip a");
      return 0;
}
int main()
{
      char *stm1;
      char *tos1;
      pid_t pid1, pid2;
      stm1 = malloc(1024 * 1024);
      if (stm1 == NULL)
      {
            perror("malloc");
            exit(1);
      }
      tos1 = stm1 + (1024 * 1024);
      pid1 = clone(process1, tos1, CLONE_NEWPID | CLONE_
      NEWNET|SIGCHLD, NULL);
      if (pid1 == -1)
```

CHAPTER 10   LEARN C PROGRAMMING SKILLS FOR VIRTUALIZATION

```
    {
        perror("clone");
        exit(1);
    }
    printf("Parent PID: %ld\n", (long)getpid());
    printf("Clone PID: %ld\n", (long)pid1);
    waitpid(pid1, NULL, 0);

    free(stm1);
    return 0;
}
```

Save the above code in clone2.c and execute it using the following commands:

```
#gcc clone2.c
sudo ./a.out
Parent PID: 50548
```
Clone PID: 50549
Child PID: 1
```
1: lo: <LOOPBACK> mtu 65536 qdisc noop state DOWN group default qlen 1000
    link/loopback 00:00:00:00:00:00 brd 00:00:00:00:00:00
```

From the above output, we can observe the following details:

- Process-1 runs with its own PID namespace; we observe its clone PID is 1, and it is not sharing a network namespace with its calling process.

- Process-1 runs with its own network interfaces and configuration; hence, we observe only one interface detail.

Start a Process with Limited Namespaces and Attach New Namespaces Later

In this example, we will run a process initially with only new PID namespaces using a clone system call. But, while running the process, it will be attached to an existing network namespace (testns1).

CHAPTER 10 LEARN C PROGRAMMING SKILLS FOR VIRTUALIZATION

For example, to set up a new network namespace (testns1), the following command is useful:

#ip netns add testns1

Then, we will attach the following process to the namespace file using setns: /var/run/netns/testns1

We do this activity using the following code:

```
#include <fcntl.h>
static int process1(void *arg)
{
    printf("PID: %ld\n", (long)getpid());
    int fd;

    printf("Before Unshare the current process%d \n",getpid());
    system("ip a");

    fd = open("/var/run/netns/testns1", O_RDONLY | O_CLOEXEC);
    if (fd == -1)
    {
        perror("open");
        exit(EXIT_FAILURE);
    }

    if (setns(fd, CLONE_NEWNET) == -1)
    {
        perror("setns");
        close(fd);
        exit(EXIT_FAILURE);
    }

    printf("Successfully the process %d attached with the existing namespace\n", getpid());
    system("ip a");
    close(fd);
    return 0;
}
```

CHAPTER 10   LEARN C PROGRAMMING SKILLS FOR VIRTUALIZATION

```c
int main()
{
    char *stm1;
    char *tos1;
    pid_t pid1;

    stm1 = malloc(1024 * 1024);
    if (stm1 == NULL)
    {
        perror("malloc");
        exit(1);
    }
    stm1 = tos1 + (1024 * 1024);

    pid1 = clone(process1, tos1, CLONE_NEWPID | SIGCHLD, NULL);
    if (pid1 == -1)
    {
        perror("clone");
        exit(1);
    }
    printf("Parent PID: %ld\n", (long)getpid());
    printf("Clone PID: %ld\n", (long)pid1);
    waitpid(pid1, NULL, 0);

    free(stm1);
    return 0;
}
```

Save the above code in clone3.c and execute it using the following commands:

```
#gcc clone3.c
#sudo ./a.out
Parent PID: 51201
Clone PID: 51202
Child PID: 1
Before Unshare the current process1
```

```
1: lo: <LOOPBACK,UP,LOWER_UP> mtu 65536 qdisc noqueue state UNKNOWN group
default qlen 1000
    link/loopback 00:00:00:00:00:00 brd 00:00:00:00:00:00
    inet 127.0.0.1/8 scope host lo
    valid_lft forever preferred_lft forever
    inet6 ::1/128 scope host
    valid_lft forever preferred_lft forever
2: eno1: <NO-CARRIER,BROADCAST,MULTICAST,UP> mtu 1500 qdisc fq_codel state
DOWN group default qlen 1000
    link/ether 84:a9:3e:71:80:39 brd ff:ff:ff:ff:ff:ff
    altname enp0s31f6
```

Successfully the process 1 attached with the existing namespace
```
1: lo: <LOOPBACK> mtu 65536 qdisc noop state DOWN group default qlen 1000
    link/loopback 00:00:00:00:00:00 brd 00:00:00:00:00:00
```

From the above output, we can observe the following details:

- Process-1 runs with its own PID namespace; we observe its clone PID is 1, and it is initially sharing a network namespace with its calling process. Hence, we observe it displays all network interfaces of the calling process host network configuration.

- Process-1 later joins the existing network namespace (testns1) successfully. Hence, it runs with its own network interfaces and configuration; we observe only one interface detail.

In this section, we will learn the following approaches to set up new processes in a virtualized environment using C programming:

Learn Setting Up and Using Control Groups

In this section, we will learn how to use Linux control groups (cgroups) for controlling and monitoring process resources such as CPU, memory, IO devices, etc. In order to use Linux cgroups, the following steps should be followed by developers.

- Set up a suitable resource cgroup
- Configure resource limits of a cgroup

CHAPTER 10 LEARN C PROGRAMMING SKILLS FOR VIRTUALIZATION

- Assign processes to a cgroup
- Monitor resources utilization of the processes belonging to the cgroup

Setting Up a Suitable Resource Control Group

On Linux, to set up a control group for a specific resource, first we should create a unique directory under the following Linux cgroups directory:

/sys/fs/cgroup/

For example, to set up a memory resource control group, we should create a unique memory cgroup (e.g., mymgrp) under the /sys/fs/cgroup/.

To set up a sample memory resource control group, we can use the following code snippets:

```
#define MEM_CGROUP_DIR "/sys/fs/cgroup/memory/mymgrp"

..
if (mkdir(MEM_CGROUP_DIR, 0755) == -1)
{
    perror("Error creating cgroup directory (may already exist)");
}
```

Configure Resource Control Group Limits

After setting up resource control groups, as we discussed in the Linux cgroups section, check and identify necessary parameters to be configured for the cgroup.

For example, to set up a memory utilization maximum limit per process group, we should create a corresponding parameter file under the memory cgroup under the /sys/fs/cgroup/mymgrp path.

To set up a memory utilization maximum limit for a memory control group as, e.g., 1 Mb, we can use the following code snippets:

```
#define MEM_LIMIT "/sys/fs/cgroup/memory/mymgrp/memory.limit_in_bytes"

fd = open(MEM_LIMIT, O_WRONLY);
if (fd == -1)
```

653

```
{
    perror("Error opening memory limit file");
    return EXIT_FAILURE;
}
unsigned int cl = 1; //Memory limit 1Mb
dprintf(fd, "%dM\n", cl);
close(fd);
```

Assign Processes to a cgroup

After setting up and configuring memory resources control group limits, we should create a processes allocation file under the memory cgroup under the /sys/fs/cgroup/mymgrp path.

For example, to assign processes (appending PIDs) under the memory cgroup, (/sys/fs/cgroup/mymgrp), the following file should be created: cgroup.procs. We can do this using the following code snippets:

```
#define MEM_CGROUP_PS "/sys/fs/cgroup/memory/mymgrp/cgroup.procs"
..

fd = open(MEM_CGROUP_PS, O_WRONLY | O_APPEND);
if (fd == -1)
{
    perror("Error opening cgroup.procs");
    return EXIT_FAILURE;
}
dprintf(fd, "%d\n", pid);
close(fd);
```

Finally, for memory utilization during a process execution, we can identify the suitable parameters supported by the corresponding cgroup and use it. For example, to display maximum memory utilization of a memory cgroup, we can use the following code:

```
system("cat /sys/fs/cgroup/memory/mymgrp/memory.max_usage_in_bytes");
```

In the next section, we will practice setting up various process and memory namespaces for experimentation and learning the usage of Linux namespaces and cgroups.

Experiment with Process and Memory Namespaces

In this section, we will practice important Linux namespaces related to process and memory. First, we will learn how to use Linux namespaces for cloning processes with their own virtual memory or sharing virtual memory. It helps you in implementing process-coordinating activities by sharing virtual memory directly. Next, we will learn how to set up isolated IPC constructs for ensuring a virtualized execution environment for process coordination activities.

By default child processes created by fork or clone share parent processes namespaces; hence, it is necessary to check and protect which namespaces can be shared. For example, if a parent process's user group permissions are shared by a child process, then the child process can have access to all private files of the parent process. Here, you will learn the importance of a new user namespace for protecting private files of parent processes by isolating user groups of parent and child processes.

Finally, you will practice how to control and monitor CPU and memory resources of a process group using Linux cgroups. Specifically, these hands-on activities help you in learning how to set up cgroups, configure cgroups, assign processes to the cgroups, and monitor resources utilization by processes.

In this section, specifically, we will do the following hands-on activities.

- Share or isolate virtual memory of processes

- Set up isolated IPC constructs for processes coordination activities

- Set up isolated user namespaces for protecting inherited files of parent process

- Set up a memory control group for limiting memory consumption by processes

- Set up CPU control group for limiting CPU resources by processes

CHAPTER 10   LEARN C PROGRAMMING SKILLS FOR VIRTUALIZATION

Hands-On Activity-1

In this hands-on activity, we will learn the default behavior of cloning processes in terms of virtual memory access and set up shared virtual memory access between processes. Mainly, we will do the following activities:

- Set up two processes using clone and execute them in order (p1->p2)
- Test access of data segment and heap segments between processes
- First execute two processes without any cloning flags, and observe the behavior in terms of virtual memory access
- Next, execute two processes with CLONE_VM flag, and observe the behavior in terms of virtual memory access
- Finally, understand the importance of CLONE_VM to share virtual memory between processes

SHARE VIRTUAL MEMORY BETWEEN PROCESSES

1. Implement these hands-on activity tasks in `clonevm.c` as follows:
2. First include the following necessary header files to do this hands-on activity:

   ```
   #define _GNU_SOURCE
   #include <sched.h>
   #include <stdio.h>
   #include <stdlib.h>
   #include <sys/wait.h>
   #include <unistd.h>
   ```

3. Set up sample data in the data segment by declaring a global variable:

   ```
   int g=100;
   ```

4. Set up sample data in the heap segment, and to provide access to the heap segment among processes, declare a global pointer variable (p):

   ```
   int *p;
   ```

5. Define process-1 sample activity as accessing data segment and heap segment data as follows:

```
static int process1(void *arg)
{
        printf("P1 PID: %ld\n", (long)getpid());
        g=g+100;
        printf("P1 accessing Parent's Data Segment:%d\n", g);
        *p=*p+1;
        printf("P1 accessing Parent's Heap Segment:%d\n", *p);
        return 0;
}
```

6. Define process-2 sample activity as accessing data segment and heap segment data as follows:

```
static int process2(void *arg)
{
        printf("P2 PID: %ld\n", (long)getpid());
        g=g+100;
        printf("P2 accessing Parent's Data Segment:%d\n", g);
        *p=*p+1;
        printf("P2 accessing Parent's Heap Segment:%d\n", *p);
        return 0;
}
```

7. In the main process, allocate a suitable stack size for both processes as follows:

```
int main()
{
        char *stm1, *stm2;
        char *tos1,*tos2;
        pid_t pid1, pid2;

        stm1 = malloc(1024 * 1024);
        if (stm1 == NULL)
```

CHAPTER 10   LEARN C PROGRAMMING SKILLS FOR VIRTUALIZATION

```
        {
                perror("malloc");
                exit(1);
        }
        tos1 = stm1 + (1024 * 1024);

        stm2 = malloc(1024 * 1024);
        if (stm2 == NULL)
        {
                perror("malloc");
                exit(1);
        }
        tos2 = stm2 + (1024 * 1024);
```

8. In the main process, set up heap segment data using pointer p, and allocate sample data inside the pointer p:

```
        p = (int*)malloc(sizeof(int));
        if (p == NULL)
        {
                perror("malloc");
                exit(1);
        }
        *p=12345;
        printf("Heap Memory: %d",*p);
```

9. Clone process-1 and process-2 using the CLONE_VM flag to share virtual memory with the main and other processes:

```
        pid1 = clone(process1, tos1, CLONE_NEWPID|CLONE_VM|
        SIGCHLD, NULL);
        if (pid1 == -1)
        {
                perror("clone");
                exit(1);
        }
        printf("Parent PID: %ld\n", (long)getpid());
        printf("Clone P1 PID: %ld\n", (long)pid1);
```

```
        waitpid(pid1, NULL, 0);
        pid2 = clone(process2, tos2, CLONE_NEWPID |
        SIGCHLD, NULL);
        if (pid2 == -1)
        {
                perror("clone");
                exit(1);
        }
        printf("Parent PID: %ld\n", (long)getpid());
        printf("Clone P2 PID: %ld\n", (long)pid2);
        waitpid(pid2, NULL, 0);
```

10. After process-1 and process-2 execution is completed, in the main process, check the data segment and heap segment contents:

```
        printf("Parent Data Segment %d\n",g);
        printf("Parent Heap Memory Segment: %d\n",*p);
        free(stm1);
        free(stm2);
        return 0;
}
```

11. Save the code in clonevm.c and execute it using the following commands:

```
#gcc clonevm.c
#sudo ./a.out
Heap Memory: 12345Parent PID: 246021
Clone P1 PID: 246022
P1 PID: 1
P1 accessing Parent's Data Segment:200
P1 accessing Parent's Heap Segment:12346
Parent PID: 246021
Clone P2 PID: 246023
P2 PID: 1
P2 accessing Parent's Data Segment:300
P2 accessing Parent's Heap Segment:12347
Parent Data Segment 300
Parent Heap Memory Segment: 12347
```

12. From the above results, observe that p1 and p2 are sharing main process data and segments.

    a. Since, we set two processes (p1->p2) to execute in order. When p1 updated the data segment variable g (100 to 200), and heap segment content using the pointer variable (12345 to 12346), these changes are reflected in p2 while accessing the data (g: 200) and heap segments (123456).

    b. Finally, after p2 updated these segments contents main process accessed the update value of g to 300 and *p as 12347.

13. Save the code in clonevm.c without CLONE_VM flag and execute it using the following commands:

    ```
    #gcc clonevm.c
    #sudo ./a.out
    Heap Memory: 12345Parent PID: 246045
    Clone P1 PID: 246046
    Heap Memory: 12345P1 PID: 1
    P1 accessing Parent's Data Segment:200
    P1 accessing Parent's Heap Segment:12346
    Parent PID: 246045
    Clone P2 PID: 246047
    P2 PID: 1
    P2 accessing Parent's Data Segment:200
    P2 accessing Parent's Heap Segment:12346
    Parent Data Segment 100
    Parent Heap Memory Segment: 12345
    ```

14. From the above results, observe that p1 and p2 are not sharing main process data and segments.

    a. Although two processes (p1->p2) to execute in order, when p1 updated the data segment variable g (100 to 200), and heap segment content using the pointer variable (12345 to 12346), these changes are not reflected in p2.

    b. Similarly, after p2 updated these segments contents main process accessed the value of g as 100 and *p as 12345 only.

From these experiments, we can understand that to enable sharing of virtual memory between them, it is necessary to set up processes using CLONE_VM. Otherwise, we should not enable CLONE_VM to avoid unnecessary sharing of data among processes.

Next we will learn how to set up isolated IPC constructs for virtualizing interprocess coordination activities.

Hands-On Activity-2

In this hands-on activity, we will learn how to isolate main process IPC constructs from the children processes created by fork. By default, children processes have direct access to their main process IPC constructs and lead to unnecessary sharing of sensitive data; this behavior can lead to security breaches between the main process and its children processes. In this hands-on activity, we will learn how to set up isolated IPC constructs between the main process and its children processes. We do the following activities:

- Set up two processes using fork and execute them in order (p1->p2)
- Set up an shared memory using an shared memory id in main process
- Test whether parent process shared memory is accessible to children process or not

SET UP ISOLATED SHARED MEMORY FOR CLONED PROCESSES

1. Implement these hands-on activity tasks in isolateshm.c as follows:
2. First include the following necessary header files to do this hands-on activity:

```
#define _GNU_SOURCE
#include <sys/ipc.h>
#include <sys/shm.h>
#include <sys/wait.h>
#include <stdio.h>
#include <unistd.h>
```

CHAPTER 10   LEARN C PROGRAMMING SKILLS FOR VIRTUALIZATION

```
#include <fcntl.h>
#include <stdlib.h>
#include <sched.h>
#define KEY 7860
```

3. Set up a shared memory in the main process using KEY:

```
int main()
{
    int shmid;
    int *shrdres;
    int size = sizeof(int);
    pid_t pid;
    shmid = shmget(KEY,size, 0666 | IPC_CREAT);
    if (shmid == -1)
    {
        perror("shmget failed");
        return 1;
    }
```

4. Attach the main process to the shared memory and set sample contents:

```
    shrdres = (int *)shmat(shmid, NULL, 0);
    if (shrdres == (int *)-1)
    {
        perror("shmat failed");
        return 1;
    }
    *shrdres=100;
    printf("Main Process ID:%d\n",getpid());
    printf("Main Process Successfully written sample contents
into shared memory: %d \n",*shrdres);
```

5. Then, before creating the children process, set up an isolated IPC namespace using the unshare system call.

CHAPTER 10   LEARN C PROGRAMMING SKILLS FOR VIRTUALIZATION

  a. It leads to a fork creating a child process and a parent process to execute in isolated IPC namespaces of the main process:

```
if (unshare(CLONE_NEWIPC) == -1)
{
        perror("unshare");
        exit(EXIT_FAILURE);
}
```

6. Create two processes using fork as follows:

```
pid = fork();
if (pid == -1)
{
        perror("fork failed");
        exit(EXIT_FAILURE);
}
```

7. In the child process, set up a shared memory for interprocess communication with the other process:

```
else if (pid == 0)
{
        shmid = shmget(KEY,size, 0666 | IPC_CREAT);
        if (shmid == -1)
        {
                perror("shmget failed");
                return 1;
        }

        shrdres = (int *)shmat(shmid, NULL, 0);
        if (shrdres == (int *)-1)
        {
                perror("shmat failed");
                return 1;
        }
        printf("%d Shared memory %d\n",getpid(),*shrdres);
```

CHAPTER 10 LEARN C PROGRAMMING SKILLS FOR VIRTUALIZATION

8. In the child process, attach to the shared memory, and without setting any value, update the contents in it:

```
*shrdres = *shrdres+300;
printf("%d Shared memory %d\n",getpid(),*shrdres);

if (shmdt(shrdres) == -1)
{
    perror("shmdt");
    exit(EXIT_FAILURE);
}
exit(EXIT_SUCCESS);
}
```

9. In the parent process, attach to the shared memory and access its content as follows:

```
else if (pid>0)
{
    wait(NULL);

    shmid = shmget(KEY,size, 0666 | IPC_CREAT);
    if (shmid == -1)
    {
        perror("shmget failed");
        return 1;
    }

    shrdres = (int *)shmat(shmid, NULL, 0);
    if (shrdres == (int *)-1)
    {
        perror("shmat failed");
        return 1;
    }
    printf("%d Shared memory %d\n",getpid(),*shrdres);
    *shrdres = *shrdres+100;
    printf("%d Shared memory %d\n",getpid(),*shrdres);
```

```
            if (shmdt(shrdres) == -1)
            {
                    perror("shmdt");
                    exit(EXIT_FAILURE);
            }
            shmctl(shmid, IPC_RMID, NULL);
            exit(EXIT_SUCCESS);

    }
    return 0;
}
```

10. Save the code in isolateshm.c and execute it using the following commands:

    ```
    #gcc isolateshm.c
    #sudo ./a.out
    Main Process ID:23781
    Main Process Successfully written sample contents into shared memory: 100
    23782 Shared memory 0
    23782 Shared memory 300
    23781 Shared memory 300
    23781 Shared memory 400
    ```

    From the results, observe the following details:

    a. The main process sets a value of 100 to the shared memory

    b. Since the child process runs with its own isolated shared memory, the shared memory contents are initialized to 0, and it is updated to 300.

    c. Then, when the parent process accesses the shared memory, it gets 300. It means the parent process is accessing the shared memory set up by the child process. Hence, on updating, the shared memory value becomes 400.

11. Save the code in `isolateshm.c` by commenting out the `unshare(CLONE_NEWIPC)` code and execute it using the following commands:

   ```
   #gcc isolateshm.c
   #sudo ./a.out
   Main Process ID:23926
   Main Process Successfully written sample contents into shared memory: 100
   23927 Shared memory 100
   23927 Shared memory 400
   23926 Shared memory 400
   23926 Shared memory 500
   ```

   From the results, observe the following details:

   a. The main process sets a value of 100 to the shared memory.

   b. Since the child process runs sharing the shared memory of the main memory, the shared memory contents are updated to 400.

   c. Similarly, when the parent or main process accesses the shared memory, then it is getting 400. Hence, on updating, the shared memory value becomes 500.

From these experiments, we can understand that to isolate IPC constructs of the main process from child processes, it is necessary to run children processes with a new IPC namespace. Otherwise, children processes can access the main process IPC constructs and lead to sharing of sensitive data and resources.

Next we will learn how to set up an isolated user namespace and test accessing protected files of the parent process.

Hands-On Activity-3

In this hands-on activity, we will learn how to isolate main process user group permissions from the children processes created by fork. By default children processes inherit parent process user permissions and lead to unnecessary sharing of sensitive files; this behavior can lead to security breaches among the main process and its children processes. In this hands-on activity, we will learn how to set up isolated user namespaces between the main process and its children processes. We do the following activities:

- Set up two processes using fork and execute them in order (p1->p2)

- Create a sensitive file (test.txt) on the host system with permissions 600. It means only the owner can read and write over the test.txt; other users do not have access to the test.txt. Note: Keep hello message in test.txt.

- Create a non-sensitive file (test2t.txt) on the host system with permissions 666. It means that all users can access test2.txt. Note: Keep hello message in test2.txt.

- First, test the two processes by isolating the user namespace and observe that a process is not able to access the test.txt. However, the process is able to access test2.txt.

- Next, test the two processes without isolating the user namespace and observe that both processes are able to access both test.txt and test2.txt.

SET UP ISOLATED USER NAMESPACE

1. Implement these hands-on activity tasks in isolateuser.c as follows:
2. First include the following necessary header files to do this hands-on activity:

```
#define _GNU_SOURCE
#include <sched.h>
#include <stdio.h>
#include <stdlib.h>
#include <fcntl.h>
#include <unistd.h>
#include <sys/stat.h>
#include <sys/wait.h>
```

CHAPTER 10   LEARN C PROGRAMMING SKILLS FOR VIRTUALIZATION

3. Set up an isolated user namespace for processes to be created in the program:

    ```
    int main()
    {
        if (unshare(CLONE_NEWUSER) == -1)
        {
            perror("unshare");
            exit(EXIT_FAILURE);
        }
    ```

4. Set up two processes using fork:

    ```
    pid_t ret=fork();
    if (ret==-1)
    {
        perror("fork");
        return 1;
    }
    ```

5. In the following process, try to access test.txt (sensitive file) and observe that during execution it does not have permission to access it due to isolation of the user namespace:

    ```
    if (ret==0)
    {
        printf("Process 1 trying to read a test file with
        permissions 600 (others are not allowed)\n");
        const char *filename = "test.txt";
        int fd;
        ssize_t bytes_read;
        char buffer[1024];
        fd = open(filename, O_RDONLY);
        if (fd == -1)
        {
            perror("Error opening file");
            return 1;
        }
        bytes_read = read(fd, buffer, 4);
    ```

CHAPTER 10   LEARN C PROGRAMMING SKILLS FOR VIRTUALIZATION

```c
            if (bytes_read == -1)
            {
                    perror("Error reading file");
                    close(fd);
                    return 1;
            }
            write(1, buffer, bytes_read);
            close(fd);
            exit(0);
    }
```

6. In the following process, try to access test2.txt (a non-sensitive file) and observe that during execution it is able to access it:

```c
        if (ret>0)
        {
                waitpid(ret,NULL,0);
                printf("Process 2 trying to read a test file with
                permissions 6664 (others are  allowed)\n");
                const char *filename = "test2.txt";
                int fd;
                ssize_t bytes_read;
                char buffer[1024];
                fd = open(filename, O_RDONLY);
                if (fd == -1)
                {
                        perror("Error opening file");
                        return 1;
                }
                bytes_read = read(fd, buffer, 4);
                if (bytes_read == -1)
                {
                        perror("Error reading file");
                        close(fd);
                        return 1;
                }
```

```
                write(1, buffer, bytes_read);
                if (close(fd) == -1)
                {
                        perror("Error closing file");
                        return 1;
                }
        }
        return 0;
}
```

7. Save the code in isolateuser.c and execute it using the following commands:

```
#gcc isolateuser.c
#/a.out
Process 1 trying to read a test file with permissions 600
(others are not allowed)
hellProcess 2 trying to read a test file with permissions 6664
(others are  allowed)
hell
```

Observe from the results that by isolating the user namespace between processes, it is possible to restrict access permissions of sensitive files or resources. Otherwise, user permissions can be inherited to the children process and the children process can access the sensitive files or resources of the main process.

Till now, we have practiced how to use process and memory-related Linux namespaces for sharing virtual memory, protecting IPC constructs, and setting user permissions for setting up virtualized execution environments for processes. Next, we will learn how to set up Linux control groups for controlling and monitoring CPU and memory resources of processes.

Hands-On Activity-4

In this hands-on activity, we will learn how to set up a memory control group and configure with a limit to restrict processes memory utilization. We do the following activities:

- Set up two processes using fork
- Set up a memory control group
- Configure limit of memory control group using the following parameter /sys/fs/cgroup/memory/mymgrp/memory.limit_in_bytes
- Append two processes to the memory control group process list
- While processes are executing monitor the memory usage using the following memory cgroup parameter: sys/fs/cgroup/memory/mymgrp/memory.max_usage_in_bytes

SET UP MEMORY CONTROL GROUPS

1. Implement these hands-on activity tasks in memcgroup.c as follows:
2. First include the following necessary header files to do this hands-on activity:

   ```
   #include <stdio.h>
   #include <stdlib.h>
   #include <string.h>
   #include <unistd.h>
   #include <sys/types.h>
   #include <sys/stat.h>
   #include <fcntl.h>
   ```

3. Define the following sample memory control group name to set up memory cgroup:

   ```
   #define MEM_CGROUP_DIR "/sys/fs/cgroup/memory/mymgrp"
   ```

CHAPTER 10   LEARN C PROGRAMMING SKILLS FOR VIRTUALIZATION

4. Define the following process group list file to assign under the memory cgroup:

   ```
   #define MEM_CGROUP_PS "/sys/fs/cgroup/memory/mymgrp/
   cgroup.procs"
   ```

5. Define the following memory configuration file to limit memory for processes under the memory cgroup:

   ```
   #define MEM_LIMIT "/sys/fs/cgroup/memory/mymgrp/memory.limit_
   in_bytes"
   ```

6. Define the following memory usage monitoring file to observe processes' memory utilization under the memory cgroup:

   ```
   #define MEM_USAGE "/sys/fs/cgroup/memory/mymgrp/memory.max_
   usage_in_bytes"
   ```

7. Start the main program by removing the memory control group directory if any exist:

   ```c
   int main()
   {
           rmdir(MEM_CGROUP_DIR);
   ```

8. Create two processes using fork:

   ```c
           for (int i=0;i<2;i++)
           {
                   pid_t pid1 = fork();
   ```

9. In each process, first set up the memory control group directory:

   ```c
                   if (pid1==0)
                   {
                           pid_t pid = getpid();
                           int fd;
                           if (mkdir(MEM_CGROUP_DIR, 0755) == -1)
                           {
                                   perror("Error creating cgroup directory
                                   (may already exist)");
                           }
   ```

CHAPTER 10   LEARN C PROGRAMMING SKILLS FOR VIRTUALIZATION

10. Under the memory control group directory, set up a process list holding file:

    ```
    fd = open(MEM_CGROUP_PS, O_WRONLY | O_APPEND);
    if (fd == -1)
    {
            perror("Error opening cgroup.procs");
            return EXIT_FAILURE;
    }
    dprintf(fd, "%d\n", pid);
    close(fd);
    ```

11. Under the memory control group directory, configure the memory limit file and assign a suitable memory limit:

    a. In this example, we are setting a 1 Mb limit for each process

    ```
    fd = open(MEM_LIMIT, O_WRONLY);
    if (fd == -1)
    {
            perror("Error opening memory
            limit file");
            return EXIT_FAILURE;
    }
    unsigned int cl = 1;
    dprintf(fd, "%dM\n", cl); //
    close(fd);
    ```

12. To test the working of the memory control group, allocate memory continuously, and during execution observe that the maximum memory allocated is under the memory control configured limit:

    ```
    printf("Running an infinite loop to consume
    CPU...\n");
    while (1)
    {
            int *p=malloc(sizeof(int)*250);
            system("cat /sys/fs/cgroup/memory/
            mymgrp/memory.max_usage_in_bytes");
    ```

CHAPTER 10 LEARN C PROGRAMMING SKILLS FOR VIRTUALIZATION

```
                    }
                }
            }
            return EXIT_SUCCESS;
}
```

13. Save the code in memcgroup.c and test it using the following commands:

    ```
    #gcc memcgroup.c
    #./a.out
    1048576
    1048576
    ..
    1048576
    ```

From the results, observe that for both processes, once they reach a maximum of 1 Mb memory allocation, no more memory is getting allocated. Hence, it is possible to restrict process-level memory utilization in a flexible manner using Linux cgroups. It helps developers to implement interesting virtualization concepts at the process level to restrict memory resources.

Next, we will learn how to set up a memory control group and use it.

Hands-On Activity-5

In this hands-on activity, we will learn how to set up a memory control group and configure it with a limit to restrict memory utilization of the processes belonging to the memory control group. We do the following activities:

- Set up two processes using fork
- Set up a memory control group
- Configure the limit of memory control group using the following parameter: /sys/fs/cgroup/memory/mymgrp/memory.limit_in_bytes

- Append two processes to the memory control group process list
- While processes are executing monitor the memory usage using the following memory cgroup parameter: sys/fs/cgroup/memory/mymgrp/memory.max_usage_in_bytes

SERVICE CHAINING USING FIFO

1. Implement these hands-on activity tasks in cpucgroup.c as follows:
2. First include the following necessary header files to do this hands-on activity:

   ```
   #include <stdio.h>
   #include <stdlib.h>
   #include <string.h>
   #include <unistd.h>
   #include <sys/types.h>
   #include <sys/stat.h>
   #include <fcntl.h>
   ```

3. Define the following sample CPU control group name to set up CPU cgroup:

   ```
   #define CPU_CGROUP_DIR "/sys/fs/cgroup/cpu/mycgrp"
   ```

4. Define the following process group list file to assign under the CPU cgroup:

   ```
   #define CPU_CGROUP_PS "/sys/fs/cgroup/cpu/mycgrp/cgroup.procs"
   ```

5. Define the following CPU scheduling period configuration file to limit CPU utilization for processes under the CPU cgroup:

   ```
   #define CPU_PERIOD "/sys/fs/cgroup/cpu/mycgrp/cpu.cfs_period_us"
   ```

6. Define the following CPU scheduling quota limit within the CPU period to limit CPU utilization for processes under the CPU cgroup:

   ```
   #define CPU_QUOTA "/sys/fs/cgroup/cpu/mycgrp/cpu.cfs_quota_us"
   ```

7. Start the main program by removing the CPU control group directory if any exist:

```
int main()
{
        rmdir(CPU_CGROUP_DIR);
```

8. Create two processes using fork:

```
        for (int i=0;i<5;i++)
        {
                pid_t pid1 = fork();
```

9. In each process, first set up the CPU control group directory:

```
                if (pid1==0)
                {
                        pid_t pid = getpid();
                        int fd;

                        if (mkdir(CPU_CGROUP_DIR, 0755) == -1)

                                perror("Error creating cgroup directory
                                (may already exist)");
                }
```

10. Under the CPU control group directory, set up a process list holding file:

```
                        fd = open(CPU_CGROUP_PS, O_WRONLY | O_APPEND);
                        if (fd == -1)
                        {
                                perror("Error opening cgroup.procs");
                                return EXIT_FAILURE;
                        }
                        dprintf(fd, "%d\n", pid);
                        close(fd);
```

11. Under the CPU control group directory, to configure the CPU scheduling period, set up the CPU scheduling period file and configure the maximum period as 10 ms:

    ```
    fd = open(CPU_PERIOD, O_WRONLY);
    if (fd == -1)
    {
            perror("Error opening cpu.cfs_
            period_us");
            return EXIT_FAILURE;
    }
    dprintf(fd, "%d\n", 10000); // 10ms period
    close(fd);
    ```

12. Under the CPU control group directory, to configure the CPU quota set set up the CPU quota file and configure the maximum CPU quota out of 10 ms as 1 ms:

    ```
    fd = open(CPU_QUOTA, O_WRONLY);
    if (fd == -1)
    {
            perror("Error opening cpu.cfs_
            quota_us");
            return EXIT_FAILURE;
    }
    unsigned int cl = 1000;
    dprintf(fd, "%d\n", cl); // 1ms quota
    close(fd);
    ```

13. To test working of CPU control group, run an infinite loop and during execution observe that the CPU utilization is limited as per CPU quota:

    ```
    printf("Running an infinite loop to consume
    CPU...\n");
    while (1)
    {
    }
    }
    ```

```
        }
        return EXIT_SUCCESS;
}
```

14. Save the above code in cpucgoup.c, and test it using the following commands:

    ```
    #gcc cpucgroup.c
    #./a.out
    ```

15. Open another terminal and use the top command to observe the CPU utilization of both processes:

    ```
    32511 root    20   0   2496   72   0 R   5.3   0.0   0:01.68 a.out
    32510 root    20   0   2496   72   0 R   5.0   0.0   0:01.69 a.out
    ```

16. Update the above code to create five processes in cpucgoup.c, and test it using the following commands:

    ```
    #gcc cpucgroup.c
    #./a.out
    ```

17. Open another terminal and use the top command to observe the CPU utilization of five processes

    ```
    32641 root    20   0   2496   72   0 R   2.3   0.0   0:00.21 a.out
    32642 root    20   0   2496   72   0 R   2.3   0.0   0:00.20 a.out
    32639 root    20   0   2496   72   0 R   2.0   0.0   0:00.18 a.out
    32640 root    20   0   2496   72   0 R   2.0   0.0   0:00.18 a.out
    32643 root    20   0   2496   72   0 R   2.0   0.0   0:00.19 a.out
    ```

Observe from the above results that all processes under the CPU group are sharing 10 ms CPU duration equally among the processes. Moreover, maximum CPU utilization per process group is limited to 10 ms only.

From the results, observe that for all processes together, once they consume a maximum of 10 ms, no more CPU scheduling period is getting allocated. Hence, it is possible to restrict process-level CPU utilization in a flexible manner using Linux cgroups. It helps developers to implement interesting virtualization concepts at the process level to restrict CPU resources.

Next, we will learn how to experiment with networking namespaces.

Experiment with Networking Namespaces

In this section, we will discuss how to set up virtual networks using Linux network namespaces and tools (iproute2). Specifically, we will discuss in detail the following concepts:

- How to set up network namespaces
- How to use iproute commands for setting up network namespaces, virtual networks, and configuring virtual networks
- Setting up a variety of virtual networks
- Hands-on activities related to running network applications using virtual networks

Learn Setting Up Network Namespaces

The Linux OS offers important features for setting up virtual networks in flexible manners. Linux network namespace is a basic feature helpful in setting up dedicated network interfaces and network protocol stacks without conflicting with the underlying physical server network interfaces and network protocol stack. Besides the Linux network namespace feature, the following tools are important for setting up virtual networks over a physical server.

- iproute2: It offers a collection of commands for setting up network interfaces, configuring network interfaces, and assigning addresses, routes, and traffic control. In this book, we use this tool for setting up network namespaces and managing them.
- If this tool is not installed on your system, you can install it using the following command:
  - `sudo apt install iproute2`
- The iproute2 is one tool for all virtual networking setup commands. Using iproute2, the following important virtual network setup tasks can be done
  - To set up network namespaces

- To set up network interfaces (virtual Ethernet (veth) devices) with network namespaces, connecting veth devices of network namespaces

- To set up virtual tunnels, bridges, and routers

- To assign IP addresses, configure routes, and set traffic control rules

Let's quickly practice how to use the iproute2 tool for virtual networks setup and testing.

Practice Using iproute2

For example, to set up a virtual network using network namespaces, the following tasks will be involved:

- Setting up network namespaces

- Configuring network namespaces with virtual Ethernet devices

- Configuring IP addresses to virtual Ethernet devices of network namespaces

- Configuring routing tables of network namespaces

- Setting up virtual eth pairs for connecting network namespaces

- Setting up virtual bridges for interconnecting network namespaces

For example, to set up a new network namespace (c1ns) the following command is used:

```
sudo ip netns add c1ns
```

To delete a new network namespace (c1ns) the following command is used:

```
sudo ip netns del c1ns
```

To set up a pair of virtual Ethernet devices (c1eth0 and c2eth0), the following command is used:

```
sudo ip link add c1eth0 type veth peer name c2eth0
```

CHAPTER 10 LEARN C PROGRAMMING SKILLS FOR VIRTUALIZATION

To configure a virtual Ethernet device (c1eth0) with a network namespace (c1ns) and make it up, the following command is used:

```
sudo ip link set c1eth0 netns c1ns
sudo ip netns exec c1ns ip link set c1eth0 up
```

To configure a loopback device (lo) and making it up with a network namespace (c1ns), the following command is used:

```
sudo ip netns exec c1ns ip link set lo up
```

To configure IP address to a virtual Ethernet devices (c1eth0) of a network namespace (c1ns), the following command is used:

```
sudo ip netns exec c1ns ip addr add 192.168.26.10/24 dev c1eth0
```

To set up a virtual bridge devices (cnbr0), which helps you to interconnect multiple networks, the following command is used:

```
sudo ip link add cnbr0 type bridge
sudo ip link set cnbr0 up
```

To interconnect two virtual Ethernet devices (c1eth0, c2eth0) using cnbr0, the following command is used:

```
sudo ip link set c1eth0 master cnbr0
sudo ip link set c2eth0 master cnbr0
```

To configure IP address for cnbr0, the following command is used:

```
sudo ip addr add 192.168.26.254/24 dev cnbr0
```

To configure a route to a network (192.168.27.0/24) for a network namespace (c1ns), the following command is used:

```
sudo ip netns exec c1ns ip route add 192.168.27.0/24 dev c4eth0
```

To check the configuration of a virtual Ethernet devices (c1eth0) of a network namespace (c1ns), the following command is used:

```
sudo ip netns exec c1ns ip address show
```

To execute a ping command using a network namespace (c1ns) the following command is used:

```
sudo ip netns exec c1ns ping -c3 192.168.27.10
```

Next we will practice setting up a variety of virtual networks using network namespaces.

Various Virtual Networks Setups

In this section, we will learn the following important virtual networks setups using network namespaces:

- Basic virtual network setup: It connects two network namespaces belonging to the same subnetwork ID.
  - If c1ns IP belongs to (192.168.24.0/24) then c2ns IP should also from the subnet: (192.168.24.0/24).
- Connect a network namespace with the underlying host
- Interconnect two network namespaces: It connects any two network namespaces belonging to different subnetwork IDs.
  - If c1ns IP belongs to (192.168.24.0/24), then c2ns IP can be from the other subnet: (192.168.25.0/24).

Basic Virtual Network Setup

In this basic virtual network setup task, we create a sample virtual network containing two network namespaces as shown in Figure 10-3 and configure it using `iproute` commands:

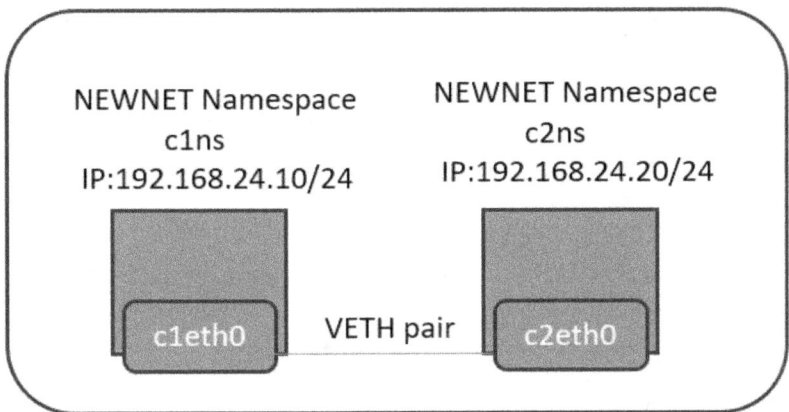

Figure 10-3. Set up a virtual network between two namespaces

First, set up two network namespaces (c1ns and c2ns) using the following commands:

```
ip netns del c1ns
ip netns del c2ns
ip netns add c1ns
ip netns add c2ns
```

Then, connect two network namespaces (c1ns and c2ns) by setting up a virtual Ethernet pair (c1eth0 and c2eth0) using the following commands:

```
ip link add c1eth0 type veth peer name c2eth0
ip link set c1eth0 netns c1ns
ip link set c2eth0 netns c2ns
ip netns exec c1ns ip link set lo up
ip netns exec c2ns ip link set lo up
```

Then, configure two network namespaces (c1ns and c2ns) virtual Ethernet (c1eth0 and c2eth0) IP addresses using the following commands:

```
ip netns exec c1ns ip addr add 192.168.24.10/24 dev c1eth0
ip netns exec c2ns ip addr add 192.168.24.20/24 dev c2eth0
ip netns exec c1ns ip link set c1eth0 up
ip netns exec c2ns ip link set c2eth0 up
```

Then, check the correctness of the virtual network setup using the following commands:

```
ip netns exec c1ns ping -c3 192.168.24.20
ip netns exec c2ns ping -c3 192.168.24.10
```

Observing from the results, ping is successful. It means we successfully set up a basic virtual network. Next, we will learn how to connect a network namespace with the host.

Interconnect Network Namespace and Host

In this virtual network setup task, we create a sample virtual network containing one custom network namespace and host network namespace as shown in Figure 10-4 and configure it using `iproute` commands:

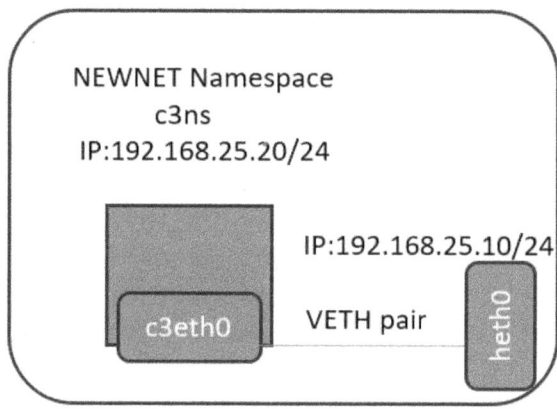

Figure 10-4. *Set up a virtual network between custom network namespace and host network namespace*

First, set up a network namespace (c3ns) using the following commands:

```
ip netns add c3ns
```

Then, connect network namespace (c3ns) and host by setting up a virtual Ethernet pairs (c3eth0 and heth0) using the following commands:

```
ip link add heth0 type veth peer name c3eth0
ip link set c3eth0 netns c3ns
ip link set heth0 up
```

Then, configure two network namespaces (c3ns and host) virtual Ethernet (c1eth0 and heth0) IP addresses using the following commands:

```
ip addr add 192.168.25.10/24 dev heth0
ip netns exec c3ns ip link set lo up
ip netns exec c3ns ip link set c3eth0 up
ip netns exec c3ns ip addr add 192.168.25.20/24 dev c3eth0
```

Then, to route IP packets from c3ns to host configure route using the following commands:

```
ip netns exec c3ns ip route add 192.168.25.0/24 dev c3eth0
```

Then, check correctness of virtual network setup using the following commands:

```
ping -c3 192.168.25.20
ip netns exec c3ns ping -c3 192.168.25.10
```

Observing from the results, ping is successful. It means we successfully connect a network namespace with a host. Next, we will learn how to interconnect two network namespaces.

Interconnect Two Different Subnet Network Namespaces

In this virtual network setup task, we create a sample virtual network containing two different subnets configured with network namespaces as shown in Figure 10-5 and configure it using the iproute commands:

CHAPTER 10   LEARN C PROGRAMMING SKILLS FOR VIRTUALIZATION

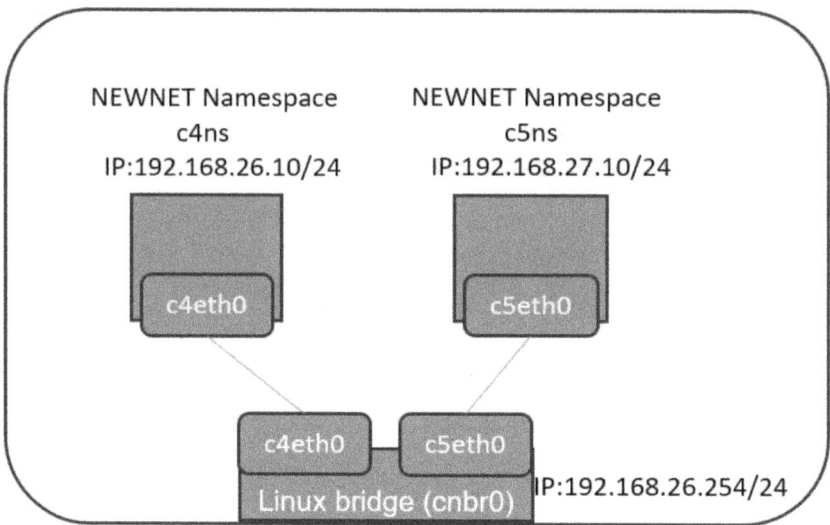

Figure 10-5. Set up a virtual network between two different subnets configured namespaces

First, set up two different subnet network namespaces (c4ns and c5ns) using the following commands:

```
sudo ip netns del c4ns
sudo ip netns del c5ns
sudo ip netns add c4ns
sudo ip netns add c5ns
```

Then, connect two network namespaces (c4ns and c5ns) by setting up a virtual Ethernet pair (c4eth0 and c5eth0) using the following commands:

```
sudo ip link add c4eth0 type veth peer name c5eth0
sudo ip link set c4eth0 netns c4ns
sudo ip link set c5eth0 netns c5ns
sudo ip netns exec c4ns ip link set lo up
sudo ip netns exec c5ns ip link set lo up
```

Then, configure two subnet network namespaces (c4ns and c5ns) virtual Ethernet (c4eth0 and c5eth0) IP addresses using the following commands:

```
sudo ip netns exec c4ns ip link set c4eth0 up
sudo ip netns exec c5ns ip link set c5eth0 up
```

```
sudo ip netns exec c4ns ip addr add 192.168.26.10/24 dev c4eth0
sudo ip netns exec c5ns ip addr add 192.168.27.10/24 dev c5eth0
```

Then, set up a virtual bridge to connect (c4ns and c5ns) using the following commands:

```
sudo ip link add cnbr0 type bridge
sudo ip link set cnbr0 up
```

Then, connect (c4ns and c5ns) interfaces with the bridge (cnbr0) using the following commands:

```
sudo ip link set c4eth0 master cnbr0
sudo ip link set c5eth0 master cnbr0
```

Then, assign a unique IP address to the bridge (cnbr0) from one of the network namespace subnet (192.168.26.0/24) using the following commands:

```
sudo ip addr add 192.168.26.254/24 dev cnbr0
```

Then, configure the route on the host to reach the other network namespace subnet (192.168.27.0/24) using the following commands:

```
sudo ip route add 192.168.27.0/24 via 192.168.26.10 dev c4eth0
```

Then, configure the route on c4ns to reach the other network namespace (c5ns) subnet using the following commands:

```
sudo ip netns exec c4ns ip route add 192.168.27.0/24 dev c4eth0
```

Then, configure the route on c5ns to reach the other network namespace (c4ns) subnet using the following commands:

```
sudo ip netns exec c5ns ip route add 192.168.26.0/24 dev c5eth0
```

Then, check the correctness of the virtual network setup using the following commands:

```
sudo ip netns exec c4ns ping -c3 192.168.27.10
sudo ip netns exec c5ns ping -c3 192.168.26.10
```

Observing from the results, ping is successful. It means we successfully set up a basic virtual network. Next, we will learn how to connect a network namespace with the host.

Hands-On Activity-1

In this hands-on activity, we will connect processes with an existing virtual network using network namespaces. Specifically, we do the following tasks:

- Set up two processes using fork and configure the process with existing network namespaces using setns
- Connect two processes with the virtual network setup given in figure
  - Connect child process with an existing network namespace cn4ns
  - Connect parent process with an existing network namespace cn5ns
- Child process ping to the parent process connected network IP
- Parent process ping to the child process connected network IP
- Inspect the results

CONNECT PROCESSES WITH AN EXISTING VIRTUAL NETWORK

1. Implement these hands-on activity tasks in nettest1.c as follows:
2. First include the following necessary header files to do this hands-on activity:

   ```
   #define _GNU_SOURCE
   #include <sys/ipc.h>
   #include <sys/shm.h>
   #include <sys/wait.h>
   #include <stdio.h>
   #include <unistd.h>
   #include <fcntl.h>
   #include <stdlib.h>
   #include <sched.h>
   ```

3. In main, set up two processes using fork:

    ```
    int main()
    {
        pid_t pid;
        pid = fork();
        if (pid == -1)
        {
            perror("fork failed");
            exit(EXIT_FAILURE);
        }
    ```

4. Connect the child process with the network namespace c4ns, and ping to the network namespace c5ns IP:

    ```
                else if (pid == 0)
                {
                    int fd;
                    fd = open("/var/run/netns/c4ns", O_RDONLY | O_CLOEXEC);
                    if (fd == -1)
                    {
                        perror("open");
                        exit(EXIT_FAILURE);
                    }
                    if (setns(fd, CLONE_NEWNET) == -1)
                    {
                        perror("setns");
                        close(fd);
                        exit(EXIT_FAILURE);
                    }
                    system("ip a");
                    system("ping -c3 192.168.27.10");
                    exit(EXIT_SUCCESS);
                }
    ```

5. Wait for the child process to complete its execution and connect the parent process with the network namespace c5ns, and ping to the network namespace c4ns IP:

```
            else if (pid>0)
            {
                wait(NULL);
                int fd;
                fd = open("/var/run/netns/c5ns", O_RDONLY | O_CLOEXEC);
                if (fd == -1)
                {
                    perror("open");
                    exit(EXIT_FAILURE);
                }
                if (setns(fd, CLONE_NEWNET) == -1)
                {
                    perror("setns");
                    close(fd);
                    exit(EXIT_FAILURE);
                }
                system("ip a");
                system("ping -c3 192.168.26.10");
                exit(EXIT_SUCCESS);
            }
            return 0;
        }
```

6. Save the above code in nettest1.c using the following commands:

```
#gcc nettest1.c
#sudo ./a.out
..
c5ns
        inet 192.168.26.10/24 scope global c4eth0
..
PING 192.168.27.10 (192.168.27.10) 56(84) bytes of data.
```

```
64 bytes from 192.168.27.10: icmp_seq=1 ttl=64 time=0.025 ms
64 bytes from 192.168.27.10: icmp_seq=2 ttl=64 time=0.067 ms
64 bytes from 192.168.27.10: icmp_seq=3 ttl=64 time=0.087 ms

--- 192.168.27.10 ping statistics ---
..
        link/ether 86:4a:16:ca:de:50 brd ff:ff:ff:ff:ff:ff link-netns c4ns
..
PING 192.168.26.10 (192.168.26.10) 56(84) bytes of data.
64 bytes from 192.168.26.10: icmp_seq=1 ttl=64 time=0.053 ms
64 bytes from 192.168.26.10: icmp_seq=2 ttl=64 time=0.066 ms
64 bytes from 192.168.26.10: icmp_seq=3 ttl=64 time=0.073 ms

--- 192.168.26.10 ping statistics ---
3 packets transmitted, 3 received, 0% packet loss, time 2036ms
rtt min/avg/max/mdev = 0.053/0.064/0.073/0.008 ms
```

From the results, we can observe that both processes are connected with existing namespaces successfully, and we can verify their IP addresses. Moreover, both processes' ping results are successful.

Next, let's learn how to run standard network applications using network namespaces.

Hands-On Activity-2

In this hands-on activity, we will connect a process with an existing virtual network namespace to run a `netcat` TCP server and test it from the host. It is similar to packing a network application with a specific network namespace and deploying it over the physical server. Specifically, we do the following tasks:

- If `netcat` tool is not installed, then first install `netcat` package using apt-get install command.
- Set up two processes using fork
- Configure the child process with an existing network namespace c3ns

CHAPTER 10   LEARN C PROGRAMMING SKILLS FOR VIRTUALIZATION

- Child process runs a TCP server over port number 1234 using netcat tool

- Parent process waits for child process to exit

- Then, from the host start netcat TCP client to connect with the TCP server running using c3ns network namespace

DEPLOY A NETWORK APPLICATION USING EXISTING NETWORK NAMESPACE

1. Implement these hands-on activity tasks in nettest2.c as follows:

2. First include the following necessary header files to do this hands-on activity:

    ```c
    #define _GNU_SOURCE
    #include <sys/ipc.h>
    #include <sys/shm.h>
    #include <sys/wait.h>
    #include <stdio.h>
    #include <unistd.h>
    #include <fcntl.h>
    #include <stdlib.h>
    #include <sched.h>
    ```

3. In main, set up two processes using fork:

    ```c
    int main()
    {
        pid_t pid;
        pid = fork();
        if (pid == -1)
        {
            perror("fork failed");
            exit(EXIT_FAILURE);
        }
    ```

CHAPTER 10 LEARN C PROGRAMMING SKILLS FOR VIRTUALIZATION

4. Connect child process with the network namespace c3ns, and run netcat TCP server over port number 1234:

```
else if (pid == 0)
{
    int fd;
    fd = open("/var/run/netns/c3ns", O_RDONLY | O_CLOEXEC);
    if (fd == -1)
    {
        perror("open");
        exit(EXIT_FAILURE);
    }
    if (setns(fd, CLONE_NEWNET) == -1)
    {
        perror("setns");
        close(fd);
        exit(EXIT_FAILURE);
    }
    system("ip a");
    system("nc -l 1234");
}
```

5. Parent process waits for child process to exit:

```
else if (pid>0)
{
    wait(NULL);
}

return 0;
}
```

6. Save the above code in nettest2.c and test it using the following commands:

```
#gcc nettest2.c
#sudo ./a.out
..
```

693

```
91: c3eth0@if92: <BROADCAST,MULTICAST,UP,LOWER_UP> mtu 1500
qdisc noqueue state UP group default qlen 1000
..
        inet 192.168.25.20/24 scope global c3eth0
```
hi
hello
how

7. Open another terminal of the host and execute the following commands to start netcat TCP client:

   a. Run the following command to connect with the TCP server running over network namespace ns3

   b. Observe that the connection will be successful

   c. Exchange sample messages

```
#nc -v 192.168.25.20 1234
Connection to 192.168.25.20 1234 port [tcp/*] succeeded!
hi
hello
how
```

From the results, we can observe that your host is connected with namespace c3ns running the TCP server successfully, and we can verify their IP addresses also. Then, TCP client and server processes are exchanging messages successfully.

Next, let's learn how to run and test a web server using network namespaces.

Hands-On Activity-3

In this hands-on activity, we will connect a process with an existing virtual network namespace and run it with its own UTS namespace to deploy a webserver using a unique hostname. Then, connect the web server from the host using hostname. It is similar to packing a web server with a specific network namespace and UTS namespaces for deploying it over the physical server. Specifically, we do the following tasks:

- If the netcat tool is not installed, then the first install the netcat package using apt-get install command.
- Set up two processes using fork.
- Configure the child process with an existing network namespace c3ns.
- Child process runs a web server over port number 9090 using netcat tool.
- Parent process waits for child process to exit.
- Then, from the host start web browser to connect with the web server running using c3ns network namespace.

DEPLOY A WEB SERVER USING NETWORK NAMESPACE AND UTS NAMESPACE

1. Implement these hands-on activity tasks in nettest3.c as follows:
2. First include the following necessary header files to do this hands-on activity:

```
#define _GNU_SOURCE
#include <sys/ipc.h>
#include <sys/shm.h>
#include <sys/wait.h>
#include <stdio.h>
#include <unistd.h>
#include <fcntl.h>
#include <stdlib.h>
#include <sched.h>
```

3. In main, start with unsharing the existing UTS namespace

```
int main()
{
    char hostname[256];
    int result = gethostname(hostname, sizeof(hostname));
```

CHAPTER 10 LEARN C PROGRAMMING SKILLS FOR VIRTUALIZATION

```
        printf("Before Unshare the current process%d hostname
        %s\n",getpid(), hostname);

        if (unshare(CLONE_NEWUTS) == -1)
        {
                perror("unshare");
                exit(EXIT_FAILURE);
        }
```

4. Set up two processes using fork:

```
        pid_t pid;
        pid = fork();
        if (pid == -1)
        {
                perror("fork failed");
                exit(EXIT_FAILURE);
        }
```

5. In the child process, first set a unique host name:

```
        else if (pid == 0)
        {
                system("hostname newname");
                result = gethostname(hostname, sizeof(hostname));
                printf("After Unshare the current process%d hostname
                %s\n",getpid(), hostname);
```

6. Then, connect the process with an existing network namespace c3ns:

```
                int fd;
                fd = open("/var/run/netns/c3ns", O_RDONLY |
                O_CLOEXEC);
                if (fd == -1)
                {
                        perror("open");
                        exit(EXIT_FAILURE);
                }
```

```
            if (setns(fd, CLONE_NEWNET) == -1)
            {
                perror("setns");
                close(fd);
                exit(EXIT_FAILURE);
            }
```

7. Then, deploy a simple web server using the netcat tool:

    a. It simply responds with hello world messages to connected web clients.

    ```
            system("ip a");
            system("echo -e 'HTTP/1.1 200 OK\nContent-Type:
            text/plain\nContent-Length: 12\n\nHello world!'
            |nc -lp 9090");

    //      exit(EXIT_SUCCESS);
        }
    ```

8. Parent process waits for child process to exit:

    ```
        else if (pid>0)
        {
            wait(NULL);
        }
        return 0;
    }
    ```

9. Save the code in nettest3.c and before executing it, save its hostname and corresponding IP address in the host machine/etc/hosts file:

    cat /etc/hosts
    192.168.25.20   newname

10. Compile and test the netest3.c using the following commands:

    a. Observe that web server starts and waits for web clients

    b. Open a web browser from the host and access the following URL: http://newname:9090

c. Observe that web server receives an HTTP request message from the browser, and it sends an HTTP response message (hello world)

```
#gcc nettest3.c
#sudo ./a.out
Before Unshare the current process25862 hostname iiitdmk-HP-
ProDesk-600-G5-MT
After Unshare the current process25863 hostname newname
..
91: c3eth0@if92: <BROADCAST,MULTICAST,UP,LOWER_UP> mtu 1500
qdisc noqueue state UP group default qlen 1000
      link/ether e2:14:27:27:c6:95 brd ff:ff:ff:ff:ff:ff link-
      netnsid 0
      inet 192.168.25.20/24 scope global c3eth0
 ..
GET / HTTP/1.1
Host: newname:9090
User-Agent: Mozilla/5.0 (X11; Ubuntu; Linux x86_64; rv:131.0)
Gecko/20100101 Firefox/131.0
Accept: text/html,application/xhtml+xml,application/
xml;q=0.9,image/avif,image/webp,image/png,image/
svg+xml,*/*;q=0.8
Accept-Language: en-US,en;q=0.5
Accept-Encoding: gzip, deflate
Connection: keep-alive
Upgrade-Insecure-Requests: 1
Priority: u=0, i

GET /favicon.ico HTTP/1.1
Host: newname:9090
User-Agent: Mozilla/5.0 (X11; Ubuntu; Linux x86_64; rv:131.0)
Gecko/20100101 Firefox/131.0
Accept: image/avif,image/webp,image/png,image/svg+xml,image/*;q=
0.8,*/*;q=0.5
Accept-Language: en-US,en;q=0.5
Accept-Encoding: gzip, deflate
```

```
Connection: keep-alive
Referer: http://newname:9090/
Priority: u=6
```

From the results, we can observe that a simple web server is deployed using an existing network namespace (c3ns) successfully, and it is accessible from the host web browser.

Summary

In this chapter, we have learned the basics of virtualization concepts using Linux features such as namespaces and control groups. As part of experimentation, we have learned how to set up completely custom namespaces, detach from existing namespaces, and attach to existing namespaces. We have learned how to limit resources for virtualized processes using Linux cgroups. As part of hands-on activities, we explored important system calls related to virtualization, such as `setns`, `unshare`, and `clone`, to set up virtualized environments through C programming. Specifically, we have learned how to set up process, memory, and network namespaces through C programming hands-on activities. In summary, these activities help you to easily grasp the concepts of process, memory, and network virtualization and acquire the necessary skills to set up virtualization environments through C programming.

I would like to thank you all for reading this book, and I believe this book helps you to practice C programming for acquiring essential skills in terms of system, networks, and cloud domains in a short time.

Index

A

abort() system, 20
access() memory layout, 115
add function, 256, 257
Application errors, 172
Arithmetic and logic unit (ALU), 4, 5
ArrayAccess() function, 175, 198, 203, 206, 208
ArrayBoundsCheck(int), 175
ArrayInfo-related assembly codes, 150, 151
Array index, 82, 86, 88, 93
Array indexing approach, 274
Array memory layout, 37
Array of pointers (ptrArr), 231
Arrays, 81, 364
    1-D array, 91, 99
    2-D and 3-D data elements, 89
    2-D array, 91, 94
    3-D array, 91, 94, 99
    6-integer elements array, 81
    benefits, 83
    binary tree implementation, 90
    character array, 81
    circular list implementation, 87
    data elements, 88
    data exchange, 84–85
    directed graphs implementation, 90
    elements, 81
    hands-on activity, 93
    indexing, 85–90
    inner loop array data elements, 92–93
    integer array, 81, 82
    logarithmic time complexity, 87, 88
    matrix handling, 88
    name and index, 82
    N-D arrays, 93
    nested loops order, 97
    pointer variable, 83
    pointers, 84
    row-major access, 96
    row-major/column-major access, 92
    variable-size arrays, 92, 98
asr() function, 164
Asynchronous programming, 440
    IPC approaches, 440
    message queue, 451
        header files, 451, 452
        loop, 455, 456
        message sender process, 451
        message structure, 454
        msgsnd, 452, 453
        rcvr.c, 453
        sample messages, 452
        sendr.c, 454, 455
        set up, 452
        signal handler, 454, 455
        testing, 453, 456
    microservices, 440

B

Best dynamic memory management practices, 281, 284, 285
32-bit computer systems, 7

INDEX

64-bit computer systems, 7
Broadcast messages sending client applications, 616
Broadcast UDP client
    accepting messages and sending replies, 618
    bcastclient.c, 616
    creating executable rudps.c, 620
    defining port number and buffer size, 617
    defining UDP socket, 617
    enabling non-blocking send and receive operations, 617
    including header files, 616
    kill broadcast server, 620
    restart broadcast server, 620, 621
    setting protocol address, 618
    setting socket option, 617
    starting client, 620
Broadcast UDP server
    accepting messages and sending replies, 614
    bcastserver.c, 613
    creating executable rudps.c, 615
    defining port number and buffer size, 613
    including header files, 613
    setting protocol address, 614
    setting socket option, 614
    starting server, 616
    UDP socket creation, 613
Buffer overflow attacks, 161, 162
8-byte alignment, 117

C

Cache coherency, 6
Call-by-reference parameter-passing approach, 229
CallByValue1 memory space, 230
CallByValue2 memory space, 230
Call-by-value parameter-passing approach, 229
callee function, 53, 54, 85, 115, 138
    memory layout, 85
    stack frame, 60
Caller functions, 77
Calloc allocation, 280
calloc function, 277–281, 294, 299–302, 306, 308, 312
C arrays, 85, 86, 91, 103, 114 *see also* Arrays
C developers, 270
Central processing unit (CPU)
    control unit (CU), 5
    general architecture and internal components, 3
C function execution procedure
    block-Level local variables, 58
    code segment, 59
    data segment memory area, 60
    developer's responsibilities, 62
    frame pointer, 61
    function-level local variables, 57
    global variables, 58, 59
    heap segment, 60
    lifetime, block-level local variables, 58
    lifetime of local variables, 58
    local variables, 57
    scope of variable, 57
    stack segment, 60–61
    static variables, 59
C functions, 51
cgroups *see* Control groups (cgroups)
Client/server crashes, 555
clock() function, 243
clone, 630, 643

Clone system call, 649
CLONE_NEWIPC, 627
CLONE_NEWNET, 627
CLONE_NEWPID, 625
CLONE_NEWUSER, 626
CLONE_NEWUTS, 626
CLONE_VM, 626
Code coverage analysis
    and static code, 183
    automated tools, 184
    compile important.c file, 190
    functions level statistics
        check, 184–185
    gcc and gcov usage, 185–188
    gcov-generated file, 193
    individual function-level code
        coverage statistics, 191
    individual lines of code execution
        statistics, 185
    main function, 190
    min function, 189
    search and min functions, 188
    search function, 188, 193
codeop file, 149–151
codeop1 file, 150
codeop2 file, 150, 151
Communication channels, 475
Compilation, 144
    dynamic linking, 144
    ELF file, 144
    gcc tools, 144
    static linking, 144
Compilation tools, 144, 145 *see also* gcc
    compilation options
Compiler, 24
    gcc tools, optimization levels, 25–26
    handle application code reliability and
        security, 26–28

    handle runtime errors, 28
        activities using gdb, 28
        linking and loading options, 29–30
        linking object files, 30–31
    major roles, 24–25
    primary role, 24
Computer system architecture
    CPU (*see* Central processing
        unit (CPU))
    CPU and IO device interactions, 6–7
    CPU cores, 3–5
    inspect system configurations on Linux
        OS, 7–11
    memory hierarchy, 5–6
Container, 625
Containerization technologies, 623
Containers deployment, 625
continue command, 201
Control groups (cgroups), 623
    assign processes, 654
    blkio cgroup, 629
    configure resource control group
        limits, 653
    controller, 627
    controlling and monitoring process
        resources, 652
    controlling/restricting resources
        usage, 627
    CPU, 628
    lightweight virtualization, 627
    memory cgroups, 628
    monitoring resources usage, 627
    network control groups, 629
    set up CPU cgroups, limiting CPU
        resources by processes, 674–678
    set up memory cgroups, limiting
        memory consumption by
        processes, 671–674

INDEX

Control groups (cgroups) (*cont.*)
    set up memory resource cgroups, 653
    steps, developers, 652
Control unit (CU), 5
COPY command, 256
C pointers
    efficient communication approach for functions, 229–230
    flexible data accessing approaches, 231
    pointers to arrays, 232–233
    pointers to structures, 233–234
C procedure-oriented programming, 44
C programmers, 45, 47
C programming
    built-in data structures, 45
        arrays, 45
        structures, 46
    built-in libraries, 47
    invoke OS services, 47
    pointers, 46 (*see* Pointers)
    procedure-oriented programming approach, 45
    responsibilities, C programmer, 47–50
CPU control groups, 628
CPU cores, 3, 4
    cache memories, 5
    clock cycles, 4
    components, 4
    controller, 4
    hardware-level threads, 4
CPU cycles, 4, 5
C strings, 100, 101, 103, 104 *see also* Strings
C structures, 112
    activities, 114–115
    alignment options, 121
    code and test, 122
    compiler attributes, 120
    C protocol stack structure, 127
    data members' memory allocation, 117–118
    data members' memory layout, 120
    data structures, 114
    data structures modeling, 123–125
    define multiple users, 113
    GoodOrg, 122
    hands-on activity, 118–119, 128
    main() function, 121
    memory layout, 113, 115, 116
    multi-key search trees, 125
    organize data members, 119
    packing structure data members, 118
    protocol implementation, 126
    protocol messages, 114, 129
    ProtocolHeader, 126
    protocols and protocol stack modeling, 126–128
    struct, 113
    structure variables, 114
    structure variables between functions, 115–117
    structure variables memory layout, 114
    time-based data structures, 114
    users' list, 112
    variables, 113
    variables memory layout, 113
C union, 132, 133
    independent protocol headers, 135
    MyProto implementation, 135–140
    program execution, 133
    protocol message structure implementation, 134
    protocol stack, 134, 135
    ProtocolStack variable size, 135
    standard TCP/IP protocol stack, 134
    unique memory organization, 134

variable memory layout, 134
variables, 133
variables and data members, 133

D

Database management
    systems (DBMS), 126
DataRangesOperations(int), 175
Developers, 471
    FIFO, 426, 427
    issues/respective solutions
        critical section and synchronization
            issues, 370, 371
        data sharing issues, 376
        false sharing, 376–378
        mutex and Conditional
            Variable, 373–375
        pthreads mutex objects, 371–373
    message queue, 433
    pipe, 421, 422
    roles, 363
    semaphores, 460, 461
    shared memory, 439
    synchronous programming, 440
disassemble command, 208
Docker, 623
Domain name system (DNS), 515
Dynamically allocated memory
    locations, 283
Dynamic Host Configuration
    Protocol (DHCP), 479, 515
Dynamic linking, 29, 30
Dynamic memory allocation, 224
Dynamic memory allocation-related
    system calls
    extending memory blocks
        dynamically, 277, 278

handling multiple blocks, 279–281
library function
    free, 276, 277
    malloc, 274–276
stdlib.h, 274
Dynamic memory allocation tasks in
    reliable manners
    hands-on activity-1, 293–299
    hands-on activity-2, 294, 300–306
    hands-on activity-3, 294, 306–312
Dynamic memory management
    benefits, 271
    C developers, 270
        powers associated, 272, 273
        responsibilities, 273, 274
    description, 270
    error handling (*see* Valgrind tools)
    handling dynamic requirements, 271
    importance of, 271

E

exec() system, 20
Executable and linking format (ELF) file,
    144, 152, 163
exit() system, 20

F

FIFOs, 410
    accessing, 411, 422
    creation, 411, 422
    developers role, 426, 427
    OS role, 411
    OUTQ FIFO file, 423
    sample C programs, 423–426
    use case, 412
    write system call, 423

INDEX

Floating point unit (FPU), 4, 5
fno-stack-protector, 26
fork, 626, 630, 643, 663, 692, 695
fork() system, 20
free function, 274, 276, 277, 281, 294, 298, 300, 301
func.c file, 63, 66
Function pointers
    basic function pointers, 256–257
    declaration and usage, 257
    declare array, 258–259
    getMemBlock, 258
    p2memf, 258
    polymorphism, 261
    polymorphism concepts and testing, 262–267
    sample functions, 259
    test() function, 259
    typedef, 258, 262
function_name, 53
Functions, 364

G, H

gcc compilation options, 150
    for linking object files, 151
        compile comlink.c, 154
        create static and dynamic libraries using gcc, 155–158
        dynamic linking, 152–153
        mdtools.c file, 159, 160
        sample C program, 153
        static *vs.* dynamic, 153
        static linking, 152
    for performance tuning
        compiler program, 145
        generate assembly-level code files, 149
        loopOpt1(), 148
        loopOpt2(), 148
        optimization levels, 145–146
        optimization.c, 146–148
        vimdiff command, 150–151
    for secured code, 161
        buffer overflow attacks, 161
        gcc –fstack-protector-strong, 162
        process memory layout, 161
        stack execution, 162–163
        stack protection, 162
        string library functions, 163
    security.c, 164
        asr() function, 164
        asr() in main() and execute code, 167
        gcc linking option, 166
        main() function, 166
        nostackexec in main, 171
        stackexec function, 165, 170–171
        stackguard function, 164, 168
        standard library functions, 169–170
        stdlib.h, string.h, and stdio.h, 165
gcc-generated code-optimized files, 150
gcc optimization levels, 145–146
gcov tool, 183–186, 188, 191, 192
gdb tool, 195
    C application stack, registers and its assembly code, 206–209
    code execution, 195–202
    disassemble, 197
    for common debugging activities, 197
    handle C application crash from its core dump file, 217–219
    handle C application runtime crash, 212–216
    Info, 197
    info break, 197

inspect C application code and
    data, 202–206
inspect C application runtime stack
    size, 209–212
print variablename, 196
reliability3.c, 198
set var variablename=value, 196
watch variablename, 196
gethostname, 633
getMemBlock, 258
GlobalFun(), 55, 56

I, J, K

impfunc.c, 68, 70
Important C system calls
    memory management tasks, 272
Interconnecting devices, 475
Internet infrastructure and components,
    474, 475
Internet service provider (ISP)
    networks, 474
Internet services, 474
Interprocess communication (IPC)
    approaches, 20, 405
    dup and dup2, 408
    FIFOs (see FIFOs)
    file handling, 407
    message queues (see Message queues)
    PIPEs (see PIPEs)
    semaphores (see Semaphores)
    shared memory (see Shared memory)
    synchronization issues, 457, 458, 471
Interprocess coordination activities, 406
Invalid memory, 284
Invalid write and Access, 292
IO Control Groups (BLKIO), 629
IO devices, 6, 7, 9, 15, 22, 38

IP address
    calculation, 480
    host addresses, 479
    network device, 479
    private, 480, 481
    public, 480
    subnet, 479, 480
IPC constructs, 35, 43, 44
IP_MULTICAST_IF option, 560
IP_TTL option, 560
iproute, 682
iproute2, 679–682

L

Library functions, 269, 271, 272
Lightweight virtualization, 624
Linux
    fork system call, 317
    lightweight processes, 315
    message queues, 413
    multiple processes, 315
    multitasking applications, 316
    process creation, 316
    pthreads library, 319
    signal handling concepts, 357
    system calls, 335, 405, 406
    threads, 316
Linux commands chaining, pipes, 441
    command execution, 444
    commands, 441
    dup system call, 443
    dup2 system call, 443
    header files, 441
    N processes, 442
    n-1 pipes, 442
    ncmdschain.c, 441
    parent and child processes, 444
    testing, 444

INDEX

Linux features
    cgroups, 623 (*see also* Control groups (cgroups))
    namespaces, 623 (*see also* Namespaces)
Linux kernel, 625
Linux OS, 2, 7, 11, 13–15, 20, 22, 23, 29
Load balancing, 605
localFun(), 55, 56

M

main() execution, 59
main() function, 62, 76, 80, 121, 139, 175
main() memory layout, 115, 116
malloc function, 274–277, 282, 293, 294, 297
mdtools.c file, 159, 160
Medium access control (MAC), 477
memalloc1.c, 295, 299
memalloc2.c, 301, 305
memalloc3.c, 307
memoryAccess(), 282, 283
memoryAccess(int N), 284
Memory access latencies, 1, 5, 6, 34
Memory access-related errors, 172–173
    gcc options, 173
        -fanalyzer, 174
        -fsanitize = address, 173
        -fsanitize = undefined, 173
    identification tool (*see* Valgrind tool)
    reliability3.c, 174, 175
        -fsanitize=address option, 174
        undefined option, 174
Memory allocation system, 269
Memory control groups, 628, 674–678
Memory management operations, 15
Memory management-related system, 270

Memory management unit (MMU), 6, 31, 36
Message queues, 412
    accessing, 428
    creation, 427
    decoupling, 412
    developers role, 433
    event-driven programming, 412
    ID, 412
    msgrcv system call, 428, 429
    msgsnd system call, 428
    OS role, 413
    sample C programs
        msgrcvr.c, 429, 431–433
        msgsndr.c, 429–431
    structure, 413
    use case, 414
move() function, 68, 69
Multilevel pointers, 226
    double pointer variables, 227
    Forward2Fun, 227, 228
    Pass3NextFun, 228
    ptr's value and address, 226
Multiprocessing, 554, 556
Multiprocessing applications, 401
Multiprocessing/multithreading programming approaches, 556
Multitasking applications, 316, 363, 370, 373, 402
Multithreaded application
    activities, 387
    first approach, 388
        issues, 392
        main function, 391, 392
        parallelsum.c, 391
    parallelsum.c
        implementation, 389, 390
        issues, 390

performance, 387, 388
second approach, 388
    issues, 393
    main function, 393
    parallelsum.c, 392
    results, 393, 394
third approach, 388
    issues, 395
    main function, 395
    parallelsum.c, 394
    results, 395
Multithreading, 554
Multithreading network applications, 557
MyProto protocol, 135–140
MyProto structure, 137

N

Namespaces, 623
  attach process
    existing user and network namespaces, 640, 642, 643
    existing UTS namespace using setns, 638, 640
    setns system calls, 636
    set up new UTS namespace, 637, 638
    unshare, 636
  clone
    attach new namespaces later, 649–652
    limited namespaces, 649–652
    multiple namespaces, 648, 649
    necessary new namespaces, 645–647
  CLONE_NEWIPC, 627
  CLONE_NEWNET, 627
  CLONE_NEWPID, 625
  CLONE_NEWUSER, 626
  CLONE_NEWUTS, 626
  CLONE_VM, 626
  detach process
    fork, 630
    network namespace using unshare, 635, 636
    parent and child processes, 630, 631
    parent process execution environment, 631
    unshare system call usage, 631, 632
    user namespace using unshare, 634, 635
    UTS namespace using unshare, 632, 634
  experiment, process and memory namespaces
    cloning processes, 655
    hands-on activities, 655
    set up isolated shared memory, cloned processes, 661–666
    set up isolated user namespace, 666–670
    share virtual memory between processes, 656–661
  kernel resources, 625
  Linux kernel, 625
  set up virtualized execution environment, 644
  virtualized execution environment, 643
NAT, *see* Network address translation (NAT)
Nested functions, 55, 56, 77–80
netcat tool, 691, 695, 697
net_cls, 629
net_prio, 630
Network address translation (NAT), 481
Network applications performance, 554

INDEX

Network control groups, 629
Network namespaces, 635, 640
    connect processes with an existing virtual network, 688–691
    deploy network application, 691–694
    deploy web server, 694–699
    iproute2, 679–682
    network interfaces, 679
    network protocol stacks, 679
    virtual networks setups
        basic virtual network setup, 682–684
        interconnect network namespace and host, 684, 685
        interconnect two different subnet network namespaces, 685–687
        set up virtual network between two namespaces, 683
NEWIPC namespace, 627
NEWPID namespace, 626
NEWUSER namespace, 626
NEWUTS namespaces, 626
next command, 200
Non-blocking server UDP implementation
    closing UDP servers' sockets, 583
    data reading readiness check, 581
    declaring variables, 579
    defining function, 579
    defining port number and buffer size, 579
    including header files, 578
    netcat UDP clients, 583
    non-blocking mode, 578
    nonbudp.c, 578
    polling task, 580
    setup procedure, 580
    terminals, 584
    testing command, 583
    testing, netcat UDP clients, 578
Non-blocking socket programming, 553
    fcntl, 565–567
    implementing non-blocking TCP/UDP servers, 565
    network application, 564
    non-blocking server TCP implementation, 568–577
    non-blocking server UDP implementation, 578–584
    TCP/UDP server, 564
    TCP/UDP sockets, 564
Non-blocking TCP server implementation
    client's connected sockets, 573
    connection request check, 572
    data reading readiness check, 571
    defining function, 569
    defining port number and buffer size, 569
    including header files, 568
    initializing connection descriptors, 571
    netcat TCP clients, 576, 577
    non-blocking mode, 568
    nonbtcp.c, 568
    polling task, 571
    program ending, 575
    set up procedure, 570
    TCP clients, 576
    testing commands, 575
    testing, netcat TCP clients, 568
    variables declaration, 569
NULL pointer, 282, 284

O

Operating system (OS), 1, 11

computational, memory and I/O
    hardware resources
    management, 12
I/O Devices Accessing Services, 12
processes communication, 12
process management activities and
    services (*see* Process
    management, OS)
process management operations, users
    program access, 15–16
process memory layout, 16, 17
program execution activity, 16
programming development and
    deployment tools, 13
responsibilities and services, 13
stack and heap segment, 17
User Interface (UI), 11
user process execution on Linux
    OS, 14–15
user program and interaction with
    Linux OS, 13
user programs execution
    services, 11, 12
OS memory management activities, 21

P, Q

Page replacement algorithms, 21
Parent and child processes
    data sharing activities, 341
    failures, 356
    file descriptors, 350–352
    importance, 340, 342
    new process execution, 341
        developers observation, 356
        failures, 356, 357
        issues, 354
        reliableps.c, 354, 355
        updated code, 355, 356
    orphan process, 342, 343
    segments, 346–348
    valgrind command
        file descriptor leaks, 352, 353
        memory leaks, 349, 350
    Zombie process, 344, 345
Parsing function, 252, 253
PCB, *see* Process Control Block (PCB)
Peripheral component interconnect
    (PCI) bus, 6
PIPEs, 409
    accessing, 419
    array, 419
    creation, 418
    data structures, 409
    descriptors, 409
    developers role, 421, 422
    OS role, 409, 410
    parent process, 419
    sample C program, 419–421
    use cases, 410
Pointers, 224, 364
    access 1-D subarrays of 2-D arrays, 244
    access 2-D subarrays of 3-D arrays, 244
    access packet structure containing
        nested structures, 249–250
    access time of arrays, simple indexing
        vs. pointers, 243
    arraysnptr.c, 243
    to array subparts, 237–238
    basic pointers, 225, 226
    basic ways to access structures, 247
    dynamic memory concepts
        implementation, 224
    efficient ways to access structure
        variable, 247–249
    integer array data structure, 234

INDEX

Pointers (*cont.*)
    minimize functions communication, 224
    to multidimensional arrays, 238–239
    multilevel (*see* Multilevel pointers)
    parse functions, 254
    parsing.c, 251, 255
    polymorphism, 225, 255
    sample protocol message, 251
    void pointers, 235
Pointers to strings
    array of array of strings, 241–242
    array of strings, 240–241
    simple string, 240
Pointer to array variable (ptr2Arr), 232, 236, 237
Pointer variables, 255, 256
Polymorphism, 255, 261, 262
Procedure-oriented programming, 52
    arguments, 54
    benefits, 52
    C function syntax, 52, 53
        function body, 53
        function signature, 53
        return type, 53
    complex evaluation function, 54
    function encapsulation and data hiding features, 55
    main(), 54
    nested functions, 55
    nested functions in GNU C, 77–80
    principles, 54
    recursive functions, 55 (*see* Recursive functions)
Process control block (PCB), 18
Process execution, 34
    application code, 34
    application data accessing paths, 35
    device drivers and device controllers, 38
    external devices access, 35
    and IO devices access-related issues, 38–40
    IPC constructs, 35
    and memory access-related issues, 35–38
    network applications access, 35
    running, 34
    waiting, 34
Process management
    developers
        assigning jobs, 324, 325
        coordination activities, 326, 327
        fork system call, 324
        interrupts, 326
        multiple processes order, 325
        process errors, 326
        process exit activities, 325
    developers considerations, 318
    fork system call, 317, 324
    interrupt handling
        arguments, 359
        developers considerations, 362
        importance, 341, 342, 357
        signals, 357, 358, 360, 361
        system call, 359
        updated code, 362
    multiple processes execution order
        activities, 331
        activities implementation, fork2.c, 332, 333
        child process, 331
        fork2.c results, 334
        parent process, 333, 334
        waitpid() waits, 331
        wait-related system calls, 331

712

N processes executable images
    activities, 336
    activities implementation, fork3.c, 337, 338
    char *const argv[], 336
    const char *file, 336
    developers considerations, 335
    execvp system call, 336
    fork3.c results, 339, 340
    parent process, 338
  parent and child processes (*see* Parent and child processes)
  process table, 341
  specific number of processes
    activities, 327
    activities implementation, fork1.c, 327, 328
    fork1.c results, 329
    overlapping processes, 330
    parent process, 329
Process management, OS
  allocate multiple processes, 17
  context switching delay, 19
  ELF file, 16
  execution process, states, 18–19
  IO management module, 22–23
  memory management approach, 21–22
  as multiple processes, 17
  PCB, 19
  process state diagram, 18, 19
  protection services to user processes, 23
  PSB, 18
  storage devices and file access, 22
  user programs, 20
Process memory layout, 33
  code segment, 32
  C program process memory layout, 32
  data segment, 32
  ELF, 31
  heap segment, 32
  memory requirements, 33
  stack and heap segments, 33
  stack segment, 33
Process memory layout-related access checkpoints
  heap segment-related access checks, 42
  interprocess communication-related access checkpoints, 43–44
  shared libraries access, 43
  shared memory access, 43
  stack segment-related access checks, 41–42
Process reliability and security issues, 40
Process runtime execution environment, 36
Process services chaining, FIFO, 445
  process-1 (fifo1.c)
    header files, 445
    mkfifo, 445, 446
    results, 448, 449
    sample messages, 446
    testing, 446
  process-2 (fifo2.c)
    loop, 447, 448
    read-only mode, 447
    testing, 448
  process-3 (fifo3.c)
    loop, 449, 450
    testing, 450
    write-only mode, 449
Programming techniques, 269
Protocol address, 478, 479
ptr2Arr2D variables, 239

INDEX

R

readelf command, 162, 163, 168, 170, 171
realloc function, 277, 278, 293
Recursive functions, 71, 75
    base conditions on input
        arguments, 71–72
    elements for N times, 74
    hrecfunc(), 75, 76
    in recfunc.c, 73
    input arguments, 72
    lrecfunc(), 75
    run executable (a.out), 77
    standard algorithms, 72–73
Reliable TCP client
    closing sockets, 596
    including header files, 594
    main section, 594
    receiving contents, 596
    rtcpc.c, 594
    sample.txt contents, 596
    TCP server connection, 595
Reliable TCP server
    child process, 592, 593
    configuring TCP server protocol
        address, 590
    confirmation message, 593
    including header files, 588
    main section, 588
    releasing socket resources, 594
    SO_KEEPALIVE option, 589
    SO_REUSEADDR option, 589
    TCP socket, 591
    waiting, infinite loop, 591
run command, 203, 207

S

sample() execution, 61, 62

sample() function, 61
Semaphores, 458
    access shared memory, 461
        child processes, 463, 464
        header files, 462
        id, 463
        parent processes, 465
        safesharing.c, 462
        sem_open, 462
        set up, 463
        testing, 465
    accessing, 460
    advantages, 459
    control processes, access shared
        memory, 466
        child processes, 468, 469
        ctrlacces.c, 467
        header files, 467
        id, 468
        parent process, 469, 470
        sem_open, 467
        set up, 468
        testing, 470
    creation, 459
    developers role, 460, 461
    lock variables, 416
    OS role, 416, 417
    post operation, 458
    sem_wait/sem_post operations, 460
    synchronization issues, 416
    use case, 417
    wait section, 458
setns, 630, 650
    set up new UTS namespace, 637, 638
    system calls, 636, 638, 643
    user and network namespaces, 640,
        642, 643
    UTS namespace, 638, 640

INDEX

Shared libraries, 33, 43
Shared memory, 414
    accessing, 434
    benefits, 414
    creation, 434
    deletion, 435
    detachment, 435
    developers role, 439
    OS role, 415
    sample C programs, 435, 436, 438
    segments, 414, 434
    use case, 415
Simple network management protocol (SNMP), 515
sizeof operator, 93
SO_BROADCAST option, 559
SO_KEEPALIVE option, 561, 587
Socket options
    address reuse options, 561
    default option values, 562, 563
    function used, 561
    network applications, 559
    network operations, 559
    network-related features, 559
    routing and related features, 559, 560
    SO_REUSEADDR option value, 563
    socket general options, 560, 561
    TCP-related options, 561
Socket programming approaches
    multiprocessing/
        multithreading, 556–559
    network applications requirements
        performance, 554
        reliability, 555
        scalability, 555, 556
    non-blocking (see Non-blocking socket programming)

socket options (see Socket options)
Socket reuse port option, 610
SO_LINGER option, 561
SO_OOBINLINE option, 561
SO_RCVBUF option, 560
SO_RCVLOWAT option, 560
SO_RCVTIMEO option, 560
SO_REUSEADDR option, 561, 587
SO_REUSEPORT option, 561, 604, 605
SO_SNDBUF option, 560
SO_SNDLOWAT option, 560
SO_SNDTIMEO, 560
Space randomization, 161, 164
Static linking, 29, 30
stdlib functions, 312
stdlib.h library, 270
StringChecks(char*), 175
String library functions, 27, 163
Strings, 100
    benefits to developers, 103
    as buffers, 104
    as character arrays, 101
    concatenation activities, 107
    inpStr to inpStr2, 106
    input string (inpStr2), 108, 109
    input string length, 110
    library functions, 105
    matching activities, 105
    memory library functions, 104
    memory organization, 101
    network applications, 104
    string.h library functions, 103
    string library functions, 104
    strprocess.c, 106
    strrchr, 111
    substring length, 109
    substrings, 111

INDEX

Strings (*cont.*)
   terminating character, 103
   tokenization, 105
   using strpbrk, 111
StructAccThrPtr, 248
struct Packet, 249, 250
Structures, 364
Structure variables, 113–115
Synchronous programming, 440

T

TCP client program structure
   general, 500, 501
   TCP socket programming,
     506, 508, 509
TCP client-server performance and reliability issues handling
   reliable delivery at application level, 586, 587
   reliable TCP client, 594–597
   reliable TCP server, 588–594
   rtcps.c with rtcpc.c testing, 597–599
   server crashes, 585
   TCP client crashes, 585, 586
   TCP connection, send and receive errors, 586
   TCP server-client connection errors and confirmation testing, 599–601
   TCP server-client connection testing, 599–601
TCP client task handling function, 557
TCP/IP layers, 475
   application layer, 476
   defines link layer, 477
   network layer, 477
   physical layer, 477
   transport layer, 476

TCP/IP stack, 475, 476
   IP addresses, 479, 480
   network devices/layers, 478
   and network interactions, 477
   protocol address, 478, 479
TCP listening socket, 565
TCP network application traffic
   monitoring and inspecting, 539
     callback function, 543, 544
     header files, 543
     insptcp.c, 543
     main function, 545, 546
     messages, 544, 545
     pcap.h library functions, 539, 540
     program structure, 540–542
     tasks, 542
     testing, 546, 547
TCP server application, 587
TCP server program structure
   general, 496, 497
   multiprocess, 498, 499
     TCP socket programming, 510, 511, 513–515
   TCP socket programming, 502, 504–506
TCP socket programming
   accept system call, 490
   bind system call, 488
   close() call, 495
   connect system call, 489–491
   C socket address structure, 487
   htons or htonl functions, 488
   IP address, 488
   listen() system call, 490
   multiprocess TCP server program
     gcc commands, 514
     iterative server, 511
     mtcps.c, 511–513

INDEX

sleep(), 514
   tasks, 510
   testing, 513, 514
port number, 488
recv() system call
   arguments, 493
   blocking mode, 493
   errors, 494
   example, 494, 495
   return value, 493
send system call
   arguments, 491
   blocking mode, 491
   errors, 492
   example, 492, 493
   return value, 491
shutdown() system call, 495
socket system call, 487
TCP client program structure
   code execution, 509
   details, 509
   itcpc.c, 506, 508
   itcps.c, 509
   tasks, 506
TCP protocol address, 487
TCP server program structure
   code execution, 505, 506
   details, 506
   itcps.c, 502, 503, 505
   tasks, 502
3-way handshake procedure, 490
TCP/UDP network application traffic, monitor and inspect
program structure
   main(), 542
TCP/UDP network applications, 553
TCP_MAXSEG option, 561
TCP_NODELAY option, 561

test() function, 259
Testing fault tolerance of UDP servers
   accepting messages and sending replies, 608
   Ctrl+C command, 610
   defining port number and buffer size, 606
   including header files, 606
   rudps.c, 606
   rudps.c creation, 609
   setting protocol address (IP+port), 607
   setting socket option, 607
   starting servers, 609
   UDP clients, 609
   UDP socket creation, 606
Testing load balancing of UDP servers
   opening terminals, 611
   receiving requests, 612
   rudps.c creation, 611
   starting servers, 611
testtools.c file, 156–158
Thread management
   assigning tasks/data to threads
      critical sections access, 367
      data dependencies, 367
      data organization, 369
      flow dependencies, 369
      synchronization approaches, 368, 369
      tasks, 367
   creation/assigning tasks
      C functions, 364
      input elements, partition, 366
      main() process, 365
      nthrds, 366
      struct, 366
      Task, 366
   data race conditions

INDEX

Thread management (*cont.*)
    critical section, 396
    datarace.c, 396, 397
    functions, 397
    helgrind option, 396
    valgrind results, 398
  developers
    multitasking application, 364
    roles, 363
  developers considerations, 323
  functions, 363
  issues/respective solutions
    critical section and synchronization issues, 370, 371
    data sharing issues, 376
    false sharing, 376–378
    mutex and Conditional Variable, 373–375
    pthreads mutex objects, 371–373
  joinable threads, 321, 322
  locking issues
    code modification, 400
    critical sections, 398, 399
    helgrind option, 398
    identification, 401
    lockingissues.c, 398
    testing, 400
    threads, 399, 400
    valgrind results, 400, 401
  multithreaded application (*see* Multithreaded application)
  N list/K threads
    activities, 383
    create threads, 385
    delete list/free memory, 386
    execution/results, 386
    linear search, 384
    main function, 385
    parallelsearch.c, 384
    search function, 384
    testing, 386
  pthread_create(), 319
    const pthread_attr_t *attr, 320
    pthread_t *thread, 319
    void *(*start_routine) (void *), 319
    void *arg, 320
  structures and pointers, 363
  thread execution, 320
  thread usage
    basicthreads.c, 379
    create threads, 382
    delete list/free memory, 382
    execution/results, 382
    functions, 378
    linear search, 380
    main() process, 381
    mean value, 381
    minimum element finding function, 379, 380
    minimum element finding procedure, 380
    search function, 379
    testing, 383
    valgrind tool/helgrind options, 396
tools.c file, 155–157
tools.o object file, 156, 157
Transmission control protocol (TCP), 473, 481
  clients, 486
  client-server application, 486, 515
  connection, 481, 483
  connection set up, 482, 483
  connection shutdown, 483
    client, 483, 484
    fields, 485, 486
    header/files, 484

server, 484
rules, 481, 482
typedef, 248, 258, 259, 262, 267

U

UDP client
    budpc.c, 533
    header files, 533
    main function, 533
    message, 534, 535
    resources, 535
    tasks, 532
    testing, 535, 536
UDP client-server performance and reliability issues handling
    broadcast messages (*see* Broadcast UDP server)
    broadcasting applications, 605
    fault tolerance, 606–610
    load balancing, 605, 610–612
UDP connection-oriented client
    cbudpc.c, 536
    main function, 536, 537
    tasks, 536
    testing, 538
UDP network application traffic
    monitoring and inspecting, 539
        callback function, 548
        header files, 547
        inspudp.c, 547
        main function, 549, 550
        pcap.h library functions, 539, 540
        program structure, 540–542
        tasks, 547
        testing, 550
        traversing, 548
        type DNS/message length, 549

UDP server
    budps.c, 530
    header files, 530
    loop, 531
    main function, 530
    resources, 532
    testing, 532
UDP socket programming
    basic system calls, 517
    chat application
        tasks, 529
    connection-oriented socket, 518, 519
    protocol address, 518
    recvfrom() system call
        arguments, 521
        blocking mode, 521
        error, 522
        messages, 522, 523
        return value, 522
        uses, 521
    sendto() system call
        arguments, 519
        blocking mode, 519
        errors, 520
        message, 520
        return value, 520
        uses, 519
    socket system call, 517
    UDP client program structure, 525, 526
        connection-oriented, 527, 529
    UDP server program structure, 523–525
unshare, 630
    network namespace, 635, 636
    user namespace, 634, 635
    UTS namespace, 632, 633
unshare system call, 631, 632, 662
until command, 201

User datagram protocol (UDP), 473, 515
    applications, 515
    drawbacks, 516
    header/fields, 516, 517
    services, 516
    uses, 515
User Interface (UI), 11
User namespace, 634, 640
UTS namespace, 632, 638, 695

V

valgrind tool, 172, 181, 269, 281
    description, 285
    dynamic code analysis, 181, 182, 286
    error summary, 183
    heap summary, 183
    important messages, 287
    leak summary, 183
    memory accessing errors, 182, 288–293
    sample program, 182, 287
valgrind (helgrind) tool, 316, 395
vfork() system, 20
vimdiff command, 150, 151
Virtual Ethernet devices, 680, 681
Virtualization concepts, 623, 630, 632, 643
Virtualization technologies, 624
Virtual machines (VMs), 624
VMs deployment, 624
VMs namespace, 626
void pointers, 235

W, X, Y, Z

wait() system, 20

GPSR Compliance

The European Union's (EU) General Product Safety Regulation (GPSR) is a set of rules that requires consumer products to be safe and our obligations to ensure this.

If you have any concerns about our products, you can contact us on

ProductSafety@springernature.com

In case Publisher is established outside the EU, the EU authorized representative is:

Springer Nature Customer Service Center GmbH
Europaplatz 3
69115 Heidelberg, Germany